OLD ENGLISH LITERATURE

Old English Literature

Critical Essays

Edited by

R. M. LIUZZA

Yale University Press   New Haven & London

Designed by James J. Johnson and set in Janson types by The Composing Room of
Michigan, Inc. Printed in the United States of America by R.R. Donnelley & Sons.

Library of Congress Cataloging-in-Publication Data

Old English literature : critical essays / edited by R. M. Liuzza.
    p. cm.
  Includes bibliographical references and index.
  ISBN 0-300-09139-7 (pbk. : alk. paper)

    1. English literature—Old English, ca. 450–1100—History and criticism.
I. Liuzza, R. M.

  PR171.O44 2001
  829.09—dc21   2001035968

A catalogue record for this book is available from the British Library.

The paper in this book meets the guidelines for permanence and durability
of the Committee on Production Guidelines for Book Longevity of the Council
on Library Resources.

10 9 8 7 6 5 4 3 2 1

Contents

Acknowledgments

I am grateful to a number of friends and colleagues for their help on this project: to Fred Robinson, who first proposed it; to Larisa Heimert at Yale University Press, who enthusiastically supported it; to a number of anonymous readers who suggested ways to improve it; to Shari Horner, Nicholas Howe, Eileen Joy, Myra Seaman, Jack Niles, Molly Rothenberg, Sharon Rowley, and John Hill, who offered advice on the selection of essays and the introduction; and to Marie Carianna of Tulane's Academic Center for Learning, Research, and Technology for help with illustrations. Editors at a number of presses were patient and generous in the negotiation of permissions to reprint these essays; I am grateful for their assistance and understanding. Most of all I am, as always, grateful to Ellen Farina, whose love and support have made all else possible.

For permission to reprint the essays in this collection, I would like to thank the authors of the individual works and the editors of the following journals and presses:

Nicholas Howe, "The Cultural Construction of Reading in Anglo-Saxon England," in *The Ethnography of Reading*, ed. Jonathan Boyarin (Berkeley: University of California Press, 1993), 58–79. © 1993 The Regents of the University of California. Reprinted by permission of the publisher.

Susan Kelly, "Anglo-Saxon Lay Society and the Written Word," in *The Uses of Literacy in Early Medieval Europe*, ed. Rosamond McKitterick (Cambridge: Cambridge University Press, 1990), 36–62. © 1990 Cambridge University Press. Reprinted with the permission of Cambridge University Press.

Sarah Foot, "The Making of Angelcynn: English Identity Before the

Norman Conquest," *Transactions of the Royal Historical Society*, 6th ser. 6 (1996), 25–49. Reprinted with the permission of the Royal Historical Society.

Katherine O'Brien O'Keeffe, "Orality and the Developing Text of Caedmon's *Hymn*," *Speculum* 62 (1987), 1–20. © 1987 The Medieval Academy of America. Reprinted by permission.

Kevin Kiernan, "Reading Cædmon's Hymn with Someone Else's Glosses," *Representations* 32 (1990), 157–74. © 1990 The Regents of the University of California. Reprinted by permission.

Clare A. Lees and Gillian R. Overing, "Birthing Bishops and Fathering Poets: Bede, Hild, and the Relations of Cultural Production," *Exemplaria* 6 (1994), 35–65. Pegasus Press, University of North Carolina, Asheville, N.C. 28804. Copyright © 1994. Used by permission of the publishers.

Stephen D. White, "Kinship and Lordship in Early Medieval England: The Story of Sigeberht, Cynewulf, and Cyneheard," *Viator* 20 (1989), 1–18. © 1989 The Regents of the University of California. Reprinted with permission of the publisher.

Stephanie Hollis, "The Thematic Structure of the *Sermo Lupi*," *Anglo-Saxon England* 6 (1977), 175–95. © 1977 Cambridge University Press. Reprinted with the permission of Cambridge University Press.

Earl R. Anderson, "Social Idealism in Ælfric's *Colloquy*," *Anglo-Saxon England* 3 (1974), 153–62. © 1974 Cambridge University Press. Reprinted with the permission of Cambridge University Press.

Jocelyn Wogan-Browne, "The Hero in Christian Reception: Ælfric and Heroic Poetry," in *La funzione dell'eroe germanico: storicità, metafora, paradigma*. Atti del Convegno internazionale di studio, Roma, 6–8 Maggio 1993. Philologia, 2nd. ed. Teresa Pàroli (Rome: Il Calamo, 1995), 323–46. © 1995. Reprinted by kind permission of the author, editor, and publisher.

Clare Lees, "Didacticism and the Christian Community: The Teachers and the Taught," first appeared as chapter 4 in *Tradition and Belief: Religious Writings in Late Anglo-Saxon England* (Minneapolis: University of Minnesota Press, 1999), 106–32. © 1999 The Regents of the University of Minnesota. Used with permission.

Roy F. Leslie, "The Editing of Old English Poetic Texts: Questions of Style," in *Old English Poetry: Essays on Style*, ed. Daniel G. Calder (Berkeley: University of California Press, 1979), 111–125. Reprinted by permission.

M. R. Godden, "Anglo-Saxons on the Mind," in *Learning and Literature in Anglo-Saxon England*, ed. M. Lapidge and H. Gneuss (Cambridge: Cambridge University Press, 1985), 271–98. © 1985 Cambridge University Press. Reprinted with the permission of Cambridge University Press.

Robert Bjork, "*Sundor æt Rune:* The Voluntary Exile of The Wanderer," *Neophilologus* 73 (1989), 119–29. © 1989 Kluwer Academic Publishers. Reprinted with kind permission from Kluwer Academic Publishers.

Margrét Gunnarsdóttir Champion, "From Plaint to Praise: Language as Cure in 'The Wanderer'," *Studia Neophilologica* 69 (1998), 187–202. © 1998 Scandinavian University Press (Universitetsforlaget). Reprinted by permission of the publisher.

Peter Orton, "The Form and Structure of *the Seafarer,*" *Studia Neophilologica* 63 (1991), 37–55. © 1991 Scandinavian University Press (Universitetsforlaget). Reprinted by permission of the publisher.

Shari Horner, "En/closed Subjects: The *Wife's Lament* and the Culture of Early Medieval Female Monasticism," *Æstel* 2 (1994). © 1994 the author. Reprinted by permission.

Sandra McEntire, "The Devotional Context of the Cross before A.D. 1000," in *Sources of Anglo-Saxon Culture*, ed. Paul E. Szarmach and Virginia Darrow Oggins (Studies in Medieval Culture 20. Kalamazoo: Medieval Institute, 1986), 345–56. Reprinted with the permission of the author and of the Board of the Medieval Institute at Western Michigan University.

Carol Braun Pasternack, "Stylistic Disjunctions in *The Dream of the Rood,*" *Anglo-Saxon England* 13 (1984), 167–86. © 1984 Cambridge University Press. Reprinted with the permission of Cambridge University Press.

Fred. C. Robinson, "God, Death, and Loyalty in *The Battle of Maldon,*" in *J. R. R. Tolkien, Scholar and Storyteller: Essays in Memoriam*, ed. Mary Salu and Robert T. Farrell (Ithaca, N.Y., 1979), 76–98. © 1979 by Cornell University. Used by permission of the publisher, Cornell University Press.

John D. Niles, "Maldon and Mythopoesis," *Mediaevalia* 17 (1994 for 1991), 89–121. © 1994 CEMERS, Binghamton University. Reprinted by permission of CEMERS.

Figures 1 and 2 in Kevin Kiernan's "Reading Cædmon's Hymn with Someone Else's Glosses" are reproduced by permission of Rosenkilde and Bagger, Ltd. Figure 3 is © 1942 Columbia University Press and is reprinted by permission of the publisher. Figure 4 is reproduced by permission of the estate of John C. Pope. Figure 5 is reproduced by permission of W. W. Norton and Co.

In some cases the essays in this volume have been slightly modified from their original form—notes renumbered in sequence and internal references changed to endnotes. No attempt has been made, however, to impose uniformity in forms of reference and citation, or to update references to works noted as "forthcoming."

Introduction

THE surviving remains of Old English literature are the flotsam and
jetsam of a vanished world, manuscripts and fragments of texts divorced from their original context, most of them second- or third-
hand copies of unknown originals, many of them saved from oblivion only
by chance or neglect. From these randomly preserved parts of a whole we
are supposed to extrapolate a fluid and living system—a spoken dialect, a
literary tradition, a moment in history—but it is sometimes difficult to
imagine how to move from these discontinuous scraps to a reconstructed
reality. The textual product reveals only traces of the process behind it, and
often seems to hide the forces of culture, history, and language that have
consciously or unconsciously shaped it. Can we make these texts speak?
And if we do, will we understand what they say?

Numerous obstacles confront us. We no longer hear the nuances of
voice and tone, or understand fully the registers of discourse, that give language so much of its meaning—in some cases we do not even know what
some of the words in a given text literally mean.[1] The difficulties of deciphering texts in another language, and of reconstructing manuscript readings from a tangle of damage and error, often leave us little time or energy
to appreciate the vivid and complex art of the works we read. Nor can we
turn to the context of these works for help in understanding them: we have
no biographical information about most authors, and only a very rough
idea when many works were written. In most cases we do not know who
first read these works or what their reactions to them might have been. Our
natural empathy as readers is often frustrated: many of the tales these works
tell and the problems they seem to solve are remote from contemporary
concerns. Notions of good and evil, concepts of community, ideas about

gender, the relations between humanity and the physical world, the sense of
the meaning of life, often seem radically different from modern ways of
thinking. On the other hand, some situations and characters seem thoroughly familiar—the recklessly brave hero on the battlefield, the mournful
woman in solitude, the pious teacher in his classroom—and yet it is likely
that we are in as much danger of misreading some texts because of this familiarity as we are of misreading others because of their remoteness and
strangeness. We might mistake our own ventriloquism for the author's
original voice.

Yet the makers of this body of surviving texts from Anglo-Saxon England, the period roughly from the seventh through the eleventh centuries,
are closer to us than the Greeks and Romans or the Biblical Hebrews, to
name just a few other cultures for whom distance and unlikeness and the
fragmented nature of surviving evidence have not proved an insurmount-
able barrier to a continued presence in our cultural imagination. The Anglo-Saxons have a claim on us by virtue of geography and language, and by
the role that the idea of the "Anglo-Saxon" has played, for better or worse,
in European and American history.[2] We have a responsibility to remember
and interpret the past, and to understand ourselves in relationship to that
past. And as one becomes familiar with the surviving manuscripts and texts,
a rough outline begins to appear; one notices certain predilictions and preoccupations, certain gaps and omissions, certain recurring themes and
striking evasions—the note of sadness for time past, for example, reverber-
ating as a kind of *continuo* underneath the theme of stability in heaven, or
the praise for the asceticism of the monastic life sounding a low descant
against the celebration of community and memory in poetic performance.
Eventually and with effort we develop a sense of what "the" Anglo-Saxons
were like (we should always use the definite article with caution, because
one of the most seductive dangers of studying a distant past is the assumption that there was one truth, one social body, one group with a single outlook; this is surely no more true of the Anglo-Saxons than it is of us today,
though time and chance have vigorously winnowed the already-sparse
body of texts that might offer evidence of cultural diversity). The works
usually read in introductory Old English classes—the prose prefaces of Alfred and Ælfric, a few lively entries in the *Anglo-Saxon Chronicle*, Wulfstan's
Sermo Lupi ad Anglos, the short poetic works known as "elegies," the
homiletic *Dream of the Rood*, the heroic *Battle of Maldon*—have become the
customary landmarks by which we navigate through Anglo-Saxon culture.
From them we can construct a sense of the people who wrote and read these
works; between them we can sketch out lines of connection, fill in some of

the blanks of other lost or unread texts, and map out, tentatively and provisionally, the foreign country that is England in the first millennium.

This work of mapping Old English literature is immeasurably assisted by the perspectives offered by contemporary literary criticism. As many of the essays in this collection demonstrate, the fragmented, authorless, ideologically charged world of Anglo-Saxon texts is a natural habitat for modern theory.[3] If scholars like Hayden White have taught us that our historical narratives are always contingent upon our present demands and desires, we now recognize that past narratives of the past, like Alfred's preface to the *Pastoral Care* or the heroic elegy *Beowulf*, are no less so—like us, the authors of these works sought to justify themselves by the stories they told about the past.[4] And if modern literary theory has made us recognize that texts are not created apart from the ideologies that promote them, nor scholarship apart from the institutional practices that enable it, we can also recognize that our own textual practices—from learning paradigms to editing manuscripts, from glossing poems to publishing anthologies of critical essays—mirror a complex politics of language and representation whose effects are already everywhere present in Old English literature.[5] Problems of vernacular textuality, interfaces of orality and literacy, discourses of secular and sacred society, dialogues of honor and sanctity colliding in the production of the self—all these complex vectors of force and influence have left their mark on the texts we read. We are more aware than ever that texts do not simply represent culture, they create it, and so we must remember as we read Anglo-Saxon literature that we are not simply looking *through* these texts at individuals and their society transparently depicted with photographic fidelity, but *at* the texts for signs of the work they once did in the culture that used them. If we can no longer take an innocently positivist stance toward the object of our work, we can at least be thankful for the odd congruence between the preoccupations of contemporary theory and the everyday practices of medieval philology.[6] The recognition of textual instability that is the hallmark of poststructuralist thought since Derrida can only make Anglo-Saxonists more attentive to the work we do in editing, glossing, translating, and establishing the material text, shoring up fragments against our ruins.

The essays in this collection offer modern readers some avenues of access to the study of Old English; focusing on the texts that are often encountered in an introductory or second-semester Old English class, they are meant to provoke discussion, answer questions, provide background, and occasionally startle the reader into appreciation for the complexity and energy of Anglo-Saxon studies. The essays take a number of approaches to their subjects and use a variety of different critical tools and vocabularies, from linguistics to psychoanalysis. Some essays provide a historical framework for general reading, while others discuss a single text in some detail. In addition to generous amounts of information and critical analysis, each essay provides an exemplary model of how contemporary readers grapple with these old, fragmented, and sometimes mysterious texts.

A number of the essays investigate common themes that are, I believe, ultimately related—the creation of English national identity, the uses of texts and the nature of literacy, the idea of the individual subject as an entity enmeshed in, yet separate from, its culture. These themes recur in these essays because they recur in the texts we read, and because they are, perhaps, the fundamental questions of all literary history: who are these people who wrote these books? What were they trying to say, and to whom? What made them write, and what consequences did this writing have? And what do we do when we assign boundaries to literary periods and group texts in anthologies and editions? Whose interests do we serve? What responsibility do we have to these texts, what obligations to our own place in history? When we engage with seriousness and reverence and humility in a deep contemplation of the literature of any vanished age, we eventually commit ourselves to a particular view of time and the self that is, ultimately, authenticating and affirming of both our shared humanity and our cultural contingency. We acknowledge the distance between ourselves and the past even as we accept the connections that inevitably bind us to the writers and readers of another age. We explore the difference between one culture and a temporally remote other, while affirming by virtue of our very exploration that there is a history of the human subject in its cultural setting whose development we can read and understand—there is a thread, however tenuous, that leads from there to here. We shape these texts by studying them, editing them, preserving them, interpreting them; they shape us no less thoroughly by the long perspective they take on our own cultural enterprises and expectations, and by the way we use them to validate, challenge, support, or escape from the present order of things.[7]

The collection begins with two essays, quite different in tone and approach, on the topic of reading and writing. These are such universal activities in modern life, so seemingly "natural" that it may be hard to imagine that the Anglo-Saxons were any different from us. Nicholas Howe's "Cultural Construction of Reading in Anglo-Saxon England" (1993) points out that our habits of reading are culturally determined; among the Anglo-Saxons and most medieval peoples, reading is a communal and social activity rather than a private, ruminative one. The very word *rædan* (from which

Modern English "read" is derived) means "to explain" or "to offer counsel" as often as it means "to interpret written characters." The oral, public, and communal act of giving counsel (*ræd*) and explaining obscurity (*rædels*) brings reading and interpretation into the heart of the social order. Bede's story of Cædmon shows one way in which reading and scriptural exegesis were conducted in a monastic setting and in a culture of restricted literacy. Cædmon's miraculous gifts, Howe points out, do not include a sudden ability to read—such a gift being apparently superfluous in the textual community of Hild's monastery. This sense of reading and writing as acts that create the community they serve should be central to our understanding both of Bede's work and of Alfred's, for both saw that unity was created not only through a common faith and a shared sense of history but also through a common language and a shared textual practice. Howe's essay reminds us that textual communities exist in many forms; we cannot assume that ways of reading and writing a thousand years ago are like our own.[8] As we read an Old English text in search of its audience, author, and context, we must remember that woven into the very fabric of its textual identity is the voice of an entire community.

We know the reading habits of the Anglo-Saxons primarily from the physical remains of their texts, from early runic inscriptions to eleventh-century vernacular homiletic anthologies, but we do not generally know how, when, by whom, or under what circumstances these texts were read. Susan Kelly's "Anglo-Saxon Lay Society and the Written Word" (1990) approaches the question of reading and writing from a perspective unfamiliar to most new students of Old English literature, the world of charters, royal writs, and government documents usually left to historians. Kelly's treatment of this material both opens a window onto a fascinating world of manuscript evidence—the textual remains of once-active ties of law, loyalty, and personal obligation—and compiles valuable information on practices of literacy, the necessary context and precondition for our interpretation of Old English literature. Charters and other pieces of documentary evidence, as Kelly presents them, preserve the outlines of social interactions and situated uses of written language, and in their remains we may discern the history of a developing reliance on records and texts. Charters, primarily ecclesiastical instruments, also reveal the close interdependence of royal bureaucracy and monastic and episcopal establishments—clerics provided the transcribers and the repositories of records, kings provided patronage and security and the grants of land that, typically, charters record. Cartularies show the slow growth of a new form of institutional and archival memory, subject both to verification and to forgery, drawn up with ceremony and deposited with solemnity in the church that thereby guaranteed its sanctity and its force.[9] From this new form of memory came, although only gradually, a new relationship between secular society and the written word. Ownership of land came to be associated with textual authority: more detailed records came to be kept of large estates and in some sense came to represent those estates—culminating in the great Norman survey of the Domesday book, which, it could be argued, is the greatest triumph of the Anglo-Saxon secular bureaucracy. We cannot understand the purpose or meaning of any Old English text until we consider the reasons for its deposition in writing and the people who might have read it; these basic questions of context and audience underlie all interpretive activity. Kelly's learned work provides absorbing and important background for our sense of the social world of Anglo-Saxon texts.

The intimate link between language and history is the subject of Sarah Foot's "Making of *Angelcynn:* English Identity Before the Norman Conquest" (1996). This exemplary historical study examines the role of Alfred the Great, king of the West-Saxons, in the forging of a national identity around the concept of a specifically "English" nation. Nations and their history are created by words, Foot suggests; new political arrangements (such as the incorporation of Mercia into the orbit of West-Saxon lordship) require new terminology to express them and new ideas about the past to explain them. Alfred's political rhetoric advanced the idea that all the Germanic people of England were one people, the *angelcynn*, or "English nation." The educational plan outlined in Alfred's prefatory letter to his translation of Gregory's *Pastoral Care* works as much to unite the disparate tribes under his sway behind a common language and cultural tradition as it does to restore Christian learning to a land that Alfred claimed had lost it. "Alfred's educational programme," Foot remarks, "could be interpreted as a conscious effort to shape an English imagination by disseminating beyond the court his ideas about the nature of 'Englishness' and his fictive interpretation of history through the works he determined the English should read." The Alfredian "nation"—Foot is careful not to use the term too narrowly and anachronistically—defined itself against outsiders (the Welsh and the Danes) by its common language, Christian religion, and shared history; this national self-portrait was, essentially, created by Alfred and his court from the examples of Bede and Gregory: "one Church, one people and one faith," as Foot describes it, "could prefigure a political unity." Alfred reinforced this unity by literary as well as political means; his promotion of English as a literary language was part of his struggle to unite the various Germanic peoples of the island under West-Saxon rule.[10] This

powerful myth survives today in our efforts to reconstruct the culture and
history of the Anglo-Saxons—many tribes and groups—largely from the
West-Saxon perspective. In that sense Alfred's political project has had a
long afterlife. Foot reminds us that language and literature, particularly
self-conscious reflections on literary history such as that found in Alfred's
preface to *Pastoral Care*, are never transparent factual representations, for
they inevitably arise from interested positions of advocacy and promote
specific political projects.

Of all such reflections on literary history, none has had more widespread dissemination than Bede's account of the poet Cædmon. This story
has become one of the touchstones of Old English literature; its account of
an unlettered cowherd who is given the miraculous gift of poetic song has
come to seem a natural place to begin almost any study of Old English poetic style or literary history. A cluster of three articles highlight different
yet equally rich approaches to this deceptively simple story. Katherine
O'Brien O'Keeffe's "Orality and the Developing Text of Caedmon's *Hymn*"
(1987) brings theories of orality (the literary and communicative practices
of societies before the adoption of writing) to a study of the practices of
manuscript copying. Ideas about oral composition have shaped our study of
individual poetry and of the literary history of the Anglo-Saxons.[11] Behind
these ideas, as important and indeed crucial as they have been, lie a great
many assumptions, too often unexamined, about the nature of reading and
textuality, poetry and performance. O'Brien O'Keeffe redirects this discourse to a study of the reception of Cædmon's *Hymn* rather than its production; she seeks the traces of orality in the "visual cues" such as lineation,
word division, and punctuation in fourteen surviving manuscript copies of
this work. "The differing use of these visual cues between Latin and Old
English will point to differences in expectations about reading Latin, an
almost purely textual language, and Old English, a living language only
newly being committed to writing." The various Latin poems in Bede's
Historia Ecclesiastica are presented with numerous visual cues to assist the
reader; the English text of Cædmon's *Hymn*, whether a marginal addition
to a Latin manuscript or an integral part of the Old English Bede, is not.
Neither word spacing, punctuation, nor capitalization help the reader deci-
pher the text. Moreover, the text of the English poem is less fixed, more
subject to variation by copyists, more likely to differ in design or wording
from other copies—the Latin is a bound text, the English a fluid work.
O'Brien O'Keeffe notes that the reading/copying of the scribes "is formula-dependent, in that the variants observe metrical and alliterative constraints, and context-defined, in that the variants produced arise within a

field of possibilities generated within a context of expectations." The variable nature of oral formulaic poetry influenced the reading and copying of this poem even after it became a written text. The text of Cædmon's *Hymn* is striking evidence for the ways in which literacy and orality were accommodated to one another in Anglo-Saxon England.[12]

Kevin Kiernan's intriguing argument in "Reading Cædmon's 'Hymn' with Someone Else's Glosses" (1990) is that we really cannot say whether the Old English *Hymn* as we have it is in fact a genuine relic of Cædmon's miraculous poetic corpus, or a bogus relic crafted from Bede's Latin paraphrase. Kiernan reminds us that Bede does not include the poem in his Latin *Historia Ecclesiastica;* he offers only a paraphrase of a few opening lines. Bede's interest is in the piety of Cædmon's life and the miracle of his gifts, not the precise words of his first poem. For most modern readers, of course, the reverse is true—out of our need for a sense of poetic origins we have promoted the nine lines of the vernacular *Hymn* to the center and moved Bede's hagiography to the margins. Examining the manuscript placement of the earliest texts of the *Hymn*, Kiernan observes that "Anglo-Saxon scribes did not view these versions, as we do today, as central texts." They are, in fact, more like glosses than carefully preserved poems, and Kiernan proceeds boldly to consider the possibility that the Old English version is indeed literally a gloss, a reverse translation of Bede's Latin paraphrase. The Old English translator of Bede who inserted a version of the *Hymn* into his text edited Bede's Latin to make the Old English verse seem at home: "the producer of the Old English *History* gave his readers in the tenth and eleventh centuries the first really believable, seeming authentic, text of Cædmon's 'Hymn' by concealing its actual history." This history is further concealed, Kiernan notes, by the text as it is published today: "for us, the endnote or marginal note, Cædmon's 'Hymn', has become the central poetic text while the old central prose text, Bede's Latin *History*, has become the endnote or the footnote." Both scholarly editions such as the *Anglo-Saxon Poetic Records* and works for the general reader like the *Norton Anthology of English Literature* offer highly selective presentations of the text, obscuring its actual history in favor of other editorial concerns, whether the presumption of an "early" West-Saxon dialect (extrapolated from various manuscript readings and the laws of historical linguistics) or the idea of oral-formulaic composition (for which Cædmon is, one might say, the poster boy). Kiernan's provocative essay reminds us how little we can objectively know about an Old English poem, how much depends upon critical history and readerly desire both in the past and in the present. The nine short lines of Cædmon's *Hymn* have done and continue to do strenu-

ous work for Old English studies, but Kiernan suggests that most of what
we think we know about this poem is built on a very unstable foundation.

Cædmon, as Bede tells it, was the first to make sacred poetry in English.
In effect it is to him, at least indirectly, that we owe the preservation of the
entire corpus of vernacular verse. As the story is usually told, however, one
central figure is overlooked or effaced: the abbess Hild, in whose monastery
the events of the story unfold. Clare Lees and Gillian Overing's challenging
essay "Birthing Bishops and Fathering Poets: Bede, Hild, and the Relations
of Cultural Production" (1994) seeks to correct this imbalance by reexam-
ining the stories of Hild and Cædmon, as told by Bede, in terms of "cultural
production"—both the production of value in the monastic system and the
assignment of value in modern scholarship. Cædmon's story is a fable of labor and literacy, education and bureaucracy, as much as it is a miracle of inspiration and an example of piety: "who sustains Cædmon, and whom, or
what, does Cædmon sustain?" Lees and Overing ask. One may answer that,
for many readers, Cædmon, an oral vernacular poet in a Latin text, sustains
the enterprise of Old English poetry by standing in for its anonymous cre-
ators, a role he apparently played in Anglo-Saxon times as he does today in
the *Norton Anthology of English Literature*. Absent in this account, Lees and
Overing point out, is the figure of Hild the abbess, whose story precedes
Cædmon's in Bede's narrative; "Bede and successive critics," they argue,
"have cast the myth of origins, literary and divine, as an ideological myth of
masculinism." Hild, a figure of considerable power and influence in her
day, is only metaphorically a "mother"; as Lees and Overing recount her
story, she is a willing participant in the monastic system's redefinition of reproduction as the (monastic) production of clergy. Her political prominence depends on her accommodation to the monastic system; her position
in Bede's narrative stresses her piety and her spiritual influence rather than
her power, and privileges the divine production of poets and prelates over
gendered human reproduction. The effacing of the prominence of women
in the spread of Christianity in England is akin, they argue, to the effacing
of the oral, vernacular, private world by the textual, Latin, public values of
Bede and later writers. The urgency of Lees and Overing's interrogation of
Bede's text is palpable—they seek to read between the lines of Bede's story,
to re-establish Hild in both history and literary history, and to appropriate
the story of Cædmon from its male-centered critical history in order to extrapolate alternative stories of the origins of Old English literature.

The importance of recognizing the position from which a text speaks
likewise informs Stephen White's "Kinship and Lordship in Early Medieval England: The Story of Sigeberht, Cynewulf, and Cyneheard" (1989).

White begins with a careful exposition of the plot of the Anglo-Saxon Chronicle entry for 757, one of the best-known stories in that work. The compact and closely told story, anomalous for the work in which it appears, has had enormous appeal for modern readers. It sketches a conflict of kinship and kingship, loyalty to family or leader, which many have likened to the stark tales of the Icelandic sagas. Such assumptions, White argues, are only loosely based on the text itself, whose conclusions are "narrower and more ambiguous" than many modern readers have expected; the Chronicle entry depicts a broad range of possible relations between a lord and his followers, including deposition (of Sigeberht) and murder (of ealdorman Cumbra) as well as suicidal loyalty. The story, White argues, is less an illustration of "the logic of loyalty" (as Cassidy and Ringler put it) and the triumph of the principle of lordship over that of kinship, than a darkly complex political conflict complicated by family ties. Distinguishing between good kin-slaying and bad becomes more difficult, more contingent on a host of factors no longer entirely recoverable to the modern reader. White suggests that modern readings of the story depend on the assumptions of nineteenth-century historiography, which postulated an historical movement in "progressive societies" from family to king, private to public, tribe to state, status to contract—in short, from forms of social order that privilege the personal to those which value the political. The story of Cynewulf and Cyneheard, he notes, does not necessarily provide evidence for this. History, he reminds us, is written by the victors, and historiography rewrites history from the privileged perspective of still other victors. "The authors and compilers of the *Anglo-Saxon Chronicle* were not passive witnesses to the events they chronicled," White argues. Our understanding of the story—even of its narrative tension and dramatic impact—depends in part on our acceptance of its ideology, the chronicler's telling of only one of many possible versions of the story.

Four essays that treat later Old English prose all address themselves, in one way or another, to the relations between religious and secular social orders. The tenth-century Benedictine revival re-established monasteries and religious life around a close alliance between court and cloister. New methods of education, new writings on the obligations of the Christian life, and a lively outpouring of homiletic and instructional prose mark the literature of this period.[13] One of the most powerful pieces of Old English prose from this era is Wulfstan's *Sermo Lupi ad Anglos*, a fiery sermon written in 1014 during a crisis of Danish invasion. Its resonant pulpit-pounding style is energetic to the point of intoxication; its stern denunciation of political and moral decline, and its accumulation of appalling detail, are meant to move its hearers to remorse and action.[14] The work is less often admired, as Stephanie Hollis notes in "The Thematic Structure of the *Sermo Lupi*" (1977), for its careful structure. Wulfstan, usually appreciated for his passionate rhetoric, is often thought to have worked by borrowing, reworking, and assembling prefabricated parts, processes that do not always lend themselves to planning and intellectual development, but Hollis returns to the surviving manuscript copies of the sermon to explore Wulfstan's structure and organization. The central theme of the sermon, which Hollis summarizes as "the nation's progression to disaster," is set out in a long opening sentence that sets the tone and suggests the structure of the rest of the sermon. By carefully distinguishing original from added readings, dependent from main clauses, conditional from declarative sentences, and by noting repetitions and variations on key words, Hollis delineates the care with which Wulfstan developed his theme. The effect of this work, she argues, is as much a product of its thoughtful structure and intellectual seriousness as of its emotionally charged subject and style.

For many modern students of Old English, the gloss to Ælfric's Latin *Colloquy on the Occupations* serves as one of the first introductions to grammar and vocabulary. Its usefulness and readability for beginning students are largely due to the fact that the Old English gloss, which of course follows the word order of its Latin text, was rearranged into idiomatic vernacular prose by Henry Sweet in his *First Steps in Anglo-Saxon* in 1897. The irony of this situation—a tenth-century monastic pedagogical work intended to introduce novices to the arcane language of Latin still does duty a millennium later to introduce students to the arcana of Old English because it was first glossed by a scribe and then later revised by an editor—has not been lost on scholars and readers.[15] Yet beneath the layers of irony and behind the apparent simplicity of the text, the *Colloquy* remains an ambiguous document, its primary questions still largely unanswered. What was the situation of its first audience? What is the purpose of its discussions of the various occupations? What social reality, if any, underlies it? What lesson (beyond the proper conjugation of the verb *loqui*) does it teach? Earl R. Anderson's "Social Idealism in Ælfric's *Colloquy*" (1974) addresses some of these questions and seeks to illuminate both the scholastic and the social purpose of this text. The debates in the *Colloquy*, Anderson notes, arise from a long intellectual background: the merchant's defense of the profit motive, the quarrels between the cook and the baker over their relative necessity to society, the whole idea of interdependent orders of society, are found in early traditions of school-debate and rhetorical exercise, and the questions they raise were discussed in works of political and moral philosophy. What-

ever they can or cannot tell us about the real lives of real Anglo-Saxons—
and the modern consensus is that they can really tell us very little—the debates in the *Colloquy* are not just grammatical exercises; in their pedagogical
setting they explore and celebrate the diverse but complementary gifts of
men. They are also, as Anderson notes, reflections of the Benedictine ideal
of a regular life of work and prayer "within the confines of an economically
self-sufficient community devoted to the service of God—a community
separate from the world but at the same time a microcosmic image of it, in
which each monastic craftsman contributes in his own way to the general
welfare." Anderson's discussion of "Benedictine idealism" helps us return
this work, so useful in the modern classroom, to its original context in the
Anglo-Saxon classroom. Remembering the world in which Ælfric wrote
encourages modern readers to recognize that his teaching of grammar carried with it an element of moral instruction.

　　The most common popular picture of the Anglo-Saxons may be that of
hearty thanes in ring-mail, feasting and drinking in the mead-hall, swing-
ing swords and hurling boasts. As with all stereotypes and sweeping gener-
alizations, there is perhaps a shred of truth in this: it is, at least, one version
of the way some Anglo-Saxons saw themselves, filtered through a coarser
modern sensibility and a late-romantic desire for heroic origins. But, as
Jocelyn Wogan-Browne points out in "The Hero in Christian Reception:
Ælfric and Heroic Poetry" (1995; slightly revised for publication here), this
is at best a distorted and partial picture of the literary landscape of the age.
In particular, Christian tradition offered alternative starting points for the
construction of the Anglo-Saxon self. Indeed, in much recent criticism "the
heroic is now more credibly seen as proceeding from within Christian culture and as having its own history of changing assimilations there." Contrasting and comparing Ælfric's *Life of Edmund* to the *Battle of Maldon* (com-
memorating a battle that was fought just a few years after Ælfric wrote his
text), Wogan-Browne notes that, despite some similarities of style and diction, the two texts are quite different in purpose and direction, social context and value. Though Ælfric's patron Æthelweard, for whom the text was
written, was himself faced with Viking attacks and the defense of his native
land, his response was to pay tribute rather than fight (like Byrhtnoth) or
face martyrdom (like Edmund); his own perception of the Germanic heroic
ethos, whatever it may have been, was filtered through a Christian sensibility and a recognition of late-tenth-century political and legal realities. Ælfric's inversion of the heroic ideal in *Edmund* can be read as a critique of the
militaristic ethos of the heroic code, but, as Wogan-Browne rightly points
out, it is not a Christian attack on an opposing and specifically Germanic

ideal of selfhood, because both the military/heroic and the pacifist/self-sacrificing ideal arise within the Christian tradition. "Ælfric subsumes and includes heroic values within a past structured not as an endless linear progression of deeds and deaths, but as shaped and typologically meaningful"; heroic action is not contrasted to Christian mercy but appropriated by it. Finally, reading *Maldon* as a curiously reticent and elegiac commemoration of that battle, Wogan-Browne speculates that Leoflæd, Byrhtnoth's daughter, was responsible for the poem's production—it may be that women, mothers and daughters and wives, were responsible for the transmission and preservation of secular poetry, while men like Ælfric reconstructed and deconstructed it in terms of public policy and spiritual formation. In the end, Wogan-Browne's essay reminds us that however large they may loom in the popular imagination, heroic codes, and all the constructions of the self built around violent self-assertion and loyalty under fire, were only a subsidiary part of the Anglo-Saxon imagination of the world, and these codes and ideals were themselves contested, constructed, and contextualized in surprising ways.

In "Didacticism and the Christian Community: The Teachers and the Taught" (1999), Clare Lees looks at how such constructions of the self were promoted through the teaching of Christian doctrine in homilies and letters, mainly in the work of Ælfric. Such teaching, she argues, created the Christian society by defining orthodoxy, prescribing and proscribing practices of devotion, and binding individuals together as a Christian community against a sinful excluded Other (pagans, heretics, Jews). The homilies of Ælfric bear witness to his mission as a teacher, his unwavering faith in the inherent rightness of orthodoxy, and his power to place his listeners as rational actors in a moral arena where their actions define them as Christians. While the meaning of his scriptural commentary is pointed toward understanding the Word of God, its purpose was directed to encouraging obedience to Christian law. The diversity of belief found in popular culture—poems, charms, folk remedies—were not tolerated by Ælfric; in his view there was one truth, manifest in everything, one human reason that allowed us to perceive it, and one church whose true members were thoroughly separate from paganism and heresy. By "relocating the literal within the spiritual," the Christian community that Ælfric preached both supercedes the individual and subsumes the family and other social organizations; as the individual becomes a believing subject, so the society becomes a Christian Body of Christ in which all are brothers, yet each retains his place in the hierarchies of class and gender. "These representatives of the Christian family, subject to the law of belief, incorporate but do not dismantle social hierar-

chies," Lees points out; " . . . the homiletic vision of the Christian community holds in place the harsh realities of Anglo-Saxon life, however charitable its moral discourse." Lees concludes her multivalent look at Christian
teaching practice by arguing that members of the Christian community are
created by action, the continual practices of correct ritual and moral virtue
that define the believer against the heathen. This ritual and action are social
in nature, not individual or personal; the self is created by its participation
in the community of faith: "there is no identity beyond the community,
which liturgical ritual confirms, or beyond the Christian behaviors that ritual maintains. . . . Belief is therefore foundational to identity in the homilies." As readers shaped by the assumptions of our own age we tend to see
the self as paramount and the community as a contingent collection of autonomous individuals, and assume this is the right and normal, indeed the
only possible, way of imagining the world. Lees reconsiders these notions
of identity and community from a different historical perspective; her arguments have important consequences for the way we consider the individual
in a medieval text, whether the historical actor, the author of a prose sermon, or the narrative "I" in a poem.

The remaining essays in this collection address themselves to Old English poetry. Much about this body of poetry remains unknowable and ir-
recoverable. We know far too little about authors and audiences, origins
and purposes, readers and reception. Moreover, the form in which we normally read these poems—the edited anthology—is dramatically different
from the form in which they were originally produced (either as performance or as a manuscript text for recitation or reading). As casual readers
we tend to take the authority of an edition on faith, trusting that what the
editor prints is what the author intended, and what the editor translates in
his glossary is what the words must have meant. This faith is, however, exactly that: a matter of trust rather than evidence. The recent interest in
electronic editions[16] suggests a desire on the part of readers and editors to
move beyond the misleading certainty of text on a page in order to present
Old English poetry in all its messy manuscript contingency. Most poetic
texts survive in only one manuscript, a copy of a lost original, whose fidelity
to its source we are unable to determine and whose coherence we are occasionally at a loss to understand. Editors are constantly called on to fill in
gaps, replace obscure readings, interpret ambiguities, punctuate, emend,
gloss, title, and in general perform all the services of mediation between a
unique and fragile original and a modern reproducible printed text.[17] The
editions we use, which are generally the place we start our reading and the
grounds on which we base our interpretations, are in fact themselves

the product of much reading and interpretation; they are the end result, not the starting point, of a long train of thought about the meaning of the text. Roy Leslie's "Editing of Old English Poetic Texts: Questions of Style" (1979) considers the importance of an understanding of poetic style in determining which readings of a manuscript text of a poem are original and which are errors. Paradoxically, our sense of Old English poetic style is itself derived from the very manuscripts whose style we are trying to analyze. Furthermore, when we talk about "style" in Old English we often mean two contradictory things—the characteristics of the poetry in general (variation, formulae, alliteration) without regard for the peculiar uses of any individual poet, or precisely these individual characteristics (the style of Cynewulf, for example, or the style of the *Beowulf*-poet) once the general qualities of OE verse have been subtracted. Style is, in other words, a difficult concept to define, much less to characterize, and still less to use as a tool for textual reconstruction.[18] Leslie reads carefully and closely, however, particularly in *The Wanderer* and *The Seafarer*, and notes places in which our sense of the poem's language and diction may lead us to suspect that the Exeter Book scribe has been unfaithful to his exemplar. An editor, Leslie notes, "has considerable powers to influence our understanding of a poem, and considerable opportunities to abuse that power." The more the reader is aware of the distance between the poem as it was written in a manuscript and the poem as we read it in an edition, and of the inescapable circularity of the processes by which our sense of the poetry is constructed, the less we will be susceptible to that abuse.[19]

It was sometimes thought in earlier days that most Old English poetry could be separated into layers of "pagan" and "Christian" composition, an early core of secular (usually heroic) values and a later shell of homiletic interpolation.[20] A poem like *The Seafarer* could be divided into two parts; the second didactic and Christian part could be discarded, as it is in Ezra Pound's translation.[21] More recent and more thoughtful readings of such poems recognize that secular and scriptural values are thoroughly interwoven, and that the influence of Latin culture and thought on vernacular poetry is deep and pervasive.[22] Malcolm Godden's "Anglo-Saxons on the Mind" (1985) demonstrates the richness of this comparative study of sources and influences in its exploration of early medieval conceptions of the mind in Latin and English prose and poetry. Threading his way through the obscure territory of early medieval psychology, clearing the thickets of near-synonyms and fine distinctions, Godden points out that two different traditions can be found in Anglo-Saxon England: the former, represented by Alcuin, Alfred, and Ælfric, reached toward a unified con-

cept of the mind and the soul, while the latter, reflected in the poetic vocabulary, emphasized the distinction between the two and connected the mind
to the passions as well as the intellect. Alcuin, he notes, differs from Augustine in his identification of the mind with the soul; this idea persists in Alfred's translation of Boethius's *De consolatione Philosophiae* and a philosophical text in Ælfric's *Lives of Saints*. This tradition specified that the human
rational capacity is identical to the immortal and divinely created spirit, capable of consciously turning to evil in the exercise of its free will. A different conception of the self can be found in the vocabulary of Old English poetry: there the word *mod* means "courage," "mind," "pride," "not so much
the intellectual, rational faculty but something more like an inner passion
or willfulness, an intensification of the self that can be dangerous." Godden
turns his investigation of these Anglo-Saxon conceptions of the self to two
of the most psychologically complex Old English poems, *The Wanderer* and
The Seafarer. There the mind is seen as a volatile and potentially destructive
inner drive, self-assertive and unruly, needing to be controlled by the conscious self, and both are distinguished from the soul that leaves the body at
death. It may be impossible to recover the conditions under which the Anglo-Saxon subject conceived itself; Godden's careful study of vocabulary,
source, and tradition, however, helps us understand not only the inner
landscape of Old English literary self-presentation, at the crossroads of native and Latin models, but also the complex cultural world in which the literature lived.

The poignant philosophical lament of *The Wanderer* is raised along one
of the most complex borders in any society, the boundary between the individual subject and the group. Much cultural crisis arises from the tensions
between the various ways individuals define themselves: by membership in
and identification with various kinds of social collectives (family, peers,
class, gender, nation), by a sense of the self as having a kind of depth in
which one might find both one's universal humanity and a poignant alienation from others, by the need to assert some distinction between oneself
and other members of a group—to stand out while fitting in. Consequently
a great deal of literary work elicits and patrols this boundary between
"subject positions" and the things to which and by which they are subjected
and positioned. Two essays examine *The Wanderer* from this perspective.
Robert Bjork's "*Sundor æt Rune:* The Voluntary Exile of The Wanderer"
(1989) suggests that the images of exile in that poem are themselves part of
a participation in a culture; even the lament for a lost world can affirm that
world, reinforcing cultural stability by the depiction of the misery of its absence. By emphasizing repetitive word patterns in the poem Bjork suggests

that the narrative persona undergoes a shift in perspective that "transforms the inferior, world-bound, essentially hopeless exile track of the Germanic world into the superior, heaven-bound, hope-filled exile track of the Christian faith." Margrét Gunnarsdóttir Champion's "From Plaint to Praise: Language as Cure in 'The Wanderer'" (1998) regards the poem as a kind of "spiritual autobiography" written at the intersection of language, culture, and the self. Modern psychoanalytical theory provides Gunnarsdóttir with an explanatory paradigm of extraordinary force and clarity for the poem's plotting out of the course of grief, "the dialectic of form and desire"— mourning for a lost lord, a lost world, a lost idiom of the self-moving from loss to acceptance to spiritual health and growth. Working through his grief by speaking, the persona of *The Wanderer* enacts the pattern of psychoanalysis, naming and creating metaphorical displacements for his objects of loss. Gunnarsdóttir argues that the classic problem of speakers and speech boundaries in the poem—there are clearly several voices, real or imagined, but their boundaries are by no means universally recognized[23]— is part of its elegiac work, the "multi-dimensional search for a consoling stability." This search moves through several levels. It begins with the commonplaces of formulaic depictions of exile, stock items in a poetic repertory that offer no access to the authentic self, "a tattered blanket hurled over the urgency of need." It continues through the perception of the fragility of cultural consolations, the realities of war and death, simultaneously embracing and rejecting the possibility of creating a stable self from the unstable values and symbols of the world. Finally, in the utterance of its stoic wisdom, Gunnarsdóttir argues that the narrative persona is empowered to symbolize, to recognize that the human subject is founded on death and loss, given urgency and authenticity by the approaching end of the world. Arguing against critics who read the poem's Christian conclusion as a simple solution to the wanderer's existential dilemma, Gunnarsdóttir writes: "This story is not conventionally progressive: it neither registers heroic conformity, like so many Norse sagas do, nor religious conversion, an insight into transcendence. Instead 'The Wanderer' is a story of self-creation, generically closer to modernist 'portraits' of the artist as cultural exile than to either heroic legend or Augustinian autobiography." The speaker does not reject his culture's offer of consolation—this would be another fragmentation into narcissism—but claims his own consolation within a broader view of the value of aesthetic speech, the "true word" that names the self and its lost home.

Peter Orton's "The Form and Structure of *The Seafarer*" (1991) begins by noting of this poem that "most of the individual sentences are easy enough to understand in isolation; the problem lies in their presentation as parts of an autobiographical narrative." Resisting the natural inclination to make sense of the poem by focusing only on its more transparent passages, Orton reads the whole poem carefully and thoroughly, working to "make sense of what is said in the order in which it is said." Doing so constrains Orton to read the poem in terms of personal development, and to reject interpretations of the early parts of the poem that rely on attitudes revealed in the later parts of the poem, as well as interpretations that depend on the nuances or connotations of words found in other contexts elsewhere in Old English literature. This ascetic hermeneutic yields interesting results; Orton's self-contained reading of the poem reveals not only the considerable gaps in the possibilities of interpretation but the surprising coherence of much of the poem's diction and character development. Setting an emblematic opposition between the life of the seafarer and the landlubber, the poem leaves deliberately vague the background and motive for the narrator's sea voyages—as often in the "elegies," we are given tantalizing glimpses of a contextualizing story. These poems seem like a collapsed narrative, a still photograph of a moving image, obliquely suggesting threads of action and event that are not developed in the text. The elegies are, as it were, soliloquies in a drama whose action takes place offstage and whose narrative trajectory the audience is forced to construct for itself. Orton's reading, however, stays close to the text, carefully sorting out the jump-cuts, psychological conflicts, and redoublings of the narrative voice, distinguishing between sections of the poem in terms of the narrator's self-projections into the past and future, the development of his efforts to "hammer out a new identity." Orton argues that the poem underwrites Christian virtue by the terms of secular society—by making the misery of a sea voyage into a form of virtue, for example, or urging his audience to gain *lof mid englum* by brave deeds against the devil. He suggests that the poem resolves its own crisis of representation by the recasting of oppositions and the repositioning of the narrator as a mediator between secular and spiritual concerns. In general, Orton's principle of reading the poem in order and at face value tends to limit allegorical or symbolic possibilities; although it may seem a harsh discipline in the face of the poem's own extravagant invitations to allegoresis,[24] this is a valuable check on our tendency to read the poem as wholly metaphorical. By staying within the poem, Orton discovers that the poem is itself about boundaries, confines, expectations, and reinterpretation: "to understand *The Seafarer* properly we need to appreciate the situation of the Anglo-Saxon outsider, the problem of self-definition that the individual faced once he stepped outside the realm of conventionally received experience, and the hold over him that traditional social values exerted."

The elegiac mood is found at almost every turn in Old English litera-ture, from *Beowulf* to the homilies to the short dramatic monologues now called "elegies" found in the Exeter Book. And yet for all the ubiquity of the elegiac tone, the meaning, purpose, and audience of the elegies is as myste-rious as ever.[25] These works appear at times to be situated between the heroic and the Christian world, between the values of the Germanic hall and the virtues of asceticism and spiritual renunciation. In them we can sense, perhaps as clearly as anywhere in Anglo-Saxon culture, the tensions and accommodations of secular and religious cultures, but our understand-ing of the meaning of these works is (as usual) hindered by our lack of knowledge about their cultural context. Among the most ambiguous of the elegies, largely because of its female first-person speaker, its cryptic vocab-ulary, and its puzzling lack of resolution (spiritual or otherwise), is the Ex-eter Book's *Wife's Lament*. Despite its lack of a spiritual or homiletic turn such as that found in *The Wanderer* and *The Seafarer,* Shari Horner suggests in "En/Closed Subjects: *The Wife's Lament* and the Culture of Early Me-dieval Female Monasticism" (1994) that this mysterious work, too, should be read from within the development of monastic culture. The poem's fe-male speaker, exiled, isolated, and consigned to some sort of wooded bar-row, is produced by a "discourse of enclosure" that recalls and reflects the conditions of female monasticism, the increasing claustration of female re-ligious in the Anglo-Saxon period. Drawing on the theories of Judith But-ler, Horner argues that the speaker is "gendered" by her very confinement and restriction; while the male speakers of *The Wanderer* and *The Seafarer* are defined by their wide-ranging and wandering—only their thoughts are fettered and contained—the speaker of *The Wife's Lament* is quite markedly immobile, free of speech but bound in body, and in this her position is strik-ingly like that of an Anglo-Saxon woman religious. Her language, Horner argues, might have registered to an early audience as akin to that of a nun; her situation might have been intelligible by analogy to the known world of cloistered women religious, her speech a kind of matins (*uhtsang*), her death-in-life a familiar trope of the enclosed religious life. Horner raises provocative questions of diction, register, connotation, and context; her re-flections on the poem can help us understand its resonances to its original audience.

For many modern readers it is not easy to enter the imaginative world of an Anglo-Saxon religious poem like *The Dream of the Rood*. Issues of sin and salvation, faith and devotion, incarnation and atonement, may seem dim and distant. Likewise the practices of medieval religion—more important, it may be argued, than its theology—are unknown or misunderstood. Sandra McIntire's "The Devotional Context of the Cross Before A.D. 1000" (1986) offers some important background to the reading of the *Dream of the Rood* and helps us understand not only what the poem means but how it fit into its early Anglo-Saxon context. Devotion to the cross, the physical memorial of the passion of Christ, was an important aspect of the early medieval church, arising from the finding of the relic of the True Cross in Jerusalem in the early fourth century: venerating the wood of the cross was part of the liturgy of Good Friday; relics of the cross were enclosed in gilded shrines which no doubt resembled the jeweled speaker of the *Dream of the Rood*; large standing stone crosses like the Ruthwell Cross were gathering points, boundary markers, and preaching posts. All believers were encouraged to make the Sign of the Cross on their bodies on every occasion; the performance of this gesture was widely held to have almost magical efficacy against the wiles of demons. McIntire also describes the "cosmological Cross," an image of the cross towering into the sky and extending across the whole world, encompassing the four directions and uniting heaven and earth. In our secular age it may be difficult to imagine the power of the Cross as a religious symbol, and so we are in danger of reading a poem like *The Dream of the Rood* in a vacuum, isolating it like a museum specimen in a glass case, appreciating its aesthetics while utterly missing its purpose and power. McIntire tries to do little more than sketch the background of this omnipresent figure in Anglo-Saxon religious life, but even the few hints she offers suggest the depth of meaning this symbol must have held for the first readers of the poem.

Carol Braun Pasternack's "Stylistic Disjunctions in *The Dream of the Rood*" (1984) reads across the borders between the poem's sections to explore the ways in which we construct meaning from moments of difference. The poem is marked by its strong parallels and repetitions within sections and by equally strong shifts in tone from one section to another. The differences between sections of this poem are so great, she notes, that many critics have been moved to ascribe the ending of the poem (after line 78) to another and later author, while other critics, more interested in unity, have discussed the echoes and parallels between different sections of the poem. Pasternack, however, returns our focus to the disjunctions in style between one part of the poem and another, boundaries which divide the poem into sections and create analogical relations of theme between them: "the verbal echoes point to the resemblances among these parts and the disjunctions demarcate them, point to the distinctions." The poem "is about the idea of the cross, presented according to several different perspectives." Drawing attention to patterns of syntax which distinguish one section from another, Pasternack shows that word-order plays a great role in the creation of poetic meaning—in the first section the subject-verb pattern is used, for example, but when the cross begins to speak the verb-initial structure predominates. Through these strongly marked sections a multiple perspective is offered to the reader: "each section provides some insight, forms one strategy by which the meaning of the Crucifixion can be approached." Pasternack's close reading of grammar and syntax suggests that the art of this luminous poem arises from within the structures of the language itself.[26]

Two final essays present different understandings of the heroic *Battle of Maldon*. This poem, as many critics have noted, seems to partake fully of the heroic ethos and tone, despite the fact that it was written, at the earliest, in the last decade of the tenth century, a time when the "heroic age," to the extent that any such time ever existed outside of the literary imagination, was a distant memory. The poet might well have called on the ideal of Christian sacrifice and death, such as that found in Ælfric's Life of St. Edmund, to infuse the defeat of Byrhtnoth and his companions with the sanctity and triumph of the martyrs' witness to the faith; he does not do so, and instead reimagines an "epic" or heroic warrior ideal from the heart of a culture steeped in the stories of Christian sacrifice. The artistry required to achieve this feat of historical reimagination is detailed by Fred C. Robinson in "God, Death, and Loyalty in *The Battle of Maldon*" (1979). Through a detailed reading of the prayer Byrhtnoth utters just before his death, Robinson argues that the poet has emphasized the terror of particular judgment—the physical struggle between angels and demons for possession of the soul at the body's death—to reinvest the moment of death with the anxiety and insecurity necessary for heroic action to have meaning. Robinson suggests that the poet alludes to the inscrutability of God's judgments throughout the poem, rendering his moral landscape with dark shadows and unseeable depths: there are no supporting angels, no comforting visions; no divine messenger appears to Byrhtnoth assuring him of his starry crown. The allusions to God that do appear generally invoke the uncertainty of His favor and the unknown quality of His control of events. "These allusions to God in the poem, along with the dying prayer of Byrhtnoth, suggest a world devoid of the certainties which orthodox Christianity is usually thought to bring and one in which heroism is achieved at a dear price and is rich with meaning." Robinson also carefully reads the speech of the Viking messenger to explore the ways in which the poet has rein-

vented the theme of loyalty, itself a kind of anachronism in the historical reality of the 990s. The messenger's divisiveness is countered by Byrhtnoth's
unifying rejoinder; the bond of loyalty imagined by the poet proceeds from
relatives to retainers to those not connected personally with their leader at
all. Loyalty is conceived in the poem as broadly national and social, not personal, and the absence of loyalty is regarded, as in Wulfstan's *Sermo Lupi*, as
both the cause and the most horrifying manifestation of social chaos. Asserting the supreme virtue of loyalty in the face of cosmic uncertainty, the
poet creates the conditions under which secular heroism again makes sense.

John Niles' "*Maldon* and Mythopoesis" (1994) notes that *The Battle of
Maldon* is a seemingly perfect blend of historical reportage and heroic lay;
the poem is artful but not *too* artful, heroic in tone and style but conforming, apparently, to historical fact. Its apparent message of honorable but
suicidal loyalty in the face of defeat has spoken powerfully to many readers
and given the poem a firm place in the literature of English militarism. To
these tendencies and traditional readings Niles offers a powerful challenge:
we are tempted to read *Maldon* as a relatively honest account of actions and
attitudes in late-tenth-century England, but Niles suggests instead that we
should understand *Maldon* as an example of myth-making, a symbolic account of and justification for the unpopular and unsuccessful policies of appeasement during the reign of Æthelred II. The defeat at Maldon, Niles
argues, was a turning point in the English fortunes against the invading
Danes. Using the evidence of the *Anglo-Saxon Chronicle* and other annals
and histories, Niles reconstructs both the consequences of Byrhtnoth's
death on England in the 990s and the impact this event must have had on
English morale and policy. Arguing that the poem was written shortly after
the battle it commemorates—Æthelred is depicted, for example, as a king
worth fighting for, his reputation not yet sullied—Niles suggests that the
poem's purpose was to present an argument in favor of the policy of paying
tribute to the Vikings. It presents this message by glorifying the death of
Byrhtnoth, which subtly suggests the wisdom of compromise: if the valiant
Byrhtnoth could not defeat the Vikings, how could anyone else? Byrhtnoth's defeat and death are presented in the vivid colors and outsized gestures of myth in order to argue a political position; the poem "uses a particular event, drawn from history though rendered schematically, as the core
of a story that gives coherent literary expression to major issues of the poet's
day." *Maldon* celebrates heroic loyalty and resistance even as it shows the futility of this doomed but glorious attitude, but it does not, Niles insists, encourage suicidal loyalty. The theme of its bloody conclusion is vengeance,
not martyrdom, "the pragmatics of violence and accommodation in a world

that was spinning rapidly out of English control." This challenging reinterpretation of *Maldon* asks us to view the poem in its historical context, to imagine the interests and ideals of its original audience, and to consider how such a poem may have functioned in its first setting.

As all the essays in this collection show, the meaning of a work of literature is never transparently *there*, waiting to be discovered by our reading like some new land awaiting an explorer. Meaning is a collaboration between a text, its historical situations (both then and now), and its readers, and any and all of these elements may be complicated, compromised, conflicted, and conditioned by factors no longer entirely discernible. We do not simply stumble upon meanings in the thickets of a text, excavate them from the underbrush and debris and deposit them, cleaned and labeled, in the museum of our interpretations. Meanings live; they move and change from different angles. Nor is it sufficient any longer simply to appropriate a few privileged elements of Old English culture to validate our own. Yet despite the fragmentary nature of the evidence, and all the gaps and discontinuities between medieval texts and our world—what has been called the "alterity" of the Middle Ages—it is still possible to make the leap in imagination from one age to another through patience, sympathy, knowledge, and attention to detail. Each of the essays in this collection offers a kind of blueprint for thinking about Old English, a model for how this imaginative leap may be carried out. Each is also a point of departure for further thought and study, new questions and methods. The related themes explored in a number of these essays may inspire reading in other Anglo-Saxon texts, from such well-known works as Bede's account of the conversion of the English or Ælfric's lives of saints to lesser-known pieces like medical recipes and works of instruction, or the eschatological poetry of *Judgment Day*, or the lovely *Advent* lyrics. The texts that make up the instructional canon of Old English are only a small part of the surviving body of material that informs our understanding of the period. Likewise these essays are only a sample of the wealth of recent scholarship on Old English. I hope that these essays may inspire readers to seek them out and, ultimately, to chart their own course through this rich and strange territory.

Notes

1. An example of how far one may go even with a lack of understanding can be found in E. G. Stanley, "Two Old English Poetic Phrases Insufficiently Understood for Literary Criticism: *þing gehegan* and *seono gehegan*," in Daniel G. Calder, ed., *Old English Poetry: Essays on Style* (Berkeley, 1979), 67–90.

2. Reflections on this topic may be found in the essays in Allen J. Frantzen and John D. Niles, eds., *Anglo-Saxonism and the Construction of Social Identity* (Gainesville, Fla., 1997).

3. For examples of Anglo-Saxonists engaged in contemporary theory, see the essays in Allen Frantzen, ed., *Speaking Two Languages: Traditional Disciplines and Contemporary Theory in Medieval Studies* (Albany, 1991).

4. Hayden White, *The Content of the Form: Narrative Discourse and Historical Representation* (Baltimore, 1987).

5. Frederic Jameson, *The Political Unconscious: Narrative as a Socially Symbolic Act* (Ithaca, 1981). For reflections on this topic in *Beowulf*, see John D. Niles, "Locating *Beowulf* in Literary History," *Exemplaria* 5 (1995), 79–109, and Carol Braun Pasternack, "Post-Structuralist Theories: The Subject and the Text," in Katherine O'Brien O'Keeffe, ed., *Reading Old English Texts* (Cambridge, 1997), 170–91.

6. For the end of positivism in medieval studies, see the essays on the so-called "new philology" in *Speculum* 65 (1990); further reflections are in Daniel Donoghue, "Language Matters," in O'Brien O'Keeffe, ed., *Reading Old English Texts*, 59–78. New directions in philology are suggested by Martin Irvine, *The Making of Textual Culture: 'Grammatica' and Literary Theory, 350–1100* (Cambridge, 1994); theories of textual editing are discussed by David Greetham, *Textual Transgressions: Essays Toward the Construction of a Biobibliography* (New York, 1998).

7. On the mutual interdependence of texts and readers in literary history, see, among others, Allen J. Frantzen, *Desire for Origins: New Language, Old English, and Teaching the Tradition* (New Brunswick, N.J., 1990).

8. Further thoughts on literacy among the Anglo-Saxons may be found in D. A. Bullough, "The Educational Tradition in England from Alfred to Ælfric: Teaching *Utriusque Linguae*," *La scuola nell'occidente latino dell'alto medioevo. Settimane di studio del Centro Italiano de studi sull'alto medioevo* 19 (1972), 453–94; Patrick Wormald, "The Uses of Literacy in Anglo-Saxon England and Its Neighbours," *Transactions of the Royal Historical Society* 5th ser. 27 (1977), 95–114, Seth Lerer, *Literacy and Power in Anglo-Saxon Literature* (Lincoln, 1991), and George Brown, "The Dynamics of Literacy in Anglo-Saxon England," *Bulletin of the John Rylands Library* 77 (1995), 109–142.

9. For more on this topic in later centuries, see M. T. Clanchy, *From Memory to Written Record*, 2d ed. (Oxford, 1993).

10. Alfred's preface is also discussed by Jennifer Morrish, "King Alfred's Letter as a Source on Learning in England in the Ninth Century," in P. E. Szarmach, ed., *Studies in Earlier Old English Prose* (Albany, 1986), 87–107. See also Janet Bately, "Old English Prose Before and During the Reign of Alfred," *Anglo-Saxon England* 17 (1988), 93–138.

11. See, most importantly, F. P. Magoun, "The Oral-Formulaic Character of Anglo-Saxon Narrative Poetry," *Speculum* 28 (1953), 446–67. See also John Miles Foley, *The Theory of Oral Composition: History and Methodology* (Bloomington, IN, 1988), 65–74, and *Oral-Formulaic Theory and Research: An Introduction and Annotated Bibliography* (New York, 1985), Alexandra Hennessey Olsen, "Oral-Formulaic Research in Old

English Studies: I," *Oral Tradition* 1 (1986), 548–606 and "II," *Oral Tradition* 3 (1988), 138–90, Roberta Frank, "The Search for the Anglo-Saxon Oral Poet," *Bulletin of the John Rylands Library* 75 (1993), 11–36, and more recently Paul Acker, *Revising Oral Theory: Formulaic Composition in Old English and Old Icelandic Verse* (New York, 1997), and the essays in A. N. Doane and C. B. Pasternack, eds., *Vox Intexta: Orality and Textuality in the Middle Ages* (Madison, 1991). Still useful are the general reflections on orality found in W. Ong, *Orality and Literacy: the Technologizing of the Word* (London, 1982), and "Orality, Literacy, and Medieval Textualization," *NLH* 16 (1984), 1–11.

12. The ideas in O'Brien O'Keeffe's article were further developed in her book *Visible Song: Transitional Literacy in Old English Verse* (Cambridge, 1990).

13. The classic study of this period remains David Knowles, *The Monastic Order in England, 940–1216*, 2d Ed. (Cambridge, 1966); see also the essays in Barbara Yorke, ed., *Bishop Æthelwold: His Career and Influence* (Woodbridge, 1988), and David Parsons, ed. *Tenth-Century Studies: Essays in Commemoration of the Millenium of the Council of Winchester and Regularis Concordia* (Chichester, 1975).

14. An interesting study of Wulfstan's preaching style in relation to its delivery is Andrew Orchard, "Crying Wolf: Oral Style and the *Sermones Lupi*," *ASE* 21 (1992), 239–64.

15. See the insightful essay of Nicholas Howe, "Historicist Approaches," in O'Brien O'Keeffe, ed., *Reading Old English Texts*, 79–100.

16. The most prominent of which is Kevin Kiernan's *Electronic Beowulf* (Ann Arbor, 1999).

17. The classic study on this topic is Kenneth Sisam, "The Authority of Old English Poetical Manuscripts," in *Studies in the History of Old English Literature* (Oxford, 1953), 29–44; see also Douglas Moffat, "Anglo-Saxon Scribes and Old English Verse," *Speculum* 67 (1992), 805–27, and R. M. Liuzza, "The Texts of the Old English *Riddle 30*," *JEGP* 87 (1988), 1–15. Further thoughts on editing may be found in E. G. Stanley, "Unideal Principles of Editing Old English Verse," *PBA* 70 (1984), 231–273; Michael Lapidge, "Textual Criticism and the Literature of the Anglo-Saxons," *Bulletin of the John Rylands Library* 73 (1991), 17–45; and Katherine O'Brien O'Keeffe, "Texts and Works: Some Historical Questions on the Editing of Old English Verse," in J. N. Cox and L. J. Reynolds, eds., *New Historical Literary Study: Essays on Reproducing Texts, Representing History* (Princeton, 1993), 54–68. The importance of punctuation is stressed by Bruce Mitchell, "The Dangers of Disguise: Old English Texts in Modern Punctuation," *RES* 31 (1980), 385–413, rpt. in Bruce Mitchell, *On Old English: Selected Papers* (Oxford, 1988), 172–202.

18. See Daniel G. Calder, "The Study of Style in Old English Poetry: A Historical Introduction," In Calder, ed., *Old English Poetry: Essays on Style*, 1–65.

19. Leslie's work on *The Wanderer* was enthusiastically analyzed by Bruce Mitchell, the most prominent scholar of Old English syntax, in several essays over the course of his distinguished career; these may be found in his *On Old English*. See particularly "Some Syntactical Problems in *The Wanderer*," 99–117, "An Old English Syntactical Reverie: *The Wanderer*, lines 22 and 34–36," 118–125; "More Musings on

Old English Syntax," 126–133, and "Linguistic Facts and the Interpretation of Old English Poetry," 152–171.

20. For the earlier history of this attitude see E. G. Stanley, *The Search for Anglo-Saxon Paganism* (Cambridge, 1975).

21. Pound's vigorous translation of *The Seafarer* is found in his *Personae* (New York, 1926), pp. 64–66. For an appreciation see Fred C. Robinson, "'The Might of the North': Pound's Anglo-Saxon Studies and *The Seafarer*," in Fred C. Robinson, *The Tomb of Beowulf and Other Essays on Old English* (Oxford, 1993), 239–258.

22. An example of this influence, and the initial inspiration for Malcolm Godden's essay reprinted below, is found in Peter Clemoes, "*Mens absentia cogitans* in *The Seafarer* and *The Wanderer*," in Derek Pearsall and R. A. Waldron, eds., *Medieval Literature and Civilization: Studies in Memory of G. N. Garmonsway* (London, 1969), 62–77. For more general discussion of source study in Old English, see Katherine O'Brien O'Keeffe, "Source, Method, Theory, Practice: On Reading Two Old English Verse Texts," *Bulletin of the John Rylands Library* 76 (1994), 51–73, and D. G. Scragg, "Source Study," in O'Brien O'Keeffe, ed., *Reading Old English Texts*, 39–58.

23. See Gerald Richman, "Speakers and Speech Boundaries in *The Wanderer*," *JEGP* 81 (1982), 469–79; rpt. in Katherine O'Brien O'Keeffe, ed., *Old English Shorter Poems: Basic Readings* (New York, 1994), 303–18.

24. See, for example, Daniel G. Calder, "Setting and Mode in *The Seafarer* and *The Wanderer*," *NM* 72 (1971), 264–75; Frederick S. Holton, "Old English Sea Imagery and the Interpretation of The *Seafarer*," *Yearbook of English Studies* 12 (1982), 208–17; John F. Vickrey, "Some Hypotheses Concerning *The Seafarer*, Lines 1–47," *Archiv für das Studium der neueren Sprachen und Literaturen* 219 (1982), 57–77, rpt. in O'Brien O'Keeffe, ed., *Old English Shorter Poems: Basic Readings*, 251–79.

25. Some definitions are offered by Anne Klinck, "The Old English Elegy as a Genre," *English Studies in Canada* 10 (1984), 129–40; a critique is found in María José Mora, "The Invention of the Old English Elegy," *English Studies* 76 (1995), 129–39.

26. Pasternack's ideas are further developed in *The Textuality of Old English Poetry* (Cambridge, 1995).

Abbreviations

ANQ	*American Notes & Queries*
ASE	*Anglo-Saxon England*
ASPR	*Anglo-Saxon Poetic Records*
BL	British Library
BMF	E. A. Bond, *Facsimiles of Ancient Charters in the British Museum*, 4 vols. (London, 1873–78)
CCSL	*Corpus Christianorum, Series Latina* (Turnhout)
ChLA	Albert Bruckner and Robert Marichal, *Chartae Latinae Antiquiores: Facsimile Edition of the Latin Charters prior to the Ninth Century*, I– (Olten and Lausanne, 1954–)
CLA	E. A. Lowe, *Codices Latini Antiquiores: A Palaeographcal Guide to Latin Manuscripts prior to the Ninth Century*, I–XI plus Supplement (Oxford, 1935–71)
CSEL	*Corpus Scriptorum Ecclesiasticorum Latinorum* (Vienna)
CUL	Cambridge University Library
EEMF	*Early English Manuscripts in Facsimile*
EETS	Early English Text Society
	o.s. Original Series
	s.s. Supplemental Series
EHD	*English Historical Documents*, I: *c. 500–1042*, ed. Dorothy Whitelock (2d ed., London, 1979)
EHR	*English Historical Review*
ES	*English Studies*

HE	Bede, *Historia Ecclesiastica Gentis Anglorum*
JEGP	*Journal of English and Germanic Philology*
L&L	*Learning and Literature in Anglo-Saxon England*, ed. M. Lapidge and H. Gneuss (Cambridge, 1985)
MÆ	*Medium Ævum*
MGH	*Monumenta Germaniae Historica*
MLN	*Modern Language Notes*
MLQ	*Modern Language Quarterly*
MLR	*Modern Language Review*
MP	*Modern Philology*
ms	manuscript
MS	*Mediaeval Studies*
N&Q	*Notes & Queries*
NLH	*New Literary History*
NM	*Neuphilologische Miteillungen*
OE	Old English
OED	*Oxford English Dictionary*
OSF	*Facsimiles of Anglo-Saxon Manuscripts*, ed. W. B. Sanders, 3 vols., Ordnance Survey (Southampton, 1878–84)
PBA	*Proceedings of the British Academy*
PG	*Patrologia Graeca*, ed. J.-P. Migne, 168 vols. (Paris, 1857–68)
PL	*Patrologia Latina*, ed. J.-P. Migne, 221 vols. (Paris, 1844–64)
PMLA	*Publication of the Modern Languages Association*
RES	*Review of English Studies*
SP	*Studies in Philology*
TRHS	*Transactions of the Royal Historical Society*

The Cultural Construction of Reading in Anglo-Saxon England

NICHOLAS HOWE

> The house was quiet and the world was calm.
> The reader became the book; and summer night
>
> Was like the conscious being of the book.
> The house was quiet and the world was calm.

IN these lines from "The House was Quiet and the World was Calm,"[1] Wallace Stevens offers a particularly modern description of reading as a private, meditative transaction between reader and book. The act of reading becomes a scene in which the reader is alone, distanced from the claims of domestic and public life. What is read is specifically a book, that is, the material form texts assume in a world shaped both by the technology of printing and by Romantic notions of the self. Thus, as Stevens says, the book as an object possesses "conscious being." Under these conditions, the poet's claim that "the reader became the book" expresses a sense of causation that turns on the double meaning of "become": the reader takes on the form of the book by suiting or complimenting it. The act of reading imposes a trance-like concentration on the reader so that "The words were spoken as if there was no book." A characteristically Stevensian trope, the "as if" of this line asserts its opposite, the inescapable presence of the book in the scene of reading. This concentration is necessary because the reader "wanted much most to be / The scholar to whom his book is true." Stevens closes the poem by claiming audaciously that "truth in a calm world . . . Is the reader leaning late and reading there."

With its chastened, even mundane, direction, "The House was Quiet and the World was Calm" asserts our shared belief that we read best alone, at night, becoming our book, desiring to be the perfect reader we honor as the "scholar." In this way, the poem would have seemed incomprehensible to a medieval reader shaped by classical practices and texts as they were absorbed into Christian culture. For it is precisely the quiet and solitude of Stevens's reader that would have disturbed a medieval reader accustomed to reading as a public, spoken act performed within what Brian Stock calls a "textual community":

> What was essential for a textual community, whether large or small, was simply a text, an interpreter, and a public. The text did not have to be written; oral record, memory, and reperformance sufficed. Nor did the public have to be fully lettered. Often, in fact, only the *interpres* had a direct contact with literate culture, and, like the twelfth-century heretic Peter Waldo, memorized and communicated his gospel by word of mouth.[2]

As the inclusion of orality proves, Stock's use of community is not primarily, if at all, metaphoric; it refers to an actual group of readers, listeners and interpreters. Under these conditions, reading and interpreting texts has the social effect of creating a community in which "individuals who previously had little else in common were united around common goals." Such a community depends upon but also in turn creates "a general agreement on the meaning of a text."[3]

This sense of reading as a communal act, so hauntingly alien to Stevens's poem, may be taken as a useful model for considering reading as a performative event in Anglo-Saxon England because it introduces the necessary dimension of shared cultural practice.[4] Later I will suggest that Stock's idea of a textual community holds for Anglo-Saxon England by examining the etymology of such Old English words as the noun *ræd* and the verb *rædan*, and also by considering various Anglo-Saxon descriptions of the scene of reading.[5] But first I want to complicate Stock's concept of textual community by examining a counterexample that in its deviation from cultural norms of reading helps us to understand better the nature of these same norms.

As Augustine describes his long journey to conversion in the *Confessions*, he frequently interposes descriptions of his rhetorical and philosophical education. These passages usually center on his encounters with great figures and, more particularly, with them as readers. Thus Augustine explains his break with the Manicheans as dating from his discovery that he had read more widely than had Faustus, the famous teacher of that sect (*Confessions*, V. 6–7). It thus seems perfectly natural that as he approaches conversion in Milan, Augustine should describe the reading practices of Ambrose, the great Catholic bishop of that city. What surprises us, however, is that Augustine does not identify the works read by Ambrose but rather describes the silent and self-contained manner of his reading. In those moments when Ambrose was not fulfilling a public role, Augustine tells us, he would refresh his body by eating and his mind by reading. But, and the full force of Augustine's *sed* must be registered, Ambrose read silently: *sed cum legebat, oculi ducebantur per paginas et cor intellectum rimabatur, vox autem et lingua quiescebant* "but when he read, his eyes followed the pages and his heart pondered the meaning, though his voice and tongue were still" (*Confessions* VI.3).[6] Augustine is careful to specify that Ambrose would read silently to himself even when others were present and might have approached him in conversation. This practice seemed so unusual to Augustine and others around him that they debated about (*discedebamus*) it and offered possible explanations for it. Perhaps Ambrose read silently so that those around him would not be able to interrupt him with questions about the meaning of the text before him. That is, Ambrose read silently to avoid functioning, in Stock's term, as the *interpres*. Or perhaps, Augustine suggests, Ambrose did so to spare his weak voice for necessary public occasions. In the end, Augustine can only assert that Ambrose must have had some good reason for reading silently.

This last comment in no way lessens Augustine's wonder at the sight of a man reading silently. For his is the wonder of a man who had spent his first forty years or so in reading aloud and in public diverse works on Roman rhetoric, Manichean doctrine, Neoplatonic philosophy, and Christian theology. This sense of wonder belongs, then, to a man who believed that the way to the truth was through the written word as performed or interpreted within a community. Whatever spiritual beliefs he held and discarded, Augustine never lost that faith in the written text. To suggest that Ambrose would have appreciated "The House was Quiet and the World was Calm" might be foolishly anachronistic, yet it reminds us not merely of the obvious point that conventions of literacy are culturally determined but also of the more necessary point that not all members of a community subscribe to such conventions at all times. Still, to the extent that he portrays Ambrose as a reader not unlike the scholar of Stevens's poem, Augustine does establish the terms of his own practice as a reader within a textual community: that it should be the speaking aloud of the written text in the company of others so that they might interpret its meaning. That such a community would produce discordant babble rather than interpretive dialogue holds only if we assume tht it had no protocols for reading as evident as the signs admonishing "Silence!" in our libraries.[7]

To move from Augustine's *Confessions* to the Old English *ræd* and *rædan* means encountering quite different conventions of culture, language, and literacy. Without denying these obvious differences, it becomes easier to make this move if we recognize that these words and their cognate forms in other Indo-European languages first denoted the act of giving counsel through speech. Recent scholarship on medieval literacy, as examplified most imaginatively in M. T. Clanchy's *From Memory to Writen Record: England, 1066–1307* (1979), Brian Stock's *The Implications of Literacy* (1983), and Rosamond McKitterick's *The Carolingians and the Written Word* (1989), also offers some assistance for considering reading practices in Anglo-Saxon England.[8] Two very recent books, both learned and subtle, focus moe specifically on pre-Conquest England: Katherine O'Brien O'Keeffe's *Visible Song: Transitional Literacy in Old English Verse* (1990) and Seth Lerer's *Literacy and Power in Anglo-Saxon Literature* (1991).[9] O'Keeffe develops a range of innovative techniques for examining manuscripts as evidence for Anglo-Saxon literacy, while Lerer draws productively on contemporary literary and literacy theory to construct a vision of that culture's "literate imagination."[10] Yet since neither constructs its argument by examining what Anglo-Saxons as members of textual communities might have meant by *ræd* and *rædan*, or by absorbing the work of contemporary ethnographers, the following study will be something of a foray into unexamined territory.[11] Perhaps the most useful of all guides for this foray is Tzvetan Todorov's salutary observation that: "Nothing is more commonplace than the reading experience, and yet nothing is more unknown. Reading is such a matter of course that, at first glance, it seems there is nothing to say about it."[12] As Todorov goes on to demonstrate, there is indeed much to say about reading literary texts. Similarly, there is much to say about the word *reading* itself, despite the fact that it seems so utterly transparent in meaning.

The significance of *rædan* can be measured both by its complex etymology and by the range of its primary meanings, because together they establish that it denoted a variety of necessary functions within Anglo-Saxon culture. In his *Indogermanisches Etymologisches Wörterbuch*, Julius Pokorny classifies the old English *rædan* with other forms sharing the Indo-European root *rē-dh-, rō-dh-, rə-dh-*, including Sanskrit *rādhnóti, rádhyati* "to achieve or accomplish" and the Common Germanic **rêdan*. Important Germanic cognates include Gothic *garēdan*, Old High German *rātan*, Old Saxon *rādan*, Old Norse *rāđa*, and Old Frisian *rêda*.[13] As the etymological note in the second edition of the *Oxford English Dictionary* explains, these Germanic cognates share the principal meanings of "to give advise or counsel," "to exercise control over something," and "to explain something obscure," such as a riddle (*OED, s.v. read*). This note adds further that only Old English and, perhaps following its lead, Old Norse extended the meaning of "to explain something obscure" to mean "the interpretation of ordinary writing." "Ordinary writing" must be distinguished from the original and specialized meaning of the Old English *writan* "to cut a figure in something" (Bosworth-Toller, *s.v. writan*, I),[14] and more specifically, "to incise runic letters in stone." These runic inscriptions do not belong to the category of ordinary writing, and thus deciphering them would have fallen under one of the original senses of *rædan*, namely, "to explain something obscure."

The transition from reading something that is obscure, such as a runic inscription, to reading a written text in Old English or Latin—the "ordinary writing" of the *OED*—is crucial to the semantic development of the Modern English *read*. But this transition must be set in a semantic context rather different from that provided by the *OED*. Among the cognates discussed by Pokorny under the root *rē-hd-, rō-dh-, rə-dh-*, but not listed in the *OED*, are a group of words that designate various forms of speech: Welsh *adrawd* "to tell or narrate" and *amrawdd* "conversation, discourse"; Gothic *rōdjan* "to speak"; Old High German *rātan* "to consult or confer with"; Old Norse *rǫða* "to speak." This set of words makes explicit what lies implicit in the other cognates listed above: that the giving of counsel, or the exercising of control, or the explaining of something obscure could only have been a *spoken* act in the cultures that used these various languages before the introduction of writing. More specifically, these words are alike in denoting speech acts that posit an audience or, in the term used in this study, a textual community. In diverse ways, giving advice and solving riddles depend on a shared set of beliefs and body of knowledge. As these functions are performed through the medium of speech rather than writing, they become public means for creating and then enlarging the bounds of a textual community.[15]

The various senses that cluster around the Common Germanic **rêdan* share these two crucial features. With them in mind, it seems slightly more comprehensible that the English word *read* acquired the sense of "to comprehend a written text." Unlike *raten*, its cognate in German, *read* has not remained within its orginal senses. It has instead been extended to occupy he semantic category that in Gothic is divided between the two verbs **rêdan* and *lisan*, and in Modern German between *raten* and *lesen*. As a result, the English word for comprehending a written text has no etymological basis in the idea of collecting or gathering together letters and words to form the text as a whole, as do *lisan, lesen*, or the Latin *legere*. That our word has no metaphoric underlay of gathering or harvesting is quite surprising, whether one considers the linguistic relations between English, Gothic, and German, or the cultural influence of Latin on English during the formative Anglo-Saxon period.[16]

Why then did the Old English not use the very common word *gad(e)rian* "to gather" as a calque, or morphemic translation, for the Latin *legere* but instead reserved it for translating the Latin *collegere* "to collect"?[17] What conditions led speakers of Old English to conceive of comprehending a written text in ways that had not to do with gathering but rather with offering counsel or solving a riddle? The answer to these questions lies in the very nature of the medieval textual community as a group bound together by the reading aloud of texts to listeners for the purpose of interpretation. In a culture unaccustomed to the written text, the act of reading would have seemed remarkably like solving a riddle. For it meant translating meaningless but somehow magical squiggles on a leaf of vellum into significant discourse, even and most remarkably into sacred scripture. What was alien, opaque, seemingly without meaning becomes familiar, transparent, and meaningful when read aloud by those initiated in the solution of such enigma.[18] Without the dimension of oral performance, reading of this sort could not be perceived by nonliterates as the solving of a mystery. The squiggles must be made to speak.[19]

The same sense of decoding appears in our contemporary use of *read* in nontextual senses, as when we speak of "reading a situation" (where reading means "interpretation" or "solution") or of "profiting from someone's reading of a situation" (where reading edges toward meaning "advice"). In such instances we are not, as might seem the case, offering a metaphorical extension of *read* from a textual to a nontextual context but rather reasserting the primary senses of the word—to solve a riddle and thereby offer advice, counsel, learning. When we speak of reading ordinary writing we are thus using one of the metaphors we live by to describe a text as an enigma that must be solved or made to yield up its meaning. Our use of reading in this sense has, I suspect, little if any conscious metaphoric intent even when appearing in the title of a work of literary analysis that promises to decode a text, such as Edward B. Irving's fine *A Reading of Beowulf*.

In tracing out the semantic development of *rædan* in Old English, it is useful to begin with a poetic collection of proverbial sayings and conventional knowledge that bears the modern editorial title of *Maxims I*.[20] This poem of more than 200 lines contains dozens of maxims about virtually all aspects of human experience. The poem is especially valuable for our purposes because it presents its contents as conventional or normative. As it

describes the desired order of things in the culture, *Maxims I* offers this series of statements: "Counsel should go with wisdom, the right with the
wise, good with the good" (*Ræd sceal mid snyttro, ryht mid wisum, / til sceal
mid tilum;* III:157, ll.22–23a).[21] This sequence establishes the relation between counsel (*ræd*) and the moral virtues of wisdom and goodness. Later
in the poem, *ræd* is set in opposition to *yfel* "evil" so that counsel becomes
the most helpful and evil the least helpful of human attributes (*Ræd biþ yttost
/ yfel unnyttost;* 160, ll.118b–119a). The public utility of counsel demands,
in the poet's vision, that it be spoken aloud and shared: "A man should speak
counsel, write secrets, sing songs, earn fame, express judgment, be active
daily" (*Ræd sceal mon secgan, rune writan, leoþ gesingan, lofes gearnian, dom
areccan, dæges onettan;* 161, ll.138–140). The poet announces that giving
counsel is an oral, public act and further defines that statement with the
following and contrasting statement that associates writing with runes,
whether in the literal sense of the runic alphabet or the metaphoric sense of
secret knowledge.[22] In an oral culture, to give counsel is of necessity to
speak and thereby to create community. This belief is explicitly stated by
the *Maxims*-poet, but the poem in which we read that statement is itself
confirmation that *ræd* as counsel or advice must be exchanged through
speech if it is to exist in a nonliterate community.

    Ræd and its derivatives are also used in the Latin-Old English glossaries
to translate various forms of *consulere* "to consider, take counsel, consult."
Thus, we find the Latin phrase *consulo tibi* glossed by the Old English
phrase *ic ræde ðe* "I counsel you."[23] and *consulta* by both *rædas* (col. 374.23)
and *geræding* (col. 383.25). The Old English *rædbora* "advice-bearer" is used
to gloss the Latin *consiliarius* "counsellor"[24] (col. 539.1) and also the Latin
jurisperitus "one skilled in law" (col. 424.5). Similarly, the Old English
rædgifa "advice-giver" could be used to gloss the Latin *consiliator* "counsellor" (col. 170.6). This evidence is particularly useful because it derives
fromglossaries that record the linguistic interface between literate Latin
culture and preliterate English culture. For Anglo-Saxon gloss-writers to
use *ræd* and the like to translate *consulere* and the like establishes that the
Old English word could often have the same sense of counsel as a public act
as did the Latin word.

    While most uses of *ræd* and related forms in Old English texts refer to
the giving of advice, a significant number of others denote the more specific
act of explaining something obscure or solving a riddle. As a major genre of
the wisdom literature so loved by the Anglo-Saxons, the riddle had considerably higher intellectual standing in early medieval England than it does
today.[25] Thus the act of solving a riddle was seen as valuable because it pro-

vided illumination, knowledge, even advice. Many of the Old English riddles found in the Exeter Book are expressed in the first-person and conclude with this challenge to the listener: "Say what I am called" (*Saga hwæt
ic hatte;* III:180–210, 229–243). These riddles quite literally demand an
oral solution. In others, the challenge takes the form of "Read what I mean"
(*Ræd hwæt ic mæne;* 229; see also Riddle 59, ll.15–19:210). As a genre, the
riddle announces itself as a statement that must be solved or read. Thus Ælfric (c. 955–1020) in his *Grammar* glosses the Latin *ænigma* "enigma" with
rædels "riddle."[26] In another Latin-Old English gloss, *rædels* appears beside
four Latin words: *coniectura, opinatio, estimatio, interpretatio* "conjecture,"
"opinion," "estimation," "interpretation"[27] which are alike in suggesting
responses to or readings of something obscure or enigmatic. This sense of
rædan is not limited to interpreting texts, though that is perhaps its most
common use. In his "Homily for Palm Sunday," Ælfric describes a blindfolded Christ who is challenged by the Jews to guess or "read" who is
touching him: *heton hine rædan hwa hine hreopode* "they commanded him to
read who was touching him."[28] In this example, the blindfolded Christ becomes a personified representation of those acts which require one to read
the obscure or difficult as a means of proving one's intellectual or spiritual
authority.

    With this sense, we reach the end of the semantic field occupied by such
cognates of the English *read* as the German *raten.* The extension of the English word to mean the interpretation of ordinary writing draws on the
senses that have already been surveyed and also, I would argue, a context
that can be situated quite precisely. While my survey of the Old English
uses of *rædan* to mean the interpretation of writing is far from exhaustive,
one interesting trend emerges from even a few examples. Put simply, the
need to translate the Latin *legere* seems to have provided the decisive impetus for the semantic extension of *rædan* in this direction. Ælfric's practice in
translating the Heptateuch from Latin into Old English near the end of the
tenth century provides a neat example for this development of *ræd* and *rædan.* In translating Exodus 18:19, *sed audi verba mea atque consilia,*[29] he offers
ac gehyr min word ond minne ræd "but hear my word and my counsel." Here,
as one would expect, *ræd* is used for *consilio.* In translating Exodus 24:7, *legit
audiente populo,* however, Ælfric offers the extended sense of *rædan: rædde his
boc þam folce* "he read his book to the people."[30] As I shall discuss in a moment, Ælfric's addition of *boc* "book" to *rædan* signals his understanding
that he is using the Old English verb in an extended and potentially confusing manner when it translates *legere.* He thus offers the explanatory, if
seemingly redundant, *boc* to help gloss this extended meaning for *rædan.*

As centers for the copying, illuminating, and interpreting of written texts, as well as the teaching of students, monasteries were quite obviously the place where the need to develop an Old English word to designate the reading of such texts was most pressing. And while Latin was the language of the monastic ideal, the vernacular had its obvious uses in the education of the young and the daily life of those monks unable to attain a working fluency in Latin.[31] One of the chief practices of monastic culture also contributed to the extension of *rædan* to translate *legere*, namely, the practice of reading works aloud, especially during meals.[32] Thus chapter 38 of the *Benedictine Rule*, easily the most important of early medieval monastic rules, prescribes that there should only be holy reading during meals: *Mensis fratrum aedentium lectio deesse non debet*,[33] or, in the tenth-century Old English version of the *Rule: Gebroðra gereorde æt hyra mysum ne sceal beon butan haligre rædinge* "nothing but holy reading shold be recited to the brothers while they are at their meals."[34] That this *lectio* or *ræding* will be drawn from a written text is established by the subsequent references in the Latin text to a *codex* and in the Old English to a *boc*. In this brief passage from the *Rule*, we see not merely the practice of reading described but also the pressing into service of a form of *rædan* to translate a form of *legere*. Related uses of *ræd/ræding* "reading" to translate *lectio*, and of *rædere* "reader" to translate lector appear elsewhere in the Old English version of the *Rule*.[35] The same translation practice may also be found in a variety of Old English works that offer glosses of Latin, such as Byrhtferth's *Manual* of the late tenth century (*ræding* = *lectio*),[36] and Ælfric's *Grammar* (*ræding* = *lectio*).[37] In his *Grammar*, a work designed to lead young students from Old English to Latin, Ælfric three times glosses the masculine *lector* with *rædere* and the feminine *lectrix* with *rædestre*.[38] The last example of this gloss is particularly noteworthy because it occurs in a list of ecclesiastical officials ranging from the *patriarcha* = *heahfæder* "patriarch" to *laicus* = *læwede mann* "layman." This use of *rædere* to mean *lector* refers specifically to the church functionary who would read aloud to the spiritual community.

The Old English *Benedictine Rule* is the translation of a Latin work, Ælfric's *Grammar* is meant for the teaching of Latin, and Byrhtferth's *Manual* digests a great deal of information from Latin texts. Each of these English works therefore offers an implicitly bilingual context, which allows readers to better understand the semantic extension of *rædan* and the like to translate *legere* and the like. In works intended to promote the growth of literacy, especially within monastic culture, there would be little need to gloss or otherwise announce the relatively new and quite technical sense for *rædan*, if only because the Old English works using the word in this manner were themselves being read aloud within a textual community of monks and students. We may see here the coalescence of the important earlier meanings of *rædan* as they concern spoken discourse, the giving of counsel, and the interpreting of obscurity, for all three are contained within the reading aloud of a work of scriptural or didactic value written in a code accessible only to the initiated.

In other Old English works of a more popular character, we find writers glossing this new sense of *rædan*. In addition to the example cited earlier from his version of the Heptateuch, we find these representative examples in the works of Ælfric (c. 955–1020): *swa swa we on bocum rædað* "as we read in books" in his *Life of St. Swithin;*[39] *swa swa hit geræd on godspelle* as the gloss for *sicut legitur in evangelio* "just as it reads in the Gospel" in his *Colloquy;*[40] and *we rædað on Christes bec* "we read in Christ's book" in his "Homily for Shrove Sunday."[41] In *The Blickling Homilies*, a popular work of the tenth century, the necessity to explain that *rædan* can mean to read a written text leads the homilist to a very explicit, even redundant, statement: *þonne we gehyron Godes bec us beforan reccean ond rædan, ond godspell secggean* "When we hear God's book explained and read to us and the gospel spoken."[42] This passage offers a brief but vivid sketch of a textual community in which God's book is heard because it is read aloud and then interpreted. All of the primary senses of *rædan* cohere in the homilist's use of the verb but in ways that still seem to have required explanation.

As the reading of written texts became more common and thus less enigmatic, the need to gloss this new sense of the verb must have diminished. A work such as Ælfric's *Grammar* points to a future in which literacy will become a more widespread and necessary skill. It is thus thoroughly appropriate that the forms Ælfric uses to illustrate first, second, and third person singular verbs should be *ego lego ic ræde, tu legis þu rætst, ille legit he ræt* "I read, you read, he reads."[43] It is grammars of Latin written for English students that will create the necessary context for this new sense of *rædan* and make it primary over time. That this new sense of reading is still not quite ours, though, is made clear by four pages in Ælfric's *Grammar* devoted to an obsessively complete conjugation of the passive verb in Latin as exemplified by *legor* "to be read." Ælfric defines the passive *legor* as *Ic eom geræd on sumum gewrite sum ðing to donne*, literally "I am advised in this writing to do something."[44] I would suggest that Ælfric's use of *rædan* here can be taken as meaning both "advise," and thus as belonging with the phrase "to do something," and also as meaning "read," and thus as belonging with the phrase "in this writing." That is, one is advised to do something by reading. More generally, there could be no better example of a passive verb than this

to offer students who were themselves being read to and who were struggling to understand the obscurities of Latin as a written language. As Lerer
observes, "Literacy for Ælfric is thus a social practice as much as it is an intellectual skill."[45] In this same spirit, Byrhtferth explains in his *Manual* that
he is writing for the benefit of *iunge mynstermen* "young monastic students"
and bids *þa boceras ond þa getydde weras* "scholars and learned men" not to be
impatient with his elementary exposition.[46] The Old English noun *bocere*
can mean "scholar," "author," "grammarian," "Jewish scribe" (*Dictionary of
Old English*, s.v. *bocere*) but most basically it means one who can *read*
books.[47] As these examples demonstrate, *rædan* belongs to the category of
key words described by Raymond Williams: "they are significant, binding
words in certain activities and their interpretation; they are significant, in-
dicative words in certain forms of thought."[48] *Rædan* belongs at the very
center of the profound cultural changes that characterize Anglo-Saxon England because in no small measure they were made possible by this new idea
of reading.[49]

Etymology and linguistic usage do not alone define cultural practice. To
understand what reading meant to Anglo-Saxons—frequently but not always clerical males[50]—we need to see how they functioned within their
various speech communities. We need, in other words, to ask what they did
if we are to gain some sense of how the word *read* continued its semantic development to include meanings that refer specifically to comprehending a
written text. There survive in Anglo-Saxon works at least two vivid descriptions of reading within textual communities. Quite fortunately these passages describe individuals of widely different class and background: the
cowherd Cædmon as told about by Bede in his *Ecclesiastical History of the English Church and People* (731), and King Alfred as told about by Asser in his
Life of Alfred (893). As the great religious history of the Anglo-Saxons and as
the period's fullest political biography respectively, these two works are culturally central and command serious attention. In each we see the act of
reading described in ways that the etymology of *rædan* can only hint at. Yet
that etymology provides a necessary reminder that reading was conducted
under largely oral conditions. In considering these passages from Bede and
Asser, it is helpful to follow Carlo Ginzburg, as he discusses the reading
practices of the French peasantry in the late eighteenth century, and ask:
"To what extent did the prevalently oral culture of those readers interject itself in the use of the text, modifying it, reworking it, perhaps to the point of
changing its very essence?"[51]

The story of Cædmon provides a classic case for studying reading practices in a culture of restricted literacy. As a cowherd in the service of a

monastery, Cædmon lives on the periphery of a literate community but he also functions each day within the established practices of his own oral culture. Indeed, the miracle associated with Cædmon could only have occurred in a setting that allowed the oral and the written to coexist and even to permeate each other. Bede relates that Cædmon would, from a sense of his own lack of talent, quietly withdraw from the banqueting hall when his turn to sing a song and play the harp approached. Put another way, Cædmon withdraws from the most established social ritual of his vernacular community. One night, after leaving the hall, he retires to the cowbarn and falls asleep to a dream in which someone calls to him by name and orders him to sing a song. Cædmon replies that he cannot sing, the authority figure repeats his command, and Cædmon asks what he should sing about. After being told to sing of God's Creation, Cædmon recites a vernacular poem that he had never heard before and that now goes by the name of "Cædmon's Hymn."[52] The nine-line poem that we have seems to be only a fragment of Cædmon's first creation, but it clearly observes the strict metrical, alliterative, and stylistic conventions of vernacular Old English poetry and is also orthodox in its Christian theology.

The next morning Cædmon tells the reeve and then the abbess of the monastery about his dream. All agree that Cædmon has been divinely inspired with the gift of poetic composition. For modern scholars, particularly those interested in oral composition, this story containsin the person of a monastic cowherd the great cultural encounter of Anglo-Saxon England between the native, vernacular culture of a Germanic people and the Mediterranean, Latin culture of the Catholic Church. In this encounter, Cædmon becomes a Christian hero by turning traditional poetics to the new and urgent purpose of propagating the faith.[53] In doing so, he seems to preserve a necessary place for orality in a culture where religious authority was increasingly defined by those who could read the written text of the Latin Bible. For scholars of a vernacularizing bias, the story of Cædmon demonstrates the survival of a traditional, indigenous poetics in the face of the cultural invasion of Christianity. The subjects of that poetry may be new, but its oral technique and audience remain largely unchanged. Framed within the narrow terms of poetic composition, this line of argument makes good sense. If we enlarge the frame to consider the ways in which Cædmon found subjects for his poetry, however, then we must conclude that his story marks the end of pure orality in Anglo-Saxon England and initiates a complex interchange between oral poetics and written texts.[54] More particularly, his story establishes that this new interchange could take place within the bounds of a textual community precisely because it was sufficiently flexible to include cowherd as well as cleric, vernacular as well as scriptural language.

Bede's account of Cædmon does not end with his "Hymn," as some strict oralists might prefer. Bede goes on to explain that the abbess and monks of the monastery set Cædmon a test to determine if his miraculous gift were limited to the creation of one short poem or could extend to other compositions: "They then read to him a passage of sacred history or doctrine, bidding him make a song out of it, if he could, in metrical form. He undertook the task and went away; on returning next morning he repeated the passage he had been given, which he had put into excellent verse" *exponebantque illi quendam sacrae historiae siue doctrinae sermonem, praecipientes eum, si posset, hunc in modulationem carminis transferre. At ille suscepto negotio abiit, et mane rediens optimo carmine quod iubebatur compositum reddidit.*[55] In the Latin, the crucial verb to designate the monks' action is *exponere* "to set forth, to expound" because it makes clear that they did not simply read aloud a scriptural passage (unfortunately not identified by Bede) but also interpreted it. The initial stage of this exposition depended, either implicitly or explicitly, on translation from Latin to the vernacular. While we cannot know whether the monks read the texts aloud first in Latin and then translated them into Old English, or simply paraphrased them into the vernacular, it remains evident that the members of this textual community recognized that they were functioning in a bilingual context. It may well be that the distinction between vernacular and Latin is at least as consequential for studying reading in Anglo-Saxon England as is the more obvious distinction between orality and literacy. For this distinction determined the sociolinguistic character of the community, especially in matters relating to its members' communicative responsibilities. As the monks expound the text to Cædmon, they incorporate him within their community and also determine that his role will be to expound the text in a different manner to a different audience. The nature of Cædmon's divine gift is thus clearly limited to his ability to transform written text as it is read aloud to him into Old English verse for oral delivery. To stress the obvious, what is not at issue is the question of Cædmon's inability to read ordinary writing. Miracles, it would seem, need only extend so far.

Having satisfied the monks of his ability, Cædmon is admitted yet more fully into the textual community. He takes monastic vows and continues to compose poetry. More specifically, he sang (*canebat*) stories taken from Genesis, from Exodus, and from elsewhere in the sacred scripture. He sang as well about the Life of Christ, from His birth to His ascension, and thus drew on the New as well as the Old Testament. While we have Old English

poems on virtually all of these subjects, none can be ascribed on internal evidence to Cædmon. Still, it is not surprising that other Old English poets
should have taken for their subjects the same biblical stories as did Cædmon. For these subjects reveal the Old English poets' understanding of the
textual community to which they have been admitted: one in which they
must disseminate the central canon of the evangelical church.

Unlike the divinely-inspired substance of his "Hymn," the subjects of
Cædmon's later poems were very much the result of human intervention.
Bede explains that the monks continued to read to Cædmon and instruct
him: "He learned all he could by listening to them and then, memorizing it
and ruminating over it, like some clean animal chewing the cud, he turned
it into the most melodious verse: and it sounded so sweet as he recited it
that his teachers became in turn his audience" *At ipse cuncta, quae audiendo
discere poterat, rememorando secum et quasi mundum animal ruminando, in carmen dulcissimum conuertebat, suauiusque resonando doctores suos uicissim audi-
tores sui faciebat.*[56] To the question why the monks did not teach Cædmon
to read, one might respond that it would have been a waste of everybody's
time. Less facetiously, one might say that the question itself reveals a misunderstanding of the nature of an early medieval textual community. Established as he was within the monastery, Cædmon had no need to read
alone and to himself. Indeed, his particular responsibility to transform
Latin text into Old English verse emphasized the skills of oral performance
rather than of reading comprehension. We must also ask if the entire question of Cædmon's inability to read is not at least partially anachronistic in
its assumption that this ability be defined strictly by our own cultural practice as readers who exist in only the most tenuous of communities. Put in
another way, one that considers ends rather than means, we can argue that
Cædmon was literate in matters of scriptural knowledge. As Stock cau-
tions, "Literacy is not textuality."[57] The question then becomes one of asking what Cædmon could not do as a poet because he could not, by our standards, read for himself. The only possible answer, I would suggest, is that
he could not have existed apart from his community. And yet, if that were
to have happened, Cædmon could not be described as a poet because he
would have no audience or community to whom he could recite his oral
compositions. The point holds both ways. Separate Cædmon from his
community as defined by those who read to him and he could not find the
content of his poems; separate him from his community as made up of
those who listened to him and he would not retain his communal validation
as a poet.

The terms of this argument may also be reversed to ask what it means that the monks of Cædmon's monastery could read, as we use the term. For even here, in considering reading as a skill reserved to an elite group pledged to spread the divine truth as contained in a Latin text, we see that reading retains its earlier cultural features. Even for this elite, reading necessarily involved the element of oral delivery, of reading aloud, and also of giving counsel or advice or, in the story of Cædmon, subject matter. To read meant to expound to other members of one's textual community. However we examine reading in Anglo-Saxon England, we cannot escape the ethnographic dimension of a community bound together by common texts. Quite simply, no Anglo-Saxon learned to read in order to read alone, late at night, in a quiet house and a calm world.

One might of course counter that we can only know about Cædmon and his textual community because we can read about it in Bede's *Ecclesiastical History*, the most learned and polished of all Latin works written in Anglo-Saxon England. In other words, we know of Cædmon only because Bede could write and expected his fellow Anglo-Saxons to read so that they could learn the religious history of themselves as a people. To this, one can only respond that Bede knew the precise nature of his own textual community. Though he lived a monastic life from early childhood, Bede did not restrict the benefits of literacy to those who belonged to that community and who could read. As he closes the preface to his *Ecclesiastical History*, he requests the prayers of those who read his work or who hear it read: *legentes siue audientes*.[58] Both readers and listeners belong in a community at once textual and spiritual, written and oral, in which intellectual and spiritual life is created through the communal interchange of reading.

This sense of reading as a communal act informs the intellectual life of King Alfred (fl. 871–899) as told by his friend and teacher, the Welsh cleric Asser. While Alfred seems to have learned to read the vernacular at the relatively advanced age of twelve, he revealed from early childhood a powerful ability to memorize Old English poetry.[59] Thus Asser describes the young Alfred memorizing an entire book of Old English poetry (*Saxonicum poematicae artis librum*) so that he might win it from his brothers in a competition sponsored by their mother. While Asser's text is somewhat murky at this point,[60] it is evident that Alfred did not himself read this book but rather memorized its contents after it was read aloud to him. To that extent, he reminds us of Cædmon, but Alfred did learn to read English in his teens and, far more impressively, Latin at the age of thirty-nine. Asser explains that Alfred learned to read and interpret Latin on a single day through divine inspiration (*divino instinctu legere et interpretari simul uno eodemque die primitus inchoavit*).[61]

At this moment, we are reminded that Asser's *Life of Alfred* owes no small debt to the conventions of hagiography.[62] Nonetheless, Alfred's mastery of Latin was a remarkable achievement, even if we explain it not by divine inspiration but by his life-long presence within a textual community. For Asser tells us that the most striking characteristic displayed by Alfred throughout his life was that of reading aloud or listening to others read aloud at all times and under all conditions (*Nam haec est propria et usitatissima illius consuetudo die noctuque, inter omnia alia mentis et corporis impedimenta, aut per se ipsum libros recitare, aut aliis recitantibus audire*).[63] If Alfred did learn to read Latin in a day, it was because he had spent much of his life preparing to read, as we mean the term, by listening to others read communally. Taken in this way, Asser's *Life of Alfred* rcords Alfred's knowing absorption of the ideas and workings of a literate culture—that is, of written texts in Old English and in Latin—before he could read for himself through membership in a textual community. Alfred, by the available evidence, never learned to write in either Latin or Old English. As Katherine O'Brien O"Keeffe puts it tellingly: "A man and a king at a transitional moment in the shift from orality to literacy, he does not write but orders Asser to do it for him."[64]

Alfred's belief in the cultural importance of reading both English and Latin shaped his educational program for his own children as well as the Anglo-Saxons as a people. Given Alfred's own belated formal education, there is something very poignant in Asser's description of the school attended by his children, both male and female, and of the books in Latin and in English that were assiduously read. The principles that guided the education of Alfred's children in their small and seemingly informal school[65] found fuller and more influential expression in the program of translations advanced by Alfred in the 890s. After defeating the Danes in 878 and consolidating his rule over the southern portion of England granted to him under the terms of the Treaty of Wedmore, Alfred devoted himself to educational reform. In his famous *Preface* to the Old English translation of Gregory's *Pastoral Care* (c. 890), Alfred delivers an impassioned if perhaps hyperbolic lament on the wretched state of intellectual life in England on his ascent to the throne in 871.[66] No one south of the Thames, Alfred claims, could then translate from Latin into English and few elsewhere on the island could do so. Those who served God at that time could not profit from the available books because they were written in Latin rather than English.

Although Alfred struggled to improve the teaching of Latin in England, he also sponsored a program of translating crucial Latin works into English. These works may not have been numerous, but together they contained the core of Latin Christianity: Gregory the Great's *Pastoral Care* and *Dialogues*, Orosius's *History Against the Pagans*, Boethius's *Consolation of Philosophy*, Augustine's *Soliloquies*, and Bede's *Ecclesiastical History*. Whether Alfred translated any or all of these works is far less important for our purposes than is his accomplishment of creating an intellectual and, it should not be forgotten, political climate of stability in which they could be translated. Moreover, as C. L. Wrenn has observed, Alfred's "impetus must have caused the writing of other prose translations in his later years" that have since been lost.[67] The importance of this translation program for the practice of reading in Anglo-Saxon England can hardly be overestimated, for it brought into the vernacular textual community a body of Latin learning in history, philosophy, and theology that would otherwise not have been accessible even to those who could read ordinary writing in the vernacular. Alfred's exemplary kingship thus extends far beyond his youthful military success. As a ruler, he was one of the lucky few to have known what to do with the peace he won in battle. Most remarkably, he recognized that his nation's political and spiritual well-being depended on a dynamic, inclusive, and thus increasingly vernacular textual community. By reading aloud to others or by hearing others read aloud to them, members of such a community might emulate the virtuous and shun the wicked as Bede had urged in the preface to his *Ecclesiastical History*. Arguably the greatest of Alfred's accomplishments was to place reading in all of its various senses—the understanding of written texts but also the giving of counsel and the understanding of obscure matters—at the heart of public life.

For all that one wishes, no study of reading in Anglo-Saxon England can end with the visionary Alfred and that last brilliant decade of his reign. Instead, one must close with the name of another Anglo-Saxon king, one not blessed with Alfred's love of learning. The last king to rule Anglo-Saxon England before its conquest by the Danish King Cnut in 1014 was the unfortunate Ethelred, literally "Noble Counsel" but nicknamed by later generations "The Unready." He was not, as one might think from this epithet, unprepared; rather, he was more immediately Ethelred "No Counsel" (*un* + *ræd*). Sir Frank Stenton has described Ethelred as a "king of singular incompetence."[68] To the extent that we think of him merely as unprepared, we mitigate his incompetence, for he was guilty of a far greater failing in an Anglo-Saxon king. He took no counsel and had no sense of his political role within the textual community. He betrayed his name and earned his epithet: Noble Counsel, No Counsel.

Much more could and should be said about reading in Anglo-Saxon England. A comprehensive semantic-field study of words relating to reading in Old English, Latin, and Old Norse would be the obvious next step, particularly if it were responsive to the larger ethnographic and sociolinguistic aspects of the topic.[69] Yet even this preliminary study makes clear that reading in Anglo-Saxon England cannot be understood by any facile opposition of orality and literacy. To quote Brian Stock one last time: "There is in fact no clear point of transition from a nonliterate to a literate society."[70] That no such point of clear transition can be located in Anglo-Saxon England is vividly illustrated by the linguistic evidence, especially when the key words are not considered only in isolation but also are placed within a larger ethnographic context. This intertwining of language and social practice provides a powerful methodology for countering what James Clifford has called "ethnographic pastoral,"[71] the belief that there was once a golden age of orality before the corrupting force of literacy made itself felt. As he acutely observes, "in the West the passage from oral to literate is a potent recurring *story*—of power, corruption, and loss" (118). It is also a story, as we are now coming to realize, that has too often distorted the practice of those who study orality and literacy either ethnographically or historically. If we are, more specifically, to understand the complex range of human acts that speakers of English have over the centuries designated as reading, we must avoid constructing visions of a lost past, just as we must avoid assuming that reading is tied inextricably to our modern and highly literate conventions. For all that we become Wallace Stevens's "scholar" as we study— alone, by ourselves, too often late at night—the historical and semantic development of reading, we should remember that *rædan* originally referred to a public, spoken act within a community.[72]

Notes

1. Wallace Stevens, *The Palm at the End of the Mind: Selected Poems and a Play*, ed. Holly Stevens (New York, 1972), 279.

2. Brian Stock, *Listening for the Text: On the Uses of the Past* (Baltimore, 1990), 37.

3. Stock, *Listening for the Text*, 37.

4. For striking parallels with reading practices in ancient Jewish culture, see Daniel Boyarin, "Placing Reading: Ancient Israel and Medieval Europe," in *The Ethnography of Reading*, ed. Jonathan Boyarin (Berkeley, 1993), 10–37.

5. I follow the standard practice of using Anglo-Saxon to designate the period of English history from the fifth through the eleventh centuries, as well as the people of that period, and of reserving Old English for the Germanic vernacular spoken then. Any consideration of the linguistic communities of Anglo-Saxon England would ide-

ally include Latin and the Scandinavian dialects introduced during the period as well as Old English.

6. Augustine, *Confessions*, 2 vols., trans. William Watts (Cambridge, Mass., 1989), I.272

7. For a portrait of such a modern textual community and its conventions of interpretive dialogue, see Jonathan Boyarin, "Voices Around the Text: The Ethnography of Reading at the Mesivta Tifereth Jerusalem," in *The Ethnography of Reading.*

8. M. T. Clanchy, *From Memory to Written Record: England, 1066–1307* (Cambridge, Mass., 1979); Brian Stock, *The Implications of Literacy: Written Language and Models of Interpretation in the Eleventh and Twelfth Centuries* (Princeton, 1983); Rosamond McKitterick, *The Carolingians and the Written Word* (Cambridge, 1989); see also Ruth Crosby, "Oral Delivery in the Middle Ages," *Speculum* 11 (1936), 88–110; Franz Baüml, "Varieties and Consequences of Medieval Literacy and Illiteracy," *Speculum* 55 (1980), 237–65.

9. Katherine O'Brien O'Keeffe, *Visible Song: Transitional Literacy in Old English Verse* (Cambridge, 1990); Seth Lerer, *Literacy and Power in Anglo-Saxon Literature* (Lincoln, 1991). These books appeared after I completed the first draft of this study. I have learned a great deal from them and have sought to integrate their findings into my work, while also recognizing the striking similarities in argument and evidence between their work and mine.

10. Lerer, *Literacy and Power,* 195.

11. Lerer, 236–37, nn. 23, 24, offers a few suggestive comments on *ræd* and also quotes the etymological discussion in the *OED s.v. read,* but he does not pursue the linguistic and ethnographic issues advanced in this study.

12. Tzvetan Todorov, "Reading as Construction," in *The Reader in the Text. Essays on Audience and Interpretation,* ed. Susan R. Suleiman and Inge Crosman (Princeton, 1980), 67–82, at p. 67.

13. Julius Pokorny, *Indogermanisches Etymologisches Wörterbuch,* 2 vols. (Bern and Munich, 1959), 1:59–60.

14. Lerer, *Literacy and Power,* 142, 167.

15. A textual community is of course embedded in a larger speech community. In the case of Anglo-Saxon England, one might argue that the most important textual communities were not those that used only Old English or Latin, but rather those that used both of these languages for the purposes of reading.

16. That the English *read* lacks this underlay also suggests that the development of *lesen* and *legere* may not be quite as natural or inevitable as seems at first glance. But that is a problem for another study.

17. See, for example, Julius Zupitza, ed., *Ælfrics Grammatik und Glossar: Text und Varianten* (Berlin, 1880; rpt., with preface by Helmut Gneuss, Berlin, 1966), 176.

18. See further O'Brien O'Keeffe, *Visible Song,* 21.

19. A similar process can be seen in the derivation of *glamour* from *grammar.* As the knowledge of written signs, grammar acquired an occult or magical aura and thus,

over time, gave rise to *glamour* in the sense first of enchantment and then of bewitching beauty (*OED, s.v. grammar*).

20. Where possible, I offer a date for the Anglo-Saxon works cited. Quite frequently, however, these dates are very approximate and should be treated with extreme caution. They are rarely so accurate as to sustain a chronologically precise argument for the semantic development of a word.

21. Citations from Old English poetry are from G. P. Krapp and E. V. K. Dobbie, *The Anglo-Saxon Poetic Records*, 6 vols. (New York, 1931–53), and are cited by volume, page and line in the text.

22. See Lerer, *Literacy and Power*, 10–17.

23. Citations in this paragraph are to Thomas Wright and Richard Paul Wülcker, eds., *Anglo-Saxon and Old English Vocabularies*. 2d ed. 2 vols. (London, 1884).

24. See also Zupitza, *Ælfrics Grammatik und Glossar*, 301.

25. Morton W. Bloomfield, "Understanding Old English Poetry," *Annuale Mediaevale* 9 (1968), 5–25; Nicholas Howe, "Aldhelm's Enigmata and Isidorian Etymology," *ASE* 14 (1985), 37–59.

26. Zupitza, 33.

27. Wright-Wülcker, col. 209.5.

28. Benjamin Thorpe, *The Homilies of the Anglo-Saxon Church . . . Containing the Homilies of Ælfric* (London, 1846; rpt. New York, 1971), II.248.

29. S. J. Crawford, ed. *The Old English Version of the Heptateuch, Ælfric's Treatise on the Old and New Testament and his Preface to Genesis* (EETS o.s. 160. London, 1922), 258. Quotations from the Vulgate are taken from *Biblia Sacra* (Madrid, 1965).

30. Crawford, *OE Heptateuch*, 272.

31. Erich Auerbach, *Literary Language and Its Public in Late Latin Antiquity and in the Middle Ages*, trans. Ralph Manheim. (New York, 1965), 283–84.

32. See W. J. Ong, *Orality and Literacy: The Technologizing of the Word* (London and New York, 1982), 74–75, and Lerer, *Literacy and Power*, 8–9.

33. John Chamberlin, ed., *The Rule of St. Benedict. The Abingdon Copy* (Toronto, 1982), 48.

34. Arnold Schröer, *Die angelsächsischen Prosabearbeitungen der Benedictinerregel* (Cassel, 1885–88), 62.

35. Schröer 18, 33–35, 62–63.

36. S. J. Crawford, *Byrhtferth's Manual*. EETS o.s. 177 (London, 1929), 100–102; see Wright-Wülcker, col. 129.37.

37. Zupitza, 206.

38. Zupitza, 48, 71, 299.

39. G. I. Needham, ed., *Ælfric: Lives of Three English Saints* (London, 1966), 78.

40. G. N. Garmonsway, ed. *Ælfric's Colloquy* (London, 1965), 39.

41. Thorpe, *Homilies of the Anglo-Saxon Church*, I.162.

42. R. Morris, ed., *The Blickling Homilies of the Tenth Century*, EETS o.s. 73 (London, 1880), 111; for similar examples see pp. 15 and 161.

43. Zupitza, 127–28.

44. Zupitza, 182.

45. *Literacy and Power*, 56.

46. Crawford, *Byrhtferth's Manual*, 132.

47. Lerer, *Literacy and Power*, 130–31, 201; for Bede as *breoma bocera* "famous scholar" see Krapp and Dobbie, VI.27.

48. Raymond Williams, *Keywords: A Vocabulary of Culture and Society*. Rev. ed. (New York, 1985), 15. Williams does not discuss *read* or any related form.

49. For the remarkable level of literacy and learning among the educated elite of Anglo-Saxon England, see Patrizia Lendinara, "The World of Anglo-Saxon Learning," in *The Cambridge Companion to Old English Literature*, ed. Malcolm Godden and Michael Lapidge (Cambridge, 1991), 264–81. For the practices of Anglo-Saxon readers, especially those of vernacular works, see O'Brien O'Keeffe, *Visible Song*, 155–87.

50. C. P. Wormald, "The Uses of Literacy in Anglo-Saxon England and its Neighbours," *TRHS*, 5th ser. 27 (1977), 95–114.

51. Carlo Ginzburg, *The Cheese and the Worms: The Cosmos of a Sixteenth-Century Miller*, trans. John and Anne Tedeschi (New York, 1982), xxii.

52. Krapp and Dobbie VI:105–6.

53. Robert W. Hanning, *The Vision of History in Early Britain: From Gildas to Geoffrey of Monmouth* (New York, 1966), 88.

54. O'Brien O'Keeffe, *Visible Song*, 46; Lerer, *Literacy and Power*, 42–60. For general studies of orality in Anglo-Saxon England, see Jeff Opland, *Anglo-Saxon Oral Poetry: A Study of the Traditions* (New Haven, 1980) and John Miles Foley, *The Theory of Oral Composition: History and Methodology* (Bloomington, Ind., 1988), 65–74. For a more specialized study on orality and pectorality, see Eric Jager, "Speech and the Chest in Old English Poetry," *Speculum* 65 (1990), 845–59.

55. Bertram Colgrave and R. A. B. Mynors, eds., *Bede's Ecclesiastical History of the English People* (Oxford, 1969), 417–19.

56. Colgrave and Mynors, 418–19.

57. Brian Stock, *The Implications of Literacy*, 7.

58. Colgrave and Mynors, 6.

59. William Henry Stevenson, ed. *Asser's Life of King Alfred* (Oxford, 1904), 19–20.

60. Simon Keynes and Michael Lapidge, trans., *Alfred the Great: Asser's Life of King Alfred and Other Contemporary Sources* (Harmondsworth, 1983), 239, n. 48.

61. Stevenson, 73.

62. See Lerer, *Literacy and Power*, 61–96.

63. Stevenson, 67.

64. *Visible Song*, 84.

65. Stevenson, 300, on *schola*.

66. For translation, see Keynes and Lapidge, *Alfred the Great*, 124–26.

67. C. L. Wrenn, *A Study of Old English Literature* (New York, 1967), 222; see further Allen J. Frantzen, *King Alfred* (Boston, 1986).

68. *Anglo-Saxon England*, 3d ed. (Oxford, 1971), 395.

69. No such study is cited in the recent and thorough survey by Vic Strite, *Old English Semantic-Field Studies* (New York, 1989).

70. Stock, *The Implications of Literacy*, 9; see also Jack Goody, *The Interface Between the Written and the Oral* (Cambridge, 1987), 293; O'Brien O'Keeffe, *Visible Song*, 190–94.

71. James Clifford, "On Ethnographic Allegory," in *Writing Culture: The Poetics and Politics of Ethnography*, ed. James Clifford and George E. Marcus (Berkeley, 1986), 98–121, at p. 118.

72. As is apparent, I write as a medievalist rather than as an ethnographer. But it is a pleasure to acknowledge my debt to ethnographic works that have shaped my thinking about reading: Keith Basso, "The Ethnography of Writing," *Explorations in the Ethnography of Speaking*, ed. Richard Bauman and Joel Sherzer (Cambridge, 1974), 425–32; Clifford, "On Ethnographic Allegory"; Joel Sherzer, "The Ethnography of Speaking," in *Linguistic Theory: What Can It Say About Reading?* ed. Roger W. Shuy (Newark, Del., 1977), 144–52; Dennis Tedlock, *The Spoken Word and the Work of Interpretation* (Philadelphia, 1983); Daniel A. Wagner, Brinkley M. Messick, and Jennifer Spratt, "Studying Literacy in Morocco," in *The Acquisition of Literacy: Ethnographic Perspectives*, ed. Bambi B. Schieffelin and Perry Gilmore (Norwood, N.J., 1986), 233–60; and Goody, *The Interface Between the Written and the Oral*. For assistance and conversation about the topic of reading, I thank Jonathan Boyarin, James N. Comas, Morris Foster, Georgina Kleege, and Fred C. Robinson. I must also thank Daniel Donoghue and Antonette diPaolo Healey for kindly reading an earlier version of this study.

Anglo-Saxon Lay Society and the Written Word

SUSAN KELLY

THE study of literacy in Anglo-Saxon England in some ways resembles the hunt for a certain elusive type of sub-atomic particle: the direct evidence for its existence is negligible but the fact that it does exist can be inferred from its perceived effect upon its environment. When we scour the primary sources for references to reading and writing, to the literacy of individuals, to basic education and book-ownership, our haul is sparse indeed. Inferences drawn from scribal competency can be suggestive, but hardly provide a sufficient basis for general analysis of the quality and extent of Anglo-Saxon literacy. The conclusions that derive from this type of material are plainly limited; they tend to reinforce the traditional view that literacy was essentially an ecclesiastical preserve, for it is impossible to demonstrate that the occasional indication to the contrary is anything more than an exception. Fortunately, the argument can be amplified by considering the problem from a rather different perspective and studying the ways in which the Anglo-Saxons utilized the written word and the extent to which writing superseded speech and memory as the standard method of conveying and storing information. This approach leads us to a rather different conclusion, for it seems to show that by the end of the period, if not several centuries before, written documentation had an important place in secular society and was used in ways which could imply a degree of literacy among certain sections of the laity.

Before we can assess the impact which literacy had on Anglo-Saxon society, it is necessary to try to establish a starting point for the investigation. The obvious answer might seem to be the seventh century, when Christianity and its attendant Latin literary culture gained a foothold in England. But it would be a mistake to see pagan Anglo-Saxon society as entirely ignorant of writing. The Anglo-Saxon settlers brought with them from Germany the runic alphabet and there survives a small corpus of runic inscriptions on stones and on portable objects, which includes examples from the pagan period and from subsequent Christian centuries. Most of these inscriptions are very short, consisting of no more than a name or a couple of words, and some seem to be gibberish, with possible magical connotations. But there is a handful of slightly longer texts, the most significant being the inscriptions on the Auzon (Franks) Casket and the lines from *The Dream of the Road* which were engraved on the Ruthwell Cross.[1]

The limited nature of the evidence makes it difficult to evaluate the importance of runes in pagan Anglo-Saxon society and the extent of runic literacy. A point of some interest is that runic characters were originally devised for engraving on wood, which is only rarely preserved from the early middle ages. The site of the mediaeval city at Bergen in Norway has yielded approximately 550 runic inscriptions on wood dating from the fourteenth century, many of them letters and everyday messages cut into small wooden sticks or tablets which were easily transported.[2] There is some evidence for rune-stick letters in Scandinavian contexts as far back as the ninth century.[3] It is possible that the early Anglo-Saxons made extensive use of rune-sticks for practical communications, but the absence of even one surviving example makes it difficult to proceed beyond speculation. We do have some evidence for familiarity with the runic alphabet among the educated classes of society. For instance, the solution to certain Anglo-Saxon riddles depends upon knowledge of runes, and the poet Cynewulf used them to attach a cryptic 'signature' to some of his works.[4] In the later part of the eighth century two runes (þ, p) were adopted into the Roman alphabet for writing words in the vernacular, in order to represent sounds in English (/θ/, /ð/, /u̯/) for which there was no Latin equivalent; this suggests that some Anglo-Saxon clerics were literate in runes.[5] There are runic legends on a number of proto-pennies (*sceattas*) from the seventh and eighth centuries and on a few pennies of late eighth- and early ninth-century date from Mercia, Northumbria and East Anglia, which indicates at the very least that some moneyers were familiar with runic script.[6] But there are signs that by the later Anglo-Saxon period runes were no longer in common use and might be regarded primarily as an exotic script with cryptic possibilities.[7]

It appears that Latin and the Roman alphabet were first introduced into the Anglo-Saxon areas of Britain by foreign missionaries from the later sixth century onwards.[8] In southern England the primary influence was from Rome and the Frankish church, but the north was effectively evangelized by missionaries from Ireland and Iona and long retained strong cultural links with these areas, even after the capitulation of the Northumbrian clergy to Roman usage at the Synod of Whitby in 664.[9] It would be interesting to consider whether the impact of literacy and the written word on early Anglo-Saxon society was appreciably different in these two areas, but the distribution of the surviving evidence makes such comparison very difficult. From southern England we have numerous documents of secular interest, mainly in the form of land-charters and law-codes. In the north and east of the country this type of documentation disappeared, presumably as a result of the upheavals of the Scandinavian settlements, and thus most of the surviving material from the earlier period of Anglo-Saxon history in these areas is concerned with purely ecclesiastical or scholarly matters.[10] It is clear that Irish scholarship was an enormous inspiration to the Northumbrian church in the seventh and eighth centuries, but is is difficult to decide whether this intellectual contact had an effect on the assimilation of the written word into Northumbrian society. A potentially important point is that the Irish ecclesiastics, like the English but unlike the Italian and Frankish missionaries, spoke a vernacular which had no basis in Latin, and were therefore accustomed to learning the literary language of the church as a foreign tongue. It is possible that this experience of bilingualism was of value to them in the training of Anglo-Saxon clerics in literary skills, and the consequence could have been that literacy had a deeper foundation in the Northumbrian church. The Irish may also have had some influence on the early development of a tradition of vernacular writing in England, although there is no clear evidence to this effect.[11] I will consider below the links between the vernacular literary tradition and lay literacy.

The primary and most accessible record of the interaction between early Anglo-Saxon society and the written word is the Latin land-charter (technically, diploma) and the associated vernacular documents which deal with land and property. We have some 1,500 such documents from the Anglo-Saxon period as a whole, and about a third of these purport to date from the ninth century or earlier.[12] Approximately 300 charters survive as 'originals', that is, written in contemporary script on separate sheets of parchment; the rest are later copies on single sheets and copies in monastic cartularies.[13] This is a significant collection of material, but it can be difficult to use. A fairly high proportion of Latin charters are forgeries or have been in some way tampered with or rewritten. It is possible that this is true for as many as a third of the extant texts, and for the earlier period the percentage of suspicious documents is higher. Some forgeries are blatant, but in other cases the fabrication or alteration can be detected only by the most subtle scholarship; sometimes it is not possible to prove one's suspicions of a document. These difficulties of establishing authenticity should not prove a deterrent against proper consideration of this type of source-material. Charters provide the most important illustration of how the secular society of Anglo-Saxon England absorbed the ecclesiastical gift of the written word.

The earliest charters with any claim to authenticity date from the 670s and come from Kent, Surrey and the kingdoms of the West Saxons and the Hwicce. Shortly afterwards comes the first surviving East Saxon charter.[14] The date of these charters has led scholars to associate the introduction of this type of document with the arrival in England in 669/70 of Theodore and Tarsus and Abbot Hadrian, together with a fresh influx of Italian clerics. But there are difficulties in accepting this view and some grounds for suggesting that the idea of the land-charter was current in England at a rather earlier date. The distribution of the earliest extant texts over such a wide area of southern England seems incompatible with a very recent introduction. So does the fact, highlighted by Chaplais, that these charters broadly conform to a basic diplomatic pattern which is unique to England, while exhibiting a range of variations within that pattern which suggests that the local charter-scribes were familiar enough with the basic model to depart from it with confidence; if the diplomatic initiative truly belonged to Theodore's time, we would expect a greater degree of uniformity.[15] Chaplais has argued in detail that the evidence points to the evolution of the Anglo-Saxon charter over a fairly long period before the date of the first surviving examples, and to the earliest Roman missionaries as the agents who introduced the concept into England. Other scholars have recently suggested that the Anglo-Saxon charter had rather more diverse origins; they point to possible instances of Frankish and even Celtic influence, and propose that the idea of charter-writing was introduced into different parts of England by different agents at different times in the late sixth and seventh centuries.[16]

Either contention requires us to account for the total disappearance of the hypothetical charters written before c. 670 and the improved rate of preservation immediately thereafter. An attractive explanation is that the earliest charters were written on papyrus, which was the normal medium for charter-writing in both Italy and Gaul in the sixty and seventh centuries. The survival rate of papyrus documents in western Europe is very poor indeed. The earliest surviving product of the papal chancery is a letter of Hadrian I dated 788; between this date and the second half of the tenth century, when the papal chancery began to use parchment, only forty papal bulls have been preserved as originals, out of the thousands that are known to have been issued.[17] Of the Merovingian charters written on papyrus, Pirenne has memorably observed, 'La rareté des actes mérovingiens ne doit . . . pas nous faire illusion. Ils ne sont que les *rari nantes* échappés au gouffre de l'oubli.'[18] The chancery of the Merovingian kings used papyrus until the later part of the seventh century, when it was phased out in favour of parchment. The available evidence points to the 670s as the period of transition: we have five originals on papyrus in the name of Chlothar III (31 October 657–10 March 673), while the first original on parchment was issued by Theuderic III in September 677.[19] It may be more than a coincidence that the earliest surviving Anglo-Saxon original is a charter of Hlothhere of Kent, issued in May 679. The close connection between the Merovingian and Kentish dynasties has long been recognized. Two kings of Kent married Merovingian princesses, and many of their descendants were given Frankish names (for instance, Hlothhere is equivalent to Chlothar). Wood has recently put a strong case for the existence of Merovingian overlordship not only over Kent but also over much of southern England in the sixth and seventh centuries.[20] This political connection could have led to the imitation in England of some Frankish administrative practices, and could perhaps have prompted the jettisoning of papyrus by Anglo-Saxon charterscribes in favour of parchment. Unfortunately, this argument is difficult to sustain. As we shall see, charters in early Anglo-Saxon England were almost certainly never written in any form of royal chancery; they seem to have been drafted and written mainly in episcopal scriptoria, at least until the early tenth century. Moreover, it should be noted that the Frankish influence detectable in the Anglo-Saxon charter is very slight. Direct imitation of the Merovingian chancery therefore seems unlikely. The papyrus predecessors of the extant diplomas must remain hypothetical.[21]

The peculiar nature of the Anglo-Saxon charter on its first appearance is sufficient in itself to suggest a period of development prior to the 670s. Superficially it seems to conform to normal diplomatic practice, but in its essentials it breaches some of the most important diplomatic conventions.[22] The most bizarre aspect is the complete absence of any outward mark of validation. There is no sign of the autograph *signa* or subscriptions of the donor, witnesses and notary which were normally found in the Italian private charter, nor of the autograph valedictions and monograms which validated papal and imperial documents. The Anglo-Saxon diploma certainly concludes with a list of the subscriptions of ecclesiastical and lay witnesses, but these are almost invariably written by a single scribe, usually the scribe of the text. This is the case whether the subscriptions are in subjective form (*Ego N consensi*) or objective form (*Signum manus N*), and in spite of regular claims in the text that the subscription was autograph (*manu propria*). There is not a single example in an Anglo-Saxon charter of a true autograph subscription. This should not be regarded necessarily as a reflection of massive illiteracy among clergy and laity. Italian diplomatic made provision for the illiterate witness, who was allowed to make his mark (usually the sign of the cross) alongside the note *signum manus N*. Both subjective and objective subscriptions in Anglo-Saxon charters are generally preceded by a cross, but not one of these can be proven to be autograph; in surviving original charters the crosses are uniform and presumably written by the scribe of the text.[23] Thus, in an apparently genuine charter datable to 697 or 712 in favour of a monastery at Lyminge, King Wihtred of Kent declares that he has made the sign of the cross because he does not know how to write (*pro ignorantia litterarum signum sancte crucis expressi*); yet all the subscription-crosses in this charter are identical.[24] The witness list of the Anglo-Saxon charter seems to represent an attempt to imitate the outward form of a regular Italian charter without regard for its legal substance. It is difficult to believe that any Mediterranean ecclesiastic could be responsible for such a travesty. Rather, in its received form the Anglo-Saxon charter seems to reflect some measure of adaptation to English conditions and perhaps the dilution of the strict diplomatic conventions at the hands of English clerics trained by Augustine and his successors. The evidence suggests that the number of Roman missionaries who travelled to England was fairly limited, and most seem to have arrived within a few years of each other at the turn of the sixth century. It is possible that the Anglo-Saxon charter acquired its unique features during the central years of the seventh century, when the original missionaries were dying out and their English disciples were taking over the episcopal chairs and scriptoria.

The early Anglo-Saxon diploma is essentially an ecclesiastical document, unlike its Italian models which originated in secular society. In its typical form it records a grant of land by a king to an individual cleric as the representative of his community or to a member of the laity who wished to use the land to found or endow a monastery. The diploma was drafted by an ecclesiastic, usually the local bishop or one of his scribes, on behalf of the beneficiary rather than the donor.[25] The conventional *formulae* employed have a strong ecclesiastical flavour, the most obvious manifestation of this being the substitution of spiritual punishments for the secular penalties threatened against those who refused to abide by the provisions of the grant.[26] The Anglo-Saxon charter reflects the desire felt by the early churchmen to have some written guarantee for their property. But what legal force could such a document have in secular Anglo-Saxon society? It was all very well for the church to assert that its own records, drawn up in pseudo-legalistic form, were proof of ownership. It was also necessary for the validity of the written word to be recognized by the laity.

This difficulty seems to have been resolved, at least in part, by incorporating the charter into a formal ceremony marked by highly visible rituals. This kind of activity is not well represented in our sources, but there are occasional references in the early charters to the transfer of a sod of earth from the estate granted and to the placing of the sod or of the charter on an altar or gospel-book.[27] There is some evidence that charters might be stored on the altar or bound into a gospel-book; certainly by the later Anglo-Saxon period and perhaps at an earlier date charters were copied into blank spaces in gospel-books.[28] In this way the charter was visibly associated with the divine. It seems likely that the document was ceremonially handed over by the donor to the beneficiary as a symbol of the transaction, and there may have been some accompanying ritual in which the donor and perhaps the witnesses touched the parchment as a formal guarantee of their testimony.[29] Some early charters have been written in two stages, the witness list having been added at a later date.[30] This suggests that the text of the charter was written out by or on behalf of the beneficiary before the ceremony, and that the witness list was added during the ceremony or subsequent to it. We have some evidence that a note of the witnesses present might be made on a separate scrap of parchment (a *scedula*) for reference when completing the charter; two such *scedulae* survive, sewn onto the parchment of original charters of the ninth century.[31] It should be noted that in one of these two cases the text and witness list of the charter were written by a single scribe apparently at the same time, which implies that when this particular document was witnessed during the conveyance ceremony the parchment itself was blank. It seems likely that, in the eyes of the laity, the transfer of land was effected and guaranteed by the rituals which marked the transaction, and that the diploma was important as a part and symbol of these ceremonies, not on its own account as a written record of the transaction. The value of a diploma as a title-deed resided less in the information which it contained than in its function as a potent symbol of ownership.

This is an important key to understanding the subsequent history of the Latin diploma in England. The churchmen seem to have achieved their aim of inspiring lay recognition of the diploma as a title-deed and thus brought about the integration of the written word into land-ownership. So successful was this manoeuvre that laymen also began to acquire written title to land. By the later eighth century we find charters in which a layman is

named as the beneficiary and in which there is no clear indication that the
land is subsequently to be used for ecclesiastical purposes. By the later Anglo-Saxon period the majority of surviving Anglo-Saxon charters are in
favour of laymen, and it seems probable that this represents only a small
proportion of the total number of such charters, since on the whole these
documents have been preserved only if at some point they entered the
archive of an ecclesiastical community. The attraction of acquiring a charter seems to have lain in the type of land tenure with which it was associated, which derived from special measures for the original endowment of
the church. Land covered by a charter was *bocland* and could be freely dis-
posed of by its owner, unlike *folcland* which was subject to the normal claims
of heirs and kindred, as well as to a number of rents and dues. The Latin
charter was a useful way of marking and guaranteeing alienable property,
and it could be transferred together with the land to a new owner.[32]

It is this last aspect of the function of the Anglo-Saxon diploma that
demonstrates the relative unimportance of its content. A very few of the
surviving single-sheet charters bear an endorsement noting the transfer of
the land and documentation from the original beneficiary to a new owner.
Thus, when a *comes* of King Cenwulf of Mercia came into possession of a
Kentish estate and its charter, recording Offa's grant of the land to an abbot
in 767, he took care to have the change of ownership noted, confirmed and
witnessed on the dorse.[33] This charter was being brought up to date to reflect the changing circumstances of ownership. But most original charters
have no such endorsement, even in cases where ownership is known to
have changed on more than one occasion. Some of the surviving records of
dispute over land show that charters might be stolen or otherwise fraudu-
lently obtained and yet still have the power of proving ownership: possession was all. A well-known eighth-century instance concerns King
Cynewulf of the West Saxons. In a document of 798 recording the end of the
dispute, we are told that King Æthelbald of Mercia granted a monastery at
Cookham with all its lands to Christ Church, Canterbury, and to safeguard
the donation sent a sod of earth and all the title-deeds to Christ Church to
be placed on the altar there. After the death of the incumbent archbishop,
the documents were stolen and given to King Cynewulf, who thereupon
converted to his own use the monastery and all its possessions.[34] It would
appear that land and charter might be transferred to new owners without
any attempt being made to alter the text of the charter to bring it into line
with the new situation. The charter was a title-deed insofar as it gave symbolic proof of ownership; the content was relatively immaterial. In cases of
dispute resort was frequently made to the testimony of witnesses, local in-

habitants or supporters who could give evidence about the previous history of the estate.[35]

In the ninth century we seem to see some change in the concept of the charter's function. One of the most important manifestations of this is the development of the boundary-clause. Previously charters had contained only an occasional and vague indication of boundaries in Latin, expressed in terms of the cardinal points of the compass. Reliance seems to have been placed on the fact that local estate-boundaries were well-known. There may have been a ceremony of 'beating the bounds' to impress them on local memories; in the earliest known original charter, datable to 679, King Hlothhere is made to assert (with a poor regard for spelling and grammar) that the land is to be held 'according to the well-known boundaries demonstrated by myself and my officers' (*iuxta notissimos terminos a me demonstratus et proacuratoribus meis*).[36] In the ninth century and later charter-scribes regularly included a detailed boundary-clause in English, which indicates that charters now functioned, at least in some respects, as true written records. It is important to note that this development involved the use of the vernacular.

From at least the beginning of the ninth century onwards, Latin diplomas came to be supplemented by an extensive range of documents in English or in a mixture of Latin and English, which included wills, leases and miscellaneous agreements. The most important of these documents were sealed royal writs, in which the king drew to the attention of the officials of the local shire court or other interested parties any new donation of land or transfer of property or privilege; this was in addition to the issue or transfer of a Latin diploma and ensured that the beneficiary's right to the land would be recognized. There is some evidence that such writs might also have been used for routine administrative matters. The earliest trustworthy examples date from the reign of Cnut, but it is possible that similar documents were in use in the tenth century and perhaps earlier. Those writs dealing with landownership represent a significant development in the use of the written word in this area. They supplied the deficiencies of the formal Latin diploma as a witness of legitimate possession, and also regularized the informal oral procedures of guaranteeing ownership by recourse to local witnesses.[37]

Rather more complex transactions involving land and property were also recorded in vernacular documents. For example, fifty-eight wills survive from Anglo-Saxon England, of which fifty-three are in English.[38] The earliest example is the will of a Kentish reeve named Abba, which survives on its original parchment and is datable to between 832 and 840.[39] Abba made elaborate provisions for future eventualities, according to whether he

were to have a child or whether his widow wished to remarry or enter a convent. His intention was to ensure that the land eventually reverted to his
kindred, but even that was not the end of his concern; he further specified
which members of his family were to receive the land in turn and what was
to become of it after their respective deaths, and finally arranged that if his
family should die out completely the estate was to pass to Christ Church in
Canterbury. Whoever held the property was to donate a regular render of
livestock and other produce to the monastery at Folkestone, and to make
extensive gifts of money to the church and to individual clerics: 'and
Freothomund is to have my sword'. On the dorse of the document appears
an additional statement by Heregyth, Abba's wife, to the effect that future
owners of an estate at Challock (probably not the land covered by Abba's
provisions) were to pay a specified annual render to the Christ Church
community. Abba's will was probably written by a Christ Church scribe; it
was witnessed by the archbishop and members of the community and
named Christ Church as the ultimate beneficiary to the land after his family: in return for this last concession, the head of the Christ Church community was to afford his protection to Abba and his heirs and to act as their
advocate. There is a definite ecclesiastical interest in Abba's arrangements,
but it is not an overriding one; the main concern of the document is the
complex provision for the future inheritance of the property within the kindred. It appears as if Abba himself recognized the value of recording this information.

Other laymen and women seem to have felt the same, for the majority
of surviving wills relate to lay bequests. Many of them are concerned with
the elaborate provisions surrounding the property of the wealthy and well
connected. Thus we have the wills of two kings (Alfred and Eadred), two
queens, an ætheling, five ealdormen and a number of other individuals
known to have been related to the royal dynasty and the nobility. An outstanding example is the early eleventh-century will of Wulfric Spott, a
member of an important Mercian family and the brother of Ealdorman
Ælfhelm, which disposes of no fewer than eighty estates scattered over
eleven counties in north-west Mercia and the southern Danelaw, as well as
an enormous amount of treasure, not to mention a hundred wild horses and
sixteen tame geldings.[40] There are also a number of wills in the name of
men and women of less exalted rank, who make rather humbler bequests.
For instance, in the middle of the ninth century Badanoth Beotting, who
seems to have been a minor official in the court of King Æthelwulf of Wessex, bequeathed to Christ Church in Canterbury his heritable land, which
amounted to only sixteen yokes of arable and meadow. Badanoth specified

that the estate was not to pass to the church until after the death of his wife and children, and that they were to pay an annual rent to the community.[41] A number of other wills, as well as some agreements affecting the immediate relations of the parties, refer to a similar arrangement: the donor pledged land to the church and (sometimes) promised an annual rent or render, on condition that his or her heirs were allowed to retain the property for their lifetimes. Such an arrangement satisfied the demands of piety while ensuring provision for dependents, and could also enlist the advocacy of a powerful ecclesiastical community on the side of the donor and family.

The mirror of such pledges was the ecclesiastical lease.[42] Documents recording tenancy arrangements survive in a number of ecclesiastical archives. The most important source is Worcester, which preserved a magnificent series of leases from the eighth century until the end of the Anglo-Saxon period, including no fewer than seventy-six in the name of Bishop Oswald (960/1–92). Oswald leased the lands of the Worcester community to his relatives, his clerics, his thegns and his followers almost invariably for a period of three lifetimes (that is, for the lifetimes of the beneficiary and two subsequent heirs). The scale of Oswald's leasing arrangements seems to have been unusual, but ecclesiastical leases were by no means a novelty in his day: the earliest surviving Anglo-Saxon lease which seems trustworthy dates from the second half of the eighth century, and the practice must have been widespread by 816 when the Synod of Chelsea attempted to limit the timespan of leases of church property to a single lifetime.[43] The larger churches could not hope to farm all their estates in demesne, and it made sound economic sense to let some of their property to free tenants in return for certain payments. The production of a written lease formalized such arrangements and gave the church some guarantee that the reversion clause would be honoured. We have records of well over a hundred Anglo-Saxon leases, probably representing only a small fraction of the total issued since these were ephemeral documents, but only a dozen survive as originals.[44] These show that, at least by the tenth century it was usual to produce such documents in the form of a chirograph. The text of the agreement was written out in duplicate or triplicate (and occasionally in quadruplicate) on one sheet of parchment and CYROGRAPHUM (or a variant) was added in large letters in the gaps between the copies. The parchment was then cut through the word CYROGRAPHUM and the separate pieces distributed to the interested parties and sometimes to disinterested churches or to the king for safekeeping and an additional guarantee. Thus both sides had a record of the agreement and if a dispute arose the copies could be compared and matched. The earliest surviving example of a chirographic lease comes from 904, but there is a possibility that a lost lease of 855 was originally drawn up in this form.[45] The chirograph may possibly have had its origin in Ireland, but it reached its greatest formal development in England.[46] It proved a remarkably efficient document and was used for a range of purposes. The reason for the popularity of the chirograph (and perhaps the motive for its invention) may have been its capacity for involving illiterate laymen in the documentary process. The production of chirographs on a regular basis perhaps indicates that secular society took a strong interest in written documentation.

Leases might be written variously in Latin or English or in a mixture of the two. Eleven of Oswald's leases are in the vernacular, but a number of these have some Latin admixture. The rest are basically in Latin, but almost all contain some sections in English, generally a boundary-clause and perhaps a sanction or notes on the conditions of the lease. Approximately a quarter also contain within the text a very brief passage in the vernacular summarizing some portion of the Latin, most commonly the date and the provision that the land was to revert to Worcester after three lives, which were the essential details. The inclusion of such a summary might indicate that the lease might be read by someone who was literate in the vernacular but not in Latin. At any rate, the casual bilingualism of these documents displays something of the linguistic attitude of the scribes who drafted them. It appears that English was not thought to be out of place, even in an important ecclesiastical record.

Other aspects of land tenure and property-ownership were covered by different types of vernacular document. Regularly we find memoranda on the exchange or purchase of land. Thus, when a Kentish nobleman named Godwine bought a piece of land from his sister, Eadgifu, the transaction was noted in a tripartite chirograph.[47] So too was an agreement imposed upon the three monastic communities in Winchester by King Edgar which involved the adjustment of their respective boundaries.[48] We also have a number of documents in both Latin and English recording the manumission of slaves. This would seem to have been essentially an oral ceremony, but the details were frequently recorded, usually in a free space in a gospel-book, as a precaution against a subsequent challenge to the freedman's status. The surviving manumissions date from the tenth century and later.[49] At least by the eleventh century written documentation had come to play a part in another important social transaction: we have two vernacular marriage agreements, from Canterbury and Worcester respectively, detailing the property arrangements made between the groom and the bride's kindred.[50] Various documents describing disputes over property and the subsequent settlements have been preserved. Sometimes these appear to be formal records of agreements; an early example is a Worcester document of 825 concerning a dispute over swine-pasture.[51] Elsewhere we find more partisan accounts, designed to be of use in a continuing quarrel; such is the description of a dispute over toll-rights in the Wantsum Channel between the two Canterbury houses, Christ Church and St. Augustine's, which consistently sets out the Christ Church point of view.[52] Many land-transactions, whether purchases, exchanges or formal settlements, were guaranteed by supporters who were willing to stand surety for the parties. Fortuitously, two lists of such sureties have survived, almost certainly the remnant of a much larger number of similar records; one of these is an extensive compilation detailing the guarantors for a series of Peterborough estates which must have been put together from scattered records and notes in the abbey's archive.[53] Alongside this we can set a long Bury St Edmunds memorandum about rents and renders which was compiled from miscellaneous material, probably shortly after the Norman Conquest.[54] We can deduce from such compilations and from the occasional fortunate Old English survival that, at least by the end of the Anglo-Saxon period, the great monastic houses kept detailed records of their estates, tenants, rents, stock and disbursements, which supplemented their formal title-deeds.[55] The king and many lay landowners might have followed the same practice; such secular records had no chance of direct survival, but they probably underlie many sections of Domesday Book.

The extent of vernacular literacy among the clergy and the laity and the implications of the use of the vernacular in formal and informal documents are issues of the greatest importance. In the tenth and eleventh centuries, English had a respected place as an alternative literary and documentary language. Some ecclesiastics composed extensively in the vernacular and many manuscripts written in this period contain vernacular texts, such as sermons, poetry and translations from Latin. English was a medium of instruction in schools and was regularly used by the draftsmen of leases and agreements and by the royal administration for sealed writs and law-codes.[56] Moreover, from the later tenth century some churchmen made successful efforts to standardize the vernacular by promoting the use of the West Saxon dialect elsewhere in the country.[57] There are signs that some members of the church might be literate in English but have difficulty reading Latin. Bishop Æthelwold of Winchester was commissioned by King Edgar and his wife to translate the Rule of St Benedict into the vernacular, apparently for a community of nuns, and several later manuscripts of the Rule are bilingual.[58]

Such toleration and encouragement of vernacular literacy as a necessary if regrettable substitute for latinity is usually traced back to the educational initiatives of King Alfred. In the much-discussed epistolary prose preface attached to his translation of Pope Gregory's *Pastoral Care*, Alfred set out his observations on the state of English literacy and outlined his plans to improve it.[59] He began by remarking on the good fortunes enjoyed by England in former times when learning was valued, and went on to complain of such a neglect of learning that hardly anyone south of the River Humber (and probably not many north of it) could understand the divine services in Latin or translate a letter from Latin into English. Indeed, Alfred professed to be unable to recollect a single person capable of these feats south of the Thames at the time when he became king. He saw the beginnings of this decline in the period before the immense devastation wrought by the Viking invaders, and speaks of churches filled with books and a great number of clerics who could not read the books because they were not written in their own language. As a remedy for the general ignorance of the clergy, Alfred decided to promote the translation of essential texts into English. Free-born young men who were otherwise unoccupied were to be taught to read such works in the vernacular, and those who were intended for holy orders could go on to study in Latin afterwards. We have the testimony of Asser that at least some part of this educational scheme was implemented; he tells how Alfred's sons and daughters were taught how to read books in Latin and how to write, in the company of the well-born children of almost the entire region and many of less distinguished birth.[60]

The validity of Alfred's remarks about the abysmal state of learning in ninth-century England has been meat for a great deal of discussion.[61] It seems likely that Alfred exaggerated to some degree in his implication that southern England was almost entirely bereft of competent latinists; the fact that he had recruited three Mercian teachers to help in his educational and literary projects implies that the tradition of Latin learning had not completely died out, at least in parts of Mercia.[62] But the available evidence suggests that the standards of Latin in the south were generally poor. Brooks has used the wealth of surviving ninth-century charters from Canterbury to suggest that, even in such an important centre, there seem to have been very few scribes able to draft a Latin charter by the middle of the century and these scribes themselves were unsure of grammar and orthography.[63] Later research has broadly confirmed this assessment and also indicated a gap in the copying of literary manuscripts in the central decades of the century.[64] Alfred seems to have been largely justified in his horror at the decline of Latin learning in ninth-century England and in his understanding

that this decline preceded the large-scale Viking attacks; Canterbury charters of the 820s show signs of weakness in Latin grammar and composition.[65] Note, however, that poor spelling and grammar are not found only
in ninth-century charters. A dreadful example is the earliest original charter, datable to 679, which was drafted in Kent while that excellent scholar,
Theodore of Tarsus, was archbishop of Canterbury.[66] But, in general, reasonable standards seem to have been achieved and maintained in the eighth
century. The subsequent breakdown in the early ninth century may have
been due in part to the attempts of the Canterbury charter-scribes to produce more ambitious and complex documents, and perhaps also to a sudden
expansion of output as a result of the extensive land-transactions engaged in
by Wulfred in his efforts to reorganize the archiepiscopal estates.[67]

Alfred's scheme to provide regular instruction for the laity in the vernacular and his sponsorship of the translation of important Latin works
seem likely to have contributed to the enthusiasm with which English was
used for literary and documentary purposes in the tenth and eleventh centuries. Moreover, his insistence that his officials set themselves to studying
on pain of losing their position may have provided a foundation for the expansion in the tenth century of the range of administrative documentation
in the vernacular.[68] But Alfred's own statement shows that vernacular literacy was already well established in England. Bede seems to have recognized
the value of English as a medium of translation, for on his deathbed he was
still working on a translation of Isidore's *De natura rerum* for the benefit of
his pupils as well as a translation of the first six chapters of St John's Gospel
for the church's use (*ad utilitatem ecclesie Dei*).[69] We have a number of
eighth- and ninth-century manuscripts containing glossaries, in which
Latin words are given an English equivalent; the main function of these
seems to have been to facilitate the study of Latin vocabulary.[70] Even before Alfred initiated large-scale translation from Latin, literary texts in English were being copied in scriptoria, although none has survived in contemporary manuscripts; we learn from Asser that Alfred's mother gave him
a volume of Saxon poems and that, as king, Alfred made a habit of reading
English books aloud.[71] In addition, the use of the vernacular for certain
types of legal document was already common in the first half of the ninth
century. As already mentioned, the earliest surviving Anglo-Saxon will on a
single sheet dates from the 830s. We have an apparently genuine English
lease dated 852 from *Medeshamstede*/Peterborough and an English record
of a dispute over swine-pasture dated 825 from Worcester.[72] Most impressive is a small group of vernacular documents from the middle of the century connected with the affairs of the Kentish nobility. This group includes

two grants of annual renders of produce to Christ Church in Canterbury and two to St Augustine's Abbey in the same city.[73] We also find a complicated agreement, datable to *c.* 871, between an ealdorman named Alfred and Christ Church: in return for a lifetime lease on an estate at Croydon, Alfred promises to bequeath another estate to Christ Church, but also makes arrangements to safeguard the position of his daughter in respect to both estates.[74] Even more interesting is a slightly earlier agreement between a widow and her husband's kinsman about land which her husband had given her, the purpose of which was to ensure that the land was not alienated from his family; the archbishop and the Christ Church community are witnesses and the charter was probably drawn up in the archiepiscopal scriptorium, but the church in no way benefits from the agreement.[75]

The use of the vernacular for such legal documents in the ninth century has been attributed to the increasing scarcity of scribes capable of drawing up a Latin charter. Brooks' work on the archiepiscopal scriptorium at Canterbury, the source of most of these ninth-century vernacular texts, seems to illustrate this tendency. At Canterbury painful efforts were made to ensure that royal diplomas granting land were still produced in Latin. But elsewhere even this last distinction may have been ignored; the evidence is a unique vernacular charter in the name of King Berhtwulf of Mercia, datable to 844 or 845, which concerns a perpetual grant of land at Wotton Underwood in Buckinghamshire.[76] This charter, which survives as an original, is seen as demonstrating 'that at least one Mercian church had already at that time to resort to producing a royal diploma in English rather than Latin, and indeed a very strange form of English at that'.[77] This example may not be as straightforward as it at first appears. We know that in the ninth century it seems to have been the normal practice for a land-charter to be drawn up in the local episcopal scriptorium, although there were occasional exceptions to this rule.[78] The Buckinghamshire estate granted by Berhtwulf would have lain in the contemporary diocese of Leicester, and the incumbent bishop, Ceolred, is one of the witnesses to this charter. In another charter, dated 844, Bishop Ceolred appears as the initial donor of an estate at Pangbourne in Berkshire, less than 30 miles from Wotton Underwood, which was subsequently granted by King Berhtwulf to the ealdormen of Berkshire; this charter, which was preserved in the archive of Abingdon Abbey, was drawn up in Latin and, although awkward in its phraseology and grammar, it conforms in most respects to the normal conventions of Latin diplomas.[79] The Pangbourne charter seems to show that the tradition of Latin charter-writing was by no means moribund in this part of the Middle Anglian diocese. It may be sensible to treat the vernacular charter concerning Wotton Underwood as an anomaly rather than a clear demonstration of declining standards of latinity. It is possible, although difficult to prove, that the document was a temporary record of the transaction for use in the conveyance ceremony and was intended to be written up in a more formal manner at a later date.[80]

The Wotton Underwood charter is the only example of a royal diploma drawn up entirely in the vernacular. In general, there was a clear distinction between royal diplomas, intended to function as title-deeds, which were invariably in Latin (although by the ninth century it was normal for a Latin diploma to incorporate some sections in English, such as a boundary-clause or a list of appurtenances and dues), and other types of document, such as wills, leases and grants of render, which might be in Latin but which were usually drawn up in English in the ninth century and subsequently. Weak ecclesiastical command of Latin is thus unlikely to be a complete explanation for the development of a strong tradition of vernacular documentation in the ninth century. The use of English had several functional advantages. In some circumstances English was far more convenient and more accurate than Latin for the type of information that had to be conveyed; this was true for the extensive lists of renders found in ninth-century Kentish documents, which involved some vocabulary for which it would have been difficult to find an exact Latin equivalent, and also for detailed boundary-clauses. Another incentive for using English may have been the need to record a verbal statement of intent or agreement.[81] Above all, the value of English lay in its accessibility to a wider public. A Latin diploma was doubly inaccessible to the uneducated. Not only did it have to be read out to them; it also required translation into the vernacular. Thus, when two letters of Pope Zacharias were presented to the Synod of *Clofesho* in 747, they were read out and then translated (*et manifeste recitata et in nostra lingua apertius interpretata sunt*); the translation may have been for the benefit of King Æthelbald of Mercia and the *principes* and *duces* who were attending the synod, but it was probably also appreciated by many of the clerics present, especially those in lower orders.[82] A document written in English could reflect more closely the oral procedures which it recorded and could be read out to the interested parties, their supporters and witnesses. While it lacked the dignity and arcane authority associated with the use of Latin, it was more functional in a secular context than any Latin document could be.

The reasons for the early development of the non-Latin vernacular as a vehicle for legal documentation must lie partly in the circumstances of early English history, which included the apparent disappearance of spoken Latin and of all vestiges of the late Roman bureaucracy; Latin was so remote from the secular side of society that greater use had to be made of the vernacular in all areas of administration and social regulation. This point is illustrated most forcibly by the surviving Anglo-Saxon law-codes. The earliest is that of King Æthelberht I of Kent and thus almost contemporary with the introduction of Latin literacy into England.[83] Bede tells us that, among the other benefits which he conferred on his people, King Æthelberht established a law-code according to the example of the Romans, which was written up in English (*Anglorum sermone*) and still observed by the men of Kent in Bede's own day.[84] Three other vernacular law-codes survive from the seventh century, two from Kent and one from Wessex.[85] It has been suggested that the reason for the use of the vernacular in this context was the inability of those clerics charged with drafting the laws to bridge the gaps in legal terminology between Latin and Old English.[86] This explanation is not convincing, since the three later seventh-century law-codes were produced in the years when Theodore and/or Hadrian were resident in Kent; they taught Roman law to their English pupils (among them Aldhelm, a West Saxon) and were presumably capable of drafting a law-code in Latin if one were required.[87] In the case of the laws of Æthelberht, the path chosen involved the Roman missionaries in an even greater difficulty than finding Latin terms for unfamiliar concepts: namely, the creation of a new literary language from an unfamiliar tongue hitherto unwritten, except in runes. The magnitude of this step should be appreciated. It involved the transformation of sound into writing and required informed decisions on spelling and grammar.

Such an initiative was unlikely to be undertaken solely to produce a law-code. It must be seen in the wider context of the progress of the Roman mission in Kent. Augustine and his companions were already worried about linguistic difficulties before they arrived in England. In order to allay their anxieties, Pope Gregory arranged that they should be joined by Frankish priests who would act as interpreters.[88] Much ink has been spent on the question of the mutual intelligibility of Frankish and English; alternatively it is possible that mercantile and political contact between Kent and Gaul and the presence of Franks at Æthelberht's court had familiarized some Franks with English (and some Anglo-Saxons with Frankish).[89] In spite of the services offered by the Franks, the Roman missionaries had little chance of success unless they quickly came to terms with the English vernacular, which was essential for preaching and for the instruction of English youths and indeed for communication with their royal patrons. It was probably in the process of teaching themselves English that they came to write down the language for the first time, perhaps in the form of glossaries. The only vernacular documents to survive from the seventh century are the four southern law-codes, but it is probable that the new literary language was also used for other material, particularly items required for the basic instruction of clerics. We can seek a parallel in the development of a written vernacular in Germany, where the missionaries (Anglo-Saxons and others) were also faced with the instruction of a people with an unwritten language: the earliest texts in Old High German are glossaries, translations of the Lord's Prayer and Creed, and prayers.[90]

The early English church had to be tolerant of the vernacular if it was to have a priesthood of any size. In his letter to Bishop Egbert, Bede remarked that he had often given the Creed and Lord's Prayer translated into English to priests ignorant of Latin, and he recommended that not only laymen but also clerics and monks with no Latin should be taught these texts in the vernacular.[91] For the church's purposes, the encouragement of vernacular literacy as a prelude to (and often a substitute for) Latin literacy was perhaps inevitable. Without an organized procedure for educating clerics, there was a risk that the expansion of the church in England would leave the priesthood swamped with non-latinists; in the eighth and early ninth centuries the shortage of teachers was probably exacerbated by the departure of so many talented scholars for Germany.[92] It may well have been the dilution rather than the decay of learning which led to the situation bemoaned by Alfred, with a clergy in general incapable of profiting from the library stocks of the churches because the books were not in English.

Basic education in the vernacular may have been available to young laymen as well as to boys intended for the priesthood. We have a little evidence from the early Anglo-Saxon period that the sons of Anglo-Saxon noblemen might attend monastic schools, apparently in some cases as an extension of the practice of sending children to be fostered in another noble household. Thus Wilfrid as a youth was entrusted to the care of a nobleman who had entered the monastery of Lindisfarne and while living there seems to have received some kind of an education, although he was still untonsured (*laicus capite*), and does not seem to have been already destined for the church. When Wilfrid himself became a bishop, noblemen sent their sons to him to be taught (*ad erudiendum*), and Stephanus makes it clear that when these boys grew up they could choose whether to become warriors or priests.[93] We have no way of estimating the proportion of laymen and women who had the benefit of such instruction or the quality and extent of the education that they received. But it seems likely that, as in the case of young men intended for the priesthood, education was bilingual and any training in the skills of literacy would begin (and sometimes end) with the vernacular. This

is the impression given by the only detailed description of the basic education of an Anglo-Saxon layman. Asser's account of the successive stages of
Alfred's progress in literacy and learning is not as coherent as we might
wish, but the outlines can be discerned. The future king remained *illittera-
tus* until his twelfth year or even later, apparently because no suitable teachers were available. Before this, however, he was an avid listener to vernacular poetry and made a habit of memorizing it. At some point his mother
promised a volume of vernacular poetry to whichever of her sons could
most quickly understand and recite it; Asser's version of this episode is confused, but it would appear that Alfred took the volume to his tutor, who
read it aloud so that he could memorize it. We next hear of Alfred's literary
capacities after he became king at the age of twenty-two. Among his many
activities he often read aloud (*recitare*) books in English (*Saxonici libri*),
while continuing to learn by heart vernacular poems. But he was distressed
by his ignorance of divine wisdom (*divina sapientia*) and the liberal arts. To
repair this he assembled a coterie of learned men who would read aloud to
him, thus allowing him to become acquainted with scholarly texts; Asser explains that he could not understand these works himself because he had not
yet begun to read anything (*non . . . adhuc aliquid legere inceperat*). On the
face of it this seems to contradict his earlier statement that the king spent
part of his time reading aloud from English books. The explanation would
seem to be that at this time the king was literate in the venacular but not in
Latin. We might also be correct to see a distinction between the general
ability to read Latin and the ability to read complex Latin texts. Asser's account gives the impression that the king could understand spoken Latin,
even if he could not read it; it is, however, possible that the scholars were
translating and explaining the texts as they read. Asser notes that it was in
the year 887 that Alfred first began to read and translate (*legere et interpretari*); here he presumably refers to works in Latin. There is no evidence that
Alfred ever learned to write, although his children were taught to do so; we
do know that the king later called upon Asser's services as a scribe to jot
down striking passages in the works that they were studying together.[94]

No doubt a small number of laymen, like Alfred, went on to understand
and even to read Latin. Alfred, in the preface to his translation of the *Pastoral Care* of Gregory, reminisces that there had previously been learned
men (*wiotan*) both within and without the church (*ægðer ge godcundra hada
ge woruldcundra*); it seems likely that he is referring to Latin learning.[95] Two
seventh-century kings were given the accolade *doctissimus* (very learned) by
Bede, although it must be admitted that both seem to have been educated
abroad.[96] Other early Anglo-Saxon kings showed enthusiasm for learning

and literature, and the study of history, involving as it did the achievements of their ancestors and peers, was especially dear to their hearts. Bede implies that King Ceolwulf of Northumbria was actively interested in the progress of the *Ecclesiastical History* and indeed had asked for a copy of it.[97] We discover from a chance reference in a letter of Alcuin that King Offa of Mercia also owned a copy of Bede's most celebrated work.[98] A continuing royal interest in history is reflected in the fact that the first literary work to be produced in the vernacular in Alfred's reign seems to have been the Anglo-Saxon Chronicle.

Vernacular poetry and the Chronicle were secular literature and, even though clerics could and did appreciate the former and may have been responsible for the latter, probably imply a secular audience.[99] Asser provides the information that volumes of Saxon poetry and English books were available before Alfred gave a boost to the written vernacular. From the ninth century we have a significant number of vernacular charters and other documents which show laymen and women taking advantage of the medium of writing to record complex agreements and arrangements about property. It appears that, even before Alfred's time, certain sections of the laity were interested in writing and written material. We cannot tell if laymen in large numbers had acquired the mechanical skills of reading and writing: the details of Alfred's education remind us that in the early mediaeval period listening, reading aloud and extensive memorization were far more important adjuncts of learning than they are today. The strong element of professionalism in the skills of literacy might make it unnecessary for the higher classes of society to practise them; instead they could call on the services of a secretary to take dictation or to read aloud books and documents. In the last resort, the case for widespread literacy in the modern sense among the early Anglo-Saxon laity must remain unproven, and it is impossible even to approach the question of whether lay familiarity with runic writing laid the foundation for reception of conventional literacy or to any extent contributed to the strength of the vernacular written tradition. Nevertheless, it seems clear that already by the ninth century the written word had been accommodated within secular society. Keynes' chapter in this volume[100] demonstrates that by the later Anglo-Saxon period the royal administration and the upper reaches of society were using writing, and especially vernacular writing, on a routine basis. No doubt this state of affairs at least in part reflects the success of Alfred's plans for lay education and his wisdom in promoting English rather than the less accessible Latin as a basis for instruction. But Alfred did not initiate the use of vernacular writing in England; rather he attempted to enlarge the scope of books available in English in order to promote learning and philosophy and to improve the calibre of the nobility. English had been used since the seventh century to record material of lay interest. The foundation for the outstanding literary activity of the later Anglo-Saxon period already existed.[101]

Notes

1. The most accessible discussion of runes and runic inscriptions is by R. I. Page, *An Introduction to English Runes* (London, 1973).

2. A. Liestøl, "Correspondence in runes," *Mediaeval Scandinavia* 1 (1968), 17–27.

3. A. Liestøl, "The literate Vikings," *Proceedings of the Sixth Viking Congress*, ed. P. Foote and D. Strömbäck (Uppsala, 1971), 69–78.

4. Riddles: Page, *Introduction*, 202–5. Cynewulf: K. Sisam, *Studies in the History of Old English Literature* (Oxford, 1953), 1–28.

5. For the date, see A. Campbell, *Old English Grammar* (Oxford, 1959), 12, 26–28, and K. Sisam, "Anglo-Saxon royal genealogies," *Proceedings of the British Academy* 32 (1953), 287–346, at 310–11.

6. Page, *Introduction*, 119–33; P. Grierson and M. Blackburn, *Medieval European coinage, I. The Early Middle Ages (5th to 10th centuries)* (Cambridge, 1986), 158, 293, and nos. 668–69, 685–6, 707–15, 1121a–c, 1236, 1479, 1482.

7. See Page, *Introduction*, 34–5, 69–70, 215; R. Derolez, *Runica Manuscripta* (Bruges, 1954), 137–69.

8. For the progress of evangelization see H. Mayr-Harting, *The Coming of Christianity to Anglo-Saxon England* (London, 1972). Augustine and his companions were preceded in southern England by Liudhard, the bishop who had accompanied the Merovingian princess Bertha to Kent on her marriage to King Ethelberht I: *Bede's Ecclesiastical History of the English People*, ed. and trans. Bertram Colgrave and R. A. B. Mynors (Oxford, 1969), 72–74 (I.25). The marriage is usually dated to before 560, which implies the presence of literate Franks in Kent for almost four decades before Augustine's arrival. It has been suggested that this was of some significance for the recording of sixth-century events in the Anglo-Saxon Chronicle: K. Harrison, *The Framework of Anglo-Saxon History to A.D. 900* (Cambridge, 1976), 121–23. There is, however, good reason to think that the marriage should be dated rather later, perhaps as late as 581: see I. Wood, *The Merovingian North Sea*, Occasional Papers on Mediaeval Topics 1 (Ålingsas, Sweden, 1983), 15–16.

9. This clear-cut division should perhaps be modified: see J. Campbell, "The first century of Christianity in England," *Ampleforth Journal* 76 (1971), 12–29 (reprinted in his collected papers, *Essays in Anglo-Saxon History* (London, 1986), 49–67). For continuing relations between Ireland and Northumbria, see K. Hughes, "Evidence for contacts between the churches of the Irish and the English from the Synod of Whitby to the Viking Age," in *England before the Conquest: Studies in Primary Sources*

Presented to Dorothy Whitelock, ed. P. Clemoes and K. Hughes (Cambridge, 1971), 49–67.

10. For an indication that the Northumbrian church did produce land-charters see Stephanus, *The Life of Bishop Wilfrid*, ed. and trans. B. Colgrave (Cambridge, 1927; paperback ed. 1985), 16; and the reference to *regalia edicta* by Bede in his letter to Bishop Egbert: in *Venerabilis Baedae Opera Historica*, ed. C. Plummer (Oxford, 1896), p. 415, and trans. *EHD*, p. 805. See also P. Chaplais, "Who introduced charters into England? The case for Augustine," in *Prisca Munimenta*, ed. F. Ranger (London, 1973), 88–107, at 101–2.

11. The problems of the Irish missionaries and their attitude to the vernacular are considered by D. N. Dumville, "*Beowulf* and the Celtic world: the uses of evidence," *Traditio* 37 (1981), 109–60, at 110–20.

12. For a general introduction to Anglo-Saxon charters, see F. M. Stenton, *Latin Charters of the Anglo-Saxon Period* (Oxford, 1955); *EHD*, 369–84; N. P. Brooks, "Anglo-Saxon charters: The work of the last twenty years," *Anglo-Saxon England* 3 (1974), 211–31. The surviving charters to the end of the reign of Edgar are edited by W. de G. Birch, *Cartularium Saxonicum*, 3 vols. and index (London, 1885–99); later charters are found only in the earlier edition of J. M. Kemble, *Codex Diplomaticus Aevi Saxonici*, 6 vols. (London, 1839–48), in vols. III, IV, and VI. The vernacular documents are well edited by F. E. Harmer, *Select English Historical Documents of the Ninth and Tenth centuries* (Cambridge, 1914), and *idem.*, *Anglo-Saxon Writs* (Manchester, 1952); *Anglo-Saxon Wills*, ed. D. Whitelock (Cambridge, 1930); *Anglo-Saxon Charters*, ed. A. J. Robertson (Cambridge, 1939; 2d ed. 1956) Three important archives exist in modern editions: *Charters of Rochester*, ed. A. Campbell, Anglo-Saxon Charters 1 (London, 1973), *Charters of Burton Abbey*, ed. P. H. Sawyer, Anglo-Saxon Charters 2 (London, 1979), *Charters of Sherborne*, ed. M. A. O'Donovan, Anglo-Saxon Charters 3 (London, 1988). The indispensable guide to the study of this material is Sawyer's handbook. For more recent work see Brooks, "Anglo-Saxon Charters," and the articles listed in the annual bibliographies in *Anglo-Saxon England*.

13. Originals and later copies on single sheets are reproduced in *BMF* and *OSF*. Facsimiles of Anglo-Saxon charters dating before *c*. 800 are to be found in *ChLA* III and IV. Charters omitted from these collections and recent discoveries appear in a British Academy volume: Simon Keynes, *A Handlist of Anglo-Saxon charters: Archives and Single Sheets* (forthcoming). On the definition of an 'original' diploma, see P. Chaplais, "Some early Anglo-Saxon diplomas on single sheets: originals or copies?," in *Prisca Munimenta*, ed. Ranger, pp. 63–87.

14. Kent—Sawyer no. 8 (=*EHD* no. 56 (679)); Surrey—Sawyer no. 1165 (=*EHD* no. 54 (672 x 674)); Wessex—Sawyer no. 1164 (=*EHD* no. 55 (670 x 676)); Hwicce— Sawyer no. 51(676); Essex—Sawyer no. 1171 (=*EHD* no. 60 (685 x 694)).

15. Chaplais, "Who introduced charters into England?," 100–101.

16. A. Scharer, *Die angelsächsische Königsurkunde im 7 und 8. Jahrhundert* (Vienna, 1982), 56–57; P. Wormald, *Bede and the Conversion of England: The Charter Evidence* (Jarrow Lecture, 1984), 14–19.

17. R. L. Poole, *Lectures on the History of the Papal Chancery down to the Time of Innocent III* (Cambridge, 1915), p. 37, and see Noble's comments in *The Uses of Literacy in Early Medieval Europe*, ed. Rosamond McKitterick (Cambridge, 1990), 85–94.

18. H. Pirenne, "Le Commerce du papyrus dans la Gaule mérovingienne," *Comptes Rendus des Séances de l'Académie des Inscriptions et Belles-Lettres* (1928), 179–91, at 183.

19. G. Tessier, *Diplomatique royale française* (Paris, 1962), p. 17. Tessier stresses that the scarcity of originals makes it impossible to be sure whether or not there was an abrupt abandonment of papyrus, but it seems certain that parchment was the normal medium for charter-writing in Gaul by the end of the seventh century. Papyrus continued to be used in Gaul until the eighth century and it seems unlikely that the changing practice of the chancery is to be explained by shortage of papyrus or interruption in the supply: see N. Lewis, *Papyrus in Antiquity* (Oxford, 1974), p. 92.

20. Wood, *Merovingian North Sea*, 12–18.

21. Note that a number of papal privileges and letters were sent to England in the seventh to ninth centuries and that none of these has survived as originals: see W. Levison, *England and the Continent in the Eighth Century* (Oxford, 1946), 24–30, and 255–57, for an ingenious reconstruction of two corrupt papal privileges, apparently transcribed from fragmentary papyrus originals.

22. See the discussion by Chaplais, "Single sheets," *passim*.

23. Bruckner has suggested that the crosses in a small number of Anglo-Saxon charters might be autograph, but his examples are not convincing: *ChLA* III, no. 186, pp. 29–31, no. 190, pp. 42–43; IV, no. 236, pp. 16–17. See, however, S. D. Keynes, *The Diplomas of King Æthelred 'the Unready', 978–1016* (Cambridge, 1980), p. 101 n. 54, for a diploma of 993 with possible autograph crosses alongside some of the subscriptions.

24. Sawyer no. 19 (=*OSF* III.1).

25. For discussion of charter-production in early Anglo-Saxon England, see N. Brooks, *The Early History of the Church of Canterbury* (Leicester, 1984), 168–70, and P. Chaplais, "The origin and authenticity of the royal Anglo-Saxon diploma," in *Prisca Munimenta*, ed. Ranger, 28–42, at pp. 36–42. The case for production of charters by a royal secretariat in the tenth and eleventh centuries is argued by Keynes, *Diplomas*. See also Keynes, "Royal Government and the Written Word in Late Anglo-Saxon England," in *The Uses of Literacy in Early Medieval Europe*, ed. McKitterick, 244–48.

26. For penalty-clauses see Chaplais, "Single sheets," 71–2.

27. See, for instance, Sawyer nos. 1164 (=*EHD* no. 55), 1258 (=*EHD* no. 79).

28. Chaplais, "The royal Anglo-Saxon diploma," 33–36. See also Roger Collins, "Literacy and Laity in Early Medieval Spain," in *The Uses of Literacy*, ed. McKitterick, p. 117.

29. Chaplais, "Single sheets," 77.

30. *Ibid.*, 83–84.

31. Sawyer nos. 163 and 293 (=*BMF* II. 9 and *OSF* III. 17). See M. P. Parsons, "Some scribal memoranda for Anglo-Saxon charters of the eighth and ninth cen-

turies," *Mitteilungen des österreichischen Instituts für Geschichtsforschung* 14 (1939), 13–32, at 15–19, 21–22.

32. For discussion of these types of land tenure, see: H. R. Loyn, *Anglo-Saxon England and the Norman Conquest* (London, 1962), 171–75; Keynes, *Diplomas*, 31–33; Wormald, *Bede and the Conversion of England*, 19–23; E. John, *Land-Tenure in Early England* (Leicester, 1960), 51–53; *idem, Orbis Britanniae* (Leicester, 1966), 64–127.

33. Sawyer no. 106 (=*BMF* I.9). Other examples of endorsements to original charters recording changes of ownership are Sawyer nos. 287 and 332 (*BMF* II.28, *OSE* I.10), but neither is straightforward. Cartulary copies of charters on occasion contain notes of changes of ownership which could be derived from endorsements, but a number of these seem unacceptable and may have been added by the cartularist or an archivist.

34. Sawyer no. 1258 (=*EHD* no. 79).

35. See J. L. Laughlin, "The Anglo-Saxon legal procedure," in *Essays in Anglo-Saxon Law* (Boston, 1876), 183–305; A. J. Kennedy, "Disputes about *bocland:* the forum for their adjudication," *ASE* 14 (1985), 175–95. Patrick Wormald has recently reassessed the place of documentary evidence in such disputes: "Charters, law and the settlement of disputes in Anglo-Saxon England," in *Settlement of Disputes*, 149–68.

36. Sawyer no. 8 (=*EHD* no. 56). See also the formal tracing of the boundaries of a Worcester estate to settle an eleventh-century dispute: Sawyer no. 1460 (*c.* 1010 x 1023).

37. For these documents see Harmer, *Writs*, and *Facsimiles of English Royal Writs to AD. 1100 Presented to Vivian Hunter Galbraith*, ed. T. A. M. Bishop and P. Chaplais (Oxford, 1957). See also J. Campbell, "Some agents and agencies of the late Anglo-Saxon state," in *Domesday Studies*, ed. J. C. Holt (Woodbridge, 1987), 201–18, at pp. 214–25, and Keynes, "Royal Government and the Written Word in Late Anglo-Saxon England," 244–48.

38. Sawyer nos. 1482–1539. Note that the Latin wills are all late copies and probably represent translations of English originals or fabrications. A number of wills appear in both vernacular and Latin versions, but invariably the vernacular text seems to be primary. A new study of Anglo-Saxon wills is being prepared as a Cambridge doctoral thesis by Kathryn Lowe: "Literacy in Anglo-Saxon England: the evidence of the wills."

39. Sawyer no. 1482. This is the earliest will on a separate piece of parchment. Sawyer no. 1500 (805 x 832) was added to a copy of the charter granting land to the testator.

40. Sawyer no. 1536 (=*EHD* no. 125). See discussion by Sawyer, *Burton Abbey*, pp. xv-xxxviii.

41. Sawyer no. 1510 (=*BMF* II.25).

42. It is probably correct to see a continuum between an individual's pledge of land to the church and an ecclesiastical lease; they may represent the same transaction from different viewpoints. Such arrangements seem likely to have a connection with the Roman concept of *precarium* and its later development in Gaul: for this, see R. La-

touche, *The Birth of the Western Economy* (2d ed., London, 1967), 24–27; M. Bloch, *Feudal Society* (2d ed., London, 1962), 164.

43. Sawyer no. 1254; *Councils and Ecclesiastical Documents Relating to Great Britain and Ireland*, ed. A. Haddan and W. Stubbs, 3 vols. (Oxford, 1871), III: 582.

44. Sawyer nos. 1270, 1281, 1288, 1326, 1347, 1385, 1393, 1394, 1399, 1405, 1417, 1487.

45. Sawyer no. 1273. See Chaplais, "Single sheets," p. 63 n. 3.

46. For the possible Irish origin of the chirograph, see B. Bischoff, 'Zur Frühgeschichte des mittelalterliche Chirographum," in *idem, Mittelalterliche Studien,* 3 vols. (Stuttgart, 1966–81), I: 118–22.

47. Sawyer no. 1473 (1044 x 1048) (=*BMF* IV.28).

48. Sawyer no. 1449 (964 x 975).

49. See *EHD*, 383–84 and nos. 140–50. No. 147 demonstrates the importance of a proof of free status.

50. Sawyer nos. 1459 (1014 x 1016), 1461 (1016 x 1020) (=*EHD* nos. 128, 130).

51. Sawyer no. 1437 (original charter lost).

52. Sawyer no. 1467 (=*BMF* IV.20).

53. *Charters*, ed. Robertson, nos. 47 (Sawyer no. 1452) and 40.

54. *Ibid.*, no. 104.

55. For instance, some early eleventh-century farm accounts from Ely survive on binding-strips: N. R. Ker, *Catalogue of Manuscripts Containing Anglo-Saxon* (Oxford, 1957), no. 88; see also nos. 6, 22, 77, 353.

56. See, generally, D. A. Bullough, "The educational tradition in England from Alfred to Ælfric: Teaching *utriusque linguae*," *Settimane di studio del Centro Italiano di Studi sull'Alto Medioevo* 19 (Spoleto, 1972), 453–94. For manuscripts written in the vernacular, see Ker, *Catalogue*.

57. H. Gneuss, "The origin of standard Old English and Æthelwold's school at Winchester," *ASE* 1 (1972), 63–83.

58. *Ibid.*, 73–74.

59. *King Alfred's West Saxon Version of Gregory's Pastoral Care*, ed. H. Sweet, EETS, o.s. 45 (London, 1871), 2–8. For a translation see S. Keynes and M. Lapidge, *Alfred the Great: Asser's 'Life of King Alfred' and Other Contemporary Sources* (Harmondsworth, 1983), 124–26.

60. *Asser's Life of Alfred*, ed. W. H. Stevenson (Oxford, 1904), 58–59 (c. 75); Keynes and Lapidge, *Alfred the Great*, 90–91.

61. See P. Wormald, "The uses of literacy in Anglo-Saxon England and its neighbours', *TRHS* 5th series 27 (1977), 95–114, and most recently J. Morrish, "King Alfred's letter as a source on learning in the ninth century," in *Studies in Earlier Old English Prose*, ed. P. E. Szarmach (Albany, N.Y., 1986), 87–107.

62. *Life of Alfred*, ed. Stevenson, 62–63; Keynes and Lapidge, *Alfred the Great*, 92–93. The ninth-century Mercian compiler of the Old English Martyrology was also a competent latinist: see J. E. Cross, "The latinity of the ninth-century Old English Martyrologist," in *Studies in Earlier OE Prose*, ed. Szarmach, 275–99.

63. Brooks, *Early History*, 164–74.

64. Papers by D. N. Dumville and M. Lapidge delivered at a symposium on "England in the ninth century" which took place at the British Museum in January 1987.

65. For example, Sawyer no. 1436 (=*BMF* II.18).

66. Sawyer no. 8. See Chaplais, "Single sheets," 65–66.

67. Wulfred's land-transactions are discussed by Brooks, *Early History*, 132–42.

68. For this see *Life of Alfred*, ed. Stevenson, 93–94 (c. 106); Keynes and Lapidge, *Alfred the Great*, 110. See Keynes, "Royal Government and the Written Word in Late Anglo-Saxon England," 226–57.

69. Cuthbert, *Epistola de obitu Baedae*, ed. and trans. Colgrave and Mynors, *Bede's Ecclesiastical History*, 582.

70. W. M. Lindsay, *The Corpus, Epinal, Erfurt and Leyden Glossaries* (Oxford, 1921); M. Lapidge, "The school of Theodore and Hadrian," *ASE* 15 (1986), 45–72.

71. *Life of Alfred*, ed. Stevenson, 20, 59 (cc. 23, 76); Keynes and Lapidge, *Alfred the Great*, 75, 91.

72. Sawyer nos. 1482, 1440, 1437.

73. Christ Church—Sawyer nos. 1195, 1197. St Augustine's—Sawyer nos. 1198, 1239.

74. Sawyer no. 1202.

75. Sawyer no. 1200; see also nos. 1196, 1199. For the relationships between these Kentish noblemen and women see Brooks, *Early History*, 147–49.

76. Sawyer no. 204 (=*OSF* I.8).

77. Brooks, *Early History*, 174.

78. See above, p. 43 and n. 25.

79. Sawyer no. 1271 (=*EHD* no. 87).

80. Compare Sawyer no. 163, discussed above, p. 44, where it seems that the parchment was blank when used in the conveyance ceremony.

81. For the importance of the verbal declaration see Sawyer no. 1462 (=*EHD* no. 135). Anglo-Saxon wills may also have originated as public statements: see discussion by M. M. Sheehan, *The Will in Medieval England* (Toronto, 1963), 3–106.

82. Haddan and Stubbs, *Councils*, III: 362.

83. *Die Gesetze der Angelsachsen*, ed. F. Liebermann, 3 vols. (Halle, 1903–16), I: 3–8; *EHD* no. 29.

84. *Bede's Ecclesiastical History*, ed. Colgrave and Mynors, 150 (II.5).

85. Kent—Laws of Hlothhere and Eadric (673–685?), Laws of Wihtred (695); Wessex—Laws of Ine (688–94). See *Gesetze*, ed. Liebermann, I: 9–14, 88–123; *EHD* nos. 30–32.

86. P. Wormald, "*Lex scripta* and *verbum regis:* Legislation and Germanic kingship from Euric to Cnut," in *Early Medieval Kingship*, ed. P. H. Sawyer and I. N. Wood (Leeds, 1977), 105–38, at p. 115.

87. Lapidge, "School of Theodore and Hadrian," 52–53.

88. *Bede's Ecclesiastical History*, ed. Colgrave and Mynors, 68 (I.23); *MGH Epp.* I: 423–24 (=*EHD* no. 162).

89. Bishop Agilbert, a Frank, declined an invitation to speak at the Synod of Whitby because he would have needed an interpreter and he had previously been dismissed by King Cenwealh because his speech was regarded as barbarous: *Bede's Ecclesiastical History*, ed. Colgrave and Mynors, 300, 235 (III.25, 7).

90. J. K. Bostock, *A Handbook on Old High German Literature* (2d ed., Oxford, 1976), especially 90–117; R. McKitterick, *The Frankish Church and the Carolingian Reforms, 789–895*, Royal Historical Society Studies in History 2 (London, 1977), 184–205.

91. *Baedae Opera Historica*, ed. Plummer, 115; *EHD*, 801.

92. See for instance the references to learned men travelling to assist Boniface in Hesse and Thuringia: *Vita Bonifatii auctore Willibaldo*, ed. W. Levison, *MGH SS i.u.s.* LVII, 34, trans. C. H. Talbot, *The Anglo-Saxon Missionaries in Germany* (London, 1954), 47.

93. *Life of Bishop Wilfrid*, ed. and trans. Colgrave, 6, 44.

94. *Life of Alfred*, ed. Stevenson, 20, 59–63, 73–75 (cc. 22–23, 76–78, 87–89); Keynes and Lapidge, *Alfred the Great*, 75, 91–93, 99–100 (and p. 239 n. 46 for discussion).

95. *Pastoral Care*, ed. Sweet, p. 2; Keynes and Lapidge, *Alfred the Great*, p. 124.

96. Colgrave and Mynors, *Bede's Ecclesiastical History*, 190 (Sigeberht of East Anglia), 430 (Aldfrith of Northumbria) (III.15, IV. 26). Sigeberht was educated in Gaul, Aldfrith in Ireland.

97. *Ibid.*, 2 (Preface). See D. P. Kirby, "King Ceolwulf of Northumbria and the *Historia Ecelesiastica*," *Studia Celtica* 14/15 (1979–80), 163–73.

98. Levison, *England and the Continent*, 245–46.

99. See discussion by P. Wormald, "Bede, *Beowulf* and the conversion of the English aristocracy," in *Bede and Anglo-Saxon England*, ed. R. T. Farrell, British Archaeology Reports, British Series 46 (Oxford, 1978), 32–95, at 42–49.

100. Simm Keynes, "Royal Government and the written Word in Late Anglo-Saxon England," in *The Uses of Literacy in Early Medieval Europe*, ed. Rosamond McKitterich (Cambridge, 1990). 226–57.

101. I should like to thank David Dumville, Rosamond McKitterick and Simon Keynes for their comments and criticism.

The Making of *Angelcynn:* English Identity Before the Norman Conquest[1]

SARAH FOOT

THERE are grounds for seeing an increasing sophistication in the development of a self-conscious perception of 'English' cultural uniqueness and individuality towards the end of the ninth century, at least in some quarters, and for crediting King Alfred's court circle with its expression. King Alfred was not, as Orderic Vitalis described him, 'the first king to hold sway over the whole of England', which tribute might rather be paid to his grandson Æthelstan.[2] He was, however, as his obituary in the Anglo-Saxon Chronicle described him, 'king over the whole English people except for that part which was under Danish rule'.[3] Through his promotion of the term *Angelcynn* to reflect the common identity of his people in a variety of texts dating from the latter part of his reign, and his efforts in cultivating the shared memory of his West Mercian and West Saxon subjects, King Alfred might be credited with the invention of the English as a political community.

This paper will consider why it was that Alfred, and after him the tenth-century West Saxon kings who creaed an English realm, chose to invent an *Angelcynn* and not the Saxonkind that might seem more obvious considering their own ethnic origins.[4] In exploring the promotion of this collective name for the politically united Anglo-Saxon peoples, I start from the premise that language is more than an important reflection of the thought of an age; it is essentially constitutive of that thought. Such ideas are only open to a people as they have the language available to express them; in other words, ideas are conditioned by the language in which they can be thought.[5]

For the year 886 the Anglo-Saxon Chronicle reported that King Alfred had occupied London and that 'all the English people (*all Angelcyn*) who were not under subjection to the Danes, submitted to him'.[6] It now seems probable that London had in fact been recovered from the Danes a few years earlier, perhaps in 883 when the Chronicle reports Alfred laying siege to the city, and that what occurred in 886 was either a retaking of the city or a ceremonial statement of the significance of London's restoration to 'English' rule.[7] Earlier in the ninth century Mercia had forcibly been brought under West Saxon rule by King Ecgberht, and in mid-century there is evidence for some co-operation between the two kingdoms.[8] But while the events of 886 may represent only a formalisation of this pre-existing alliance, the rhetoric by which they are described serves to construe this as a formative moment in the creation of a united West Saxon/Mercian realm. The ceremony is coupled with the submission of the Mercian ruler Æthelred (to whom charge of the city was entrusted) and his acceptance of an ealdordom, and may also have coincided with his marriage to Alfred's daughter Æthelflæd.[9] According to Asser the joining of Wessex and Mercia was a new union, voluntarily entered into: 'all the Anglo-Saxons—those who had formerly been scattered everywhere and were not in captivity with the Danes—turned willingly to King Alfred and submitted themselves to his lordship'.[10]

The adoption of a new political terminology to reflect the new hegemony of Wessex over the western Mercians is, as Janet Nelson has recently argued, particularly apposite.[11] It was from this time that Alfred was styled in charters *rex Angul-Saxonum*, rather than the more usual West Saxon title of *rex Saxonum*, and from this point in his narrative that Asser adopted the same style to describe the king.[12] Alfred clearly now considered himself licensed to act on behalf of more than his West Saxon subjects; in making an agreement with the Viking ruler of East Anglia, Guthrum, he spoke of himself as acting on behalf of all the counsellors of the English: *ealles Angelcynnes witan*.[13] The discourse here is not, however, simply such as that used by any ruler consolidating a new political realm. Certainly Alfred's record of military success demonstrated the wisdom of Mercian acceptance of his rule, but he could have continued to ensure the physical safety of his subject peoples without compromising their separateness. What the Alfredian rhetoric does is to advance the notion that all the Germanic subjects of the West Saxon king were essentially one 'Englishkind'. The common identity of the West Saxons, Mercians and the men of Kent as the *Angelcynn* was defined by the West Saxon court machine specifically with reference to their otherness from those subject to Danish rule (and from the Welsh from whom Alfred had also received submission),[14] and their common cause under one leader in opposition to the Danes, but also more generally in the sense of one people with a common heritage, one faith, and a shared history.[15]

The role of King Alfred in the development of a sense of English individuality will be examined by exploring the ways in which the Germanic inhabitants of pre-Conquest Britain described themselves and were described by outsiders.[16] The separate and individual identity of the different kingdoms of pre-Conquest Britain was clearly important to their rulers, and it is important to recognise that the apparent use of a consistent vocabulary for the English people does not prefigure any sense of political unity among the Anglo-Saxons before the late ninth century.[17] However, examination of contemporary linguistic usage can be a valuable key to concepts of the past, particularly in the sphere of naming. Not only are the words chosen by one culture to express its ideas one sign of its own distinctive and individual thought, but the collective names adopted by communities play a significant part in the process of the formation of their identity.[18]

Robert Bartlett has argued that medieval ethnicity was a social construct rather than a biological datum, being determined primarily by cultural distinctions which have the potential to evolve differently in changing circumstances.[19] He cites the example of Regino of Prüm who, writing *c.* 900, offered four categories for classifying ethnic variation: 'the various nations differ in descent, customs, language and law'.[20] Although Regino placed *genus* not *lingua* as the first of his categories, racial differences were generally considered less relevant in the formation of concepts of nationhood in the middle ages than cultural qualities such as customs, language and law. The imiportance of linguistic bonds in forging collective identity was recognised by many medieval writers.[21] In an insular context, Bede distinguished the peoples of Britain (Britons, Picts, Irish and English) by the languages which they spoke.[22] Following Bede in part, Alcuin drew attention to the role of language together with lineage: 'famed Britain holds within her bounds peoples divided by language and separated by race according to their ancestors' names'.[23] In accentuating the potential of the written language—*Englisc*—to bind together his subjects as the *Angelcynn*, Alfred showed how the promotion of the common tongue they shared might be useful in overriding the inheritance of political and ancestral separateness in the creation of a new identity.[24]

The word *Angelcynn* is first found in one Mercian charter of the 850s from Worcester, where it was used to distinguish those of English origin from foreigners and was apparently synonymous with the Latin *Angli*.[25] But it becomes common only in the last two decades of the ninth century when it appears in a variety of texts associated with the Alfredian court, notably in works which were part of the king's programme of educational reform and revival. This implies that it was not chosen unwittingly but, together with the subject matter of the texts themselves, it was part of an attempt to promote a nascent conception of one people. It was as the *Angel-cynn* that Alfred described his subjects in the letter which he circulated to his bishops with his translation of Pope Gregory's *Regula pastoralis*. Recalling how formerly 'there were happy times then throughout the *Angelcynn*', Alfred appealed to the collective memory of his people, reminding them of their shared past and of the consequences of their failure to abstract themselves from worldly affairs to apply the wisdom given by God: 'Remember what punishments befell us in this world when we ourselves did not cherish learning or transmit it to other men.'[26] His solution was to urge his bishops to assist him in teaching 'all the free-born young men now among the *Angelcynn*' to read English, for which project he was translating, or arranging to have translated 'into the language that all can understand, certain books which are the most necessary for all men to know'.[27] These texts, as has long been recognised, were not chosen randomly, but together constituted a programme of study which if mastered would serve to restore Christianity among the English aristocracy, which in the king's opinion had declined so far, notably through their loss of understanding of Latin, that God had sent the Danes as divine punishment.[28]

In this prefatory letter to the *Regula pastoralis* the king showed his sensitivity to the power of language and its potential for conveying wisdom, as well as an awareness of the benefits which earlier societies had drawn from the use of their own vernaculars: 'then I recalled how the Law was first composed in the Hebrew language, and thereafter, when the Greeks learned it, they translated it into their own language and other books as well'.[29] Language offers understanding, and understanding gives knowledge of the Law, and hence knowledge of God. The text above all others which gave Alfred's officials knowledge of the kind of wisdom they needed to fulfil their duties was, as Simon Keynes has noted, the king's law-code.[30] Here Alfred portrayed himself as a law-giver firmly rooted within an historical tradition;[31] quoting the law of Moses and earlier laws from each of the kingdoms over whom he now had lordship, he claimed not to be making new law, but to be restoring to his newly united peoples the law that they had lost. This is made explicit in the historical introduction which the king appended to his own law-book, where he begins with a collection of passages of Mosaic law, mostly taken from Exodus and beginning with the Ten Commandments, before moving on to consider how Old Testament law for the Jews was modified for Christian nations, and then the earlier medieval history of law-giving.[32]

Afterwards when it came about that many peoples had received the faith of Christ, many synods of holy bishops and also of other distinguished counsellors were assembled throughout all the earth, and also throughout all the *Angelcynn* (after they had received the faith of Christ)... Then in many synods they fixed the compensations for many human misdeeds, and they wrote them in many synod-books, here one law, there another. Then I, King Alfred, collected these together and ordered to be written many of them which our forefathers observed, those which I liked; and those which I did not like I rejected with the advice of my counsellors and ordered them to be differently observed. For I dared not presume to set in writing at all many of my own, because it was unknown to me what would please those who should come after us. But those which I found, which seemed to me most just, either in the time of my kinsman King Ine, or of Offa, king of the Mercians, or of Æthelberht (who first among the *Angelcynn* received baptism), I collected herein and omitted the others.

Alfred was appropriating his subject peoples' separate—Christian—pasts to his own ends. The law he now gave to the *Angelcynn* was not one of his own creation but an amalgam of the collected laws of previous kings of Kent, Mercia and Wessex. Alfred was legislating here overtly in the tradition of a Christian king, against an historical background of Old Testament law-giving (and in the light of a contemporary Frankish commitment to written laws and to the collection of law-codes).[33] He was showing the Anglo-Saxons how similar their laws were to those of Ancient Israel and also inviting them to remodel themselves as a new Chosen People.[34] Bede had conceived of the *gens Anglorum* as the new Israel, but Alfred went further: he purported to restore a state that had formerly existed, equivalent to the state of Israel restored after the Babylonian captivity, not to create a new unitary structure of diverse peoples brought together under one Christian law.[35] Previous Anglo-Saxon kings had extended their realms by military force in order to encompass people from different *gentes*, but had not thereby either made themselves into 'emperors' or indeed defined their own kingship other than by reference to their own *gens:* although he had taken control of the previously independent kingdoms of the Hwicce, the South Saxons and of Kent, removing or demoting their own kings, and he had some authority in Surrey, Essex and East Anglia, Offa was never described in contemporary documents as other than *rex Merciorum*.[36] Where Alfred was innovative was in his attempt to make his West Saxon and Mercian peoples into one *gens* (the *gens Anglorum* or *Angelcynn*) using his programme of educational revival and reform to encourage among his subjects an idea of their single past history. Appealing to their memory of shared experience and common law he sought to persuade them that he was restoring the English, whereas, albeit following a model provided by Bede, he was inventing them.[37]

The creation of a newly named people subject to one lord, loyalty to whom was forcibly imposed by oath,[38] might be understood in the narrow sense of the imposition of a politically defined nationhood by a cultural elite, in this case the royal court, over a wider population, an identity which could never have been exclusive nor taken priority over pre-existing, more local, allegiances. One might therefore dismiss Alfred's notion of Englishness as representative only of a restricted kind of political identity with no broader relevance beyond the rarefied circles of Alfred's immediate entourage. It might, nevertheless, at least within that confined group surrounding the king, resemble a primitive attempt at creating a single *gens*. Alfred's primitive 'nation', created out of political necessity, would to some extent conform to Gellner's definition of nationalism (articulated exclusively in relation to modern states) as 'primarily a principle which holds that the political and national unit should be congruent'.[39] But the Alfredian 'nation' was also defined in terms of its difference from the other (here clearly understood to be both the Christian Welsh and, more significantly, the pagan Danes) in which context Peter Sahlin's comments, although again made in a modern context, seem pertinent: 'national identity like ethnic or communal identity is contingent and relational: it is defined by the social or territorial boundaries drawn to distinguish the collective self and its implicit negation, the other'.[40] However, while there are clearly some echoes, in placing loyalty to the primitive state too high up the agenda and apparently minimising the importance of other possible communities or identities any modern nationalist model is too exclusive for ninth-century circumstances. The creation of one political unit at this period was hindered by the fissiparous nature of the early Anglo-Saxon state, and the vigour of regional separatism—the distinctiveness of Mercia and, later, in the tenth century, of Northumbria continued to be articulated far beyond the establishment of unified rule from Wessex. There was, as Wormald has shown, no Alfredian England.[41] But, in agreeing that there was no potential for uniting the polities, must we also accept that there was no putative conception of Englishness?

Alfred's educational programme could be interpreted as a conscious effort to shape an English imagination by disseminating beyond the court his ideas about the nature of 'Englishness' and his fictive interpretation of history through the works he determined the English should read. Drawing attention to Asser's account of the king's learning of 'Saxon songs' (*carmina Saxonica*) in his childhood and his urging their memorisation on his entourage, Janet Nelson has stressed the distinctively Saxon vernacular and aristocratic cultural inheritance which Alfred wished to emphasise.[42] While this might suggest a specifically (West) Saxon focus to Alfred's endeavours, other aspects of his programme demonstrate the wider transmission of his ideas to his Kentish and Anglian (Mercian) subjects as well, through the use of the vernacular, which breadth is encompassed by Keynes and Lapidge's translation of Asser's *libri Saxonici* as English books.[43] Alfred was not only reminding all of his aristocracy that they shared a cultural tradition (in which they might more actively participate if they reacquired the wisdom they had lost)[44] but asserting that their common cultural ethic arose from their common origins and a shared history.[45]

The historical element of the curriculum Alfred devised is striking: not only were Orosius's Histories against the Pagans and Bede's Ecclesiastical History translated into Old English at this time, but it must be in the context of this wider programme that the compilation of the Anglo-Saxon Chronicle was commissioned.[46] The Chronicle and the Old English Bede could both be seen as instruction for the English, the *Angelcynn*, in their shared inheritance of a common history. One of the themes of Bede's History, as I shall suggest further below, was the promotion of a sense of unity and common cause among the Germanic Christian peoples of Britain; where Bede wrote of a Christian *gens Anglorum*, his Mercian translator spoke of *Ongelcynn* or *Ongelþeode*.[47] Together this historical literature gave the English a myth—a story with a veiled meaning—of their common origins; the Anglo-Saxon Chronicle in particular is a history with an inner hermeneutic. It is not propaganda for one dynasty;[48] the Chronicle does not present, in the way that Bede did, the history of one people in a linear progression with a beginning, a middle and an end: there are indeed too many beginnings in the Chronicle. But, despite its annalistic form, it is a continuing and developing narrative.[49] The separate beginnings of Alfred's subject peoples are brought to one end: that of unitary rule from Wessex. It hard not to see the chronicler's statement about the general submission of 886 as the climactic moment of the achievement of this end to which the whole was directed, although the story continues thereafter: the *Angelcynn* have had multiple early histories, but will have one future, together. The inclusion of the different origin-myths for the separate early kingdoms illustrates the distinctiveness of each people; their ethnic diversity and the particular circumstances in which each group arrived in Britain gives each people its own traditions and culture; the genealogies for each royal line provide a record of each separate ruling dynasty.[50] Yet despite the differences in each kingdom's past history, they all share certain common features and ultimately theirs is a collective history.

In anthropological terms this might be called an instrumental ethnicity, a group identity based on the political circumstances of the moment, a subjective process for defining a collective group.[51] In this case one useful model, despite its failure to consider pre-modern societies, is that of Benedict Anderson's *Imagined Communities*.[52] Alfred was indeed trying to shape the English imagination; by collating and presenting a coherent historical whole he invented an English community, implanting into the minds of his people a personal and cultural feeling of belonging to the *Angelcynn*, the English kind. Alfred presented his subjects with an idea partly shaped by Bede, partly of his own devising, and he adopted a self-conscious way of promoting it through the educational reform-programme. Despite the differences in scale, this is similar to Anderson's argument about the importance of the mass production of print as a formative process in the creation of imagined nations. It is significant that Alfred used the vernacular in order that his ideas might be most accessible.[55] While the texts he thought 'most necessary for all men to know' would not have been accessible to as wide an audience as that theoretically possible in a print culture, Alfred was aiming at a socially and geographically wide readership—'all free-born young men now among the English'—who were to be reached through the participation of all of the king's bishops in his extended realm. The notion of a common English identity was certainly dreamt up in the rarefied, scholarly atmosphere of Alfred's court, but it was from the outset intended for a wider audience. One might wish to question the likelihood of the notion penetrating to the wider mass of the semi-free peasantry, but the obligation of general oath-taking suggested by the first chapter of Alfred's law-code might indicate that it was to the broader group of those subjects who swore the oath that the rhetoric of Englishness was directed.

Alfred was thus manipulating the history of the Anglo-Saxon peoples to create among his own subjects a sense of cultural and spiritual identity, by invoking a concept of Englishness particularly dependent on the Christian faith. It was the loss of faith (notably through the loss of that knowledge which had given previous generations access to the wisdom of Christian writings) which had led the English to the brink of collapse and brought so many of their ethnic as well as spiritual compatriots into captivity under a foreign, and pagan, people. For all the obvious (and patently far from coincidental) advantages for the new regime, this was more than simply a rationale for the political domination of Wessex over Mercia. How original was it?

That divine vengeance might be anticipated if sin were not corrected was scarcely a novel idea; divine displeasure was indeed the most frequently adduced explanation for any disaster.[54] Nor was Alfred the only writer to make direct association between Viking raids and divine displeasure:[55] in 839 his father Æthelwulf had written to the Frankish emperor, Louis the Pious, warning that if men did not quickly repent and return to Christian observance pagan men would lay waste their land with fire and sword.[56] While other writers of this period looked to spiritual renewal, and improvement in individual religious observance,[57] Alfred's perception that the root of the evil lay in his subjects' ignorance, rather than in their lack of faith, led to his adoption of the innovative remedy of vernacular education.

In apparently including Bede's Ecclesiastical History among those Latin works translated as part of his vernacular programme, Alfred acknowledged the debt which he owed to Bede for the invention of a concept of the English.[58] For Bede, the Anglo-Saxon peoples, though separated by the diversity of their political arrangements, were united by their shared Christian faith into one *gens Anglorum* in the sight of God: it was as English Christians that the faithful should identify themselves to St Peter. As Patrick Wormald has argued, it was Bede who gave the idea of Englishness its particular power; Bede demonstrated that the Church not only created but named this new communal identity and made the *gens Anglorum* a people with a covenant, like Israel.[59]

For Bede, the semblance of unity was created by the existence of one language distinguishing the Germanic settlers of Anglo-Saxon England from their British, Irish and Pictish neighbours. His sensitivity to the role of language in defining ethnic groups was stressed at the beginning of his history, where he also introduced the idea that the Latin of the Bible had the potential to unite these differences.[60]

> At the present time there are five languages in Britain, just as the divine law is written in five books, all devoted to seeking out and setting forth one and the same kind of wisdom, namely the knowledge of sublime truth and of true sublimity. These are the English, British, Irish, Pictish as well as the Latin languages; through the study of the scriptures, Latin is in general use among them all.

One of Bede's intentions in writing his History was to demonstrate that, despite their separate ethnic and political origins, the Anglo-Saxons had been brought together into one *gens* by the unifying power of the Christian faith, transmitted to them by Rome. His summary of the state of Britain at the time when he was writing reinforces this view that religion could act as a binding force: it is as one united, Christian people that the relationship of the English with their non-Germanic neighbours (Picts, Irish and Britons) is defined.[61]

Part of what Bede had aimed to illustrate was the process by which a 'national' Church was created; as he traced the establishment of separate sees in each individual kingdom—the framework around which the History was structured—he stressed not a series of distinct institutions for each individual people but the making of a single Church, subject to Rome. The high point of his narrative was the primacy of Archbishop Theodore, 'the first of the archbishops whom the whole English Church consented to obey'.[62] Not only was this the first time when the separate churches of the individual kingdoms were united under one authority, but Theodore was the first person to whom all of the English offered any sort of authority. Although Bede's was an argument about spiritual authority not about political power, there was a potential political dimension to his historical vision, as is demonstrable from his list of kings who held *imperium*, or wide-ranging power.[63]

> In the year 616 Æthelberht of Kent entered upon the eternal joys of the heavenly kingdom. He was the third English king to rule over all the southern kingdoms which are divided from the north by the river Humber and the surrounding territory; but he was the first to enter the kingdom of heaven. The first king to hold the like sovereignty— *imperium*—was Ælle, king of the South Saxons; the second was Ceawlin, king of the West Saxons; the third, as we have said, was Æthelberht, king of Kent; the fourth was Rædwald, king of the East Angles, who while Æthelberht was still alive acted as military leader of his own people. The fifth was Edwin, king of the Northumbrians, the nation inhabiting the district north of the Humber. Edwin had still greater power and ruled over all the inhabitants of Britain, English and Britons alike, except for Kent only. He even brought under English rule the isles of Angelsey and Man which lie between England and Ireland and belong to the Britons. The sixth to rule within the same bounds was Oswald, the most Christian king of the Northumbrians, while the seventh was his brother Oswiu, who for a time held almost the same territory.

The context of this celebrated passage is Bede's obituary for Æthelberht of Kent, and the chapter includes material from a variety of sources, much of it probably deriving from Canterbury. It is not, however, necessary to presume that the list itself derives from Canterbury,[64] and there may be a case for attributing its construction to Bede himself, bearing in mind the importance to him of the unity of the *gens Anglorum*. This is not to argue either that there was, or that Bede was claiming that there was, one quasi-imperial office, ranking above the kingship of an individual kingdom, held by certain figures between the late fifth and seventh century, which passed from one king to another depending on their relative superiority.[65] Bede seems merely to have been hinting that, just as one faith and one language *can* unify disparate groups, so, bearing in mind the demonstrable unity provided by the centralising authority of the Church, *could* a single political authority serve as one means of binding otherwise distinct political groups into a common cause: the promotion of the true faith and the making of a people with a single, Christian identity. That such an argument might be translated further in the ninth century by a dynasty which found itself in possession of a power exceeding that of any of its West Saxon predecessors, and that it might (having itself only newly come to power) look to Bede's account for an historical justification or parallel for its own pretensions, seems entirely natural. What Alfred can be seen to have recognised is the potential for his own purpose of the model invented by Pope Gregory and promoted by Bede: one Church, one people and one faith could prefigure a political unity, an ideal which might be made real by a king with sufficient power and ideological energy to promote it.

In making the one nation he created English (and not Saxon) Alfred perpetuated the name for that people coined by Bede. Bede did not invent the term, nor was he unique among Anglo-Saxon writers in using it to define the Germanic people of Britain collectively, but he did use it more consistently than his contemporaries.[66] The author of the Whitby Life of Pope Gregory wrote of the pope's role in ensuring the salvation of the *gens Anglorum* and once made reference to the *sudrangli*, meaning apparently the the people south of the Humber.[67] Boniface's letters frequently alluded to the characteristics of the English race, although he also noted their kinship with the continental Saxons; similarly Bishop Torhthelm of Leicester wrote to Boniface on hearing of the success of his continental Saxon mission, to rejoice at the conversion of *gens nostra*.[68] The anonymous Lindisfarne Life of Cuthbert referred to the bishops of the Saxons, while Stephen, hagiographer of Wilfrid, wrote of both *Angli* and *Saxones*.[69] To outsiders, the Germanic inhabitants of the former Roman Britain did interestingly seem to have a single identity, but it was a Saxon one, they were *Saxones*. The Celtic peoples of Britain consistently called their Germanic neighbours Saxons (a usage which persisted into the modern period).[70] The term Saxon was similarly used by most of the non-insular authors who described affairs in Britain in the fifth and sixth centuries such as the Gallic Chronicler of 452 and Constantius, author of the Life of St Germanus,[71] and this terminology continued to be used in the seventh century.[72]

At variance with all these early external authorities is the sixth-century

Byzantine historian Procopius, who in describing the island of *Brittia* spoke of the three populous nations to inhabit the place, each with a king set over it, these nations being the *Brittones* (named from the island), the *Frisiones*, and the *Angiloi (Αγγιλοι)*.[73] Procopius's information about Britain was presumably obtained from the group of *Angiloi* whose presence he recorded among a legation sent from the Frankish king to Constantinople *c.* 550, making a claim for Frankish hegemony over the island.[74] One might question how accurately Procopius recorded (and translated) the language used by these foreign enemies, were it not that Pope Gregory adopted the same term, *Anguli*, to described the Germanic inhabitants of Britain. It is not impossible that Gregory's nomenclature was influenced either by Procopius or by the general currency of the term at the Imperial court in Constantinople, where Gregory is known to have been papal apocrisarius *c.* 578–585.

All of Pope Gregory's letters about the mission to Kent referred to the people as the Angles, including those written after he had received some direct information about affairs in Britain and so might have known that this was not the most appropriate term, certainly not for the people whom Æthelberht ruled.[75] These texts associated with Gregory are not, however, consistent in the retention of the third syllable added by Procopius; the brief biography of Gregory in the *Liber pontificalis* referred to the pope's sending of missionaries *ad gentem Angulorum*, but his verse epitaph stated that he had converted the *Anglos* to Christ.[76] The extra syllable makes more plausible the 'not Angles but angels' pun (and in reporting the famous story of the boys in the Roman slave-market the anonymous Whitby hagiographer of Gregory indeed described them as *Anguli* although Bede termed them *Angli* in his own account).[77] In the letter which he wrote in July 598 to Eulogius, bishop of Alexandria, where he described the success of the Augustine's mission, however, Gregory provided an alternative explanation for the name English, referring to the missionaries whom he had sent to the *gens Anglorum in mundo angulo posita*.[78]

Gregory's adoption of the *Angli/Anguli* label, wherever he had obtained it, would have had little influence had it not been taken up by Bede and via his writings gradually acquired a wider currency. A shift is noticeable in the language used by continental writers to describe the Germanic peoples of Britain from the eighth century, perhaps as Bede's Ecclesiastical History began to circulate on the continent through the influence of English missionaries, but there is little consistency of practice, the two names, Saxon and English, being used synonymously.[79] For example Alfred's father Æthelwulf was variously described in the Annals of St-Bertin as king of the En-

glish, of the Anglo-Saxons, of the west English as well as king of the West
Saxons.[80] The author of the miracles of St Wandrille appears to have
viewed Britain as inhabited by only one people (the *gens Anglorum*) although having multiple kings; he reports how at some time between 858
and 866 the *praefectus* of Quentovic, Grippo, was sent by Charles the Bald
on a mission *in insula Brittannica ad reges gentis Anglorum*.[81] That there was
an association between the Germanic inhabitants of Britain and the continental Saxons was by no means forgotten; Boniface could write to all the
Angli in the eighth century urging them to pray for the conversion of
the Saxons, 'because they are of one blood and one bone with us',[82] and in
the tenth century the marriage of Edith, sister of King Æthelstan, to the
Saxon king Otto was seen as a reassertion of familial ties between the two
peoples, as well as providing the Saxon dynasty with an opportunity to benefit from a more ancient kingship.[83]

It thus appears that before the eighth century the seaborne attackers of
Roman Britain and the peoples who settled the south-eastern part of the island in the sub-Roman period were seen generically by outsiders as *Saxones*.
Bede also talked of the *aduentus Saxonum*, even though he sought to describe the salvation of the *gens Anglorum*. The fact that there was one term
in general usage before Bede's time suggests that the Germanic inhabitants
of Britain were perceived from the outside as one community with a recognisable identity and distinction from their neighbours. The created notion
that this community should be named the *Angli* came gradually to be recognised on the continent from the eighth century, but the consistency of usage found in the earlier period does not persist, except in the Celtic-speak-
ing areas, where the Germanic peoples of Britain remained Saxons.

King Alfred's vision of one people united through a shared history,
common faith and opposition to the Danes under a single rulership might
have found outward celebration in the ceremonies to mark the general submission of 886, but can scarcely have met without opposition. Those reluctant to accept the concept of the newly created identity or unwilling to accept West Saxon overlordship had, however, few independent means of
articulating their alternative perceptions or preferences (or, at least, few are
recorded). The Alfredian programme was indeed in part an exercise in controlling knowledge, encompassing as it did 'those books most necessary for
all men to know'. Those attracted to Alfred's court were not exclusively English. According to Asser 'foreigners of all races came from places near and
far', some in search of money, others looking for a lord of proven ability:
'many Franks, Frisians, Gauls, pagans (*viz* Danes), Welshmen, Irishmen
and Bretons subjected themselves willingly to his lordship, nobles and

commoners alike'.[84] There were others of 'English' birth who failed to perceive the benefits to be gained from obedience to King Alfred. A charter of
Alfred's son, Edward the Elder, dated 901, provides the history of an estate
in Wiltshire, recording that it had previously been forfeited by an ealdorman, Wulfhere, 'when he deserted without permission both his lord King
Alfred and his country (*patria*) in spite of the oath which he had sworn to
the king and all his leading men. Then also, by the judgment of all the
councillors of the *Gewisse* and of the Mercians he lost the control and inheritance of his lands.'[85]

Such acquiescence as there was in the unified rule created by Alfred did
not extend beyond his death to the automatic acceptance of his heirs.
Within Wessex Alfred's son, Edward the Elder, faced a challenge from his
cousin, Æthelwold.[86] The predominantly West Saxon sources imply that
the arrangements for the control of the parts of Mercia not under Danish
control remained as they were (direct control of the kingdom rested in the
hands of Ealdorman Æthelred and his wife Æthelflæd, but under King Edward's overall authority)[87] and Edward continued in his charters to use the
royal style his father had adopted: 'king of the Anglo-Saxons'.[88] There is no
record in the surviving sources of any objection to these arrangements beyond 903 (although the Mercian Register hints at disquiet when Edward
assumed rulership of Mercia on his sister's death in 918),[89] but acceptance
of the necessity for Mercian and West Saxon collaboration against a common threat is not sufficient ground for arguing for widespread noble acquiescence in the fusion of the two kingdoms, or the loss of the separate identities of their peoples.

The notion of one English nation continued to have a currency throughout the tenth century and might seem to have had a wider applicability
following the unification of England under West Saxon rule first by King
Æthelstan and particularly in the time of King Edgar. Ælfric showed signs
of national pride in writing *c.* 1000 that 'the English nation (*angelcynn*) is not
deprived of God's saints when in England lie buried such holy people as this
sainted king [Edmund], and the blessed Cuthbert and St Æthelthryth in
Ely. . . There are also many other saints among the English nation (*on an-
gelcynne*).'[90] Did Ælfric attribute to Alfred a responsibility for making this a
single people greater than that inherent in his defeat of their enemy, the
Danes?[91] He certainly knew of 'the books which King Alfred wisely translated from Latin into English', specifying of these only a *Historia Anglorum*,
presumably the translation of Bede's History not now thought to have been
translated by Alfred personally.[92] To an outsider in the eleventh century,
the English did look to be one people; Cnut wrote to his subjects as 'the

whole race of the English' (*totius gentis Anglorum*), and in the preface to the version of his laws which he brought before an assembly at Oxford in 1018, Cnut sought to 'establish peace and friendship between the Danes and the English and put an end to their former strife'.[93] The referent of the term has, however, shifted since Alfred's day. Alfred's English were the Christian people of Kent, Wessex and western Mercia;[94] the English whom Cnut conquered included not only the East Anglians and Northumbrians but men of Danish parentage, born or settled in England. The Normans also saw the people they had conquered as one English *gens*.[95]

Although some continued to perceive the Anglo-Saxon peoples as one nation, and to use the term English to describe them into the eleventh century, this does not demonstrate a linear development of an Alfredian notion of English nationhood through the tenth century, nor the perpetuation of the shared memory that Alfred had sought to cultivate. The potential to unite all the Englishkind under one rule became a reality temporarily only in the reign of King Æthelstan, and permanently only from the time of Edgar. The tenth-century West Saxon kings frequently saw themselves as kings of the English (*rex Anglorum*) but not uniquely or exclusively so; their authority ranged more widely, encompassed peoples of greater ethnic diversity and might extend to governorship of Britain.[96] A grant of King Eadred's of 946 reported that king's consecration to 'sovereignty of the quadripartite rule' on the death of his brother, Edmund, who had 'royally guided the government of kingdoms of the Anglo-Saxons and Northumbrians, of the pagans and the Britons'.[97] It may be that regional separatism was too sensitive an issue to be ignored by southern kings often seen as unwelcome foreigners in Mercia, let alone Northumbria; the problems of imposing unitary rule from the south were considerable, and the loyalty of these regions to Wessex was never certain.[98]

Where there was any notion of the existence of Englishness among the nobility even in Wessex, let alone Mercia or Northumbria, it is likely to have been perceived as only one of a number of possible communities of identity. Those who might at times have defined themselves as English would simultaneously recognise other loyalties: to their king, to their lord, to a village, to a region. Distance from the West Saxon court (or from Canterbury) might alter conceptions of Englishness substantially. Alliance with Scandinavian 'enemies' looked attractive at various times to archbishops of York, and the members of the northern Mercian and Northumbrian nobility.[99] Nevertheless, it does appear that one collective identity of Englishness had an enduring currency through the pre-Conquest period, transcending the significant separation brought about by the existence of a multiplicity of different political organisations and ethnic groups among the Anglo-Saxons. Alfred's promotion of the *Angelcynn* as a people with a shared past united under West Saxon rule fostered an awareness that English self-consciousness lay in more than their acknowledgement of a common Christianity centred on Canterbury. Patrick Wormald has already shown how useful the notion of Englishness was to be in the evolution of the early English state; it is worth exploring whether the notion has any potential for the examination of other spheres of pre-Conquest history.[100]

The force of this sense of a common identity is striking, notably its prevalence in sources at least from Bede's time onwards, coupled with the fact that it was clearly recognisable to outsiders. That 'a strong sense of a common unity as a people is not incompatible with a highly particularised local identity' has been demonstrated by the current President of the Society in relation to eleventh- and twelfth-century Wales. Professor Davies has shown that the Welsh defined their common unity in terms of a common descent, the invention of a common mythology to create their identity, a common language and literary tradition, and much that was common in law, together with the coining of names to given themselves a consciously constructed identity as compatriots.[101] This argument—that one can have cultural, legal and linguistic unity without political unity—is equally valid for the pre-Norman English. Alfred's achievement lay in his realisation that by harnessing and focusing these three forms of identity through an appeal to a common memory, and by imposing a cultural hegemony he was able to provide a retrospective and self-consciously historical explanation for the creation of a fourth, national, consciousness. In that sense, while Bede invented the English as a people in the sight of God,[102] they were made one nation by 'Alfred of the English, the greatest treasure-giver of all the kings [Bishop Wulfsige] has ever heard tell of, in recent times, or long ago, or of any earthly king he had previously learned of.'[103]

Notes

1. I owe a particular debt of gratitude to Michael Bentley, Julia Crick, David Dumville, Simon Loseby and Janet Nelson all of whom read the text of this paper in draft and made numerous suggestions for its improvement.

2. *The Ecclesiastical History of Orderic Vitalis*, ed. M. Chibnall (6 vols., Oxford, 1968–80), II.241; quoted by S. Keynes and M. Lapidge, *Alfred the Great: Asser's 'Life of King Alfred' and Other Contemporary Sources* (Harmondsworth, 1986), 46. For King Æthelstan (whose extended realm was a temporary creation, not surviving his death) see D. N. Dumville, *Wessex and England from Alfred to Edgar* (Woodbridge, 1992), ch.

4. It was a foreign conqueror, the Danish king, Cnut, who described himself as *ealles Engla landes cyning:* I Cnut, prologue, ed. F. Liebermann, *Die Gesetze der Angelsachsen* (3 vols., Halle, 1903–16), I.278–307, at 278; transl. *English Historical Documents, I, c. 500–1042,* ed. D. Whitelock (2nd edn, London, 1979) [hereafter *EHD*], no. 49, 454. See P. Wormald, '*Engla lond:* The Making of an Allegiance', *Journal of Historical Sociology,* VII (1994), 1–24, at 10.

3. Anglo-Saxon Chronicle, *s.a.* 900; *MS A,* ed. J. Bately (*The Anglo-Saxon Chronicle: A Collaborative Edition,* ed. D. Dumville and S. Keynes, III (Cambridge, 1986)) [hereafter ASC], 61; *EHD,* no. 1, 207.

4. On the adoption of collective names see A. D. Smith, *The Ethnic Origins of Nations* (Oxford, 1986), 22–4. See also P. Wormald, 'Bede, the *Bretwaldas* and the Origins of the *gens Anglorum*', in *Ideal and Reality in Frankish and Anglo-Saxon Society,* ed. P. Wormald *et al.* (Oxford, 1983), 99–129, at 103–4.

5. For discussion in an Anglo-Saxon context of the relationship between a culture's ideas and the language in which they are expressed see M. Godden, 'Anglo-Saxons on the Mind', in *Learning and Literature in Anglo-Saxon England,* ed. M. Lapidge and H. Gneuss (Cambridge, 1985), 271–98, at 286. A helpful introduction to the wider issue of the role of language in the making of history is N. Partner, 'The New Cornificius: Medieval History and the Artifice of Words', in *Classical Rhetoric and Medieval Historiography,* ed. E. Breisach (Kalamazoo, Mich., 1985), 5–59, especially 25–40; also N. Partner, 'Making up Lost Time: Writing on the Writing of History', *Speculum,* LXI (1986), 90–117, at 94–8.

6. ASC, *s.a.* 886, ed. Bately, 53: 'Þy ilcan geare gesette ælfred cyning Lundenburg, 7 him all Angelcyn to cirde, þæt buton Deniscra monna hæftniede was, 7 hie þa befæste þa burge æþerede aldormen to haldonne'. Transl. *EHD,* 199.

7. That London was recovered before 886 is suggested by the numismatic evidence, which has been interpreted to mean that Alfred was minting his London-monogram pennies earlier in the 880s than 886: M. A. S. Blackburn, 'The London Mint in the Reign of Alfred', in *Kings, Currency and Alliances: The History and Coinage of Southern England, AD 840–900,* ed. M. A. S. Blackburn and D. N. Dumville (Woodbridge, forthcoming). For the significance of the ceremonies of 886 see J. Nelson, 'The Political Ideas of Alfred of Wessex', in *Kings and Kingship in Medieval Europe,* ed. A. Duggan (London, 1993), 125–58, at 154–5.

8. The Chronicle reported for 825 that Ecgberht had defeated the Mercians at Wroughton, and for 829 that he conquered the kingdom of the Mercians and everything south of the Humber: ASC, *s.a.* 823, ed. Bately, 41; *s.a.* 827, ed. Bately, 42; transl. *EHD,* 185–6. Evidence for increased understanding between the two kingdoms is apparent in the reign of Æthelwulf (who married his daughter to the Mercian king, Burgred, and assisted him in an expedition against the Welsh in 853) and during the 840s when the West Saxon and Mercian coinages were closely related: Keynes and Lapidge, *Alfred the Great,* 12.

9. Keynes and Lapidge (*Alfred the Great,* 228 n. 1) have argued that Æthelred accepted Alfred as his lord as early as 883, on the evidence of a Worcester charter S 218

[S = P. H. Sawyer, *Anglo-Saxon Charters: An Annotated List and Bibliography* (London, 1968)], but this could now be fitted into the new chronology for the taking of London in that year.

10. Asser, Life of King Alfred, c. 83, ed. W. H. Stevenson, *Asser's Life of King Alfred* (Oxford, 1904; new impression, 1959), 69; transl. Keynes and Lapidge, *Alfred the Great*, 98.

11. Nelson, 'The Political Ideas', 134–5.

12. As Nelson has pointed out, although Asser described Alfred as 'ruler of all the Christians of the island of Britain, king of the Anglo-Saxons' in the preface to his Life of the king, he did not use that style again until describing events after the formal submission of 886: Nelson, 'The Political Ideas', 155. For the adoption of the royal-title *rex Angul-Saxonum* in Alfred's charters see Stevenson, *Asser*, 149–52; Whitelock, 'Some Charters in the Name of King Alfred', in *Saints, Scholars and Heroes*, ed. M. H. King and W. M. Stevens (2 vols., Collegeville, Minn., 1979), I.77–98; Keynes and Lapidge, *Alfred the Great*, 227–8 n. 1; Nelson, 'The Political Ideas', 134 n. 42.

13. Alfred-Guthrum treaty; ed. Liebermann, *Die Gesetze*, 1.126–9; transl. in Keynes and Lapidge, *Alfred the Great*, 171–2. Alfred might alternatively have here been asserting his right to act on behalf of the Angles (namely the Mercians), not just the West Saxons for whom he already spoke as king, which message could have had a similar propaganda value. But the text of the treaty goes on to distinguish Danishmen (*Deniscne*) from Englishmen (*Engliscne*), and I understand the *Angelcynn* mentioned here to incorporate all those in Kent and Wessex as well as the Mercian Angles. The treaty is customarily dated to 886 (capture of London) x 890 (death of Guthrum): Keynes and Lapidge, *Alfred the Great*, 171. Dumville has, however, challenged this view and argued that the treaty should rather be dated to 878: *Wessex*, ch. 1.

14. Asser, Life of Alfred, ch. 80, ed. Stevenson, 66; transl. Keynes and Lapidge, *Alfred the Great*, 96.

15. Keynes and Lapidge, *Alfred the Great*, 38–41.

16. Important in shaping my ideas has been S. Reynolds, 'What do we Mean by Anglo-Saxon and the Anglo-Saxons?', *Journal of British Studies*, XXIV (1985), 395–414.

17. The development before the Conquest of the notion of an English (as opposed to a Saxon, or Anglo-Saxon identity) has been examined by Patrick Wormald in various articles: 'Bede, the *Bretwaldas*'; 'The Venerable Bede and the "Church of the English"', in *The English Religious Tradition and the Genius of Anglicanism*, ed. G. Rowell (1992), 13–32; '*Engla Lond*: The Making of an Allegiance', *Journal of Historical Sociology*, VII (1994), 1–24; 'The Making of England', *History Today* (February 1995), 26–32.

18. Godden, 'Anglo-Saxons on the Mind', 286; Smith, *Ethnic Origins*, 23.

19. R. Bartlett, *The Making of Europe* (London, 1993), 197. See also P. Geary, 'Ethnic Identity as a Situational Construct in the Early Middle Ages', *Mitteilungen der Anthropologischen Gesellschaft in Wien*, CXIII (1983), 15–26, at 18–20.

20. Regino, letter to Archbishop Hatto of Mainz (ed. F. Kurze, *Regionis Prumien-*

sis Chronicon, MGH, SRG (Hanover, 1890), xix–xx): 'sicut diuersae nationes populo-rum inter se discrepant genere, moribus, lingua, legibus'. W. Kienast (*Die fränkische Vasallität* (Frankfurt, 1990), 270–1 n. 900) has noted that Regino's definition of na-tional characteristics is similar to the famous opening sentence of Caesar's Gallic War: 'Gallia est omnis diuisa in partes tres . . . Hi omnes lingua, institutis, legibus inter se differunt' (Gaul is a whole divided into three parts . . . All these differ from one an-other in language, institutions and laws); Caesar, The Gallic War, I.1 (ed. and transl. H. J. Edwards (London, 1917)). I am grateful to Professor J. L. Nelson for drawing this reference to my attention.

21. Bartlett, *The Making of Europe*, 198–204.

22. *Bede's Ecclesiastical History of the English People*, ed. and transl. B. Colgrave and R. A. B. Mynors (Oxford, 1969) [hereafter *HE*], I.1, at 16–17. John Hines has com-mented on the significance of Bede's recognition of the existence of a single English language: 'The Becoming of the English: Identity, Material Culture and Language in Early Anglo-Saxon England', *Anglo-Saxon Studies in Archaeology and History*, VII (1994), 49–59, at 51. The extent to which Bede's language was at variance from that of other writers of his time is explored further below; see also Wormald, 'Bede, the *Bret-waldas*', 120–3.

23. *Alcuin: The Bishops, Kings and Saints of York*, ed. and transl. P. Godman (Oxford, 1982), lines 501–2: 'in se quod retinet famosa Britannia gentes / diuisas linguis, pop-ulis per nomina patrum'. Alcuin's statement owes something to *HE*, III.6 (ed. and transl. Colgrave and Mynors, 230–1): 'omnes nationes et prouincias Brittaniae, quae in quattuor linguas, id est Brettonum Pictorum Scottorum et Anglorum diuisae sunt'.

24. Alfred preface to the Old English *Regula pastoralis*, ed. D. Whitelock, *Sweet's Anglo-Saxon Reader in Prose and Verse* (rev. edn, Oxford, 1967), 4–7, at 5; transl. Keynes and Lapidge, *Alfred the Great*, 124–6 at 125: 'So completely had learning de-cayed among the *Angelcynn*, that there were very few on this side of the Humber who could comprehend their services in *Englisc*.'

25. S 207, a charter of Burgred of Mercia dated 855 by which he granted the min-ster at Blockley to the church of Worcester, freeing it from various obligations includ-ing that of lodging all mounted men of the English race (*& ealra angelcynnes monna*) and foreigners, whether of noble or humble birth, which freedom was to be given for ever, as long as the Christian faith might last among the English (*apud Anglos*). That the term *Angelcynn* had been coined before Alfred's time (possibly long before its first recorded written usage) does not detract from my central argument that Alfred har-nessed the word to his own particular ends.

26. Alfred, prose preface, ed. Whitelock, 5; transl. Keynes and Lapidge, *Alfred the Great*, 125. Compare also Alfred's preface to his translation of Psalm xiii, ed. J. W. Bright and R. L. Ramsay, *Liber Psalmorum: The West Saxon Psalms* (Boston and Lon-don, 1907), 24; transl. Keynes and Lapidge, *Alfred the Great*, 158: 'When David sang this thirteenth psalm, he lamented to the Lord in the psalm that in his time there should be so little faith, and so little wisdom should be found in the world. And so does every just man who sings it now: he laments the same thing in his own time.' See also

T. A. Shippey, 'Wealth and Wisdom in King Alfred's *Preface* to the Old English Pastoral Care', *EHR*, XCIV (1979), 346–55; for the interest taken in Alfred's prefatory letter by Anglican reformers andother scholars in the second half of the sixteenth century see R. I. Page, 'The Sixteenth-Century Reception of Alfred the Great's Letter to his Bishops', *Anglia*, CX (1992), 36–64, at 37–41.

27. Alfred, prose preface, ed. Whitelock, 6; transl. Keynes and Lapidge, *Alfred the Great*, 126.

28. Compare Alfred's translation of Psalm ii:12, ed. Bright and Ramsay, 3, transl. Keynes and Lapidge, *Alfred the Great*, 154: 'Embrace learning lest you incur God's anger and lest you stray from the right path.' Although in his Life of the king Asser depicted Alfred's thirst for learning as driven primarily by personal aspiration (for example, Life of Alfred, chs. 76–8, ed. Stevenson, *Asser*, 59–63; transl. Keynes and Lapidge, *Alfred the Great*, 91–3), the final chapter of Asser's Life makes explicit the broader application Alfred envisaged: ch. 106, ed. Stevenson, *Asser*, 92–5, transl. Keynes and Lapidge, *Alfred the Great*, 109–110. S. Keynes, 'Royal Government and the Written Word in Late Anglo-Saxon England', in *The Uses of Literacy in Early Medieval Europe*, ed. R. McKitterick (Cambridge, 1990), 228–57, at 230–1.

29. Alfred, prose preface, ed. Whitelock, 6; transl. Keynes and Lapidge, *Alfred the Great*, 125.

30. Keynes, 'Royal Government', 231–2.

31. Wallace-Hadrill ('The Franks and the English: Some Common Historical Interests', in his *Early Medieval History* (Oxford, 1975), 201–16, at 216) noted the relevance to Alfred of Bede's statement (*HE*, II.5) that Æthelberht of Kent had established with the advice of his counsellors a code of laws after the Roman manner, which had been written down in English to be preserved, and drew attention also to the example of ninth-century Frankish law collections.

32. Alfred, Laws, introduction §49.7–9; ed. Liebermann, *Die Gesetze*, I.44–6; transl. Keynes and Lapidge, *Alfred the Great*, 163–4.

33. J. L. Nelson, 'Literacy in Carolingian Government', in *The Uses of Literacy*, ed. McKitterick, 258–96, at 263.

34. Wormald, 'The Venerable Bede', 25. For the Franks' perception of themselves as a chosen people, a new Israel, see J. L. Nelson, 'Kingship and Empire in the Carolingian World', in *Carolingian Culture: Emulation and Innovation*, ed. R. McKitterick (Cambridge, 1994), 52–87, at 55–6; for ninth-century Frankish use of the exemplary world of the Old Testament see J. M. Wallace-Hadrill, 'History in the Mind of Archbishop Hincmar', in *The Writing of History in the Middle Ages*, ed. R. H. C. Davis and J. M. Wallace-Hadrill (Oxford, 1981), 43–70, at 49–51.

35. For Bede's conception see Wormald, 'The Venerable Bede', 23–4. Alcuin had drawn a parallel between the sack of Lindisfarne in 793 and the sack of Jerusalem and destruction of the Temple by the Chaldeans, which led to the Israelites' Babylonian captivity: *Epistola* 20, 3d. Dümmler, *MGH, Epistolae Karolini Aevi*, II.57 transl. *EHD*, no. 194. I am grateful to Dr Judith Maltby for suggesting the parallel with the Babylonian captivity to me.

36. S. Keynes, 'Changing Faces: Offa, King of Mercia,' *istory Today*, XL (November 1990), 14–19. A small group of Worcester charters does give more grandiose titles to Æthelbald of Mercia: S 94, 101, 103, and S 89 (trans. *EHD*, no. 67) in which Æthelbald is called *rex sutangli* and in the witness list, *rex Britanniae*. Although this charter might be compared with the statement Bede made about the extent of Æthelbald's power south of the Humber (*HE*, V.23), these titles are not adopted by other scriptoria of the period and may reveal more of the aspirations of Worcester draftsmen than the Mercian king's own perceptions of his rule.

37. This point was noted by Gaimar, who in his *Estoire des Engleis* (written *c.* 1140) attributed to King Alfred the responsibility for making the Anglo-Saxon Chronicle as a history of the English: *L'estoire des Engleis by Geffrei Gaimar* (Anglo-Norman Text Society, 1960), vv. 3443–50. I am grateful to John Gillingham for drawing this point to my attention and for allowing me to see his forthcoming paper 'Gaimar, the Prose *Brut* and the Making of English History'.

38. Alfred, Laws, §1.2, ed. Liebermann, *Die Gesetze*, I.46. Carolingian parallels are particularly apt here, for example Charlemagne's imposition of a general fidelity oath in 789 after the revolt of Hardrad (*Duplex legationis edictum*, c. 18, *MGH, Capitularia*, I, no. 23, 63) and his insistence in 802 that all over the age of twelve should promise to him as emperor the fidelity which they had previously promised to him as king: *MGH, Capitularia*, I, no. 33, ch. 2, 92. See now M. Becher, *Eid und Herrschaft: Untersuchungen zum Herrscherethos Karls der Großen* (Sigmaringen, 1993), especially chs. ii and iv.

39. E. Gellner, *Nations and Nationalism* (Oxford, 1983), at 1, and 53–62. More sympathetic to the idea that national sentiment might exist in pre-modern nations is A. D. Smith, *National Identity* (Harmondsworth, 1991).

40. P. Sahlins, *Boundaries: The Making of France and Spain in the Pyrenees* (Berkeley and Los Angeles, 1989), 271. Compare also E. Hobsbawm (*Nations and Nationalism since 1780* (Cambridge, 1990), 91): 'there is no more effective way of bonding together the disparate sections of restless peoples than to unite them against outsiders'. And L. Colley, 'Britishness and Otherness: An Argument', *Journal of British Studies*, XXXI (1992), 309–29.

41. Wormald, 'The Making of England'.

42. Asser, Life of King Alfred, ch. 76 (ed. Stevenson, 59); J. L. Nelson, 'Wealth and Wisdom: The Politics of Alfred the Great', in *Kings and Kingship*, ed. J. Rosenthal, *Acta* XI 1984) Binghampton, N.Y., 1986), 31–52, at 44.

43. Keynes and Lapidge, *Alfred the Great*, 91. Compare Asser, Life of Alfred, ch. 75 (ed. Stevenson, *Asser*, 58, transl. Keynes and Lapidge, *Alfred the Great*, 90) which refers to the school established by the king where books were carefully read in both languages, in Latin and English: *utriusque linguae libri, Latinae scilicet et Saxonicae*. Nelson was also referring to the relevance to Kentishmen and Mercians of the wisdom which Alfred sought to foster: 'Wealth', 45.

44. Nelson, 'Wealth', 45.

45. One is reminded here of Anthony Smith's definition of ethnic communities as

'named populations with shared ancestry myths, histories and cultures, having an as-sociation with specific territory and a sense of solidarity': *The Ethnic Origins of Nations* (Oxford, 1986), 32. Also Colley, 'Britishness', p. 317.

46. That the translation of Bede's Ecclesiastical History into Old English, al-though not made by the king himself, might be datable to Alfred's reign was argued by D. Whitelock, 'The Old English Bede', *Proceedings of the British Academy*, XLVIII (1962), 57–90; reprinted in her collected papers *From Bede to Alfred* (Aldershot, 1980), no. viii. Her opinion is shared by Keynes and Lapidge, *Alfred the Great*, 33. While I would argue that the compilation of the Anglo-Saxon Chronicle was part of King Al-fred's wider scheme for the invention of a sense of shared identity among his subjects, others have sought to separate the compilation of annals from the late ninth-century West Saxon royal court both chronologically: A. Thorogood, 'The Anglo-Saxon Chronicle in the Reign of Ecgberht', *EHR*, XLVIII (1933), 353–63, and geographi-cally: F. Stenton, 'The South-Western Element in the Old English Chronicle', *Preparatory to Anglo-Saxon England*, ed. D. M. Stenton (Oxford, 1970), 106–15; J. Bately, 'The Compilation of the Anglo-Saxon Chronicle, 60 BC to AD 80: Vocabu-lary as Evidence', *Proceedings of the British Academy*, LXIV (1978), 93–129.

47. *The Old English Version of Bede's Ecclesiastical History of the English People*, at, for example, I.xiii, IV.ii, V.xxiii (ed. T. Miller, 4 vols., Early English Text Society, original series XCV–XCVI and CX–CXI (London, 1890–8), part i, 54, 258, 478–80). The word *Angelcynn* occurs in a number of annals in the A manuscript of Anglo-Saxon Chronicle before 886, used in relation to the English people as a whole (*s.a.* 443, 597, 787 and 836, ed. Bately, 17, 25, 39, 43) and of the English school in Rome (*s.a.* 874, ed. Bately, 49).

48. *Contra* R. H. C. Davis, 'Alfred the Great: Propaganda and Truth', *History*, LVI (1971), 169–82; and J. M. Wallace-Hadrill, who saw the Chronicle as 'a reflection of urgent political need not of a people, but a dynasty': 'The Franks and the English in the Ninth Century: Some Common Historical Interests', in *Early Medieval History* (Oxford, 1975), 201–16, at 210–11.

49. I differ here from H. White in his analysis of early medieval annals: *The Con-tent and the Form: Narrative Discourse and Historical Representation* (Baltimore, Md., and London, 1987), ch. 1. On medieval writers' use of linear narrative see also Part-ner, 'The New Cornificius', 42–3. I am grateful to Michael Bentley for discussing these ideas with me at length; I intend to pursue some of these thoughts about the Chronicle in a forthcoming paper.

50. For consideration of the use of genealogy in the assertion of political unity in the early middle ages see D. N. Dumville, 'Kingship, Genealogies and Regnal Lists', in *Early Medieval Kingship*, ed. P. H. Sawyer and I. N. Wood (Leeds, 1977), 72–104 (reprinted in Dumville's collected papers: *Histories and Pseudo-Histories of the Insular Middle Ages* (Aldershot, 1990), no. xv).

51. P. Amory, 'Ethnographic Culture and the Construction of Community in Os-trogothic Italy, 489–554' (Ph.D thesis, University of Cambridge, 1994), 8–11; Geary, 'Ethnic Identity', 24–6.

52. B. Anderson, *Imagined Communities: Reflections on the Origin and Spread of Nationalism* (2nd edn, London, 1991), especially chs. 2–3.

53. In an East Frankish context one might compare here the promotion of the German vernacular by Louis the German: J. M. Wallace-Hadrill, *The Frankish Church* (Oxford, 1983), 333–4.

54. Gildas had laboured this point in portraying the pagan attacks of Germanic peoples on Britain as a reflection of God's anger with the Christian British: *Gildas: The Ruin of Britain and Other Works*, ed. and transl. M. Winterbottom (London and Chichester, 1978). See R. W. Hanning, *The Vision of History in Early Britain* (London, 1966), chs. 2–3. For consideration of the same themes in the Second Viking Age see M. Godden, 'Apocalypse and Invasion in Late Anglo-Saxon England', in *From Anglo-Saxon to Early Middle English: Studies Presented to E. G. Stanley* (Oxford, 1994), 130–62.

55. For example the letters written by Alcuin following the first Viking raid on Lindisfarne in June 793: *Epistolae*, 16–21, ed. E. Dümmler, *Epistolae Karolini Aevi* II, MGH, Epistolae, IV (Berlin, 1895); and see D. A. Bullough, 'What Has Ingeld to do with Lindisfarne', *Anglo-Saxon England*, XXII (1993), 93–125, especially 95–101. Among ninth-century texts see the Synod of Meaux and Paris, 845–6 (ed. W. Hartmann, MGH, *Concilia*, III (Hanover, 1984), 60–132 at 82); quoted by S. Coupland, 'The Rod of God's Wrath or the People of God's Wrath? The Carolingian Theology of the Viking Invasiions', *Journal of Ecclesiastical History*, XLII (1991), 535–54, at 537 n. 6; and the *Translatio et miracula S. Germani*, chs. 2–4 (ed. G. Waitz, *MGH, SS*, xv.1 (Hanover, 1887), at 10–11). I owe this last reference to Janet Nelson.

56. *Les Annales de Saint-Bertin, s.a.* 839, ed. F. Grat *et al.* (Paris, 1964), 29; transl. Nelson, 43. The danger which Viking attacks presented to the continuance of the Christian faith in England was noted by various outsiders in the ninth century; see my 'Violence against Christians? The Vikings and the Church in Ninth-Century England', *Medieval History*, I.3 (1991), 3–16, especially 9–10.

57. The capitulary of Pîtres, 862 (ed. A. Boretius and V. Krause, *MGH Capitularia* II, no. 272), for example describes how 'tumults have arisen, wretchedly stirred up both by pagans and by those calling themselves Christians, and . . . terrible calamities have spread through this land'. Attention is drawn to the individual sins of the Franks for which reason 'we have been exiled from the land of the living'. The remedy proposed is clear: 'in the destruction around us God has revealed to us what we should understand about the devastation within us, so that, having understood, we should return to him and believe'. I am grateful to Dr Simon Coupland for allowing me to quote from his translation of this capitulary.

58. For the attribution of the Old English Bede to Alfred's reign see above n. 46 and D. Whitelock, 'The Prose of Alfred's Reign', in *Continuations and Beginnings: Studies in Old English Literature*, ed. E. G. Stanley (London, 1966), 67–103, at 77–9 (reprinted in her collected papers *From Bede to Alfred*, no. vi).

59. Wormald, 'The Venerable Bede', 21, 24. Compare also N. Howe, *Migration and Mythmaking in Anglo-Saxon England* (New Haven and London, 1989), 49–71.

60. Bede, *HE*, I.1, 16–17. For the significance of dialectal variants within Old En-

glish as markers for the separate identities of different Anglo-Saxon kingdoms see Hines, 'Identity', 55–7.

61. Bede, *HE*, V.23, 558–61.

62. Bede, *HE*, IV.2, 332–3. The making of a single *ecclesia Anglorum* had clearly been Pope Gregory's original intention; see for example his advice to Augustine about the consecration of new bishops: *HE*, I.27, 86.

63. Bede, *HE*, II.5, 148–51.

64. That Bede obtained this list second-hand has been argued by, among others, B. Yorke, 'The Vocabulary of Anglo-Saxon Overlordship', *Anglo-Saxon Studies in Archaeology and History*, II (British Archaeological Reports, British series XCII, Oxford, 1981), 171–200, at 195–6, and S. Fanning, 'Bede, Imperium and the Bretwaldas', *Speculum*, LXVI (1991), 1–26, at 25. For other arguments that Bede himself compiled this list see S. Keynes, 'Rædwald the bretwalda', in *Voyage to the Other World: The Legacy of Sutton Hoo* (Minneapolis, Minn., 1992), 103–23, at 109–10 (and for a fuller survey of other secondary opinion ibid. nn. 44–7, pp. 119–20), and N. Higham, *An English Empire: Bede and the Early Anglo-Saxon Kings* (Manchester, 1995), 49.

65. Bede's intent here has been somewhat obscured by the use of the word *bretwalda* in the Anglo-Saxon Chronicle *s.a.* 827 (recte 829) in relation to the power held by the West Saxon king, Ecgberht, following his conquest of the kingdom of the Mercians and everything south of the Humber. Ecgberht was said by the chronicler to have been the eighth king who was *brytenwalda* (*bretwalda* uniquely in the A manuscript of the Chronicle), the previous seven being those named by Bede in *HE* II.5. But where Bede had envisaged a wide-ranging kind of power, the chronicler appears to have conceived of an office, or wide rulership. The form *bretwalda* (meaning ruler of Britain, from *bret-* 'Briton' and *-walda* 'ruler' or 'king') is attested only in the A manuscript of the Chronicle and is unlikely to represent the original spelling. Other manuscripts have different forms: *brytenwalda* or *brytenwealda* (BDE), *bretenanwealda* (C). Here *bryten* might be a noun meaning 'Britain', but it might alternatively be an adjective *bryten* from the verb *bretoan* 'to break', or 'disperse'; so *brytenwalda* might mean simply 'wide ruler'. See Whitelock in *EHD*, 186 n. 2; Keynes, 'Rædwald the Bretwalda', 111.

66. Wormald, 'Bede, the *Bretwaldas*', 122–3; for a semantic discussion of Bede's use of the word 'Angle' see Wormald, 'The Venerable Bede', 21–3.

67. Anonymous, *Liber beatae Gregorii papae*, chs. 6, 12, 18, ed. and transl. B. Colgrave, *The Earliest Life of Gregory the Great* (2nd edn, Cambridge, 1985), 82–3, 94–5, 102–3.

68. Boniface, *Epistola* 46, ed. M. Tangl, *Die Briefe des heiligen Bonifatius und Lullus*, MGH, Epistolae selectae, 1 (Berlin, 1916), p. 74; and compare *Epistolae* 33, 73, 74, 78, ed. Tangl, *Die Briefe*, 57–8, 150–2, 156, 169 and 171. Torhthelm's letter is preserved with Boniface's correspondence: *Epistola* 47, ed. Tangl, *Die Briefe*, 76.

69. Anon., *Vita S. Cuthberti*, IV.1, ed. and transl. B. Colgrave, *Two Lives of St Cuthbert* (Cambridge, 1940), 110–11. References to the English or *gens Anglorum* are found in *The Life of Bishop Wilfrid by Eddius Stephanus*, chs. 6, 11, 41, ed. B. Colgrave (Cambridge, 1927), pp. 14–15, 22–3, 82–3; to the *Saxones:* chs. 19, 21, pp. 41, 43.

Stephen also quoted a letter of Wilfrid's in which he described his country of origin as *Saxomia:* ch. 30, p. 60. A letter of abbot Hwætberht's to Pope Gregory II quoted by Bede in his *Historia abbatum* similarly described England as *Saxonia: Historia abbatum,* ch. 19, ed. C. Plummer, *Venerabilis Baedae Opera Historica* (2 vols., Oxford, 1896), I.383, and note II.368. M. Richter, 'Bede's *Angli:* Angles or English?', *Peritia,* III (1984), 99–114, at 105. In a letter to Pope Zacharias Boniface described himself as born and raised *in transmarina Saxonia: Epistola* 50, ed. Tangl, *Die Briefe,* 84.

70. Richter, 'Bede's *Angli*', 105–7; Wormald, 'Bede, the *bretwaldas*'; 122; L. Colley, *Britons: Forging the Nation 1707–1837* (2nd edn, London, 1994), 13.

71. Gallic Chronicle of 452, ed. T. Mommsen, *MGH, Auctores Antiquissimi,* IX (Berlin, 1892), 660; Constantius, Life of St Germanus, chs. 17–18, ed. W. Levison, *MGH, SRM,* VII (Hanover, 1919–20), 263, 265.

72. Wormald, 'Bede, the *Bretwaldas*', 122. Much of this ground was explored by E. A. Freeman, *History of the Norman Conquest* (3rd edn, 2 vols., Oxford, 1877), I.533–48, who argued that the Germanic inhabitants of pre-Conquest England ought to be described as the English, not as the Anglo-Saxons.

73. Procopius, *History of the Wars,* ed. and transl. H. B. Dewing (5 vols., London, 1914–28), VIII.xx.4–8.

74. Procopius, *Wars,* VIII.xx.8–10. R. Collins ('Theodebert I, "Rex Magnus Francorum"', in *Ideal and Reality,* ed. Wormald, 11–12) ascribed this legation to the time of Theudebert, who died in 548, but Ian Wood (*The Merovingian North Sea,* 12 and 23 n. 77) has argued rather that it should be dated to *c.* 553. For the likelihood that the Franks did have some hegemony over southern England see further I. Wood, 'Frankish Hegemony in England', in *The Age of Sutton Hoo,* ed. M. Carver (Woodbridge, 1992), 235–41, at 235, and I Wood, *The Merovingian North Sea,* (Alingsas, 1983), 12–14. Robert Markus has suggested that Pope Gregory's mission to the English might have been conceived on the presumption of continued Frankish domination of southern England as part of a plan for the revitalisation of the Frankish church: 'Gregory the Great's Europe', *TRHS,* 5 ser., XXXI (1981), 21–36, at 26–7.

75. H. Chadwick, 'Gregory the Great and the Mission to the Anglo-Saxons', *Gregorio Magno e il suo empo,* Studia Ephemeridis 'Augustinianum' XXXIII (Rome, 1991), 199–212, at 199–200.

76. *Liber pontificalis,* ed. L. Duchesne (2 vols., Paris 1886–92), I.312: '. . . misit eos in praedicationem ad gentem Angulorum ut eos conuerteret ad dominum Iesum Christum'. Gregory's epitaph is preserved by Bede, *HE,* II.1, 132, and John the Deacon in his Life of Gregory, IV.68 (*Patrologia Latina,* ed. Migne, LXXV, col. 221 C).

77. *Liber beatae Gregorii papae,* ch. 9, p. 90: 'Cunque responderent, "Anguli dicuntur, illi de quibus sumus," illed dixit, "Angeli Dei".' Compare also ch. 13, p. 94, where the insertion of the additional syllable looks like an error in the transmitted text: 'Thus the name of the Angli, with the addition of the single letter *e* means angels': *ergo noman Angulorum, si una e littera addetur, angelorum sonat;* had the name originally been given as *Anguli,* the letter *e* would need to be substituted, not added. Bede's account of the same story is found in his *HE,* II.1, 134–5.

78. *S. Gregorii Magni, Registrum Epistularum*, VIII.29 (ed. D. Norberg, *Corpus Christianorum, series Latina* CXL–CXLA (Turnhout, 1982)), CXLA.551. The same pun is made by Widukind: *Res Gestae Saxonicae*, I.8 (ed. G. Waitz, MGH, Scriptores III (Hanover, 1839), 419–20): 'Et quia illa insula in angulo quodam maris sita est, Anglisaxones usque hodie uocitantur.'

79. Richter, 'Bede's *Angli*', 113. See for example *Annales Regni Francorum, s.a.* 786 and 808 (ed. F. Kurze, MGH, SRG (Hanover, 1895), at 73 and 127); Einhard, *Vita Karoli Magni*, ch. 25 (ed. G. Waitz, MGH, SRG ius 25 (Hanover, 1911), 30).

80. Annals of St-Bertin, *s.a.* 839, 855, 856, 858 (ed. Grat *et al.*, 28, 70, 73, 76): *rex Anglorum, rex Anglorum Saxonum, rex occidentalium Anglorum* and *rex occidentalium Saxonum.* The same text, *s.a.* 862 termed Æthelwulf's son, Æthelbald *rex Anglorum*, ed. Grat *et al.* 87. In a ninth-century confraternity book from the northern Italian monastery of Brescia Æthelwulf appears among a list of pilgrims with the appellation *rex Anglorum*, having presumably visited the house during his visit to Rome in 855/6: Rescia, Biblioteca Queriniana, MS G.VI.7, fo. 27v: H. Becher, 'Das königlich Frauenkloster San Salvatore/Santa Giulia in Brescia im Spiegel seiner Memorialüberlieferung', *Frühmittelalterliche Studien*, XVII (1983), 299–392, at 377. I owe this reference to Janet Nelson.

81. *Ex miraculis S Wandregisili*, ed. O. Hodder-Egger, MGH Scriptores XV (Hanover, 1887), 408–9; quoted by P. Stafford, 'Charles the Bald, Judith and England', in *Charles the Bald: Court and Kingdom*, ed. M. Gibson and J. L. Nelson (2nd edn, Aldershot, 1990), 139–53, at 142.

82. Boniface, *Epistola* 46, ed. Tangl, *Die Briefe*, 74.

83. K. Leyser, 'The Ottonians and Wessex', in his *Communications and Power in Medieval Europe: The Carolingian and Ottonian Centuries*, ed. T. Reuter (London, 1994), 73–104, at 74–5. See also E. Van Houts, 'Women and the Writing of History in the Early Middle Ages: The Case of Abbess Matilda of Essen and Aethelweard', *Early Medieval Europe*, I (1992), 53–68, at 57 and 63–4. The so-called *Leges Eadwardi confessoris*, dating from the mid-twelfth century, also preserve a remnant of a sense of common descent and interests between English and Saxons, directing that Saxon visitors should be received as if brothers, for they are born 'from the blood of the *Angli*, that is to say from *Engern*, a place and region in Saxony, and the English from their blood; they are made one people, one kind': ch. 32 C, ed. Liebermann, *Die Gesetze*, I.627–72, at 658; transl. Leyser, 'The Ottonians', 74.

84. Asser, Life of Alfred, chs. 101, 76, ed. Stevenson, *Asser*, 87, 60; transl. Keynes and Lapidge, *Alfred the Great*, 107 and 91.

85. S 362, transl. *EHD*, 100. Discussed together with other instances of disloyalty to Alfred by J. L. Nelson, '"A Kind Across the Sea": Alfred in Continental Perspective', *TRHS*, 5th series, XXXVI (1986), 45–68, at 53; and by S. Keynes, 'A Tale of Two Kings: Alfred the Great and Æthelred the Unready', *ibid.* 195–217, at 206. For further evidence of reluctance to promote Alfred's plans see Asser, Life of King Alfred, chs. 91 and 106, ed. Stevenson, *Asser*, 77, 93–4; transl. Keynes and Lapidge, *Alfred the Great*, 101, 110.

86. The Chronicler reported not only that Essex submitted to Æthelwold, and that he was later joined by the East Anglian Vikings and a Mercian prince, but that Edward had some difficulty in holding his own army together, having to send seven messengers to the men of Kent who persisted in lingering behind against his command: Anglo-Saxon Chronicle 903. Æthelwold's revolt has been discussed by Dumville, *Wessex*, 10.

87. This has been argued by Simon Keynes on the basis of a group of charters issued in 903 and by references in S 396 (*EHD*, 103) and S 397 issued in 926 to 'the order of King Edward and also of Ealdorman Æthelred along with the other ealdormen and thegns': 'A Charter of Edward the Elder for Islington', *Historical Research*, LXVI (1993), 303–16. In other charters, however, Æthelred and Æthelflæd made grants without reference to Edward: S 221, 224–5; see P. Stafford, *Unification and Conquest: A Political and Social History of England in the Tenth and Eleventh Centuries* (London, 1989), 25–6.

88. S. Keynes, 'The West Saxon Charters of King Æthelwulf and his Sons', *English Historical Review*, CIX (1994), 1109–49, at 1148–9. The West Saxon chronicle described Æthelred as an ealdorman, but the tenth-century writer of a Latin chronicle based on a lost version of the Anglo-Saxon Chronicle termed him *rex* (*Chronicle of Æthelweard*, ed. A. Campbell (Edinburgh, 1962), 49–50), and Asser described Æthelred's power in terms similar to those he used of the Welsh kings who submitted to Alfred: Asser, Life of Alfred, ch. 80, ed. Stevenson, *Asser*, 66–7; transl. Keynes and Lapidge, *Alfred the Great*, 96. See Stafford, *Unification*, 26.

89. The Mercian Register for 919 reported that Æthelred's daughter was deprived of all authority in Mercia and taken into Wessex: *Two of the Saxon Chronicles Parallel*, ed. C. Plummer (2 vols., Oxford, 1892–9), I.105; trans. Whitelock, *EHD*, 217.

90. Ælfric, *Passio Sancti Eadmundi Regis et Martyris*, quoted by C. Fell, 'Saint Æðelþryð: A Historical-Hagiographical Dichotomy Revisited', *Nottingham Medieval Studies*, XXXVII (1994), 18–34, at 18.

91. *The Old English Version of the Heptateuch: Ælfric's Treatise on the Old and New Testament and his Preface to Genesis*, ed. S. J. Crawford (London, 1922), 416–17; transl. Dumville, *Wessex*, 141: 'In England too kings were often victorious because of God, as we have heard tell—just as King Alfred was, who fought frequently against the Danes until he gained victory and thus protected his people; similarly Æthelstan, who fought against Anlaf and slaughtered his army and put him to flight—and afterwards with his people he [Æthelstan] dwelt in peace.'

92. Whitelock, 'The Prose of Alfred's Reign', 69.

93. Cnut's letter to the English of 1027, ed. Liebermann, *Die Gesetze*, I.276–7 at 276, transl. Whitelock, *EHD*, no. 53. I Cnut prologue, ed. Liebermann, *Die Gesetze*, I.278–307 at 278; transl. *EHD*, no. 47.

94. Interesting in this context is the Chronicle's (alliterative verse) annal for 942, which, describing King Edmund as lord of the English and protector of men, recounts how he 'overran Mercia and thereby redeemed the Danes, previously subjected by

force under the Norsemen, for a long time in bonds of captivity to the heathens': ASC 942, ed. Bately, 73; transl. Whitelock, *EHD*, no. 1, 221.

95. G. Garnett, '"Franci et Angli": The Legal Distinctions between Peoples after the Conquest', *Anglo-Norman Studies*, VIII (1986), 109–37; R. W. Southern, *Medieval Humanism and Other Studies* (Oxford, 1970), 135–8. See also J. Gillingham, 'The Beginnings of English Imperialism', *Journal of Historical Sociology*, V (1992), 393–409. In some senses, however, Northumbria was virtually a separate state *c.* 1100: W. E. Kapelle, *The Norman Conquest of the North: The Region and its Transformation, 1000–1135* (London, 1979), 11–13.

96. Numerous tenth-century royal charters style kings as 'king of the English and of the people round about', and the witness lists to these grants reveal the presence at the West Saxon court of Northumbrian and often Welsh princes. For the articulation of imperial pretensions in the charters of Æthelstan and his successors see Dumville, *Wessex*, 149, 153–4, and N. Banton, 'Monastic Reform and the Unification of Tenth-Century England', in *Religion and National Identity*, ed. S. Mews (Oxford, 1982), 71–85, at 72–3 and 80–1.

97. S 520, transl. *EHD*, no. 105; for discussion of this group of alliterative charters see Whitelock, *EHD*, 372–3. Similarly the early tenth-century coronation *ordo* granted West Saxon kings government of two or three nations: C. E. Hohler, 'Some Service Books of the Later Saxon Church', in *Tenth-Century Studies*, ed. D. Parsons (London and Chichester, 1975), 60–83, at 67–9. For Edgar's imperial coronation at Bath in 973 see Banton, 'Monastic Reform', 82. The pledge made to Edgar at Chester by six British kings in the same year was reported only in the northern recensions of the Chronicle: ASC 973 DE, ed. Plummer, I.119; transl. Whitelock, *EHD*, 228. In the more elaborate account of this ceremony given by John of Worcester, Edgar is reported to have declared afterwards to his nobles 'that each of his successors would be able to boast that he was king of the English, and would enjoy the pomp of such honour with so many kings at his command': *The Chronicle of John of Worcester II: The Annals from 450–1066, s.a. 973*, ed. and transl. R. Darlington *et al.* (Oxford, 1995), 424–5.

98. D. Whitelock, 'The Dealings of the Kings of England with Northumbria in the Tenth and Eleventh Centuries', in *The Anglo-Saxons*, ed. P. Clemoes (Cambridge, 1959), 70–88; N. Lund, 'King Edgar and the Danelaw', *Mediaeval Scandinavia*, IX (1976), 181–95; Keynes, 'A Tale of Two Kings', 206–8.

99. Lund, 'King Edgar', 189–92; W. M. Aird, 'St Cuthbert, The Scots and the Normans', *Anglo-Norman Studies*, XVI (1993), 1–20, especially 3–4 and 6–9.

100. I hope to pursuethis further in a thematic consideration of the history of the English before the Norman Conquest.

101. R. R. Davies, *Conquest, Coexistence and Change: Wales 1063–1415* (Oxford, 1987), 15–20.

102. Wormald, 'The Venerable Bede', 24.

103. Wulfsige, bishop of Sherborne, preface to his translation of Gregory's *Dialogues;* transl. Keynes and Lapidge, *Alfred the Great*, 188.

Orality and the Developing Text of Caedmon's *Hymn*

KATHERINE O'BRIEN O'KEEFFE

THE modern editorial practice of printing Old English poetry one verse to a line with a distinct separation between half-lines distracts attention from a well-known and important fact, that Old English poetry is copied without exception in long lines across the writing space.[1] Normal scribal practice does not distinguish verses, reserving capitals and points for major divisions of a work.[2] In manuscripts of Latin poetry, however, quite another practice holds. Latin verses copied in England after the eighth century are regularly transmitted in a formal familiar to modern readers: verses are set out one to a line of writing, capitals begin each line, and often some sort of pointing marks the end of each verse. The regularity of this distinction in copying practice and the difference in the nature and level of the graphic conventions used for verse in the two languages imply that such scribal practice was deliberate and was useful and significant for contemporary readers.

Caedmon's *Hymn* is the earliest documented oral poem in Old English. Although the manuscripts of the *Hymn* have been examined to analyze Old English dialects, to describe oral formulae, and to establish a text of the poem, almost no attention has been paid to the variety of ways in which the text is set out.[3] This variety of formatting and the poem's origin as an oral composition make Caedmon's *Hymn* an especially rewarding work to study. Because the poem is found in fourteen manuscripts copied in England from the eighth through the twelfth centuries, representing two manuscript environments and two dialects, it provides much evidence about the transformation of a work as it passes from an oral to a literate medium, about the consequent development of a text in Old English, and about the presuppositions underlying the way a text was to be read.[4]

My study of Caedmon's *Hymn* approaches the issue of orality and literacy in Old English verse from the viewpoint of the reception rather than the composition of a work. While arguments about the composition of Old English poetry have provided much valuable information on orality in Anglo-Saxon England, they have not been conclusive, since the presence of formulae in verse (a critical element in defining oral character) is ambiguous evidence at best.[5] It may thus be useful to examine the survival of orality from the opposite quarter—the contemporary reception of poetic works. If the voices are silent, perhaps the manuscripts may be made to speak.

Three assumptions underlie the argument I will make about the manuscript evidence of Caedmon's *Hymn*. The first is that orality and literacy are "pure" states only in theory. In fact, cultures and individuals find themselves on a continuum between the theoretical end points of orality and literacy.[6] My second assumption is that the appearance of a work in manuscript provides no assurance that the work was conceived of as a "text" in the modern sense or even originally written (as opposed to composed orally). My third, and perhaps most important, assumption is that the movement from orality to literacy involves the gradual shift from aural to visual reception and that such a shift is reflected in the increasing spatialization of a written text.[7]

This third point requires some further explanation. In an oral situation, communication takes place within a discrete time. That the listener must be present when the speaker performs is only one aspect of the intense temporality of the speech act. Emphasis, clarity, surprise, and suspense all depend on the speaker's modulation of his speech in time. When a work is written, however, its tempo no longer depends on the speaker or writer.[8] In fact, tempo virtually disappears. Surprise and emphasis, and most especially clarity, now depend on the transformation of temporal modulations into space. Irregular pauses in the stream of speech become conventionalized by more or less regular spaces between "words."[9] Dots and marks indicate special status for portions of text; scripts and capitals indicate a hierarchy of material and meaning.[10] Literacy thus becomes a process of spatializing the once exclusively temporal, and the thought-shaping technology of writing is an index of the development of this process. The higher the degree of conventional spatialization in the manuscripts, the less oral and more literate the community.

The manuscript records of Caedmon's *Hymn* have much to tell us about the reception of the poem throughout the Old English period. In the West-Saxon translation of the *Historia ecclesiastica*, Caedmon's *Hymn* is part of the main text; in the Latin text it is a gloss to the paraphrase of the *Hymn*. It survives in two dialects of Old English and in several centuries of manuscripts. In short, the *Hymn* offers a range of evidence sufficient for the study of formatting practices in Old English and Latin poetry over a considerable period of time. The extralinguistic markers to examine are location of text on the page, lineation, word division, capitalization, and punctuation. The differing use of these visual cues between Latin and Old English will point to differences in expectations about reading Latin, an almost purely textual language, and Old English, a living language only newly being committed to writing.[11]

1

From the eighth century on, Latin poetry in England was copied in lines of verse.[12] Because this technique is so commonplace to the reader of modern verse, the significance of such a shift in formatting is easily overlooked. But the developing convention of copying Latin poetry spatially by lines of verse underlies an important step in using spatial and nonverbal cues (especially capitals and punctuation) to assist readers in their tasks. As information in a text shifts from purely linguistic to partially visual, verse becomes increasingly chirographically controlled and its formatting increasingly conventional.

The *Historia ecclesiastica* contains verses in hexameters, elegiac distichs, and epanaleptic distichs, each of which invites different types of spatial organization to distinguish its metrical form from the surrounding prose.[13] In their treatment of these verses, the manuscripts of the *Historia ecclesiastica* written in England document the incorporation of a complex set of visual cues to present Latin verse in writing. Those of the eighth century show considerable fluidity and experimentation in the formatting of verse, while the eleventh-century manuscripts (none from the ninth or tenth centuries survive) exhibit highly consistent and conservative layouts.

Five manuscripts of the *Historia ecclesiastica* written in England in the eighth century survive: Leningrad, Saltykov-Schedrin Public Library, Q.v.I.18 (*CLA* 11, no. 1621); Cambridge, University Liberary, KK.5.16 (*CLA* 2, no. 139); London, British Library, Cotton Tiberius A.xiv (*CLA* Suppl., no. 1703); London, British Library, Cotton Tiberius C.ii (*CLA* 2, no. 191); and Kassel, Landesbibliothek, 4° Theol. 2 (*CLA* 8, no. 1140). Most scholars of the manuscripts have assigned priority to CUL KK.5.16, which is usually dated to 737, but recently M. B. Parkes has cogently argued that the Leningrad manuscript is conceivably older and closer to Bede's scriptorium.[14] In addition to these two early Northumbrian manuscripts are Tiberius A.xiv, a mid-eighth-century copy of Leningrad Q.v.I.18, probably also written at Wearmouth-Jarrow, and Kassel 4° Theol. 2, a fragmentary manuscript written in several small Northumbrian hands of the second half of the century.[15] Tiberius C.ii dates to the second half of the eighth century and is most probably southern.[16] While the first three manuscripts transmit the M text, Tiberius C.ii and Kassel 4° Theol. 2 transmit the C text, the version represented by all later English manuscripts.[17]

In these early manuscripts of the *Historia ecclesiastica*, verse is formatted spatially according to the complexity of verse form. Of the six poems in the *Historia*, Bede's epanaleptic alphabetic acrostic distichs on St. Etheldreda, "Alma deus trinitas" (4.20 [18]), is the most complex, and for these verses all the manuscripts use capitalization, lineation, and punctuation to highlight alphabet, repetition, and distichs. The Leningrad manuscript's treatment of these verses is instructive: as the manuscript closest to Bede's scriptorium, it illustrates the early development of Insular minuscule and of graphic conventions. For the verses on Etheldreda, Scribe D carefully distinguishes the visual features of the hymn.[18] A capital initial at the margin and a fresh line signal the beginning of each distich. While the two verses of the distich are run on within the column, a comma-shaped sub-distinctio separates hexameter and pentameter lines.[19] The hymn ends with heavy punctuation. In a similar fashion, Tiberius A.xiv, probably a copy of Leningrad Q.v.I.18, uses layout to highlight both verse form and alphabetic acrostic, beginning each distich on a fresh line with a colored initial.

The hurried and rather careless scribe of CUL KK.5.16 is exceptionally careful with Bede's hymn. The capital initial of "Alma" is of the sort reserved for the beginnings of chapters. Each distich begins with a capital initial. The unusual care taken in spacing between the last word of a distich and the following capital initial, as well as the consistent pointing between distichs, suggests that the scribe was mindful of the visual dimension of Bede's demanding hymn. The treatment of the hymn in Tiberius C.ii shows some uncertainty over method but a clear intent to produce a visual display. To highlight the alphabetic acrostic, the scribe placed each large initial in the margin, dotting and coloring many of them. His intention seems to have been to give two column lines to each distich. However, the overrun of the last word of the prose introduction necessitated dropping each epanaleptic clause to the line below, breaking the visual symmetry. With this practice, whenever a distich ends mid-column, the scribe uses two hair strokes to separate the completed distich from the following squeezed-in line end.[20] While the scribe's effort to highlight the alphabetic acrostic obscures the epanalepsis, his mixed result shows that he conceived of the distich as a visual unit.

In the eighth-century manuscripts, verses in distichs show some ambivalence in the choice of layout. The two epitaphs of book 5, on Caedwalla (5.7) and Theodore (5.8), are useful examples. CUL KK.5.16 writes the verses in long lines but distinguishes each verse with a capital initial, and remaining scribal punctuation marks verse length, not grammatical divisions. Tiberius C.ii employs a different format for each epitaph. In that on Caedwalla, the scribe highlights verse lines at the expense of the distich by beginning each verse line with a capital in the margin. However, in the following epitaph on Theodore, the scribe emphasizes the distich instead, beginning lines 1 and 3 in the margin. For these epitaphs, Scribe D in Leningrad Q.v.I.18 appears to be experimenting with combinations of techniques. The first distich of Caedwalla's epitaph is written across the column, and heavy punctuation separates the two verses. Lines 3–10 each begin at the margin, and lines 11–24 revert to presentation in distich form. In the latter format, each distich begins with a capital initial; in line format, each verse begins with a capital. In the two excerpts Bede quotes from Theodore's epitaph there is a similar ambivalence about the technique of lineation. The poem begins with a capital, and lines 1 and 2 each begin at the margin. The following two lines, however, are run on. In the second set of verses, following "ultimi hi," lines 5 and 6 run on but lines 7 and 8 begin at the margin.[21] Spacing between verses is clear, and each line of verse was apparently pointed by a distinctio.

The epitaph on Wilfrid (5.10) in simple hexameters, shows the least complexity in graphic display. Scribe D writes the first verses in long lines (though separating each verse by a sub-distinctio), but shifts method to begin verses 4 through 20 at the margin with a capital. While both Kassel 4° Theol. 2 and Tiberius A.xiv format this epitaph in lines of verse, Tiberius C.ii distinguishes verses with capital initials only. CUL KK.5.16 distinguishes the first two lines with capital initials and terminal punctuation, but then discontinues the practice.[22]

The eighth-century manuscripts of the *Historia ecclesiastica* show a clear intent to provide visual cues to aid in reading the verses in the text. At the simplest level, this purpose is served by pointing. At its most complex, graphic interpretation involves capitalization and the fitting of verses into the columnar lines. This practice becomes fixed in the manuscripts of the following centuries. No English manuscripts of the *Historia ecclesiastica* survive from the ninth of tenth centuries, and from the eleventh century, to my knowledge, only six manuscripts remain. In these manuscripts, layout for

poetry is highly consistent. The graphic representations of the poetry in
the *Historia* in Oxford, Bodleian Library, Bodley 163 (Ker. no. 304, xi in.), is
typical of the other surviving eleventh-century manuscripts: Oxford, Bodleian Library, Hatton 43 (Ker, no. 326, xi in.); Cambridge, Trinity College,
R.7.5 (early eleventh century); Winchester Cathedral, 1 (Ker, no. 396, xi[1]);
London, British Library, Royal 13.C.v (second half of the eleventh century); and Durham, Dean and Chapter Library, B.II.35 (late eleventh century). Verses (except for the hymn in 4.20 [18]) are written across the
writing space but are carefully distinguished by pointing.[23] Prosper's epigram (1.10) begins with a large red capital, and black capitals begin the next
two distichs. Punctuation reinforces that structure with a low point to separate verses of the distichs and a high point as terminal punctuation for the
distich.[24]

Each verse of Gregory's epitaph (2.1) begins with a red capital.[25] The
pointing has been considerably altered, though originally the system must
have consisted of high and low points. This practice is followed as well for
the epitaphs of book 5.[26] The hymn on Etheldreda (4.20 [18]), however, is
written in lines of verse with the size of script reduced. Each verse begins
with a red rustic capital initial.[27] Present terminal punctuation for each line
is a punctus versus, but the tail of the versus is in much lighter ink. The
original system probably used a low point to mark the caseura and a high
point for terminal punctuation. This system, by highlighting each line of
verse, obscures the alphabetic acrostic which begins each distich. The
twelfth-century manuscripts examined for this study consistently write the
poems in lines of verse.[28]

Although there is room for variation in the use and ornamentation of
capitals, the manuscript tradition carefully distinguishes the verses in the
Historia ecclesiastica from the surrounding prose. Pointing and capitalization
mark off lines of verse, not sense or breath pauses. The evidence points to
an awareness that Latin required extralinguistic cues to help the reader
work through the verse.[29] The methods used to distinguish Latin verse
were not adopted in the written record of Old English poetry. An examination of manuscripts containing the surviving records of Caedmon's *Hymn*
may suggest some reasons for this difference.

2

Caedmon's *Hymn* travels in two textual environments, as a marginal addition to the account of Caedmon's miraculous composition in the *Historia ecclesiastica* (4.24 [22])[30] and as an integral part of the West-Saxon translation

of the *History*. Its promotion from margin to text proper is consonant with the other modifications the Old English translator made in the Latin text. His inclusion of Caedmon's *Hymn* necessitated as well some rearrangement of the Latin material, for example the omission of the paraphrase and Bede's apology for the Latin translation. In the context of these changes, the anonymous translator affirmed his faith in the version of Caedmon's *Hymn* which he transmitted by introducing with the words: "þara endebyrdnes ðis is." An examination of the twelve Latin manuscripts in which Caedmon's Hymn appears offers evidence on the status of the text, the conventions of copying Old English poetry, and practices of word division and punctuation. From these we may make inferences about practices of reading.

Dobbie divided the extual tradition of Caedmon's *Hymn* into two main lines, the "aelda"/"ylda" group and the "eorðu" group, which he then sub-divided by dialect.[31] Each of these groups has two Northumbrian witnesses, though the copies of the Northumbrian "eorðu" version are Continental and too late to be useful to this study. The two Northumbrian records of the "aelda"/"ylda" group, Leningrad Q.v.I.18 and CUL KK.5.16, are, however, the earliest witnesses to the text of Caedmon's *Hymn* and as such are of crucial importance.

In many ways, as records of the *Historia ecclesiastica*, CUL KK.5.16 and Leningrad Q.v.I.18 are very different. The latter is a particularly careful copy of the text. Outside of errors in the sources quoted by Bede (and thus, probably, in the originals), there are only six errors in the text written by Bede, and these errors are minor.[32] Given the length of the *Historia*, the high accuracy of Leningrad Q.v.1.18 argues that its copying was close to the author's draft. Leningrad Q.v.I.18 is also a handsome copy of the text, and the individual work done by four Wearmouth-Jarrow scribes shows a high level of concern for calligraphy in the manuscript as a whole.[33] The stints of the first two scribes, which supply the first eight quires, are clearly later than the work of scribes C and D, and, Parkes argues, were added to make up for loss from the original state of the Leningrad manucript. The work of scribes C and D may thus well be the oldest witness to the text of the *Historia ecclesiastica* in existence. Early scholars, of Leningrad Q.v.I.18 thought that the system of numerals in the margin, a dating device which yields the year 746, provided a terminus a quo for the manuscript.[34] The marks, however, are in the ink of a corrector,[35] making the date of the CD portion earlier than 746. This issue assumes particular significance, since scribe D added Caedmon's *Hymn* at the bottom of fol. 107r.

Scribe D wrote Caedmon's *Hymn* in three long lines across the bottom margin of fol. 107r. Whether he added it at the time of writing or at some point afterwards is impossible to determine. It is clear that he did not alter his usual arrangement of twenty-seven lines per column to accommodate the *Hymn*. Functionally, the *Hymn* is a gloss to Bede's Latin paraphrase in 4.20 [18]. The hand is Insular minuscule, and though just as precise as that in the Latin columns, much smaller. The *Hymn* begins with a capital *N*, there is no other capital, and the only point occurs after "all mehtig."[36] The orthography and spacing of the words in the *Hymn* show characteristic attention to detail. Word division is as scrupulous as in the Latin text. While separation of free morphemes is possible, no words are run on.

In the Latin text of the *Historia ecclesiastica*, where the Leningrad manuscript is deliberate, measured, calligraphic, and accurate, CUL KK.5.16 is hurried, uncalligraphic, and imprecise. Ornament is lacking; the scribe wrote his Insular minuscule in long lines across the writing space, leaving only very narrow margins. Punctuation is spare, and the spacing, though not cramped, is not kind to a reader. Spacing between words is about the same size as spacing between letters within words, and the Latin text often appears to be a series of undifferentiated letters. There is, however, a considerable difference between the scribe's work on the *Historia* and his execution of Caedmon's *Hymn* on the first three lines of fol. 128v, a sort of addendum to the text of the history.[37] Like Leningrad Q.v.I.18, CUL KK.5.16 begins with the *Hymn*'s only capital letter. The word division of the *Hymn* is actually better than that of the Latin text. The scribe runs together "nu scylun," and splits "hefaen ricaes" and "middun geard." Word separations are limited to free morphemes. His orthography is highly consistent as well, although "dryctin" is consistent by correction, and the scribe varies "hefaen" with "heben." The point which occurs after "scepen" (l. 6) is the only point in the text of Caedmon's *Hymn* in CUL KK.5.16.

The inclusion of Caedmon's *Hymn* by the original scribes in both CUL KK.5.16 and Leningrad Q.v.I.18 suggests that from earliest times Caedmon's *Hymn* was considered a worthy companion to the Latin account of Caedmon's miracle. Its appearance in Leningrad Q.v.I.18, a manuscript from Wearmouth-Jarrow very close to the author's copy, and the discipline obvious in its script, spacing, and orthography speak to the care which the Old English poem was thought to merit. Equally, that it is recognized as verse, but not marked off as such by the techniques used by the same scribe for Latin verses, strongly suggests that such graphic marking was perceived to be redundant. Given its scribal origin, the quality of the copy of Caedmon's *Hymn* in CUL KK.5.16, otherwise a hastily written production, argues a self-consciousness about writing the Old English verses not apparent in the Latin.

The six surviving eleventh-century English copies of the *Historia ecclesi-astica*—Oxford, Bodleian Library, Bodley 163; Oxford, Bodleian Library, Hatton 43; Cambridge, Trinity College, R.7.5; Winchester Cathedral, 1 (all manuscripts of the early eleventh century); London, British Library, Royal 13.C.v; and Durham, dean and Chapter Library, B.II.35 (both late eleventh century)—while grouped as C versions, preserve different strands of the textual tradition.[38] Hatton 43 transmits a very accurate text, quite close to that of the eighth-century southern C version, BL Cotton Tiberius C.ii, though not a copy.[39] According to Plummer, Bodley 163 is a copy of the carelessly executed Winchester 1.[40] These two manuscripts (part of a "Winchester" group) share alterations in the chronology of 5.24 with the "Durham" group (headed by Durham B.II.35) but show a northern con-nection by the presence of Aethelwulf's poem on the abbots of a northern English monastery.[41] Royal 13.C.v (Gloucester?) transmits a C text which nonetheless shares some readings with BL Cotton Tiberius A.xiv, an M text.

All six of these manuscripts were originally copied without Caedmon's *Hymn*. Only Hatton 43, Winchester 1, and Bodley 163 contain the *Hymn*, and in each case the copying of the *Hymn* into the *Historia ecclesiastica* was done at least a quarter-century later than the writing of the Latin text.[42] This circumstance and the wide selection of textual strands attested by the surviving eleventh-century copies suggests that Caedmon's *Hymn* did not travel integrally with the text in any one textual tradition. The addition of the *Hymn* to Hatton 43, Bodley 163, and Winchester 1 would seem to have been fortuitous.

Especially interesting is the disparity in date between the copying of the text of the *Historia ecclesiastica* in Hatton 43 (which Ker dates to xi in.) and that of the *Hymn* (which Ker dates to xi²). The color of ink for the addition is similar to that used for many corrections. The placement of the *Hymn* is interesting as well. It is written in four long lines at the bottom of fol. 129r. The scribe has keyed the *Hymn* to the Latin paraphrase by a *signe de renvoi* and has drawn a box around the text. The location of the text here is similar to that in Leningrad Q.v.I.18. One wonders what kind of exemplar the scribe of the addition had before him.[43]

In any event, Hatton 43 preserves the most orthographically pure text of Caedmon's *Hymn* in the *Z version, although it is later than either Win-chester 1 or Bodley 163. On the basis of the textual relations between Win-chester 1 and Bodley 163, Dobbie thought it probable that Caedmon's *Hymn* in Bodley 163 was copied from the Winchester manuscript. The in-dependence of Caedmon's *Hymn* from the copying of the Latin text makes this circumstance unlikely. Winchester 1 is a peculiar manuscript. Caedmon's *Hymn* is copied in the upper right outer margin of fol. 81r with a *signe de renvoi* to the text. The copying is careless,[44] but apart from some orthographic differences, Winchester differs from *Z only in the substitution of "word" for "ord." Given the copyist's carelessness, it is probable that this variant is unique to Winchester. About the text of the *Hymn* in Bodley 163 we can conclude little, save that this version has "gehwylc" rather than "gehwaes." On this basis it can be placed confidently in the *Z group. The few remaining letters of the *Hymn* in the left margin of fol. 152v survive a considerable attempt made to erase it.[45]

The copies of Caedmon's *Hymn* in the twelfth-century manuscripts show a comparable independence of the *Hymn* from the Latin text. Of the four manuscripts which transmit the *Hymn*,[46] only Oxford, Magdalen College, lat. 105, and Oxford, Bodleian Library, Laud Misc. 243, have the text in the hand of the original scribe. Ker describes the hand of the *Hymn* in Hereford Cathedral P.v.1 as "contemporary." The *Hymn* in Oxford, Lincoln College, lat. 31, was added by one of the correctors.[47]

While Magdalen 105 and Hereford P.v.1 belong to the same textual group, that of the common text in southern England, they transmit different versions of the *Hymn*. The version in Magdalen 105 is the standard *Z text of the "aelda"/"ylda" group. Hereford is peculiar in transmitting a corrupt "eorðu" text, which comes either from Laud Misc. 243 or its examplar. Laud. Misc. 243 transmits a "Gloucester" version of the history but its text of the *Hymn*, thoroughly corrupt, derives from an *AE text (i.e., it was copied from the version in the West-Saxon *History*).

The version of the *Hymn* in this manuscript needs further examination. At issue is the nature of the transmission of Caedmon's *Hymn* in Laud Misc. 243. Dobbie favored Frampton's conclusion[48] that Laud Misc. 243 is a transcript from memory, on the basis that the appending of "halig scyppeod" at the end of the poem could not have been done by a scribe with a correct copy before him. This argument might be persuasive were it not for the presence of other errors of a purely graphic nature, that is, the dittography of "herian herian," the spelling "scyppeod,"[49] and the impossible syntax caused by the omission of "or astealde." Despite Dobbie's assertion to the contrary,[50] it is quite possible that the transposition of "halig scyppeod" could have been made from a "correct" copy. This is far more likely than the memorial transmission of so corrupt a text, especially since the corruption violates the alliteration, the main means of aiding correct memorial transmission.

The copyist who added Caedmon's *Hymn* in Hereford Cathedral P.v.1 reproduced the error with "scyppeod" and introduced one of his own, "drihtent." However, he corrected the syntax caused by the missing "ord astealde" by omitting the whole phrase "swa . . . drihten" (ll. 3b–4a). Once again, we see Caedmon's *Hymn* included in the Latin text by chance. The text was obviously not in Hereford's exemplar for the *Historia*, and at some point along the line either the scribe of Laud Misc. 243 or the scribe of his exemplar departed from his Latin text to use the *Hymn* from a West-Saxon translation of Bede's history. The final twelfth-century manuscript to be considered, Lincoln College, lat. 31, also adds Caedmon's *Hymn* from another examplar. The text of the *Historia ecclesiastica* in Lincoln 31 is in the "Burney" group of manuscripts, but it has been collated with and corrected from the "Digby" group, from which the corrector added the West-Saxon version of Bede's *Death Song*.[51]

The change of hand in the copying of the *Hymn* in all but Magdalen 105 and the peculiar Laud Misc. 243 suggests that the inclusion of Caedmon's *Hymn* in the eleventh and twelfth centuries is fortuitous. This inference is strengthened by the fact that these copies containing the *Hymn* are largely from different textual groups. No group is identifiable by the presence of the *Hymn*. Caedmon's *Hymn* did not, in fact, normally travel with the *Historia ecclesiastica*. The circumstances of its including indicate that the *Hymn* appears in the *Z version as a gloss with its own discrete textual tradition. Given the various lines of descent represented by its host text, it is surprising that the West-Saxon "ylda" text is in the good shape it is. That this is so argues that Caedmon's *Hymn* in the *Historia ecclesiastica* became textual fairly early, that is, became a *written* poem in a relatively modern sense. A possible objection to this conclusion might be that the *Z group dates from the eleventh and twelfth centuries, and thus one migh expect the text to be fossilized. The best answer to this objection is an examination of the five surviving manuscripts of the West Saxon translation of the *Historia ecclesiastica*. With the exception of Oxford, Bodleian Library, Tanner 10, these are eleventh-century productions. An examination of the state of their records of the *Hymn* should demonstrate that something other than age is responsible for the fixity of the text in *Z.

There are five witnesses to the text of Caedmon's *Hymn* as it was contained in the West-Saxon translation of the *History*: Oxford, Bodleian Library, Tanner 10 (Ker, no. 351, x[1]); Oxford, Corpus Christi College, 41 (Ker. no. 32, xi[1]); Cambridge, University Library, KK.3.18 (Ker, no. 23, xi[2]); and London, British Library, Cotton Otho B.xi (Ker, no. 180, x med.), now thoroughly burnt, but whose readings survive in the sixteenth-century transcript by Nowell in London, British Library, Add. 43,703. The transcript is useless as evidence for orthography, punctuation, spacing, and mise-en-page, since Nowell was hardly xerographic in his reproduction of the text. Certain readings: "ne" (for "nu"), "eorþū" (for "eorþan"), "eode" (for "teode"), "finū" (for "firum") are clearly the visual mistakes of a sixteenth-century transcriber. However, one variant, "weoroda" (l. 3a), is useful to the study of the relationships among the five manuscripts. "Weoroda" can only have been an original reading, since it is highly improbable that a nonnative speaker would by accident produce a likely and grammatical variant.

Miller's examination of the manuscript tradition of the West-Saxon *History* established that the West-Saxon texts of the *History* as a whole derive from the same original translation.[52] In this light, the extensive variation shown by these copies, apart from orthographic differences, is remarkable and demands consideration. In the nine lines of the *Hymn*, *AE contains seven variations, all of which are grammatically and semantically appropriate. In the variations *nu/nu we; weorc/wera/weoroda; wuldorfaeder/ wuldorgodes; wundra/wuldres; gehwaes/fela; or/ord; sceop/gescop* we see a dynamic of transmission where the message is not embellished but where change within the formula is allowed. The variations in the *AE version are that much more startling by contrast with the record of the *Z texts. In the five manuscripts of this West-Saxon version traveling with the *Historia ecclesiastica* there is only one nonorthographic variant, "word" in Winchester 1. How can this difference be accounted for? The likeliest explanation would be independent translation, but this has been demonstrated not to be the case on other grounds.[53] The *Z and *AE groups each descend from one original. The dating of the copies would not appear to be significant either, since the core of variables in *AE lies in the eleventh-century manuscripts, and the eleventh-century records of *Z are extremely stable. Nor is there compelling evidence that an unusual wave of scribal incompetence is responsible for the variants. There is, however, one circumstance not accounted for—the textual environment. The *Z group travels as a gloss to the Latin paraphrase in the *Historia ecclesiastica*. The *AE version, on the contrary, finds its place in the vernacular redaction of Bede's story of Caedmon. Since the only variable circumstance in the transmission of *Z and *AE is textual environment, I would suggest that the variability of text in *AE is a consequence of its environment in a purely vernacular text, a vernacular whose character as a living language kept it close to the oral status which until fairly recently was its only state.

When we examine the variations in these five records of the West-Saxon version, we see in the despair of the textual editor palpable evidence of a fluid transmission of the *Hymn* somewhere between the formula-defined process which is an oral poem and the graph-bound object which is a text. We see a reading activity reflected in these scribal variants which is formula-dependent, in that the variants observe metrical and alliterative constraints, and which is context-defined, in that the variants produced arise within a field of possibilities generated within a context of expectations.[54] The reading I am proposing is reading by suggestion, by guess triggered by key words in formulae. It is a method of reading which is the natural and inevitable child of an oral tradition only recently wedded to the possibilities of writing. Variance in an oral tradition is made inevitable by the subjectivity of the speaker (and hearer) but is constrained by impersonal meter and alliteration. The writing of a poem acts as a very powerful constraint on variance, and in the face of such constraint, the presence of variance argues an equally powerful pull from the oral.

The process of copying manuscripts is rarely simply mechanical. Given the normal medieval practice of reading aloud, or at least subvocalizing, the scribe likely "heard" at least some of his text.[55] And copying done in blocks of text required the commission of several words or phrases to short-term memory.[56] The trigger of memory is responsible for various sorts of contamination,[57] as seen, for example, in the importation of Old Latin readings into the copying of the Vulgate Bible. Quite another sort of memory trigger is responsible for "Freudian" substitutions in a text.[58] Here the substitutes, if syntactically correct, are usually not semantically or contextually appropriate.

The presence of variants in Caedmon's *Hymn*, however, differs in an important way from the appearance of memorial variants in biblical or liturgical texts. Both sorts depend to some degree on memory, but the variants in Caedmon's *Hymn* use memory not to import a set phrase but to draw on formulaic possibility. Reception here, conditioned by formulaic conventions, produces variants which are metrically, syntactically, and semantically appropriate. In such a process, reading and copying have actually conflated with composing.[59] The integral presence of such variance in transmitting the *Hymn* in *AE argues for the existence of a transitional state between pure orality and pure literacy whose evidence is a reading process which applies oral techniques for the reception of a message to the decoding of a written text.[60] Caedmon's *Hymn* shows us neither purely literate nor memorial transmission,[61] but a tertium quid whose nature remains to be explored.

3

To this point, the argument about the varying degrees of fixity in the text of Caedmon's *Hymn* has focused on evidence offered by textual transmission. The practices of punctuation displayed in the paraphrase of the *Hymn* and in the *Hymn* itself in the manuscripts under consideration offer a different kind of evidence to support the argument about fixity in the text, reading, and visual cues.

In reviewing Table 1, displaying the punctuation of the Latin paraphrase of the *Hymn*, one cannot help but be struck by the regularity of pointing in these records. The pointing in the fullest case separates the *Hymn* into three major clauses (beginning "nunc . . . "; "quomodo . . . "; "qui . . . "), which are in turn subdivided. In the first case points separate the variations on the direct object, in the second and third they distinguish dependent clauses. These points are grammatical markers, and if they function as breath pauses, they do so only secondarily.[62] The table shows unanimity in marking the main clauses, save for CUL KK.5.16, the hastily executed eighth-century M text. The marking of objects or dependent clauses also shows little variety.

The pointing of the Old English *Hymn* shows no such uniformity. From

TABLE I   Pointing in the Latin Paraphrase of Caedmon's *Hymn*

	Placement of Points by Clause[1]							
Manuscripts	*caelestis*	*creatoris*	*illius*	*gloriae*	*deus*	*extitit*	*tecti*	*creavit*
Leningrad Q.v.I.18	x	x	x	x	x	x	x	x
CUL KK.5.16						x		
Tiberius C.ii		x				x	x	x
Tiberius A.xiv	x	x		x	x	x	x	x
Cambridge Trinity R.7.5	x		x	x		x	x	x
Winchester 1	x	x		x	x	x	x	x
Hatton 43	x		x	x		x	x	x
Bodley 163	x	x		x	x	x	x	x
Royal 13.C.v	x	x	x	x	x	x	x	x
Laud Misc. 243	x		x	x	x	x	x	x
Magdalen 105	x	x	x	x	x	x	x	x
Lincoln 31	x		x	x	x	x	x	x
Cambridge Trininty R.5.27	x	x		x	x	x	x	x
Hereford P.v.1	x		x	x	x	x	x	x

[1]The punctuation follows the last word of the clause.

an examination of Table 2, several observations may be made. The only larger agreement in punctuation is a terminal point which marks off the *Hymn* as a whole. Even here, there is not unanimity, for neither CUL KK.5.16 nor, more significantly, Bodleian Library Hatton 43 supplies terminal points.[63] Caedmon's *Hymn* divides into three main clauses (beginning "nu . . ." "he . . ."; "þa middangeard . . ."). The first contains three variations on the direct object (or on the subject in versions without "we") and the subordinate "swa" clause. The second is a simple main clause with a variation on the subject. The third is a complex sentence with OSV structure and nested variations on subject and object. Of all the records of the *Hymn* under consideration, only Tanner 10 provides a consistent grammatical pointing terminating each main clause. As might be expected, the *AE group shows great variety. One might note especially the difference in pointing between CUL KK.3.18 and its probable exemplar. The later manuscript clearly added points to separate the variant objects, but pays no attention to the full stop wanting after "onstealde." The *Z group shows, predictably, both a higher incidence of punctuation and a higher incidence of agreement within itself. The system of punctuation in Hatton 43, in many ways the best record in the group, is similar to that in the Latin paraphrase of the *Hymn*. Hatton 43 divides the *Hymn* into two statements ("nu . . . astealde"; "he . . . aelmihtig"),

TABLE 2 Pointing in Caedmon's *Hymn*

	Placement of Points by Clause (Expressed in Half-Liners[1])																	
Manuscripts[2]	1a	1b	2a	2b	3a	3b	4a	4b	5a	5b	6a	6b	7a	7b	8a	8b	9a	9b
Leningrad Q.v.I.18																		x
CUL KK.5.16										x								
Tanner 10					x					x								x
CCCC 41													x					x
OxCCC 279																		x
CUL KK.3.18			x			x					x							x
Hatton 43	x	x	x	x			x				x				x			
Winchester 1		x						x										x
Laud Misc. 243	x		x	x							x							[x][3]
Hereford P.v.1											x							[x][3]
Magdalen 105	x	x	x	x			x				x							x
Lincoln 31	x	x	x	x			x				x	x	x					x

[1]In each case where punctuation occurs, a point follows the last word of a half-line.
[2]Bodley 163 is not considered here because it is too badly damaged to discern pointing.
[3]In Laud Misc. 243 and Hereford P.v.1, 6b is placed at the end of the *Hymn*.

though the final point is missing. These statements are further divided, the first by object variant and the dependent "swa" clause. The second separates two variants on the main clause, both depending on "gesceop." This scheme is followed by Magdalen College, lat. 105 (with terminal punctuation); Lincoln College, lat. 31, adds points after "bearnum" and "scyppend" while omitting the point after "drihten." Winchester 1, Laud Misc. 243, and Hereford P.v.1 are predictably idiosyncratic.

There are several issues here, and these are best examined in Dobbie's manuscript groups, beginning with the last, *Z. Just as an examination of mise-en-page and textual descent in *Z established the high degree of fixity in the text, so its frequent use of punctuation as an extralinguistic signal confirms that fixity as a movement from the subjectivity of the speaker to the objectivity of the graph committed to vellum. Yet the Old English records show a high variability in pointing as compared with Latin records of the paraphrase copied in the same time period.

*AE shows an idiosyncrasy in punctuation consonant with the variability it shows in the transmission of the *Hymn*. While pointing in Tanner 10 can be analyzed as "grammatical," such a pattern is lacking in the other three extant *AE records. Most interesting are the relationships between Oxford, Corpus Christi College 279, and CUL KK.3.18. Whether KK.3.18 is a copy of the Oxford manuscript's exemplar or of the manuscript itself, we see an acute case of the spontaneous nature of Old English pointing. In this group one might make a case for pointing as breath markers.

The group comprised of CUL KK.5.16 and Leningrad Q.v.I.18 stands apart from the West-Saxon versions in several ways. Its antiquity, its closeness to Wearmouth-Jarrow, the exquisite care lavished on its copying (even for the hurried CUL KK.5.16) make the record it transmits of supreme importance. What we see are systems of pointing in Latin and Old English at variance with one another. Even discounting CUL KK.5.16 as a careless copy, and hence of little use for argument, we have the testimony of Leningrad Q.v.I.18, where the Latin text and Caedmon's *Hymn* are both written by Scribe D. The copy of Caedmon's *Hymn* in the Leningrad manuscript is a very careful and correct record in the same way as the text of the *Historia ecclesiastica* is careful and correct. Yet the pointing of the Latin paraphrase is copious while the pointing of the Old English poem is limited to a purely formal terminal point. The points, so useful in Latin, are missing precisely because they were redundant in Old English, unnecessary either for scansion or sense. In the early copies of the *Hymn*, the omission of pointing, a visual cue for decoding, is a powerful indication of the still strongly oral component in the *Hymn*'s transmission and reception.

The records of Caedmon's *Hymn* show that the status of the *Hymn* as text and the degree of fixity of the text depend on the environments of the *Hymn*, whether Latin or Old English. When the *Hymn* travels as a gloss to the *Historia ecclesiastica*, the text is subject to little variation, while those records of the *Hymn* which are integrated in the West-Saxon translation of the *History* show a high degree of freedom in transmission. Examination of the conventions of lineation and punctuation in Latin and Old English poetic texts within the *History* demonstrates a considerable variation in conventions for each language. Lineation and, certainly, pointing for poetry are necessary extralinguistic cues which assist the reader in decoding the Latin text. These conventions are uniformly applied. The Old English *Hymn*, however, is never displayed graphically by metrical line, nor does punctuation distinguish lines or half-lines or act consistently as a marker of grammatical divisions.

The transmission and reception of Caedmon's *Hymn* have several implications for the larger understanding of literacy in Anglo-Saxon England and for our own reading of Anglo-Saxon poetic works. The differing level and nature of extralinguistic cues in Latin and Old English imply that Caedmon's *Hymn* was read with different expectations, conventions, and techniques than those for the Latin verses with which it traveled. Techniques of reading Old English verse which allowed the incorporation of "formulaic" guesses into the written text represent an accommodation of literacy, with its resistant text, to the fluidity of the oral process of transmission. The evidence suggests that for Caedmon's *Hymn*, at least, an oral poem did not automatically become a fixed text upon writing and that under certain conditions the "literate" reception of the text had a considerable admixture of oral processes. This demonstrable accommodation of literate to oral in the manuscript records suggests a starting place for future investigation into the features of a transitional state between pure orality and pure literacy in the reception of a poetic text. An investigation of the formatting conventions, pointing, and variants in Old English verse in multiple copies, especially *Solomon and Saturn*, the poems of the *Anglo-Saxon Chronicle*, and the metrical Preface and Epilogue to Alfred's translation of the *Pastoral Care*, should provide further information about the growth of literacy and the development of a text in Anglo-Saxon England.

Notes

1. The Metrical Epilogue to the *Pastoral Care* in Oxford, Bodleian Library, Hatton 20, beginning at the top of fol. 98v, is laid out in an inverted triangle. The com-

mendatory verses, "Thureth," in London, British Library, Cotton Claudius A.iii, fol. 31v, are similarly formatted, but in each case the arrangement of the words actually works against the sense of the verse.

2. See N. R. Ker, *Catalogue of Manuscripts Containing Anglo-Saxon* (Oxford, 1957), pp. xxxiii–xxxvi. The use of points and capitals in the greater part of the corpus of Old English poetry is infrequent and irregular. For an exemplary discussion of pointing practice in the Exeter Book see Craig Williamson, ed., *The Old English Riddles of the Exeter Book* (Chapel Hill, 1977), pp. 12–19 and 35–48, esp. p. 16. A notable exception to common practice is Oxford, Bodleian Library, Junius 11, whose half-lines are generally, if not systematically, pointed. See Ker, *Catalogue*, no. 334, p. 408. Other manuscripts containing more or less regularly pointed verse are: London, British Library, Cotton Tiberius B.i, fols. 112–15v (Ker, no. 191, s. xi med.); Oxford, Bodleian Library, Junius 121, fols. 43v–52r, 53v (Ker, no. 338, s. xi [3rd quarter]); Cambridge, Corpus Christi College, 201, pp. 161–67 (Ker, no. 49, s. xi in.) and pp. 167–69 (Ker, s. xi med.); and London, British Library, Cotton Julius A.ii, fols. 136–44 (Ker, no. 158, s. xii med.). The verse which occurs in these late manuscripts is largely translation from biblical or liturgical sources.

3. See especially Donald K. Fry, "The Memory of Caedmon," in *Oral Traditional Literature: A Festschrift for Albert Bates Lord*, ed. John Miles Foley (Columbus, 1981), pp. 282–93, and "Caedmon as Formulaic Poet," in *Oral Literature: Seven Essays*, ed. Joseph J. Duggan (Edinburgh, 1975), pp. 41–61. Jeff Opland, *Anglo-Saxon Poetry: A Study of the Tradition* (New Haven, 1980), examines Bede's account and understanding of the "miracle" (pp. 112–29). Dobbie's careful study (*The Manuscripts of Caedmon's Hymn and Bede's Death Song* [New York, 1937]) provides some "diplomatic" transcriptions of versions of Caedmon's *Hymn*. These are broken into half-lines and are printed with modern spacing of words. I note errors in his record of manuscript punctuation below. M. B. Parkes, in *The Scriptorium of Wearmouth-Jarrow*, Jarrow Lecture (n.p., 1982), examines some implications of the writing of Caedmon's *Hymn* in Leningrad, Public Library, Q.v.I.18, and in Cambridge, University Library, KK.5.16.

4. I omit from consideration the versions of the *Hymn* in Dijon, Bibliothèque Municipale, 574 (12th c.); Paris, Bibliothèque Nationale, lat. 5237 (15th c.); and Cambridge, Trinity College, R.5.22 (14th c.). The first two are products of Continental scribes; the last is English, but too late to be useful to this study.

In terms of numbers of manuscripts, Bede's *Death Song* is the most attested Old English poetic text, surviving in Northumbrian dialect in twelve Continental manuscripts (9th through 16th c.) and in thirty-three Insular manuscripts transmitting the West-Saxon version (12th c. and later). However, for evidence of the native reading and copying of an Old English poetic text, Bede's *Death Song* is unsatisfactory on several grounds. Of the twelve copies of the Northumbrian version, two are early (9th and 11th c.), but all are copied by foreign scribes whose careful but mechanical copying tells us little about reading practice in Old English. The West-Saxon copies of Bede's *Death Song* descend from the same original copy (Dobbie, *Manuscripts*, p. 115), and the unanimity of these records is a tribute to the accurate copying of scribes whose familiarity with Old English is, nevertheless, questionable (Dobbie, p. 115). While the Insular copies of Bede's *Death Song* offer some parallel for my contentions about transmission of the *Z group of Caedmon's *Hymn* (see below, p. 14), the manuscripts of Bede's *Death Song* do not provide the rich evidence offered by Caedmon's *Hymn* for native English copying and reading in the eighth, tenth, and eleventh centuries.

5. On the evidence of formulae for oral composition see Francis P. Magoun, Jr., "The Oral-Formulaic Character of Anglo-Saxon Narrative Poetry," *Speculum* 28 (1953), 446–67. Larry D. Benson's much-cited reply, "The Literary Character of Anglo-Saxon Formulaic Poetry," *PMLA* 81 (1966), 334–41, at p. 334, n. 4, argued that Old English poetry was composed within a "lettered tradition." The assumptions of "orality" and "literacy" behind both arguments are called into question by the verse of Aldhelm, a superbly literate author whose Latin verse is, nonetheless, formulaic. See Michael Lapidge, "Aldhelm's Latin Poetry and Old English Verse," *Comparative Literature* 31 (1979), 209–31.

6. See Franz H. Bäuml, "Varieties and Consequences of Medieval Literacy and Illiteracy," *Speculum* 55 (1980), 237–65, at p. 239 on the inadequacies of the definition of medieval literacy as the ability to read and write Latin. One documents as an index of the early growth of literacy in England see M. T. Clanchy, *From Memory to Written Record: England 1066–1307* (London, 1979), p. 97 and p. 183.

7. Walter J. Ong, *Orality and Literacy: The Technologizing of the Word* (London, 1982), pp. 117–23.

8. Of writing, Isidore of Seville observes, "Litterae autem sunt indices rerum, signa verborum, quibus tanta vis est, ut nobis dicta absentium sine voce loquantur. [Verba enim per oculos non per aures introducunt.] Vsus litterarum repertus propter memoriam rerum. Nam ne oblivione fugiant, litteris alligantur. In tanta enim rerum varietate nec disci audiendo poterant omnia, nec memoria contineri. Litterae autem dictae quasi legiterae, quod iter legentibus praestent, vel quod in legendo iterentur." W. M. Lindsay, ed., *Isidori Hispalensis episcopi Etymologiarum siue originum libri XX* (Oxford, 1911), 1.3.1–3.

9. On the functional difference between the spoken and written word see Bäuml, "Varieties," pp. 247–48. See also Jacques Derrida, *Of Grammatology*, trans. Gayatri Chakravorty Spivak (Baltimore, 1976), pp. 30–73, esp. p. 39.

10. Until M. B. Parkes's book on medieval punctuation appears, see Edward Maunde Thompson, *An Introduction to Greek and Latin Paleography* (Oxford, 1912), pp. 55–64, for an overview of arrangement of text, punctuation, and accents. For early conventions of punctuation to mark the colon, comma, and periodus, see Isidore, *Etymologiae* I.20.1–6. Patrick McGurk, "Citation Marks in Early Latin Manuscripts," *Scriptorium* 15 (1961), 3–13, discusses scribal practices for distinguishing quoted material.

11. On the significance of layout and punctuation in prose and poetic texts see M. B. Parkes, "Punctuation, or Pause and Effect," in *Medieval Eloquence: Studies in the Theory and Practice of Medieval Rhetoric*, ed. James J. Murphy (Berkeley, 1978), pp. 127–42, esp. p. 130, n. 14. In "The Influence of the Concepts of *Ordinatio* and *Compi-*

latio on the Development of the Book," in *Medieval Learning and Literature: Essays Presented to Richard William Hunt*, ed. J. J. G. Alexander and M. T. Gibson (Oxford, 1976), pp. 115–41, Parkes examines the integral connection of "the structure of reasoning" and the physical appearance of books (at p. 121). Chirographic control of learned Latin is discussed in Ong, *Orality and Literacy*, pp. 112–14.

12. Helmut Gneuss, "A Preliminary List of Manuscripts Written or Owned in England up to 1100," *Anglo-Saxon England* 9 (1981), 1–60, lists ten eighth-century manuscripts written in England which contain verse. In addition to the manuscripts of the *Historia ecclesiastica* discussed below, manuscripts containing verse are: Cambridge, Corpus Christi College, 173 (*CLA* 2, no. 123, Sedulius); Vatican City, Biblioteca Apostolica Vaticana, Pal. lat. 235 (*CLA* 1, no. 87, Paulinus of Nola); Leningrad, Saltykov-Schedrin Public Library, Q.v.XIV.1 (*CLA* 11, no. 1622, Paulinus of Nola); Leningrad, Saltykov-Schedrin Public Library, Q.v.I.15 (*CLA* 11, no. 1618, Aldhelm); Miskolc, Zrinyi Ilona Secondary School, *s.n.* (*CLA* Suppl., no. 1792, Aldhelm). Formatting varies from the old practice in CCCC 173 of separating verses by point to the newer practice in Leningrad Q.v.I.15, which writes Aldhelm's *Enigmata* in lines of verse. By the tenth century, English manuscripts of Latin verse are consistently formatted in lines of verse with redundant initial capitals and points at the ends of lines.

13. Those in simple distichs are: Prosper's brief epigram against Pelagius (1.10) and the epitaphs on Gregory the Great (2.1), Caedwalla (5.7), and Theodore (5.8). Bede's own hymn on Etheldreda (4.20 [23]) is an epanaleptic alphabetic acrostic, and Wilfrid's epitaph (5.19) is in hexameters. I follow throughout the chapter numbers in B. Colgrave and R. A. B. Mynors, eds., *Bede's Ecclesiastical History of the Englis People* (Oxford, 1969). G. R. Blakley, Department of Mathematics, Texas A&M University, provided many useful observations on the scansion of these verses.

14. Peter Hunter Blair, ed., *The Moore Bede: An Eighth Century Manuscript of the Venerable Bede's "Historia ecclesiastica gentis Anglorum" in Cambridge University Library (KK.5.16)*, EEMF 9 (Copenhagen, 1959), p. 28; Peter Hunter Blair, "The Moore Memoranda on Northumbrian History," in *Early Cultures of North-West Europe*, ed.C. Fox and B. Dickins (Cambridge, Eng., 1950), pp. 245–57. See especially D. H. Wright, review of Blair, *The Moore Bede*, *Anglia* 82 (1964), 110–17. Parkes, *Scriptorium*, pp. 5–6, supports arguments advanced by E. A. Lowe, "A Key to Bede's Scriptorium," *Scriptorium* 12 (1958), 182–90. Lowe's further argument on the copying of the colophon on fol. 161 ("An Autograph of the Venerable Bede?" [*Revue bénédictine* 68 (1958), 200–202]) is disputed by Paul Meyvaert, "The Bede 'Signature' in the Leningrad Colophon," *Revue bénédictine* 71 (1961), 274–86, and by D. H. Wright, "The Date of the Leningrad Bede," *Revue bénédictine* 71 (1961), 265–73.

15. On Cotton Tiberius A.xiv see Colgrave and Mynors, *Ecclesiastical History*, pp. xlvi–xlvii. On Kassel 4° Theol. 2 see T. J. M. Van Els, *The Kassel Manuscript of Bede's "Historia ecclesiastica gentis Anglorum" and Its Old English Material* (Assen, 1972), pp. 6–18, 26.

16. Sherman M. Kuhn, "From Canterbury to Lichfield," *Speculum* 23 (1948),

591–629, at pp. 613–19, and "Some Early Mercian Manuscripts," *Review of English Studies*, n.s. 8 (1957), 355–74, at pp. 366–68, suggests a Mercian provenance. But see Kenneth Sisam, "Canterbury, Lichfield, and the Vespasian Psalter," *Review of English Studies*, n.s. 7 (1956), 1–10, 113–31, who questions his criteria. D. H. Wright, review of *The Moore Bede*, p. 116, suggests St. Augustine's. See also Helmut Gneuss, "Zur Geschichte des MS. Vespasian A.I," *Anglia* 75 (1957), 125–33.

17. Colgrave and Mynors, *Ecclesiastical History*, follow Plummer's distinction of a C text and a later M text (p. xli on versions of the C text). Charles Plummer, *Venerabilis Baedae historia ecclesiastica gentis Anglorum, historia abbatum, epistola ad Ecgberctum una cum historia abbatum auctore anonymo*, 2 vols. (Oxford, 1896), 1:lxxx–cxxxii.

18. On the stints of the scribes see O. Arngart, ed., *The Leningrad Bede: An Eighth Century Manuscript of the Venerable Bede's "Historia ecclesiastica gentis Anglorum" in the Public Library, Leningrad*, EEMF 2 (Copenhagen, 1952), p. 18, and Parkes, *Scriptorium*, pp. 6–11.

19. I have not been able to see Leningrad Q.v.I.18 and am wary of making any argument about scribal pointing on the basis of the facsimile, especially since some repointing has been done. However, the comma-shaped point is characteristically early.

20. As a result of considerable repointing in the manuscript, each distich now appears marked by a punctus versus, but original punctuation is by medial point.

21. Bede quotes two sections of the epitaph: the opening and the closing four lines. Kassel Landesbibliothek, 4° Theol. 2 and BL Cotton Tiberius A.xiv both write these epitaphs in lines of verse.

22. The formatting for verses in 1.10 and 2.1 raises questions beyond the scope of this paper. For a full account see my "Graphic Cues for the Presentation of Verse in the Earliest English Manuscripts of the *Historia ecclesiastica*," in preparation.

23. The practice in the eleventh-century manuscripts of the *Historia ecclesiastica* of running verses across the writing space and using only capitals and points to separate verses is a throwback to much earlier practice, probably owing to pressures of space. In this period, manuscripts of poetry are always formatted spatially in lines of verse.

24. Hatton 43 begins each verse with a capital.

25. Winchester 1 points each verse, but capitalization is inconsistent. BL Royal 13.C.v writes the epitaph in lines of verse beginning with line 4. Durham B.II.35 distinguishes hexameters with capital initials and separates all verses by a point on the line of writing.

26. For the epitaph in 5.7, Winchester 1 and Royal 13.C.v follow this practice. Hatton 43 points at the end of each verse but uses capitals inconsistently. The practice in Trinity R.7.5 is impossible to ascertain because the original punctuation has been erased. For the epitaph in 5.8, Royal 13.C.v and Trinity R.7.5 point at the end of each line of verse. Winchester 1 capitalizes by distich, omitting the capital for line 1. Hatton 43 has a capital for "hic" only. For Wilfrid's epitaph in 5.19, Trinity R.7.5 follows Bodley 163's practice of separating verses by marking them with high and low points. Royal 13.C.v and Hatton 43 change formats here and write the epitaph in lines of verse introduced by capital initials. Winchester 1 separates all lines by punctus versi

but is inconsistent with capitals. Durham B.II.35 formats these in lines of verse, beginning each distich with a capital initial and marking each line with a terminal point.

27. Hatton 43 follows this practice. Winchester 1 begins each distich with a capital, writes the poem in lines of verse through *M*, and then reverts to long lines. Royal 13.C.v. and Trinity R.5.7 begin each distich with a capital and run the verses across the space.

28. Given the number of twelfth-century English copies, I have limited my discussion to a consideration of those English manuscripts which contain Caedmon's *Hymn*. Examination of most of the other twelfth-century English manuscripts of the *Historia ecclesiastica* revealed that the pattern of verse presentation discussed here holds.

29. See Parkes, "Pause and Effect," p. 139, on the scribe's awareness of the needs of his audience.

30. The exception is the late manuscript, Cambridge, Trinity College, R.5.22 (14th c.), where Caedmon's *Hymn* has been copied into the main text.

31. Dobbie, *Manuscripts*, p. 48, prints a stemma. He defines four groups. For the "aelda"/"ylda" text, the Northumbrian witnesses are CUL KK.5.16 and Leningrad Q.v.I.18 [M-L]; the West-Saxon members of this group [*Z] are: Oxford, Bodleian Library, Hatton 43 and Bodley 163; Oxford, Lincoln College, lat. 31; Oxford, Magdalen College, lat. 105; Winchester Cathedral, 1; Cambridge Trinity College, R.5.22. For the "eorðu" text the West-Saxon members [*AE] are: Oxford, Bodleian Library, Tanner 10; London, British Library, Cotton Otho B.xi; Oxford, Corpus Christi College, 279; Cambridge, University Library, KK.3.28; Cambridge, Corpus Christi College, 41. The peculiar Oxford, Bodleian Library, Laud Misc. 243, and Hereford Cathedral, P.5.1, are in this group. The two Continental manuscripts form the *Y group.

32. Colgrave and Mynors, *Ecclesiastical History*, pp. xxxix–xl, xliv.

33. Parkes, *Scriptorium*, p. 11.

34. Olga Dobiache-Rojdestvensky, "Un manuscrit de Bède à Léningrad," *Speculum* 3 (1928), 314–21, at p. 318, makes this argument. O. Arngart revises his initial agreement with this position (*Leningrad Bede*, pp. 17–18) in "On the Dating of Early Bede Manuscripts," *Studia Neophilologica* 45 (1973), 47–52, where he argues that the calculations are Bede's own and thus useless for dating.

35. Lowe, "Key," rejects the significance of "746" on the basis of the difference in ink. While admitting Meyvaert's arguments on the possible forgery of the colophon ("'Signature,'" p. 286), Parkes (*Scriptorium*, p. 26, n. 35) questions the priority of CUL KK.5.16.

36. Dobbie, *Manuscripts*, p. 17, prints a point after "astelidae." This point is visible neither on the fascimile (O. Arngart, *The Leningrad Bede*) nor on the photograph of fol. 107r which M. B. Parkes kindly showed me.

37. See A. H. Smith, ed., *Three Northumbrian Poems* (New York, 1968; rpt. 1933), pp. 20–22, who summarizes views of earlier scholars and accepts the view that the scribe of the Latin text also wrote Caedmon's *Hymn*. Soo too Blair, *Moore Bede*, p. 29. Ker, *Catalogue*, no. 25, describes it as a "contemporary addition."

38. Colgrave and Mynors, *Ecclesiastical History*, p. xli.

39. The other early manuscript, Cambridge, Trinity College, R.7.5, is sufficiently close to BL Tiberius C.ii to suggest that it is a copy (Colgrave and Mynors, *Ecclesiastical History*, p. li).

40. Plummer, *Historia ecclesiastica*, 1:cxviii–cxix. Ker. *Catalogue*, no. 396, calls them "closely related."

41. See Colgrave and Mynors, *Ecclesiastical History*, pp. xlix–li.

42. Kerr, *Catalogue*, dates Caedmon's *Hymn* in Hatton 43 to xi^2 (no. 326), in Winchester 1 to xi med. (no. 396), and in Bodley 163 to xi med. (no. 304).

43. The only surviving texts transmitting the Northumbrian dialect (and hence the earlier version) of Caedmon's *Hymn* are M texts. At what point Caedmon's *Hymn* was added to a C text is impossible to determine. Dobbie does note that *Z derives directly from a Northumbrian version of the *Hymn* (*Manuscripts*, p. 47).

44. On the second line, "heri" is dotted for omission; "metoddes" has the first *d* dotted; "heofen" has been corrected by the addition of an *o* over the second *e*.

45. Could we know when this was done, we might learn something about the eraser's vision of the relationship between text and *Hymn*.

46. These four twelfth-century manuscripts are only a fraction of the twelfth-century English manuscripts extant. See Colgrave and Mynors, *Ecclesiastical History*, pp. xlvi–lxi.

47. On the relationship between the text of the *History* ("Burney" group) and the additions and corrections from the "Digby" group, see Dobbie, *Manuscripts*, pp. 88–89, and Colgrave and Mynors, *Ecclesiastical History*, p. liv.

48. M. G. Frampton, "Caedmon's Hymn," *Modern Philology* 22 (1924), 1–15, at p. 4.

49. Dobbie, *Manuscripts*, p. 41, claims that photostats indicate that the *o* in "scyppeod" had been partially erased to make it look like an *n*. Upon examination of the manuscript I could see no evidence of erasure or scraping. The vellum is quite smooth.

50. Dobbie, *Manuscripts*, p. 43.

51. Dobbie, *Manuscripts*, pp. 37, 88–89.

52. Thomas Miller, ed., *The Old English Version of Bede's Ecclesiastical History*, 2 vols., EETS 95, 96, 110, 111 (London, 1890–98), 1:xxiii–xxiv.

53. Miller, *Old English Version*, 1:xxiv–xxvi.

54. On the "grammar" of formulae see Berkley Peabody, *The Winged Word* (Albany, 1975).

55. Henry John Chaytor, "The Medieval Reader and Textual Criticism," *Bulletin of the John Rylands Library* 26 (1941–42), 49–56.

56. Martin L. West, *Textual Criticism and Editorial Technique* (Stuttgart, 1973), pp. 20–21.

57. On the role of memory in various sorts of textual corruption in Latin classical texts see Louis Havet, *Manuel de critique verbale appliquée aux textes latins* (Paris, 1911, rpt. Rome, 1967), items 1082–97.

58. R. M. Ogilvie, "Monastic Corruption," *Greece and Rome*, 2nd ser., 18 (1971), 32–34; Sebastiano Timpanaro, *The Freudian Slip: Psychoanalysis and Textual Criticism*, trans. Kate Soper (London, 1976).

59. On the intrusion of oral processes into what he terms "pre-literate written transmission" of medieval music see Leo Treitler, "Oral, Written, and Literate Process in the Transmission of Medieval Music," *Speculum* 56 (1981), 471–91, at p. 482.

60. Bäuml, "Varieties," p. 246, n. 23, notes that without functional dependence on literacy, the ability to write does not imply recognition of the fixity of a text.

61. See Alan Jabbour, "Memorial Transmission in Old English Poetry," *Chaucer Review* 3 (1969), 174–90. My argument is particularly in conflict with his comments on pp. 181–82.

62. On the various practices of pointing for verse and prose see Parkes, "Pause and Effect," p. 130, esp. n. 14.

63. Dobbie, *Manuscripts*, p. 39, incorrectly prints a terminal point.

Reading Cædmon's "Hymn" with Someone Else's Glosses

KEVIN S. KIERNAN

Aᴄᴄᴏʀᴅɪɴɢ to the Venerable Bede, our first reliable English historian, English literature had a miraculous origin in the late seventh century in a religious somniloquy by an illiterate cowherd named Cædmon. Writing at least a half century after the miracle, Bede represents Cædmon's Old English "Hymn" in only a Latin paraphrase in his *Historia Ecclesiastica Gentis Anglorum*. Our earliest vernacular versions of the "Hymn" appear, not as part of Bede's text, but rather as notes later appended by scribes to two eighth-century manuscripts of the *Historia Ecclesiastica*.[1] From its humble start as a marginal, secondary text, the vernacular "Hymn" first worked its way into the central, primary text by means of a tenth-century Old English translation of Bede's entire *History*.[2] It continued to appear, nonetheless, as a marginal text from the eleventh to the fifteenth century in Latin manuscripts of Bede. Nowadays scholars are generally convinced that we have inherited by this process authentic witnesses of Cædmon's debut as a poet; in fact, they print the "Hymn," in both scholarly editions and general anthologies, as *the* central text, with Bede's *Historia Ecclesiastica* relegated to the margins. The textual history of Cædmon's "Hymn" provides an unmiraculous case history of how re-productions of literary texts both purposely and unintentionally re-present our past.

Bede tells the story of Cædmon in book 4, chapter 24 of his *Historia Ecclesiastica*.[3] Anglo-Saxonists feel sure that everyone knows and remembers this story, in modern translation needless to say, but it will still be useful to represent it here in summary form as our point of departure. We all realize of course that Bede's Latin will lose some of its dignity in the process.

Cædmon was a layman who worked on an estate near the monastery of Whitby in Northumbria. Sometimes at parties (*in convivio*) his fellow workers would agree among themselves to liven things up by singing songs in turn. Yet whenever he saw the *cithara* coming his way, Cædmon would always duck out, not knowing any songs whatsoever. One night, when it is his turn anyway to take care of the cattle, he escapes to the stables, where he falls asleep and is urged by a visitor in a dream to sing about Creation. He complies, and Bede gives us a Latin paraphrase of his "Hymn": "Nunc laudare debemus auctorem regni caelestis, potentiam Creatoris," and so on. Before resuming the story, Bede makes it clear that he is giving "the sense but not the order of the words which [Cædmon] sang as he slept. "For," Bede says, "it is not possible to translate verse, however well composed, literally from one language to another without some loss of beauty and dignity." Following this somewhat academic intermezzo, Cædmon wakes up with the "Hymn" on his mind and, poetically inspired, adds some more verses to it. Cædmon then tells his boss the reeve about his gift, and the reeve takes him to Abbess Hild at the monastery for advice. After determining that God had granted him a special grace, Hild persuades Cædmon to join the monastery, where he launches a productive career, in the cloistered context of Whitby, as an oral composer of devout verse.

As far as we are concerned, this concludes the story of our first English poet. Writing ecclesiastical, not literary, history, however, Bede finishes his story differently. Many of our literary historians fail to tell the rest of the story, that our first poet opposed "with a flaming and fervent zeal" anyone who failed to submit to the monastic rule and that he died like a saint, predicting the exact hour of his death (*EH*, 418–21). These are not the highpoints of his career for us.

At this proto-stage in English literary history, at any rate, all we had inherited of our first poet's oeuvre was Bede's Latin paraphrase of Cædmon's oral performance while he dreamed.[4] Scholars have not inquired too deeply into the exact nature of Bede's source, no doubt because Bede specifies that he translated the short version Cædmon sang in his dream, not the longer one produced the next morning when Cædmon "added more verses in the same manner, praising God in fitting style."[5] As his Latin translation attests, moreover, Bede never had any intention of preserving the original Old English version. To put it bluntly, English literature did not for Bede fit into the grand scheme of things. Where, then, did we get our vernacular text? In light of its first preserved manifestation in a Latin paraphrase made more than a half century after the original illiterate dream, it is no small part of the overall miracle that Cædmon's "Hymn" has come down to us *in Old English* in seventeen Bede manuscripts dating from the eighth to the fifteenth century. As wondrous as it may seem, moreover, new printed renditions continue to appear in the twentieth century. By taking a look at the manuscript tradition, we can perhaps learn something about our own cædmonian dreams in the age of print.

Unfortunately, looking at this particular manuscript tradition is not a spectacle for casual observers. It too must begin, of course, more than a half century after Cædmon's oral performances, sleeping or waking, and it ends a couple of centuries closer to us than to Cædmon. By sorting the manuscripts in a variety of inconsistent ways, we find that there is a Northumbrian group of manuscripts and a West Saxon group, provided we remember that West Saxon is a generic literary dialect in late Old English times; there is an early Northumbrian group of two and a different, very late, twelfth- and fifteenth-century, Northumbrian group of two; there is as well a fairly early "West Saxon" or "Alfredian" group, and a distinct, somewhat later and longer-lived group, also called West Saxon.[6] Perhaps the most basic division revolves around the variant readings, *ælda* (*ylda* in the West Saxon manuscripts) and *eorðan*, both deeply fixed in the manuscript tradition. Two Northumbrian and six late West Saxon manuscripts agree that Bede's Latin cliché, *filiis hominum*, exactly glosses "the sons of men," *ælda barnum* or *ylda bearnum*, coming authentically from Cædmon,[7] while two Northumbrian and seven West Saxon manuscripts agree that Cædmon sang an extraordinary phrase, "the sons of the earth," *eorðan bearnum*, which Bede blandly glossed with a cliché.[8] Of the ten manuscripts dating from Old English times, five belong to the *ælda barnum* or "sons of men" group, including the two eighth-century Northumbrian and the three late-eleventh-century West Saxon manuscripts, always with the West Saxon spelling, *ylda*, for Northumbrian *ælda*.[9] The remaining five, belonging to the *eorðan bearnum* or "sons of the earth" group, are the tenth- and eleventh-century West Saxon versions in the Old English translation of the *Ecclesiastical History*.

Fairly soon, it seems, after Bede's death in 735 some of his near contemporaries provide us with the first extant vernacular versions of Cædmon's "Hymn" by adding them to the two eighth-century manuscripts of the Latin *Historia Ecclesiastica*. The Leningrad Bede almost certainly derives from Bede's own monastery of Jarrow, while the Moore Bede may well have some connection with its twin monastery at Wearmouth.[10] Like the related eleventh-century *ylda* manuscripts, neither of these eighth-century versions of Cædmon's "Hymn" was ever part of Bede's Latin text nor of the original design of the manuscripts. The central, overriding interests of early Northumbrian Christianity had the effect of literally marginalizing the English text of Cædmon's "Hymn," for it was the idea of the "Hymn," not its language, dialectal idiosyncrasies, or even textual authority that was important in the context of the conversion of pagans. It is perhaps no coincidence that there was a resurgence of Latin manuscripts of the *Historia Ecclesiastica* and a return to the "marginalized" text of Cædmon's "Hymn" during the eleventh century, when a well-established Anglo-Saxon Church again faced the task of converting pagans and apostates, this time among the Anglo-Danes and Scandinavian immigrants in the newly subsumed Danelaw. In both contexts, at any rate, an English version of Cædmon's "Hymn" would not have been a burning priority.

There were conceivably many reasons, including the love of one's own language, for individual scribes to transmit an English text of the "Hymn" in the margins of a Latin manuscript of the *Historia Ecclesiastica*. But in view of the unusually large number and overall uniformity of the surviving marginal texts, there must have been some institutional support for the practice—the propagation of copy texts, for example, for monastic libraries with Latin Bede manuscripts already in their collections.[11] One motive particularly appropriate for manuscripts coming from Jarrow and Wearmouth must have been to strengthen the authority of Bede. What better way of showing Bede's special veracity, or the prestige of a particular Bede manuscript, than by providing the source of his paraphrase in an endnote, as the Moore manuscript does? Mastering its source in high scholarly fashion, the scribe even adds the comment "Primo cantauit cædmon istud carmen," "Cædmon first sang *that* song."[12] Yet it would be wrong to conclude that the marginal notes were themselves meant to carry the authority they paradoxically add to the Latin Bede manuscripts. A closer look at the way the Moore manuscript produces the text of the "Hymn" as an endnote can help put all the marginal notes in perspective.

A single scribe produced the Moore *Historia Ecclesiastica* using what Peter Hunter Blair has justly described as "an Anglo-Saxon minuscule of austere beauty" (*MB*, 15). The text ends on fol. 128r25 with a formal *Explicit* in red, but four lines, obviously written by the same scribe, are added at the bottom of the page with annals for the years 731–34, citing events that occurred after Bede completed his work but before he died. Turning the page, one is immediately struck by the reduced size of the script in lines 1–3, the Old English text of the "Hymn," and in line 4, which begins with the attribution to Cædmon (fig. 1). The small scale of these four lines sharply contrasts with the usual size of the script, which resumes in lines 5–12 for some chronological notes known as the "Moore Memoranda."[13] The contrasting scale alone should tell us that the chronological notes, like the main text

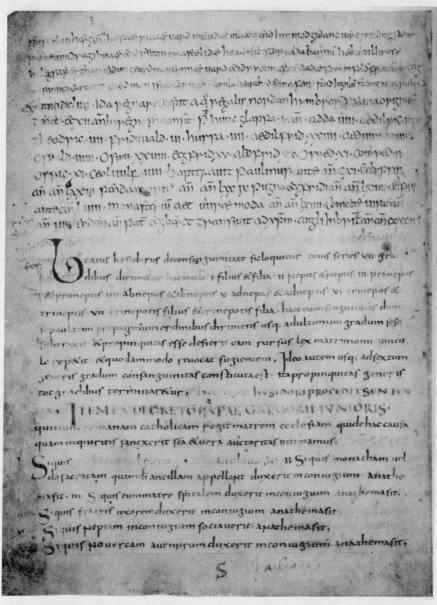

Figure 1. The Moore Bede, fol. 128v. From *The Moore Bede*, ed. Peter Hunter Blair, Early English Manuscripts in Facsimile, vol. 9 (Copenhagen, 1959). Reproduced by permission of Rosenkilde and Bagger, Ltd.

of the *Historia Ecclesiastica*, had more prestige than Cædmon's "Hymn." The reduced size of the script for the "Hymn" reminds one of a gloss rather than a main text, and indeed in line 4 the scribe adds three apparently random glosses of hard Latin words—*arula hearth, destina feur-stud, Iugulum sticung*—only the first two of which appear anywhere in Bede. The glosses apparently mean "hearth," "fire-proof stud," and "pig killing," judging by the meager information about these Old English words in our dictionaries, and at first glance would seem to have more to do with a pig roast than with epoch-making poetry.[14] Strangely careful not to waste any space on a page that presumably was blank when lines 1–4 were written, the scribe also squeezes in "nota rubrica," "mark in red," at the end of line 4, apparently a reminder to someone to rubricate the manuscript.[15] Today we wouldn't dream of printing such trivial items next to Cædmon's "Hymn."

As we can plainly see from this manuscript, as well as from all the ones that add Cædmon's "Hymn" to the margins of Bede's *Historia Ecclesiastica*, Anglo-Saxon scribes did not view these versions, as we do today, as central texts. Figure 2, for example, shows the other early Northumbrian copy of the "Hymn" from the Leningrad manuscript. As in the case of the Moore Bede, this vernacular text of the "Hymn" was added to its manuscript, too, at a later time.[16] The possibility that the Old English versions we have inherited in this way began as glosses, or reverse translations of Bede's Latin paraphrase, warrants more attention than it has yet received.[17]

The suspicion that all of our versions ultimately derive from the tenth-century Alfredian translation of Bede was in fact brought up repeatedly in the nineteenth century.[18] Richard Wülker argued the case most effectively in 1876, showing why he thought the Northumbrian version at the end of the Moore manuscript was only a dialectal transliteration of the West Saxon version from the Alfredian Bede.[19] His arguments, however, were insecurely based on inadequate representations of the "Hymn" and its manuscript setting before a facsimile was available. As a result, Julius Zupitza effectively demolished his theory by citing the internal dating of the Moore version of Cædmon's "Hymn" in 737, about a century and a half before King Alfred came along.[20] Wülker later conceded that the Northumbrian version in the Moore manuscript (the Leningrad version had not yet been discovered) was written in the eighth century, long before the Alfredian translation.[21] His concession, however, does not eliminate the possibility that the earliest Northumbrian version might be a reverse translation of Bede's Latin paraphrase. As David Dumville has recently observed, "There must be room for the conjecture that we have only nine lines of the Old English because that is all Bede gave in his Latin prose rendering: in

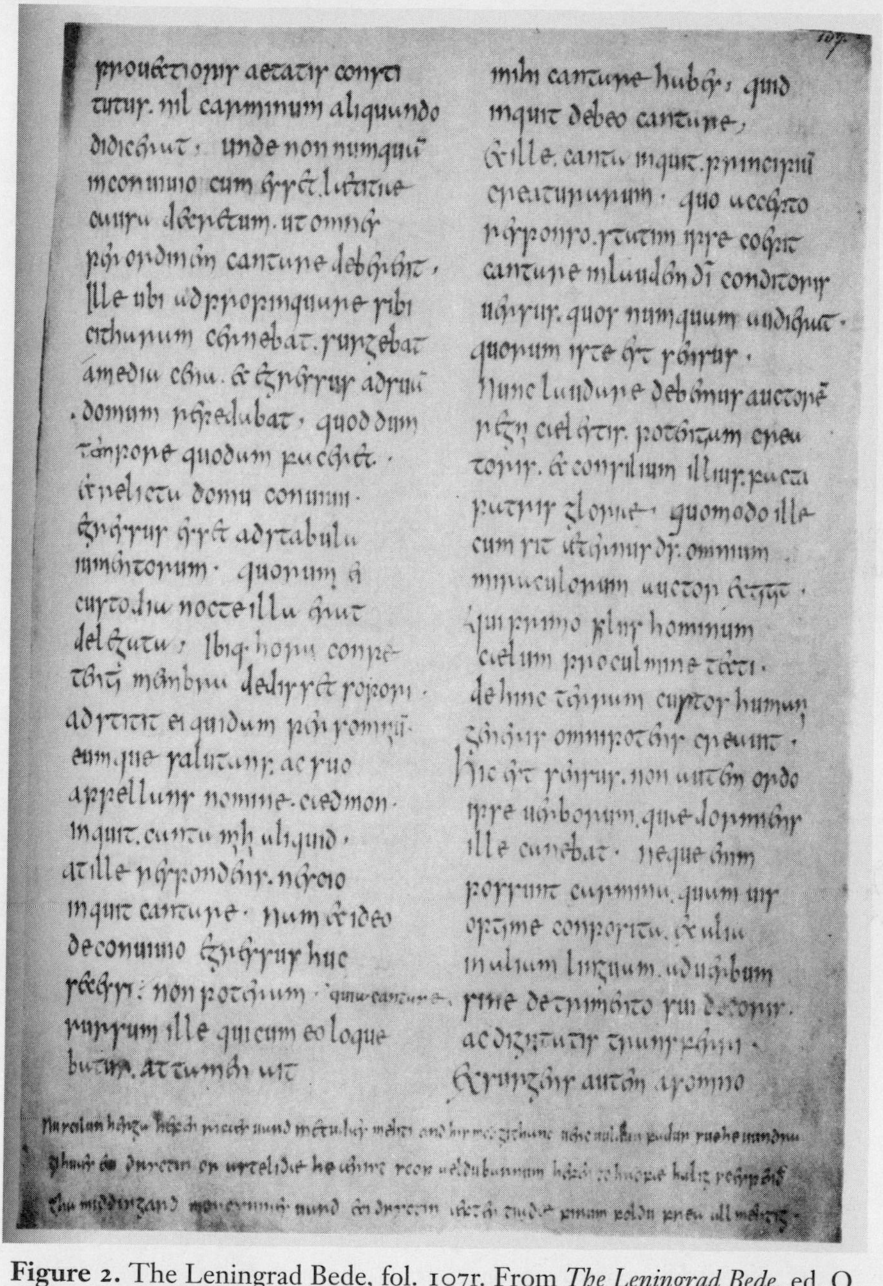

Figure 2. The Leningrad Bede, fol. 107r. From *The Leningrad Bede*, ed. O. Arngart, Early English Manuscripts in Facsimile, vol. 2 (Copenhagen, 1952). Reproduced by permission of Rosenkilde and Bagger, Ltd.

short, the Old English is at least as likely to be a poetic rendering of Bede's Latin as the source of his words; otherwise we could have expected more of the poem to have been given by the person who added these nine lines at the end of the Moore manuscript."[22]

One way of approaching the question is to scrutinize Bede's claim that he was unable to translate the "Hymn" word for word into Latin. If he had made a literal translation of the vernacular text that has come down to us, Bede would have ended up with the following text:

Nunc debemus laudare   regni caelestic auctorem,
Nu scylun hergan   hefaenricaes uard,

Creatoris potentiam   et illius consilium,
metudæs maecti   end his modgidanc,

facta Patris gloriae: quomodo ille miraculorum omnium,
uerc uuldurfadur   sue he uundra gihuaes,

[*cum sit*]   *aeternus Deus,   auctor exstitit,*
eci dryctin   or astelidæ;

qui primo tecti   hominum filiis
he aerist scop   aelda barnum

caelum pro culmine,
heben til hrofe,   [*haleg scepen,*]

dehinc terram   humani generis Custos
tha middungeard   monocynnæs uard;

    creavit
[*eci dryctin   aefter*] tiadæ

        omnipotens.
[*firum foldu,   frea*] allmectig.

The glosses show that Bede would have been able to "paraphrase" the "Hymn" word for word: "Nunc debemus laudare regni caelestis auctorem, Creatoris potentiam et illius consilium, facta Patris gloriae: quomodo ille miraculorum omnium, cum sit aeternus Deus, auctor exstitit, qui primo tecti hominum filiis caelum pro culmine, dehinc terram humani generis Custos creavit omnipotens." The result may not be classical Bedan prose, but it is perfectly intelligible Medieval Latin, following the pattern of the vernacular, and after all, Bede was supposedly translating an Old English poem.[23] But if Bede actually paraphrased this version of Cædmon's "Hymn," why did he precisely translate phrase by phrase for two-thirds of the poem and then leave out three half-lines of verse, *haleg scepen*, line 6b; *eci dryctin*, line 8a; and *firum foldu*, line 9a; as well as the two alliterative staves, *æfter* in line 8b and *frea* in line 9b? It seems especially strange for him to omit the new epithets for God, *haleg scepen* and *frea*, and to eliminate all the alliteration, the most salient feature of the verse. It is difficult to appreciate how Bede might think the inclusion of these things would spoil his translation.[24] If we take the position, instead, that an enterprising Anglo-Saxon myth maker translated Bede's Latin into Old English, we can see that he (or she) translated *all* of Bede's Latin version and, compelled by the meter, boldly added a few half-lines and provided the necessary alliteration.

The scribes who added the "Hymn" as footnotes or marginal notes all use the smaller script characteristic of glosses, which first become prevalent in Anglo-Saxon England during the eighth century, around the time of Bede.[25] Elsewhere, interlinear continuous glosses ultimately end up as Old English poems in, for example, the Kentish "Hymn," the psalms of the *Paris Psalter,* and the *Meters of Boethius.*[26] With all due respect to the memory of Cædmon, it would not have taken a major poet to turn Bede's paraphrase into the "Hymn" that has come down to us. As we have seen, a glossator with no poetic skills at all would have ended up with about two-thirds of the poem's locutions, all metrically viable after the Latinate inversions had been turned around, from *Nu [we] scylun hergan (Nunc laudare debemus)* in line 1 to *eci dryctin (aeternus Deus)* in line 8, simply by making a straightforward interlinear or marginal gloss. With Bede's caveat before him about the difficulty of translating poetry word for word, an intelligent glossator familiar with the conventions of Old English poetry could finish the job in *his* sleep. The same argument holds for Bede's translation from Cædmon to Latin, perhaps, but the exceptional occurrence of *scylun,* "must," without the personal pronoun *we,* corresponding to Bede's *debemus,* strongly suggests that the gloss moved from Latin to English.[27]

The vicissitudes of a living oral tradition give us plausible ways of explaining some substantive variations in the text of Cædmon's "Hymn." However, the extraordinary retention of the reading *sculon,* "must," still without the pronoun *we,* in tenth- and eleventh-century manuscripts in the otherwise distinct *eorðan* group, convinces me that the Old English poem must have descended from eighth-century Northumbrian to late West Saxon as a changing written text, not an oral one. The oral tradition would not have perpetuated a formula native speakers could not understand, whereas the manuscript tradition did in fact perpetuate it, with the help of an accurate scribe, in what is considered the best copy of the Alfredian Bede, Bodleian Library MS Tanner 10. The scribe of Corpus Christi College Oxford MS 279 first copied "Now must," too, but then corrected the traditional blunder in his copy text to "Now *we* must," a graphic illustration of what a native speaker of Old English ought to make of a first-person-plural verb without a first-person-plural pronoun.[28] This brave scribal correction of what we call "a deep-seated corruption" may also show how late scribes of the Old English Bede felt free to make intelligent revisions of Cædmon's "Hymn." As Katherine O'Brien O'Keeffe has observed about the tenth- and eleventh-century *eorðan* manuscripts, "In the variations . . . *weorc/wera/weoroda; wuldorfaeder/wuldorgodes; wundra/wuldres; gehwaes/fela; or/ord; sceop/gescop* we see a dynamic of transmission where the message is not embellished but where change within the formula is allowed" (15). We can sensibly attribute these variations to the "dynamic of *translation*" brought about by King Alfred's native cultural program at the end of the ninth century.

Public relations in the Middle Ages in fact associated the English translation of Bede's *Historia Ecclesiastica* with King Alfred himself. Although scholars now agree that all five of our manuscripts of the Old English Bede descend from a Mercian, rather than an Early West Saxon, archetype, it remains more than likely that Alfred's reforms directly inspired the original translation.[29] We know by definition that the Latin source was in front of the translator, and we may safely surmise from the well-attested manuscript tradition that many of these copies already contained Old English translations of Cædmon's "Hymn" in the margins. With a copy of the Latin Bede and an Old English translation of the "Hymn" from the *ælda/ylda* group in the margins, we can easily explain the later development of the *eorðan* group of manuscripts. If he recognized that the marginal version of Cædmon's "Hymn" was no more than a metrical, paraphrasing gloss of Bede's Latin paraphrase, the Old English translator would have had the incentive to rework these materials. Encouraged by Bede's comment that he was providing only a paraphrase of Cædmon's "Hymn," and not deterred by the clearly unauthoritative glosses in the margins, the first Old English translator of Bede's *Historia Ecclesiastica* was free to produce a new and more compelling version of Cædmon's "Hymn" than the copy text provided.

This late Old English translator of Bede takes some wise liberties with the Latin source. In the story of Cædmon, for instance, the phrase *in convivio* comes out as *in gebeorscipe*, "at beer parties," and the *cithara* becomes the familiar Anglo-Saxon *hearp*, or "harp." For our purposes, of course, the most important changes in this part of the Old English Bede are the ones directly relating to the new production of Cædmon's "Hymn." As we have already seen, the translator made his own metrical paraphrase more credible by rendering the biblical phrase *filius hominum* with the entirely original phrase *eorðan bearnum*, "the sons of the earth."[30] But he also made three big changes that for the first time accorded extraordinary authority to the original text of the "Hymn" by implying that Bede himself transmitted it in its original form. First, the translator renders Bede's disclaimer *iste est sensus*, "this is the general sense" of the "Hymn," with the far more purposeful words *þære endebyrdnesse þis is*, "this is its proper disposition." Second, he replaces Bede's Latin prose paraphrase of the "Hymn" with a vibrant Old English poem no one had ever seen in the margins of the *Historia Ecclesiastica*. And third, the translator completely omitted Bede's subsequent commentary: "This is the sense but not the order of the words which [Cædmon] sang as he slept," Bede had said. "For it is not possible to translate verse, however well composed, literally from one language to another without some loss of beauty and dignity." In these three changes, the producer of the Old English *History* gave his readers in the tenth and eleventh centuries the first really believable, seemingly authentic, text of Cædmon's "Hymn" by concealing its actual history.

I would like to leave the manuscript tradition of Cædmon's "Hymn" at this juncture, as it is about to drift off into the later Middle Ages, and look briefly at the printed tradition of the text in the multi-tiered institution of academia today. There were, of course, many texts produced in manuscript and print in the long interim that have helped shape our modern editions. What is immediately remarkable today is that the text has descended to fully fledged Anglo-Saxonists in only two "standard" editions, the prestigious, early Northumbrian, or "Bedan" version and the prestigious, "early" West Saxon, or "Alfredian" version, with copious footnotes to both recording the multitudinous variants from all the other manuscripts (fig. 3).[31] There is, most remarkably, no sign of the Latin or Old English prose of Bede's *Historia Ecclesiastica* in these standard editions. The poem alone now comes to us handsomely bound, in this example as part of the six-volume set of *The Anglo-Saxon Poetic Records*. For us, the endnote or marginal note, Cædmon's "Hymn," has become the central poetic text while the old central prose text, Bede's Latin *History*, has become the endnote or the footnote.

The text of Cædmon's "Hymn" also descends to us in what is called "normalized" spelling, idealized linguistic forms meant to help students learn the largely unattested Early (with a capital *E*) West Saxon dialect of Old English associated with King Alfred (fig. 4).[32] This new version of the "Hymn," reconstructed in "normalized" Early West Saxon from the two early Northumbrian versions, is prominently centered on the page, while a modern translation of most of Bede's Latin prose account of Cædmon's story is marginalized in the commentary at the back of the book. Notice in the textual footnotes that John Pope has introduced no fewer than ten vari-

CÆDMON'S HYMN

WEST SAXON VERSION

Text from MS. Tanner 10 (T), with variants from the other MSS. (for the sigla, see Introd., pp. xcv–xcvii)

Nu sculon herigean heofonrices weard,
meotodes meahte and his modgeþanc,
weorc wuldorfæder, swa he wundra gehwæs,
ece drihten, or onstealde.
5 He ærest scop eorðan bearnum
heofon to hrofe, halig scyppend;
þa middangeard moncynnes weard,
ece drihten, æfter teode
firum foldan, frea ælmihtig.

106

Cædmon's Hymn 1 Nu] Ne C; Nu we with we added above the line O; Nu we
Ca B H W Bd₁ Ln Mg Tr₁ Ld₁ Hr sculon Lñ; sculon B
sculon] sceolon Ca Ld₁ Hr; sculun Ln; sceolon Tr₁ herigean]
scyllon O; sculun O H Bd₁ Ln Mg Hr; herian heri with heri underlined for
hergean C; herian O H Bd₁ Ln Mg Hr; herian heri with second herian underlined for
deletion W; herian herian with second herian underlined for deletion Ld₁;
herion Tr₁ heofonrices] heofonrices Tr₁ 2 meotodes] metodes C O
Ca B; metoddes with first d dotted beneath for deletion W; metudes H Bd₁
Ln Mg Tr₁ Ld₁ Hr meahte] mihte C O Ca B W Mg Tr₁ Ld₁ Hr; myhte
H Bd₁; michte Ln and] Ond C modgeþanc] modgebonc C O 3
weorc] weoroda C; wera with a altered from o O; wera Ca; wurc H Bd₁ Mg
wuldorfæder] wuldorgodes B; wuldorfæder Tr₁; wuldorfæder with o altered
from u H; wulder fæder Ld₁ Hr wundra gehwæs] wuldres gehwæs Ca;
wundra fela B; wundra gehwylc H W Mg; wundra gehwylc Ln Tr₁; wundra
i...-ylc with y altered from i Bd₁ 3b-5a wundra . . . He] Not in Hr
4 ece] eche Ln drihten] dryhten O or onstealde] Not in Ld₁, which adds
þa before he. l. 5 or] oörd with d added above the line O; ord Ca B H
Bd₁ Ln Mg Tr₁; word W onstealde] astealde B H W Bd₁ Ln Tr₁;
astalde Mg 5 He] Hu (or Nu?) Tr₁ ærest] æres Ca; ærust Ln; erust
Tr₁; i:ræst W scop] scop C; gesceop O H Bd₁; bescipp Ca W Mg Ln Tr₁
eorðan] With e crowded in after the rest had been written Ca; eorþa C; eorðe
Ld₁ Hr; ylda H W Bd₁ Ln Mg Tr₁ bearnum] An erasure of two or
three letters after this word O 6 heofon] heofen with the second e dotted
beneath for deletion and o written above it W hrofe] rofe Ca W Mg
halig scyppend] Ld₁ and Hr omit this half-line here but insert halig scyppend
at the end of the poem after frea ælmihtig scyppend] scypend C;
(Continued at foot of p. 107.)

BEDE'S DEATH SONG

NORTHUMBRIAN VERSION

Text from MS. 254, St. Gall (Sg), with variants from the other MSS. (for the sigla, see Introd., pp. ci–cii)

Fore thaem neidfaerae naenig uuiurthit
thoncsnotturra, than him tharf sie
to ymbhycggannae aer his hiniongae
huaet his gastae godaes aeththa yflaes
5 aefter deothdaege doemid uueorthae.

Bede's Death Song 1 Fore] fere Z thaem] ti'e Sg; thae Ba; the Ad₁
Kl₁ Mu Kl₃ Hk V Z Ad₃ Me; see Note neidfaerae] neidfare Ad₁; neidfaere
Kl₁; neydfaere Mu; neidfacre Kl₃ Hk V Z Me; neidfacere Ad₃ uuiurthit
vuiurthit Mu 2 thoncsnotturra] toncsnotturra Kl₃; thonesnotturra
Kl₃; thoncsnothturra Ad₃ tharf] With t added above the line Sg; thars
Mu; chraf Kl₃; thraf Hk V Z Ad₃; traf Me sie] sig Hk Ad₃ 3 to] tho
Kl₃ ymbhycggannae] ymbhycgganne Ba; ymbhicggannae Kl₃; ymbhicg-
gannae Kl₃ V; ymbhycgganne Hk Z Ad₃ Me hiniongae] With a added
above the line Sg; hyniongae Kl₃ 4 huaet] huaex Kl₃ Hk V Z Ad₃ Me
gastae] gaste Ad₁ Kl₁ Mu Kl₃ Hk V Z Ad₃ Me godaes] godeles Kl₃ Hk
V Z Me; godoles Ad₃ aeththa] aëhtha Sg Ba 5 aefter] aester Ad₁
Kl₁ Mu Kl₃ Hk V Z Ad₃ Me deothdaege] deothdaege Kl₃ Hk V Z Ad₃ Me
doemid] doemud Ad₁; doemnt Kl₁ Mu; doemit Kl₃ Hk V Z Ad₃ Me
uueorthae] With a added above the line Sg; uueorthe Ad₁ Kl₁ Kl₃ H₃ V Z
Ad₃ Me; vueorthe Mu

107

(Continued from p. 106.)
scippend W 7 þa middangeard] ða middongeard O; þe middangeard
B; middangearde H Ln Mg Tr₁; middanear... .W; :.... :. .;dane₃;de
Bd₁ moncynnes] mancynnes B W; mancynnes H Bd₁ Mg; mankynnes
Ln Tr₁ weard] The letter e erased after this word Ln 8 ece] eche Ln
drihten] dryhten O; drihlt Ca; drihtent Hr æfter] æff Ca; epter Tr₁;
efter Hr teode] An erasure of one letter (d?) after o O; eode C; tida H W
Bd₁ Ln Mg Tr₁ 9 firum] fira C; fyrum B W Ld₁; fyrii Hr; pirum Tr₁
foldan] With n added above the line O; on foldum H W Bd₁ Ln Mg Tr₁; on
foldum Ld₁ Hr frea] euca Tr₁ ælmihtig] ælmyhtig H; ealmihti W;
elmihtig Tr₁; Ld₁ and Hr add halig scyppeod (so l. 6b) after ælmihtig

Figure 3. From *The Anglo-Saxon Minor Poems*, ed. Elliot van Kirk Dobbie, *Anglo-Saxon Poetic Records*, vol. 6 (New York, 1942), 106–7. © 1942 Columbia University Press. Reprinted by permission of the publisher.

Cædmon's Hymn

The Hymn Normalized in West-Saxon Spelling
Based on the Northumbrian Version of MSS M and L

Nū sculon herian   heofon-rīċes Weard,
Metodes meahta   and his mōd-ġeþanc,
weorc Wuldor-Fæder,   swā hē wundra ġehwæs,
ēċe Dryhten,   ōr astealde.
Hē ærest scōp   ielda bearnum
heofon to hrōfe,   hāliġ Scieppend;
þā middan-ġeard   mann-cynnes Weard,
ēċe Dryhten,   æfter tēode—
fīrum foldan   Frēa ælmihtiġ.

Substantive variants in MS T (Bodleian Library, Tanner
10, f. 100), the best of the West-Saxon texts, included in the
Old English version of Bede's *Historia Ecclesiastica*:
4 onstealde. 5 eorðan *for* ielda.

Spelling variants in T compared with the normalized text:
1 herigean. 2 meotodes. meahte. 4 drihten. 5 sceop.
6 scyppend. 7 moncynnes. 8 drihten.
Among variants in some of the later copies are: 1 we
before sculon. 4 ord *for* or. 5 gesceop *for* scop.

4

Figure 4. From *Seven Old English Poems*, ed. John C. Pope, 2d ed. (New York, 1981), 4. Reproduced by permission of the estate of John C. Pope.

ants in his reconstructed Early West Saxon text from Bodleian Library MS
Tanner 10, "the best of the West-Saxon texts." Of the two "substantive variants" the most radical is the change in line 5b of *eorðan* to *ielda*, a spelling
of West Saxon *ylda* displaying the Early West Saxon shibboleth, *ie*. As Pope
says in his preface, this *ie* spelling is the "most conspicuous mark of Early
West Saxon" (viii). Indeed, without it, we wouldn't be able to tell that the
reconstructed text was Early West Saxon at all: seven of the remaining
"Early" spellings occur in one or more of the surviving West Saxon manuscripts of the "Hymn"; the other two variant spellings are found in other
West Saxon manuscripts. Despite its conspicuousness, *ielda* occurs nowhere in the three-million-word corpus of Old English prose and verse,
not to mention any of the manuscripts of Cædmon's "Hymn."[33] In contrast, the well-attested late West Saxon spelling, *ylda*, occurs often in Old
English, eight times in the phrase "the sons of men," in such divergent texts
as *Genesis, Daniel, Beowulf,* the *Paris Psalter,* the *Menologium,* and *A Prayer.*
As we have seen, it is not only a cliché but a loan translation of a Latin biblical cliché, *filiis hominum*. The translation *ylda bearnum* occurs six times in
the six different copies of Cædmon's "Hymn" found in the context of the
Latin *Historia Ecclesiastica*.

   In many ways, the most interesting and influential reproduction of the
text of the poem today can be found in anthologies for general readers. As if
by some miracle of literary history, Cædmon's "Hymn" now appears as the
first English text produced in the 2,616-page first volume, fifth edition, of
the ubiquitous *Norton Anthology of English Literature*.[34] Quite properly, the
Norton editors try to give their general readers a simple, straightforward
account of the prevailing critical position about the "Hymn." Thus they
present it in the immediate context of "An [*sic*] Ecclesiastical History of the
English People," without raising any questions about the antiquity, priority, or authenticity of the Old English poem. "The story we reprint," they
say, "preserves what is probably the earliest extant Old English poem. . . .
Bede tells how Cædmon, an illiterate cowherd employed by the monastery
of Whitby, miraculously received the gift of song, entered the monastery,
and became the founder of a school of Christian poetry" (19). They especially stress the idea that Cædmon, contrary to Bede's insistence that "he
was not taught the art of song by men or by human agency but received this
gift through heavenly grace," was an oral-formulaic poet:

> Cædmon was clearly an oral-formulaic poet, one who created his
> work by combining and varying formulas—units of verse developed
> in a tradition transmitted by one generation of singers to another. In

this respect he resembles the singers of the Homeric poems and oral-formulaic poets recorded in the twentieth century, especially in the Balkan countries. Although Bede tells us that Cædmon had never learned the art of song, we may suspect that he concealed his skill from his fellow workmen and from the monks because he was ashamed of knowing "vain and idle" songs, the kind Bede says Cædmon never composed. Cædmon's inspiration and true miracle, then, was to apply the meter and language of such songs, presumably including pagan heroic verse, to Christian themes.[35]

In their efforts to distill an extremely complicated textual history and to introduce students to oral-formulaic theory, the editors have created a diminutive Old English monster. As a result, by looking more closely at this extraordinary production, we can get some idea of how we sometimes unintentionally rewrite literary history (fig. 5).

The modern English translation effectively hides the unprecedented combination of languages, dialects, manuscripts, and versions in the Norton reproduction. Under the big general heading of "Old English Literature" the Norton first prints a modern English translation of "Anglo-Latin Literature," Bede's story of Cædmon. We can recognize the source by Bede's remarks introducing and then commenting on his Latin paraphrase of Cædmon's "Hymn." Yet these remarks by Bede can appropriately apply only to his Latin paraphrase, not to what we are supposed to think of as Cædmon's original Old English poem. Having studied the manuscript tradition, moreover, we know that none of the Anglo-Saxon Latin manuscripts contains an integrated copy of the Old English "Hymn," only marginal copies. The Norton silently integrates its copy from the Old English Alfredian translation in Bodleian Library MS Tanner 10. The manuscript is hard to recognize at first glance because *eorðan* is for some reason emended to **ielda*,[36] which even in its attested forms of *ælda* and *ylda* only occurs in marginal copies in Old English manuscripts.

While performing their awesome, traditional duty of inaugurating all of English literature, the nine strange lines of Cædmon's "Hymn" are made stranger by the modern English glosses and the huge caesuras, which unintentionally present the poem as if it should be read in columns, each with a left justified margin, like the footnotes at the bottom of the same page, rather than from left to right, like Old English poetry. An unsuspecting reader, an undergraduate taking a survey course in English literature, for example, or perhaps even a specialist in romanticism teaching the survey, can by an amusing coincidence make almost as good sense out of the text by reading the modern glosses in "column one" (all the a-verses) first, and then *mancynnes Weard* (heaven's or mankind's Guardian), depending on the alliteration required. This formulaic style provides a richness of texture and meaning difficult to convey in translation. As Bede said about his own Latin paraphrase of the *Hymn*, no literal translation of poetry from one language to another is possible without sacrifice of some poetic quality.

Several manuscripts of Bede's *History* contain the Old English text in addition to Bede's Latin version. The poem is given here in a West Saxon form with a literal interlinear translation. In Old English spelling, æ (as in Cædmon's name and line 3) is a vowel symbol that has not survived; it represented both a short *a* sound and a long open *e* sound. þ (line 2) and ð both represented the sound *th*. The large space in the middle of the line indicates the caesura. The alliterating sounds that connect the half-lines have been italicized.

From An Ecclesiastical History of the English People

[*The Story of Cædmon*]

Heavenly grace had especially singled out a certain one of the brothers in the monastery ruled by this abbess,[1] for he used to compose devout and religious songs. Whatever he learned of holy Scripture with the aid of interpreters, he quickly turned into the sweetest and most moving poetry in his own language, that is to say English. It often happened that his songs kindled a contempt for this world and a longing for the life of Heaven in the hearts of many men. Indeed, after him others among the English people tried to compose religious poetry, but no one could equal him because he was not taught the art of song by men or by human agency but received this gift through heavenly grace. Therefore, he was never able to compose any vain and idle songs but only such as dealt with religion and were proper for his religious tongue to utter. As a matter of fact, he had lived in the secular estate until he was well advanced in age without learning any songs. Therefore, at feasts, when it was decided to have a good time by taking turns singing, whenever he would see the harp getting close to his place,[2] he got up in the middle of the meal and went home.

Once when he left the feast like this, he went to the cattle shed, which he had been assigned the duty of guarding that night. And after he had stretched himself out and gone to sleep, he dreamed that someone was standing at his side and greeted him, calling out his name. "Cædmon," he said, "sing me something."

And he replied, "I don't know how to sing; that is why I left the feast to come here—because I cannot sing."

"All the same," said the one who was speaking to him, "you have to sing for me."

1. The Abbess Hilda (614–680), a grand-niece of the first Christian king of Northumbria, founded Whitby, a double house for monks and nuns, in 657 and ruled over it for 22 years.

2. Oral poetry was performed to the accompaniment of a harp; here the harp is being passed from one participant of the feast to another, each being expected to perform in turn.

Figure 5. From *The Norton Anthology of English Literature*, ed. M. H. Abrams et al., 5th ed., vol. 1 (New York, 1986), 20–21. Reproduced by permission of W. W. Norton and Co.

"What must I sing?" he said.

And he said, "Sing about the Creation."

At this, Cædmon immediately began to sing verses in praise of God the Creator, which he had never heard before and of which the sense is this:

Nu sculon *h*erigean Now we must praise	*h*eofonrices Weard heaven-kingdom's Guardian,
Meotodes *m*eahte the Measurer's might	and his *m*odgeþanc and his mind-plans,
weorc Wuldor-Fæder the work of the Glory-Father,	swa he *w*undra gehwæs when he of wonders of every one,
*e*ce Drihten eternal Lord,	or onstealde the beginning established. [3]
He ærest sceop He first created	*i*elda[4] bearnum for men's sons
*h*èofon to hrofe heaven as a roof,	*h*alig Scyppend holy Creator;
ða *m*iddangeard then middle-earth	moncynnes Weard mankind's Guardian,
*e*ce Drihten eternal Lord,	æfter teode afterwards made—
*f*irum *f*oldan for men earth,	Frea ælmihtig Master almighty.

This is the general sense but not the exact order of the words that he sang in his sleep; for it is impossible to make a literal translation, no matter how well-written, of poetry into another language without losing some of the beauty and dignity. When he woke up, he remembered everything that he had sung in his sleep, and to this he soon added, in the same poetic measure, more verses praising God.

The next morning he went to the reeve,[5] who was his foreman, and told him about the gift he had received. He was taken to the abbess and ordered to tell his dream and to recite his song to an audience of the most learned men so that they might judge what the nature of that vision was and where it came from. It was evident to all of them that he had been granted the heavenly grace of God. Then they expounded some bit of sacred story or teaching to him, and instructed him to turn it into poetry if he could. He agreed and went away. And when he came back the next morning, he gave back what had been commissioned to him in the finest verse.

Therefore, the abbess, who cherished the grace of God in this man,

3. I.e., "established the beginning of every one of wonders."
4. The later manuscript copies read *eorþan*,

"earth," for *ælda* (West Saxon *ielda*), "men's."
5. Superintendent of the farms belonging to the monastery.

proceeding to "column two" (the b-verses). Here is Norton's "Hymn," following this naive or otherwise carefree procedure:

> Now we must praise
> the Measurer's might,
> the work of the Glory-Father,
> eternal Lord,
> He first created
> heaven as a roof,
> then middle-earth
> eternal Lord,
> for men earth,
> heaven-kingdom's Guardian
> and his mind-plans,
> when he of wonders of every one . . .

It gets a little clumsy at this point, but by reading it in the educated
way, overcoming the Norton format, one comes upon this clumsiness
sooner:

> Now we must praise   heaven-kingdom's Guardian,
> the Measurer's might   and his mind-plans,
> the work of the Glory-Father,   when he of wonders of every one . . .

But take a closer look at this unfortunate formatting of the Nortonian text.
Despite the slightly larger print of the Old English text, it is the modern
English version that unintentionally governs the layout, from the gigantic
caesuras to the spacing between words in the Old English text. Like an Anglo-Saxon interlinear gloss, individual Old English words, not an edited
text, are written above the modern English text, which alone is punctuated
to give sense to its words. Having begun in our earliest manuscripts as a
marginal gloss of a Latin paraphrase and having achieved an apotheosis as a
central text at least twice in its polyglossarial history, Cædmon's "Hymn"
has ended up in the Norton Anthology at least looking like the most prestigious gloss in all of English Literature. When the editors fix the formatting of Cædmon's "Hymn" in a future edition, they will have the salutary
chance to see again, to re-vise, the way our ancient and modern reproduc-
tions re-present our past.
gloss

Notes

A version of this paper was read in 1989 at Texas A & M University as part of a conference on "(Re)producing Texts/(Re)presenting History," sponsored by the Interdisci-

plinary Group for Historical Literary Study. I would like to thank Barrett Watten for exceptional help in preparing this article for publication.

1. From dubious internal evidence the Moore Bede (Cambridge University Library MS Kk.5.16) is usually dated in the year 737 and the Leningrad Bede (M. E. Saltykov-Shchedrin Public Library MS Q.v.I.18) in 746. For a discussion of these dates see Kevin S. Kiernan, "The Scribal Deconstruction of 'Early' Northumbrian," *ANQ* 3 (1990): 48–55.

2. Thomas Miller, ed., *The Old English Version of Bede's Ecclesiastical History of the English People*, 4 vols., Early English Text Society, o.s., nos. 95, 96, 110, 111 (1890–98; reprint ed., Millwood, N.Y., 1978–88).

3. Bertram Colgrave and R. A. B. Mynors, eds., *Bede's Ecclesiastical History of the English People* (Oxford, 1969), hereafter cited in the text as *EH*.

4. Early scholars credited Cædmon with composing many other extant Old English poems. In fact, the eleventh-century Bodleian Library MS Junius 11, one of the four great Old English poetic codices, was formerly known as the Cædmon Manuscript, and it still carries this inscription in its current binding. The facsimile by Israel Gollancz is likewise entitled *The Cædmon MS of Anglo-Saxon Biblical Poetry: Junius XI: In the Bodleian Library* (Oxford, 1927).

5. Bede was neither old enough nor near enough to Whitby to record the miracle in the stables. John Pope seems to leave open the possibility that someone else was on the scene. He says, "Since Bede makes it plain that Cædmon was unable to read and write when he entered the monastery, and gives no indication that he learned to do so later, we may assume that the hymn was first recorded by someone else, quite possibly during Cædmon's lifetime if not on the occasion of the alleged miracle"; *Seven Old English Poems*, 2nd ed. (New York, 1981), 51; all references to Pope are from this edition. Bede also makes it plain that Cædmon's second oral performance of the "Hymn" was different from the first, all encouraging one to wonder about the exact age and authenticity of our extant version(s).

6. See E. V. K. Dobbie, *The Manuscripts of Cædmon's Hymn and Bede's Death Song* (New York, 1937), 10–48. "Alfredian" in this context refers to the group of five manuscripts preserving the Old English translation of Bede's *Ecclesiastical History*, apparently made by a Mercian scholar working for Alfred. As Dobbie says, "I am using the term 'West Saxon' here, in accordance with the general custom, to indicate all the non-Northumbrian texts of the Hymn, without prejudice to the probable Mercian origin of the Alfredian Bede" (22, n. 31).

7. The two eighth-century Northumbrian manuscripts are the Moore (*ælda*) and Leningrad (*aeldu*) texts. Of the six late (tenth-to-fourteenth-century) West Saxon manuscripts (with the spelling *ylda* for *ælda*), all except the fourteenth-century manuscript contain the "Hymn" as a marginal addition.

8. The five tenth- and eleventh-century manuscripts of the Alfredian Bede all preserve the "Hymn" in the main translation. The two late (twelfth- and fifteenth-century) Northumbrian manuscripts both incorporate the Old English version of the "Hymn" in the Latin Bede.

9. The best recent discussion of the manuscript tradition is Katherine O'Brien O'Keeffe, "Orality and the Developing Text of Cædmon's *Hymn*," *Speculum* 62 (1987): 1–20.

10. See E. A. Lowe, "A Key to Bede's Scriptorium: Some Observations on the Leningrad Manuscript of the 'Historia Ecclesiastica Gentis Anglorum,'" *Scriptorium* 12 (1958): 182–90. Colgrave and Mynors suggest that the scribe of the Moore Bede "was on a visit to Wearmouth or Jarrow, or had the loan of a copy from there in his own monastery for a limited time"; *Ecclesiastical History*, xliv. It is worth noting that the scribe goes out of his way to mention the founding of Wearmouth in the "memoranda" at the end of the manuscript (fol. 128v11).

11. M. B. Parkes has recently drawn attention to urgent requests from Boniface in 746 and 747, indicating "a heavy demand for Bede's work on the continent"; "The Scriptorium of Wearmouth-Jarrow," Jarrow Lecture (1982), 15.

12. *The Moore Bede, Cambridge University Library MS Kk.5.16*, ed. Peter Hunter Blair, Early English Manuscripts in Facsimile, no. 9 (Copenhagen, 1959), fol. 128v4; hereafter cited in the text as *MB*.

13. See Peter Hunter Blair, "The *Moore Memoranda* on Northumbrian History," item 6 in *Anglo-Saxon Northumbria*, ed. M. Lapidge and Peter Hunter Blair (London, 1984), 245–57.

14. In fact all three glosses derive from the text of Bede if Hunter Blair is right that *Iugulum* was listed for the finite forms of *iugulare*, "to slaughter"; *Moore Bede*, 13, n.14.

15. The same scribe apparently wrote "rubricaui rubrica numeros," "I have rubricated the numbers in red," in the left margin, beginning at 128v12. Explaining this note, Hunter Blair observes that the chapters were later numbered "in red ink in the margin throughout the manuscript"; *Moore Bede*, 28.

16. To my knowledge no one has noticed that the "Hymn" was added by a different scribe with similar but not identical handwriting. The distinguishing feature is the truncated descender on the letters *f, p, r,* and *s,* compared to the long descender on the letter *g*. In the main text, with exactly the same space between lines, the descender on these letters is invariably long and spiky. For the view that the handwriting is identical, see for example O. Arngart, *The Leningrad Bede: An Eighth Century MS of the Venerable Bede's Historia Ecclesiastica Gentis Anglorum in the Public Library, Leningrad*, Early English Manuscripts in Facsimile, no. 2 (1952), 30; and A. H. Smith, ed., *Three Northumbrian Poems* (New York, 1968), 19.

17. Arngart reflects the current view. "Suffice it to say," he says, "that it is now recognized to be the original of Bede's Latin paraphrase, not as was once maintained an Anglo-Saxon translation of the passage in the Latin text"; *Leningrad Bede*, 30–31. Bruce Mitchell briefly raises strong evidence to the contrary when he says, "One can see that, if the Latin version with *debemus* had come first, *scylun* alone could be explained as a careless gloss for it; compare *Coll 253 wyllap wesen wise*, Latin *uolumus esse sapientes*." But he immediately dismisses this possibility; "Cædmon's *Hymn*, Line 1: What Is the Subject of *Scylun* or Its Variants?" in *On Old English* (London, 1988), 92.

18. John Lingard first proposed this theory in 1806 in *The Antiquities of the Anglo-*

Saxon Church. "The Anglo-Saxon verses are found in King Alfred's translation of Bede," Lingard said, "and are generally supposed to have been transcribed by that prince from some ancient copy. I think it, however, equally probable, that they were the composition of the royal translator." For convenience I cite from the later American edition, based on the 1810 British edition (Philadelphia, 1841), 316.

19. Richard Wülker, "Ueber den Hymnus Caedmons," *Beiträge zur Geschichte der deutschen Sprache und Literatur* (Tübingen) 3 (1876): 348–57. Wülker notes that in 1851 Benjamin Thorpe also argued that the "Hymn" from the Alfredian Bede was a "retranslation" of Bede's Latin paraphrase (352–53).

20. Julius Zupitza, "Über den Hymnus Cädmons," *Zeitschrift für deutsches Altertum und deutsche Literatur* 22 (1878): 210–23.

21. Richard Wülker, *Grundriss zur Geschichte der angelsächsischen Litteratur* (Leipzig, 1885), 117–20.

22. David Dumville, "'Beowulf' and the Celtic World: The Uses of Evidence," *Traditio* 37 (1981): 148. Dumville is mistaken that Dobbie and Hunter Blair thought that the "Hymn" was added by another scribe (148, n. 182). E. V. K. Dobbie says it was added "apparently by the same scribe who wrote the text of Bede"; *The Anglo-Saxon Minor Poets*, Anglo-Saxon Poetic Records, no. 6 (New York, 1942), xcv. Hunter Blair concurs, referring to "the seeming identity of handwriting with the remainder of the manuscript"; *Moore Bede*, 27.

23. The only peculiar constructions involve the verbs, especially *tecti*, which Bede places after *pro culmine.*

24. Wülker agreed with Zupitza in 1885 that these parts of the text were left out because, as Bede said, "it is not possible to translate verse, however well composed, literally from one language to another without some loss of beauty and dignity"; see *Grundriss*, 119–20.

25. See Henry Sweet, ed., *The Oldest English Texts*, Early English Text Society, o.s., no. 83 (1885; reprint ed., Oxford, 1966), for editions of eighth-century glosses.

26. M. C. Morrell, *A Manual of Old English Biblical Materials* (Knoxville, Tenn., 1965), observes that "if the Old English metrical psalms really have an Anglian origin, they belong then to that first flowering of Christian piety that had its centers in the north, and the tradition of metrical translation is even older than the tenth-century Benedictine Reform" (149).

27. It is easy to explain *scylun* as a careless gloss of *debemus*, but hard to account for a native speaker like Cædmon omitting the identifying pronoun. Mitchell reveals that there is no acceptable evidence supporting the editors' view that "*we* could be unexpressed at the beginning of a poem in which it does not occur and in which there was therefore no first person grammatical referent"; "Line 1," 90.

28. A second Alfredian Bede, BL Cotton MS B.xi., supposedly read *Ne sculon*, "not must," but this part of the manuscript was destroyed in the Cotton fire of 1731. This misreading in fact comes from a sixteenth-century transcript, now BL Additional MS 43, 703, by Laurence Nowell, who presumably conflated *Nu* and *we* in the Cotton text.

29. See Simon Keynes and Michael Lapidge, *Alfred the Great* (New York, 1983), 29, 33–34; and Allen Frantzen, *King Alfred* (Boston, 1986), 8.

30. According to Dobbie,

> The evidence of other poems would . . . favor *ælda barnum* as the original reading of the Hymn at this point, for this formula is found not only frequently in Anglo-Saxon, but in the other Germanic dialects as well, whereas *eorðu bearnum* (or *eorðan bearnum*) is, so far as I know, unexampled elsewhere. And, though we cannot be quite rid of the possibility that *eorðu* was the original reading of the Hymn in 1.5, the weight of the evidence favors the conclusion that *ælda barnum*, as found in the original of M and L and in the *hominum* of the Latin text of Bede, were the words written [*sic*] by Cædmon himself.

Manuscripts, 48; Dobbie is not the only scholar to forget that Cædmon was illiterate.

31. These "standard" Bedan/Northumbrian and Alfredian/West Saxon editions are presented in the same way in Smith's *Three Northumbrian Poems* (38–41) and Dobbie's *Anglo-Saxon Minor Poems* (105–6).

32. The reconstructed dialect is more romantically than rigorously founded on characteristic spellings in unrelated manuscripts of texts closely linked to Alfred's cultural reform. As Campbell says, "The 'Early West Saxon', which has come to be regarded as a grammatical norm, is based on the Parker MS. of the *Old English Chronicle* from the beginning to 924, the two oldest manuscripts of Ælfred's translation of Gregory's *Cura Pastoralis*, and the Lauderdale MS. of Ælfred's translation [*sic*] of Orosius"; *Old English Grammar*, 8–9.

33. Antonette diPaolo Healey and Richard L. Venezky, *A Microfiche Concordance to Old English* (Newark, Del., 1981).

34. *The Norton Anthology of English Literature*, ed. M. H. Abrams et al. (New York, 1986), 19–22.

35. This modern analysis of the miracle is indebted to Fred Robinson and Bruce Mitchell, who likewise say the "Hymn" "attests to a minor miracle of literary history that cannot be denied: in these polished verses Cædmon demonstrated that the ancient heroic style was not incompatible with Christian doctrine and hence was worthy of preservation"; *A Guide to Old English*, 4th ed. (Oxford, 19886), 204. Bede would doubtless be chagrined to learn that modern readers rationalized his miracle as our first literary hoax.

36. The inspiration for the Norton conflation is presumably Pope's "The Hymn Normalized in West-Saxon Spelling Based on the Northumbrian Version of MSS M and L," *Seven Old English Poems*, 4, the only other place I know of where **ielda* and Bodleian Library MS Tanner 10 can be found together. The grave accent on the *e* of *heofon* (line 6a) and the spelling *ða* for *þa* are minor errors in transcription of the Tanner MS, not odd features of some other West Saxon manuscript.

Birthing Bishops and Fathering Poets: Bede, Hild, and the Relations of Cultural Production

CLARE A. LEES and
GILLIAN R. OVERING

OUR title refers to two events in Old English literary history, both of which originate with Bede in his *Ecclesiastical History*.[1] According to Bede, Hild is worthy of memory at least in part because, as celebrated Abbess and Mother of the dual foundation of Streonæshalch or Whitby, she created an environment of spiritual instruction that produced five bishops. Twentieth-century historians, following Bede, also remember Whitby as a virtual "nursery of bishops," to borrow, as others have, Frank M. Stenton's evocative phrase.[2] The second event recalls an even better known literary moment when Bede bequeaths his society, and subsequent scholarly readers, the account of the so-called first English poet, Cædmon, often known as the Father of English poetry. Allen J. Frantzen describes this in an equally evocative phrase as a "birth" of Christian Anglo-Saxon poetry.[3]

The two events are, of course, connected in this trio of names—Bede, Hild, Cædmon—but their connections reveal an unequal hierarchy. Bede authors and creates both moments, but it is Hild who is the abbess of the monastery that produces Cædmon and five bishops. Yet scholarship tends to remember these two events separately. Putting Bede's two moments side by side (as they appear in *EH* 4.23 and 24), we examine the cultural activities represented in the two accounts, and re-presented by the institution of Anglo-Saxon scholarship, as gendered ones. We might express this as follows: Bede (the man) fathers Cædmon (poets/poetry/sons) while Hild (the woman) mothers bishops/men.

The gender asymmetry suggested by the events of Hild's "Life" and Cædmon's miracle is a familiar binarism of patriarchy: women reproduce, men produce. This fundamental binarism (one that might be fruitfully added to those proposed by Frantzen), moreover, still informs much Old English scholarship.[4] When literary history remembers Cædmon's "Hymn" as the originary event of English poetry, it tends to forget Hild—as a direct consequence of Bede's structuring of the event. Three recent critical expositions, for example (by Kevin S. Kiernan, Martin Irvine, and Seth Lerer), each of which has insights into our rereadings of Bede's account, do not address Hild's active participation in the miracle.[5] Historians, on the other hand, remember Hild but equally fail—though for different reasons—to examine her role in Cædmon's miracle. Indeed, Hild has been enjoying something of a renascence in academic circles. She has been the subject of one detailed study of her "Life," by Christine E. Fell, and often features in works on women in Anglo-Saxon England as well as in studies of the role of women in early monastic history.[6] In this way, Hild has been added to the growing pantheon of outstanding women of history previously silenced by androcentric scholarship. The success of the approach, however, is also its weakness. The principal source of our information about Hild is, of course, Bede, but in recent feminist studies we see Bede's role in disseminating and shaping her history downplayed in favor of a recontextualized focus on women. The all too obvious conclusion is that the different research paradigms of traditional historiography, literary history, and feminist scholarship shape the subjects that they investigate.

It is not necessary, however, to choose between silencing Hild and hearing Bede, or vice versa; we wish to avoid a duplication of binary choices that set critical paradigms in a competitive relationship. We are not concerned with chastising Bede, critics, or historians for selective amnesia or partial recall. Instead we re-investigate the dynamic of Bede and Hild by connecting these two figures within the larger framework of their relation to cultural production. We remember what conventional (i.e., non-feminist) scholarship and patriarchal authors (i.e., Bede) forget, silence, or erase and we suggest a different model for future feminist scholarship.

If relations of production may be understood as the "relations in which means of production (both the objects upon which labor power works and the instruments that work on these objects) stand to the agents of production (individual human beings, institutions, corporations etc.)," as Britton Harwood suggests, we explore how this dynamic may be modified and specified to describe both cultural production in the Anglo-Saxon period, and the ways in which scholarship produces and reproduces that culture.[7] "Culture" in this period involves a variety of means and forms of agency, and of degrees of access to, alienation from, and control over these: it concerns, for example, developments in literacy and education; production of manuscripts; production and maintenance of a scribal labor force, a church bureaucracy, and personnel. It also concerns the founding, building, and managing of a monastery—from its layout to its work force (ecclesiastical and secular). As the history of the swineherd-turned-poet Cædmon makes abundantly clear, "culture" encompasses the provision made for those laborers and the stories told about them. Who sustains Cædmon, and whom, or what, does Cædmon sustain?

We begin, therefore, with an examination of how women are represented in originary moments of cultural production, using Bede, Hild, and Cædmon as a test case, and raise some theoretical questions and issues prompted by the specifics of this historicized instance.[8] We then use our reconstruction of these literary events as paradigmatic narratives that offer the possibility of theorizing the relations of gender in the production of culture in early Anglo-Saxon society, and of discovering new questions and directions for future research. We historicize such originary narratives in order to situate their power and to theorize the continued production of their meaning in contemporary critical discourse. In other words, we have one eye firmly on the past and the other firmly on the present: we wish to appropriate the patriarchal myth of the origins of Old English poetry and to suggest alternative ways of understanding this origin. Our emphasis is not so much on new information (the stories of Bede, Hild, and Cædmon are, after all, often rehearsed) but on new ways of interpreting it.

1. Engendering Originary Narratives

"... quam omnes qui nouerant ob insigne pietatis et gratiae
    matrem uocare consuerant."

"... and all who knew her piety and grace called her mother."

—EH 4.23

It is not hard to see how Bede's account of Cædmon has been invested with all the power of an originary narrative by institutional Anglo-Saxon scholarship: both Frantzen and Kiernan have drawn attention to the critical paradigms through which the account is conventionally read. As Frantzen points out, Bede himself presents the narrative as one of origins and, to judge by the reception of the "Hymn" in Anglo-Saxon England, the Anglo-Saxons also invested it with considerable power.[9] But these three moments —the "original" authorial moment, the evidence for its reception in Anglo-Saxon England, and its subsequent reception by Anglo-Saxonists—are not synonymous, though there is a discernible tendency to map one on top of the other (i.e., the critical approach on top of its "history"). Each moment is invested with particular desires, which are themselves part-products and part-producers of contemporary concerns and issues: that is to say, literary events are complex and overdetermined. What has been neglected by recent analyses is the significance of such events for our understanding of the interplay of gender and desire in the production of their meaning.

Above all, Bede's desires are those of the Christian writer who interprets the human history of the Church in England according to the paradigm of sacred history. Cædmon's story, as an account of the origins of sacred poetry, is incorporated into, and embrace by, the Word. The social power of this "eventful" narrative derives from the ways in which Bede's account makes manifest the Word of God in a Christian community, emblematized as the monastery of Whitby. Bede's sacred desires are necessarily mediated via literary genres, and his story thus discovers an intersection of sacred master narrative, generic form, and his own desire and talent as narrator. One obvious way to make manifest the power of God is to use the miracle narrative, and the narrative of Cædmon stresses the miraculous. Cædmon is the vessel through which God's ways are revealed to men, but Cædmon is no saint in this not-quite-hagiographical narrative. Nor is his story that of the first poet's first inspiration and the first poem. Cædmon's song is divinely inspired, as Bede emphasizes, and he draws others to the faith by singing Christian songs which have the power to move, perhaps even to convert. This is a powerful originary moment in the history of English Christianity—the moment when the native (Germanic) traditions of oral song-making are allied with the subject of Christianity and harnessed for the faith. Others could sing before Cædmon, but only Cædmon, divinely inspired and remaining illiterate, sings *Christian* songs.

Bede's narrative certainly shaped, even produced culture. The combination of the status of Bede as a native Anglo-Saxon *auctor* and the "Hymn" as a product of Christian and native traditions seems to have been highly influential. Bede's Latin *History* was translated into Old English in the ninth century, and is conventionally associated with Alfred's court, while the Latin continues to function as a source of authority for later Old English writers such as Ælfric.[10] More importantly, the "Hymn" enjoyed a wide dissemination. Old English versions of the "Hymn" date from shortly after Bede's account, copied into the margins of the *History* and elsewhere a total of twenty-one times (with some significant variations between the copies) —a figure which speaks for itself when the majority of Old English poems survive in only one version.

The manuscript copies of the Latin and English versions of the "Hymn" offer some explanations for this popularity. As Katherine O'Brien O'Keeffe has demonstrated, scribes gradually find ways of assimilating this oral poem to the highly literate textual culture of the later Anglo-Saxon period by developing methods of formatting and punctuation unique to Old English poetry.[11] These scribes, in other words, preserve and commemorate the poem by reversing the processes of its oral composition. Bede is, after all, very precise about Cædmon's methods of composition. He is a song-maker who relies on his memory to transform a sacred text into poetry with a Christian message. Many of the Old English versions are separate from their context in Bede, written in margins or in one case at the end of the manuscript (a nice *post scriptum*). Thereby, they acquire a quasi-independent status—materially severed from both authors, Bede and Cædmon. The reception of the "Hymn" in the Anglo-Saxon period is thus one which recuperates the poem linguistically for the vernacular: to Bede's Latin paraphrase is added an Old English version (or versions), marked in the manuscripts as textually separate from the Latin narrative. The Latin and Old English are contiguous, not projected one on top of the other.

Bede's celebrated remarks about his individual stylistic preferences and priorities in refusing to translate the poem (". . . for it is not possible to translate verse, however well composed, literally from one language to another without some loss of beauty and dignity," *EH* 4.24) underline an authorial honesty, or perhaps self-consciousness, that marks his narrative as a particular instance of a master narrative. His paraphrase is a Latin graphic trace of an originally vernacular oral song. For all its power as an account of the first moment in Anglo-Saxon Christian poetry, however, Bede's narrative is simultaneously one of loss. The paraphrase in Latin—the prestige language of Christian culture—only makes the reader more aware of the vernacular poem that it supplants and that the Old English versions seek to redeem. Bede identifies ancient traditions with emerging institutions and his text produces a reordering, a re-membering in terms of his priorities and desires, which inevitably involves a forgetting.

Historians and literary critics also inevitably bring their own desires to Bede's account of Cædmon. In reconstructing this story of English Christianity as an event of English literature or on the other hand of history, certain lacunae in Bede's account gain prominence. To the traditional historian testing the authenticity of Bede's miraculous narrative, the Cædmon story offers the challenge of defining history or hagiography, fact or fiction. This is a laudable enterprise: time and again, Bede has been demonstrated to be, in our terms, a reliable historian using scholarly methods of documentary or witness testimony wherever possible. But reading for "facts" only exposes the lacunae of this particular text. For who was Cædmon and where is the rest of his poetry? We know nothing of Cædmon save that his name is probably British. In spite of Bede's long list of Cædmon's compositions, we know nothing of his poetry save for the copies of the "Hymn," which Bede does not even give in the original language. As the only authority capable of verifying this problematic narrative (just who is Cædmon without Bede?), Bede ensures himself a place at the originary moment, which is an *a priori* moment of cultural production—enacted between Cædmon and God, channeled through Bede. This is also a classically patriarchal moment, where poetry is exchanged between men and the Father (God) via the human father (Bede). The myth of origins turns out to be an ideological myth of masculinism.

Where the historian is frustrated by the paucity of evidence, the literary critic has a field day. To judge both from the regular critical output on the story and the "Hymn" as well as from the number of times the "Hymn" has been anthologized, Bede's story of Cædmon and his poem is a critical best-seller. The attractions are self-evident. The structure of Bede's story resembles mythical accounts of the beginnings of poetry from different cultures (Scandinavian, for example) to add to his mythical story of Hengest and Horsa and the origins of the Anglo-Saxons (*EH* 1.15). The literary critical story begins with this premise and emphasizes that the origins of English poetry are coterminous with a repositioning of the relationship between a Christian Latin culture and a Germanic oral one. The paradigm reads Bede's story using, in microcosm, the binarisms of Anglo-Saxon culture and Old English literature—Christian/Germanic, literate/oral. This story is familiar: the scene is staged between the old (the Germanic or British illiterate laborer, Cædmon) and the new (the Christian scholar, Bede). The new triumphs by incorporating the old within its ideology, just as Pope Gregory recommended to Augustine (*EH* 1.30). Embedded within this paradigm of successive stages of conquest and domination, made palatable by myths of progress and voluntary cultural submission, are the many ambivalences, deceptions, and remetaphorizations which attend and disguise the violence of the overlay of one order of cultural representation upon another.

In mapping our critical desires for origins on top of a text which is itself concerned with origins, Bede's narrative neatly becomes the site for many of our most treasured assumptions about Anglo-Saxon culture and Old English literature. The literary critical story acknowledges Bede's narrative as originary and it therefore depends on the inter-relatedness of narrative and poem. The popularity of both text and poem derives in large measure from the simple fact that we cannot go beyond the text: *there is nothing before Bede; we do not know who Cædmon was.* Our role as reader is that of witness to the beginnings of English poetry, blessed by the Church, and authored by one of the greatest scholars of the Anglo-Saxon period. In short, we are required as readers to stand witness to a miracle. It is therefore not surprising that this is also a story which gives priority to Bede and to the mysterious Cædmon embedded ineluctably in his account. This is the power of originary narratives. But, as we have already argued in our discussion of the "Hymn," such moments are also moments of loss. What is omitted in the conventional literary reconstruction of Bede's account is Hild.

Bede's originary moment is fraught with apparently competing narratological agendas (the sacred, the literary genre, the cultural-political) which displace and overlay each other in a series of successive accommodations and appropriations. But, while the master narrative is rewritten and its elements rearranged by those who follow Bede, its trajectory remains unchanged in that the demands of all of these narrative structures offer no place for a different conception of agency. Bede's originary moment is also, as we have seen, a political instance—then and now. Frantzen explores eloquently how Bede presents a "cultural thesis" that privileges, by a series of appropriations, literate Christianity as a consolidating cultural force over the pagan oral past. Moreover, the power of Bede's originary significance, Frantzen also points out, "is entirely the creation of those who came after him."[12] As culture is produced and reproduced in this redrawing of oppositions, it is not surprising that Hild's absence is simply reconfigured and female agency unaccounted for, but this absence does offer a new perspective on the so-called dichotomies of the period—Christian/pagan, oral/literate —and the myth of a "barbaric" past replaced by, even gracefully (i.e., with God's grace) assumed into a more progressive future. These patterns of realignments of oppositions assume a decidedly non-dichotomous, even a unified force, from a feminist perspective.

However literary readers have chosen to recreate the drama of Bede's moment, whatever critical methodology they use to elicit a reading, the principal actors—Bede, Cædmon, and God—remain the same. What is striking about these readings is their masculinity: Bede's drama lays claim to literature for men as well as for Christianity. His is a patriarchal myth of literary creation which imitates the first Christian myth: the first song created by Cædmon is a "Hymn" of Creation sung to the Father of Creation— Bede's account fathers the first Christian poem. The feminist reader is required to stand witness to a miracle whose very grounds for belief are an exclusively masculine model of authorship. Striking too is the weight of criti-

cal silence that is complicit in reconstructing this patriarchal myth. The
fourth actor in Bede's narrative is Abbess Hild, the abbess in charge of
Cædmon's monastery, the woman who acts as the ultimate arbiter for the
veracity of Cædmon's miracle, the woman responsible for advising Cædmon to take monastic vows and for facilitating his continued work as a
Christian poet by ordering him to be instructed in the events of sacred history. But Bede does not name Hild in his account of Cædmon, nor does the
Old English translation[13] and, in fact, she is already dead in the narrative
logic of the *History*, since her life ends as his begins; her obituary precedes
his story. Hild's death issues the moment of the birth of poetry, and is itself
a direct product of Bede's twinned desires in writing—as a Christian man,
and as a Christian hagiographer.

In fact, Hild is twinned with Cædmon in a number of respects. Her
"Life" (*EH* 4.23), a more pronounced hagiography than Cædmon's, prefaces and parallels his, and like Cædmon, although to a more radical extent,
she is displaced by Bede in the miraculous account of Christian poetry.
Elided in Cædmon's history, she is, however, given her own but here she is
displaced by the trope of mother of the monastery, and by the genre of hagiography. Bede's narrative is framed by Hild's decision to dedicate her life
to God at the age of thirty-three (perhaps a purely symbolic age), and by his
account of the manner of her death in 680, which is duly accompanied by a
number of premonitory visions. Within this hagiographical frame, the key
details of Hild's life, according to Bede, emerge. Born of noble, perhaps
even royal parents (Breguswith and Hereric) in Northumbria, and also related to the royal house of East Anglia, Hild was baptized by Paulinus at the
same time as Edwin, the first Christian Northumbrian king. She seeks
monastic life in exile at Chelles with her sister, Hereswith, but is recalled
before leaving by Aídán. Her first position as abbess is at Hartlepool, but
thereafter she founds and presides over the influential double monastery of
Whitby, "teaching them to observe strictly the virtues of justice, devotions,
and chastity, and other virtues too, but above all things to continue in peace
and charity." She directs the nuns and monks in a careful program of scriptural study—Bede tells us that five monks later become bishops while a
sixth, Tatfrith, died before he could be consecrated—and acted as advisor
to kings and princes.[14] So remarkable were her achievements, Bede tells us,
that all who knew her called her "Mother."

We have already pointed out some ways in which Bede and successive
critics have cast the myth of origins, literary and divine, as an ideological
myth of masculinism. When Bede insists on Hild's ubiquitous maternity
(an idea perpetuated by twentieth-century critics), we are prompted to ex-

amine this construction of the maternal role more closely. Bede theorizes the maternal here as nurturing, which is paradoxically synonymous with Hild's active production of the clergy.[15] But the power to translate reproduction into cultural production is denied in that Hild is alienated not only from her labor, but also from her gender and her clerical "progeny." She is alienated too from her own mother, Breguswith, whose dream predicts her daughter's subsequent spiritual achievements. Maternity is doubly appropriated when it is thus emptied of its gendered force and specificity and reabsorbed into the masculine economy as a means of production under masculine control. In fact, Bede effectively "gets the birth out" of this construction of maternity, removing the specifics of female presence and experience, and sterilizing it, as it were, for clerical metaphorical use. Moreover, we must stress Hild's own participation in this dynamic: the procreation of culture may be remetaphorized as masculine but in producing clerical "progeny," indeed, in "appropriating" Cædmon's poetic talent in the service of patriarchal Christianity,[16] Hild is also reproducing patriarchy, and producing the means which alienate her from her labor. We are confronted with one of the paradoxical aspects of Hild's relation to cultural production, a point we will take up at greater length in part two of this essay: the more actively she participates in the production of patriarchal culture, the more passively she is constructed by the cultural record.

That Hild had in reality both access to and a degree of autonomous control over the means of cultural production has been well documented. "We cannot think of Whitby without thinking of Hild," states Blair, discussing the importance of Whitby as a center for learning in the seventh century. Blair's article, though posthumous and partly reconstructed from his notes, is a fine example of traditional historical research, which carefully recreates Hild's life and the foundation of Whitby by piecing together information from Bede with other historical sources. He then considers the famous Synod of Whitby, the story of Cædmon, and the role of Whitby as a "nursery" for bishops.[17] In other words, Bede's "Life of Hild" in book 4, chapter 23 is supplemented by information either found elsewhere in the *History* or by other sources—as in the case of Hild's royal successors, Ælfflæd and Eanflæd. Blair fashions a narrative of Whitby in which Hild figures as important in the major institutions and events of her age; this is complemented by that of Christine Fell, who offers the kind of detailed story paradigmatic of contemporary historical research into Hild. Scholars such as Jane Chance and Joan Nicholson develop another story by uncovering Hild's relationship with other exemplary aristocratic women, nuns and queens, in early Anglo-Saxon society.

This valuable research is an important way of remembering Hild but let's be quite clear about Bede's biography. Neither Eanflæd nor Ælfflæd—the two royal women and nuns closest to Hild—are mentioned in his "Life." Nor is the Synod of Whitby, which is arguably the most important event in seventh-century Church history and is discussed by Bede earlier (*EH* 3.25). Even in the context of the development of the English Church, these "omissions" are startling: the continued prosperity of Whitby after Hild's death is largely due to Ælfflæd (who was dedicated to the monastery by her royal father, Oswiu of Northumbria, at the age of one, *EH* 3.24) and her mother Eanflæd. In fact, Bede's narrative of Hild's political contacts mentions only her relationships with men—unless one counts her mysterious connection to the "first English nun," Heiu, who was dead before Hild's appointment to Hartlepool. Hild was certainly present at the Synod held in her own monastery, where she voted for the pro-Celtic side, as Bede and the *Life of Wilfrid* suggest,[18] but Bede does not refer to the Synod in her "Life." Strictly speaking, of course, these are not "omissions" since Bede covers them in other sections of the *History*, but the structure of his "Life" excludes them—suppresses them, perhaps—in favor of a focus on her piety.

Conspicuously absent from Bede's "Life of Hild" is any trace of what we may assume with good reason to be the forceful physical and verbal presence of this politically prominent woman. Interestingly, this silencing of voice and presence raises issues similar to those in the development of literacy, suggesting that the "disappearance" of the oral trace of Cædmon's "Hymn" and of female presence might be usefully jointly theorized, a more general observation to which we shall return later. Hild's specific disappearance, however, is clearly a matter of Bede's desires in recreating her story. Bede credits Hild with influence in the political events of her time but only with an unspecified reference to the fact that kings and princes as well as "ordinary people" sought her advice. *Which kings, which princes?* we might ask. What Bede stresses instead is Hild's fostering of learning at Whitby. Again the nurturing element of the maternal role is highlighted, but the "real woman" is nowhere to be found: her actual connection to political power, social change, and the realities of cultural production are unidentified and unacknowledged. The proof of Whitby's excellence is the fact that it fostered five bishops, all of whom are named, unlike those aristocrats who sought her advice—Bosa, Ætla, Oftfor, John of Beverly, and Wilfrid of York—and two of whom are given their own narratives in the *History* (5.2–7; 19). Mother, founder, educator, *not* principal actor: this is how Bede chooses to remember Hild.

Just how influential was Bede's "Life of Hild" in the Anglo-Saxon pe-

riod? Unlike other saints, both male and female, in the early Anglo-Saxon
church—Cuthbert, Oswald, or Æthelthryth, for example—there is little
evidence for a wide-spread Anglo-Saxon cult. She is commemorated in
only one calendar (Willibrord's), included in only one martyrology (the
ninth-century *Old English Martyrology*) and her death is briefly noted in the
Anglo-Saxon Chronicle.[19] Evidence for a lost *Life* of Hild, presumably written at Whitby, is suggested by the wording of her entry in the *Old English
Martyrology*.[20] Otherwise, bearing in mind the fragmentary and accidental
nature of material that survives, Hild disappears without trace, to reappear
post-Conquest in a few regional liturgies and calendars.[21]

It is clear, therefore, that Hild deserves to be rescued from Bede and afforded her own place in history. The question is, just what kind of a place?
In rewriting her history, we should beware of silencing the patriarchal desires of her hagiographer—desires that are equally evident in Bede's account of Cædmon. A comparison between the two accounts sharpens our
point: removed from the "primal" scene of cultural production in the account of Cædmon, Hild is given a different nurturing role in the production of Christianity in her "Life." Metaphorically at least, Bede and Cædmon produce while Hild reproduces. Bede, after all, goes out of his way to
stress Hild's role as "mother" in her "Life." But as "mother to all," emptied
of female presence and political force, Hild may be creator and originator
of none: her power to create and to produce is initially dissipated and then
specifically forgotten.

The gender asymmetries present in the reconstruction of originary
events are played out again by scholarship, literary or historical. The conventional historical account argues that Cædmon's story, with Hild as his
patron, demonstrates that Whitby must have been a center of vernacular as
well as Latin learning.[22] Leaving aside the essential mystery of Cædmon at
the heart of this narrative, several other questions remain unasked, even by
those historians writing about women: what was Hild's role as patron? what
does it mean to call Hild the patron of Cædmon? how does Bede write of
Hild's participation in Cædmon's story? In contrast, the conventional literary critical account reads *as* Bede, bearing witness to his miraculous story of
Cædmon and ignoring his story of Hild. In each case, Hild suffers, only
partially remembered by history, repressed by literary critics. There is no
better example of the implicitly gendered stance of originary narratives
than Bede's silence about Hild. She is granted a supporting role in his account, giving center stage to Cædmon; but contemporary critics have been
reluctant to grant her even this. It is all too easy to forget Hild when thinking of Cædmon. Women have no place at the beginning of English poetry,

it would seem. Nor do they have much of one in the institutionalized narratives of contemporary scholarship on this subject.

Crudely speaking, those scholars who remember Hild reconstruct her history, her *historia;* those who remember Cædmon, reconstruct the literary myth of Christian poetry in which Hild is given little role to play. But Hild bridges these two worlds, revealing and questioning the inadequacies of our own disciplines that sever the literary from the historical. For the feminist reader, the historical approach to Hild might appear to be the most fruitful. Hild has at least a place in the historical record, even if it is a place which needs to address the patriarchy of her hagiographer. But this methodology risks diminishing her role in the Cædmon story, as Bede does, and leaves unanswered our questions about her role as patron. Moreover, Bede does not just relegate Hild to the margins by refusing to name her; he silences her textually by the more radical method of "killing" her. To be sure, Bede praises Hild in her own story, but the Mother of the monastery is only the Abbess of poetry. Can we recuperate, or rather revive, Hild as a literary figure *and* an historical figure?

2. The Gendered Paradigm of Cultural Production: Complicit Mothers, Implicit Fathers

Without Hild there would be no Cædmon. Without Bede, however, we would remember neither Hild nor Cædmon. In the patriarchal world of the seventh century, the three figures of Bede, Cædmon, and Hild are more inextricably intertwined than in modern rewritings. Hild is a woman of her age and there is no indication that she escaped it even as abbess. Frantzen calls attention to the alacrity with which Cædmon is "whisked" into the monastery by Hild, and to her ability to spot a new protegé, concluding that her role contributes to the appropriation of the artist.[23] Indeed, as we have suggested, her promotion of Cædmon in the interests of patriarchal Christianity invokes her complicity in her own appropriation, her own removal from the cultural record. Perhaps these are reasons why we have been reluctant to look too deeply into her story. At present, it seems that one branch of feminism seeks to recuperate and redeem the forgotten women of history; a second seeks to define and, thereby, redefine the representation of women in the arts; while a third addresses the equally important project of understanding patriarchy. In order to find an interpretive framework that can embrace all three projects and realign the narratives of Hild, Bede, and Cædmon, we need to look more closely at the theory of cultural production embedded in Bede's account.

In the masculinist myth that is Cædmon's story, the process of creating songs is doubly suppressed in favor of the product, the "Hymn." First, the man who creates the "Hymn" does so in a miraculous dream, which names him. Second, the woman who facilitates this process remains unnamed throughout, defined only by institution (the "Abbess") and by non-anaphoric pronouns. The account thus privileges divine composition over human agency, product over process, Bede over Cædmon, and both Bede and Cædmon over Hild. The emphasis on divine production expels gender—this is a "birth" without a birth. We see the same movement repeated in Hild's "Life." Hild's moral worth (as mother) is emphasized at the expense of her fostering (as mother) literacy but also of her evident political power (as at the Synod of Whitby); and both these cultural and political functions are displaced by the metaphor of "mothering" bishops. Another "birth" without a birth. These narratives of culture, in other words, emphasize product over process as examples of how the complex of birth and nurture is appropriated and downplayed by Bede. The question then arises: how can we recuperate the *processes* of cultural production to understand a specifically female contribution and reconstruct the business of these women's lives? Is there a way to put the "birth"—the physical realities of women's experience—back into the paradigm? We could ask, for example, exactly what it means to say that a woman "founded a monastery": did she design it, dig the foundations (as did Saints Seaxburg and Landrada according to their *vitae*);[24] or raise the money to buy the land (as did Hild apparently)?[25] Similarly, what is implied by the title of abbess—what does it mean to say that a woman "ran a monastery"[26]—did she teach, produce manuscripts,[27] fundraise, oversee the necessary agricultural and domestic systems? Some women, it appears, did many of these things, and much historical work outlines the individual contributions of "exceptional" religious women, but the larger issue of how these contributions to the production of culture were valued within a masculine economy remains to be addressed: at what points and for what reasons are women's apparent control over and access to the means of production subsumed within and replaced by patriarchal modes of production.

In sum, we are asking different questions about women's work, about women's relation to their labor and to the social economy in which it is exchanged, and about those forms of cultural representation, especially those which "write" material culture, via which we construct this historical relationship. Jane Tibbetts Schulenburg provides a starting point for our enquiries with her examination of female religious life from a variety of sociopolitical viewpoints that range from the conditions of female sanctity to policies of cloistering and patterns of monastic donation. Her summary is useful:

> This early period in Frankish Gaul and Anglo-Saxon England was an especially positive age in the development of women's monasticism. It was a time when royal and ecclesiastical authority was weak and decentralized. Political and economic power was situated within royal and aristocratic households and easily accessible to women. Society was essentially "open" and fluid. It was an era of relative peace and prosperity. It was also an age of new beginnings—a time of necessity during which the Church was becoming established and was not yet highly organized, reformed, or right-minded. In this milieu, women's practical assistance was especially valued. Female religious were accepted as partners, friends, sisters, and collaborators in the faith. . . . Unfortunately, with the reform movements and their emphasis on ascetic piety and clerical celibacy, the initial appreciation of women's active participation in the Church was lost and replaced by an atmosphere of heightened fear and suspicion of female sexuality.[28]

Although we will question the implications of a "Golden Age" of female monasticism, Schulenberg outlines key aspects of the broader cultural discussion in which we aim to contextualize Hild and her work: first, the connections between women's status and labor and stages of social development; then, the developing distinctions between public and private from the point of view of both gendered labor and domain.[29] England in the seventh century was still loosely comprised of individual kinship-based aristocratic kingdoms, awaiting the later development of a centralized monarchy and movement toward a civil state. Marxist historians and feminist anthropologists would agree overall that the rise of the civil state leads historically to a substantial decrease in the power and the visibility of women, whether they are placed in the monastic or secular spheres, and to the devaluation and privatization of the domestic sphere.[30]

Many developments in female monasticism in the Anglo-Saxon period neatly and illuminatingly parallel this anthropological theoretical overview. The changing requirements for female sanctity, for example, document how the early emphasis on the public presence and political acumen of the saint later gives way to the promulgation of her domestic virtues. Consider too the specific effects of policies of strict active enclosure on female monastic communities.[31] While we might examine more closely the degree of female autonomy within the double monastery,[32] the abbess' more literal domestic confinement increases her answerability to the abbot and provides an instance of the consolidation of kinship-based (whether matrilineal or patrilineal) societies under the advancing civil state. The new isolation of and emphasis on the "household" as social unit, as opposed to the more problematically diffuse (and harder-to-tax) kin-group, gives the male head of household, whether social or religious, power to control female production.[33]

Recent studies of material culture offer clear spatial images of a similar pattern, but raise additional questions about the relative status of monastic women within the overall development of restrictions on women as a sex and as a class. In her analyses of male and female monastic household layouts in the later medieval period (which raise the possibility of analogous work on the Anglo-Saxon period), archaeologist Roberta Gilchrist argues that spatial organization and design layout of the household "are both generated by and active in perpetuating a societal ideal" and that "[i]n this model, gender domains would be formulated by the kinship structures specific to a social and economic mode of production."[34] In general, nuns' cloisters were more difficult of access from the surrounding precincts than were the male counterparts, but Gilchrist also notes a specific difference: "In nunneries the *dorter*, the communal sleeping area of the nuns was the most secluded. In the monasteries, the chapter house, the heart of the community where daily business was transacted, was the most inaccessible to the external secular world."[35] Although the seclusion of the male monastic place of business might be variously theorized, the inaccessibility of the female sleeping quarters suggests an analogy to the restrictive privatization of the domestic sphere. Gilchrist argues against one contemporary feminist view that celebrates the monastic life as freedom from sexualized domestic oppression, asserting that "medieval nuns were contained within a private domain, not dissimilar to that of their secular counterparts, which emphasized their chaste fidelity as Brides of Christ."[36]

Clearly, the archaeological analysis of gender domains has much to contribute to expanding our literal and symbolic understandings of women's movement and activities, but it also can help to diagram the developments in their connections to modes of production. The spatial containment of women, Gilchrist contends, is an indication of rank and status, and here we might place the active female monastic cloister on a par with the middle-class Victorian woman's parlor: in both cases their architectural segregation demonstrates the "surplus labour of women who are alienated from their role in economic production."[37] Schulenburg also reminds us that denial of access to certain spaces is parallel to denial of access to cultural production when she catalogues the Carolingian reform councils' strict exclusion of women from "sacred space," now designated as "public." This exclusion from the public sphere contrasts with the purported freedom of the "undifferentiated space of the great hall."[38]

As we map out and attempt to understand the cultural and economic terms of a hypothesized decline in women's rights and freedoms in the Anglo-Saxon period, we must also try to describe the "height" from which they fell, and return to the "Golden Age" hypothesis, which is still a major force in feminist histories of monasticism.[39] What, if anything, was materially different in the condition of women and in their relation to cultural production in the early period, when Hild apparently ruled at Whitby, travelled freely, and voiced her opinions in public at important religious and political events?

Schulenburg, for example, makes the point that the transitional social "fluidity"—when lines of power had not yet been rigidly drawn up—and the decentralization of political and religious authority in early English society allowed women greater access to and control over means of production, whether cultural or agricultural. Public and private spheres coalesced in the "undifferentiated space" inhabited by the politically powerful family and women moved freely within this space. This view is supported by anthropologists Stephanie Coontz and Peta Henderson, who emphasize class as well as gender distinctions in describing the developing civil state's cooptation of forms of authority: "The new public, hierarchical nature of authority put an end to the informal and delegated powers that aristocratic women had exercised by virtue of their family position."[40] Aristocratic status and operational kinship ties are here assumed to be necessary bases for women's realization and exercise of power, and could bear greater emphasis. Any discussion of female monasticism throughout the period should but too rarely does entail a consideration of class. Hild and her peers are not only women: they are, for the most part, high-ranking women. Moreover, the specific status of the aristocratic woman within a patriarchal social system has been variously theorized by feminist critics interested in the coincidental developments of gender and class oppression. Broadly speaking, the aristocratic woman may be perceived as having different interests and hence consciousness that separate her from lower class women, and these differences obscure the commonality of oppression of both men and women of the lower class; or, rather, the lines may be drawn somewhat differently:

> . . . the contradiction is between some men and *all* women as a social group. There are no contradictory interests among women in either kin-corporate or aristocratic class society. Aristocratic women do not share the socio-economic status of aristocratic men, as they do not have independent access to the means of production. . . . Like high-

ranking servants, aristocratic women are artificially attached to the class of their husband or father, while in fact they belong to the dominated classes of society, even if they are not conscious of this.[41]

Hild's own consciousness of her specific relation to, and degree of complicity in, patriarchal modes of production, and how she might have valued and perceived her own labor are, of course, the most mysterious questions in our enquiry. And the best answer we can give is to keep asking questions of the existing cultural record. Instead of celebrating the aristocratic woman's exercise of power, we can critically examine the conditions of the exercise, and remember the contradictions and tensions generated by the very conditions of her status.

Kinship, therefore, is one area of research where we can continue to question the cultural record and define more particularly the parameters of the new feminist myth of a "Golden Age" of female monasticism. We can, for example, look at some of the royal mothers represented by Bede, and review the series of conversion scenarios that are scattered throughout the *History.* The conversion of the Kentish kingdom provides the first, and perhaps most fundamental example. Augustine, arriving in Kent to convert the English, finds a royal family already sympathetic to Christianity to the extent that Bertha, the Frankish wife of Æthelberht I, is a Christian (1.25). Bede, however, does not stress the importance Bertha might have had in this Kentish court, in spite of the fact that Bertha and Æthelberht are the parents of quite a remarkable dynasty of Christian saints—mainly female saints—that link Kent with Northumbria and Mercia.[42]

A similar process is evident to a more marked extent in Bede's account of the conversion of the Northumbrian kingdoms. Edwin's conversion was certainly facilitated by his marriage to Æthelberht's daughter, the Christian Æthelburg, who brings Paulinus with her and whose daughter Eanflæd was one of the first to be baptized in Northumbria (*EH* 2.9). Bede takes pains to record the two papal letters that urge conversion on Edwin, both the one written to the king, and the one addressed to Æthelburg, which emphasizes the importance of true Christian marriage and her role in Edwin's conversion (2.10, 11). Yet the real drama of Edwin's conversion—the well-known accounts of Edwin's dream and of the advice of the high priest Coifi—excludes Æthelburg altogether (2.12–14). The conversion of kings, as we might expect, is of far greater importance than the conversion of queens—however much we might wish to speak of the "power of women through the family."[43] In the case of the conversion of the West Saxons, Bede tells us that Oswald of Northumbria was present at Cynigils's baptism, and cemented the alliance by taking Cynigils's daughter as his wife, but Bede does not tell us her name (3.7), and similar dynamics are present in the subsequent accounts of the conversions of the Middle Angles (3.21) and the South Saxons (4.13), where both queens were already Christian—the women's religious correctness was less important to Bede than the dynastic allegiances cemented by these newly Christian kings.

It has become conventional among feminist historians to point to the kinship ties of the royal women who, as abbesses, nuns, and saints, achieve a considerable degree of prominence in this period. Hild herself is closely associated with the royal families of both Northumbria and East Anglia, and her monastery of Whitby even more closely tied to the royal house of Edwin (the church there provides the royal burial ground; Eanflæd retires there, and Ælfflæd succeeds after Hild, *EH* 3.24). Whitby seems to have taken some pains to tie Edwin to its other benefactor, Gregory, and this may have influenced the dominance of his cult over Hild's.[44] Royal monasteries do indeed stay in the family (in more ways than one), and the connections that we seek between these remarkable women may in fact obscure the evident political interests of the royal families. It is possible to piece together a considerable network of female contacts and kinship affiliations for the early period of Anglo-Saxon monasticism, but each series of connections needs examination on its own merits. While we may balk at the description of "high-ranking servant," the status and power of such aristocratic women is clearly coopted in the service of patriarchy.[45]

Female monasticism is above all a partnership between royal and ecclesiastical interests—at least as it is presented in the historical accounts. The royal women, we might assume, derived considerable benefit from their kinship affiliations, not simply to protect property interests, but perhaps to cement an alternative female caste, principally comprising mothers and daughters. Given the patriarchal structuring of such accounts, however, the aristocratic caste may be a ghetto.

By looking more closely at women's writing in the period, this issue of an alternative female caste/ghetto can be defined against patriarchal versions of women's experience. Texts written by women are few and far between in Anglo-Saxon England, but there does exist a notable series of Latin letters written by women both in England and on the continent, the majority of which are addressed to Saint Boniface. Critical discussion has mainly concentrated on the (supposedly inferior) Latin rhetoric of these letters, although it has largely neglected the complementary issue of the extent to which female voices and experience may be obscured by such institutionalized forms of writing.[46] More importantly, the letters constitute a body of evidence for female attitudes toward kinship with relevance for our understanding of a female dynasty of mothers and daughters. The women in these letters are often concerned about the loss of kinship ties and seek to replace them with spiritual ties, using virtually the same language.[47] In epistle 13, Ecgburg laments her separation from her sister, Wetburga (who is in Rome), and the death of their brother, Oshere; she turns to Boniface for spiritual consolation. In epistle 14, a letter jointly written by a mother, Eangyth, and her daughter Bugge, to Boniface, to discuss a possible voyage to Rome (eventually undertaken by Bugge, after the death of her mother), the alienation of women from kin is even more pronounced: the letter stresses that the women have neither son, nor brother, nor father, nor uncle. Leoba's first extant letter to Boniface, epistle 29, shows her to be in a similar predicament and offers an interesting solution. This letter, which also shows Leoba keen to have advice about her poetic skills, recounts how she has lost both father and mother and is therefore writing to her distant relative, Boniface, to claim fraternal as well as spiritual ties. Leoba, in fact, subsequently joins Boniface's mission. The contrast of Leoba's situation with that of Berhtgyth as described in the latter's correspondence with her brother Baldhard, from whom she is apparently permanently estranged, is pointed.[48] It is hard to escape the conclusion that women, exiled from their kin for whatever reasons, seek the solace of real exile and the life of the ascetic, or *peregrinus*. In fact, several of the women who did join Boniface in such an exile were actually related to him, like Leoba.[49] Hild too originally wished to join her sister at Chelles, and it would appear that this was the closest kin she had.[50]

The evidence of these letters, however tentative, suggests an alternative way of interpreting the notion of a separate female caste within Anglo-Saxon monasticism and within its evident patriarchy. The saintly royal women maintain the family, even within their cloistered environment, and their family maintains them, with an eye firmly on dynastic interests. These monasteries and the cults of royal women are supported financially by their families and descendants, within the ideology of the Christian ruling family—be it Northumbrian, Kentish, Mercian, or West Saxon. They remain Anglo-Saxon mothers, whether literally, spiritually or both, and they mother patriarchal dynasties that in many cases promote the spread of, or help maintain, Christianity. Interpreted in this light, it is possible to understand the cultural importance of suppressing mothering. What we witness in Bede's account of Hild's role is an appropriation and a rewriting of mothering, a re-inscription of the feminine within the parameters of patriarchy.

Hild's specific situation once again raises larger general questions when we consider the implications of this re-inscription, and the many places that we may find "mothering" or literal and metaphorical forms of female experience rewritten throughout the period. Whether we read Bede's gendered accounts of Hild and Cædmon as unique or as paradigmatic of the ways in which Anglo-Saxon writers constructed events of cultural production, we can ask the same question of men's writing that we asked of women's: to what extent do institutionalized forms of rhetoric condition and require the re-inscription of the feminine? Asser's celebrated account of Alfred learning vernacular poetry from his mother, Osburh (which is itself paralleled by the continental example of Theodoric's daughter, Amalasuntha, and her plans for the education of her son, Alaric) offers an important counterpoint to our discussion of Hild.[51] Asser's masculinist enterprise emphasizes Alfred's precocious mental skills, revealed in competition with his brothers, and Asser omits Osburh's name.[52]

The formal demands of the hagiographic genre where women's deaths take precedence over their lives can be addressed in similar fashion. Saints' lives say as much, if not more, about the spiritual and cultural preoccupations of their hagiographers and intended readers as they do about their ostensible subjects, and Bede's "Lives" of Ælthelburg and Æthelthryth are cases in point.[53] The narrative process of isolating (in cloister or on pedestal) the female saint obscures, as we have already suggested, her relationships with other women, which in turn obscures the possibility of reconstructing women's experience of kinship. In her discussion of the later Anglo-Saxon royal female saints, for example, Susan Ridyard notes some ways in which the hagiographer casts saintly mothers and daughters or sisters in a competitive relation to each other, vying for greater degrees of piety, as in the cases of the mother, Werburg, and the daughter, Eormenhild, or the sisters, Seaxburg and Æthelthryth. Working from these hagiographical sources, Ridyard herself construes the mother-daughter, sister-sister relationship as either political or spiritual, paying little attention to other ways of constructing kinship and connections between women, as her discussion of Edith and her mother, Wulfthryth, indicates.[54]

Furthermore, the hagiographical emphasis on virginity and spiritual maternity conceals and devalues, according to Julia Kristeva, not only real connections between women but also the value of reality—including its threatening aspect to both men *and* women—of physical maternity. She calls particular attention to the arrogation of the maternal function by male mystics as a basis for cultural forms of arrogation of the maternal principle;

other forms of appropriation of the female body for the cultural and political purposes of patriarchal religion have been well documented by recent
research in the later medieval period, especially by Karma Lochrie.[55] In the
light of these new symbolic frameworks, which theorize the appropriation
of the female body, we could ask what happens to the bodies themselves.
We might reexamine the implications of, for example, the eminently
"displaced" body of Saint Edburga, one of the most famous (i.e., most
recorded) women of our period. She is not only disinterred on several occasions but also divided up, the parts of her body signifying equally political
and divine protection—the edge, however, goes to those who host the
greater part:

> Although she has been divided into two shares in her relics, yet her
> virtue abounds in every particle: it offers a superiority to the nuns of
> Winchester, since the greater part of her body is there, while the oft-
> recited glory of her heavenly miracles gives lustre to the monks of
> Pershore.[56]

Ridyard questions the veracity of this account, suggesting that it was written "to provide the Pershore relics with a history."[57] Whether or not this is
in fact the case, it is precisely our point that such stories and such metaphors
comprise the cultural record, and *do* contribute to writing the history of
women's bodies and experiences.

   We return, finally, to a question we raised in the first part of this essay:
to what degree might the suppression and rewriting of feminine process
parallel the "disappearance" of the oral trace? How far is it the case that Anglo-Saxon accounts of the production of texts suppress process? Can we
usefully conceptualize these forms of suppression or absence in similar
ways? The complexity with which accounts of the cultural record are
overdetermined is evident from the ways other Anglo-Saxon male writers
present the act of writing. In many cases—Asser, Alfred and Ælfric spring
to mind—the product that is the text takes precedence over the process of
composition.[58] Masculinity is associated with, and subordinate to, the fin-
ished product, it would appear; a point that is borne out of Bede's structuring of Cædmon's story.

   One striking parallel to Bede's treatment of Hild is Aldhelm's *Enigma*
30, concerning the letters of the alphabet. Although Aldhelm borrows the
basic idea from Isidore, Katherine O'Brien O'Keeffe points out that the
"metaphorical development is all his own."[59] Here the instruments of literacy are constructed as women *sine voce*, as "seventeen voiceless sisters" who
nonetheless offer "ready words" to those who know how to use/read them.

In a number of Aldhelm's *enigmata*, O'Keeffe discovers a pattern where the ignorant instrumentality of the vehicle of literacy begins to emerge: the bookcase in *Enigma* 89 "stuffed with books, can learn nothing from them. Though dead, it has innards which are pregnant (*praecordia gestant*) with volumes it can never enjoy." O'Keeffe's discussion focuses on the silencing of the processes of orality, and calls attention to the violence inherent in these metaphorical forms of silencing and appropriation—an imaging of violence, moreover, which she suggests is an English addition to the Latin tradition. That these silenced "vehicles" of literacy become feminized, however, is of particular interest to our argument, as is the idea of the erosion and effacement of presence before the onset of a written cultural record, which itself erodes the issue of female literacy.

"But every technology exacts its price," O'Keeffe writes. "The power to preserve is gained at the cost of the intimacy of words. Through writing, words, divorced from oral source and substance, are conveyed by silence and absence. Writing becomes a technology of alienation."[60] While we do not want to fall prey to either a privileging of, or nostalgia for, voice and presence, nor would we want to isolate or victimize the feminine, it seems that such images and accounts resonate with our discussion of the *processes* by which the "disappearance" of Hild is culturally enacted. When we struggle to hear or reconstruct Hild's voice at the great Synod of Whitby, for example, we might remember O'Keeffe's suggestion that "[i]n the oral world, knowledge is gained and displayed in verbal struggle."[61] Furthermore, the notion of the codification of the processes of literacy might be paralleled to the development of public/private divisions within society: it appears as difficult to codify the scribal relationship to the text in an oral/literate transitional period as it is the actual power of women in the periods of social transition that we have outlined above, but our ways of thinking about each issue may prove profitably interchangeable at the levels of metaphor and process.

In conclusion, it has been our aim to introduce and initiate questions in this essay rather than offer a program for solutions. If contemporary scholars and historians, following in the wake of all who knew her in Bede's time, continue to call Hild "mother," then let us do so with a heightened sense of the term, and of the complexities of its cultural determination. Let us name Hild, and her social role, advisedly, within the context and confines of the cultures that produced her and continue to produce her, and let us continue to construct a broader understanding of relations of cultural production in the Old English period and subsequently that would seek to hear how she might name herself.

Notes

1. Bertram Colgrave and R. A. B. Mynors, ed. and trans., *Bede's Ecclesiastical History of the English People* (Oxford: Clarendon, 1969). This text will be cited as *EH* followed by book and chapter numbers.

2. Frank M. Stenton, "The Historical Bearing of Place-Name Studies: The Place of Women in Anglo-Saxon Society," reprinted in *New Readings on Women in Old English Literature*, edited by Helen Damico and Alexandra Hennessey Olsen (Bloomington: Indiana University Press, 1990), 79–88, at 79; see also Peter Hunter Blair, *An Introduction to Anglo-Saxon England* (Cambridge: Cambridge University Press, 1959), 25; Patrick Sims-Williams, *Religion and Literature in Western England, 600–800*, Cambridge Studies in Anglo-Saxon England 3 (Cambridge: Cambridge University Press, 1990), 102.

3. Allen J. Frantzen, *Desire for Origins: New Language, Old English, and Teaching the Tradition* (New Brunswick, NJ: Rutgers University Press, 1990), 142.

4. Frantzen, *Desire for Origins*, 18–20.

5. Kevin S. Kiernan, "Reading Cædmon's 'Hymn' with Someone Else's Glosses," *Representations* 32 (1990): 157–74; Martin Irvine, "Medieval Textuality and the Archaeology of Textual Culture," *Speaking Two Languages: Traditional Disciplines and Contemporary Theory in Medieval Studies*, ed. Allen J. Frantzen (Albany: SUNY Press, 1991), 181–210, at 197–99; Seth Lerer, *Literacy and Power in Anglo-Saxon Literature* (Lincoln, NE: University of Nebraska Press, 1991), 30–60. Arguing that he is realigning "the study of Cædmon by situating it in the narrative trajectory of Book 4" (33), Lerer relates Bede's narrative of Cædmon to his account of Imma (*EH* 4.22), thus eliding the chapter on Hild altogether. Lerer's account of Bede's interest in the signifying power of Christian letters as opposed to the dead letters of the Imma narrative is indeed important, but Bede's book 4 is also arguably the book of female abbesses, as we suggest below, note 53.

6. Christine E. Fell, "Hild, Abbess of Streonæshalch," *Hagiography and Medieval Literature. A Symposium*, ed. Hans Bekker-Nielsen, Peter Foote, Jørgen Højgaard Jørgensen and Tore Nyberg (Odense: Odense University Press, 1981), 76–99. See also Jane Chance, *Woman as Hero in Old English Literature* (Syracuse, NY: Syracuse University Press, 1986), 53–64; Joan Nicholson, "*Feminae gloriosae:* Women in the Age of Bede," *Medieval Women*, ed. Derek Baker, Studies in Church History, Subsidia 1 (Oxford: Basil Blackwell), 15–29; Jo Ann McNamara and Suzanne Wempel, "The Power of Women Through the Family in Medieval Europe, 500–1100," *Feminist Studies* 1 (1973): 126–41, and "Sanctity and Power: The Dual Pursuit of Early Medieval Women," *Becoming Visible: Women in European History*, ed. Renate Bridenthal and Claudia Koonz (Boston: Houghton Mifflin, 1977), 90–118.

7. Britton J. Harwood, "The Plot of *Piers Plowman* and the Contradictions of Feudalism," in *Speaking Two Languages*, ed. Frantzen, 91–114 (n21).

8. *Anglo-Saxon Women and the Church*, by Stephanie Hollis (Woodbridge, Suffolk: Boydell, 1992), came too late to our attention to be considered here, although we

strongly recommend that it be read in conjunction with this essay. Our thesis complements but does not replicate Lerer's in *Literacy and Power in Anglo-Saxon Literature*,
which does not address the question of female engagement in the production of literacy, nor examine female access to the social structures and institutions empowered by
literacy. While there is as yet no detailed study of this phenomenon in the Anglo-
Saxon period, see the summaries of basic information by: Sims-Williams, *Religion and
Literature*, 184–242; Christine E. Fell, *Women in Anglo-Saxon England* (Oxford: Basil
Blackwell, 1984), 109–29, and "Some Implications of the Boniface Correspondence,"
in *New Readings on Women in Old English Literature*, ed. Damico and Olsen, 29–43; Patrizia Lendinara, "The World of Anglo-Saxon Learning," *The Cambridge Companion
to Old English Literature*, ed. Malcolm Godden and Michael Lapidge (Cambridge:
Cambridge University Press, 1991), 264–81, especially 270–71; and Janet Nelson,
"Women and the Word in the Early Middle Ages," *Women in the Church*, ed. W. J.
Sheils and Diana Wood, *Studies in Church History* 27 (1990): 53–78. For a useful survey of female literacy in the Carolingian period that emphasizes the possibility that
women acted as a conduit for education within the aristocratic family, see Rosamond
McKitterick, *The Carolingians and the Written Word* (Cambridge: Cambridge Univer-
sity Press, 1989), 223–27.

9. Kiernan, "Reading Cædmon's 'Hymn'" and Frantzen, *Desire for Origins*, 142.

10. Dorothy Whitelock, "The Old English Bede," *Proceedings of the British Academy* 48 (1962): 57–90, at 58–78, but see Janet M. Bately, "Old English Prose Before
and During the Reign of Alfred," *ASE* 17 (1988): 93–138, at 103–4.

11. Katherine O'Brien O'Keeffe, "Orality and the Developing Text of Cædmon's
Hymn," *Speculum* 62 (1987): 1–20; and *Visible Song: Transitional Literacy in Old English
Verse*, Cambridge Studies in Anglo-Saxon England 4 (Cambridge: Cambridge Uni-
versity Press, 1990), 23–46.

12. Frantzen, *Desire for Origins*, 144.

13. Thomas Miller, ed. *The Old English Version of Bede's Ecclesiastical History of The
English People*, Part I.2. EETS 96 (Oxford: Oxford University Press, 1959), 342–48.

14. Sims-Williams, *Religion and Literature* (185), discusses the slender evidence
for the sixth, Tatfrith, who died before he could be consecrated bishop.

15. Hild is never referred to as a virgin by Bede, and her more usual designation is
by institution, "Abbess": for a speculative discussion of Bede's reasons, see Fell, "Hild,
Abbess of Streonæshalch," 78–81. Fell also calls attention to Bede's "untypical com-
pliment that all who knew her called her mother" (86), which is echoed by Eddius
Stephanus in his *Life of Wilfrid*: "matre piissima" (Bertram Colgrave, ed. *The Life of
Bishop Wilfrid by Eddius Stefanus* [Cambridge: Cambridge University Press, 1927, repr
1985], 20). This detail is not found in the account of Hild's life in the *Old English Martyrology*, which also omits discussion of her educational role at Whitby; see J. E. Cross,
"A Lost Life of Hilda of Whitby: The Evidence of the *Old English Martyrology*," *The
Early Middle Ages, Acta* 6 (1979): 21–43. Although "mother" is a conventional appellation for an abbess, Bede's accounts of other female abbesses, such as Æthelburg (*EH*
4.7–11), have a different resonance; see note 53 below.

16. Quoted from Frantzen, *Desire for Origins*, 142.

17. Peter Hunter Blair, "Whitby as a Centre of Learning in the Seventh Century," *Learning and Literature in Anglo-Saxon England: Studies Presented to Peter Clemoes on the Occasion of His Sixty-Fifth Birthday*, ed. Michael Lapidge and Helmut Gneuss (Cambridge: Cambridge University Press, 1985), 3–32, at 3 and 25.

18. Colgrave, *The Life of Bishop Wilfrid*, 20–21.

19. Fell, "Hild, Abbess of Streonæshalch," 87–88. The identification of Hild with one Hildeburh (possibly the full form of Hild's name according to Fell, ibid., 78) in the litany of saints in London, B.L., Cotton Galba A. xiv, edited by Michael Lapidge in *Anglo-Saxon Litanies of the Saints*, Henry Bradshaw Society 106 (London: Boydell, 1991), 168, is mere speculation on present evidence.

20. Cross, "A Lost Life of Hilda of Whitby."

21. The post-Conquest evidence is surveyed by Fell, "Hild, Abbess of Streonæshalch," 88–94, to which should be added the seventeenth-century *Life*, apparently translated from the *Nova Angliae Legendum* into English by Thomas Astley; see C. Horstmann, ed. *The Lives of Women Saints of Our Contrie of England, also some other Liues of Holie Women Written by Some of the Auncient Fathers*, EETS 86 (London: Trübner, 1886), 56–58.

22. The frequently rehearsed evidence for Latin learning at Whitby—the earliest *Life of Gregory*, Ælfflæd's Letter to an unknown abbess of Pfalzel, and the archaeological presence of styli and book-clasps—is conveniently summarized by Sims-Williams, *Religion and Literature*, 185–86, in his account of the scholarly Oftfor, who left Whitby to join Theodore's school at Canterbury.

23. Frantzen, *Desire for Origins*, 142.

24. Jane Tibbetts Schulenburg, "Female Sanctity: Public and Private Roles, ca. 500–1100," in *Women and Power in the Middle Ages*, ed. Mary Erler and Maryanne Kowaleski (Athens: University of Georgia Press, 1988), 102–25, at 110.

25. Blair, *An Introduction to Anglo-Saxon England*, 148; Fell, "Hild, Abbess of Streonæshalch," 85. While the evidence for Hild's acquisition of land for Whitby is ambiguous (*EH* 3.24), it is perhaps worthy of note that the Old English translation states that she "gebohte tyn hida lond hire in æhte in þære stówe" (Miller, *Old English Version of Bede*, 236, lines 31–32). Many early monasteries were founded by royal grants of land: for examples, see Sims-Williams, *Religion and Literature*, 92–97, 103–4.

26. The extent of female governance of these early foundations is difficult to establish since, for one thing, the practice of following a particular rule was not firmly instituted in England until the tenth-century Benedictine Reform: Whitby, for example, stipulated the commonality of all possessions (*EH* 4.24), which does not appear to have been the case at Much Wenlock (Sims-Williams, *Religion and Literature*, 117–18). Although the *Regularis concordia*, edited by Dom Thomas Symons (London: Thomas Nelson, 1953), one of the principal policy documents of the tenth-century reforms, is written for both monks and nuns, it is notoriously vague on provisions for female religious life, as is indicated by the revisions that replace "abbot" with "abbess" in the fragment in Ms. Cambridge, Corpus Christi 201. Post-Conquest evidence is

more suggestive. Heloise, for example, notes that the Rule of Benedict can only be fully observed by men and accordingly requests that Abelard provide a rule for the nuns at the Paraclete; see J. T. Muckle, "The Letter of Heloise on Religious Life and Abelard's First Reply," *MS* 17 (1955): 240–81, at 242. Abelard's reply, while insisting on the authority of the abbess in her community (and suggesting that it is the role of the chantress to copy books, or make suitable arrangements for copying), is equally insistent that ultimate authority rests not with the abbess, but with her male superiors, the abbot and male ecclesiasts; see T. P. McLaughlin, "Abelard's Rule for Religious Women," *MS* 18 (1956): 241–92.

27. Anglo-Saxon evidence for female teachers and scribes is also hard to interpret. Hild is certainly praised as an instructor, but it remains unclear who actually educated Cædmon. Evidence from the "Boniface" correspondence, discussed below, is relevant here; it is edited by Michael Tangl, *Die Briefe des Heiligen Bonifatius und Lullus*, MGH, Epistolae Selectae I (Berlin, 1955), and translated by E. Kylie, *The English Correspondence of Saint Boniface* (London, 1911). Boniface's letter (epistle 35) to Eadburg—possibly Abbess of Wimborne or Thanet, according to Sims-Williams, "An Unpublished Seventh- or Eighth-Century Anglo-Latin Letter in Boulogne-sur-Mer MS 74," *MÆ* 48 (1979): 1–22—asks her to copy Peter's Epistles in letters of gold and thanks her for other gifts of books and vestments, but does not illuminate us as to who did the copying. It is perhaps significant that we have no named female scribes—in contrast to the continental evidence cited by B. Bischoff, "Die Kölner Nonnenhandschriften und das Skriptorium von Chelles," *Mittelalterlichen Studien* I (Stuttgart, 1966), 16–34, and McKitterick, *Carolingians and the Written Word*, 257. Evidence such as Aldhelm's *De virginitate* for the nuns at Barking, or the provisions made by Jerome in his Letter to Laeta, a popular text for female education in the early Middle Ages according to M. L. W. Laistner (*Thought and Letters in Western Europe A.D. 500–900* [1931; reprinted Ithaca: Cornell University Press, 1957], 47–48), suggests at least the notion of a separate curriculum for women. We are on firmer ground with the examples of female ownership of books (for example, Cuthswith's ownership of Jerome's commentary on Ecclesiastes, discussed by Sims-Williams, *Religion and Literature*, 190–91); readers (particularly in the cases of early prayer books—the Harley Fragment and the Book of Nunnaminster); and correspondence, as in the "Boniface" letters discussed below—though even here we might ponder the significance of the male postscript by a certain Ealdbeorht to epistle 13 (he is also known from epistle 129), which may indicate that he was the scribe of both these female-authored letters (Sims-Williams, ibid., 224–25).

28. Schulenburg, "Women's Monastic Communities, 500–1100: Patterns of Expansion and Decline," *Signs* 14 (1988–89): 261–92, at 291–92.

29. Schulenburg also raises the interesting and as yet largely unresearched issue of women's relation to rural/urban and peacetime/wartime economies (ibid., 290).

30. Recent studies develop Engels's evolutionary perspective on the decline of women's rights and the parallel emergence of social hierarchies; Friedrich Engels, *The Origin of the Family, Private Property and the State* (New York: International, 1972). For

examples, see Rayna R. Reiter, ed. *Towards an Anthropology of Women* (New York: Monthly Review Press, 1975); S. Ortner and H. Whitehead, eds., *Sexual Meanings: The Cultural Construction of Gender and Sexuality* (Cambridge: Cambridge University Press, 1981); and Stephanie Coontz and Peta Henderson, "Property Forms, Political Power, and Female Labour in the Origins of Class and State Societies," *Women's Work, Men's Property*, ed. Coontz and Henderson (London: Verso, 1986), 108–55.

31. See Schulenburg, "Female Sanctity: Public and Private Roles, ca. 500–1100," and "Strict Active Enclosure and its Effects on the Female Monastic Experience," in *Medieval Religious Women 1: Distant Echoes*, ed. John A. Nichols and Lillian Thomas Shank (Kalamazoo: Cistercian Publications, 1984), 51–86.

32. Male priests, of course, were essential to these communities since only they could perform the necessary sacerdotal duties. Consider also the evidence for relationships between bishops and female religious: for example, Ælfflæd, who benefited from the advice of Bishop Trumwine, is also closely associated with Bishop Wilfrid (as is Eanflæd, her mother, and Æthelthryth; see Colgrave, *The Life of Bishop Wilfrid*, 6–9, 40–47); Hild herself is at least initially guided by Bishop Aídán (*EH* 4.23). The account of Wimborne in the *Life of Leoba* by Rudolf of Fulda stresses the extraordinary measures that the first abbess, Cuthburh, took to exclude even bishops; see Rudolph of Fulda, G. Waitz, ed., *Vita Leobae*, MGH, Scriptorium 15, pt. 1, 118–31, and the translation by C. H. Talbot, *The Anglo-Saxon Missionaries in Germany* (London: Sheed & Ward, 1954). For a survey of the degrees of strain in the relationship between the early abbesses and the bishops, see Sims-Williams, *Religion and Literature*, 138–43. While Archbishop Theodore of Canterbury rules in favor of dual monasteries since they are the established practice in England, there is a touch of reluctance in the wording of his decision; see Arthur West Haddan and William Stubbs, ed. *Councils and Ecclesiastical Documents Relating to Great Britain and Ireland*, 3 (1871; reprinted Oxford: Oxford University Press, 1964), 195. Outside the ecclesiastical sphere, it is important to stress that these women appear to have been dependent, at least in part, on royal grants to found their monasteries in the first place. Ælfflæd, for example, is dedicated to God by her father, Oswiu, together with twelve grants of land for foundations in Deira and Bernicia (*EH* 3.24); see also note 25 above. If we add this tentative evidence to the evident patriarchal slant of the cultural record, it is hard indeed not to consider these women instrumental in promoting their patriarchal religion.

33. For further discussion of this point, see Coontz and Henderson, "Property Forms, Political Power," 150–53. Many early "family" monasteries enjoyed ecclesiastical tax-immunities that clearly defined the status of the house relative to royal and episcopal obligations. The advantages of such immunities were mixed since other obligations were expected in return; see Sims-Williams, *Religion and Literature*, 134–37, for an introductory summary.

34. Roberta Gilchrist, "The Spatial Archeology of Gender Domains: A Case Study of Medieval English Nunneries," *Archeological Review from Cambridge* 7 (1988): 21–28, at 22.

35. Ibid., 26.

36. Ibid., 27. For alternative views, see Marilynn Desmond, "The Voice of Exile: Feminist Literary History and the Anonymous Anglo-Saxon Elegy," *Critical Inquiry* 16 (1990): 572–90; Jane Marie Leuke, "The Unique Experience of Anglo-Saxon Nuns," *Medieval Religious Women 2: Peaceweavers*, ed. Lillian Thomas Shank and John A. Nichols (Kalamazoo: Cistercian Publications, 1987), 55–65; Joan Nicholson, "*Feminae gloriosae*"; McNamara and Wempel, "The Power of Women Through the Family," and "Sanctity and Power."

37. Gilchrist, 25.

38. Schulenburg, "Female Sanctity," 115 and 104.

39. Judith M. Bennett has recently offered a critique of this governing concept for the later Middle Ages; see "Medieval Women, Modern Women: Across the Great Divide," *Culture and History 1350–1600: Essays on English Communities, Identities and Writing*, ed. David Aers (Detroit: Wayne State University Press, 1992): 147–75.

40. Coontz and Henderson, "Property Forms, Political Power," 151.

41. Ibid., 142.

42. D. W. Rollason, *The Mildrith Legend: A Study in Early Medieval Hagiography in England* (Leicester: Leicester University Press, 1982), 9–14.

43. Quoted from McNamara and Wempel's title, "The Power of Women Through the Family in Medieval Europe, 500–1100."

44. As argued by Rollason, *Saints and Relics in Anglo-Saxon England* (Oxford: Blackwell, 1989), 115.

45. Quoted from Coontz and Henderson, "Property Forms, Political Power," 142. In this connection, consider the example of the Mildrith legend, painstakingly reconstructed by Rollason, *The Mildrith Legend*. Æthelberht I and Bertha of Kent are the parents of a royal dynasty, well-known for its super-abundance of saints, many of whom are women. In this network, we detect the political strategies of an aggressively ambitious family, actively forging links with the kingdoms of Northumbria and the Mercians, as well as the East Anglians. Indeed, as Rollason points out (41), the peculiarly genealogical character of the Mildrith legend, particularly in its pre-eleventh-century phase, serves the interests of the dynasty above and beyond the saintly royal women (many of whom were mothers) who distinguish its line. Similar strategies are also at work in the later royal cults of the West Saxon royal families investigated by Susan J. Ridyard, *The Royal Saints of Anglo-Saxon England: A Study of West Saxon and East Anglian Cults* (Cambridge: Cambridge University Press, 1988). The cults of Edburg, Edith of Wilton, and the revival of the cult of Æthelthryth of Ely (which also celebrates Seaxburg and Eormenhild) owe more to the complex interests of the interests of the royal families and the Church, than to their importance as sacred royal women (96–97, 169, 179–96). It is intriguing to note that the *Lives* of these royal women (many of which survive in post-Conquest recensions—a fact that may be more significant than Ridyard is inclined to suggest) appear to play down their aristocratic connections (see, for example, 82–92).

46. The "Boniface" correspondence is edited by Michael Tangl and translated by E. Kylie (see note 27 above). The debate between Peter Dronke, *Women Writers of the*

Middle Ages: A Critical Study of Texts from Perpetua to Marguerite Porete (Cambridge: Cambridge University Press, 1984), 30–35, and Fell, "Some Implications of the Boniface Correspondence," *New Readings on Women in Old English Literature*, 29–43, centers on the extent to which these letters may be read as personal, private, and emotional, or formal, public, and rhetorical. Further research, however, is required to establish just how conventional is their language and to what extent this rhetoric can be said to be gendered. For example, how formulaic is the Saxon nun Huneberc's extreme self-deprecation as she sets out to arrogate a "masculine prerogative" and write the life of a saint, as documented by Schulenburg, "Saints' Lives as a Source for the History of Women, 500–1100," in *Medieval Women and the Sources of Medieval History*, ed. Joel T. Rosenthal (Athens: University of Georgia Press, 1990), 285–320, at 295. For a recent assessment of the Latinity of epistle 13, by Ecgburg, in comparison with that of Burginda, see Sims-Williams, *Religion and Literature*, 211–42, who describes both as "beginner's essays" (242).

47. The burden of the loss of kin is not exclusive to the female letters of the Boniface mission: the letter written by Lull, Denehard, and Burghard to Abbess Cyneburg (Ep. 49) offers the deaths of mother, father, and other kin as a reason for joining the mission. The most dramatic example of rhetorical and affective "play" with kinship ties is surely that of Heloise: "Domino suo immo patri, coniugi suo immo fratri, ancilla suo immo filia, ipsius uxor immo soror, abaelardo, Heloisa" (edited by J. T. Muckle, "The Personal Letters Between Abelard and Heloise," *MS* 15 [1953]: 47–94, at 68): "To her lord, or better, her father; to her husband, or better, her brother; his handmaid, or better, his daughter; his wife, or better, his sister—to Abelard, Heloise," translated by Peter Dronke, *Women Writers*, 112.

48. For discussion, see Dronke, *Women Writers*, 30–32. The stylistic connections between Berhtgyth's letters and the expression of exile and isolation in the so-called Old English Elegies are noted by Dronke (31) and by Fell ("Some Implications of the Boniface Correspondence," 40), but would merit further investigation.

49. In addition to Leoba, who claims kinship with Boniface on her mother's side, we might add Tecla, Abbess of Kitzingen, also related to Leoba; see Wilhelm Levison, *England and the Continent in the Eighth Century* (1946; reprinted Oxford: Clarendon, 1966), 76–77. Fell, "Some Implications of the Boniface Correspondence," 39, points out that Boniface refers to Leoba, Tecla, and Cynehild as "daughters," suggesting that this indicates their youth relative to Boniface; we note in addition that the term replaces the evident close relations between Leoba and Tecla. Cynehild does not seem to be related to either of these women, but she is the maternal aunt of Lull, whose daughter is Berhtgyth of the Berhtgyth-Baldhard correspondence.

50. Aristocratic women often sought spiritual instruction abroad in the seventh century. Bede explains that there were few English monasteries at the time (*EH* 3.8), and cites the examples of Sæthryth, step-daughter of Anna of East Anglia and Æthelburg his daughter, both of whom become abbesses of Faremoutiers-en-Brie. Æthelburg's niece, Eorcengota, was also a nun at Faremoutiers. In the same account, Bede also mentions Chelles (founded by the English wife of Clovis II, Balthild), where

Mildrith is said to have studied as well as Hild's sister, Hereswith (Rollason, *The Mildrith Legend*, 11), and Andelys-sur-Seine. The traffic may not have been all in one direction, however, since the later *Life* of Bertila, first Abbess of Chelles, describes how she sent men, women, and books to England in response to a request from the Saxon kings for assistance in founding monasteries. It is possible that Liobsynde, the apparently Frankish-named first abbess of Much Wenlock, was one of Bertila's mission; see James Campbell, "The First Century of Christianity in England," reprinted in *Essays in Anglo-Saxon History* (London: Hambledon Press, 1986), 49–67 at 58. As is well known, the English practice of double monasteries is closely related to that of similar houses in Gaul upon which it may be modelled; early examples appear also in Spain (Campbell, 61).

51. For the continental evidence, see C. P. Wormald, "The Uses of Literacy in Anglo-Saxon England and Its Neighbours," *Transactions of the Royal Historical Society*, 5th series, 27 (1977): 95–114, at 98 and 105.

52. See William Henry Stevenson, ed., *Asser's Life of King Alfred* (1904; reprinted Oxford: Clarendon, 1959), 20. Asser's lack of interest in Osburh's name at this other moment of cultural production is also regularly rehearsed in twentieth-century critical accounts: see, for example, Simon Keynes and Michael Lapidge, ed. and trans., *Alfred the Great* (Harmondsworth: Penguin, 1983), 14. Janet Nelson, however, has recently noted Asser's silencing of the female voice in her "Women and the Word in the Early Middle Ages," 71–72. Seth Lerer's suggestive analysis of the masculinist assumptions of Asser's narrative, while stressing his appropriation of Alfred's instruction and the transition from what Lerer calls the "mother tongue" of the vernacular to the paternal *auctoritas* of Latin education and Christian culture (*Literacy and Power*, 61–96), neither names Osburh nor explores her participation in Alfred's education. We can go further than Lerer does (at 78) in exploring the connections between intellectual and "manly skills" of, for example, hunting that are emphasized by Asser: such associations seem to point more in the general direction of the *topoi* of arms and letters, *translatio studii* and *translatio imperii*, so familiar in later medieval works forging a patriarchal *auctoritas* for the educated aristocrat; see Ernst Robert Curtius, *European Literature and the Latin Middle Ages*, trans. Willard R. Trask (London: Routledge, 1953), 29, 384, 178–79. In addition to the continental example of Amalasuntha, Dhuoda's *Liber Manualis* provides a rare and important example of a mother writing an instructional work for her aristocratic son, translated by James Marchand, "The Frankish Mother: Dhuoda," in *Medieval Women Writers*, ed. Katharina M. Wilson (Athens: University of Georgia Press, 1984), 1–29.

53. In addition to the brief notices of the deaths of Eorcongota and Æthelburg of Faremoutiers-en-Brie (*EH* 3.8), Bede gives only three full female "Lives" in the *History*: Hild, Æthelburg, and Æthelthryth, all in book 4, which is arguably the book of the abbesses. Each narrative is governed by the generic constraints we have seen in Hild's story, as we might expect, and each focuses on woman's death rather than her life—arguably to an even greater extent than the male "Lives." All three women are abbesses of dual foundations (Whitby, Ely, Barking), although Bede

does not stress this dimension of monastic life in the early period: indeed, it is possible that the majority of monasteries in England at this time were dual—the fullest discussion remains Mary Bateson, "Origin and Early History of Double Monasteries," *Transactions of the Royal Historical Society* 13 (1899): 137–98. Æthelburg of Barking, like Hild, is known as "mother," but delimited as "instructress of women" (her convent was founded by her brother, Bishop Eorconwald, also founder of the monastery of Chertsey, *EH* 4.7). Æthelthryth of Ely, distinguished by her miraculous virginity through two marriages at the expense of her royal connections (a point that Ælfric subsequently also emphasizes in his version of her *Life*, ed. Walter W. Skeat, *Ælfric's Lives of Saints*, vol. 1, EETS 76, 82 [Oxford: Oxford University Press, 1966], 435, lines 37–41), is said to have conducted her community in motherly fashion (*EH* 4.19). As with Hild, then, the trope of mothering is deployed in such a way as to favor product over process, since both Bede and Ælfric are vague about the force and practice of such maternal instruction. Bede's accounts of Hild and Cædmon are directly followed by an example of the antithesis of the well-run foundation in his narrative of the burning of the monastery at Coldingham, which is also governed by an abbess, Ebba (*EH* 4.25). The contrast with the foundations of Barking, Ely, and Whitby could not be clearer, with Bede stressing the moral lesson of Coldingham, where the nuns in particular are singled out for their immodest and inappropriate behavior and where a monk, Adamnan, is instrumental in trying to remedy the situation. But what really sets Bede's strategies into relief, perhaps, is a comparison with the continental *Life of Leoba* (*Vita Leobae*) written by Rudolf of Fulda (ed. Waitz, trans. Talbot). Though largely a pastiche of earlier hagiographic motifs, most often associated with male saints (and perhaps this is the point), Rudolf's picture is of a woman instrumental in providing instruction for other women and teachers in the province of her own foundation and, even more importantly, so distinguished by her learning she corrects the nuns who were reading to her in her sleep. It is Leoba who writes to Boniface asking for advice about her compositional skills, and encloses a short Latin poem for comment (epistle 29).

54. Ridyard, *Royal Saints of Anglo-Saxon England*, 91, 142–44.

55. Julia Kristeva, "Stabat Mater," *Tales of Love*, trans. Leon S. Roudiez (New York: Columbia University Press, 1987), 234–63; Karma Lochrie, "The Language of Transgression: Body, Flesh, and Word in Mystical Discourse," *Speaking Two Languages*, ed. Frantzen, 115–40.

56. *Vita Edburge*, cited by Ridyard, *Royal Saints of Anglo-Saxon England*, 19.

57. Ibid., 130.

58. For Asser, see Lerer (*Literacy and Power*, 86–88), who discusses the concept of the "absent" author in the creation of Alfred as a writer. Alfred's use of the conceit of the poet paradoxically erased and written by his poetry is elegantly explored by James W. Earl, "King Alfred's Talking Poems," *Pacific Coast Philology* 24 (1989): 49–61. Ælfric presents a slightly different authorial persona: see, for example, the first Prefaces to the *Catholic Homilies*, where Ælfric is subordinate both to the Fathers whom he "translates" and to his ecclesiastical and lay patrons, while providing a series of pre-

scriptions for the correct use of the homilies; see *Ælfric: Sermones Catholici*, ed. Benjamin Thorpe (reprinted Hildesheim: Georg Olms, 1983), 1:1–3.

59. *Visible Song: Transitional Literacy in Old English Verse*, 53–54.

60. Ibid., 52.

61. Ibid., 54.

Kinship and Lordship in Early Medieval England: The Story of Sigeberht, Cynewulf, and Cyneheard

STEPHEN D. WHITE

IN an unusually lengthy entry[1] for the year 757, the *Anglo-Saxon Chronicle* recounts a complex and well-crafted story, which the chronicler and his contemporaries presumably found interesting, dramatic, and perhaps even instructive and which modern scholars have never tired of retelling.[2] The story opens in 757,[3] when Sigeberht, because of his "wrongful" acts, was deprived of his kingdom by Cynewulf and the councillors of the West Saxons.[4] Sigeberht, who, like Cynewulf, was supposedly descended from Cerdic,[5] retained control over Hampshire, perhaps as an underking.[6] But later, after killing an ealdorman named Cumbra, who had long stood by him,[7] Sigeberht was first driven into the Weald by Cynewulf and then killed at the village of Privet by a swineherd, who thereby avenged the death of ealdorman Cumbra.[8]

After fighting many battles with the Britons,[9] Cynewulf decided, in 786, to expel from his kingdom an *aetheling* named Cyneheard, who, as Sigeberht's brother, may well have been recognized as the present king's kinsman.[10] During his campaign against the *aetheling* Cynewulf visited *Meretun*,[11] where he stayed in a lodge with a mistress of his, while a small retinue[12] remained in a nearby hall.[13] After news of Cynewulf's whereabouts somehow reached Cyneheard, the *aetheling* led his followers against the king and killed him before the king's retainers could aid him. These royal retainers then confronted Cyneheard, who offered each of them "money and life,"[14] presumably in return for their political support.[15] Rejecting the *aetheling*'s offer, the king's followers attacked him and, except for one British hostage,[16] were all killed in what was evidently a hopeless attempt to avenge Cynewulf.[17]

The next morning, after barricading themselves in the stronghold at *Meretun*, Cyneheard and his men confronted a second, larger group of Cynewulf's followers, led by ealdorman Osric and a royal thane called Wiferth.[18] The *aetheling* offered his adversaries "money and land on their own terms," if they would grant him the kingdom.[19] In addition, either Cyneheard or Cyneheard's men indicated that at least some of Cynewulf's followers had kin in Cyneheard's band and would not desert him.[20] Whatever the significance of the second statement,[21] neither it nor Cyneheard's previous offer induced any of Cynewulf's men to abandon the battlefield. Instead, the king's followers then declared that "no kinsman was dearer to them than their lord [i.e., Cynewulf]" and that "they would never follow [their lord's] slayer [i.e., Cyneheard]."[22] Cynewulf's men then "offered their kinsmen [in Cyneheard's band] that they might go away unharmed."[23] Cyneheard's followers replied that they would give this offer no more heed than Cynewulf's other followers had given on the previous day to Cyneheard's similar offer to them.[24] No other ways of avoiding a battle or limiting its scope were proposed. In the ensuing encounter, Cyneheard and his followers were all killed, except for an ealdorman's godson.[25] Perhaps some members of Cynewulf's party perished as well.[26]

Although it is unclear why such a long, elaborate story appears in a chronicle whose other entries for this century never exceed a couple of lines,[27] the interest of modern scholars in the story is easily explained. Students of early English literature have studied it closely, partly because it resembles passages from Icelandic sagas[28] and partly because it treats, in a rhetorically effective way, a major theme in early medieval literature—the loyalty of warriors to their leaders.[29] The story has also been closely examined by political and social historians.[30] Although the most cautious of them indicate that the values expressed in the story were entirely traditional and in no way progressive,[31] many others claim that by favorably portraying warriors who were willing to fight and kill their own kin in order to support or avenge their lord, the chronicler's story provides what one scholar calls "a pointer" clearly designating the path of later English political and social development.[32] They have used it to show, for example, that at least by 786, "the ties between lord and man exceeded those of blood relationship"[33] and that although "the claims of kindred were still recognized" at this time, "they were, if necessary, subordinated to the superior claims of lordship."[34] In the opinion of certain historians, the story of Cynewulf and Cyneheard signals the "victory of the lordship principle over the kindred tie."[35]

On closer inspection, however, the precise significance of this well-known tale seems much less clear than many scholars have claimed. In fact, the chronicler never comes close to articulating the rule that obligations to a lord invariably outweigh or supersede obligations to kin. Nor does the story show that in behaving as they did at *Meretun*, the followers of Cynewulf or Cyneheard were conforming to any such rule or to anything resembling a "code." Lacking clear textual support, conventional readings are based largely on far-reaching assumptions about early medieval English society, law, and political development and about the most plausible ways of explaining political behavior. Because these assumptions are not necessarily supported either by the story of Cynewulf and Cyneheard or by other evidence, they should be identified and queried.

*   *   *   *   *

Any conclusion or lesson that contemporaries were expected to draw from the chronicler's entry for 757 was narrower and more ambiguous than the one extracted by many modern scholars. To see why this text does not provide clear evidence of the preeminent status of lordship in eighth-century England, we should first examine the early parts of the story, which concern Cyneheard's brother Sigeberht, and only then consider the two famous battles of 786 between the followers of Cynewulf and Cyneheard.[36] In the chronicler's account of Sigeberht's fall, the principle of lordship does not consistently prevail and is not assigned absolute preeminence. The story opens, after all, with an attack on a lord by his own followers. Although the story of Sigeberht's fall from power certainly does not indicate that warriors were considered free to disobey, abandon, or betray their chiefs whenever they wished, it clearly suggests that a man's obligations to his lord were not thought to be absolute: when weighed against other considerations, these duties were sometimes set aside.

Moreover, unless a transcendent legal code systematically regulated relations between lords and followers in eighth-century England, the chronicler's statement that Sigeberht was deposed for his "unjust" and "wrongful" acts does not imply that a lord forfeited his legal claim on the loyalty of his followers *only* when he committed specific, wrongful acts, as determined by a formal legal process. Instead, if Sigeberht's so-called deposition involved only "a hint" of constitutionalism,[37] then the chronicler's account of it shows that although a lord in eighth-century Wessex had a claim, recognized by custom, on the loyalty of his followers, followers could sometimes justify the abandonment of their lord by means of an "officializing strategy"[38] whose customary force was well recognized.

In other words, there were two equally plausible ways of simultaneously representing and evaluating Sigeberht's fall from power. On the one hand, Sigeberht, ealdorman Cumbra, and Sigeberht's other loyal followers could have claimed that a good lord had been foully betrayed by evil followers, who had then tried to justify their treachery by blackening their lord's reputation.[39] In condemning Sigeberht's enemies, they could have appealed, at least implicitly, to the principle that warriors owed loyalty to their lords.[40] On the other hand, Cynewulf and his allies, like the chronicler himself, presumably justified Sigeberht's deposition by citing the wrongful acts that this king had supposedly committed. They thereby invoked, at least indirectly, the principle that a lord who acted wrongfully lost his claim on his followers' loyalty. The only difference in status between the two arguments was that the second one was advanced by the victorious political faction.

Like the account of Sigeberht's deposition, the chronicler's statement that Sigeberht killed ealdorman Cumbra, who had long supported him, also bears on the question of how contemporaries conceptualized the relations between followers and lords. If a transcendent legal code governed such relations and dictated the behavior of Cynewulf's and Cyneheard's followers in 786, then we should be able to determine whether, under the same code, Sigeberht acted lawfully in killing Cumbra. If we cannot attain this objective, we can conclude that the episode in question is not necessarily consistent with conventional interpretations of our story, which depend on the view that lordship was an absolute determinant of political action, except in cases where lords had previously lost their authority by violating the code.

On the one hand, if we argue that Sigeberht was justified in killing Cumbra, as Cynewulf was in overthrowing Sigeberht, then we could bolster our previous hypothesis that the mutual obligations of lord and follower were far from absolute. Under certain circumstances, one party to this sort of bilateral relationship could renounce the other and turn against him. This conclusion, however, is hard to reconcile with the view underlying conventional readings of the story that a warrior's obligations to his lord were inviolable and therefore took precedence, in all cases, over that warrior's other duties. According to Cassidy and Ringler, for example, a contemporary audience would have assumed that

> a man's loyalty to his lord is everything: that he must sacrifice his life
> for him if need be, and avenge his death at any cost—even at the cost
> of ignoring the other cardinal loyalty of the Germanic world, loyalty
> to one's kin. . . . All the characters in this little tale are faithful to *the
> heroic code* and make the "correct" choice. Hence, the story is not only
> exemplary, but also perfectly clear: the *logic of loyalty* makes the behav-

ior of the actors and the sequence of events patterned and predictable.[41]

However, if the obligations of followers to lords or lords to followers could
sometimes be set aside, then the political struggles recounted by the chronicler become less logical and less predictable. The mere fact that Cynewulf
was the lord of certain warriors who fought against Cyneheard's band at
Meretun in 786 will not fully account for the decision of these men to
avenge their king by fighting their kin.

On the other hand, if we argue that it was wrong and unlawful for Sigeberht to kill his follower Cumbra, but proper and lawful for some of
Cynewulf's followers to kill their own kin in order to avenge their lord, we
must provide grounds for distinguishing in this way between the killing of
Cumbra and the killing of Cyneheard's followers. Even though the chronicler himself makes this distinction by obliquely condemning the killing of
Cumbra and implicitly glorifying Cynewulf's men for avenging their lord,
this author's written text is not a definitive, impartial, or complete statement of law or custom. Instead, it presents only one of several different stories that could have been told about Sigeberht, Cynewulf, and Cyneheard.
If passages about lords who killed followers or followers who killed lords do
not reveal the defeat of the lordship principle, it is not obvious why a passage about warriors who fought their kin to avenge their lord necessarily
demonstrates the superiority of lordship to kinship.

An analysis of Cumbra's death, moreover, should consider both the
rhetorical and the normative contexts that the chronicler has created for
this episode. Clearly, this author wished to portray Sigeberht unfavorably.
Having claimed that, as king, Sigeberht had acted wrongfully, the chronicler then suggests that, as lord, the deposed king betrayed one of his followers. Without describing the killing of Cumbra, the author provides
grounds for condemning it by noting that this ealdorman had long stood by
Sigeberht. If he thereby invoked implicitly a norm that lords should not kill
their *loyal* followers, he did so under specific circumstances for a specific
polemical purpose. What his text provides, therefore, is not a general statement of early English law, but further evidence indicating that an effective
way of vilifying a lord and exonerating his enemies was to represent him as
killing or injuring a faithful follower.[42]

This kind of invective could not have succeeded unless the chronicler's
audience acknowledged that lords should not kill or otherwise mistreat
their loyal followers; but its success also depended on the audience's willingness to agree with the chronicler (and presumably with Cumbra and

Cumbra's avenger) that Sigeberht had no valid grounds for killing this particular follower. Because we have already seen that people could sometimes justify a royal lord's deposition by his followers, we can assume that under certain circumstances, people could also justify the killing of a follower by his lord. The question is whether those circumstances were clearly articulated in rules that were legally binding and that formed a coherent system or code. If early medieval custom consisted of an articulated system of rules that were routinely applied to particular cases, then, at least in theory, it could have provided unambiguous answers to questions about when a lord and follower could justifiably attack one another. But if early English custom is better represented as a set of vaguely articulated norms or principles with no systematic and generally accepted method of relating one principle to another or of applying norms to practice, then this body of custom could have provided no obvious and conclusive way of deciding whether acts such as Sigeberht's deposition or the killing of Cumbra were fully legitimate.[43]

At first glance, the passage about Sigeberht's death at the hands of a swineherd seems to support the traditional reading of the chronicler's entry. Here, the chronicler portrays a loyal follower who avenges his fallen lord by trekking through the Weald to cut down a descendant of Cerdic; and by implicitly justifying this killing, the text may show that a lord's followers had a binding obligation to avenge him.[44] This way of interpreting the chronicler's interpretation of Sigeberht's death, however, is open to several objections. First, instead of serving primarily to celebrate a follower who did his duty by avenging his lord, this passage portrays the final degradation of a bad lord, who, in isolation, met an ignoble death. Contemporaries, moreover, might well have remarked on the social status of Cumbra's avenger. Indeed, our own view of Sigeberht's death would change radically if we knew that only the swineherd was prepared to avenge Cumbra. In this case, an account of Sigeberht's death could easily have emphasized the *failure* of Cumbra's kin or most distinguished followers to take vengeance on Sigeberht.[45] Furthermore, if the deposed Sigeberht had, in fact, lost all his political backing after killing Cumbra, then the vengeance taken on him loses much of its heroic glamor. Killing an outcast must have been relatively easy and involved little risk of provoking an immediate retaliatory attack on the outcast's slayer.[46] If taken at face value, the story of Sigeberht's death can be cited in support of the conventional interpretation of the chronicler's entry. But the significance of this episode starts to look more problematic as soon as we realize that our author told only one of several possible stories about Sigeberht's death and used it to dramatize and justify this king's downfall. All chroniclers both select and shape the events they record in accordance with their own political outlooks; and the authors and compilers of the *Anglo-Saxon Chronicle* were not passive witnesses to the events they chronicled.[47]

For the purpose of assessing the political significance of lordship and kinship, the famous conclusion to the story is also more ambiguous than conventional interpretations of it suggest.[48] Consider, first, the composition of Cynewulf's and Cyneheard's followings. The fact that certain followers of Cynewulf were kinsmen of certain followers of Cyneheard[49] may suggest that lordship was more politically and legally potent than kinship was. The magnetic force of lordship, it seems, could pull apart a kin group and place kinsmen on opposing sides of a conflict.[50] In addition, the kinship tie between the leaders of the two bands[51] can be cited as evidence that even the ruling family of the kingdom "was divided against itself."[52]

On the other hand, an examination of the same evidence from a different perspective yields a different conclusion. The *failure* of the *aetheling*'s followers to support the king can be used as evidence of how limited Cynewulf's powers of lordship really were. Cynewulf, we could argue, could not command the loyalty of all warriors from the important kin groups of his realm. Some of the king's followers, moreover, had previously abandoned Cynewulf in favor of Cynewulf's enemy, the *aetheling*,[53] and the *aetheling* himself, under one interpretation, had rebelled against his royal lord.[54]

With respect to the relative importance of lordship and kinship, evidence about the nature of the conflict between Cynewulf and Cyneheard is also disconcertingly ambiguous. If we choose to view this conflict simply as a struggle between rival lords, each with his own following, then we must obviously treat lordship as the crucial factor determining the alignment of political forces at *Meretun* and dismiss kinship as a subsidiary or even irrelevant principle of political association. However, if we shift our focus by fixing on the close kinship between Sigeberht and Cyneheard, we can view the conflict of 786 between Cyneheard and Cynewulf as part of a feud that had been in progress intermittently at least since the time of Sigeberht's deposition and in which family solidarity played a significant role,[55] especially if we allow for the possibility that both Cynewulf and Cyneheard had kinsmen among their followers.[56] If we fix our gaze on the kinship connections between Cynewulf, on the one hand, and both Sigeberht and Cyneheard, on the other, we can regard the battles of 786 as parts of an intrafamilial royal feud,[57] revealing, among other things, that family solidarity within the ruling house of Wessex was important, but not all-powerful. Because these three ways of representing and, in a sense, explaining the conflict between Cynewulf and Cyneheard all seem accurate and yet incomplete and because all of them, in one form or another, were available both to the chronicler and to the historical actors themselves, it begins to look as though the political issues raised at *Meretun* cannot be neatly reduced to a simple question about whether kinship or lordship was preeminent.

Even the celebrated negotiations following Cynewulf's death can be reinterpreted so as to raise questions about conventional readings of the story. In seeking the support of the first group of royal followers in return for "money and life," Cyneheard was acting from a position of strength, since this group must have been considerably smaller than his own;[58] as an experienced leader, he must also have known something about the values of warriors. Nevertheless, he still thought he had a chance of gaining support from men whose lord he had just killed. Why else should he have offered to spare men who, if allowed to live, would have felt compelled to kill him in order to fulfill their obligation to avenge Cynewulf? Once again, our story reveals a more fluid political culture than the conventional interpretation allows for.

Upon learning that kinsmen of theirs were supporting the *aetheling*, members of Cynewulf's second band did not abandon their conflict with Cyneheard.[59] But neither did they ignore Cyneheard's message about the composition of his following, which made them pause before taking vengeance on every warrior implicated in killing their lord. In fact, by offering to let their kinsmen leave Cyneheard "unharmed," these royal followers were indicating their willingness to let their relatives escape vengeance, at least for the time being; and they did so without precipitating any protest by other royal followers or by the chronicler himself. In other words, a warrior's obligation to avenge his lord could sometimes be qualified to the point where some of the lord's slayers might escape vengeance entirely.[60] In fighting against each other, moreover, followers of Cynewulf and their kin in Cyneheard's band were not really renouncing, in general terms, the claims of kinship and acknowledging the superior claims of lordship. Instead, under specific political conditions, members of each of these two groups were fighting against specific kinsmen, who were not necessarily their close relatives[61] and who had previously broken with them, in a sense, by joining a rival following.[62] Furthermore, any followers of Cyneheard who were also kinsmen of the *aetheling* were not renouncing kinship ties; instead, after trying to avert a battle in which they would have to fight their kin, they were simply choosing to honor one kinship tie rather than another.[63]

Finally, we reach several important questions about the actions taken by Cynewulf's and Cyneheard's followers. First, why did followers of Cynewulf who had kin with Cyneheard reject Cyneheard's offer? And why was their own counteroffer to these same kinsmen rejected as well? Second, did the decisions of these warriors conform to established law or custom? Did these men behave properly and lawfully? Instead of responding to Cyneheard's offer by asserting that their legal duty to their dead lord outweighed their legal obligations to their kin, Cynewulf's followers simply said, first, that no kinsman was dearer to them than their fallen lord, and, second, that they would never follow their lord's slayer.

The first statement indicates nothing about how a man should act when duties to his lord conflicted with his obligations to kin; it served only to undercut Cyneheard's implicit suggestion that a warrior should not or would not attack his own kin even to avenge his lord. The second statement by Cynewulf's followers shows that by accepting Cyneheard's offer, they would have been committing an act that another English storyteller, the *Beowulf*-poet, represented as being particularly shameful. A decision on their part to become Cyneheard's followers would probably have seemed even more blameworthy than that of the Danes in *Beowulf*, who reluctantly made a truce with their lord's slayer, Finn, the king of the Jutes. The agreement between Finn and the Dane's new leader, Hengest, took the following form:

> Finn declared to Hengest with oaths deep-sworn, unfeigned, that he would hold those who were left from the battle in honor in accordance with the judgment of his counsellors, so that by words or by works no man should break the treaty *nor because of malice should ever mention that, princeless, the Danes followed the slayer of their own ring-giver, since necessity forced them. If with rash speech any of the Frisians should insist on calling to mind the cause of murderous hate, then the sword's edge should settle it.*[64]

This passage indicates that for a contemporary audience, the crucial point about Cyneheard's offer was that anyone who accepted it would have been following the slayer of his own ring-giver.

Because Cynewulf's followers were being asked to take a specific and disgraceful political action, their decision to refuse Cyneheard's offer and attack him has no clear bearing on the question of whether, in general, lordship or kinship was the more powerful principle of political association. Moreover, the fact that they offered a safe-conduct to their kin in Cyneheard's band shows that in this encounter kinship was not a negligible force. Instead of choosing in an abstract and legalistic way between loyalty to kin and loyalty to lord, these men had to answer three specific questions about how to deal with a specific political crisis. First, should they accept the *aetheling*'s offer, fail to avenge Cynewulf, and take the shameful step of following Cynewulf's slayer? In effect, they answered this question in the negative. Second, was their duty to avenge their lord so broad and compelling that they had to kill Cyneheard's entire band, including their own kin? This question, too, they implicitly answered in the negative.

Finally, in trying to avenge Cynewulf, were they prepared to kill specific kinsmen who had helped to kill Cynewulf and were following Cynewulf's slayer and who had refused their own kin's offer of safe-conduct? In effect, Cynewulf's followers answered this question affirmatively. But because they did not deduce this affirmative answer from a general rule or principle about the relative strengths of lordship and kinship, they must have reached their decision through a process very different from the one posited by various modern scholars. According to the conventional interpretation, Cynewulf's followers were following a legal rule when they chose to fight and kill all members of Cyneheard's retinue. Under the interpretation proposed here, these men made political, as opposed to legal, decisions and in doing so were merely guided by norms that did not dictate their decisions but that they and the chronicler probably found useful in retrospectively explaining and justifying those decisions.

Even though the chronicler never explicitly judged these decisions, he clearly approved of what happened at *Meretun* in 786. Many modern scholars have approved as well, because in their view the warriors in question were conforming to a "code" in which legal obligations to a lord superseded every other legal obligation. "For a contemporary audience," according to Mitchell and Robinson, "the violence and tragedy of the feud between Cynewulf and Cyneheard would have been transcended by the reassuring fact that the ideal prevailed: on both sides men made the heroic choice, and they chose right."[65] But is it certain that contemporaries would have universally expressed unqualified approval *whenever* warriors avenged their lords by killing their own kin? To answer this question affirmatively requires more optimism and less irony about politics than the best medieval poets and story-tellers expressed.

The chronicler's entry for 757 portrays, against a historical background of enduring political strife, warriors who were enmeshed in dense, complex networks of potentially conflicting duties to kin and to lords and who had to make choices that required them to reinterpret, slight, ignore, set aside, or directly violate some of these obligations. Political decisions of this kind were full of poetic interest,[66] precisely because they could be used to draw attention to "irresolvable" conflicts.[67] Although the chronicler presumably wished to celebrate at least some of the warriors who fought at *Meretun*, he

presents only one story-teller's retrospective, ideological view of past political processes that had once been open to different readings.

In the statement of Cynewulf's followers that they would not follow
their lord's slayer, in the claim that Sigeberht was deposed for his wrongful acts, and, perhaps, in the chronicler's entire story, what we find are
not statements of, or allusions to, sovereign legal enactments, but evidence
of what Pierre Bourdieu calls "officializing strategies." Such ideological
strategies, he points out, are essential to effective group action in societies
in which no political institution monopolizes the legitimate use of force,
because when successfully employed, they "transmute 'egoistic,' private,
particular interests . . . into disinterested, collective, publicly avowable, legitimate interests."[68] In analyses of early English politics, these polemical
strategies have to be reckoned with and should not necessarily be treated as
mere cloaks for the pursuit of private advantage, especially when they seem
to have led men to their deaths. Nevertheless, they cannot properly be regarded as clear-cut evidence about the principles underlying or dictating
political action. Even the chronicler, though pursuing "officializing strategies" of his own, reveals that Cynewulf, Cyneheard, and their followers, as
well as Sigeberht and Cumbra, were not automatons who made political
decisions simply by consulting a code or rule-book.

Although the conventional reading of our story lacks a solid textual
basis, it accords well with broad assumptions about early English society
and political development. Even though these assumptions may have been
largely discarded by recent historians,[69] they retain influence, especially in
literary commentaries. In particular, the claim that the chronicler's story
reveals the triumph of lordship over kinship is supported by the presuppo-
sition that in early medieval England, kinship was always weak and grew
weaker still, as lordship gained importance. The conventional reading also
rests on the questionable assumptions that legal rules in early medieval England can be clearly distinguished from other kinds of norms and that, because political behavior is normally the product of obedience to legal rules,
political narratives, such as the chronicler's entry, provide evidence of legal
rules at work. Finally, the conventional reading is also based on the pre-
supposition that early English history can be accurately represented as a
process by which a society whose prehistoric forerunners on the Continent
were once organized solely on the basis of kinship evolved relatively rapidly
after the age of settlements into a society which was organized around lordship and in which kinship had been gradually reduced to a merely social and
emotional, as opposed to a legal and political, force.[70] If these assumptions
about kinship, lordship, law, and political development are abandoned or

substantially qualified, then the conventional reading of our text loses much of its remaining credibility.

Since the late nineteenth century, various historians have, in effect, laid the groundwork for the conventional reading of our text by emphasizing the alleged weakness of kinship in early medieval England and by noting, in some cases, the rapidity with which a rise of lordship undermined what was already an attenuated kinship system. F. W. Maitland argued that, because early English blood-feuds and settlements to feuds involved, not unilineal descent groups, but rather bilateral kindreds, which, by their very nature, could have had no enduring corporate existence, the early medieval family could not have held land communally or constituted the basic unit of early English society.[71] A little later, H. M. Chadwick argued that as "the primitive sanctity of the family was giving way," lordship or "personal allegiance" became the "dominant" principle of English political organization.[72] Phillpotts extended Maitland's argument about the early English kindred by claiming that because the kindred's only legal function was to engage in feuding, which ceased to be a legitimate activity after the time of Edmund, kinship in England must have quickly lost what little legal significance it had once possessed.[73] Although Stenton conceded that early English society was "knit together" by kinship,[74] he claimed that the composition of family groups was "very loose and indefinite," that kinship never dominated legal administration,[75] and that even coresidential kin were "in law a mere group of individuals which could at any time be dissolved by the action of its members."[76]

Lancaster later concluded that early English kinship

> seems to have been less rigid than has frequently been thought; the circle of effective kin smaller; the lack of descent groups probable, despite patrilineal bias; the stability of marriage uncertain; and the corporateness of landholding and residential units unproven.[77]

Loyn has seconded these conclusions. Noting that Germanic settlers in England lacked a complex kinship system comparable to the ones described in early Norwegian and Welsh laws,[78] he claimed that "the formal institutional life of the kin was atrophied, if not stifled at birth, by the strength of territorial lordship and Christian kingship."[79] In early medieval England, he concluded, "kinship and kindred principles are strong socially but hesitant in their own legal right."[80] In law, according to Loyn and others, the future belonged to lordship.[81]

Arguments of this kind have often proved valuable in undermining the view that "the most potent force which held [early English] society together was not any authority of government, whether elective or hereditary, but the primary bond of blood relationship" between members of corporate kin groups based on "agnatic relationship."[82] By relentlessly attacking this hypothesis, which Chadwick said was "generally" held in 1907,[83] scholars have effectively demonstrated that Anglo-Saxon England was never a society in which virtually all significant legal and political obligations took the form of duties to kin;[84] they have also shown that, with respect to kinship organization, early medieval England differed from its forerunners on the Continent, from certain other medieval European societies, and from many non-European societies as well.[85]

None of these arguments, however, comes close to demonstrating that kinship was a negligible force in early English politics or that warriors, as a group, did not attach to kinship the kind of binding legal force they attributed to lordship. The finding that ties to close kin were stronger than ties to distant kin, that feuds were carried on by cognatic kindreds with "indefinite" boundaries, and that feuding groups included nonkin, as well as kin,[86] does not imply that kinship ties were weak;[87] at most, this evidence shows only that such ties were *relatively* weak, when viewed in certain kinds of comparative contexts.

It is also misleading, at best, to argue for the weakness of kinship ties in early medieval England on the grounds that they were relatively weaker than such ties supposedly were in the factitious, pre-migration Germanic society that historians sometimes use as a reference point for discussions of later Germanic societies. If historians postulate the existence of a primitive Germanic society in which kinship ties were sacred and entailed inviolable and inviolate obligations, they can then cite any subsequent failure to honor these ties as evidence of a decline of kinship, rather than as instances of conflicts and contradictions that inevitably arise in certain kinds of societies. Such arguments, however, rest on the fallacious assumption that in societies where all political obligations are represented as duties to kin, these duties are always observed.[88]

Furthermore, even if true corporate kin groups never existed in early medieval England, bilateral kindreds, *pace* Maitland, could have acted as quasi-corporate groups for certain purposes.[89] In addition, the fact that blood-feuds were waged down into the eleventh century[90] suggests that kinship long retained importance as a basis for recruitment to political groups. Although no fully articulated system of landholding by family communities seems to have existed in early medieval England,[91] documented customs barring landholders from alienating certain kinds of land away from kin[92] are clearly inconsistent with a purely individualistic system of land tenure.[93] If kinship served as an idiom of social classification that people could use to justify decisions about the allocation of important material resources, it must have had more than merely emotional or social force.

Furthermore, the claim that kinship, unlike lordship, lacked "legal," as opposed to "emotional" or "social," significance rests on the dubious assumption that in this period, legal and social norms can be readily distinguished from one another. If historians simply assume that royally promulgated dooms constituted legal rules, whereas norms articulated in other ways were not legally binding, then they can easily show that, legally, duties to lords came to supersede duties to kin, because dooms treat lordship more fully than kinship and were sometimes designed to undermine the legitimacy of certain kinship obligations.[94] This argument depends on the assumption that the codes were both fully authoritative and complete statements of English law. If we abandon this view of Anglo-Saxon law codes, then we can, at most, treat dooms relating to kinship or lordship as articulating, in partial form, one of several competing ideologies about what people owed their lords and their kin.[95]

One implication of this argument is that the conflict that Cynewulf's followers experienced between their wish to avenge their lord and their wish to avoid harming their own kin may not have differed significantly from the conflict that a warrior probably experienced when two different kindreds to which he belonged were engaged in a feud and demanded his support.[96] The two conflicts will appear different, only if we treat kinship and lordship as mutually antagonistic principles of political organization, each of which was clearly dominant during a different stage of political development. The alternative, proposed by various historians, is to treat kinship and lordship as coexisting, if not complementary, methods of representing, structuring, activating, and legitimating certain kinds of political relationships[97] and to leave open the question of precisely how kinship and lordship ties were related to one another at specific junctures in the history of particular communities.

By treating eighth-century norms about kinship and lordship merely as guides to proper behavior that were not integrated into a complete, coherent, and authoritative system,[98] we can better interpret and explain political actions such as the ones taken by the followers of Cynewulf and Cyneheard. Instead of assuming that these men were obeying legal rules, we can imagine a relationship between norm and practice similar to the one posited by Bourdieu. Insisting that "the precepts of custom . . . have nothing in common with the transcendent rules of a juridical code"[99] and are "very close to sayings and proverbs,"[100] he asserts that "'customary rules' preserved by the group memory are themselves the product of a small batch of schemes enabling agents to generate an infinity of practices adapted to endlessly changing situations, without those schemes ever being consti-tuted as explicit principles."[101] He also argues that "the rules of customary law have some practical efficacy only to the extent that, skillfully manipu-lated . . . they 'awaken,' so to speak, the schemes of perception and appreci-ation, in their incorporated state, in every member of the group."[102] Under this interpretation of so-called customary law, norms that enjoined war-riors to avenge their lords, to avoid following their own lord's slayer, or to support their kin will retain a place in analyses of earlier medieval politics, but not as absolute determinants of political practice.

* * * * *

Explicitly or implicitly, conventional interpretations of the story of Cyne-wulf and Cyneheard articulate several familiar and interrelated themes in modern historical writing on earlier European history: the decline of kin-ship and family; the rise of contractual lordship; and the rise of the state. Previous commentators on this text often imply that although there had once been a time when Germanic warriors valued kinship more highly than lordship, this time, in England, had passed by 786. Under this interpreta-tion, men who supposedly chose lord over kin at *Meretun* were not simply making a politically expedient or personally agreeable choice; they were conforming both to the law of their own society and to an important law of historical development. Instead of allowing their kinship status to dictate their political behavior, they made political decisions mandated by their contractual relationships with their lord and, in doing so, put aside consid-erations of personal sentiment and paid allegiance to established authority.

Relying on an inaccurate reading of the chronicler's text, proponents of this interpretation have themselves paid allegiance to a developmental the-ory proposed by Sir Henry Maine. In 1861, he wrote:

> The movement of progressive societies has been uniform in one re-spect. Through all its course, it has been distinguished by the gradual dissolution of family dependency and the growth of individual oblig-ation in its place. The individual is steadily substituted for the Family as the unit of which civil laws take account.[103]

Maine then identified "Contract" as "the tie between man and man which replaces by degrees those forms of reciprocity in rights and duties which have their origins in the Family."[104] After noting how much progress Eu-ropean societies had achieved in distancing themselves from societies based on the family, Maine enunciated his famous conclusion that "the movement of progressive societies has hitherto been a movement *from Status to Contract*."[105] If stripped of its reference to "progressive societies," this pronouncement about the general direction of European political development over several millenia may be more right than wrong. But the dangers of using it as an infallible guide to every twist and turn in earlier English history should, by now, be obvious. At the very least, it seems implausible to locate the definitive appearance of a society founded primarily on contract, not in the industrialized world of modern capitalism, but in the wilds of an eighth-century kingdom.

Notes

1. I received valuable help from Elizabeth A. R. Brown, Kate Gilbert, William I. Miller, and Patrick Wormald, none of whom bears any responsibility for errors I have doubtless made.

2. For the Old English text, see *Two of the Saxon Chronicles Parallel*, ed. Charles A. Plummer, 2 vols. (Oxford 1899) 1.46–49, which gives the A-text (the Parker MS) and the E-text (the Laud MS) in full, with variant readings from the B-, C-, and D-texts in the footnotes. The F-text gives only a brief note on Cynewulf and Cyneheard, 1.46 n. See also *The Anglo-Saxon Chronicle: A Collaborative Edition*, ed. David Dumville and Simon Keynes, 3: *MS A*, ed. Janet M. Bately (Cambridge 1986) 36–37, and 4: *MS B*, ed. Simon Taylor (Cambridge 1983) 25–26. References in this article are to the reedited version of the Old English text in Bruce Mitchell and Fred C. Robinson, *A Guide to Old English, Fourth Edition Revised with Prose and Verse Texts and Glossary* (1986; repr. Oxford 1987) 192–195 (abbreviated henceforth as MR, followed by line numbers).

For translations into modern English, which often differ from one another on crucial points, see, for example, Francis P. Magoun, "Cynewulf, Cyneheard and Osric," *Anglia: Zeitschrift für englische Philologie* 57, n.s. 45 (1933) 361–376 at 375–376; C. L. Wrenn, "A Saga of the Anglo-Saxons," *History* n.s. 25 (1940) 208–215 at 210–211; Charles Moorman, "The 'A.-S Chronicle' for 755 [*sic*]," *Notes and Queries* 199 (1954) 94–98 at 95; Tom H. Towers, "Thematic Unity in the Story of Cynewulf and Cyneheard," *Journal of English and Germanic Philology* 62 (1963) 310–316 at 311–312; Francis Joseph Battaglia, "*Anglo-Saxon Chronicle* for 755 [*sic*]: The Missing Evidence for a Traditional Reading," *PMLA* 81 (1966) 173–178 at 174; *English Historical Documents, c. 500–1042*, ed. and trans. Dorothy Whitelock, ed. 2 (New York 1979) 175–176; and *The Anglo-Saxon Chronicle*, ed. and trans. Dorothy Whitelock, with David C. Douglas and Susie I. Tucker (London 1961) 30–31.

On the later incorporation of the story chronicles or histories by such authors as Henry of Huntingdon, Florence of Worcester, Symeon of Durham, the monk of Abingdon, Aethelweard, William of Malmesbury, Roger of Wendover, and Geoffrey Gaimar, see Plummer 2.44–47; Alexander Bell, "Cynewulf and Cyneheard in Gaimar," *Modern Language Review* 10 (1915) 42–46; William Hunt, "Cynewulf," in *Dictionary of*

National Biography, ed. Leslie Stephen and Sidney Lee (Oxford 1917) 5.372; Battaglia 176, 177; Frederic G. Cassidy and Richard N. Ringler, *Bright's Old English Grammar and Reader*, ed. 3, second corrected printing (New York 1971) 139–142 passim; Whitelock, *Documents* 175 and nn. 4, 9.

3. Although the entry in the manuscripts is for the year 755, editors routinely assume that it treats a sequence of events beginning in 757 and ending in 786; Whitelock, *Documents* (n. 2 above) 124, 175 n. 5; Whitelock, *Chronicle* (n. 2 above) xviii, xxiii, 30 n. 5; Magoun (n. 2 above) 361, 368; Battaglia (n. 2 above) 173 n. 1; Dumville and Keynes (n. 2 above) 3.36–39, 4.25–27.

4. "Her Cynewulf benam Sigebryht his rices ond Westseaxna wiotan for unryhtum dædum, buton Hamtunscire": MR 1–2. Having become king in 756, Sigeberht ruled for only a year or so: Plummer (n. 2 above) 1.46; Whitelock, *Documents* (n. 2 above) 75. On Cynewulf, see Whitelock, *Documents* 21; Frank Stenton, *Anglo-Saxon England*, ed. 2 (1947; repr. London 1962) 174, 203, 207, 214; P. H. Sawyer, *From Roman Britain to Norman England* (New York 1978) 106. Some commentators have assumed that an established constitutional body formally deposed Sigeberht: Plummer (n. 2 above) 2.44; Magoun (n. 2 above) 368, 375. Wormald takes the more plausible position that this episode merely "has a hint of 'constitutional' procedures": Patrick Wormald, "The Age of Offa and Alcuin," in James Campbell et al., *The Anglo-Saxons* (Oxford 1982) 101–131 at 115.

5. The D- and E-texts of the *Chronicle* explicitly identify Sigeberht as Cynewulf's kinsman (*maeg*): Whitelock, *Documents* (n. 2 above) 175 n. 6; Cassidy and Ringler (n. 2 above) 139 n. Although other versions omit this detail, they state of Cynewulf and Sigeberht's brother, Cyneheard, that "hiera ryhtfæderencyn gæþ to Cerdice": MR 42–43. Whereas Magoun (n. 2 above) suggests that these kinship ties were unimportant (363 and n. 3), Battaglia (n. 2 above) attaches great significance to them (176–177).

6. See Magoun (n. 2 above) 368 and n. 4, 369 and nn. 1, 2.

7. ". . . he hæfde þa [Hampshire] oþ he ofslog þone aldormon þe him lengest wunode": MR 2–3. Commentators generally identify this ealdorman as Cumbra, who is named a few lines later: Plummer (n. 2 above) 2.44–45; Magoun (n. 2 above) 365 and n. 3, 369; Mitchell and Robinson (n. 2 above) 193; Cassidy and Ringler (n. 2 above) 139. The passage just quoted does not clearly indicate when Cumbra became associated with Sigeberht or when the latter killed the former.

8. "Ond hiene þa Cynewulf on Andred adræfde, ond he þær wunade oþ þæt hiene an swan ofstang æt Pryfetes flodan; ond he wræc þone aldormon Cumbran": MR 3–6. This passage does not indicate how quickly the swineherd avenged Cumbra. On Privet(t) or Privetsflood in Hampshire, see Magoun (n. 2 above) 369 and n. 5; and Cassidy and Ringler (n. 2 above) 139.

9. "Ond se Cynewulf oft miclum gefeohtum feaht uuiþ Bretwalum": MR 6–7. On Cynewulf's campaigns, see Wrenn (n. 2 above) 214; A. F. Major, *Early Wars of Wessex* (Cambridge 1913) 79, 81.

10. "Ond ymb xxxi wintra þæs þe he rice hæfde, he wolde adræfan anne æþeling se

was Cyneheard haten; ond se Cyneheard wæs þæs Sigebryhtes broþur": MR 7–9. XXXI is an error for XXIX: Mitchell and Robinson (n. 2 above) 193; Whitelock, *Documents* (n. 2 above) 175 n. 9. Although this passage suggests that the king initiated the conflict with the *aetheling*, who may simply have posed a threat to him (Towers [n. 2 above] 315), Cynewulf may have attacked Cyneheard because the latter was engaged in a revolt: Magoun (n. 2 above) 374; Stenton (n. 3 above) 207; Peter Hunter Blair, *Roman Britain and Early England, 55 B.C.–A.D. 871* (New York 1963) 251; Rosemary Woolf, "The Ideal of Men Dying with Their Lord," *Anglo-Saxon England*, ed. Peter Clemoes (hereafter ASE) 5 (1976) 63–82 at 71. On the position of an *aetheling* in this period, see David N. Dumville, "The Aetheling: A Study of Anglo-Saxon Constitutional History," ASE 8 (1979) 1–34, esp. 14–17.

11. Most scholars identify *Meretun* or *Merantun* with Merton in Surrey: Magoun (n. 2 above) 367; Cassidy and Ringler (n. 2 above) 140 n.; Mitchell and Robinson (n. 2 above) 193. One suggests Merton in Devonshire: Wrenn (n. 2 above) 214. Another proposes Martin in Hampshire: H. P. R. Finberg, *The Formation of England, 550–1042* (1974; repr. Frogmore, St. Albans 1976) 104.

12. "Ond þa geascode he þone cyning lytle werode on wifcyþþe on Merantune": MR 9–10. On the size of this force, see n. 17 below.

13. According to one reconstruction, "the *bur* stands inside the stronghold (*burh*) but is separate from the main hall, where the King's retinue is housed. The entire compound is surrounded by a wall and is entered through a *gatu* (ll. 27, 36) in the wall. The *bur* is entered through a *dura* (1. 13)"; Mitchell and Robinson (n. 2 above) 193. On the *bur*, see also P. V. Addyman, "The Anglo-Saxon House: A New Review," ASE 3 (1974) 273–307 at 304; and Kathryn Hume, "The Concept of the House in Old English Poetry," ASE 3 (1974) 63–74.

14. "Ond hiera se æþeling gehwelcum feoh ond feorh gebead": MR 19–20.

15. Cyneheard's offer to the first group of royal followers, like his later offer to the second group, may well have been made on condition that the members of the first band would acknowledge him as king: Woolf (n. 10 above) 70. But it is impossible to determine how closely the two offers resembled one another.

16. On the British hostage, see Plummer (n. 2 above) 2.46; Magoun (n. 2 above) 365 and n. 2; Mitchell and Robinson (n. 2 above) 194. Treating him as the central character in the entire story, Moorman identifies him both with the swineherd who avenged Cumbra by killing Sigeberht and with the "ealdorman's godson," who survived the second battle of 784 and who, under this interpretation, was the godson of ealdorman Cumbra, not ealdorman Osric: Moorman (n. 2 above) 97. On this implausible theory, see Towers (n. 2 above) 313–314.

17. Since the first group of Cynewulf's followers was evidently smaller than Cyneheard's force, the *aetheling* could not have made his offer out of desperation: see, e.g., Woolf (n. 10 above) 70. More controversial is the question of just how large these bands were. Relying on an entry for 786 (corrected from 783 or 784) from the A-, C-, D-, and E-texts (Plummer [n. 2 above] 1.52, 53; Whitelock, *Documents* [n. 2 above] 180), several scholars claim that Cynewulf's first band consisted of 84 men, plus the

British hostage: Magoun (n. 2 above) 371 and n. 1, 366 and n. 4; Wrenn (n. 2 above) 214; Moorman (n. 2 above) 96. However, because the entry just cited is ambiguous, others have maintained that the *aetheling*'s force, not the king's first band, numbered 84 men: Cassidy and Ringler (n. 2 above) 140; Battaglia (n. 2 above) 174 n. 7; Finberg (n. 11 above) 104.

18. The passage summarized here can be rendered in various ways: Whitelock, *Documents* (n. 2 above) 176 n. 4; Mitchell and Robinson (n. 2 above) 194. On Osric and Wiferth, see Magoun (n. 2 above) 366, 367.

19. "Ond þa bebead he him hiera agenne dom feos ond londes, gif hie him þæs rices uþon": MR 28–29. Cyneheard may have been offering men in Cynewulf's second band a privilege similar to the one known in Scandinavia as "self-doom": Plummer (n. 2 above) 2.46; Wrenn (n. 2 above) 215; Cassidy and Ringler (n. 2 above) 141; Mitchell and Robinson (n. 2 above) 194. Alternatively, the *aetheling* may simply have been offering "liberal terms": Magoun (n. 2 above) 373 n. 1.19.

20. ". . . ond him cyþde þæt hiera mægas him mid wæron, þa þe him from noldon": MR 29–30. On the question of whether the verb *cyþde* (third person singular) should be amended to *cyþdon* (third person plural), which is found in several manuscripts (Plummer [n. 2 above] 1.48), see Whitelock, *Documents* (n. 2 above) 176 n. 5.

21. According to one commentator, "Cyneheard, realizing that he cannot defeat the [second] party, pretends that a great many of Cynewulf's thanes, among them some of Osric's kinsmen, have come over to his side. . . . In reality, of course, he has only the one hostage": Moorman (n. 2 above) 97. For convincing criticisms of this argument, see Towers (n. 2 above); and, above all, Battaglia (n. 2 above), 175–178.

22. "Ond þa cuædon hie þæt him nænig mæg leofra nære þonne hiera hlaford, ond hie næfre his banan folgian noldon": MR 30–32.

23. "Ond þa budon hie hiera mægum þæt hie gesunde from eodon": MR 32–33.

24. "Ond hie cuædon þæt tæt ilce hiera geferum geboden wære þe ær mid þam cyninge wærun. Þa cuædon hie þæt hie hie þæs ne onmundun 'þon ma þe eowre geferan þe mid þam cyninge ofslægene wærun'": MR 33–36. It is impossible to determine in what respects, precisely, the two offers resembled each other.

25. On the godson, whose godfather is normally identified as ealdorman Osric, not ealdorman Cumbra, see Magoun (n. 2 above) 366 and n. 3, 374; and n. 16 above.

26. On the size of the forces at *Meretun*, see n. 17 above.

27. On the striking differences between this story and other eighth-century entries in the *Chronicle*, see Plummer (n. 2 above) 2.44; Magoun (n. 2 above) 361–362; Wrenn (n. 2 above) 213. On the question of how the story came to be inserted into the *Chronicle*, see Magoun 3;74–375; Wrenn; Whitelock, *Documents* (n. 2 above); Cassidy and Ringler (n. 2 above) 138.

28. See Magoun (n. 2 above) 361; Wrenn (n. 2 above); C. E. Wright, *The Cultivation of Saga in Anglo-Saxon England* (London 1939) 26, 78–80; R. W. McTurk, "'Cynewulf and Cyneheard' and the Icelandic Sagas," *Leeds Studies in English* n.s. 12 (1981) 81–127.

29. In addition to the works of Magoun, Wrenn, Moorman, Towers, Battaglia,

Cassidy and Ringer, and Mitchell and Robinson cited in n. 2 above, see Ruth Water-house, "Theme and Structure of 755 *Anglo-Saxon Chronicle*," *Neuphilologische Mit-teilungen* 70 (1969) 630–640; and earlier discussions cited in Magoun. According to Mitchell and Robinson, the chronicler's story "exemplifies one of the cardinal virtues of Germanic society in the heroic age: unswerving loyalty to one's sworn leader, even when that loyalty is in conflict with claims of kinship": Mitchell and Robinson 192; see also 136. In defending a "traditional reading" against Moorman, Battaglia makes valu-able observations that were not fully incorporated into subsequent discussions.

30. See, for example, Blair (n. 10 above) 251–252; Peter Hunter Blair, *An Intro-duction to Anglo-Saxon England* (Cambridge 1962) 209–210; Hector Munro Chad-wick, *The Heroic Age* (Cambridge 1912) 349, 351; idem, *The Origins of the English Peo-ple*, ed. 2 (Cambridge 1924) 26–29, 158, 165–173; idem, *Studies on Anglo-Saxon Institutions* (Cambridge 1905) 363; R. W. Chambers, *England before the Norman Con-quest* (London 1928) 174, 176–178; Finberg (n. 11 above) 104; D. J. V. Fisher, *The An-glo-Saxon Age, c. 400–1042* (1973; repr. Hong Kong 1976) 130–131; R. H. Hodgkin, *A History of the Anglo-Saxons*, ed. 3, 2 vols. (London 1921) 2.393–395; Hunt (n. 2 above); D. P. Kirby, *The Making of Early England* (New York 1967) 148; Lorraine Lan-caster, "Kinship in Anglo-Saxon Society," *British Journal of Sociology* 9 (1957) 230–250, 359–377 at 375; H. R. Loyn, *Anglo-Saxon England and the Norman Conquest* (1962; repr. New York 1963) 298; Charles Oman, *England before the Norman Conquest* (New York 1910) 335–336, 338–339; Stenton (n. 3 above) 208 and n. 3; Dorothy Whitelock, *The Beginnings of English Society*, ed. 2 rev. (Harmondsworth 1972) 32, 37–38; Woolf (n. 10 above) 70–71; and Wormald (n. 4 above) 115. Hunt (n. 2 above) and Magoun (n. 2 above) cite older discussions of the story by historians. Karen Ferro, "The King in the Doorway: The *Anglo-Saxon Chronicle*, A.D. 755," in *Kings and King-ship*, ed. Joel T. Rosenthal, Acta 11 (Binghamton 1986 for 1984) 17–30 appeared too late to be considered in the present article.

31. Stenton claimed only that the story was "famous" for "the loyalty" shown to Cynewulf and Cyneheard by their followers: Stenton (n. 3 above) 208. To Finberg, the tale simple revealed that "the ideals of the heroic age were not dead in [eighth-century] Wessex": Finberg (n. 11 above). Woolf anticipated part of the present argu-ment when she claimed the Cynewulf's men refused to follow Cyneheard because "to a thegn death is preferable to ignobly entering the service of his lord's slayer": Woolf (n.10 above) 70. Wormald illuminates the story by noting that " a dynastic feud" lies behind it: Wormald (n. 4 above) 115.

32. Loyn (n. 30 above) 298.

33. Magoun (n. 2 above) 373 n. 2.

34. Fisher (n. 30 above) 130.

35. Loyn (n. 30 above) 298. Whitelock, after first using the story to show only that warriors felt obliged to support or avenge their lords (Whitelock, *Beginnings* [n. 30 above] 32), later cited it as evidence that "when the claims of the lord clashed with those of the kindred, the idea becomes established during the centuries after the con-version that the duty to the lord comes first": ibid. 37; see also 38. After stating that in

the second battle of 784, "the bond between lord and man had proved stronger than the ties of kinship when the two came into conflict with each other," Blair adds that "there is some reason for thinking that this may have become generally so": Blair (n. 10 above) 252.

Other commentators claim that the followers of Cynewulf and Cyneheard behaved in a way that was both proper *and* traditional. In Plummer's opinion, "the tie of the comitatus supersedes that of the kin": Plummer (n. 2 above) 2.46. According to Oman, the story illustrates "the Old English ideal of chivalry, the boundless fidelity due from the sworn member of the war-band to his lord": Oman (n. 30 above) 221. According to Lancaster, the story reveals that "men who chose lord over kin were highly regarded": Lancaster (n. 30 above) 375. Kirby cites the entry as evidence that the relationship between lord and man was "the most honourable of which Anglo-Saxon society could conceive": Kirby (n. 30 above) 148. Blair treats the story as "a perfect example" of how the ideals of Germanic warriors were realized in practice: Blair (n. 30 above) 210. Kirby interprets the story as "a striking demonstration of the over-riding claims of lordship": Kirby (n. 30 above) 130. For similar views expressed by historians of literature, see Magoun (n. 2 above) 373 and n. 2; Cassidy and Ringler (n. 2 above) 138–139; Mitchell and Robinson (n. 2 above) 136, 192.

36. Emphasizing the unity of the chronicler's entry, both Moorman (n. 2 above) and Battaglia (n. 2 above) closely examine the episodes antedating 784.

37. See n. 4 above.

38. On "officializing strategies," see below at n. 68.

39. According to Battaglia, Cyneheard's followers in 786 would have viewed Sigeberht's deposition in this way: Battaglia (n. 2 above) 177.

40. On the implicit invocation of norms, see John L. Comaroff and Simon Roberts, "The Invocation of Norms in Dispute-Settlement: The Tswana Case," in *Social Anthropology and Law*, ed. Ian Hamnett (London 1977) 77–112; Comaroff and Roberts, *Rules and Processes: The Cultural Logic of Dispute in an African Context* (Chicago 1981) 70–106; and Simon Roberts, *Order and Dispute: An Introduction to Legal Anthropology* (Harmondsworth 1979) 171–172. On rules, see also Sally Falk Moore, *Social Facts and Fabrications: "Customary" Law on Kilimanjaro, 1880–1980* (Cambridge 1986), esp. 38–91.

41. Cassidy and Ringler (n. 2 above) 138–139; italics added. Mitchell and Robinson summarize important provisions of "the code of the *comitatus*" as follows: "While his lord lived, the warrior owed him loyalty unto death. If his lord were killed, the warrior had to avenge him or die in the attempt. The lord in his turn had the duty of protecting his warriors. He had to be a greater fighter to attract men, a man of noble character and a generous giver of feasts and treasures to hold them": Mitchell and Robinson (n. 2 above) 136.

42. For a more elaborate example of the same strategy, see the passage about Heremod in *Beowulf*, lines 1709–1722. Lords could also be discredited, for example, by references to stinginess or sexual misbehavior.

43. In one form or another, this view of earlier medieval law appears in: S. F. C.

Milsom, "Law and Fact in Legal Development," *University of Toronto Journal* 17 (1967) 1–19; Fredric L. Cheyette, "Suum Cuique Tribuere," *French Historical Studies* 6 (1970) 287–299; Paul R. Hyams, "Trial by Ordeal: The Key to Proof in the Early Common Law," in *On the Laws and Customs of England: Essays in Honor of Samuel E. Thorne*, ed. Morris S. Arnold et al. (Chapel Hill 1980); Patrick J. Geary, "Vivre en conflit dans une France sans état: Typologie des mécanismes de règlement des conflits (1050–1200)," *Annales E.S.C.* 42 (1986) 1107–1133; Susan Reynolds, *Kingdoms and Communities in Western Europe, 900–1300* (Oxford 1984) chap. 1; and Stephen D. White, *Custom, Kinship, and Gifts to Saints: The Laudatio Parentum in Western France, 1050 to 1150* (Chapel Hill 1988) chap. 3. For a somewhat similar view of early, if not later, Anglo-Saxon law, see Patrick Wormald, "The Uses of Literacy in Anglo-Saxon England and Its Neighbours," *Transactions of the Royal Historical Society* ser. 5, 27 (1977) 95–114; idem. "*Lex scripta and Verbum regis:* Legislation and Kingship from Euric to Cnut," in *Early Medieval Kingship*, ed. P. H. Sawyer and I. N. Wood (Leeds 1977) 105–138; idem, "Charters, Law and the Settlement of Disputes in Anglo-Saxon England," in *The Settlement of Disputes in Early Medieval Europe*, ed. Wendy Davies and Paul Fouracre (Cambridge 1986) 149–168.

44. Although Woolf questions the conventional claim, based mainly on Tacitus's *Germania* and "The Battle of Maldon," that an early medieval English warrior was expected to die with his lord, she argues that a man was still obliged to avenge his lord's death sooner or later: Woolf (n. 10 above) 72 and passim.

45. If the passage in question shows that "*even* a swineherd recognized the obligation of taking vengeance upon one who had killed his own lord" (Blair [n. 10 above] 252; italics added), why does the text not portray followers other than the swineherd who recognized that obligation? To demonstrate that in this particular episode, "the logic of loyalty makes the behavior of the actors and the sequence of events patterned and predictable" (Cassidy and Ringler [n. 2 above] 139), one would have to explain how anyone could have predicted that a swineherd would have avenged an ealdorman.

46. Moorman believes that Sigeberht's slayer reappears in the story (see n. 15 above) but never asks whether he became a target for vengeance by his victim's kin or followers.

47. On the political purposes that the *Chronicle* may have served, see the works cited in Whitelock, *Documents* (n. 2 above) 123 n. 2 and 140. Although Whitelock denies that this work "was written as propaganda," she never demonstrates that it was a value-free record of events: *Documents* (n. 2 above) 123, 140. Along with Natalie Zemon Davis, "we can agree with Hayden White that the world does not just 'present itself to perception in the form of well-made stories'": Natalie Zemon Davis, *Fiction in the Archives: Pardon Tales and Their Tellers in Sixteenth-Century France* (Oxford 1987) 3, citing Hayden White, "The Value of Narrativity in the Representation of Reality," in W. J. T. Mitchell, ed., *On Narrative* (Chicago 1981) 23.

48. Battaglia (n. 2 above) anticipates several of the arguments advanced below.

49. Ibid. 177.

50. Moorman claims that any followers of Cyneheard whose kinsmen followed

Cynewulf must have "broken blood-ties": Moorman (n. 2 above); see also Towers (n. 2 above) 313 and n. 7; Battaglia (n. 2 above) 175.

51. See n. 5 above.

52. Battaglia (n. 2 above) 177; Wormald (n. 4 above) 115.

53. See Magoun (n. 2 above) 370, 373.

54. See Moorman (n. 2 above) 97; Wrenn (n. 2 above) 215.

55. In attacking Cynewulf at *Meretun*, Cyneheard may have been trying to avenge Sigeberht's deposition: Wrenn (n. 2 above) 214.

56. See Battaglia (n. 2 above) 177.

57. Ibid. 177–178; and Wormald (n. 4 above) 115.

58. See n. 17 above.

59. On the question of how many royal followers had kin with Cyneheard, see Battaglia (n. 2 above) 176–177.

60. By arguing that Cynewulf's followers made the offer of safe-conduct partly "to spare themselves the *emotional* conflict of fighting blood relatives," Magoun does his best to minimize the political or normative significance of the conflict: Magoun (n. 2 above) 373.

61. In many societies where cognatic kindreds are found and play an important political role, obligations to distant kin are often weaker than obligations to close kin: J. D. Freeman, "On the Concept of the Kindred," *Journal of the Royal Anthropological Institute* 91 (1961) 192–220; repr. with deletions in *Kinship and Social Organization*, ed. Paul Bohannan and John Middleton (Garden City, N.J. 1968) 255–272 at 265–266.

62. See n. 50 above.

63. Battaglia (n. 2 above) 177.

64. *Beowulf, the Donaldson Translation: Backgrounds and Sources: Criticism*, ed. Joseph Tuso (New York 1975) 20, lines 1095–1105. On the relationship of this passage to our text, see Woolf (n. 10 above) 69–71.

65. Mitchell and Robinson (n. 2 above) 201.

66. See, for example, Whitelock, *Beginnings* (n. 30 above) 39.

67. Stanley B. Greenfield and Daniel G. Calder deviate from the conventional interpretation of the story when they claim that it "depicts with political overtones the irresolvable conflicts between *comitatus* loyalty and blood relationships": *A New Critical History of Old English Literature* (New York 1986) 60.

68. Pierre Bourdieu, *Outline of a Theory of Practice*, trans. Richard Nice (1977; repr. Cambridge 1982) 40; see also 38–43.

69. See, e.g., the chapters by Campbell, John, and Wormald in Campbell (n. 4 above).

70. For a lucid discussion of early Germanic kinship, see Alexander Callendar Murray, *Germanic Kinship Structure: Studies in Law and Society in Antiquity and the Middle Ages*, Pontifical Institute of Medieval Studies, Studies and Texts 65 (Toronto 1983).

71. Frederick Pollock and Frederic William Maitland, *The History of English Law before the Time of Edward I*, ed. 2 (1898), reissued with a new introduction and select bibliography by S. F. C. Milsom, 2 vols. (Cambridge 1968) 2.240–260, esp. 2.240–

245. Maitland was wrong in assuming that because feuds were carried on by cognatic kindreds, other social activities must have been carried on by kin groups constituted in the same way. See T. M. Charles-Edwards, "Kinship, Status and the Origins of the Hide," *Past and Present* 56 (1977) 3–33, esp. 16 and n. 25; Lancaster (n. 30 above) 372–373; H. H. Meinhard, "The Patrilineal Principle in Early Teutonic Kinship," in *Studies in Social Anthropology: Essays in Memory of E. E. Evans-Pritchard,* ed. J. H. M. Beattie and R. G. Lienhardt (Oxford 1975) 1–29; and Murray (n. 70 above) passim.

72. Chadwick, *Heroic Age* (n. 30 above) 347, 348.

73. Bertha Surtees Phillpotts, *Kindred and Clan in the Middle Ages and After: A Study in the Sociology of the Teutonic Races* (Cambridge 1913) repr. in extract as "The Germanic Kindreds," in *Early Medieval Society,* ed. Sylvia L. Thrupp (New York 1967) 3–16 at 7.

74. Stenton (n. 4 above) 311–312.

75. Ibid. 313.

76. Ibid. 314.

77. Lancaster (n. 30 above) 376.

78. H. R. Loyn, "Kinship in Anglo-Saxon England," ASE 3 (1974) 197–209 at 197–198.

79. Ibid. 209.

80. Ibid. 207. Later, according to Loyn, "kinship remained immensely strong in ordinary social life," but "steady pressure was diminishing the legal sanctions attributable to kinship": ibid. 199.

81. See, e.g., Whitelock (n. 30 above) 38–39; Fisher (n. 30 above) 132; Finberg (n. 11 above) 230; Loyn (n. 30 above) 292, 298.

82. Hector Munro Chadwick, *The Origin of the English Nation* (Cambridge 1907) 154.

83. Ibid. 154.

84. On societies of this kind, see, for example, Morton H. Fried, *The Evolution of Political Society: An Essay in Political Anthropology* (New York 1967) chaps. 1–3; and Marshall Sahlins, *Tribesmen* (Englewood Cliffs, N.J. 1968).

85. Scholars attempting to place English kinship in a comparative European context should note Peter Sawyer's contention that "the solidarity of kin-groups" *throughout* early medieval western Europe has been "exaggerated": "The Bloodfeud in Fact and Fiction," in *Tradition og Historie-Skrivning,* Act Jutlandica 63. Humanistick serie 61 (Aarhus 1987) 27–38 at 27; italics added.

86. See Sawyer (n. 85 above) 35–36.

87. In these respects, English kindreds do not seem to have differed dramatically from those studied by anthropologists: Freeman (n. 61 above) 260–262, 263–266.

88. On conflicts between a person's obligations to different kin, see, e.g., Max Gluckman, "The Peace in the Feud," in his *Custom and Conflict in Africa* (Glencoe, Ill. 1955) 1–26; idem, *The Judicial Process among the Barotse of Northern Rhodesia,* ed. 2 (Manchester 1967) 20–24; P. H. Gulliver, *Social Conflict in an African Society: A Study of the Arusha: Agricultural Masai of Northern Tanganyika* (Boston 1963) 240–258; Jane

Fishburne Collier, *Law and Social Change in Zincantan* (Stanford 1973) 169–179; Roberts (n. 40 above) 55–56, 160.

89. See Roger M. Keesing, *Kin Groups and Social Structure* (New York 1975) 15; and Freeman (n. 61 above) 271. Murray incorporates this view of cognatic kindreds into his discussion of early Germanic kinship: Murray (n. 70 above) 4, 8, 24–25.

90. See Whitelock (n. 30 above) 47; Dorothy Whitelock, *The Audience of Beowulf* (Oxford 1951) 16–17; Loyn (n. 30 above) 294–295.

91. See Loyn (n. 78 above) 207; Lancaster (n. 30 above) 359, 376.

92. Loyn (n. 78 above) 207; Pollock and Maitland (n. 71 above) 2.254–255.

93. Loyn is right to draw "a vital distinction . . . between land subject to customary testamentary obligation within the kin and land owned by the kin": Loyn (n. 78 above) 207; see also Pollock and Maitland (n. 71 above) 2.2–17, 260–313. Nevertheless, the existence of so-called familial restraints on a landholder's power of alienation may imply that his kin had birthrights to some of his land (but see Pollock and Maitland 2.248–255) and/or that a custom broadly similar to the later French *retrait lignager* can be found in early medieval England: see Jack Goody, *The Development of the Family and Marriage in Europe* (Cambridge 1983) 105, 107, 111, 120–123, 141, 142. French historians have routinely associated familial restraints on alienation with a system of landholding in which a landholder's kin had rights of some kind in his land: see White (n. 43 above) chap. 1.

94. Whitelock 132, Loyn, Fisher 132, Kirby 142–143 (all n. 30 above); William Ian Miller, "Choosing the Avenger: Some Aspects of the Bloodfeud in Medieval Iceland and England," *Law and History Review* 1 (1983) 161–204 at 170–171. On the failure of early dooms to treat kinship obligations fully, see Loyn 292–293.

95. Miller (n. 94 above) 170–171.

96. Ibid. 173.

97. See, e.g., Eric John, "The Age of Edgar," in Campbell (n. 4 above) 160–191 at 168–169; J. M. Wallace-Hadrill, "The Bloodfeud of the Franks," in his *The Long-Haired Kings* (1962; repr. Toronto 1982) 125 n. 3.

98. Interestingly enough, the obligation of warriors to avenge their lords goes unmentioned in Old English law codes.

99. Bourdieu (n. 68 above) 16.

100. Ibid. 17.

101. Ibid. 16.

102. Ibid. 17.

103. Henry Sumner Main, *Ancient Law: Its Connection with the Early History of Society and Its Relation to Modern Ideas*, ed. 10 (Boston 1963) 163.

104. Ibid. 163.

105. Ibid. 165; Maine's italics.

The Thematic Structure
of the *Sermo Lupi*

STEPHANIE HOLLIS

*S*ERMO *Lupi ad Anglos* has attracted far more attention by its subject
matter than have other Wulfstan sermons, because its apparent topicality is of interest to students of the Old English period. Like all
Wulfstan's sermons, though, it has been chiefly esteemed for its forceful oratory—it is this sermon, indeed, which is responsible for his reputation as a
fiery orator in the Old Testament vein. Most readers have praised it more
enthusiastically than Sir Frank Stenton did, when he stated that it 'makes its
effect by sheer monotony of commination'.[1] But even its admirers have regarded it as little more than a stringing together of the nation's sins and
tribulations which impresses by the horrific accumulation of detail.[2] Such a
view, it will be argued, is a drastic oversimplification. The *Sermo Lupi* presents a number of closely related themes, and the catalogues are but one aspect of the development of these themes. Certainly the seemingly inex-
haustible fashion in which Wulfstan heaps up specific instances of the
nation's iniquities and misfortunes contributes much to the force of his in-
ductment, but the sermon is neither formless nor repetitive. On the contrary, it is the most skilfully and tightly constructed of all his sermons.

The intellectual coherence and thematic complexity of the *Sermo Lupi*
have been obscured not only by a too exclusive concentration on its oratorical force but also by the currently accepted analyses of the process of its
composition. Professor Whitelock has described the sermon largely in
terms of a haphazard compilation and adaptation of earlier material:

> To a fair amount of material from Ethelred's codes Wulfstan added an
> introductory passage made up of phrases from his eschatological ser-
> mons, especially XIII [Napier], and this homily supplied also his pas-
> sage on the decay of kinship and some isolated phrases elsewhere.

There is also a general similarity between the list of calamities in the *Sermo ad Anglos* and that in xxviii [Napier], a free translation and expansion of *Leviticus* xxvi. For his other additions, Wulfstan seems to have drawn on his experience of conditions in England . . . Finally, he has added a normal homiletic conclusion.[3]

Professor Bethurum regards the EI version[4] as the end product of a series of revisions incorporating Wulfstan's afterthoughts (like Professor Whitelock, she considers BH, the shortest version, to be the earliest):

> The revised homily as represented in C was again revised by the addition of EI 65–7, 85–91, 145–6, 160–73, and 176–90. The first passage contains an echo of vii and, like the second, is a strong rebuke to lust. Both of these additions may have been occasioned by a particular event which came to Wulfstan's attention . . . The long list of sinners in 160–73 is reworked from earlier homilies, and Wulfstan may have seen its appropriateness after he had written the first draft of his sermon. The last passage is on the responsibility of the English for their plight . . . and was suggested by a passage in one of Alcuin's letters . . . It is possible that Wulfstan discovered this letter of Alcuin's late, or discovered it in his notes . . . and thought it an apt addition.[5]

In my view the EI version is the most satisfactory exposition of the sermon's themes. This superiority might appear to favour the theory that this version represents the final stage of a process of gradual expansion. But EI differs principally from BH in the inclusion of two passages referring to the Danish attacks (EI 200–28 and 176–90), and, as I understand the sermon, both passages are crucial to the development of its themes. Their absence from BH also destroys the structural pattern discernible in EI. Further, a consideration of the verbal linking in the sermon suggests that these two passages, as well as certain others in EI but not in BH, are original (particularly EI 65–7 and 160–73). It is my belief, then, that an examination of the themes and structure of the EI version calls into question the theory that it represents the latest of the three versions written by Wulfstan. Other arguments in support of the view that BH and C are abridgements of EI I have set out elsewhere.[6]

The following discussion is based on MS I,[7] which is much earlier than E and contains corrections in Wulfstan's handwriting.[8] But while I regard MS I as substantially representative of the earliest version, I do not consider that it reproduces exactly the sermon as it was first composed. EI 79–83 and 85–91 appear to be additions, for not only are both out of keeping with their context, but also, immediately before beginning the sentence at 85–91, the scribe of MS I made a false start on the sentence which now follows this passage; and this suggests to me that he was copying a version which Wulfstan had revised at this point. Further evidence that Wulfstan re-worked this particular section is the addition, in MS I only, of a phrase (79–80) in his handwriting.[9] Also I accept that certain phrases which are peculiar to manuscripts other than I are original. All of these, with the exception of C 49–56, are short. They include '7 Æþelred man dræfde ut of his earde', which is in BH (71) only and must be regarded as original.[10] It should be stressed that these remarks on the textual variants are not exhaustive—in particular, I reserve judgement on the expansions at EI 145–6, BH 39–40 and C 75, 110, 112 and 160–1. I wish only to suggest that consideration of the sermon's themes and structure can help to establish the status of the variants.

The central theme of the sermon can be summarized as the nation's progression to disaster. It is outlined, as is usual in Wulfstan's work, in the opening sentence. This sentence describes a process of dual deterioration. It begins with a categorical statement that the world is rapidly moving to its end: 'Leofan men, gecnawað þæt soð is: ðeos worold is on ofste, 7 hit nealæcð þam ende' (7–8). The swift passage of time is immediately and inseparably linked to the deterioration of the world: '7 þy hit is on worolde aa swa leng swa wyrse' (8–9). *Wyrse* can be applied either to sins or to afflictions. Hence the deterioration referred to could be either the increase in tribulations, described in the scriptures as signs of the last days, or the moral degeneration of man traditionally believed to accompany the deterioration of the macrocosm in the sixth age.[11] The clause which follows shows that the two types of deterioration are causally connected: '7 swa hit sceal nyde for folces synnan [fram dæge to dæge] ær Antecristes tocyme yfelian swyþe' (9–10). It may be objected that, since *wyrse* is ambiguous, this clause is simply a description of the growth of sin. I interpret it, however, as meaning that the accumulation of afflictions gathers momentum from the nation's sins, since, according to the Bosworth-Toller dictionary, *yfelian* with an impersonal pronoun as subject applies only to the deterioration of 'things or circumstances'. Further, the culmination of the process is described in the final clause as '7 huru hit wyrð þænne egeslic 7 grimlic wide on worolde' (10–11). This must be a reference to the afflictions of Antichrist's reign, because 'egeslic 7 grimlic' is inappropriate to the description of sin.

The opening sentence echoes certain parts of other eschatological sermons by Wulfstan, but I would not describe it as 'made up of phrases almost identical with some in the eschatological sermons'.[12] It is not only that none of the sentences cited by editors contains expressions comparable with the first and final clauses; the description is misleading because the opening sentence of the *Sermo Lupi* is the only single sentence in Wulfstan's work which gives a complete and dramatically realized account of the process of deterioration. Its series of similarly constructed clauses linked by 'and', each advancing the argument or the chronology by one stage, gives an impression of steady accumulation. The clause lamenting the terror of Antichrist's reign, the culmination of the process described, is felt to constitute a climax, because it is the last of a number of clauses having the same pattern. It is also marked as an oratorical climax by the exclamatory *huru*. The BH and C versions give an incomplete and stylistically less effective account of the process, because they omit the final clause lamenting the ultimate disaster which overtakes the world.

The complete and dramatic description of the process of deterioration in the opening sentence of the *Sermo Lupi* marks an advance in Wulfstan's conception of the last days. In his early eschatological sermons, particularly Bethurum III and V, he had asserted that the unprecedented tribulations of the last days are a punishment for immense sins. In the *Sermo Lupi* the retributive process is conceived dynamically. Antichrist's reign is presented not as the ultimate horror foreshadowed by manifold tribulations but as the climax of a progressive growth of afflictions which is proportionate to the increasing quantity of sin. That this was in Wulfstan's mind in his opening sentence is borne out by an analysis of the sermon as a whole.

It is also borne out by the phrase 'fram dæge to dæge' which the E version includes after *synnan* and which I accept as an authentic reading. The phrase echoes a sentence in Bethurum 1b:[13] 'And us þincð þæt hit sy þam timan swyðe gehende, forðam þeos woruld is fram dæge to dæge a swa leng swa wyrse' (22–4). Here also it evidently does not mean only 'daily' but involves the idea of a progression, more particularly an increase. In the *Sermo Lupi* 'fram dæge to dæge' can be taken to refer either to the increase in afflictions or to the increase in sins. This ambiguity of reference, I believe, is intentional, in line with the ambiguity of reference, to which I have already drawn attention, in the word *wyrse*. Because the central emphasis of this sermon is on a cumulative process, when Wulfstan uses *dæghwamlice* in referring to the sins of the nations a few lines later, he immediately adds 'ihte yfel æfter oðrum' (15–16). The link between the two references to the cumulative process in the first few lines is enforced by the verbal repetition of both *dæg* and *yfel* (cf. 'yfelian swyþe' in the first sentence).

Ultimately, since it is an essential part of God's fixed plan for the universe, the deterioration of the world which ends in the reign of Antichrist and the last judgement is inevitable. Wulfstan's opening sentence states this

categorically ('ðeos worold is on ofste, 7 hit nealæcð þam ende . . . 7 swa hit
sceal nyde . . . yfelian swyþe'). If, however, punishments accrue in proportion to the sins of man, the reign of Antichrist may also be postponed by a
diminution of man's sins. It follows from this that the fulfilment of the
prophecies of the last days is contingent upon the actions of mankind.
There is therefore a remedy. This, however, is not immediately mentioned.
The opening sentence is followed by a description which demonstrates the
validity of the assertion that the world grows worse because of mankind's
sins (11–18). It is the sins and tribulations of the past that receive attention
here, the causal connection being emphasized by 'And we eac forþam' (17).
Both the sins and the punishments are described in extreme terms ('(to)
fela', 'manege' and 'ealles to wide gynd ealle þas þeode'). By stressing the
immensity of the sins already committed and asserting that these have ac-
cumulated over a long period, Wulfstan keeps before his audience the
warning that the end of the world is close at hand, since the first sentence
indicates that the proximity of Antichrist's reign is measurable in terms of
both the amount of sin and the amount of affliction.

In the process of demonstrating the nation's progression to ultimate
disaster, Wulfstan introduces the possibility of amelioration. The concept
is first introduced in a negative form, 'And næs a fela manna þe smeade
ymbe þa bote' (14–15), the negative constituting one of the sins of the past.
It then appears in a conditional clause attached to the statement that punishment has resulted from sin, the play on the meanings of *gebidan* ('endured' and 'expected') emphasizing the contrast between the afflictions of
the past and the improvement which could eventuate: 'And we eac forþam
habbað fela byrsta 7 bysmara gebiden, 7 gif we ænige bote gebidan scylan,
þonne mote we þæs to Gode earnian bet þonne we ær þysan dydan' (17–20).
In the following sentence the relation between sin and affliction is summarized in one clause, which is balanced by another dealing with repentance.
A conditional clause referring to improvement completes the sentence:
'Forþam mid miclan earnungan we geearnedan þa yrmða þe us onsittað, 7
mid swyþe micelan earnungan we þa bote motan æt Gode geræcan gif hit
sceal heonanforð godiende weorðan' (20–3). An entire sentence is then devoted to the concept of improvement: 'La hwæt, we witan ful georne þæt to
miclan bryce sceal micel bot nyde, 7 to miclan bryne wæter unlytel, gif man
þæt fyr sceal to ahte acwencan' (23–5). In this manner the emphasis of the
opening lines gradually moves from the inevitability of a progression culminating in disaster to the conditional possibility of improvement (note the
conditional clauses in 18, 22–3 and 25). The sentence at 23–5 forms the
rhetorical climax of the introduction, the exclamatory *La hwæt* and the un-

usually figurative expression giving stylistic prominence to this didactically important point. The play on the meaning of *bot* is thematically significant, for it unifies the concept of repentance with the improvement repentance could effect in the nation's fortunes. It first meant 'repentance' in 'næs a fela manna þe smeade ymbe þa bote' (14–15); then in the next two occurrences (18 and 22), as the context suggests, 'remedy' in the sense of 'assistance'. In 'to miclan bryce sceal micel bot nyde' (23–4) *bryce* may mean either 'fracture' (since the following parallel clause is obviously figurative) or 'violation', so that *bot* in this instance may signify both 'cure' and 'recompense'.

The opening lines present the relation between sin and repentance, as well as the relation between sin and punishment, in terms of progressive intensification. In his first reference to remedy Wulfstan indicates that efforts to obtain it must increase ('þæs to Gode earnian bet þonne we ær þysan dydan' (19–20)), and the point is then elaborated (20–3, quoted above). The exact balancing of the constituent elements of the two main clauses in this elaborating sentence, violated by the addition of *swyþe* in the second clause to emphasize that efforts to improve must exceed the nation's sins, suggests that repentance is capable of cancelling out the sins and bringing about the amelioration described in the final conditional clause. Whereas this sentence employs parallel main clauses to equate sin and repentance, parallel noun phrases within a noun clause are employed at 23–5 to repeat the equation ('to miclan bryce sceal micel bot nyde, 7 to miclan bryne wæter unlytel'). The grammatical compression heightens the antithetical nature of the two concepts and the power which repentance has to cancel out sins, especially in 'to miclan bryne wæter unlytel', in which opposites are directly opposed by the reduction of the verb and adverb.

In sum, the sermon's opening sentence asserts that disasters multiply in time and culminate in the reign of Antichrist as a result of the daily growth in sins. The fixity of this pattern of events is illustrated by reference to past experience, but the possibility of improving the situation gradually achieves prominence (7–25). Repentance is therefore shown to be urgently necessary, for it assumes the aspect of the sole factor capable of modifying the rapid progression to ultimate disaster. It is on the need for repentance that the remainder of the first section turns (25–52).

In Wulfstan's view, repentance must take the form of the restoration of *lagu* and *riht*. The swift onward movement to destruction can be turned back only by a reversal of the course of action which, he states early in the sermon the nation is currently pursuing: 'And næs a fela manna þe smeade ymbe þa bote swa georne swa man scolde, ac dæghwamlice man ihte yfel æfter oðrum 7 unriht rærde 7 unlaga manege ealles to wide gynde ealle þas þeode' (14–17). At 25–7 he asserts the need for repentance, echoing *lagu* and *riht*, the words which he had used earlier with negative affixes: 'And micel is nydþearf manna gehwilcum þæt he Godes lage gyme heonanforð georne [bet þonne he ær dyde] 7 Godes gerihta mid rihte gelæste.' The phrase 'bet þonne he ær dyde', only in E, is in line with the continuing insistence on the need for a renewal of righteousness. The need for repentance is also asserted in 'Ac soð is þæt ic secge, þearf is þære bote' (37–8), which repeats the *þearf* of *nydþearf* in the earlier assertion (26), which itself picks up *nyde* from the preceding exclamatory sentence equating sin and repentance (23–5). The need for repentance is evident because of the apocalyptic nature of the corruption. Christians have become worse than heathens (27–37). The emphasis of the Old Testament prophets on the oppression of the poor, widows and orphans[14] is echoed here to signalize the definitive nature of the nation's corruption (42–7). Instead of righteousness and the rule of law (both secular and divine) Wulfstan finds in his people the rule of *unriht* and *unlagu*—the words *riht* and *lagu*, on their own or in compound words or with negative prefixes, are repeated constantly throughout this indictment of the nation's sins. God's judgement, perhaps God's ultimate judgement of the people, is inevitable. This Wulfstan states in a sentence which, in its reference to *bysmor* and *byrst*, echoes his earlier insistence on the causal connection of sin and punishment (17–18): 'And þæs we habbað ealle þurh Godes yrre bysmor gelome, gecnawe se ðe cunne; 7 se byrst wyrð gemæne, þeh man swa ne wene, eallre þysse þeode, butan God beorge' (49–52). The last words, however, emphasize God's grace ('butan God beorge'). God has established not only the pattern, with which the sermon is concerned, of an inevitable deterioration of the world and an inevitable disastrous end, but also a pattern of redemption and atonement for sin.[15] It may well be that 'Uton creopan to Criste 7 bifigendre heortan clipian gelome 7 geearnian his mildse', apparently so unlike Wulfstan and recorded only in the peroration of the C version (167–8) is authentic.

In 7–52, then, we have a sustained exposition of the sermon's themes, linked by verbal repetition, of which the thematically significant instances have been noted. The section *could* be subdivided after the sentence at 23–5, because there is a shift of emphasis at this point. This exclamatory sentence marks the climax of Wulfstan's remarks on the possibility of improvement and is followed by a consideration of the need for repentance. But the division is blurred by the sentence initiator 'and', which enforces the continuity of sense, and by the repetition of *micel* and *nyd*. The section could be further subdivided before 'Ac soð is þæt ic secge, þearf is þære bote' (37–8), which marks the end of the series of comparisons (27–37) supporting the assertion that there is need for every man 'þæt he Godes lage gyme heonan-forð georne [bet þonne he ær dyde] 7 Godes gerihta mid rihte gelæste' (25–7) and introduces the catalogue of various transgressions against *riht* and *lagu*. But the repetition of *riht* and *lagu* which is prominent throughout 37–49 begins in the sentence at 25–7, which is itself an echo of 'unriht rærde 7 unlaga manege' (16). It is the repetition of *riht* and *lagu* in combination which suggests that the passage in C at 49–56 formed part of the original sermon, for without it the introductory indictment concludes with a reference to *lagu* only ('7, hrædest is to cweþenne, Godes laga laðe 7 lara for-sawene' (EI 48–9)). If, however, the C passage is admitted, the summing up phrase is immediately preceded by a reference to both *lagu* and *riht*: 'forðam unriht is to wide mannum gemæne 7 unlaga leofe' (C 56). These words provide not only a satisfactory completion of the verbal patterning begun in 'unriht rærde 7 unlaga manege' (EI 16) but also a clear statement of one of the sermon's themes, namely the nation's perverse preference for evil instead of good, which is hinted at in 'And næs a fela manna þe smeade ymbe þa bote swa georne swa man scolde, ac dæghwamlice man ihte yfel æfter oðrum 7 unriht rærde 7 unlaga manege ealles to wide gynd ealle þas þeode' (14–17).

I take the sentence at 49–52 to conclude the introductory section not merely because it is a rhetorically effective climax but because it completes the exposition, returning the argument to the point reached at 17–18 ('And we eac forþam habbað fela byrsta 7 bysmara gebiden'), taking up once more the words *byrst* and *bysmor* and coming to rest in the reference to God and his grace. At the same time, however, it serves as a bridge, because, as is evident from *Forþam* (53), it is the inception of the account of the nation's sins which follows. A bridge of this sort is characteristic of this particular sermon. Normally units of sense in Wulfstan's sermons, each unified by a particular verbal or syntactic patterning and internally linked by sentence initiators such as 'and', are isolated from one another.[16] Here, however, the boundaries of the rhetorical units are blurred because of the forward carrying nature of the theme.

The introductory section is a paradigm of the sermon as a whole. In very general terms, the sermon consists of passages describing the sins of the nation alternated with accounts of tribulation, the two being linked by statements which draw attention to the cause and effect relationship. Towards the end of the sermon the possibility of improvement is gradually reintroduced and an exhortation to repent forms its conclusion. The dynamic historical pattern described is reflected in the sermon's dynamic structure. The same pattern structures both historical time and the time it

takes to deliver the sermon. Punishment follows sin inexorably, and the catalogues of the nation's sins grow longer and the accumulation grows more
rapid as the afflictions described grow more terrible. The passages dealing
with the nation's afflictions are at 53–9, 100–28 and 174–89. The sentence
at 189–90 links the last of these to the exhortatory peroration. The passages dealing with the nation's sins, after the introductory section, are at
59–99 and 129–73. I shall examine first the accounts of afflictions.

The opening section of the sermon, as I have intimated, refers to the
nation's afflictions simply as 'fela byrsta 7 bysmara' (18) and as 'bysmor
gelome' in a passage (49–52) which also threatens that 'se byrst wyrð
gemæne'. The first account of afflictions (53–9) provides a detailed catalogue of the tribulations which the nation has suffered. Wulfstan begins by
reiterating the point that these afflictions are the result of the nation's sins:
'Forþam hit is on us eallum swutol 7 gesene þæt we ær þysan oftor bræcan
þonne we bettan, 7 þy is þysse þeode fela onsæge' (53–4). The reference to
the nation's sins, which is reminiscent of the metaphor 'to miclan bryce
sceal micel bot nyde', calls attention to the fact that the nation has accelerated, instead of slowing down, its course to destruction ('we ær þysan oftor
bræcan þonne we bettan'). Consistent with this is the statement at 55–9
that the nation has not prospered, but has suffered many afflictions. As editors have noted, the passage is similar to one in Bethurum XIX describing
the punishment which befalls the disobedient nation and one in Bethurum
V listing the calamities of the last days.[17] Though a number of the details
transform the description into a more specific reflection of contemporary
ills, its significance for Wulfstan, and possibly for his audience, may have
resided in the intimation it gives of the approaching end of the world, for
strife among nations is a sign of the second coming, and disease and un-
fruitfulness are a symptom of the earth's decline in its last age.[18] In the light
of the sermon's themes the reference to the duration and extent of the afflictions ('nu lange inne ne ute' and 'on gewelhwylcan ende') and the insistence on their intensity and frequency ('oft 7 gelome', 'swyþe þearle',
'swyþe' and 'foroft') are also intimations of the proximity of Antichrist's
reign.

The second account of afflictions (100–28) is concerned with one particular kind. Wulfstan depicts the degraded state to which the English people as a whole and their leaders in particular have been reduced by their enemies. He begins with a rhetorical question calling attention to the extent
of the humiliations suffered by the English: 'And la, hu mæg mare scamu
þurh Godes yrre mannum gelimpan þonne us deð gelome for agenum
gewyrhtum?' (100–1). The extent of the humiliations, so excessive that

nothing beyond it could be conceived, is suggestive of the impending conquest and possible destruction of the nation. The magnitude of degradation
is manifested in various ways. The Vikings' exaction of wergeld for a thrall
by unjust application of the law and the powerlessness of an English thane's
kinsmen to avenge injuries received from a thrall (101–6) reveal the unnatural supremacy of thrall over thane. This injury at the personal level is
linked, both in substance and by verbal repetition, with the reference to the
Vikings' exaction of tribute at the national level (106–8). Similarly the description of the thrall who 'his hlaford cnyt swyþe fæste 7 wyrcð him to
þræle' (117–18) is parallel to the description of the Vikings leading the English into captivity, particularly if we take *gewelede togædere* to refer not to
þas þeode but to *þa drafe cristenra manna*, so that the Christians, like the cap-
tured thane, are bound (120–2). The powerlessness of the English thane is
equally manifest when he has to witness the humiliation of his women without interfering (113–17). The culminating sentences (123–8) draw attention to the fact that the continual insult, instead of being avenged on the of-
fender, is compounded by the payment of tribute.

   The third passage referring to afflictions (174–89) consists of an historical parallel with the English conquest of the Britons which is meant to
make the audience see that the present perilous state of the nation is unprecedented. After citing Gildas's explanation for the destruction of the
Britons Wulfstan states: 'Ac utan don swa us þearf is, warnian us be swilcan;
7 soþ is þæt ic secge, wyrsan dæda we witan mid Englum þonne we mid
Bryttan ahwar gehyrdan' (186–9). If, for the magnitude of their sins, the
Britons were exterminated, the fate of the English nation, whose sins,
Wulfstan insists, are immeasurably greater than any reported of the Britons,
must also be immeasurably worse. What he has in mind must be the imminent reign of Antichrist, a fate far worse than national extermination. The
drawing of this historical parallel becomes possible because of the principle, pervasive in the sermon, that punishment is proportionate to sin. The
imminent historical event is the conquest of England by the Vikings, which
for Wulfstan coalesces with the eschatological event. The coming of the
Vikings is the coming of the reign of Antichrist, predicted in the opening
sentence (7–11). Wulfstan's presentation of the Vikings as antichrists
whose victory establishes the reign of the arch-enemy appears to be without parallel in Old English homiletic literature, but to him the equation of
Viking rule with the reign of Antichrist would have been a logical inference.
He asserts frequently in his work that heathenism is the worship of the
devil,[19] and the similarities between the reign of a heathen king and that of
Antichrist would have been obvious to him.[20] The equation of Viking vic-

tory with the rule of Antichrist is prefigured earlier in the sermon. In the account of the humiliations they inflict on the English (100–28) the Vikings are depicted not simply as the enemies of the English nation but as the opponents of *cristendom* and the oppressors *cristenra manna* (102 and 121). Their supremacy is presented as an inversion of order, for, as I have noted, instances of the humiliations suffered by the English Christians at the hands of the heathen Vikings are juxtaposed with instances of the reversal of social rôles. This association of the rule of Antichrist with an inversion of order is characteristic of Wulfstan, for Antichrist is depicted elsewhere in his sermons (particularly in Bethurum ix) as the inverter of all that is true and right. The theme of inverted order can be traced even further back in the sermon, for the employment of parallelism at 102–6, 110–12 and 125–6 to demonstrate the superiority of the Vikings recalls the series of antithetical sentences near the beginning (27–37), which contrast the heathens' scrupulous observance of religious duties with the sacrilegiousness of the English Christians. The inversion of expected order in the early passage is brought out particularly clearly in the use of *Godes þeowas* to refer to Christian clergy and *gedwolgoda þenan* to describe heathen priests, for the terms emphasize the unnatural pre-eminence of those who adhere to falsehood.[21]

It is the passages not in the BH version, then, EI 100–28 and 176–90, which provide an indication of accumulating disaster. Without them the body of the sermon contains no intimation of the coming reign of Antichrist which is referred to in the opening sentence as the culmination of the process of deterioration. Close links with the surrounding text also support the view that these passages are original. The passage at 100–28 is linked to the preceding unit by the repetition of *Godes yrre* (the phrase first occurs at 98–9) and to the following unit by the repetition of the root word *limp-* (*gelimpum* (127) and *mislimpe* (129)). The end of the passage at 176–90 is linked to the exhortatory peroration by the repetition of *þearf*. The beginning of the passage has no close verbal links with the preceding sentence, but this sentence's exhortation to guard against complete destruction ('Ac la, on Godes naman utan don swa us neod is, beorgan us sylfum swa we geornost magan þe læs we ætgædere ealle forweorðan' (174–6)) is supported only if we admit the threat of conquest contained in 176–90.

Although the passages that are concerned with the nation's sins (59–99 and 129–73) are recognizably different from one another in subject matter, their progressive accumulation of sins is indicated predominantly by stylistic devices. What is stressed is the magnitude of evil, both qualitatively and quantitatively, and the length of time during which it has prevailed. This emphasis conforms with the sermon's introduction which establishes that the approach of the end of the world can be measured by the passage of time and the increase in man's sins. The sermon refers constantly to the sins of the past as well as to those of the present, and the frequency of words such as *oft*, *foroft* and *gelome* makes it clear that the process of deterioration is already far advanced. On numerous occasions Wulfstan describes sins as having been committed by all, or almost all, members of the nation, and a number of phrases such as 'gynd ealle þæs þeode', 'innan þysse þeode', 'on æghwylcan ende', 'æghwær mid mannum' and 'ealles to wide' draw attention to the extent to which unrighteousness has spread throughout the nation. The employment of a hyperbolic style throughout the sermon is an index of the extremity of the nation's sins; the treachery in the land, for instance, is described as 'ealra mæst hlafordswice se bið on worolde' (73). The extremity of the nation's sins is also underlined when Wulfstan asserts at the end of his preliminary indictment of the nation's treachery 'do mare gif he mæge' (70) and when he states towards the end of a long recital of sins (61–99) 'And git hit is mare 7 eac mænigfealdre þæt dereð þysse þeode' (95–6).

The abundant intensifying words and phrases in the accounts of the nation's sins (and afflictions) can be seen not as mannerisms but as one of the stylistic devices employed to give expression to Wulfstan's conception of the approach of Antichrist. Intensifiers such as *swyþe*, *ealles to gelome*, *georne* and *to fela* occur, of course, in sermons which are dissimilar to the *Sermo Lupi* in theme. It is noticeable, however, that they occur only sporadically in purely expository sermons like Bethurum XII. They are a prominent stylistic feature only in sermons which, like Wulfstan's early eschatological ones and the *Sermo Lupi*, deal with extreme situations.

The first account of the nation's sins (59–99) deals with treachery. More precisely it could be described as an indictment of faithlessness, since it is informed by Wulfstan's consciousness that men have broken faith with God as well as with their fellow men. The second account (129–73) reveals the total perversity of the nation's values. In both passages Wulfstan employs cumulative and repetitive grammatical structures to suggest the rapid proliferation of the nation's sins. In the first account word pairs, one of the features of Wulfstan's style most frequently remarked on, occur as infrequently as they do in the introductory section.[22] Here, as well as in the introduction, it is primarily sentence and clause structures which are repeated and compounded, and normally each sentence or clause is limited to the description of only one particular sin. For instance, Wulfstan begins his account of treachery with a sentence describing the decay of kinship. It opens with a full clause, followed by another three, which, with the exception of the second which adds *hwilum*, are each reduced to conjunction, subject and object: 'Ne bearh nu foroft gesib gesibban þe ma þe fremdan, ne fæder his bearne, ne hwilum bearn his agenum fæder, ne broþor oþrum' (61–3). The next sin is also described in a full clause followed by reduced clauses containing further instances: 'ne ure ænig his lif ne fadode swa swa he scolde, ne gehadode regollice, ne læwede lahlice' (64–5). The second account (129–73), unlike the first, contains main clauses which consist almost entirely of lists of the names of sins and sinners, mostly linked in pairs (or occasionally larger groups) by alliteration and rhyme of various kinds and joined by conjunctions. Three consecutive main clauses near the beginning introduce long catalogues of this kind (131–46). Thus 'And eac syndan wide' (138) and 'And eac her syn on earde' (141–2), each introducing a new main clause (or sentence), do not mark, as one might expect, respites from the relentless catalogues of sins, but mark further advances in the accumulation of the nation's evil-doing. The more expository style of 147–59 provides a welcome relief, but in the EI version the lull serves only to enhance the force of the climactic indictment (160–6). In this passage, the last detailed indictment, various kinds of repetition and compounding occur. The five main clauses following the introductory sentence ('Her syndan þurh synleawa . . .') each begin with the words *Her syndan*. The five clauses have the same syntactic structure and the repeated conjunction 'and' links them. They form successive catalogues, for the subject of each clause consists of a list of nouns denoting sinners. In these catalogues too there is repetition of sound, the verbal groups being linked by verbal repetition and rhyme of various kinds.

In the sermon as a whole, then, the growth of sin is indicated by stylistic variation. The theme of 'aa swa leng swa wyrse' is embodied in the development of the sermon, because it progresses from a gradual accumulation of sins to the rapid enumeration of a multitude. In crudely didactic terms the development of the sermon is highly effective, for an emotionally stirring climax is reached in the account of the nation's sins shortly before the culminating threat of destruction and the concluding call for repentance. The series of catalogues of sinners which is peculiar to the EI version (160–6) is essential to the sermon's effectiveness, for it constitutes a climactic 'lift' after the description in 147–59. It is similar to the list of those condemned to hell in other Wulfstan sermons, particularly Bethurum XIII, and its associations for those who were familiar with Wulfstan's work would be entirely appropriate to this sermon's concern with the apocalyptic nature of the nation's sins. The passage (160–73) which includes these catalogues is one of those held to have been added after Wulfstan first wrote the sermon, because it is not in BH. Stylistic considerations can be adduced on both sides of the argument. On the one hand, the repeated *her syndan* echoes sentence openings earlier in the section ('And eac syndan wide' and 'And eac her syn on earde'), and the words *synleawa* and *gelewede* in the first sentence provide a verbal link with the immediately preceding sentence ('lewe nellað beorgan' (159)), in which the figure of speech is introduced. On the other hand, the fact that the absence of the passage results in two adjacent sentences each containing *beorgan* (BH 115 and 117) could be thought to support the view that the passage has been skilfully grafted on. I am of the opinion that it is original because of the thematic importance of 160–6 and, as I shall explain below, of 166–73 too.[23]

Both passages dealing with sins demonstrate the devil's influence on the nation, which appropriately foreshadows his imminent reign as Antichrist. The accounts of the nation's sins, then, reveal the devil's corruption of the land from within, just as the accounts of tribulations reveal that it is besieged from without by the powers of darkness. The account of the nation's 'tealte getrywða' (59–99) elaborates the assertion in the second sentence of the sermon that the devil has deluded the nation for many years and that the absence of *getreowþa* is widespread: 'Understandað eac georne þæt deofol þas þeode nu fela geara dwelode to swyþe, 7 þæt lytle getreowþa wæran mid mannum, þeah hy wel spæcan, 7 unrihta to fela ricsode on lande' (11–14). Faithlessness and untruthfulness are stated to be tenets of Antichrist in Bethurum IX (130–3) and the concealment of evil under fair appearances is particularly associated with the influence of the arch-deceiver (IX, 107–28). It is the pretence and deception which attend treachery that Wulfstan emphasizes in his indictment of the nation's 'tealte getrywða' (especially 67–70). As Professor Whitelock remarks, 'The frequency of references to treachery is one of the most striking features of the records of this period',[24] but Wulfstan's allusions to the prevalence of treachery are not simply a reflection of the contemporary situation. They are a significant aspect of the presentation of his eschatological theme, for they reveal that the influence of Antichrist is already clearly discernible.

Most of the instances of treachery Wulfstan cites in the first account of sins involve the betrayal of kinsmen, but his account of the nation's faithlessness does not merely contain instances of the violation of social order arising from the flagrant disregard of human loyalties; it includes deeds which are directly contrary to the will of God which is, ideally, reflected in the laws which govern social order.[25] There is, as he states, 'ungetrywþa micle for Gode 7 for worolde' (71–2), for kings, who represent Christ on earth, have been betrayed in various ways (71–8) and Christians are sold to the nation's enemies (83–4, 85–91 and 92–4). The passages which I regard as additions (79–83 and 85–91, including the marginal addition in Wulfstan's handwriting in MS I (79–80)) are tangential elaborations on the religious aspect of faithlessness. If they are omitted, there emerges a passage linked by verbal and syntactic repetition in the manner characteristic of the *Sermo Lupi*:

> And godsibbas 7 godbearn to fela man forspilde wide gynd þas þeode . . . 7 cristenes folces to fela man gesealde ut of þysan earde nu ealle hwile. And eal þæt is Gode lað, gelyfe se þe wille . . . Eac we witan georne hwær seo yrmð gewearð þæt fæder gesealde bearn wið weorþe 7 bearn his modor, 7 broþor sealde oþerne fremdum to gewealde. 7 eal þæt syndan micle 7 egeslice dæda, understande se þe wille.

It might be easier to adduce a motive for the addition of 80–3 if one knew precisely what Wulfstan meant by alluding to the destruction of holy places 'þurh þæt þe man sume men ær þam gelogode swa man na ne scolde', but in the case of 85–91, the motive, I suggest, is evident. Because the theme of this passage is 'tealte getreowða', Wulfstan's reference to the sale of Englishmen to heathens presents the offence as a betrayal of family bonds. The fact that the sale of *any* Christian to the enemy is *also* contrary to God's will is only implied in the reference to the sale 'cristenes folces' (83–4), which in itself is a violation of the brotherhood of Christians. At 85–91 Wulfstan broadens his theme to draw attention to the sacrilegious aspect of the sale of Christians, though he links it with the indictment of the betrayal of kinsmen by alluding to the ties of blood which bind God and man in his reference to those who are 'bought with Christ's blood'. This generalization is parallel to the marginal addition of 'toeacan oðran ealles to manegan þe man unscyldige forfor ealles to wide' (79–80) to 'And godsibbas 7 godbearn to fela man forspilde wide gynd þas þeode.'

Because the indictment of the nation's faithlessness is a revelation of its opposition to the will of God, it is an indictment of a specific instance of the pervasive *unriht* in the land, which, in combination with the prevalence of *unlagu*, is described in the introductory section (25–49). The equation of treachery and *unriht* is made in the sentence which opens this account of the nation's sins: 'forþam on þysan earde wæs, swa hit þincan mæg, nu fela geara unriht fela 7 tealte getrywða æghwær mid mannum' (59–61). The nation's opposition to the will of God is established at the very beginning of the sermon as a manifestation of the workings of the arch-enemy, for the second sentence mentions *unriht* in connection with the influence of the devil: 'Understandað eac georne þæt deofol þas þeode nu fela geara dwelode to swyþe, 7 þæt lytle getreowþa wæran mid mannum, þeah hy wel spæcan, 7 unrihta to fela ricsode on lande' (11–14). Elsewhere in his sermons Wulf-stan expresses the view that Antichrist turns men to his contrary law from the teachings of God.[26] Here, in the use of the verb *ricsode*, there is a sug-gestion that the nation has not simply abandoned *riht* but is already gov-erned by evil. A suggestion of rule by unjust and wicked laws, an inversion of order comparable to the reign of Antichrist himself, is contained also in 'unriht rærde 7 unlaga manege', a little later (16). The suggested erection of a law contrary to the law of God is made apparent in the account of the na-tion's treachery only in the EI version, where Wulfstan states: 'Ac worhtan lust us to lage ealles to gelome, 7 naþor ne heoldan ne lare ne lage Godes ne manna swa swa we scoldan' (65–7). The phrase 'worhtan lust us to lage' identifies the contrary law to which the nation adheres as Antichrist's, for it is he who teaches, in opposition to Christ, 'þæt gehwa his luste georne ful-gange'.[27]

The total perversion of the nation's values, depicted in the second ac-count of sins (129–73), is the logical outcome of acceptance of the devil's teaching. This account opens with an assertion that considerations of morality have been abandoned in favour of the proliferation of sin, ex-pressed in a clause with a negative verb followed by a main clause beginning with *ac* (129–38), a pattern which in both thought and expression recalls the opening of the first account of sins: in that passage (61–70) the same point is made in a series of negative clauses followed by a main clause be-ginning with *ac*; this sequence of clauses, in its turn, stylistically echoes the opening of the first account of tribulations (55–6), which is also con-structed on the *ne . . . ac . . .* pattern, the *ac* clause containing an account of the proliferation of tribulations comparable with the list of sins in the open-ing of the second account of sins. But the opening of the second account of sins recalls too the first reference to repentance (14–17), a sentence, also constructed on the *ne . . . ac . . .* pattern, which shows the extent of the devil's success in deluding the nation, in that it has rejected the means of remedying its perilous situation and has instead accelerated the progression to disaster through sin.

With the allusion to the nation's disregard of mortality in the second account of sin, a notion which figured in the introductory section, but gradually disappeared, being subsumed in the juxtapositioning of evil and its consequences. The notion of repentance slowly attains prominence throughout the description of the climactic character of the nation's sins. The first catalogues of sins (131–46) are followed by the assertion that men are more ashamed of good deeds than of evil ones (147–8) and by elaboration of this point (149–59). In the EI version Wulfstan returns to this thought (166–8) after a further recital of the nation's iniquities (160–6). In this version the rhetorical unit containing the indictment of the nation's sins is not followed, as are others in the sermon, by a detailed description of retribution. Before he deals with the imminence of the nation's defeat, Wulfstan exhorts the nation to consider its ways and guard against destruction, alluding only in passing to the great disasters which have been the consequence of sin (169–73). This is his first direct call for improvement. Having shown that the process of deterioration, of both man and his world, is already far advanced, he here emphasizes the shortness of time which remains and the magnitude of repentance which is required. After the concluding words of the reference to the destruction of the Britons ('wyrsan dæda we witan mid Englum þonne we mid Bryttan ahwar gehyrdan' (187–9) have implied that retribution is already long overdue and have thus given a last reminder of the need for haste, repentance finally becomes the subject of a lengthy passage consisting of imperatives instructing the audience in the form amendment must take (190–202).

One finds, then, that within the rigid structural pattern of the sermon, which alternates accounts of sins and punishments, a modification is suggested in the increasing prominence attained by the notion of repentance. The pattern is finally broken by the exhortations to repent. The sermon as a whole provides a conceptual framework which is intended to persuade its audience that repentance is urgently necessary and desirable, for the structure embodies the relentless progression of events to ultimate disaster and repentance emerges as the sole means of altering the course of events. Thus the exhortatory peroration, though an almost standard feature of Wulfstan's sermons, is an essential structural element of the *Sermo Lupi* as the culminating point of its themes.

It is the references to repentance in the second account of sins, however, which contain the clearest depiction of the nation's total perversity. Its perverted morality indicates the approaching triumph of Antichrist, for it has accepted evil as good. Wulfstan states twice that the nation repents of good deeds instead of evil ones (147–8 and 163–9). This perverse attitude, he explains (149–56), stems from the multitude's hatred and ridicule of God's followers. This explanation clearly reveals what is implicit in the introductory section: that evil men have power over the nation. The nation is beset within, as well as without, by the forerunners of Antichrist, those whom Wulfstan, in Bethurum 1b, calls 'antichrists', leading others into sin, and 'limbs' of Satan, in large numbers ushering in the reign of Antichrist by persecuting and seducing the righteous. This revelation that the nation is in the grip of antichrists makes it highly probable that the phrase 'Godes wiðersacan' in BH and C at the beginning of the third sentence in this section ('And eac her synd on earde a Godes wiðersacan apostatan abroðene' (C 140)) is original. This phrase, which clearly underlines the presence of God's opponents, is given as the translation of Antichrist in Bethurum 1b: '*Anticristus* is on Læden *contrarius Cristo*, þæt is on Englisc, Godes wiðersaca' (7–8).

Wulfstan's presentation of the nation's attitude to repentance involves more than a demonstration of moral blindness, of the acceptance of good as evil. Repentance, as the introductory section establishes, particularly by the play on *bot*, is the means of remedying the nation's situation. By being ashamed to repent of evil deeds the nation rejects the available remedy and continues on its path to inevitable destruction. Such a wilful pursuit of destruction involves blindness to the full enormity of the consequences. The nation's foolish perversity is revealed by a comparison of those who shun penance with those who refuse to seek a cure for their injuries before it is too late: 'ac for idelan onscytan hy scamað þæt hy betan heora misdæda, swa swa bec tæcan, gelice þam dwæsan þe for heora prytan lewe nellað beorgan ær hy na ne magan, þeah hy eal willan' (157–9). The figurative equation of a state of sin with injury (or disease) is carried over into the next sentence, which indicates an urgent need for remedy: 'Her syndan þurh synleawa, swa hit þincan mæg, sare gelewede to manege on earde' (160–1).

This demonstration of the foolish perversity of the nation's position is a summing up, in religious terms, of the view of English policy which Wulfstan expresses in his account of the humiliations inflicted by the Danes: 'Ac ealne þæne bysmor þe we oft þoliað we gyldað mid weorðscipe þam þe us scendað. We him gyldað singallice, 7 hy us hynað dæghwamlice. Hy hergiað 7 hy bærnað, rypaþ 7 reafiað 7 to scipe lædað' (123–7). Here the exact parallelism of the second sentence, and the initial placing of the object in the first sentence, which thus divides naturally into two halves, enforce a recognition of the contrast between the insult received and the response made to it. The full absurdity of the nation's policy is evident in these sentences, for they show that it perversely follows a course of action which benefits only its enemies and contributes to the furthering of its own destruction. The passage is preceded by an explicit statement of the nation's moral blindness: 'Oft twegen sæmen oððe þry hwilum drifað þa drafe cristenra manna fram sæ to sæ ut þurh þas þeode gewelede togædere, us eallum to woroldscame, gif we on eornost ænige cuþon [oððe a woldan] ariht understandan' (120–3). The phrase added in C and E may well be authentic, for the imputation of wilful refusal to see the truth, added to the imputation of inability to distinguish good and evil, accords with Wulfstan's castigation of the moral perversity of the nation in his second account of sins.

Wulfstan's depiction of the nation as blind to the realities of its moral and political situation has similarities to the description of the last days in II Thessalonians 11.9–12, in which the second coming is said to take place after 'operationem Satanae, in omni virtute, et signis, et prodigiis mendacibus, et in omni seductione iniquitatis iis qui pereunt; eo quod charitatem veritatis non receperunt ut salvi fierent. Ideo mittet illis Deus operationem erroris, ut credant mendacio, ut judicentur omnes qui non crediderunt veritati, sed consenserunt iniquitati.' Wulfstan's belief that the nation has been blinded to the truth by the influence of the devil accounts for expressions such as 'gecnawe se ðe cunne', 'gelyfe se þe wille' and 'þeh man swa ne wene'[28] and for his insistence that what he speaks is the truth ('gecnawað þæt soð is' (7) and 'soð is þæt ic secge' (37 and 187)) and that what he recounts is plain to see ('swutol 7 gesæne').[29] Expressions such as these are customarily described as 'set phrases' characteristic of Wulfstan's style. Nowhere else, however, are they used as abundantly as in the *Sermo Lupi*, where they are particularly appropriate to the theme; and a belief in the moral obtuseness of mankind in the last days may underlie his use of them elsewhere.

For all its topicality, we may conclude, the *Sermo Lupi* is essentially an eschatological sermon in which Wulfstan presents his most fully developed view of the last days. The eschatological daily increase in sins which he elaborates has a scriptural basis and can be seen as relating to contemporary conceptions of the microcosm and macrocosm, but, by causally relating the increase in calamities to the increase in sins, Wulfstan achieves a highly schematized conception of a twofold deterioration. The reign of Antichrist becomes, not a prophecy fulfilled at a fixed time according to God's will, as it is in other sermons, but the culmination of a process for which mankind is responsible. For this reason Wulfstan warns his audience not merely to prepare for the last judgement but to repent in order to stave off the terror of Antichrist's reign. The incentive to repentance inherent in Wulfstan's presentation of the last days in the *Sermo Lupi* is a particularly powerful one, since the reign of Antichrist is identified with the conquest of the nation by its enemies.

The *Sermo Lupi* is unique not only in its conception of the nature of the last days but also because its structure embodies its theme so ingeniously. The sermon has an intellectual structure as well as a rhetorical one. It enforces recognition of the truth of Wulfstan's opening assertion that the world is progressing inexorably to disaster, for the accounts of retribution are so organized that there is a progression from a general catalogue of calamities to a threat that the conquest of the nation is imminent. The growth of sin is indicated by the hyperbolic style, by insistence on its spread throughout the nation and by a cumulative listing of sins whose pace accelerates towards the end of the sermon. Within this framework repentance is made to appear urgently necessary and desirable, for it can modify the process of deterioration, which the sermon shows is already far advanced. The call for repentance has particular force, because it follows the most emotionally stirring sections of the sermon, the threat of destruction by the nation's enemies and the highly rhetorical lists of sinners (133–47 and 160–6).

It is not simply by verbal impressiveness and impassioned catalogues of the nation's sins and afflictions, then, that Wulfstan endeavours to persuade his audience to repent. The thematic framework in which the recital of the nation's iniquities and sufferings is placed and the manner in which the theme is developed and embodied in the sermon's structure constitute its didactic force and reveal Wulfstan's skill and originality as a sermon writer. The 'horrific accumulation of vivid detail',[30] it may be noted, although the most obvious feature of his commination, is by no means his only technique to describe the nation's woes and offences. Considering the limited nature of his immediate subject matter, the variety of styles and techniques in the sermon is not the least of Wulfstan's achievements. His indictment of the nation's sins ranges from the antithetical sentences contrasting Christian and heathen religious observances at 27–37 to the alliterative and rhyming word pairs at 133–47 and 160–6. In recounting the nation's afflictions he employs an *exemplum* as well as alliterative word pairs and describes the humiliations of the English in concrete detail (100–28).

Notes

1. F. M. Stenton, *Anglo-Saxon England*, 3rd ed. (Oxford, 1971), p. 460.

2. Notable exceptions are Professor Clemoes's analyses of two passages in which he describes their style, especially their regular rhythm, as phases in the expression of a continuously developing, thematic sequence of thought. For references, see below, n. 15 and 23.

3. *Sermo Lupi ad Anglos*, ed. Dorothy Whitelock, 1st ed. (London, 1939), p. 17; but cf. 3rd ed. (London, 1963), pp. 36–7. All subsequent references are to the 3rd edition.

4. On the three versions, BH, C and EI, see *The Homilies of Wulfstan*, ed. Dorothy Bethurum (Oxford, 1957), pp. 22–4; for their text, see pp. 255–75. All my citations of text refer to this edition by line number.

5. *Ibid.* pp. 22–3.

6. Stephanie Dien, '*Sermo Lupi ad Anglos:* The Order and Date of the Three Versions', *NM* 64 (1975), 561–70. I am indebted to Professor Clemoes who, since the publication of the 1975 article, has drawn my attention to two articles (cited below, n. 8, and 20) which bear on the arguments contained in it.

7. London, British Library, Cotton Nero A. i. For a facsimile of the whole manuscript see *A Wulfstan Manuscript*, ed. Henry R. Loyn, EEMF 17 (Copenhagen, 1971). I quote from the EI version (as printed by Bethurum), enclosing in square brackets readings peculiar to manuscripts other than I.

8. See Neil Ker, 'The Handwriting of Archbishop Wulfstan', *England Before the Conquest: Studies in Primary Sources Presented to Dorothy Whitelock*, ed. Peter Clemoes and Kathleen Hughes (Cambridge, 1971), pp. 315–31, esp. 321–4. I do not agree with Bethurum (*Homilies*, pp. 23–4) that this occurrence of Wulfstan's handwriting clinches the argument in favor of EI being the last of the three versions.

9. 112r. See Ker, 'Handwriting', p. 322, and Whitelock's textual notes, *Sermo Lupi*, p. 57.

10. See Bethurum, *Homilies*, p. 22, and Whitelock, *Sermo Lupi*, p. 5. As noted by J. C. Pope in his review of Bethurum, *Homilies* (*MLN* 74 (1959), 338–9), it is surprising that Wulfstan did not make good this defect in I.

11. See J. E. Cross, 'Aspects of Microcosm and Macrocosm in Old English Literature', *Studies in Old English Literature in Honor of Arthur G. Brodeur*, ed. Stanley B. Greenfield (Eugene, Oregon, 1963), pp. 1–22.

12. Whitelock, *Sermo Lupi*, p. 47 (n. to 4–8); see also Bethurum, *Homilies*, p. 356 (n. to 7–10).

13. For other parallels see Whitelock, *Sermo Lupi*, p. 47 (n. to 4–8).

14. The interpretation of *cradolcild* as a reference to the orphaned is perhaps slightly strained, but, since mention is made of the other two of the three categories of people which the prophetic books name as those needing special protection, it seems appropriate to recall that the child sold into slavery would probably be separated from one or both of its parents. Wulfstan's reworking of extracts from Isaiah in Bethurum xi reveals his familiarity with this aspect of the prophetic books.

15. On 37–52, cf. Peter Clemoes, *Rhythm and Cosmic Order in Old English Christian Literature*, an Inaugural Lecture (Cambridge, 1970), pp. 21–3.

16. The existence of rhetorical units in this sermon is pointed out by Roger Fowler, 'Some Stylistic Features of the *Sermo Lupi*', *JEGP* 65 (1966), 14–17. He does not appear, however, to consider that the whole of a Wulfstan sermon can be divided into units each linked internally by lexical and syntactic repetition, and he does not relate the stylistically defined units to divisions in subject matter.

17. See Bethurum, *Homilies*, p. 360 (n. to 55–61) and Whitelock, *Sermo Lupi*, pp. 53–4 (n. to 56 ff.).

18. See Cross, 'Microcosm and Macrocosm', pp. 5–15.

19. See particularly Bethurum xii and vi.

20. On Wulfstan's views of the Christian king, see Dorothy Bethurum Loomis,

'*Regnum* and *Sacerdotium* in the Early Eleventh Century', *England Before the Conquest*, pp. 129–45, esp. 136–8. Strictly speaking, of course, Cnut was king of a heathen people rather than a heathen king: it would appear that the distinction was not one that interested Wulfstan at this point of his career.

21. Wulfstan's usual term for priests is *Godes þenan*, but *Godes þeowas* is a more inclusive term (see Whitelock, *Sermo Lupi*, p. 50 (n. 32)). He would have been particularly conscious of the irony of the term *gedwolgoda þenan*, since he attempted to 'improve the standing of the clergy by awarding thane's rank to celibate priests' (Bethurum, *Homilies*, p. 357 (n. to 33–4)).

22. See 66, 69, 70–1, 95–6 and 99.

23. On 160–9 cf. Peter Clemoes, 'Late Old English Literature', *Tenth-Century Studies, Essays in Commemoration of the Millenium of the Council of Winchester and 'Regularis Concordia'*, ed. David Parsons (London and Chichester, 1975), pp. 103–14 and 229–32, at 113–14.

24. Whitelock, *Sermo Lupi*, p. 55 (n. to 73).

25. The view that secular law should correspond to God's law is evident in the enumeration of the duties of the king in *Polity* as well as in Bethurum xxi.

26. See particularly Bethurum ix, 107–end.

27. Bethurum ix, 131–2.

28. See 50, 51, 84–5, 95, 99 and 107–8.

29. See 53, 98, 128 and 168.

30. C. L. Wrenn, *A Study of Old English Literature* (London, 1967), p. 241.

Social Idealism in Ælfric's *Colloquy*

EARL R. ANDERSON

Ælfric's *Colloquy*[1] is, of course, first and foremost, a dialogue between a master and his pupils to give practice in the use of Latin at a conversational level. The pedagogic intention of the work is evident from the interlocutors' habit of lingering over commonly used words in various grammatical forms: for example, in a few opening lines (2–11) the deponent *loqui* appears as *loqui, loquimur, loquamur* and *loqueris*, together with the noun *locutio*, and within a little more than fifty lines (66–119) we find seven forms of the verb *capere*, two of them occurring four times each and one twice. Yet, equally certainly, this colloquy has more to it than just schoolboy exercises in declensions and conjugations. It has escaped the oblivion that has been the lot of its more humdrum fellows who—to use Garmonsway's personification—were assigned the rôle of literary Cinderellas, labouring 'in obscurity in monastic classrooms to help boys learn their lessons'.[2] It has long been acclaimed for its realism and for its 'sociological picture of the occupational strata'[3] of Anglo-Saxon society; and, in our own day, Stanley B. Greenfield has called attention to its literary merits, 'its fine organization and structure, dramatic in effect, with its pairing and contrasting, for example, of the king's bold hunter and the independent, timid fisherman . . . and with its lively disputation toward the end about which occupation is most essential'.[4] In the present study I hope to demonstrate that it also draws on a background of ideas and that its longevity is partly due to this ingredient. After all, Ælfric's work as a whole is intellectual in character and his various writings are related to one another as parts of a plan systematically pursued, as has been suggested by Sisam[5] and reiterated by Clemoes in an admirable metaphor:

Its controlling idea was universal history with Christ's redemption of man at its centre. The conception which moulded Ælfric's writings was in fact that which moulded the Gothic cathedral later. His main structure, as it were, consisted of two series of homilies combining Temporale and Sanctorale, later extended and completed with more Temporale homilies. *De Temporibus Anni*, the *Grammar* and *Colloquy*, and his letters for Wulfsige and Wulfstan and to the monks of Eynsham buttressed this edifice; *Lives* and Old Testament narratives enriched it with stained glass windows; 'occasional' pieces such as the *Letter to Sigeweard* gave it the synthesis of sculpture on the West Front.[6]

All the same, in a work as elementary in purpose as the *Colloquy* ideas in a developed form are not to be expected. They are likely to be at their simplest and, indeed, may remain no more than mere implications. What, then, are some of them?

Eric Colledge has suggested an influence from St Augustine's *Enarratio in Psalmum LXX* for the dialogue between the master and the merchant, in which the merchant defends his profit motive in buying goods abroad and selling them at a higher price in England (149–66). As Colledge points out, Ælfric, in allowing his merchant to justify his profit as the means of providing for himself and his wife and family, adopted Augustine's position that the merchant deserves compensation for his labour, provided that this, and not greed, is his motive.[7] It may be also that, in putting into the merchant's mouth the point that mortal danger, and sometimes shipwreck and loss of goods, is involved in earning his honest profit (155–7), Ælfric was aware of the Roman satirists' position, represented in Horace, Juvenal and Persius,[8] that merchants who undergo maritime perils are motivated by avarice, for his merchant's point of view is, in effect, a denial of this charge.[9]

It is likely that Ælfric's treatment of the baker and the cook was influenced by a tradition of using the merits of these crafts as a topic for school debate. An early example is Vespa's poem, *Iudicium coci et pistoris*, which belongs to the fifth century or earlier[10] and, if Raby is correct in characterizing it as a 'school piece which gives the opportunity for a rhetorical setting forth of the merits of each trade, with proper mythological allusions',[11] more than likely merely followed the conventions of an already existing tradition. As its title suggests, Vespa's *Iudicium*[12] presents a debate between a cook and a baker as to whose occupation is the more useful. The poem proceeds along lines familiar in debate literature: there is a balanced contention on a single subject, each side of the argument is presented with equal force and the outcome is decided by a third party or *iudex*. The *iudex* in this case is Vulcanus, who, as the source of fire, is qualified to understand both sides of the question. Weighing the arguments of each contender, he concludes that flesh and bread are both necessary to sustain life, that the cook and the baker are equals and that their quarrel is neither necessary nor desirable. Direct influence of Vespa on Ælfric is unlikely, since there is no evidence that his poem was known in England,[13] and, in any case, there are more differences than similarities between his treatment of the cook and the baker and Ælfric's. But the school tradition that Vespa represents is another matter. The baker and the cook are juxtaposed in the *Colloquy* and it is in the master's words to the baker that the validity of a craft is called into question for the first time: 'Quid dicis tu, pistor? Cui prodest ars tua, aut si sine te possimus uitam ducere?' (185–6). And the note of contention increases when, instead of addressing the cook directly as he does all the others, the master asks a question about him which demands, and receives, an answer in self-defence:

> Quid dicimus de coco, si indigemus in aliquo arte eius?
>   Dicit cocus: Si me expellitis a uestro collegio, manducabitis holera uestra uiridia, et carnes uestras crudas, et nec saltem pingue ius potestis sine arte mea habere. (192–6)

But the master is not prepared to accept this as an answer and the cook has to try again:

> Non curamus de arte tua, nec nobis necessaria est, quia nos ipsi possumus coquere que coquenda sunt, et assara que assanda sunt.
>   Dicit cocus: Si ideo me expellitis, ut sic faciatis, tunc eritis omnes coci, et nullus uestrum erit dominus; et tamen sine arte mea non manducabitis. (197–202)

Argument of this sort does not enter into the master's dealings with any other craftsman.

Debate as to the usefulness of baker and cook is but a particular application of a more general tradition of school debate over the relative merits of various crafts and callings, as represented, for instance, in a fragment from Carolingian times, *De navigio et agricultura*.[14] Influence from this wider tradition comes to the fore when the master asks the monk whether there is a wise counsellor among his companions and, on being told that there is, assigns to this counsellor the role of *iudex*: 'Quid dicis tu, sapiens? Que ars tibi uidetur inter istas prior esse?' (211–12). The counsellor's decision in favour of the ploughman as the primary secular craftsman does not go unchallenged: a smith and a carpenter each states his own claim, the smith being answered by the counsellor and the carpenter being challenged by the smith. The result of such difference of opinion is an appeal to all concerned for reconciliation, agreement and diligence in fulfilling one's calling that is similar in kind to the judgement of Vespa's Vulcan:

> Consiliarius dicit: O, socii et boni operarii, dissoluamus citius has contentiones, et sit pax et concordia inter uos, et prosit unusquisque alteri arte sua, et conueniamus semper apud aratorem, ubi uictum nobis et pabula equis nostris habemus. Et hoc consilium do omnibus operariis, ut unusquisque artem suam diligenter exerceat, quia qui artem suam dimiserit, ipse dimittatur ab arte. Siue sis sacerdos, siue monachus, seu laicus, seu miles, exerce temet ipsum in hoc, et esto quod es; quia magnum dampnum et uerecundia est homini nolle esse quod est et quod esse debet. (233–43)

We may safely conclude that elements of a school debate tradition concerning crafts have entered into Ælfric's handling of the colloquy form. Perhaps he was merely following precedent; perhaps he made the combination for the first time himself.

In his views on occupational specialization, Ælfric probably was influenced by the topos of the God-given 'gifts of men', a medieval commonplace having its *loci biblici* in such texts as I Corinthians xii.8–10 and Ephesians iv.8 but probably best known through Gregory's *Homilia IX in Evangelia* on the parable of the talents.[15] Ælfric sometimes used this topos with considerable freedom. For instance he seems to echo it in a discourse on tithes when expanding a statement by Caesarius of Arles, 'De negotio, de artificio, de qualicunque operatione vivis, redde decimas':[16] 'Ælcum men þe ænige tilunge hæfð, oððe on cræfte, oððe on mangunge, oððe on oðrum begeatum, ælcum is beboden þæt hy þa teoðunge Gode glædlice syllan of heora begeatum oððe cræftum þe him God forgeaf.'[17] In the *Colloquy* the topos is not specifically formulated, but it is surely implied in the advice to each man to practise his particular profession, just quoted: 'Et hoc consilium do omnibus operariis . . . nolle esse quod est et quod esse debet' (237–43).

The 'siue sis sacerdos, siue monachus, seu laicus, seu miles' (240–1) depends on a view of society like that expressed in the threefold classification 'oratores laboratores et bellatores', which Ælfric used in a piece appended to his *Passio Sanctorum Machabeorum*[18] and in his *Letter to Sigeweard* ('On the Old and New Testament').[19] Since both these writings were later in composition it may well be that the *Colloquy* lacks their specific formulation because the unidentified source on which they were based had not yet come

into Ælfric's hands.[20] But that his view of society was the same before he acquired this new material as it was afterwards is shown by the counsellor's
verdict in the *Colloquy* that the primary secular occupation was the ploughman's (219): just so, in the piece appended to the *Passio Machabeorum* '*laboratores* synd þa þe urne bigleofan beswincað' and their type is *se yrðlincg*[21]
and in the *Letter to Sigeweard* '*Laboratores* sind þe us bigleofan tiliað, yrðlin-
gas 7 æhte men to þam anum betæhte'.[22] Evidently the ploughman is
thought to fulfil most completely the function of the *laborator* in the social
ideal of the three mutually supporting estates. Incidentally, Ælfric's three
treatments of the topos are nicely complementary in that in the *Passio
Machabeorum* it is the *oratores*, as warriors who fight against spiritual foes,
that are in the forefront of attention, in the *Letter to Sigeweard* it is the *bellatores*, who defend the kingdom, and in the *Colloquy* it is the *laboratores*, who
provide for the material needs of society.

While the ploughman's craft is recognized as the most essential secular
occupation, even greater importance is attributed to the *oratores* in the
counsellor's answer to the question, 'Que ars tibi uidetur inter istas prior
esse?' (211–12). Probably he reflects a common medieval view when he
claims that 'mihi uidetur seruitium Dei inter istas artes primatum tenere,
sicut legitur in euangelio: "Primum querite regnum Dei et iustitiam eius, et
hec omnia adicientur uobis"' (213–16). But more particularly his answer is
in accord with the emphasis on monasticism which was especially marked at
the time Ælfric was writing and with the emphasis, within monasticism, on
the liturgical life. It is noteworthy that the same scriptural text (Matthew
VI.33; cf. Luke XII.31) is used in St Benedict's instructions concerning the
characteristics of the abbot: 'Ante omnia, ne dissimulans aut paruipendens
salutem animarum sibi commissarum ne plus gerat sollicitudinem de rebus
transitoriis et terrenis atque caducis, sed semper cogitet, quia animas sus-
cepit regendas, de quibus et rationem redditurus est. Et ne causetur de mi-
nori forte substantia, meminerit scriptum: *Primum quaerite regnum dei et
iustitiam eius et haec omnia adicientur uobis*' (II. 33–5).[23] Similarly, the conception of the *seruitium Dei* as one of the *artes*, or crafts, is reminiscent of
Benedict's chapter on the instruments of good works, which closes with the
statement, 'Ecce haec sunt instrumenta artis spiritalis' (IV. 75). The instruments of good works, such as obedience, humility and chastity, are tools
borrowed from God, to be used with care in the 'workshop' and returned
on the Day of Judgement (IV. 76–8), just as the tools of manual labour are
to be used with care and returned to the monastic storehouse at the end of
the day.

The Benedictine Rule is, indeed, the most important and pervasive influence on the *Colloquy*, although it is impossible to tell how far this influence was transmitted directly through Ælfric's familiarity with the Rule itself and how far it resulted from his experience of monastic practices at Winchester and other reformed monasteries in southern England. C. L. White, noting the strength of Ælfric's Benedictine associations, recognizes in the last part of the *Colloquy*, especially in the *horarium* (266–78), an expression of the Benedictine ideal of order in a well-regulated life;[24] but it has not been pointed out that the influence of the Rule extends also to the dialogue on crafts. Earlier scholars, apparently failing to see the importance of rôle-playing in the *Colloquy*, thought that the *pueri* actually belonged to the social orders indicated by their crafts, thus providing evidence for 'an amazing diffusion of education among all classes, boys in all the different occupations, ploughboy, gamekeeper . . . merchant, learning Latin of a secular master side by side with a young monk'.[25] Although this view is now discarded, it is still generally assumed that the dialogue on crafts refers to daily life outside the monastery walls. According to C. L. Wrenn, for example, Ælfric treats of 'the ordinary happenings of rustic daily life and occupations' by having each boy 'assume the character of a rural worker—ploughman, smith, fisherman, etc.'. Similarly, G. K. Anderson considers that the *Colloquy* gives the sociologist a 'rare chance to see the common Anglo-Saxon people at work'.[26] Although this more recent sociological view seems plausible enough, quite another possibility is suggested by Garmonsway, who writes that the oblates' dialogue on crafts is 'based on their own observation of the manifold activities of a monastic house'.[27] Garmonsway's position is justified first by the fact that the various crafts described in the *Colloquy* were commonly practised in and around the monastic enclosure, and second by the fact that colloquies typically dealt with subjects 'sensibly related to the many and varied activities of a monastic house', only occasionally ranging beyond its walls.[28]

If we accept Garmonsway's position, it is possible for us to see the unifying theme of the *Colloquy* as an expression of the Benedictine monastic ideal, derived from the Rule, of an orderly and well-regulated life within the confines of an economically self-sufficient community devoted to the service of God—a community separate from the world but at the same time a microcosmic image of it, in which each monastic craftsman contributes in his own way to the general welfare. Earlier English monachism, exemplified by Guthlac and Cuthbert, had been heavily influenced by Celtic—and ultimately Antonine—ideals, stressing the ascetic struggle of the individual for spiritual perfection. By the time of Ælfric, however, the Benedictine ideal of monasticism had become secure in many parts of England, with its stress on the community rather than on the individual, and on the communal *seruitium Dei* rather than on personal asceticism.[29] The ideal of a self-sufficient community is evident in ch. LXVI of the Rule: 'Monasterium autem, si possit fieri, ita debet constitui, ut omnia necessaria, id est aqua, molendinum, hortum uel artes diuersas intra monasterium execeantur, ut non sit necessitas monachis uagandi foris, quia omnino non expedit animabus eorem' (LXVI. 6–7). Some manuscripts include a *pistrinum* in the catalogue of necessary utilities.[30] Besides water, the mill, garden and bakery, Benedict elsewhere mentions the kitchen, the cellar and the office (XLVI) and devotes a chapter to the maintenance of tools used in various crafts (XXXII). In the chapter on manual labour (XLVIIII) it is clear that the monks are expected to devote much of their time to work, including field work, for idleness is the enemy of the soul, and the presence of monastic artisans, possessed with special skills, is attested in the chapter *De artificibus monasterii* (LVII), which warns the craftsmen against pride and establishes the policy for hiring their services outside the monastery.

It is obvious, of course, that not all the craftsmen of the *Colloquy* are represented as monks. The merchant has a family to support (163–6), the hunter is a servant of the king (53–5), and the ploughman is a serf on monastic lands (35).[31] The shepherd, faithful to his lord (41–2), and the oxherd, whose duties supplement those of the ploughman (44–7), seem to be servants of the monastery rather than monks; however, there is no reason why the other interlocutors could not be monks skilled in specific crafts: the cobbler, salter, baker, cook, smith and carpenter, particularly, all attest their usefulness to the *collegium* to which they belong. It is difficult to say whether or not the fisherman and fowler could be monks, but it is worth noting that fish was so important to the monastic economy that fishponds were maintained even if there was a river nearby.[32] In any case, whether or not all the craftsmen are monks is of little importance. The main point of the dialogue on crafts is that each member of the fraternity helps the others by his craft: 'et prosit unusquisque alteri arte sua' (235). Each craftsman contributes to Ælfric's little society in order to make that society self-sustaining, in accordance with the Benedictine ideal.

From a modern point of view, we might be tempted to see Ælfric's expression of the Benedictine ethos in the *Colloquy* as an early English Utopia, especially when we reflect that St Benedict, in the Rule, combines a practical Roman talent for government with a profound Christian idealism.[33] The true spirit of the *Colloquy*, however, is not Utopian but pedagogic. In keeping with the spirit of Benedict's request that the Rule be read frequently in the community so that the brethren may not excuse themselves on grounds of ignorance (LXVI. 8), in the *Colloquy* Ælfric offers his pupils a picture of the Rule in its practical application. Thus the demand for correct Latin usage and pronunciation, which was enforced by whipping boys who made mistakes in the oratory (*Regula* XLV), finds expression in the children's request to the master 'ut doceas nos loqui latialiter recte, quia idiote sumus et corrupte loquimur' (*Colloquy* 1–3). The use of corporal punishment for children, to which Benedict devotes a chapter (XXX; cf. XXVIII and XLV), is evident in Ælfric's community, where the boys find it necessary to learn their lessons (7–10) and behave circumspectly (279–83) in order to escape whipping. The master's final advice to his pupils, admonishing them to obedience, reverence and seriousness in all places, especially in the oratory, the cloister and the study (308–15), reflects the spirit of obedience and humility which permeates the Rule (cf. V, VI and VII).

Finally, the children's special dietary allowances and dormitory accommodation, which of course reflect monastic practices in Ælfric's day, are ultimately based on the Rule. *Quadripedum carnes* were forbidden to monks (*Regula* XXXIX); however, the oblate is allowed meat 'quia puer sum sub uirga degens' (*Colloquy* 285–6), in accordance with special provisions for youth, old age and illness (*Regula* XXXVI and XXXVII). After cataloguing the variety of foods available in the monastery (*Colloquy* 285–9), the oblate's assertion that 'Non sum tam uorax ut omnia genera ciborum in una refectione edere possim' (292–3) reflects Benedict's stipulation that only two dishes be served at any one meal (*Regula* XXXVIIII. 1–4); and the boy's claim that he is not a glutton (*Colloquy* 295–7) is in keeping with the general spirit of Benedict's chapter *De mensura ciborum*. The restriction on wine, reserved for the old and wise, and forbidden to those who are young and foolish (*Colloquy* 300–2), accords with Benedict's warning that 'uinum apostatare facit etiam sapientes' (*Regula* XL. 7). The oblate's statement that he sleeps 'in dormitorio cum fratribus' (*Colloquy* 304) accords with the dormitory arrangements described in the chapter *Quomodo dormiant monachi*, where there is even a provision for children predisposed to sleep late in the morning (*Regula* XXII; cf. *Colloquy*, 305–7). These parallels between the *Colloquy* and the Rule, whether they result from direct or indirect transmission, indicate that even the minor details of Ælfric's composition are thematic.

At the beginning of their lesson the oblates ask their master for instruction and practice only in correct Latin usage, not caring about the subject of their discourse, provided only that it would not be idle or shameful (1–6); but the master has more to offer than correct grammar and pronunciation. The disciples' gradual induction into wisdom takes place in three stages, the first two marked off by 'false closures' and the third by the master's concluding advice. In the first and longest phase (1–243) the dialogue on crafts develops into a debate over which craft is most essential. The dispute is resolved, probably not without influence from the commonplaces of the 'gifts of men' and the 'three estates' but more especially as an expression of the Benedictine ideal, by an affirmation of the need for a harmoniously unified society which is devoted to the service of God and in which each craftsman works in his own way for the benefit of the whole. In the second phase (244–60) the oblates have revised their educational goals upwards. They are now willing to study diligently to acquire not only a knowledge of correct Latin usage but also wisdom 'quia nolumus esse sicut bruta animalia, que nihil sciunt, nisi herbam et aquam' (250–1). Nevertheless an abstract discussion of the quality of wisdom would be beyond their comprehension. As in the dialogue on crafts, in the third phase (261–315) the master must guide his pupils toward an expression of spiritual wisdom in simple and practical terms. The Benedictine ideal of order and the *seruitium Dei* thus find expression in the *horarium* (268–78), and the discussion of the boys' food, drink and sleeping arrangements (284–307) shows in practical terms how an individual benefits from life in a self-sufficient community whose members work together for the common good. By combining an all-pervasive Benedictine idealism with the practical needs of language instruction Ælric produces a work of art—simple but not pedestrian, thoughtful and yet lively and witty—that is altogether worthy of one of England's most learned and creative teachers.[34]

Notes

1. Ed. G. N. Garmonsway, 2nd ed. (London, 1947); all references are to this edition.

2. Garmonsway, 'The Development of the Colloquy', *The Anglo-Saxons: Studies in some Aspects of their History and Culture presented to Bruce Dickins*, ed. Peter Clemoes (London, 1959), p. 249. On the humble origins of the colloquy as a genre, probably descending from the fourth-century *Ars Grammatica Dosithei Magistri*, see *ibid.* p. 252.

3. Stanley B. Greenfeld, *A Critical History of Old English Literature* (New York, 1965), p. 52. See, e.g., W. Cunningham, *Growth of English Industry and Commerce* (Cambridge, 1890–2) 1, 131; A. F. Leach, *Educational Charters and Documents* (Cambridge, 1911), p. xvi; Leach, *Schools of Medieval England* (Cambridge, 1915), p. 91; G. G. Coulton, *Social Life in Britain* (Cambridge, 1919), p. 54; and A. Cruse, *The Shaping of English Literature* (New York, 1927), p. 70. For a discussion of the earlier views of the sociological significance of the *Colloquy*, see ed. Garmonsway, pp. 14–15.

4. Greenfeld, *History*, p. 52.

5. Kenneth Sisam, *Studies in the History of Old English Literature* (Oxford, 1953), p. 301.

6. P. A. M. Clemoes, 'The Chronology of Ælfric's Works', *The Anglo-Saxons*, ed. Clemoes, pp. 245–6.

7. Eric Colledge, 'An Allusion to Augustine in Ælfric's *Colloquy*', *RES* n.s. 12 (1961), 180–1. The importance of Augustine's *Enarratio in Psalmum LXX* in medieval thought has been observed by J. W. Baldwin, in *The Mediaeval Theories of the Just Price*, Trans. of Amer. Philosophical Soc. n.s. 49 (1959), pt 4, esp. 12–16, and in *Masters, Princes and Merchants: the Social Views of Peter the Chanter and his Circle* (Princeton, 1970) I, 262–4 and II, 185–6, nn. 17, 18, 19 and 20.

8. All these were curriculum authors in Europe in the early Middle Ages; see E. R. Curtius, *European Literature and the Latin Middle Ages*, trans. W. R. Trask (London, 1953), p. 49. There is positive evidence that Horace was read at Winchester in Ælfric's time (see M. Lapidge, 'Three Latin Poems from Æthelwold's School at Winchester', *ASE* 1 (1972), 109); but there is no certain evidence for the study of Juvenal and Persius in late-tenth-century England.

9. Horace, *carm.* 1.1.13–17 and 3.1.25–6; *serm.* 1.4.25–32; and *epist.* 1.1.42–58 and 1.6.31–8; Juvenal, *sat.* 14.256–302; and Persius, *sat.* 5.132–60; cf. *sat.* 6.75–80. For the Roman satirists' views on merchants, see Ethel Hampson Brewster, *Roman Craftsmen and Tradesmen of the Early Empire* (Menasha, Wisconsin, 1917), pp. 30–9. The position of the Roman satirists was adopted by St. Ambrose, and much later by Peter the Chanter, who was fond of quoting Horace on this subject; see Baldwin, *Masters, Princes and Merchants* I, 263 and II, 185, n. 12.

In the event of a shipwreck, a merchant could lose everything he had, for it was customary in the early Middle Ages for the prince to seize whatever cargo remained, although earlier Roman law had protected the surviving owners or their heirs; see *ibid.* I, 247–8.

10. F. J. E. Raby (*A History of Secular Latin Poetry in the Middle Ages*, 2nd ed. (Oxford, 1957) I, 45) associates the poem with the third century. The only evidence for dating the poem, however, is the fact that it appears in the Codex Salmasianus, a collection of Latin poetry of the sixth century and earlier. Vespa's poem must have been written therefore by the sixth century, but no more certain date is possible. For the text see *Anthologia Latina*, ed. A. Riese (Leipzig, 1869 70) I. 1, 140–3.

11. *Secular Latin Poetry* I, 45.

12. 'Vespae Iudicium coci et pistoris iudice Vulcano' in ed. Riese.

13. Vespa's name does not appear in J. D. A. Ogilvy, *Books Known to the English, 597–1066* (Cambridge, Mass., 1967).

14. Monumenta Germaniae Historica, Poetae Latini Aevi Carolini 4. 1, 244–6.

15. J. E. Cross, 'The Old English Poetic Theme of *The Gifts of Men*', *Neophilologus* 46 (1962), 66–70.

16. Caesarius of Arles, *Homilia XVI, De Decimis*, Migne, Patrologia Latina 67, col. 1079.

17. *Homilies of Ælfric, a Supplementary Collection*, ed. John C. Pope, Early Eng. Text Soc. 259–60 (London, 1967–8), II, 808, lines 99–102.

18. *Ælfric's Lives of Saints*, ed. Walter W. Skeat, EETS o.s. 76, 82, 94 and 114 (London, 1881–1900), II, 1120–4, lines 812–62.

19. *The Old English Version of the Heptateuch, Ælfric's Treatise on the Old and New Testament and his Preface to Genesis*, ed. S. J. Crawford, EETS o.s. 160, repr. (London, 1969), 71–2, 'On the Old and New Testament', lines 1204–20.

20. I owe this observation to Peter Clemoes.

21. Ed. Skeat, lines 815 and 819.

22. Ed. Crawford, lines 1208–9.

23. *Benedicti Regula*, ed. Rudolph Hanslik, Corpus Scriptorum Ecclesiasticorum Latinorum 75 (Vienna, 1960); all references are to this edition.

24. Caroline Louisa White, *Ælfric, a New Study of His Life and Writings* (Boston, 1898), pp. 40–3; cf. *Regula* IX–XIX. For the Benedictine ideal of order see Dom David Knowles, *The Monastic Order in England*, 2nd ed. (Cambridge, 1963), pp. 448–53; Dom Cuthbert Butler, *Benedictine Monachism*, 2nd ed. (London, 1924), pp. 275–90; T. F. Lindsay, *Saint Benedict: his Life and Work* (London, 1949), pp. 114–32; and J. C. Dickinson, *Monastic Life in Medieval England* (London, 1961), pp. 103–9.

25. Leach, *Educational Charters and Documents*, p. xvi.

26. C. L. Wrenn, *A Study of Old English Literature* (London, 1967), pp. 70–1 and 228; George K. Anderson, *The Literature of the Anglo-Saxons*, 2nd ed. (Princeton, 1966), pp. 316 and 353.

27. Ed., p. 14.

28. 'Development of the Colloquy', pp. 255ff. The various activities of the monastic household are well documented: see Dom Justin McCann, *The Rule of Saint Benedict*, 3rd ed. (Latrobe, Penn., 1950), pp. 304–16 and 361–6; R. H. Snape, *English Monastic Finances in the Later Middle Ages* (Cambridge, 1926), p. 13; J. Evans, *Monastic Life at Cluny* (Cambridge, 1927), pp. 67 and 84; Edouard Schneider, *The Benedictines* (London, 1926), pp. 86–101; and Knowles, *Monastic Order*, pp. 466–7.

29. *Ibid.* pp. 682–5.

30. Ed. Hanslik, p. 157, note to LXVI. 6.

31. For serfdom on monastic lands see John Chapman, *St Benedict and the Sixth Century* (London, 1929), pp. 147–75.

32. D. H. S. Cranage, *The Home of the Monk* (Cambridge, 1934), p. 62.

33. Gustav Schnürer, *Church and Culture in the Middle Ages*, trans. George J. Undreiner (Paterson, N.J., 1956), I, 159ff.

34. I am indebted to Stanley B. Greenfield for his encouragement, and to Peter Clemoes for his guidance, in the composition of this paper.

The Hero in Christian Reception: Ælfric and Heroic Poetry

JOCELYN WOGAN-BROWNE

IT may seem perverse to pursue the investigation of Germanic heroic paradigms and functions by first focussing on the work of Ælfric.[1] But if we are to consider the society in which most of the surviving Anglo-Saxon poems are copied and so preserved for us, it is in a sense even more perverse *not* to consider him. The bulk and influence of his work and his profound innovativeness in English traditions of composition are in many ways the single largest literary presence of the landscape within which *The Battle of Maldon* and *Brunanburh* are composed, and in which the extant copies of most of the heroic and scriptural verse in Old English were made. Ælfric uses a significant lexical and stylistic range and much linguistic and metrical innovativeness. In both formal and thematic terms, this major Christian writer's attitude to heroic tradition is a matter of some interest in getting a broad picture of how heroic poetry was received and where it might be positioned in the society which preserves it, even if, here, this can only be briefly sketched by means of a few selected instances.

The Germanic hero bulks so large in our formative sense of Old English literature that, even after all the work of recent decades on scriptural, typological, devotional and lyric verse, it can still be difficult to remember how small a part, proportionately, of Old English literary production is constituted by heroic verse. In her study of the *miles Christi* tradition, Joyce Hill has pointed out how, in current standard histories such as Pearsall's survey of Old and Middle English, heroic poetry is assumed as the ground of Old English literary composition. Writers are supposed as constantly referring to heroic poetry either to re-endorse and invoke its values or to transfer its valency to counter-heroic models, "to fulfill the potential of the heroic style by diverting it from useless fictions to profitable truths".[2] In this model, a writer born in the tenth or eleventh century would, as it were, absorb *Maldon* and its heroicising account of a tenth-century leader's death with his mother's milk and would learn only later on in a clerical education how to turn the heroic to Christian purpose in producing, for example, an account of a saintly king's death such as Ælfric's *Oswald*. Moreover, he would be working in conscious reaction to *Maldon*, rather than writing in an established Christian framework in which *Maldon* was one possible and perhaps rather specialized stylistic strand. The heroic would, if only by pointed rejection, still be the motor and source of the writing.

Some such conceptual opposition informs the terms in which the question of Ælfric's use of heroic traditions and paradigms was first importantly raised many years ago by Dorothy Bethurum: Ælfric, she claimed in her 1932 article on his *Lives of the Saints*, very skilfully establishes "a connection between the saints and the early Germanic heroes, with the idea of replacing the latter by the former, but clothing the story of the saints in a form familiar to his heroes".[3] There has been much work on Ælfric since and it would be surprising nowadays to find anyone agreeing with Bethurum's statement of the issues. In early modern work on Old English poetry, Germanic pagan heroism and the search for origins was privileged over the tenth and eleventh century society in which it has principally been preserved. Seeking paganism everywhere, early scholarship invested a great deal in an oppositional binary model of heroic [Germanic] versus saintly [Latin] heroes and heroisms.[4] More recent scholarship has attended to the ways in which, far from being a pagan society with a Christian top-dressing, the society of the Vercelli, Junius, and Exeter codexes is one of established Christianity and Christian assumptions. Rather than an alternative or opposition to Christian culture, the heroic is now more credibly seen as proceeding from within Christian culture and as having its own history of changing assimilations there. In the poetry of the earlier period, Professor Pàroli has argued, difference can be appropriately emphasized and "si deve . . . distinguere attentamente tra la materia essenziale del poema e alcune interpretazioni posteriori in esso contenute".[5] In the later period, as Roberta Frank has argued in her study of changing Anglo-Saxon assimilations of the past, tenth-century poems "set up no unresolvable contradictions between piety and the heroic life", and such argument may well be extended even to the mutual relations of heroic and non-heroic writing and genres in the tenth and eleventh century.[6] It would therefore be surprising to find Ælfric constituting his ethos of heroism in reaction to Germanic ideals as constructed in Old English heroic verse.

Nevertheless, if the formal and thematic features of late Old English

prose and late Old English verse are considered, it is at once possible to see
why Bethurum felt compelled to make reference to the heroic tradition,
even if that now seems part of an overvaluation of heroic verse's centrality
in the context of Old English literary production as a whole. Ælfric's *Life of
King Edmund*, for instance, was written over a century later than the king's
death (869) and about three years before the battle of Maldon (i.e. c. 988):

> . . . "to bysmore synd getawode
> þas earman landleoda . and me nu leofre wære
> þæ ic on feohte feolle . wið þam þe min folc
> moste heora eardes brucan. . . .
> Þæt ic gewilnige and gewisce mid mode .
> þæs ic ana ne belife æfter minum leofum þegnum
> . . . [þe] wurdon . . .
> færlice ofslægene fram þysum flot-mannum .
> Næs me næfre gewunelic þæt ic worhte fleames .
> ac ic wolde swiðor sweltan gif ic þorfte
> for minum agenum earde."
>
> (ll. 64–7, 74–5, 77–80)[7]

"shamefully treated are / the poor people of this nation and I would
now rather / fall in battle, provided that my people / might enjoy their
land . . . This I heartily desire and wish / that I may not remain behind
alone after my beloved thanes . . . [who] have been . . . suddenly
slaughtered by these seamen. / It was never my custom to take to
flight / and I would rather perish if I must / for the sake of my own
land."

Though Ælfric is using Abbo of Fleury's life of Edmund, one might at first
glance be surprised that a Latin source should be in question at all.[8] We see
a leader engaged in defiance on behalf of his people and land. The passage
invokes loyalty to the death between a leader and his people ("þæt ic ana ne
belife æfter minum leofum þegnum", l. 75); the defence of territory ("eard",
ll. 67, 80); scorn for dishonourable flight ("Næs me næfre gewunelic þæt ic
worhte fleames", l. 78). Edmund's stance as leader here would in many ways
seem fittingly responded to by the behaviour ascribed to Byrhtnoth's retainers at Maldon:

> "Þa gyt on orde stod   Eadweard se langa
> gearo and geornful   gylpwordum spræc
> þæt he nolde fleogan   fotmæl landes
> ofer bæc bugan   þa his betera leg."
>
> (*Maldon*, ll. 273–6)[9]

"Still in the van stood Edward the Tall / ready and eager: with vaunt-
ing words / he said that he would not flee a foot's length of territory /
or retreat while his leader lay fallen."

Although Ælfric's half-lines are on average at least one syllable longer than
those of *Maldon*, and although the stress and alliteration positions vary
somewhat from the staples of heroic poetry, the passage could be viewed, in
Sievers' scheme, as a rather loose series of predominantly A-type half-lines,
with an unusually large amount of anacrusis (not inconceivable in late
heroic verse).[10] Some of the lexis is shared with heroic verse (eg *sweltan*, l.
79, *fleam*, l. 78, cf. *Maldon*, l. 293, l. 81 etc.); some is close to that of heroic
verse (*landleoda*, l. 65, cfr. *landmanna, flotmanna* in the poetic corpus).[11] The
provenance of the account, according to Ælfric's Prologue (as also his
source), is an oral battle report by Edmund's sword-bearer, told to a king
(Athelstan) in the hearing of a bishop (Dunstan), and re-told by that bishop
to a distinguished visiting cleric (Abbo), before being turned into rhythmical prose by Ælfric. This is the kind of transmission process we might well
posit for *Maldon* if, as was once thought, it were a direct account of the battle composed shortly after it had taken place according to the reports of
eyewitnesses or participants: a heroicising account of battle which had a
core of oral transmission followed by literary elaboration.[12]

Edmund's death is nonetheless very different from earlier heroic verse
and different also from *Maldon*. On closer inspection, the idea that Ælfric
might be invoking comitatus bonds and heroic readiness to die cannot be
sustained. Although Ælfric has changed the idiom of Edmund's speech (in
Abbo of Fleury's *vita*, it is heightened with echoes of Virgil's first and ninth
Eclogues), he does not rewrite it into a invocation of Germanic and heroic
defence of territory and people.[13] In line 76 (omitted above), Edmund worries about his people being slaughtered in their beds, not on the battle
field.[14] He himself does not die fighting, but refusing to fight. He throws
away his weapons and is beaten, pierced with arrows, and executed by the
Vikings (ll. 101–26) in a manner conformed by Ælfric to Christ's passion
rather than to any secular heroic agon. The social relations and values of
the Germanic heroic ethos (vengeance, treasure-giving, loyalty for example) are not present.[15]

Ælfric's text is one of the many saints' lives he produced for Æthelweard
and Æthelweard's son Æthelmær.[16] Like Ælfric (who had been formed in
Bishop Æthelwold's Winchester), Æthelweard was allied with the royalist
ecclesiastical reform party.[17] He lived not only amidst internal struggles
over church and secular property in the wake of tenth-century reform, but

with the necessity of dealing with external raids from an enemy seen as heathen. Æthelweard was ealdorman of the Western shires until his death (in either 998 or 1002), and one of the three major negotiators in the payment of tax to the Vikings in, probably, 994.[18] Ælfric's translation was thus written for a patron who, near the time of its composition, had himself to face the problem of Viking attacks and how to deal with them almost as urgently as Byrhtnoth, ealdorman of East Anglia.

The defence of one's 'eard' was at the centre of a late tenth- and eleventh-century nobleman's obligations. Richard Abels has shown that "the obligation to serve the king in arms rested in the eleventh century upon a dual foundation of land tenure and lordship."[19] Holding their lands from the king, nobles such as Æthelweard and Byrhtnoth would have had rights of jurisdiction over their estates, but an obligation to serve the king on campaign (as would the lower-ranking fyrdmen who answered to them). One of Cnut's laws gives a landowner "se ðe land gewerod hæbbe on scypfyrde and on landfyrde" the right to hold his land and to dispose of it as he pleased at death, while Æthelred's laws state that one who has deserted the royal host or broken the king's peace while in the field will forfeit his land. A warrior who deserts out of cowardice was to lose life and property but a man falling in battle by the side of his lord would have his heriot payment remitted and his heirs would succeed to his land.[20]

In tenth and eleventh-century social structures there is, then, a version of the lord and retainer bond central to heroic verse, but it is a Christian society's system of obligation and its terms of loyalty are common to legal and doctrinal discourses and to social history, rather than a prerogative of heroic poetry. Loyalty is mediated through the important shared term of 'eard' in a way that looks at least as feudal as Germanic.[21] 'Eard' [territory] and 'eðel' [native land, homeland] are enormously resonant words, frequently found in the heroic poetry and frequently found also in Ælfric's works.[22] In the quotation above from *Edmund*, for instance, the word is used with great resonance in association with the idea of standing one's ground, defending people and 'eard' (ll. 67, 80) from the men of the 'flot' (l. 77). We do not, that is, need a Germanic heroic ethos to account for the importance of the collaborative defence of 'eard' in such a society, and in so far as social structures are theorized, they are Christian theorizations. For both the ecclesiastical poet and his noble lay patron, theories of civil structure, military obligation and kingship are formed within a Christian framework seen both as enduring and of specific informing relevance to contemporary dilemmas and experiences. Biblical and hagiographic thinking on 'eard' and 'eðel' and the conduct of leaders must have seemed urgently relevant to a troubled present, the more so for providing a range of models which validated defence both by combat and through the refusal of combat. Germanic ideals, despite their compatibility with some of the ealdorman's responsibilities for his 'eard' and the king's for his 'eðel', may have seemed one rather narrow mode of response rather than a paradigm to which primary reference could be made. Perhaps, in this context, they even suggested a past of regrettable relevance to the present. If Ælfric's patron Æthelweard is indeed the author of the Chronicle written for his cousin Matilda, abbess of Essen, his sense of the Germanic past focusses on destructive conquest rather than on the heroic:

> "Quin etiam de priscorum aduentu parentum a Germania in Brittanniam, tot bella tot caedes uirorum, classiumque periclitationem gurgite oceani non paruam, in subpositis paginulis facilius inuenire potes exemplar."

> "In the following pages you can very easily find by way of example so many wars and slayings of men and no small wreck of navies on the waves of ocean, especially with reference to the arrival of our ancestors in Britain from Germany."[23]

In this Chronicle's account of the genealogy of English kings and his own ancestry, Æthelweard (if it is his work) displays no very strong interest in Sceaf and he uses this name without reference to Beowulf.[24] His association of the Germanic and the strife-torn lends support to the view that for him as for Ælfric, the rhythms and diction of heroic verse may have encoded a militarism capable of justification and nobility, but capable too, when *only* militaristic, only 'Germanic,' of being otiose as well as potentially impious.

Unlike Byrhtnoth, ealdorman of Essex, and equally, unlike Edmund, King of East Anglia, Æthelweard in the 990's was not defending his territory by dying for it, but by paying tribute. It might therefore be tempting to see Ælfric as responding correctively and polemically on behalf of a pious aristocrat such as Æthelweard to a 'hawkish' militarism on the part of some of the lay nobility among his audience to whom fighting the viking attacks seemed the best medium-term policy.[25] In that case, perhaps, Bethurum's argument could be inverted and we might see Ælfric not as invoking the heroic but critiqueing it. As Katherine O'Brien O'Keefe comments, the thematic inversions of his *Edmund* are striking.[26] In a text so close to the date of the Maldon battle, they could almost be read as a pointed commentary on the poem, had it then existed. A leader dies for his people, rather than a body of retainers dying for their leader; the concept of vengeance is replaced by that of sacrifice; a refusal to fight which is neither flight nor cowardice is displayed and a tactical decision which is unheroic (or at least, unByrhthnothian) is shown to be laudable.

Yet such a reading would probably be mistaken if it saw Ælfric's *Edmund* for Æthelweard as Christian opposition to the anonymous poet's *Maldon* for heroic Germanic Byrhtnoth. Byrhtnoth will historically have been more like Æthelweard than like a heroic Germanic warleader. Both were of the reforming monastic and monarchical party, and Byrhtnoth, who had no son, was an even more munificent patron (of Ely and other monastic houses) than Æthelweard.[27] The two ealdormen will have had a shared ethical and political framework, even if they at times pursued different policy options within it. Although Byrhtnoth was the subject of heroicising verse and Ælfric's patron the commissioner of scriptural and hagiographic texts, we do not need to suppose the heroes of *Edmund* and *Maldon* as constituted by the model of heroic/Christian opposition. In Ælfric's work, Christian traditions supply their own critique of militarism and it is extremely (and in this context, significantly) difficult to prove that he anywhere makes specific use of heroic verse that could be called distinctively Germanic and unaccounted for by the traditions and images of Christian thought about war.

On several occasions in his writing career, Ælfric reworked the same or similar materials for different audiences of secular and religious men. His treatment of martial themes and heroism for his varying audiences can be pursued in his lives of Martin, the soldier-saint who renounces fighting for Caesar in favour of Christ. Ælfric's earlier and much longer life is part of the Second Series of his *Catholic Homilies* (henceforth *CH*), completed by 995 if not earlier, and was written for clerical and liturgical use, while his later and shorter version in the *Lives of Saints* (henceforth *LS*) made monastic commemorations available to his lay patrons and was completed by 1002.[28]

The textual history of these lives allows us to see Ælfric at work in some detail. As Zettel has shown, Ælfric used a hagiographic dossier for his lives of Martin rather than (as used to be thought) reading a range of documents concerning the saint over a long period.[29] The fullest version of this dossier is more closely represented at this point by Oxford, Bodleian Library, MS Bodley 354 than the Cotton-Corpus legendary.[30] It is thus possible to follow Ælfric's reworking closely in, for example, the critical moment when Martin's renunciation of fighting for Caesar in favour of fighting for Christ is presented in the two versions. There are slight but significant differences, not accountable for by the source. In the Bodleian manuscript the text of Alcuin's *Epitome of Sulpicius* makes no detailed mention of weapons at the relevant point, but makes the saint's speech a general contrast of serving the God of heaven versus fighting for the emperor on earth:

> "Christi ego miles sum; pugnare mihi non licet . . . si hoc . . . ignauiae adscribitur, non fidei, crastina die ante aciem inermis adstabo et in nomine Domini Iesu, signo crucis, non clipeo protectus aut galea, hostium cuneos penetrabo securus".[31]

> "I am Christ's soldier: it is not permitted to me to fight . . . if this . . . is ascribed to cowardice, and not faith, I shall stand tomorrow unarmed in the battle, and in the name of the Lord Jesus, with the sign of the cross, unprotected by shield or sword, I shall safely make my way through the enemy's battle-formation".

In Ælfric's earlier English version for churchmen, the weapons Martin is abandoning are given in specific detail:

> 1   ac cwæð þæt he wolde Criste ðeowian
>   on gastlicum gecampe æfter his cristendome.
>   Ða cwæð se wælhreowa þæt he wære afyrht
>   for ðan toweardan gefeohte, na for Criste eawfæst.
> 5   Ða andwyrde Martinus unforht ðam casere
>   'Ic will ðurhgan orsorh ðone here,
>   mid rode-tacne gewæpnod, na mid readum scylde,
>   oððe mid hefegum helme, oþþe heardre byrnan'".
>   (*CH*, vol. 2, p. 502)[32]

> "but he said that he would serve Christ / in spiritual battle in accordance with his Christianity. / Then the cruel tyrant said that he was afraid / of the forthcoming fight, not reverent towards Christ. / Then Martin, unafraid, answered the emperor, / 'I will pass without fear through the enemy host, / armed with the sign of the cross, not with a red shield / or with heavy healm or hard byrnie'".

In Ælfric's second version for his lay patron, the weapons are less detailed, though the organizing military metaphor for spiritual combat is more explicit:

> "ic eom godes cempa ne mot ic na feohtan .
> Ða gebealh hine se casere . and cwæð þæt he for yrhðe
> þæs to-weardan gefeohtes . na for eawfæst-nysse
> hine sylfne æt-brude swa þam campdome .
> Ac martinus unforht to þam manfullan cwæð .
> Gif ðu to yrhðe þis telst . and na to ge-leafan .
> nu to mergen ic stande on mines drihtnes naman
> ætforan þam truman . and ic fare orsorh

> mid rode-tacne gescyld . na mid readum scylde .
> oðð mid helme þurh þæs here werod".
>
> (*LS*, ll. 106, 111–15)[33]

"'I am God's champion, I may not fight.' / Then the emperor swelled with rage and said that it was on account of cowardice / about the forthcoming battle and not because of piety / that he thus withdrew himself from the fighting. / But Martin, unafraid, said to the evil man, / 'If you count this as cowardice and not faith / now, tomorrow I will stand in my Lord's name / before the battle-line, and I will go fearlessly / protected with the sign of the cross, not with red shield / or helmet, through the enemy host'".

Both versions retain the rhetorically and thematically important contrast of "rode-tacne" and "readum scylde" (*CH*, l. 7, *LS*, l. 114), but as represented by Ælfric for monks, Martin will not use his red shield, heavy helmet, or hard byrnie (*CH*, ll. 7–8), while, represented for laymen, he will not fight with red shield and helmet (*LS*, ll. 114–5). In the source, the helmet and shield of the *CH* version are present in Sulpicius' *galea* ('[leather] helmet') and *clipeo*, but not their affective adjectival freighting. Ælfric's use of a 'red' shield must be prompted by the adjective's value, in a line of considerable rhetorical heightening, for the alliteratively-underlined contrast with "rode-tacne". (In a similar way, in the *LS* passage, Ælfric underlines the 'scyld' of line 114—for Sulpicius' *clipeo* and *cuneos*—with the internal rhyme of the verbal and nominal forms). In the balancing of the alliterating 'rod' and 'read' there is, further, a kind of visual pun: the *r*ood is *r*ed with Christ's blood, Christ's blood is a shield for humanity.[34]

It seems unlikely that Ælfric was trying to evoke a historical picture of Frankish soldiery for the *CH* audience, but if he were, there is no evidence to suggest that the Frankish foot troops (among whom the saint is serving at this point in the narrative) used red shields or that Ælfric could have thought they did.[35] Neither does Ælfric seem to be concerned to evoke contemporary battle array and equipment.[36] There are no red shields in the extant Anglo-Saxon poetic corpus, while the shieldwall, so important in *Maldon*, is precisely what Ælfric does *not* take from his source's "cuneos" here.[37] If any specific military associations were present to Ælfric as prompting or licensing the adjective, they are as likely to have been Roman traditions mediated through Carolingian texts as Germanic: the circular bronze Roman *clipeo* may well have been thought to be red, particularly if one were familiar with it through Carolingian traditions of manuscript illustration.[38] Rather than specifically Germanic heroics, the contrast here is between militarism in general and Christ's self-sacrifice.

In the *CH* version Ælfric also adds a byrnie (l. 8 in my lineation above) to the armour mentioned in Sulpicius. This was not standard English equipment until Æthelred's heriot decrees of 1008 (too late for either *CH* or *LS*).[39] As an ordinary soldier in the late Roman legions, Martin seems aware of a great deal more body armour than he would be if he were fighting in 991 at the battle of Maldon (where, as Nicholas Brooks has argued, nothing is said of helmets, and, with the possible exception of Byrhtnoth's "reaf", only the Vikings have byrnies).[40] Helm and byrnie are frequently collocated in the earlier heroic poetry, notably in *Beowulf*, but also in Old English scriptural verse such as *Judith*.[41] The force of the collocation in Ælfric's use here stems from its adjectival inversion of qualities normally regarded as virtues in weapons. Compared with the freedom, clarity and confidence with which Martin stands under his lord Christ's banner, a clumsy burdensomeness is evoked: "mid *hefegum* helme oþþe *heardre* byrnan" (*CH*, [relineated] l. 8). This looks temptingly like a mock-heroic line, but cannot confidently be said to contain more than the most general reminiscence. Though we have here a formula found in *Beowulf*, it does not bring with it precise Germanic heroic connotations so much as a general secular militarism. (Ælfric is not at this point using the figure of spiritual armour, but his primary association for the collocation of helm and byrnie could as well have been the Pauline *lorica* as any poetic use).[42] Even where the context is very favourable (with Ælfric, like a latter-day Alcuin, mocking militarism for the benefit of monks) and where there is lexical overlap, it cannot be claimed that Ælfric is doing more than opportunistically and occasionally rhetoricising secular militarism: he is not reformulating a heroic Germanic ethos.

Ælfric's mock heroics, if they are that, concerning the weapons abandoned in Martin's decision to serve Christ rather than Caesar are most fully detailed in the earlier *CH* version of the life.[43] In the later *LS* version, composed for the reading of pious magnates such as Æthelweard and Æthelmær, the point is much less sharply made (see ll. 113–5 above). In the later life, Ælfric presents many more of the miracles and shows the saint to be a powerful wonder worker: the earlier life keeps the miracles to a token couple and allows Martin's background and military career to bulk much larger. The earlier Life, designed for church use, is more overtly related to military heroism than the second which was provided for pious lay reading: Ælfric, that is, provides more of the soldier for preaching purposes and more of the saint for lay readers interested in monks' reading. Once again, the model of opposed heroic and Christian paradigms is inadequate to the interwoven themes of spirituality and martiality in Ælfric's writings and in the interests of his audience. Soldiering and saintliness can both produce the witness to human faith and loyalty disclosed in suffering: "hu þegenlice hi þrowodon", as Ælfric writes in his life of the forty Cappadocian soldier martyrs.[44] Within the framework of late Anglo-Saxon Christian thought, Germanic heroism is not an alternative paradigm, so much as a shade or strand of response, subsumed into a reality more comprehensively addressed by a Christian sense of history.

Though Martin and Edmund, as saints, may throw down the weapons of worldly militarism, Christian theory as used by Ælfric nonetheless provides for present military necessity. In West Mercia, Ælfric was less affected by the raids of the 990's than Byrhtnoth and Æthelweard in the East and South, but he cannot have been unaware either of increased viking successes or of the extent to which his audience faced strategic and ethical dilemmas in relation to them. A Christian typological sense of history structures his work, but is not incompatible with, and indeed includes, a pragmatic sense of present tactical relevance. In discussing Ælfric's homily on Judith, Ian Pringle has argued that this text's preoccupation with chastity is not incompatible with Ælfric's account of his own homily in the *Letter to Sigeweard* as an example of how "ge eower eard mid wæpnum beweriæn wið onwinnende here".[45] For Ælfric, military and spiritual responses are equally necessary and are connected: the viking raids succeed in so far as, and because, the monastic system does not totally fulfill its own aims. As Pauline Stafford comments, "military problems are seen as an outcome of failure to live up to the image of Christian kingship".[46] This argument is suggestive for the very large proportion of Ælfric's vernacular writings for lay audiences which concerns soldier-saints, martyr-kings, and the leaders of the Old Testament.

Of these texts, the one which reads most like a mirror for princes who have to decide when to engage the enemy and how to fight ethically—and the one that has most fighting in it—is Ælfric's paraphrase, in the *Lives of the Saints*, of the biblical narrative of the Maccabees, also produced for Æthelweard.[47] This text offers a more extended sense of how Ælfric subsumes and includes heroic values within a past structured not as an endless linear progression of deeds and deaths, but as shaped and typologically meaningful.

Though produced for a Western ealdorman who had chosen the opposite course to Byrhtnoth of Essex as a response to enemy raiding, Ælfric's version of the Maccabees is replete with stylistic allusion and accounts of battle which make it read at moments like *Maldon* itself. Judas Machabeus adopts a "scynende byrnan" (84/279) and fights all his battles with a sword

seized from the impious Appollonius: "þæt wæs mærlic wæpn" (876/296).
Judas prays to God to guide the course of battle ("to-bryt nu ðas hæðenan",
90/371) and encourages his troops against enemies repeatedly portrayed as
pagan despoilers of home territory:

> "Ðas cumað to us swylce hi cenran syndon
> and willað us fordon . and awestan ure land"
> (86/312–3)

"In this way they come to us as though they are braver / and they
want to destroy us and lay waste our land".

> "Hi slogon þa togædere unslawe mid wæpnum
> and þær feollon ða hæþenan fif ðusend ofslagene"
> (90/375–6)

"They joined battle then together fast with weapons / and then five
thousand of the heathen fell slain there".

The rallying speech with which Judas faces his last battle, apart from its
slightly longer lines, is even more reminiscent of *Maldon* than the life of St.
Edmund:

> "Ne ge-wurðe hit na on life . þæt we alecgan ure wuldor
> mid earh-licum fleame . ac uton feohtan wið hi .
> and gif god swa fore-sceawað . we sweltað on mihte
> for urum gebroðrum butan bysmorlicum fleame".
> (110/660–63)

"Let it never happen in [our] life that we lay aside our glory / with
cowardly flight: but let us fight against them / and if God so foreor-
dains, we shall perish in [our] strength / for our brothers without
cowardly flight".

The chief difference between Judas and the Byrhtnoth of *Maldon* here is
that Judas thinks of glory in terms of 'wuldor' (used principally in scriptural
verse) rather than being 'lofgeorn'.[48] Ælfric is extremely careful about the
legitimation of Judas' battles: they are always fought with reference to God,
taken up as requests for help, or responses to attack (92/385–96), rather
than as acts of aggression: they are always against unregenerate heathen
and always exemplary of Judas' role as "Godes ðegen" (112/686). Victory,
when it comes, as Judas says, is always from heaven ("se sige bið symle of heofonum", 86/311). While Ælfric here endorses loyalty between warriors,
kin-groups and overlords and is quite clear that Judas overcomes his enemies with weapons (102/536), Ælfric is also prepared to omit or evade implications of the source material in order to present Judas' campaigns as jus-

tified and to preserve the line between legitimated killing and vengeance. No matter how violently and extensively Judas slaughters civilian non-combatants, they turn out to have been heathen and so really fighting on the devil's side anyway. So for example in the case of the city of Ephron (I *Macc.* 5:46, unnamed in Ælfric, 94/440), Judas' army prays for a peaceful passage, but when it has proven necessary to slaughter the inhabitants they are 'the heathens' ("þa hæðenan", 96/449) and no longer 'the citizens' ("ða burhware", 96/444). Vengeance on "ðam fulum hæðenum" (84/269) is permissible: it is part of Judas' virtue that he defended and cleansed his native land ("todræfde þa arleasan . and his eðel gerymde", 84/283). Vengeance is nonetheless defined as fighting *against* heathens rather than *for* one's lord, and a strict Christian military discipline is used in this war. When Judas' troops fight in his absence and take spoil without permission they are portrayed as tempted to covetousness and are slain in battle (96/458–464). Judas does not allow this plunder to be kept, but sends it to Jerusalem as an offering for his troops' souls (96/468–71). Like the figure of the virtuous pagan, he intuits beliefs that would be revealed in the grace of redemption: he understands "æwfæstlice" ('religiously', 98/472) that all will be resurrected (hence the point of his offering), but also that true believers will have "þa selestan gife" (98/478).

In this text, then, Ælfric is careful not to legitimate vengeance even as he leaves conceptual room for loyalty between warriors and to their overlords, and for the legitimate defence of territory against heathen invasion. Having so carefully selected and presented from his source material, he finally offers a framework which would render impossible any simple legitimation of modern war by reference to Judas. Judas was "godes ðegen" (112/686) who most often fought against conquerors in defence of [his] people and has illustriously performed mighty deeds in defence of his kinsmen ("mærlice gefremode", 112/678, "for his freonda ware", 112/677) while remaining holy ("halig", 112/681). This is because he "æfre wan for willan þæs ælmihtigan" (112/683). In a dispensation particular to the Old Law ("on þam dagum", 112/684), Judas was permitted to defeat his enemies ("alyfed to alecgenne his fynd ./ and swiþost ða hæðenan", 112/684–5), but the literal fighting of God's ancient people is to be interpreted figuratively as a foreshadowing of the unmilitaristic holy men, the fighters of the New Testament. Their battles against vices and devils figure a more important permanent strife, and constitute the framework within which literal and historical military values can be judged. Judas' career of slaughter in defence of 'eard and eðel' does not license military aggression by contemporary late tenth-century and eleventh-century ealdormen in any easy way.

Points of conduct pertaining to military leadership are firmly framed in a specifically Christian sense of history: Judas was permitted to defeat his enemies and especially the heathen under the Old Law, but "Crist on his tocyme" (112/688), says Ælfric, has taught us a different ethic, that of spiritual fight against invisible enemies.

Only within this interpretative framework does Ælfric make his famous concluding acknowledgment of the demands of the *bellum iustum*, defining just war as "rihtlic gefeoht wið ða reðan flotmenn" (114/708).[49] A measure of the care with which Ælfric summarizes the implications of the Maccabee narrative for an ethical late Anglo-Saxon society is his use of the Isidorean model of social functions, the tripartite division of "laboratores, oratores, bellatores" (120/814) as a further reflection on the biblical narrative. Here, in a manner compatible with late Anglo-Saxon social structures and obligations, he explains that *bellatores* have the function of defending towns and territory ("ure burga healdað ./ and urne eard be-weriað wið onwinnendne", 122/817–8), but that the greater struggle is that of the monks who fight "wið þa ungesewenlican deofla" (122/824). In Ælfric's account, then, the warrior is, properly, an instrument of God's policy; Christian typological thinking allows Judas to be both 'woruld cempa' and 'godes þeowan' in the same act. In the same way, particular historical territories ('eard') and peoples ('eðel') are embraced within the typology of the promised land, as it applies to nations' destinies and individual souls, but this is not incompatible with simultaneous ethical reference to pressing strategic problems of the 'eard' and 'eðel'.[50]

What would Ælfric or Æthelweard have thought of *The Battle of Maldon*, supposing them to have heard it? How, indeed, would that friend to Ely, Ramsey, and the monastic party, Bryhtnoth himself, have reacted to such a poem? Would he have preferred, perhaps, Byrhtferth of Ramsey's view of him as a Maccabean fighter "defending himself on right and left" (I *Maccabees* 6:45)?[51] Perhaps, for late tenth and eleventh century abbots and magnates, *Maldon* would have seemed rather irrelevant, a leisure-time pursuit of polite literature rather than a source of ethical thought about the concerns of the day. (If so it would become yet another irony of literary history that Ælfric should be an agent, via Laȝamon's reading of him, for the transmission of stylistic features which would be richly used in the Anglo-Norman world's continuing reception of Germanic and Christian heroic paradigms. Something of the themes and style of *Maldon* would re-echo in the thirteenth-century's looser and longer alliterative line as Uther Pendragon and Arthur defended 'eard and eðel').[52]

Meditating on the reception context of *Maldon* sharpens the question of

whose interests are served, and how, by the poem's composition. If we suppose it, in accordance with the preceding argument, *not* to be a major part
of the ethical and doctrinal thinking with which the leaders of the day met
their moral and strategic dilemmas, what other features of the poem stand
out? It is less clerical and bookish than other late works such as *Brunanburh*
and the *Anglo-Saxon Chronicle* poems. If it evokes an older heroism, it is not
an antiquarian poem. It has a high degree of affective and encomiastic commemoration, it focusses on the central figure's conduct but accommodates
his relations, retainers and allies, while marginalizing those not loyal to
him. It is, if not reticent, at least ambiguous over whether or not Byrhtnoth
committed a tactical error, and it shows him making a Christian death. Far
from being interested in battle strategy and military tactics for their own
sake, it procedes in a series of vignettes and images, focussing constantly on
the elegiac and emotive content of battle and its rhetoric. The question of
who may be interested in commissioning it seems best answered by considering Byrhtnoth's own family. Byrhtnoth and his wife Ælfflæd were child-
less, and no sons succeeded the dead ealdorman. Dorothy Whitelock some
time ago suggested that Ælflæd commissioned the poem, though this suggestion has not made much headway against recent tendencies to see the
poem as much later than the battle.[53] But Byrhtnoth did, by some other li-
aison than his marriage with Ælfflæd, have a daughter, Leoflæd. Unmentioned in her mother's or aunt's will (her mother left property to ealdorman
Æthelweard's son, Æthelmær), she was probably illegitimate. But she made
a good marriage, and inherited something from her father, and later, her
husband.[54] Byrhtnoth's daughter would better fit with a lapse of time between the battle and the poem.

As Professor Frank reminds us, women may have commissioned and
made the Bayeux tapestry. The *Encomium Emmae* was probably commissioned by a woman, and the life of Edward the Confessor was probably
commissioned by his wife Edith.[55] Like their Continental contemporaries
and their Anglo-Norman successors, noblewomen of the late tenth and
eleventh centuries were among the most important patrons of artistic work
in their society. In the state of our knowledge of *Maldon's* dating, one can
only speculate, but it would seem well worth while, in considering the reception of the poem, to keep in view the women of the noble families concerned with its events. Byrhtnoth had no male heirs: his daughter Leoflæd
had one son who became a monk at Ely, and three daughters, one of whom
lived in some form of female community and wove and embroidered
church vestments (some of which are mentioned in Ely's twelfth-century
inventory).[56] In late Old English culture as in the high middle ages more

generally, the social configuration of women of high birth with access to clerics and their resources is responsible for a great deal of vernacular literature, including the commemorative and frequently lineage-oriented genres of historiography and hagiography.

I suggested earlier that the model by which Anglo-Saxons imbibed heroic poetry with their mother's milk needs some revising, at least in terms of its implications and contexts. But King Alfred himself testifies to the important role of mothers in early education, and perhaps we need only revise the model so far as to see Anglo-Saxon children in noble families picking up heroic poetry if not at the breast then at the knee—from the people who were both their mothers and its patrons. In a culture where the language of public affairs and ethical decision-making is that written by an Ælfric for an Æthelweard, commemoration of the secular hero, for all his association with the thematics of prowess and male-male obligations, may yet find its most appropriate context in the ceremonies and commemorations of noble families organized by noblewomen.

Notes

1. It is a pleasure to record my gratitude to Professor Teresa Pàroli, Professor Italo Signorini, and Dr. Maria Elena Ruggerini, the organisers of the Convegno internazionale di studio on 'L'eroe germanico: storicità, metafora, paradigma'. In addition, together with colleagues in the Liverpool Centre for Medieval Studies, I owe a great deal to Professor Pàroli for the energy and generosity with which she has fostered the research exchange between the Università di Roma, "La Sapienza" and the University of Liverpool, and for this too I am very grateful to her.

2. Joyce Hill, *The Soldier of Christ in Old English Prose and Poetry*, "Leeds Studies in English", 12 (1981), pp. 57–80 (p. 57) (quoting Pearsall).

3. Dorothy Bethurum, *The Form of Ælfric's Lives of Saints*, "Studies in Philology", 29 (1932), pp. 515–33 (p. 533).

4. See E. G. Stanley, *The Search for Anglo-Saxon Paganism*, Cambridge and Totowa, N.J. 1975; Allen J. Frantzen, *Desire for Origins: New Language, Old English and Teaching the Tradition*, New Brunswick, N.J. 1990, esp. chapters 2 and 3.

5. Teresa Pàroli, *Santi e demoni nelle letterature germaniche dell'alto medioevo*, in *Santi e demoni nell'alto medioevo occidentale*, Settimane di studio del Centro italiano di studi sull'alto medioevo, 36, Spoleto 1989, pp. 411–498 (p. 496).

6. *The* Beowulf *Poet's Sense of History*, in *The Wisdom of Poetry: Essays for Morton Bloomfield*, ed. L. D. Benson and Siegfried Wenzel, Medieval Institute Publications, Kalamazoo, Michigan 1982, pp. 53–65 (p. 63).

7. *Life of St Edmund*, in *Aelfric's Lives of Saints*, ed. W. W. Skeat, EETS OS 76 82, 94, 114 (Trübner 1881–85; repr. as two volumes London, Oxford University

Press for EETS, 1966), vol. 2, pp. 318–20 (henceforth quoted by line number in the text).

8. For Abbo's *vita*, see Michael Winterbottom, ed., *Three Lives of English Saints*, Pontifical Institute of Medieval Studies, Toronto 1972, pp. 67–87. For discussion of Ælfric's treatment of his source, see Cecily Clark, *Ælfric and Abbo*, "English Studies", 49 (1968), pp. 30–36. Lapidge and Winterbottom suggest that the text of Abbo's *Passio sancti Eadmundi* in Paris, MS BN lat. 5362 is "arguably a copy of a hagiographical commonplace-book compiled by Ælfric himself" (Michael Lapidge and Michael Winterbottom, eds., *Wulfstan of Winchester: the Life of St Æthelwold*, Oxford 1991, pp. cxlviii–ix).

9. D. G. Scragg, ed., *The Battle of Maldon*, Manchester 1981, pp. 65–6.

10. On Ælfric's prose style, especially his rhythmical alliteration, see J. C. Pope, ed., *Homilies of Ælfric: A Supplementary Collection*, 2 vols., EETS O.S. 259, 260, London 1967, 1968, vol. 1, Introduction, pp. 105–36; Frances R. Lipp, *Ælfric's Old English prose Style*, "Studies in Philology", 66 (1969), pp. 689–718); Sherman M. Kuhn, *Was Ælfric a Poet?*, "Philological Quarterly", 52 (1973), pp. 643–62.

11. Jess B. Bessinger, *A Concordance to the Anglo-Saxon Poetic Records*, Ithaca, N.Y. 1978, s.v. *landmanna, flotmanna*.

12. See for example, E. V. Gordon, ed., *The Battle of Maldon*, London 1937, pp. 4–5, 21–2.

13. Winterbottom, *Three Lives*, p. 74, ll. 6–11.

14. "þe on heora bedde wurdon mid bearnum . and wifum . [ofslægene]", 318/76.

15. See Michael Cherniss, *Ingeld and Christ: Heroic Concepts and Values in Old English Poetry*, The Hague and Paris 1972, for 'loyalty, vengeance and treasure' as characteristics of heroic verse (Cherniss' insistence on two separate poetic traditions of Germanic and Christian and his argument that Old English poetry develops by poets gradually becoming free of pre-Christian concepts and values, with *Maldon* as a kind of heathen survival [p. 255] is less convincing: a secular poem in a Christian society with a Germanic past is not the same thing as a Germanic poem).

16. Skeat, *Lives of Saints*, Preface, p. 4. On Æthelweard and Æthelmær see Milton McC. Gatch, *Preaching and Theology in Anglo-Saxon England: Ælfric and Wulfstan*, Toronto 1977, pp. 48–9. On Æthelmær as founder of Eynsham, see A. J. Robertson, *Anglo-Saxon Charters*, Cambridge 1956, p. 386 (n. to p. 144, l. 4).

17. Eric John, *The World of Abbot Ælfric*, in *Ideal and Reality in Frankish and Anglo-Saxon Society: Studies Presented to J. M. Wallace-Hadrill*, ed. P. Wormald and D. A. Bullough, Oxford 1983, pp. 300–16, esp. pp. 302–3: Pauline Stafford, *Church and Society in the Age of Ælfric*, in *The Old English Homily and Its Backgrounds*, ed. Paul F. Szarmach and Bernard F. Huppé, Albany, N.Y. 1978, pp. 11–42, esp. p. 16.

18. Æthelweard's first undoubted signature as ealdorman is in 976. He probably became the senior of the four ealdorman following Byrhtnoth's death in 911 and the death of Ealdorman Æthelwine in 992 (E. E. Barker, *The Anglo-Saxon Chronicle Used by Æthelweard*, "Bull. Inst. Hist. Research", 40 [1967], p. 86). The Parker Chronicle gives the date of the tax as 911 but it was more probably 994 (A. Campbell, ed., *The Chronicle of Æthelweard*, London and Edinburgh 1962, pp. xiii-xiv).

19. *Bookland and Fyrd Service in Late Saxon England*, "Anglo-Norman Studies", 7 (1984), pp. 1–19 (p. 2).

20. *Ibid.*, pp. 2, 5.

21. Abels argues that these systems of obligation cannot properly be called either 'Germanic' or 'feudal': "just as English law on the eve of the Conquest was a hodge-podge of archaic custom and royal innovation" varying according to locale, so the defence of the realm looked back to "the war-bands of seventh-century rulers such as Oswald and Oswiu and to the 'New Model' army of Alfred and his successors" and "depended on a system that had developed organically over the centuries and which reflected the military history of England" (*Bookland and Fyrd Service . . .*, p. 2).

22. 'Eard' occurs 76 times in the poetry (7 times in *Beowulf* alone), and is collocated 9 times with 'eðel', twice with 'æðelinga', and once each with 'ealdordom', 'eorlscipe', 'eðelriht', 'eðelwyn', 'ealdres', 'ealdor', 'eorlas'; while 'eðel' occurs 51 times (see Bessinger, *Concordance*, s.v. *eard, eðel*). For Ælfric, 'eard' is associated with the promised land and with notions of territory to be defended or (biblically) conquered: see Antonette diPaolo Healey and Richard L. Venezky, *A Microfiche Concordance to Old English*, Toronto 1980, s.v. *eard, earde, eðel* for Ælfric's numerous uses.

23. Campbell, *Chronicle of Æthelweard*, p. 1.

24. K. Sisam, *Anglo-Saxon Royal Genealogies*, "Proceedings of the British Academy", 39 (1953), pp. 287–348 (pp. 317–20).

25. Eric John argues that paying tribute must have seemed a more feasible strategy in 994 (when Æthelweard went with Bishop Ælfheah and ealdorman Ælfric to arrange payment to the Danes) than it did by 1016 when a whole series of further payments had still not achieved English aims. The battle of 991 was only *retrospectively* perceived as the turning point after which what had at the time seemed a series of separate and manageable Danish raids became visible as a decline in English power (*War and Society in the Tenth Century: The Maldon Campaign*, "Transactions of the Royal Historical Society", 27 [1977], pp. 173–95, esp. pp. 174, 190).

26. Katherine O'Brien O'Keefe, *Heroic Values and Christian Ethics*, in *The Cambridge Companion to Old English Literature*, ed. Malcolm Godden and Michael Lapidge, Cambridge 1991, pp. 107–125 (p. 116).

27. The two ealdormen not only had similar positions and responsibilities but closer ties, since Æthelweard's son, Æthelmær, endowed his foundation of Eynsham in part with lands left to him by his kinswoman, Ælfflæd, Byrhtnoth's wife (see Campbell, *Chronicle of Æthelweard*, p. xvi). For Byrhtnoth's donations to Ely, see *Liber Eliensis* ed. E. O. Blake, Camden 3rd ser., 92, London 1962, pp. 133–6, 158 (discussed by Blake, pp. 422–3). Byrhtnoth is praised in the *Liber Eliensis* for resisting those who, after the deaths of King Edgar and Bishop Æthelwold, wanted to expel the monks and recall the canons (Blake, p. 134).

28. For the dating and relative chronology of the Second Series of *Catholic Homilies* and *Lives of Saints* see P. Clemoes, *The Chronology of Ælfric's Works*, in *The Anglo-Saxons: Studies in Some Aspects of Their History and Culture Presented to Bruce Dickins*, ed. P. Clemoes, London 1959, pp. 212–47 (pp. 243–4). Ælfric apparently wrote an early,

perhaps rather hasty version of the life of Martin in his *Catholic Homilies* II (*CH* XXXIX) for Æthelweard, who had already taken an interest in *CH* (*see* Clemoes, *Chronology*, p. 226, n. 4, and K. Sisam, *Studies in the History of Old English Literature*, Oxford 1953, repr. 1962, pp. 148–98, esp. pp. 160–61) and requested more. In *LS*, Ælfric supplies Æthelweard with the more specialized lives of the saints "þe mynster-menn mid heora þeningum betwux him wurðiað" (Skeat, *Lives of Saints*, p. 4). M. R. Godden, *The Development of Ælfric's Second Series of Homilies*, "English Studies", 54 (1973), pp. 209–16 argues that the Second Series [i.e. *CH* II] is "addressed less to the congregation and more to the clergy than the First Series" (p. 216). Clemoes, *Chronology*, p. 220, sees the *LS Martin*, like the *Forty Soldiers* (*LS* XI) and *Edmund* (*LS* XXXII), as designed for non-liturgical use: appropriately, in a series undertaken for noble lay-men such as Æthelweard and Æthelmær, they could be used for pious reading at any time.

29. Patrick H. Zettel, *Saints' Lives in Old English: Latin Manuscripts and Vernacular Accounts: Ælfric*, "Peritia", 1 (1982), pp. 17–37 (pp. 24–7). See also Zettel, *Ælfric's Hagiographic Sources and the Latin Legendary Preserved in BL MS Cotton Nero E i + CCC MS 9 and Other Manuscripts*, D. Phil. thesis, Oxford 1979, pp. 265–70.

30. Zettel (*Ælfric's Hagiographic Sources . . .* , pp. 99–109, pp. 265–70) argues that Oxford, Bodleian Library, MS Bodley 354 better represents the fullest version of the Martin dossier used by Ælfric than the Cotton-Corpus legendary because the latter probably lacked Alcuin's *Epitome* of the Sulpicius *Vita* and other items used by Ælfric, but that there were items lacking in this dossier which *were* present in Ælfric's major source of his saints' lives, i.e. his exemplar of the Cotton-Corpus legendary. On the Cotton-Corpus legendary see further Teresa Webber, *Scribes and Scholars at Salisbury Cathedral c. 1075 - c. 1125*, Oxford 1992, p. 70.

31. Sulpicius, *Vita S. Martini*, C. Halm, *Sulpicii Severi libri qui supersunt*, Corpus Scriptorum Ecclesiasticorum Latinorum I, Vienna 1866, repr. Hildesheim 1983, p. 114, collated with MS Bodley 354, f. 41v; see also Zettel, *Ælfric's Hagiographic Sources . . .* , p. 313, n. 35.

32. Benjamin Thorpe ed., *Sermones Catholici*, London 1844–46, repr. Hildesheim 1983, vol. 2, no. XXXIX, p. 502 (relineated from Thorpe's prose typography).

33. Skeat, *Lives of Saints*, vol. 2, no. XXXI, p. 226. Judith Gaites, *Ælfric's Longer Life of St. Martin and its Latin Sources: A Study in Narrative Technique*, "Leeds Studies in English", 13 (1982), pp. 23–41, includes a more extensive study of *LS* XXXI in re-lation to Sulpicius' *Vita* (though without benefit of the research on the source text subsequently published by Zettel).

34. For Ælfric's interest in devotion to the cross, see Eric John, *The World of Abbot Ælfric*, pp. 310–11; Barbara Raw, *Anglo-Saxon Crucifixion Iconography and the Art of the Monastic Revival*, Cambridge 1990, pp. 175–7 and p. 181.

35. On Frankish armour see P. E. Cleator, *Weapons of War*, London 1967, pp. 93–7; for diagrams of shield design and insignia listed in the fifth century *Notititia dignita-tum*, see Phil Barker, *The Armies and Enemies of Imperial Rome: Organisation, Tactics, Dress, and Weapons, 150 BC to 600 AD*, Goring by Sea 1972, pp. 54–5 (there is no ex-

ample of a Frankish foot-troop having red shields though some have red elements among their three or more colours).

36. Nicholas Brooks, *Weapons and Armour*, in *The Battle of Maldon, AD 991*, ed. D. G. Scragg, Oxford and Cambridge, Mass. 1991, pp. 208–19 (pp. 214–5).

37. Richard Abels, *English Tactics, Strategy and Military Organization in the Late Tenth Century*, in Scragg, ed., *Maldon AD 991*, pp. 143–55 (p. 149).

38. For example, the *Psalterium Aureum* (St. Gall, c. 890 AD), where Roman soldiers are shown with red shields with green subdivision markings (see Paul Martin, *Armour and Weapons*, tr. René North, London 1968, pl. 1, facing p. 4.

39. Brooks, *Weapons and Armour*, p. 217.

40. Brooks, *Weapons and Armour*, pp. 216–7. (For the argument that, if a byrnie is to be understood by 'reaf' at l. 161 in *Maldon*, it may be Offa's, not Byrhtnoth's see John C. Pope, *Offa and the Battle of Maldon*, in *Heroic Poetry in the Anglo-Saxon Period: Studies in Honor of Jess B. Bessinger*, ed. Helen Damico and John Leyerle, Kalamazoo, Michigan 1993, pp. 1–27, esp. p. 27).

41. Bessinger, *Concordance*, s.v. *helm, byrnan*.

42. Pauline spiritual armour (the breastplate of faith and love and the helmet of the hope of salvation, I *Th.* 5:8) is inappropriate when Martin is despising literal armour. This figure of thought is, however, common (occurring in this manuscripts *Martin* material at f. 83v: "ad pugnam fidei armatus galea ut lorica iusticie accinctur", f. 83v, combining *Eph.* 6:14 and 1 *Th.* 5:8).

43. M. R. Godden, *Ælfric's Changing Vocabulary*, "English Studies", 61 (1980), pp. 206–23, shows that Ælfric continuously experimented with lexis and suggests that in the Second Series of Catholic Homilies Ælfric uses a more elaborate and 'artificial' style, than in the First Series ("written as if addressed directly to a lay congregation", p. 221).

44. Skeat, *Lives of Saints*, vol. 1, no. XI, pp. 238–60 (p. 238/3).

45. Ian Pringle, *Judith: The Homily and the Poem*, "Traditio", 31 (1975), pp. 83–97 (p. 85) quoting S. J. Crawford, ed., *The Old English Version of the Heptateuch*, EETS o.s. 160, London 1922; rev. N.R. Ker, London 1969, p. 48). See also Ælfric's comment on the disruption by "multis iniuriis infestium piratarum" in the preface to *CH II* (ed. Jonathan Wilcox, *Ælfric's Prefaces* (Durham, 1994), 111/12–13.

46. Stafford, *Church and Society* . . . , p. 27 and see Pringle, *Judith* . . . , pp. 89–91.

47. Skeat, *Lives of Saints*, vol. 2, no. XXV, pp. 66–120 (henceforth referenced by page and line number in the text).

48. Bessinger, *Concordance*, s.v. *lofgeorn, wuldor*.

49. "A just fight against the cruel seamen". This passage is discussed by J. E. Gross, *Oswald and Byrhtnoth: A Christian Saint and a Hero who is Christian*, "English Studies", 46 (1965), pp. 93–109 (p. 93).

50. In his *Letter to Sigeweard* on his translations of the Old Testament, Ælfric himself underlines these points: the *Letter* summarizes Ælfric's fundamentally typological interpretation of the Maccabees as a kingroup who successfully fought "wið ðone hæðene here", seeking to drive them out "of þam earde, þe heom [the Maccabees]

God geaf" (Crawford, ed., *Heptateuch*, p. 49). Judas is seen as intuiting God's grace when he decides to call on God for help against the heathen enemies with which God punishes the sins of his people (p. 50). The *Letter* also reiterates the function of *bellatores* as being those who defend, but, in the New Testament dispensation, do not do so *sine cause* (p. 72). Ælfric further mentions that he had translated the book of Joshua for "Æþelwearde ealdormen" (p. 32), and explains Joshua's historical action of leading his people into Israel and winning it as a type of the Savior leading his people into the promised land and, eschatologically, into heaven (pp. 32–3). Here, says Ælfric, one may see the great wonders of God fulfilled in actuality ("Godes micclan wundra mid weorcum gefremode", p. 32, Laud MS).

51. Michael Lapidge, *The Life of St. Oswald*, in Scragg, *Maldon, AD 991*, pp. 51–8 (p. 53, p. 58, n. 16).

52. P. J. Frankis, *Laʒamon's English Sources*, in *J. R. R. Tolkien, Scholar and Storyteller: Essays in memoriam*, ed. M. B. Salu and R. T. Farrell, Ithaca, N.Y. 1979), pp. 64–75 (pp. 64–9). For an example of the defence of 'eard' and 'eðel' reminiscent of Ælfric's *Edmund* see *Laʒamon's Arthur: The Arthurian Section of Laʒamon's Brut*, ed. and tr. W. R. J. Barron and S. C. Weinberg, Harlow 1989, p. 28, ll. 9748–9754.

53. *English Historical Documents I, c. 500–1042*, London 1955, 2nd ed., London 1979, p. 319. John McKinnell, *The Date of* The Battle of Maldon, "Medium Ævum", 44 (1975), pp. 121–32 reviews the arguments and proposes c. 1020 or later: his argument for the dating has been questioned, (see Donald Scragg, The Battle of Maldon, in Scragg ed., *Maldon AD 991*, pp. 15–36 (p. 32, and p. 36 n. 14) but other recent work has also supported a date some time after the battle (see Earl R. Anderson, The Battle of Maldon: *A Reappraisal of Possible Sources, Date and Theme*, in *Modes of Interpretation in Old English Literature: Essays in Honour of Stanley B. Greenfield*, ed. Phyllis R. Brown, Georgia R. Crampton, and Fred C. Robinson, Toronto 1986, pp. 247–72).

54. Margaret Locherbie-Cameron, *Byrhtnoth and His Family*, in Scragg, ed., *Maldon AD 991*, pp. 253–62 (pp. 255–6); see also her *Byrhtnoth and His Sister's Son*, "Medium Ævum", 57 (1988), pp. 159–71.

55. Roberta Frank, Quid Hinieldus cum feminis: *The Hero and Women at the End of the First Millennnium* in *La funzione dell'eroe germanico: storicità, metafora, paradigma*. Atti del convegno internazionale di Studio, Roma 6–8 maggio 1993. Philologia, 2. ed. Teresa Pàroli (Rome, 1995), pp. 7–25 (pp. 10–13). On the possible connection between the *Encomium Emmae* and *Maldon see* Anderson, Maldon: *A Reappraisal . . .*, pp. 256–260. For the commissioning of the *Encomium*, see Alistair Campbell ed., *Encomium Emmae Reginae*, Camden, 3rd ser., vol. 72, London 1949, Introduction, p. xix, and Prologue, p. 4. For the Life of Edward the Confessor see Frank Barlow, ed., *The Life of King Edward*, London 1962, 2nd edit., Oxford 1992, p. xxii, p. 4.

56. Locherbie-Cameron, *Byrhtnoth and His Family*, p. 256.

Didacticism and the Christian Community: The Teachers and the Taught

CLARE A. LEES

S CHOLARLY tradition," remarks Roberta Frank, "wants us to speak well of the works we study; there would be little point in talking about something that was not beautiful and truthful, not 'interesting.'"[1] As for works, so, too, periods. Although Anglo-Saxonists may disagree about the emphases of their interpretations of the Benedictine reforms, the late tenth century is usually characterized with good reason as a "golden age."[2]

The contribution of the vernacular homilies to this "cultural renascence"[3] of the intellectual and cultural achievements of the Anglo-Saxons, while appreciated, is nonetheless underestimated. The homiletic corpus offers the strongest evidence in the period for the maintenance of a Christian discourse in the vernacular. This discourse has its own tradition-dependent rules that reiterate the truth of the faith, its aesthetic conventions, and its use of time. That is, this discourse has its own history. At the same time, vernacular religious writing offers a specific perspective on the events of the tenth century; past, present, and future are located within the moral frame of the Christian present. That present is in harmony with a Christian worldview, which is a product of, and comment on, the events of the age of the vernacular homily. Homiletic discourse not only has its own history, but that history is itself part of the history of the late Anglo-Saxon period. As *Tradition and Belief: Religious Writing in Late Anglo-Saxon England* demonstrates, Ælfric is in large measure responsible for the perception of the mid-tenth-century phase of the reform as a "golden age."

The relation of homiletic discourse to the "golden age" of the late Anglo-Saxon period centers on its didacticism, yet the moral ideals and performativity of this writing appear to stand in the way of understanding its particular historical nature. At its most superficial, didacticism is taken to

mean moral teaching; the prior views and behaviors of the taught are assumed to be modified by the teacher in the process of instruction. For
homilists and hagiographers alike, Christian didacticism and its traditions
offer the only view, the only legitimate perspective on truth, and thus the
only moral paradigm for behavior. Outside Christianity lies heresy, apostasy, paganism, and error. In other words, didacticism operates from within
the traditions of this discourse to maintain and apply its truths, which are
those of the Christian Anglo-Saxon world of the late tenth and early
eleventh centuries. To underestimate the importance of this discourse to
the "golden age" of its period is thus to underestimate the social power of
its truth claims, and thereby to ignore a large body of evidence for how the
Anglo-Saxon Christian elite viewed and represented their world.

Two other, broader perspectives that cross the divide of the late Anglo-
Saxon and post-Conquest periods nuance our understanding of the implications of vernacular didacticism for assessing the "golden age" of late Anglo-Saxon England. First, for historians such as R. I. Moore, the years 950
to 1250, which incorporate a substantial part of the late Anglo-Saxon period, see the formation of a persecuting society across Western Christendom.[4] Second, in even conventional accounts of the Middle Ages, these
same years are singled out as witnessing the beginning of the formation of
concepts of the individual.[5] Such conventional accounts have been taken
further in recent, hotly debated, scholarship that identifies the Gregorian
reforms and those of the Fourth Lateran Council of 1215 as witnessing a
historical shift in the formation of subjectivity. From the twelfth century
onward, in short, we begin to recognize the characteristics of the modern
subject.[6] These two "master narratives" of the formation of a persecuting
society and of the invention of the subject are not mutually exclusive (they
are in fact interdependent), and both have considerable implications for our
understanding of late Anglo-Saxon England.

By including late Anglo-Saxon England by date if not by detailed analysis in the emergence of persecution evidenced across medieval societies,
Moore challenges us to refine notions of the late Anglo-Saxon "golden
age," but not without reason. On the one hand, fears of Arianism haunt the
period, and the laws (secular and canonical), the penitentials, and the homilies all regularly proscribe heresy and heathenism while prescribing chaste
heterosexual behavior.[7] On the other, this period can hardly be documented as one of systematic, habitual, or widespread persecution of individuals and groups according to the familiar later medieval formulation of
unbelief (Jews, heathens, and heretics); sexuality (for example, sodomites);
or physical disease (lepers). But, Moore argues, neither can the persecution

so characteristic of later medieval societies be ascribed only to a sudden increase in the numbers of Jews, lepers, or sodomites in the West or to a concomitant rise in popular discrimination against these groups. Moore suggests instead that the conditions governing the emergence of systematic persecution in the later medieval period should include the exercise of political opportunism by the ruling classes and the reformation of the institutional structures of the church.[8] In this regard, the ecclesiastical reforms of the tenth century lay the groundwork for the later Gregorian revolution and the rise of the persecuting society. These later reforms also lay the groundwork for the formation of the modern subject, especially in their emphasis on confession.[9]

Late Anglo-Saxon England is thus located at the intersection of two contrasting narratives: the first celebrates the achievements of the English church as part of a cultural "golden age," and the second regards these very achievements as symptoms that help predict the later formation of a Western Christian society characterized by persecution. This second narrative intersects with a third, which currently disregards the Anglo-Saxon period altogether by locating the emergence of the modern subject in the twelfth century and later. The rise of vernacular didacticism in late Anglo-Saxon England provides important evidence for rethinking the interrelation of these narratives by concentrating on the regulatory function of Christian teaching.[10] Instruction in the vernacular homilies maintains the idea of a Christian society in England largely by means of systematic classification of groups and by definitions of knowledge, behavior, and identity. These definitions, which are included in the necessary conditions for the emergence of persecution according to Moore, provide the cohesive forces of an English Christian society, within which the subject is located and identified as Christian and from which all other subjects and forms of knowing are expelled.

Narratives about the persecuting society and the formation of the subject also ask Anglo-Saxonists to reflect on the discipline's assumptions about patterns of cultural assimilation and identity more generally. Following Bede, who takes his cue from Gregory's guidelines for the conversion, critical accounts of the long history of the English church are narratives of assimilation and integration, whereby paganism is smoothly if unevenly converted to Christianity. This developmental model culminates in the Benedictine reforms and the "golden age." As Bede also emphasizes, however, religious assimilation, whether of non-Christians or of different modes of Christianity, causes both real and symbolic violence. The roles of conflict and of social power in producing cultural syncretism merit closer analysis. In the early period of Anglo-Saxon history, the massacre of Welsh monks at Bangor and the controversy over the dating of Easter are classic examples of the clash of religious traditions.[11] The conversion of Danish leaders after the Viking incursions in the ninth and tenth centuries; the notorious, though often ignored, massacre of Danes on Saint Bride's Day in the early eleventh century; and the conflicts within the clergy over the Benedictine reforms themselves should also give us pause for thought.[12] These conflicts are radically different from the systematic pursuit of heresy in the later medieval period, however. With the exception of the specters of Pelagianism and Arianism, the social fact of heresy is famously absent from the history of the Anglo-Saxon period, although canon law, the penitentials, and, as we shall see, the homilies bear witness to its symbolic importance.[13] The project of Anglo-Saxon Christianity primarily addresses the dangers of heathenism and apostasy, as my study of Ælfric's *De falsis diis* and Wulfstan's *Sermo Lupi* in *Tradition and Belief*, ch. 2, indicates. As far as we know, vernacular discourses of the other—the Jew, heathen, or heretic—are largely symbolic and ideological methods of educating a Christian society.[14] Since the place where these ideologies are both explored and maintained is the vernacular homilies, their didactic purchase on the Christian subject is of major importance.

I begin, therefore, with an examination of didacticism and its production of the Christian truths whereby both community and individual subject are defined. There is only one law, to which all Christians are subject, and there is only one faith in which all participate. Such a reading of the homilies qualifies and historicizes contemporary critical assumptions about popular religion in late Anglo-Saxon England, as exemplified by Ælfric's homily for the Feast for the Circumcision in his First Series of the *Catholic Homilies*.[15] Fidelity to the law of Christianity necessarily defines the other as abject. The abjected Jew, leper, heretic, or sodomite is associated by scholars of the later medieval period both with systemic persecution and with the invention of the modern subject. The final section argues that Anglo-Saxon homilies, however, bear witness to the formation and regulation of a moral discourse about community, identity, and subjectivity largely ignored by both Anglo-Saxonists and later medievalists.[16] The interest, as Frank might put it, of the Anglo-Saxon "golden age" in relation to the homilies resides in the emergence of institutional discourses about Christian community and identity.

Didacticism and Christian Reason

Fundamental to homiletic writing is its pastoral intent. The pastoral mission informs the didactic aesthetic of religious prose and its use of conventions of time, both of which frame notions of moral knowledge and behavior, as demonstrated in *Tradition and Belief*. But aesthetics and salvation history only begin the project of understanding didacticism as a mode of instruction. Religious didacticism encodes several assumptions about its intended audience, conceived both as a social group—the Christian community—and as individuals belonging to that group—the Christian or "Christianus." Didacticism assumes that the individual—literate or illiterate—is educable, and that education is a socially and institutionally regulated process of conscious rational instruction in the traditions of Christian knowledge. In Anglo-Saxon England, this method of instruction in the vernacular has its origins in the Alfredian reforms of the ninth century, which are aimed largely at the upper classes and the clergy. Vernacular religious writing of the late tenth and early eleventh centuries is more ambitious: by intellectual argument and moral practice, it aims to direct the behavior of all Christians, who are defined as individual subjects by virtue of their relation to the Christian community. Didactic writing in Anglo-Saxon England addresses the individual as a moral actor amenable to reason to a more complex extent than any other discourse of this period. It is the use of Christian reason in addressing this moral agent that is most at odds with modern understandings of the educational process.[17]

One major barrier to understanding the role of didacticism in a traditional society like Anglo-Saxon England is historical. Modern theories of education, like modern practices, are not articulated with reference to one single tradition of knowledge and one system of reason (quite obviously, there is now no such unified tradition within Christianity). Nor is education conceived of as primarily moral. In Anglo-Saxon England, formal Christian education is restricted to the clergy and the aristocracy; as a privilege of the few, instruction is socially stratified and predominantly in Latin. Apart from the evidence for monastic and court schools, the only institutional provision for vernacular education and the only conceptualization of its necessity occurs within the vernacular homilies.[18] Vernacular education is a matter of assimilation into the ideals of a Christian society and is aimed at a much wider social segment than Latin education—a necessary consequence of the pastoral mission. Ælfric is alone among the vernacular writers in realizing the scope, though not necessarily the importance, of this mission.

Vernacular homilists like Ælfric are not primarily educational theorists, nor are they theologians, politicians, or even, for the most part and excepting Wulfstan, lawmakers. The homilies offer no full-fledged theory of didacticism, nor is Anglo-Saxon England the age of the *ars praedicandi*.[19] A sensitive reading of the homiletic corpus, and of Ælfric's works in particular, however, enables the reconstruction of the importance of moral education from a variety of perspectives. The homilies are very explicit about their intentions, even if hard evidence of how the homilies were received is slender and limited only to copying, editing, and manuscript reception. Nevertheless, to emphasize the educational content of vernacular sermons makes sense only if its goals are also emphasized. These are directed toward understanding God and the necessity of worship in a process that hinges on the relation between forms of knowing and forms of action. Hence the emphasis in the homilies on the individual as a rational actor. As Ælfric comments in one of the Easter sermons from the Second Series of the *Catholic Homilies* (*Alius sermo de die Paschae*), Christian knowledge brings understanding, but that understanding must be transformed into action:[20]

> Be ðison we magon tocnawan. þæt us is twyfeald neod on boclicum gewritum; Anfeald neod us is. þæt we ða boclican lare mid carfullum mode smeagan. oðer þæt we hi to weorcum awendan.[21]

> [Regarding this, we may know that there is for us a twofold need in scriptural writings. Our first need is that we consider with careful mind bookish doctrine; the other is that we turn it into works.]

The dual goal of understanding and acting is the major contribution of vernacular religious writing to the continuing project of maintaining a Christian society in England. This goal is quite distinct from those supported by the canons, laws, and penitentials. The aesthetics of religious prose and its structuring according to Christian notions of time also serves these objectives. For a writer like Ælfric, vernacular prose style is modeled on and revelatory of the divine order of the world. As Ælfric here suggests, Anglo-Saxon Christian didacticism is performed within a framework of knowledge, belief, and action.

Alasdair MacIntyre's study of justice and reason in tradition-dependent systems of knowledge helps define more precisely the historical difference of Christian education in the early medieval period. Within this system (heavily dominated by Augustinian Christianity), reason is a process of justification.[22] As Ælfric's *De falsis diis* demonstrates, belief is confirmed by a reasoning process that refers back to those beliefs and judgments about knowledge and action that have already been produced by the tradition. Belief is prior to reason, which reason confirms with the aid of divine grace. Reason supports, directs, and continues to direct belief by means of a process that aims to deepen apprehension of the divine. Reason thereby defends the mysteries central to Christianity. Knowledge so produced confirms the truth of belief, as defined against falsity, and demands obedience to it.

In this pre-Cartesian world of Anglo-Saxon preaching, Ælfric is exemplary only to the extent that he rationalizes and maintains the preaching mission more systematically than any other vernacular writer. It may be that he was uniquely situated to do so. As monk and later abbot, Ælfric did not attain the institutional prominence of his teacher, Æthelwold, within the church, nor did he enjoy the status of official royal adviser, as did Wulfstan. Neither engaged on the momentous tasks of reforming monastic practice, ecclesiastical administration, and the liturgy nor burdened by legislative administration and the vexed political situation of the early eleventh century, Ælfric appears to have embraced his Christian mission enthusiastically and obediently. English preaching is shaped by Ælfric's historical situation, confirming the more general insight that traditions are produced by specific sociocultural formations. How Ælfric conceptualizes preaching and how he produces Christian knowledge in accordance with his understanding of the pastoral mission have radical consequences for our understanding of religion in Anglo-Saxon England.

Ælfric's English homilies, like other vernacular homilies of the period, provide access to the body of knowledge that is Scripture, but that access is limited. Scriptural lections are recited in Latin before translation into English for commentary in the homily or sermon, although this practice is hardly systematic.[23] Translations from Scripture outside the homiletic tradition, such as Ælfric's own translation of parts of the Heptateuch,[24] or the anonymous West-Saxon Gospels,[25] are the exception rather than the rule. Debates about the implications of a vernacular Bible for a lay audience have yet to be widely articulated, although Ælfric expresses concern about these implications for a clerical audience in his preface to the translation of Genesis.[26] In the homilies, however, interpretation of Scripture in the vernacular is strictly controlled by the preacher, who is himself governed by the rules whereby knowledge is produced in a tradition-dependent system. Ælfric's evident fidelity to the prior authority of the Latin exegetical tradition[27] is again unique only in the extent to which he pursues and demonstrates that fidelity with his systematic exploitation of his sources.

The art of exegesis is that interpretation is endless, of course, but it is misleading to view spiritual interpretation as analogous to literary interpretation. All meanings are directed toward knowing a God who is finally unknowable. Moreover, Christian learning in the homilies is produced by a system of sharply defined reciprocal hierarchies that bind teacher to taught. In drawing on these conceptual hierarchies to structure his implied vernacular congregation, Ælfric is indeed extending the reach of Christian knowledge beyond monastery and court but, *pace* Jonathan Wilcox,[28] he is no democrat. Spiritual interpretation produced by a tradition-dependent system of knowledge rationalizes belief, which it mandates as true and which provides the matrix for behavior. Obedience to the truth that is Christian law limits interpretation by defining all other interpretation as false—heathen or heretical. Reason is not only a process of justification, but of defining and enforcing the limits of Christian knowledge and action.

The homilies situate both community and individual subject as Christian by means of didactic instruction in rational belief. Instruction is not merely intellectual but psychological, dependent on the faculties of memory, will, and understanding.[29] Desire for Christian knowledge, which is both assumed and created by the homilies, is governed by a prior understanding of the will (in the Augustinian sense); education of the will directs the believer toward God and thereby toward obedience to God's truth in thought and deed. The individual cannot advance along the path toward God on his or her own, however, because the will is understood to be irreparably fallen. Only God's grace can repair the will. Understood in this light, Ælfric's comment that he translates the teachings of the Church Fathers into English trusting in divine grace ("ic truwige ðurh godes gife";[30] is utterly conventional, but no less true. His homilies construct a community of learning in which training the individual will is the primary concern.

Didacticism in the homilies is therefore a discipline guided by tradition-dependent knowledge of Scripture and aided by grace. This discipline is active, embracing mind and body, understanding and action, as Ælfric reminds us, and focuses on the apprehension of a truth that is always beyond the self. Alien to the post-Cartesian mind in its insistence that false beliefs represent, in MacIntyre's words, "a failure of the mind, not of its objects," Christian education in the homilies rests on the premise that it is the "mind which stands in need of correction."[31] Teaching corrects ignorance, which can otherwise lead to false truth. Ælfric summarizes the position neatly (and alliteratively) in his Second Series homily for Rogationtide, *Feria secunda. Letania maiore:*[32]

> Læwede menn behofiað. þæt him lareowas secgon. ða godspellican lare. ðe hi on bocum leornodon. þæt men for nytennysse misfaran ne sceolon.[33]

> [Layfolk require that teachers tell them the gospel doctrine, which they learned in books, so that men should not err through ignorance.]

Teachers learn from books their doctrine and instruct the taught through the oral genre of preaching—learning becomes telling. This justification of the hierarchical process of didactic instruction is derived in the homily from Christ's discussion of the first two commandments (Matthew 22:36–40).[34] Both teacher and taught are enjoined by the first commandment to love God, despite their different duties and responsibilities within the Christian hierarchy. Obedience to God's truth holds the Christian community together by means of the virtue of humility. Humility is central to the process of instructing the fallen will. The second and complementary commandment—"Lufa ðinne nextan. swa swa ðe sylfne" (Love your neighbor as you do yourself; 180/4–5)—relates the ethical obligations of the Christian community to love one another to teaching's emphasis on action: "Ne fremað cristenum menn. þeah he fela god wyrce. buton he symle hæbbe. ða soðan lufe on him" (It benefits not a Christian man, though he performs many good works, unless he always has true love in him; 180/16–18). Love and humility—the products of the Law—are the prerequisites of successful learning and action. How far these virtues extend is one way of defining the limits of Christian community, as we shall see.

Ælfric's emphasis on the virtues of love and humility in acquiring knowledge and acting on its basis indicates that the transmission of Christian knowledge entails a psychological transformation of what we now call the self. Humility is incumbent upon both preacher and congregation in their reciprocal relation toward knowledge. An ignorant preacher cannot correct an ignorant believer, as Ælfric is fond of saying, and teaching is useless unless the mind of the believer is ready to receive it.[35] Ælfric's homilies, according to the Latin preface to the First Series, are written with the explicit intention of reaching the hearts ("ad cor peruenire")[36] of the believing English for the benefit of their souls. These are not empty conventions. Vercelli VII, for example, for which no Latin source has yet been identified, leaves us in no doubt of the significance of learning for the Christian self:

> Butan tweon, lar is haligdomes dæl, ך ealles swiðost gif hio hyre gymeleste framadrifeð ך ælce gitsunge afyrreð ך þyssa woruldlicra þinga lufan gewanige ך þæt mod to Godes lufan gehwyrfeð, ך gedet þæt hit ealle ða lustfulnesse þysses andweardan lifes onscunað. Soðlice sio lar mid geswince hio sceal þa forenemnedan þing forðbringan.[37]

> [Without doubt, learning is part of holiness, and most of all if it drives away carelessness, expels every avarice, diminishes love of worldly things, turns the mind toward love of God, and brings it about that we shun all the desires of this present life. In truth, with work learning shall bring forth all these aforementioned things.]

Learning is defined here as an active sacred labor, couched in the conventional terms of patristic psychology; the lesson of virtue leads one toward the love of God ("to Godes lufan") and away from sin and worldly desires.

The English homilies offer ample evidence for this psychic disciplining of mind and body. The most frequent analogy is that of food, so clearly mediated by the importance of the Eucharist. Food serves the body as instruction feeds the soul; without instruction, the will fails in its search for God, as exemplified in Ælfric's First Series homily for the first Sunday in Lent:[38]

> Swa swa þæs mannes lichama leofað be hlafe: swa sceal his sawul lybban be godes wordum: þæt is be godes lare. þe he þurh wisum mannum on bocum gesette; Gif se lichama næfð mete. oððe ne mæg mete þicgean. þonne forweornað he Ᵹ adeadað: swa eac seo sawul gif heo næfð þa halgan lare: Heo bið þonne weornigende. Ᵹ mægenleas; þurh þa halgan lare. heo bið strang Ᵹ onbryrd to godes willan;[39]

> [Just as man's body lives by bread, so shall his soul live by God's word, that is by God's doctrine, which he has set in books through wise men. If the body has not food, or cannot eat food, then it weakens and dies: so too the soul, if it has not holy doctrine, it will be weakening and without virtue. By holy doctrine it will be strong and stimulated to God's will.]

The homology between body and soul—feeding and regulating the body and feeding and regulating the mind—is fundamental to Anglo-Saxon didacticism, and a reminder that both body and soul are the material effects of specific practices. Just as the body is perfected after death by resurrection, so too will be knowledge and wisdom, Ælfric points out in his First Series homily, *De Dominica oratione*.[40] Perfect wisdom is the goal of the didactic process, which cannot be attained before death and without grace. The believer strives to perfect the body in emulation of Christ; so too must the acquisition of learning, of the Word itself, be right, correct, and without blemish.

The historical difference of Anglo-Saxon Christian teaching thus resides not merely in its vehicle—preaching—nor in its psychology, but above all in its rationale for transmitting the truth of its knowledge, which is the basis for belief and action.

Popular Religion:
Ælfric's First Series Homily on the Circumcision

Unquestioning obedience to the truth of one particular belief system looks suspiciously irrational to a modern, post-Enlightenment mind. MacIntyre reminds us, however, that reason has its own history. Ælfric's reformist emphasis on the cohesion of obedience, love, and truth in teaching—a product of his monastic training—can be matched by less systematic, though no less commonplace, remarks about teaching throughout the homiletic corpus. As will be abundantly clear by now, it is precisely the commonplace nature of these remarks that is important as an index of the traditions of didacticism. The homilists tell us no less than we expect (and scholars trained to enjoy the understatement of the poetry may balk at the explicitness of the prose).

Ælfric's First Series homily on the Circumcision[41] provides an exemplary opportunity to observe Christian teaching in action, confirming the general observations about didacticism with which this chapter began. The purpose of didactic writing is to offer a rationale for Christian knowledge and action. Each feast day provides analogous rationales, which are specific to the liturgical readings for that day. These rationales are produced from the meanings for that day generated by traditional Christian exegesis. The homilies both elaborate and exemplify that knowledge for the vernacular congregation and provide the framework whereby truth is discerned and falsity defined. All knowledge and action is governed by this process, which situates the individual in relation to truth and, as a result, produces the Christian subject in terms of a communal identity. There is thus only one subject in Christian didacticism—the believer, who is subject to the continuing discipline of believing, and hence knowing. The nonbeliever—heathen or Jew—is abjected by this same process, as are his or her practices.

Charms, medicinal recipes, poetry, and other material artifacts, by contrast, offer evidence for a more culturally diverse world of belief than the Christian homilies. This evidence appears to confirm narratives of cultural assimilation built upon the evidence of the conversion. In pursuit of the details of this syncretism, Karen Jolly argues for a model of popular religious belief that integrates the world of the homilies with that of the charms.[42] That Anglo-Saxon culture has room for a variety of beliefs and practices, however, is less important—because well known—than how we analyze the relation between them. This relation is above all a matter of perspective, as Jolly points out. In constructing a model of popular religion that incorporates the charms with the evidence of the homilies (though not the laws or penitentials), Jolly's perspective is both synthetic and symbiotic. Diversity and contradiction live side by side in a strikingly modern way in this "holistic world-view" (19) of popular beliefs. Accommodation of non-Christian beliefs turns out to be the achievement of the English church. Yet before we turn from the homilists to other cultural sources for their evidence of religious practices not quite so dogmatically Christian, we need to be confident of the homiletic evidence itself. What Jolly's argument downplays is the homiletic emphasis on the truth of its beliefs.[43]

Viewed from the perspective of the homiletic evidence, two issues reframe this debate about the popularity of popular religion in Anglo-Saxon England. Both issues hinge on the didactic nature of the homilies. The first involves analysis of the relation of the homilies to what Jolly calls formal religion and I have been calling the institution of the church. Homilies in general are aimed at an audience broader than that of the upper reaches of the clergy and aristocracy, but this does not mean that their audience is conceived as an undifferentiated "mass" or populace. Nor can we usefully include the institution of the church in a larger pattern of cultural belief without also emphasizing the power of this institution to create and govern those beliefs.[44] As I have already argued, the homilists present their pastoral mission as a hierarchical and unequal relation of knowing, however reciprocal this relation may be. That is, didacticism is based on an unequal power relation. This ideological view of the Christian community complements what we know of Anglo-Saxon society in general, with its sharp differentiation between class or rank and its definitions of the duties and responsibilities appropriate to each.

The second issue of didacticism in relation to the popularity of Anglo-Saxon beliefs involves the homilists' commitment to reason and the Christian truth it confirms—a force radically underestimated by Jolly. For the homilists there is one truth and one rationale for it. Logically, therefore, there is only one popular religion—that of Anglo-Saxon Christianity. All other beliefs are necessarily false, even when presented as mere practices. From the perspective of the homilies, an alternative model of popular religion makes no sense. In consequence, the relation of Christianity to other beliefs of the period must be understood as dialectical and conflicted.

Ælfric's homily on the Circumcision usefully demonstrates how late Anglo-Saxon didactic writing contests belief in terms of the truth of Christian knowledge and practice. This homily for New Year's Day, as those familiar with *Sir Gawain and the Green Knight* will also recall, is often cited for its evidence of popular, nonorthodox Anglo-Saxon Christian practices also associated with the first day of the new year. Such a reading, however, ignores the main body of the homily, which is in fact one of Ælfric's more characteristic texts in terms of genre.[45]

The Circumcision homily begins by rehearsing the lection for the day in both Latin and Old English—Luke 2:21, on the circumcision and naming of Christ—and then offers a commentary on it, derived largely from

Bede's homily for the same day, as Wilcox notes.[46] The circumcision of
Christ recapitulates in the New Testament the covenant of God with Abraham in the Old—the first man circumcised by God's command. The distinctions between the Old and the New, between literal and spiritual observance of the law, and between Jew and Christian are thus the homily's main
themes. Reason is the process by which such distinctions are made, and it
is these distinctions that provide the intellectual justification for Ælfric's rejection of nonorthodox beliefs and practices in the latter part of the
homily.[47] In short, the truth-value of Christianity in the homily is contested on the efficacy of its knowledge as opposed to the knowledge of other
practices, which include those of the Jews as well as those of non-Christian
Anglo-Saxons.

    In the exegetical tradition, the circumcision of Abraham is a literal sign
("tacen"; 224/22) of the covenant. Circumcision for all boys on the eighth
day after their birth fulfills the covenant, enabling the house of Abraham to
flourish in its generations. This first marking of the body as God's is accompanied by the practice of divine renaming: Abram ("healic fæder," high
father) is renamed Abraham, father of nations ("manegra þeoda fæder");
Sarai, meaning "my leader" ("min ealdor"), is renamed Sarah ("Sarra"),
"leader" ("ealdor") and mother of all believing women (225/33–40). God's
blessing on the house of Abraham is signified by a mark, a new name, and
the promise of genealogy and generation. The circumcision of Christ,
which manifests Christ's fidelity to the Old Law, heralds the transformation
of that law and the accompanying shift in spiritual interpretation and observance, which ushers in Christianity by rejecting Judaism (225). Baptism
and the practice of spiritual circumcision fulfills for the New Law the
promise of circumcision in the Old (225–26).

    Ælfric is at equal pains in this section of the homily (224–28) to explain
what circumcision means in the Old and New Law, using the familiar exegetical modes of literal and spiritual interpretation. Although literal circumcision is forbidden under the New Law, only by reference to its practice can the practice of spiritual circumcision—its spiritual analogy—be
understood. This point requires patient explication of the processes of spiritual signification, which provide justification for fidelity to the law: "ac gif
hit him dyslic þince þonne cide he wið god þe hit gesette: na wið us þe hit
secgað" (but if it seem foolish to anyone let him chide God, who established
it, not us, who say it; 226/85–227/86). Human reason ("menniscum gesceade"; 227/91) is the rationale for obedience to God's law: "For ði sealde
god mannum gescead þæt his sceoldon tocnawan heora scyppend: ᴣ mid
biggenge his beboda þæt ece lif geearnian" (Therefore God has given men

reason, so that they should acknowledge their Creator, and by obedience to his commandments, earn eternal life; 227/95–97).

Circumcising the body as a literal sign of the covenant is replaced by the spiritual, though no less material, discipline of excising vice from both body and mind in the New Law. This exhaustive regulation of the self is programmatic and transformative. Only once achieved can the believer merit the name of Christian (cf. Isaiah 65:15, 62:2) and join the family of Abraham in true faith ("æfter soþum geleafan"; 228/114):

> Ne sceole we for ði synderlice on anum lime beo ymbsnidene· ac we sceolon ða fulan galnysse symle wanian.] ure eagan fram yfelre gesihðe awendan.] earan from yfelre heorcnunge· urne muð fram leasum spræcum. handa fram mandædum· ure fotwylmys fram deadbærum siðfæte· ure heortan fram facne; Gif we swa fram leahtrum ymbsnidene beoð þonne bið us geset niwe nama. swa swa se witega isaias cwæð; God gecigð his þeowan oþrum naman; Eft se ylca witega cwæð; ðu bist geciged niwum naman. þone ðe godes muð genemnode: Se niwa nama is cristianus. þæt is cristen;   (227/102–10)

> [Nor should we be circumcised in only one limb, therefore, but we must continually diminish foul lust, and turn our eyes from evil sight, and our ears from evil hearing, our mouths from false speaking, hands from wicked deeds, our footsteps from the deadly path, our hearts from guile. If we are thus circumcised from sins then will a new name be given us; as the prophet Isaiah said, "God will call his servants by another name." Again the same prophet said, "You will be called by a new name that the mouth of God has named." That new name is "Cristianus"; that is, Christian.]

To be Christian is to be thoroughly circumcised from sin in a process that enacts to excess the circumcision or marking of the body under the Old Law. The practice of spiritual circumcision replaces the visible sign with the invisible, and signals Christian identity by means of a new collective name and a new family in the kin of Christ. Ælfric thus uses the Feast of the Circumcision to explore how Christian identity is maintained by the excision of sin—a practice that depends on redefining Jewish practices. Spiritual circumcision anchors how divine law resignifies identity and family.

As the second half of the homily (228–31) demonstrates, spiritual knowledge derived from an exegesis of scriptural circumcision does not tolerate other meanings and practices associated with this day. Supplementing his primary source, Bede, with Bede's scientific teaching,[48] Ælfric begins this section with a discussion of when the new year should commence. Correct knowledge is thus the overarching theme of the homily, whether it be the correct meaning of circumcision or of when the year begins. The custom that holds that the Feast of the Circumcision on New Year's Day (January 1) is also the first day of the year is contested by Christian knowledge, which offers custom no basis in tradition. Here Ælfric swiftly demonstrates the application of Christian learning by surveying the evidence for the various dates of the beginning of the year among the Romans, Hebrews, and Greeks, as well as in Anglo-Saxon calendars and liturgical books. He thereby distinguishes between rational knowledge and customary practice, both Christian and non-Christian. Correct Christian knowledge demands that the first day be that when the world was created. That day, according to the traditions of the Bible and its Christian exegesis, is March 18. The creation of the seasons on the fourth day is calculated as March 21—the Feast of Saint Benedict—and is confirmed by natural knowledge of the rebirth of the seasons. Nature is also subject to God's law.

This remapping of the seasons by the processes of Christian reason and knowledge is analogous to the remapping of the body in the first part of the homily. In the first part of the homily, the body of the Jew is replaced by that of the Christian; in the second, all calendars are replaced by the Christian. Knowledge is governed by analogy and similitude—by microcosm and macrocosm—and Ælfric's thematic emphasis on reason connects what initially appears to be two disparate parts of a homily associated only by date.[49]

Reiteration of the calculation of the Christian calendar by tradition and the subjugation of natural law to that calculation, moreover, provides Ælfric with the most correct justification for arguing against non-Christian Anglo-Saxon practices for the same day.[50] Divination, regulation of travel and action according to the lunar calendar, observance of Monday as the first day of the week, and the distinction between those animals that enjoy God's blessing and those that do not are all antitheses of Christian observances for the same day (229–30). Ælfric is firm on this point. Christian belief is the only rational knowledge, and the law of divine creation demystifies the rule of nature such that Ælfric imputes natural phenomena associated with the lunar calendar to its workings, rather than to the power of non-Christian charms.

By these arguments, Ælfric continues the emphasis in the first half of the homily on what it means to be Christian by outlining what it means to be Christian and Anglo-Saxon in the second: "Nis þæs mannes cristendom naht þe mid deoflicum wiglungum his lif adrihð: he is gehiwod to cristenum menn. ꝺ is earm hæþengylda" (The Christianity of the man who drives his life according to devilish charms amounts to nothing; he has the form of a Christian but is a wretched heathen; 230/186–88). The crucial distinctions in the homily are thus those between Christian and Jew, Christian and heathen, where Jew and heathen are synonymous. Indeed, it is these analogies that also account for the elision of women in the process of exegesis; their role in the restructuring of the Christian family is only briefly mentioned. Sarah, Abraham's wife, is a figure for female obedience, humility, and modesty (228/118–20), yet this figure is undeveloped, subsumed instead under the more general interpellation of the Christian.[51] In short, by exploring the role of reason as a faculty that perceives distinctions, Ælfric leaves us in no doubt of the extent and limits of Christian knowledge and identity.

To speak of a popular religion in Anglo-Saxon England that accommodates both the Christian subject and the abjected other, who may entertain a variety of beliefs and practices, is thus nonsensical (that is, irrational) from the perspective of the homilists. This is not to deny the existence of such subjects, of course, of whom the evidence of the charms, material culture, and the poetry leaves us in no doubt, but rather to emphasize that the attitude of Ælfric toward them is rational (in the traditional Christian sense), uncompromising, and contestatory. Just as the Jews are rejected by Christianity, as is abundantly evident from this homily, so too are all other formations of belief. Equally important, the homily offers us a glimpse of the processes of definition and distinction whereby Christian identity is formed and maintained. Crucial to these definitions is the contrast between those groups of abjected others and the collectivity of Christian identity-as-community. Ælfric follows standard homiletic practice in referring to the Christian group as "we," contrasted with the third-person pronouns used to refer to Jews and heathens alike. The vernacular homilies in general are rich in such evidence for how Christianity interpellates the Christian.

Christian Community, Family, and Didactic Identity

He that loveth father or mother more than me is not worthy of me: and he that loveth son or daughter more than me is not worthy of me. And he that taketh not his cross and followeth after me is not worthy of me.

—MATTHEW 10:37–38

As Christ points out to his disciples in the context of the injunction to preach (Matthew 10:7), Christianity commands the reorientation of familial bonds toward God. Ælfric's Circumcision homily turns on the significance of this reorientation. Through the practice of spiritual circumcision and baptism, the believer joins the Christian family in fulfillment of the covenant between Abraham and God and receives a new name. By these means, the Christian subject enters history.

Ælfric exemplifies the transformation of the individual into a believing subject in his First Series homily on John the Baptist: "Ac se þe his þeawas mid anmodnysse þurh godes fylste swa awent. he bið þonne to oþrum menn geworht. oþer he bið þurh godnysse. ⁊ se ylca þurh edwiste" (But he who with the help of God so changes his practices with a resolute mind, he will be made another man; another will he be in goodness, and the same in matter).[52] Belief in Christianity makes a new subject through the acquisition of virtue ("godnysse"), which entails mental discipline in the presence of God's grace; the material body, however, remains the same. Underlying this process are the distinctions between the visible and the invisible, the literal and the spiritual, the Old and the New, also used by the Circumcision homily. These distinctions chart the significatory process of Christian typology. In fulfillment of the pastoral mission, didacticism endlessly emphasizes the spiritual power of language under the New Law. Rituals such as baptism and the mass also offer ample evidence of this power, where what is real is defined by the presence of God's grace and the Word incarnate.

The implications of this process of relocating the literal within the spiritual are profound for understanding the analogies between Christian body, self, family, and community, which have been already discussed as conventional analogies for the didactic process. When Ælfric speaks of believers united in Christ's body (following Paul), as he does repeatedly in the homilies, this is no mere metaphor, but a description of the Church itself. The world of the spirit redefines that of the letter; the metaphor of incorporation shifts and amplifies the referent. Unity in Christ's body *is* unity in the Church, and the Church is no metaphor. At the heart of didacticism is the Word incarnate, Christ, in whose body all faithful are joined. Fidelity to the Word identifies the individual with a community of learning, which embraces both literate and unlearned in their pursuit of God's will. The knowledge desired by this community is the attainment of wisdom, aided by the gift of the spirit—"for þan ðe word is wisdomes geswutelung" (because a word is a sign of wisdom).[53] In consequence, Anglo-Saxon homilies chart the familiar process of distinguishing social and familial bonds from Christian ones, which are similarly social and familial, but are located within institutional structures of belief. Extensive obligations to kin, so treasured by students of the poetry and so evident from the secular laws, take on a different character in the light of Christian meanings for family.

By sublating the family into the Christian "familia," concepts associated with family and body are resignified. Ælfric addresses his brothers in Christ as "mine gebroðra" (my brothers) and uses the pronoun "we" to refer to this Christian family, which redefines and transcends other familial bonds according to the obligations of love or "caritas." Ælfric elucidates these meanings in his First Series homily on the Lord's Prayer, *De Dominica oratione*:[54]

> God is ure fæder þi we sceolon ealle beon on gode gebroþru. ꝺ healdan þone broþerlican bend unforodne þæt is þa soþan sibbe. swa þæt ure ælc oþerne lufige swa swa hine sylfne. ꝺ nanum ne gebeode þæt he nelle þæt man him gebeode; Se þe ðis hylt he bið godes bearn ꝺ crist ꝺ ealle halige men þe gode geþeoð beoð his gebroðru. ꝺ his gesweostru;[55]

> [God is our father; therefore we must all be brothers in God and keep the brotherly bond unbroken, that is, the true peace, such that each of us love another as himself, and command to none that which he would not that another command to him. He who obeys this is a child of God and Christ and all the holy who thrive to God are his brothers and his sisters.]

This extract from Ælfric's *De Dominica oratione* offers a compelling vision of the idealized Christian community, which incorporates all ranks of society: "for ði nu ealle cristene men ægðer ge rice. ge heane. ge æþelborene ge unæþelborene. ꝺ se hlaford ꝺ se ðeowa ealle hi sind gebroðra ꝺ ealle hi habbað ænne fæder on heofonum" (and so now all Christians, whether high or low, noble or ignoble of birth, and the lord and the slave, all are brothers, and all have one Father in heaven; 326/40–42). Membership in this fraternal community, however, is limited, as Ælfric stresses when he discusses the second commandment in his Second Series homily, *Letania maiore*:[56] "On ðam oðrum bebode. we habbað gemet. þæt we oðerne lufian swa swa us sylfe. þa ðe þurh geleafan. us gelenge beoð. and ðurh cristendom. us cyððe to habbað" (In the second commandment we have a limit, that we love another as ourselves, those who through faith are related to us, and through Christianity have kindred with us). The virtue of charity, in other words, applies only to those who believe and are known to believe. Charity is a measure of the Christian community, and does not extend beyond it (as is equally clear from Ælfric's Circumcision homily).

These representations of the Christian family, subject to the law of belief, incorporate but do not dismantle social hierarchies. The inequalities of Anglo-Saxon society remain intact, strengthened by the ideals of a community of believers that is defined repeatedly as hierarchical and unequal. The possibility of a more equitable redistribution of social power is uncountenanced precisely because of this hierarchy, within which only moral change is articulated. Social and familial relations within Anglo-Saxon Christianity are conceived of as a series of fixed states or ranks, each with their own moral duties and responsibilities, specific to secular or ecclesiastical spheres. Moral responsibility is classified according to rank, gender, and marital state. When morality colludes with political fact, powerful mystifications are operating.

As *De Dominica oratione* and *Letania maiore* spell out in their representations of the social vision of the Christian community, the rich remain rich, the poor, poor. Enumerating the states or ranks of society, *Letania maiore* goes further:[57] both rich and poor are bound to one another by their obligations of charity in the case of the former and patience in the case of the latter; similarly, the slave serves his master, the married man is faithful to his legal wife, the wife obeys her husband, and the child obeys its parents (while punishment is an appropriate method of teaching virtue); a good king has a benign paternal relation to his people and is responsible for their moral well-being, but this homiletic enumeration of social roles and responsibilities offers no role for a queen. Reasonable moral behavior—the virtue of moderation—binds one group to another.

Such preaching promotes a conservative social vision elaborating a Pauline view of Christianity, as Godden points out.[58] It is also Paul's teaching, whether directly or indirectly, that lies behind much of Ælfric's preaching on marriage and chastity, as explored in chapter 5. Similarly, Paul's influence on Christian meanings for circumcision is a strong reminder of how Christian society is constructed by resignifying Jewish practices while expelling Judaism itself. The Christian community is thus regulated from without as well as from within, as is equally evident from Ælfric's discussion of the healing of the leper (Matthew 8:1–4) in his First Series homily for the Third Sunday after Epiphany.[59]

The leper's disfigured body is a mark of a disfiguring faith: "laðlic bið þæs hreoflian lic mid menigfealdum springum. ꝺ geswelle. ꝺ mid mislicum fagnyssum. ac se inra mann þæt is seo sawul bið micele atelicor gif heo mid mislicum leahtrum begriwen bið" (loathsome is the body of the leper with many ulcers and swellings, but the inner man, which is the soul, is much more terrible, if it is steeped in various vices).[60] Like the diseased body, which is expelled from the community until it is healed, so too the diseased soul must be healed through confession and penitence. Only Christ may heal, and only the priest may regulate inner and outer health, whether by spiritual cure or excommunication: "Swa sceal don se gastlicra sacerd. he sceal gerihtlæcan godes folc ꝺ þone ascyrian. ꝺ amansumian fram cristenum mannum þe swa hreoflig bið on manfullum þeawum þæt he oþre mid his yfelnysse besmit" (So must the spiritual priest do, he must put right God's people and separate and excommunicate from Christian men he who is so leprous with sinful practices that he soils another with his wickedness; 244/ 79–82).

As these examples suggest, Ælfric's Pauline vision of Christian society as the Body of Christ is a strong moral endorsement of the social inequities of Anglo-Saxon society, maintaining its fixed boundaries by reference to the abject figures of Jew, pagan, or leper. The church supports social inequities by regulating moral behavior within a society already conceived of as hierarchical and Christian; that is, not Jewish or pagan. The homiletic vision of the Christian community holds in place the harsh realities of Anglo-Saxon life, however charitable its moral discourse.

The example of the sacerdotal power of confession also reminds us that teaching is similarly reciprocal and hierarchical; Ælfric in particular is sensitive to the limits and asymmetries of this relation between teacher and taught. His homilies repeatedly guard against heterodoxy, heresy, and heathenism, and draw a line between that knowledge which is appropriate for the laity and that which is inappropriate.[61] At the same time, none of the homilists exclude the ranks and duties of the clergy from their descriptions of the Christian community—they are, after all, integral to it. Preaching is the duty of bishops and masspriests, as the homilies repeatedly emphasize, and the role of preacher is held up to scrutiny as a moral ideal within homiletic discourse. "Lange sceal leornian. se ðe læran sceal. and habban geðincðe. and þeawfæstnysse. þy læs ðe he forlæde. ða læwedan mid him" (Long shall he who shall teach learn, and have authority and obedience, lest he mislead the laity along with himself), as Ælfric puts it in *Letania maiore*[62]—a homily that particularly stresses the importance of correct learning for the clergy. While Ælfric does not elaborate upon the specific duties of the clergy in regard to preaching to the extent that he does in his Pastoral Letters,[63] he leaves his homiletic congregation in no doubt of the dangers of clerical ignorance.

Justice, however, belongs to God (and the church). Ælfric tends to avoid in his homilies the somber accounts of the fates of the fallen teachers in hell so vividly depicted by the homilist of Blickling Homily IV (for the Third Sunday in Lent). In the Blickling version of the apocryphal *Visio Pauli*, the priest who is slow to perform his duties is condemned to "þære fyrenan ea, & to þæm isenan hoce" (to the fiery river and the iron hook), and the bishop who fails in charity is bound with chains of fire, thrust into the river of hell, and denied God's mercy.[64] By contrast, Ælfric's analogous

account of hell, the vision of Furseus authorized by Bede, does not focus
quite so explicitly on the tortures of fallen clergy.[65] In general Ælfric promotes instead the positive ideals of preaching and the sacerdotal duties of
the priesthood, fortified by images of the Old Testament prophets and the
evangelism of Christ, the apostles, and the early martyrs such as Stephen.
Whether by reference to apocryphal stories of hell or by homiletic rein-
forcement of the didactic ideals of the clergy, the homilies avoid explicit
mention of the regulation of clerical abuses by the church, evident from
canon law and the Pastoral Letters. The obligations of tithing, almsgiving,
fasting, and confession are similarly regularly mentioned by both reformist
and anonymous homilists, especially in the Lenten homilies and often in
contexts that emphasize the mutual obligations of priest and community,
but specific details of these practices are sparse.[66] The reciprocal relation
between teacher and taught represented in the homilies does not disturb or
analyze the balance of power, whether in secular or clerical spheres; it
maintains it.

Definitions of the roles of Christian teacher in relation to the broader
meanings of Christian community have the added felicity of bringing into
focus Ælfric's own self-presentation as a preacher. As is well known, Ælfric
is rare among the vernacular writers of the Anglo-Saxon period for his provision of prefaces, in Latin and Old English, to his major works: the *Catholic
Homilies*, the *Lives of Saints*, his *Grammar*, his translation of Genesis, the *Ad-
monitio ad filium spiritualem*, the *Vita S. Æthelwoldi*, and his Pastoral Letters.[67] Not since the vernacular letters and prefaces of Alfred, whom Ælfric
expressly admired, is an "I" identified with a particular individual used with
such authority and apparent selfhood. Joyce Hill has recently pointed out,
however, that the Pastoral Letters were not issued in Ælfric's name, but
were composed for the secular clergy on the authority of the bishops acting
in the tradition of the Benedictine reform. She concludes that "in consequence Ælfric avoided the process of self-identification within the public
text through which, as we have seen, he laid claim to the tradition elsewhere."[68] The point is well taken. There is a startling difference between
the conventions of authority used by Ælfric in the letters and in the homilies.

In addition, the unique information that Ælfric offers about himself in
the prefaces to the *Catholic Homilies*, for example, does not identify him
with modern ideas of authorship, but with those associated with the patristic concept of an "auctor," whose work as writer and translator has the authority of tradition and thus commands respect and obedience[69]—whence
Ælfric's concern with theological accuracy, the avoidance of error, and

his insistence on accurate copying in these prefaces. What bears further emphasis, however, is the extent to which Ælfric fashions his identity in the *Catholic Homilies* from longstanding conventions about preachers and teachers in the Christian tradition more generally. While Ælfric's concern with orthodoxy sets him apart from the homilists of collections such as Vercelli and Blickling and his opening sentences in the prefaces to the *Catholic Homilies* proclaim his affiliation with the reform tradition, Ælfric is nevertheless working within the general didactic conventions shared by other vernacular homilists. Seen in this light, Ælfric does not stand within one tradition (the reformist) so as to comment upon another (the anonymous), but uses homiletic tradition to embrace, incorporate, and thereby naturalize any sense of competition and conflict within it.[70] The identity of Ælfric as preacher is subject to this idea of tradition, and his self-representation is therefore alert to the nuances of institutional authority and genre.

It is perhaps because of Ælfric's alertness to genre and authority that the English preface to the First Series of the *Catholic Homilies* begins in a manner reminiscent of the later *accessus ad auctores*.[71] The preface identifies the author, his authority, and his reasons for undertaking the task of composition—the dangers of ignorance—and locates this task in the tradition of moral education in English first undertaken by Alfred.[72] Yet, within the space of some fourteen lines, the preface shifts genre by turning into a homily, thus appropriately introducing the homiliary itself. Indeed, this section of the preface was reissued as a separate (short) homily on the end of the world and the coming of the Antichrist, a theme common throughout the homiletic corpus.[73] In the context of the preface, however, this "homily" has different work to do: it is a sustained examination of the importance of preaching in relation to the preacher himself.

The theme of the Last Days, composed of a pastiche of verses from the familiar scriptural source (Matthew 24:21, 5, 24, 22), elaborates the rationale for teaching: "Gehwa mæg þe eaðelicor þa toweardan costnunge acuman ðurh godes fultum. gif he bið þurh boclice lare getrymmed. for ðan ðe ða beoð gehealdene þe oð ende on geleafan þurhwuniað" (Everyone can withstand the coming temptation more easily, if he is strengthened by scriptural learning, because those who persist in faith until the end shall be preserved).[74] Indeed Matthew 24:14 urges preaching in the Last Days and may well be the impetus for Ælfric's associations here. Instruction in the interpretation of the scriptural signs of the Last Days enables the believer to distinguish between the true (Christ) and the false (Antichrist). But competence in interpretation is always mediated by the clergy, who enact the gospel injunction from Christ to instruct and to provide by their behavior an example of that instruction. This urgent, ever-present need for doctrinal instruction produces the teacher as a matter of necessity. However, the teacher is neither unique individual nor specific author in either medieval or modern senses, in spite of references to an "I" or "we." Ælfric represents himself instead as an exemplary teacher supported by his affinities with scriptural tradition, which he underscores (175–77) with references to both Old Testament prophets (Ezekiel 3:18–19 or 33:8–9 and Isaiah 58:1) and New Testament apostles (1 Corinthians 3:9). Using such affinities, Ælfric is indeed the teacher as obedient to the tradition:

> For swylcum bebodum wearð me geðuht þæt ic nære unscyldig wið god. gif ic nolde oðrum mannum, cyðan [oþþe þurh tungan] oþþe þurh gewritu ða godspellican soðfæstnysse þe he sylf gecwæð. J eft halgum lareowum onwreah;[75]

> [From such commands it seemed to me that I should not be guiltless before God if I did not wish to make known to other men [either by voice] or by writing the evangelical truth that he himself said, and then revealed to holy teachers.]

It may well be that this conclusion to the preface, with its series of quotations on the moral importance of teaching from both Old and New Testaments, is aimed specifically at the clergy. Ælfric's own identity is similarly informed by the same traditional expectations. Nothing in the preface contradicts the general representation of the preacher outlined in the other homiletic examples already discussed. In the homilies, that representation is primarily the moral ideal of the instructor specific to ecclesiastical rank, whose knowledge is matched by his actions, and it is in the light of such a conventional ideal and with the support of God's grace that Ælfric's homiletic identity is constructed. The rationale for preaching and the conceptualization of the preacher as holy teacher emerge in performance—as the preface becomes homily.

Acting Christian?

The differences between Ælfric's authorial personae in, for example, the prefaces to the *Catholic Homilies* and in the Pastoral Letters might lead us to assume a distinction between self and representation, between an authentic personhood and convention. In one guise or another, whether as a concept to be dismantled, challenged, or affirmed, the notion of the self as a marker of an authentic, true, or natural identity is foundational in modern Western culture,[76] whence the seemingly endless debates about identity politics that inform much recent thinking. Ironically, in reconceptualizing the subject as performative, postmodern critics such as Judith Butler have arrived at a notion of the self not dissimilar from Ælfric's own representations.[77] Modern sensibilities can therefore accommodate the possibility that there is no self that hides behind an assumed facade of convention; in fact, we might say that Ælfric's personae are authentic in their conventionality. In his prefaces, Ælfric always names himself in relation to networks of authority and in terms of generic conventions of letters or prefaces—"alumnus adelwoldi beneuoli et uenerabilis presulis" (student of the benevolent and venerable prelate Æthelwold)[78] or "Ælfric gret eadmodlice Æðelweard ealdorman" (Ælfric humbly greets Æthelweard ealdorman),[79] for example. These personae, however, are rare in Anglo-Saxon religious writing. Far more troubling to modern theories of identity is the dominance of the first person plural, "we," in the homilies. The believer is not interpellated by personal name in the Circumcision homily, but by the collective noun Christian. The homiletic use of the Christian "we" suggests that, in the history of subjectivity, there are periods when concepts of self are not synonymous with those of individual identity; rather, individual identity is located within social systems of class and community. In the late Anglo-Saxon period, neither the self nor the individual are the foundational categories for what is deemed true, essential, or authentic; that category is inhabited instead by God.

The project of didacticism in the homilies is the maintenance of the Christian as Christian—as a member of the Christian community. This project is achieved by instruction in a body of knowledge (Scripture and patristic commentary), which defines the Christian against the non-Christian, and by the exercise of virtue, which defines Christian behavior as a continual process of the attainment of belief in thought and deed. Didactic teaching, in short, is aimed at an intellectual apprehension of a preexisting system of knowledge, which is maintained by action and defines identity. Although these actions are performed by individuals, their meaning and validity as authentic and true Christian actions are conferred on the individual only in relation to the congregation or community. Ritual actions—baptism, attendance at mass, prayer, confession, penance, and charity (in the specific senses of almsgiving and tithing)—are central to Christian identity and therefore central to the pastoral mission.

Obedience to God's law is manifested by the maintenance of Christian rituals and is the justification for them. Despite the fact that we may prefer other, more immediately material, explanations for the practice of tithing, for example, the homilies make it clear that the ideology of tithing is obedience to the law.[80] Obedience is the hallmark of Christian identity; as both origin and consequence of knowledge, and both justification and form of action, obedience is an enactment of a truth not grounded in an individual, but in a socially structured system of belief.

The social nature of ritual is emphasized throughout the homilies by denying the tremendous barriers between lay and clerical participation in terms of liturgical and pastoral roles. Vercelli Homily XII for the second day of Rogationtide, to take one example, demonstrates the powers of incorporation into the community invested in ritual behavior.[81] A season for tithing, fasting, and prayer, Rogationtide in this homily is distinguished by specific communal actions that manifest service to God:

> Þonne wið þon gesette us sanctus Petrus syðþan ꞃ oðerra cyricena eal-
> dormen þa halgan gangdagas þry, to ðam þæt we sceoldon on Gode
> ælmihtigum þiowigan mid usse gedefelice gange ꞃ mid sange ꞃ mid
> ciricena socnum ꞃ mid fæstenum ꞃ mid ælmessylenum ꞃ mid halegum
> gebedum. ꞃ we sculon beran usse reliquias ymb ure land, þa medeman
> Cristes rodetacen þe we Cristes mæl nemnað, on þam he sylfa þro-
> wode for mancynnes alysnesse.[82]

> [Then later Saint Peter and leaders of other churches established for
> us the three holy Rogation days, so that we should serve Almighty
> God with our fitting procession and with songs and with attendance
> at churches and with fasting and with alms and with holy prayers. And
> we should carry our relics around our land, the worthy crucifix of
> Christ which we call the cross of Christ, on which he himself suffered
> for the redemption of mankind.]

Individual actions such as prayer, fasting, alms—none of which are specific only to Rogationtide—combine with communal action appropriate to this liturgical season—the processions, singing, attendance at church, and the carrying of relics. These behaviors mark individual church and geographic place with the universal symbols of Christian history and worship. The conventional signs of Christianity—the cross, the Gospels, relics, litanies of the saints (228/18–29/39)—derive their meaning in relation to the specific rituals of the season, located in time and place. Worship of the saints offers protection "ge on þas tid ge on aeghwylce" (both at this time and at all time; 228/38–39), and the carrying of the Gospels symbolizes knowledge of Christ's story, his conquest of the devil through fasting, and the mysterious (that is to say, mystified) power of the Christian knowledge, which is greater than "ænig man æfre aspyrigan mæge oððe gecnawan mæge" (any man may ever explore or know; 229/28). In the same way, the offerings of cattle, land, wood, and goods at this season signify worship, honoring God for the salvation of those in the past, present, and future (229/33–37).

These ritualized actions, which enact belief in the forms of Christian knowledge both specific to this feast and to Christianity in general, ensure the presence of the divine in each and every congregation at the moment of enactment. That is to say, worship in the name of God sanctions and transforms the communal instant into a moment of divinity, recalling and reworking the words of Christ himself: "We þonne syndon nu gesamnode. We gelyfað in dryhtnes naman. He is us betweonum on andweardnesse" (We are now gathered together. We believe in the Lord's name. He is among us now; 229/49–50; cf. Matthew 18:20). Like the homiletic section of Ælfric's first preface to the *Catholic Homilies*, this homily is performative; it gathers together all the behaviors appropriate for this day into one text and restages them for and in the presence (and present) of the congregation. The homily's rhetorical power culminates in this transformative moment of divine presence, which structures its emotional charge as a form of the "timor Domini," the fear of the Lord. Quoting from Psalm 110:10 (228/54) for its scriptural authority, "timor Domini" is the origin of wisdom, of scrutiny of the self, and of desire. Desire is transformed into zeal ("onbyrdnes"), through which virtue flourishes and vice is conquered (229/51–58). Fear of the Lord is thus the foundational emotion produced by ritual behaviors for Rogationtide and its guarantor, as the conclusion stresses:

> Nu we gehyrdon, men ða leofestan, hu god is þæt we hæbben dryhtnes egesan. Secan we symle mid ondrysnum egesan þa halgan reliquias dryhtnes⁊ þyllicre gesamnunge. ⁊ þonne huru getilien we þæt we þonne ða halgan lare godspelles gehyren þæt hio fæste wunige on ussum modgeþancum. (230/72–76)

> [Now have we heard, beloved men, how good it is that we have fear of the Lord. Let us always seek with venerable fear the holy relics of the Lord and such gatherings. And then indeed let us so strive when we hear the holy teaching of the gospel that it remain fast in our minds.]

Ritual action in the presence and place of the congregation is fostered by learning to produce, maintain, and celebrate the individual believer as member of a socially stratified community whose ideological reach transcends both space and time. But the individual, though subsumed into the Christian community, remains a moral agent, whose mental discipline is entailed by these continual reenactments of belief. The Christian is always in performance, in the act of becoming.

Acting suggests a role assumed by the individual for a specific purpose. Ritual similarly implies a sense of self separated from and transformed by action. As many anthropologists argue, social meanings and named emotions forged in the process of ritualized behavior are distinct to that ritual and not to the individual.[83] Acting Christian in the homilies, however, does not permit such distinctions between self and society. There is no identity beyond the community, which liturgical ritual confirms, or beyond the Christian behaviors that ritual maintains. Nor is there a concept of self that authenticates ritual, which is instead authenticated by Scripture, its liturgical enactment, and God. In Vercelli XII, it is the presence of God that ushers in fear; fear, the "timor Domini," structures pyschic identity and the struggle of the soul for virtue. Acting Christian is thus synonymous with being Christian.

This interpellation of the Christian by ritual and knowledge is thus closer to Butler's sense of the performative processes by which identity is assumed than to concepts of acting or anthropological theories of ritual.[84] There are, however, key differences. Christian identity is produced by belief in God, which both structures and confirms the individual as Christian. Vercelli Homily XII reminds us that belief is a continuous psychic process, or struggle, which is fortified by zeal, humility, and obedience and which maintains Christian identity in the face (or fear) of a transcendental subject, God. Failure to believe results in abjection, both within the moral individual and without, where reside the pagan, the excommunicant, the leper, or the Jew. In short, the making of a Christian is a highly conscious social process, which is the result of training, discipline, and learning—the product of Christian didacticism so evident in homiletic literature. It is crucial to grasp that identity so produced is essentialist in terms of belief rather than privileged in terms of performances of sex or gender, as Butler argues. Belief is therefore foundational to identity in the homilies, which has important consequences for our understanding of sex and gender in the concepts of the Christian.[85]

What does the project of Christian didacticism in the Anglo-Saxon "golden age" offer students of the later medieval phenomena of the persecuting society and of the formation of the modern subject? First, these homilies confirm that being Christian is intimately bound to not being Christian—didacticism is aimed at the incorporation of the believer into the Christian community and the abjection of other forms of belief. This same ideological process is later used to persecute the Jews and to prosecute heresy. In Anglo-Saxon England, however, the abjection of the Jew is a figure for the abjection of the pagan, just as the prosecution of the sodomite in the penitentials is a means of maintaining chaste heterosexuality, as Frantzen points out.[86] At the same time, it is clear that these structures of belief are emergent in late Anglo-Saxon England, whose symbolic project is more the establishment of a Christian society in England than its defense against other ideological challenges. The signal achievement of the homilies is thus to persuade their audience of the truth of Christianity by means of traditional forms of reason and knowledge; this is a truth increasingly taken for granted (and thus increasingly threatened) by later medieval formations.

Second, there is an identity assumed by the Christian prior to the twelfth century. Christian identity in the homilies is, however, communal to a radical extent; it contests traditional Anglo-Saxon communities of kinship obligations, while reconfirming the sometimes threatening social hierarchies of service to lord or superior by reference to their Christian equivalents. Church or congregation replaces hall, and the social power of king or lord is annexed to that of Christianity, whose moral and intellectual strength becomes a principle of social organization by virtue of this relation. Being Christian—acting in its name—entails duties and responsibilities appropriate to social rank or class. The insistence on classification and division of identity in the homilies confirms social hierarchies—being Christian means being Christian and a king, thane, or slave. Christianity is a thoroughly social system. The imbrication between social inequlities and Christian responsibilities predicts the essential conservatism of Anglo-Saxon Christian society, and thus obscures the fact that there is a choice. As later Christian communities, and individuals, discover, there are other ways of organizing Christian society, other, sometimes more utopic, "golden ages."[87]

Moreover, by virtue of membership in Christian community—a community that subsumes the ties founded on place and time—the individual is both produced and authenticated, though this authenticity must be tried time and again on moral grounds. The homilies are fundamental evidence for the formation of the Christian as moral agent in the early medieval period. This final point has been obscured, I think, by the insistence of interiority as a defining moment in the formation of the modern subject. Individuals, however, live in groups and identify with them; the collective Christian community in the homilies rests on the formation of a collective moral conscience in which all, as individuals, share. The vocabulary of this moral conscience is that of sin and virtue, and no homily is without it (Vercelli XII is exemplary in this regard). To argue that there is no interiority in the Anglo-Saxon period is to argue that the language of sin and virtue resists internalization, which is equally belied by later developments such as the importance of confession in the history of the formation of the subject. One measure of the "golden age" of Anglo-Saxon Christianity, therefore, is the extent to which the Christian Anglo-Saxon subject is interpellated and maintained as a member of a group with his or her own moral conscience; these are the preconditions for the later "invention" of the individual.

Notes

This essay appears in a slightly different form as chapter 4 of *Tradition and Belief: Religious Writing in Late Anglo-Saxon England* (Minneapolis, 1999), 106–32.

1. Roberta Frank, "Germanic Legend in Old English Literature," in *The Cambridge Companion to Old English Literature*, ed. Malcolm Godden and Michael Lapidge (Cambridge, 1991), 88–106, at p. 88.

2. This is especially characteristic of art-historical studies of the period; see, for example, Janet Backhouse, D. H. Turner, and Leslie Webster, eds. *The Golden Age of Anglo-Saxon Art, 966–1066* (London, 1984).

3. Stanley B. Greenfield and Daniel G. Calder, *A New Critical History of Old English Literature* (New York, 1986), 68.

4. R. I. Moore, *The Formation of a Persecuting Society: Power and Deviance in Western Europe, 950–1250* (Oxford, 1987). Moore argues in broad strokes, largely to counter a historiographical emphasis that views persecution as "natural" to this period without inquiring into its processes. While his arguments need testing against the individual instance, they have yet to be substantially challenged.

5. Cf. Colin Morris, *The Discovery of the Individual, 1050–1200* (New York, 1972; rpt. Toronto, 1987).

6. The critical literature is long and complex. Michel Foucault's *History of Sexuality*, vol. 1 (tr. Robert Hurley; New York, 1980), esp. 3–73, has been instrumental in furthering the debate, as have recent studies on gender and the troubadours, esp. Sarah Kay, *Subjectivity in Troubadour Poetry* (Cambridge, 1990) and "The Contradictions of Courtly Love and the Origins of Courtly Poetry," *Journal of Medieval and Early Modern Studies* 26 (1996), 209–53. This debate is contested from a variety of perspectives on the terrain of the fourteenth century as a direct response to a widespread postmedieval assumption that the "subject" was invented in the early modern period. For a useful introduction, see David Aers, "A Whisper in the Ear of Early Modernists; or, Reflections on Literary Critics Writing the 'History of the Subject.'" In *Culture and History, 1350–1660: Essays on English Communities, Identities, and Writing*, ed. David Aers (Detroit, 1992), 177–202; see also Aers, *Community, Gender, and Individual Identity: English Writing, 1360–1430* (London and New York, 1988); David Aers and Lynn Staley, *The Powers of the Holy: Religion, Politics, and Gender in Late Medieval English Culture* (University Park, Penn., 1996); and Lee Patterson's essays on the Wife of Bath and the Pardoner in *Chaucer and the Subject of History* (Madison, 1991), 280–321 and 367–421.

7. Proscription and regulation of sexual behavior has attracted more attention than idolatry (a capital sin) or heresy, both of which are regularly proscribed in the pentitentials. For discussion of sexuality, see Allen J. Frantzen, *The Literature of Penance in Anglo-Saxon England* (New Brunswick, N.J., 1983), and more explicitly, "Between the Lines: Queer Theory, the History of Homosexuality, and Anglo-Saxon Penitentials," *Journal of Medieval and Early Modern Studies* 26 (1996), 255–96. Sexual behavior and heresy are the subjects of Ælfric's Letter to Wulfsige (ed. B. Fehr, *Die Hirtenbriefe Ælfrics* (Bibliothek der angelsächsichen Prosa 9. Hamburg, 1914; rpt. with introduction by Peter Clemoes, Darmstadt, 1964), 1–34). The subjects of heathenism, heresy, and idolatry in ecclesiastical and civil law merit further analysis, though it is clear that these are regular concerns of the monarchy and the church throughout the period, with proscriptions against heathenism resurfacing in the late Anglo-Saxon period, largely as a result of the presence of the Vikings in England. *Wulfstan's Canons of Edgar* (ed. Roger Fowler, London: EETS 266, 1972) is a good witness to the kinds of proscriptions made throughout the later period, because of its inclusion of earlier clauses (as is habitual for the laws); see, for example, paragraphs 16 and 18. See also V Æthelred and II Cnut (tr. Dorothy Whitelock, *English Historical Documents c. 500–1042*, vol. I; London, 1955, 405.1, 420.5).

8. Moore, *Formation of a Persecuting Society*, 66–99 and 124–53.

9. While annual confession is mandated by the Fourth Lateran Council, both private and public confession and penance are already assumed in practice by the homiletic literature of the late Anglo-Saxon period; see Frantzen, *Literature of Penance*, 122–74.

10. Although this essay begins this process of refining our historical understanding of the late Anglo-Saxon period by using the homilies, its evidence needs to be assessed in relation to the laws and the penitentials of this period in particular. Few have yet challenged the glow of the "golden age," although Eric John, "The World of Abbot Ælfric," in *Ideal and Reality in Frankish and Anglo-Saxon Society*, ed. Patrick Wormald, Donald Bullough, and Roger Collins (Oxford, 1983), 300–316, offers some unsentimental perceptions about Ælfric's theology.

11. Bede recounts the massacre of the monks at Bangor at the hands of Athelfrith in fulfillment of Augustine's prophecies that unless they accept English custom for religious practices (including the dating of Easter), they would suffer death at their hands (*Bede's Ecclesiastical History of the English People*, ed. Bertram Colgrave and R. A. B. Mynors; Oxford, 1969, II, 2). The ideological contest between the Irish and the English (Roman) Christians, which largely took the form of the controversy over the dating of Easter, is well known.

12. Simon Keynes, for example, argues that "there might be good cause if not to applaud then at least to condone rather than to deplore the making of payments to the Vikings and the massacre of St. Brice's Day" (*The Diplomas of King Æthelred "The Unready,"* 978–1016. Cambridge, 1980, 208). For the disputes between the regular and monastic clergy, see the Old English account of Edgar's establishment of monasteries (generally agreed to be by Æthelwold), excerpts from which are conveniently translated in Whitelock, *English Historical Documents*, 846–49.

13. A full study of the regulation of heresy in the canons and religious literature of the period is a desideratum for future research. Ælfric is still warning of the dangers of Arianism in the late tenth century; his First Series *De fide catholica* spells out the death of Arius in ways intended to recall that of Judas; see Peter Clemoes, ed., *Ælfric's Catholic Homilies: The First Series Text* (Oxford: EETS ss 17, 1997; abbreviated hereafter as *ÆCHom I*), 342–43.

14. Hermann's study of *Elene, Andreas*, and *Judith* in *Allegories of War: Language and Violence in Old English Poetry* (Ann Arbor, 1989) is one of the few to foreground the ideological importance of Judaism in Anglo-Saxon literature.

15. Ed. Clemoes, *ÆCHom I*, 224–31.

16. Where community is concerned, the only study of any detail has concentrated on the poetry, not the prose; see Hugh Magennis, *Images of Community in Old English Poetry* (Cambridge, 1996).

17. Mark Miller, "Displaced Souls, Idle Talk, Spectacular Scenes: *Handlyng Synne* and the Perspective of Agency," *Speculum* 71 (1996), 607–32, similarly points out that the role of the agent in later medieval penitential discourse has been underestimated by historians of subjectivity.

18. The most recent survey of the evidence is Martin Irvine, *The Making of Textual Culture: "Grammatica" and Literary Theory, 330–1100* (Cambridge, 1994), 272–460. Ælfric's *Grammar* (ed. J. Zupitza, *Ælfrics Grammatik und Glossar*. Berlin, 1880; rpt. 1966), the Pastoral Letters (ed. Fehr, *Die Hirtenbriefe Ælfrics*), and the *Colloquy* (ed. G. N. Garmonsway; London, 1939) all bear witness to the late-tenth, early-eleventh-century emphasis on the need to educate regular and monastic clerics. The evidence of standard Late West Saxon is also a measure of the reach of standardized vernacular education among the clergy; see Helmut Gneuss, "The Origin of Standard Old English and Æthelwold's School at Winchester," *ASE* 1 (1972), 63–83.

19. For an introduction, see James J. Murphy, ed. *Three Medieval Rhetorical Arts* (Berkeley, 1971), xvii–xx. For a fuller discussion, see H. Leith Spencer, *English Preaching in the Late Middle Ages* (Oxford, 1993), 78–133 (on medieval views of preaching) and 228–68 (on sermon form).

20. For Alfric's Latin source (Gregory), see Cyril Smetana, "Ælfric and the Early Medieval Homiliary," *Traditio* 15 (1959), 163–204, at 198.

21. Malcolm Godden, *Ælfric's Catholic Homilies: The Second Series Text* (London: EETS ss 5, 1972; abbreviated hereafter as *ÆCHom II*), 162/55–58.

22. Alasdair MacIntyre, *Whose Justice? Which Rationality?* (Notre Dame, 1988), 146–63.

23. These readings are often invisible in the critical editions, especially in Thorpe's 1844 edition of the *Catholic Homilies* (*The Homilies of the Anglo-Saxon Church. The First Part, Containing the Sermones Catholici or Homilies of Ælfric*. 2 vols. rpt. Hildesheim, 1983). cf. Clemoes, *ÆCHom I*. For full citations, see A. S. Cook, *Biblical Quotations in Old English Prose Writers* (London, 1898), *Biblical Quotations in Old English Prose Writers: Second Series* (London, 1903), and A. S. Napier, "Nächtrage zu Cook's *Biblical Quotations in Old English Prose Writers I, II, III*," *Archiv für das Studium*

der neueren Sprachen und Literaturen 101 (1898), 309–24, 102 (1899), 29–42, and 107 (1901), 105–6. Godden supplies all pericopes to the Second Series in his 1979 edition. For discussion of the vernacular homiletic translations of the Old Testament, see Richard Marsden, *The Text of the Old Testament in Anglo-Saxon England* (Cambridge, 1995), 395–443.

24. Ed. S. J. Crawford, *Ælfric's Exameron Anglice: or, The Old English Hexameron* (Bibliothek der angelsächsischen prosa 10. Hamburg, 1921); cf. Marsden, *Text of the Old Testament in Anglo-Saxon England.*

25. Ed. R. M. Liuzza, *The Old English Version of the Gospels*, vol. 1 (Oxford: EETS o.s. 304, 1994).

26. Jon Wilcòx, *Ælfric's Prefaces* (Durham, 1994), 116–19; cf. 37–44.

27. Joyce Hill, "Ælfric and Smaragdus," *ASE* 21 (1992), 203–37.

28. *Ælfric's Prefaces* 21.

29. See *Tradition and Belief*, ch. 3.

30. Clemoes, *ÆCHom I*, 174/48–49.

31. MacIntyre, *Whose Justice? Which Rationality?*, 357.

32. For discussion of this homily, see Malcolm Godden, "Money, Power, and Morality in Late Anglo-Saxon England," *ASE* 19 (1990), 41–65, at 56–59. The source—a Latin legend for the martyrdom of Saints Peter and Paul—was identified by J. E. Cross, "The Literate Anglo-Saxon: on Sources and Disseminations," *PBA* 58 (1972), 26–28, 33–36.

33. Godden, *ÆCHom II* 180/1–3.

34. Cf. Godden, *ÆCHom II* 180–82.

35. Clemoes, *ÆCHom I* 360/150–52.

36. Clemoes, *ÆCHom I* 173/9–10.

37. D. G. Scragg, ed., *The Vercelli Homilies and Related Texts* (Oxford: EETS 300, 1992), 134/1–6.

38. For Ælfric's source (Gregory's homily for the same day in the homiliary of Paulus Diaconus), see Smetana, "Ælfric and the Early Medieval Homiliary," 187–88. For other examples of this common analogy, see the First Series homilies on the Lord's Prayer, *De Dominica oratione* (*ÆCHom I* 329), and for mid-Lent Sunday (275–80), an exegesis of the miracle of the five loaves.

39. *ÆCHom I* 267/52–268/57.

40. *ÆCHom I* 332/195–200.

41. *ÆCHom I* 224–31.

42. Karen Louise Jolly, *Popular Religion in Late Saxon England: Elf Charms in Context* (Chapel Hill, 1996), esp. 71–98.

43. I differ from Jolly by emphasizing the importance of truth as a law in the homilies rather than as an exemplification of right or wrong practices (see her comments in *Popular Religion*, 87).

44. Jolly, 18–24. Jolly's emphasis on crossing binary divisions needs to be complemented by an analysis of how those divisions actually operate in the homilies and of the social forces at work in them.

45. Jolly, 87–88. For a more nuanced reading of this homily, see Wilcox, *Ælfric's Prefaces*, 26–27.

46. *Ælfric's Prefaces*, 26.

47. *ÆCHom I* 228–31.

48. Smetana, "Ælfric and the Early Medieval Homiliary," 185.

49. Jolly, *Popular Religion*, for example, describes Ælfric as going "off on a tangent" in the second part of the homily (87), while most commentators see the homily as divided into two parts (Wilcox, *Ælfric's Prefaces*, 26–27; Smetana, "Ælfric and the Early Medieval Homiliary," 185).

50. The word *rihtlicost* (most correct) is repeated almost as often as *gescead* (reason) in this homily.

51. Althusser's concept of interpellation (Louis Althusser, *Lenin and Philosophy and Other Essays*, tr. Ben Brewster; New York, 1971, 127–86), the process whereby the individual is "hailed" or subjected by an ideological discourse, or an ideological state apparatus, as Althusser puts it, although often rightly critiqued for its idealism and ahistoricist impulses (e.g., Jorge Larrain, *The Concept of Ideology*; Athens, GA, 1979, 154–64), is nevertheless a useful way of approaching the relation of the individual to the group in Christianity (Althusser's own examples include the church).

52. *ÆCHom I* 385/166–68. For the sources to this homily (Gregory and Bede in the homiliary of Paulus Diaconus), see Smetana, 190–91.

53. *ÆCHom I* 384/140–41.

54. For Ælfric's use of Augustine in this homily, see Max Förster, "Über die Quellen von Ælfrics exegetischen Homiliae Catholicae," *Anglia* 16 (1894), 33.

55. *ÆCHom I* 327/47–52.

56. *ÆCHom II* 181/10–12.

57. *ÆCHom II* 183–89.

58. "Money, Power, and Morality in Late Anglo-Saxon England," 56–57.

59. Ælfric names his source as Haymo; for discussion, see Smetana, 186.

60. *ÆCHom I* 242/44–47.

61. As is evident throughout his writing, but see especially his First Series English preface (*ÆCHom I*, 174–77).

62. *ÆCHom II* 183/111–13.

63. Cf. Joyce Hill, "Monastic Reform and the Secular Church: Ælfric's Pastoral Letters in Context," in Carola Hicks, ed., *England in the Eleventh Century* (Stamford, 1992), 106–16.

64. R. Morris, ed., *The Blickling Homilies* (London: EETS 58, 63, 73, 1874–80; rpt. 1 vol., 1967), 43.

65. But see *ÆCHom II* 195–96. Ælfric's attitude toward the *Visio Pauli* is discussed in Malcolm Godden, "Ælfric and the Vernacular Prose Tradition," in P. Szarmach and B. Huppé, eds., *The Old English Homily and its Backgrounds* (Albany, 1978), 100–101. The fullest discussion of the *Visio* is that by Charles D. Wright, *The Irish Tradition in Old English Literature* (Cambridge, 1993), 106–74.

66. In even the most explicit homilies, tithing remains a general obligation, as in Blickling IV, and is implemented in law only in the tenth century. See Rudolph

Willard, "The Blickling-Junius Tithing Homily and Caesarius of Arles," in Thomas A. Kirby and Henry Bosley Woolf, eds., *Philologica: The Malone Anniversary Studies* (Baltimore, 1949), 65–78; see also Ælfric's First Series homily for the First Sunday in Lent (*ÆCHom I* 272–74). The relation of tithing to chastity is discussed in *Tradition and Belief*, chapter 5.

67. All in Wilcox, *Ælfric's Prefaces*.

68. Joyce Hill, "Ælfric, Authorial Identity and the Changing Text," in D. Scragg and P. Szarmach, eds., *The Editing of Old English* (Cambridge, 1994), 177–89, at 183.

69. Cf. Wilcox, *Ælfric's Prefaces*, 70–71.

70. Mary Clayton, *The Cult of the Virgin Mary in Anglo-Saxon England* (Cambridge, 1990), 260–65, comes to a similar conclusion on the basis of her analysis of the Marian homilies.

71. Alfric's prefaces in fact offer useful precursors to the concepts of authorship explored by A. J. Minnis, *Medieval Theories of Authorship: Scholastic Literary Attitudes in the later Middle Ages* (London, 1984).

72. *ÆCHom I* 174.

73. See *Tradition and Belief*, ch. 3. This preface was reissued to form an addition to the First Series homily for the First Sunday in Advent in Cambridge, Corpus Christi College 188 (N. R. Ker, *Catalogue of Manuscripts Containing Anglo-Saxon* (Oxford, 1957) 43, art. 43), and as a short homily in Cambridge, Corpus Christi College 178, Bodleian Library, Junius 121, and Bodleian Library, Hatton 115 (Ker 41, art. 12; 338, art. 34; and 332, art. 28, respectively). For a brief discussion, see Wilcox, *Ælfric's Prefaces*, 68.

74. *ÆCHom I* 175/67–79.

75. *ÆCHom I* 176/119–21; cf. Wilcox, *Ælfric's Prefaces*, 110/76–80.

76. For an important critique of postmodernist theories of the subject, the political power of authenticity, and the importance of historical analysis, see Jonathan Dollimore, *Sexual Dissidence: Augustine to Wilde, Freud to Foucault* (Oxford, 1991), 39–73.

77. Judith Butler, *Bodies that Matter: On the Discursive Limits of "Sex."* (New York, 1993).

78. *ÆCHom I* 173/3.

79. W. W. Skeat, ed. *Ælfric's Lives of Saints* (London: EETS 76, 82, 94, 114, 1881–1900; rpt. 2 vols. 1966), 1, 4/35; cf. Wilcox, *Ælfric's Prefaces*, 120/1.

80. As explained by Ælfric in his First Series homily for Lent, for example (*ÆCHom I* 273–74), and discussed further in *Tradition and Belief*, chapter 5.

81. Other homilies await detailed analysis of their use of ritual and include Ælfric's First Series homily for Lent (*ÆCHom I* 273–74), the Feast of the Purification of Mary (256–57), and Palm Sunday (296–98). For general discussion of Ælfric's use of the liturgy, see Christopher A. Jones, "The Book of the Liturgy in Anglo-Saxon England," *Speculum* 73 (1998), 659–702.

82. Scragg, *The Vercelli Homilies*, 228/12–18.

83. My comments on ritual and its relation to the individual follow the critique of Talal Asad, *Genealogies of Religion: Discipline and Reasons of Power in Christianity and Is-*

lam (Baltimore, 1993), 126–35. Addressing monastic discipline in particular, Asad argues that rites did "not simply evoke or release universal emotions, they aimed to construct and reorganize distinctive emotions," which are "the product not of mere readings of symbols but of processes of power" (134).

84. Butler, *Bodies that Matter*, 1–23. For a related critique of Butler's use of performativity in a reading of *Elene*, see Clare Lees, "At a Crossroads: Old English and Feminist Criticism," in Katherine O'Brien O'Keeffe, ed., *Reading Old English Texts* (Cambridge, 1997), 159–67.

85. See *Tradition and Belief*, ch. 5.

86. Frantzen, "Between the Lines."

87. As Aers and Staley brilliantly point out in *The Powers of the Holy*, using the examples of Chaucer, Langland, and Julian of Norwich.

The Editing of Old English Poetic Texts: Questions of Style

ROY F. LESLIE

S tylistics has not hitherto played a systematic or important part in the
solution of editorial problems in Old English poetry. However, considerations of style may be used to augment linguistic factors in an attempt to produce a text that represents as closely as possible an editor's apprehension of the original work. However diverse their approaches to the
editorial task, this has been the aim of most editors; from the eighteenth to
the early twentieth century, editors allowed themselves great latitude and
thereby brought conjectural emendation into disrepute.[1] This practice was
characterized by what George Kane describes as "excessive subjectivity, an
identification with the author leading to the assumption that the editor perfectly commanded [the author's] style, or a supersession of author by editor."[2] Such excesses led Eugene Vinaver to determine, "on strictly objective
grounds, what considerations *should* dictate the editor's choice, and how far
he is entitled to in emending his text."[3] He then outlines the mechanisms of
scribal transcription, which are capable of producing no fewer than six
types of emendable error. He maintains, however, that no matter how
strongly an editor may condemn his text on rational grounds, he has to
leave it intact at those points at which it is possible that the author, not the
scribe, is responsible for it. Vinaver defines the task of the editor as a *partial*
reconstruction of the lost original and states that he must aim not at restoring the original work in every particular, but merely at lessening the damage done by the copyists.[4]

In reaction to conjectural emendation, a number of editors of Old English texts had already adopted a conservative attitude toward their texts
before the date of Vinaver's article. However, their defense of the authority
of Anglo-Saxon scribes had been excessive and had occasioned Kenneth

Sisam's inquiry into the accuracy of transmission of Old English poetry;[5] he examines those few poetic texts which occur in more than one manuscript, and concludes that in three of them the tenth-century texts show no attempt to reproduce the archaic or dialectal forms and spellings of the earlier copies. He provides evidence from proper names to demonstrate slipshod copying. He also points out that the difference between a better reading and a worse is a matter of judgment, that to support a bad manuscript reading is in no way more meritorious than to support a bad conjecture, that a bad manuscript reading, if defended, looks like solid evidence for the defense of other readings. Sisam does, however, also remind us that manuscripts are our primary witnesses.[6]

My own editorial approach is empirical, with a bias in favor of the text, knowing that it may well be unreliable, but aware also that it is the only foundation we have. I am ready to change the text only as a last resort, bearing in mind the temptations that beset an editor to prefer his own readings on insufficient textual evidence. One must agree with Kane when he urges that we be bolder on occasion;[7] however, in editing *Piers Plowman* he had checks and balances that single-text editors do not possess. But an editor of a unique text must be doubly sure that he is being bold with good reason and avoid emendation where the text as it stands makes perfectly good sense. An example of this kind is the manuscript reading *oft* in *The Wanderer* 53, which occurs in a context that is notoriously difficult to interpret; the word is regularly emended to *eft*, "back, again," though it is possible to make sense of the passage using the manuscript form *oft*, "often."[8]

Before we attempt to show, in detail, how stylistics may have a bearing on editorial practices, it is worth noting that the corpus of Old English poetry is small and consists, for the most part, of unique manuscripts which contain many *hapax legomena*. Punctuation is sporadic and, where it does occur, may be used for purposes other than to mark off syntactical units. Word division sometimes appears arbitrary and may obscure meaning. The text is written continuously, like prose, and in any case the verse is in a form unfamiliar to modern readers. For all these reasons, few statements about the literary or the linguistic aspects of a poem can be made with absolute certainty. This is especially true of characteristics of style, which are often difficult to pinpoint and gain agreement on; for although scholars will agree that such things as variation and parallelism exist, they will not always agree about the particular application of them. One critic's variation may be another's parallelism and a third's multiple objects. We therefore do not yet have a clear enough conception of stylistic norms in Old English poetry to make them reliable as criteria for emendation by themselves. What we must do in the meantime is to yoke them with other factors which point in a given direction, or use them as best we can when other factors cancel each other out.

Modern editors have, in fact, yoked literary, if not specifically stylistic evidence, to linguistic factors to an increasing extent. This has given rise to a problem about priorities. For instance, in several places in their edition of *The Wanderer*, Dunning and Bliss suggest that decisions should be made on literary rather than on linguistic grounds.[9] Bruce Mitchell has contested the validity of their proposal, claiming that they have let literary considerations outweigh not linguistic arguments but linguistic facts.[10] For Mitchell, a linguistic fact is "a statement which limits [the editor's] choice of interpretations; for example, that a particular metrical pattern is impossible, that a given inflexional ending is unambiguous, that the word being discussed means 'x' and not 'y,' that a conjunction expresses a particular relationship, . . . or that a certain word order is found only in principal clauses."[11] We should certainly not underestimate these constraints within which we must operate, and my own predilection would assuredly not be to make an editorial decision in deliberate defiance of them. However, incontestable linguistic facts are rare and, as they stand in the manuscript, may appear to be incompatible with each other. An editor may, therefore, be forced to emend on semantic or syntactical grounds. His case for emendation is strengthened, however, if a weak and ambiguous passage becomes a stylistically, as well as linguistically, satisfying one thereby. One such circumstance occurs in *The Wanderer*:

> Swa cwæð eardstapa   earfeþa gemyndig,
> wraþra wælsleahta,   winemæga hryre.[12]   (6–7)

We have two unambiguously genitive nouns, *earfeþa* and *wraþra wælsleahta*, dependent on *gemyndig*, which also takes the genitive in all other similar constructions occurring in Old English poetic texts. A third element, the noun phrase *winemæga hryre* (7b), is semantically linked to these two, but it cannot be parallel to them, dependent on *gemyndig*, as one might reasonably expect, because *hryre* is not in the genitive. Nora Kershaw's suggestion that we should read *hryre* as a loose causal or comitative dative, would appear to reconcile these two incompatible linguistic facts.[13] But her suggestion is a counsel of despair, stylistically divorcing the last phrase from its neighbors and providing a weak grammatical explanation.

However, if we emend *hryre* to the genitive *hryres*, we have three parallel expressions whose increasing emotional intensity is reflected by their increasing semantic and grammatical weight, from the simple noun, *earfeþa*, through the modified noun, *wraþra wælsleahta*, to the final phrase, *wine-mæga hryre*. I believe that we may reasonably posit authorial or scribal error at this point, on two counts. First, there is the remoteness—at the end of the next line—of the phrase from *gemyndig*. Second, the corpus of Old English poetry contains many phrases that consist of a noun in the genitive plus *hryre*, and in these phrases *hryre* is almost invariably in the oblique case. It would appear that the habitual use of the dative formula had led the author or scribe to overlook the necessity here of using the genitive.

I stated above my view that editors should normally emend only as a last resort, but that we should take George Kane's advice and be bolder on occasion. A case in point is a passage in *The Seafarer*, where the decision to emend the unique compound *cearselda* (5b) may be made largely on stylistic grounds:

> siþas secgan,   hu ic geswincdagum
> earfoðhwile   oft þrowade
> bitre breostceare   gebiden hæbbe
> gecunnad in ceole   cearselda fela.[14]   (2–5)

One must balance the fact that some kind of sense can be made of the word as it stands, with the improvement in clarity of meaning that follows from the simplest of emendations that can be made to an Old English word, namely the alteration of *d* to *ð*.

Cearselda is usually translated "abodes of care / suffering / sorrow." Ida L. Gordon refers to *meduseld*, "mead-hall," (*Beowulf* 3065) as a parallel;[15] but *meduseld* is not a true parallel, for the first element refers to "mead" and not to an abstract concept such as "grief," as it does in the closer parallel, *dreorsele*, "desolate hall" (*The Wife's Lament* 50). There are, however, semantic difficulties with the verb *cunnian*, "to experience" which, in marine contexts, always refers to the sea itself, not to what is on it, as in *The Seafarer: þæt ic hean streamas / sealtyþa gelac sylf cunnige*, "so that I myself should experience the tumult of the waves" (34–35); or in the closer parallel to this particular passage in *Andreas:*

> Swa gesælde iu,   þæt we on sæbate
> ofer waruðgewinn   wæda cunnedan.[16]   (438–40)

On the other hand, if we make the emendation of *d* to *ð*, to give *cearsēlða*, with a long *ē* in the second syllable, we have the Anglian equivalent of West-Saxon *cearsǣlða*, which would mean "experiences of care." Although this compound does not occur elsewhere, we may note that *heardsǣlþ*, "hard fate," "misfortune," is listed in Bosworth-Toller, and note also the occurrence of *earfoðsælig* "unblessed," *heardsælig* "unfortunate," and *wansælig* "miserable," "evil." If we adopt *cearsēlða* in the *Seafarer* passage, we find ourselves with two interwoven patterns of three variants each, one of verbal expressions on the theme of endurance (*þrowade, gebiden hæbbe* and *gecunnad*), and one of nominal expressions on the theme of times of anxiety (*geswincdagum, earfoðhwīle* and *cearsēlða*). We then have a passage strikingly similar in impact to *Deor:*

> Welund him be wurman   wræces cunnade,
> anhydig eorl   earfoþa dreag,
> hæfde him to gesiþþe   sorge ond longaþ.[17]   (1–3)

So far I have shown how considerations of style can come to the aid of an editor in elucidating meaning in individual phrases. I turn now to the wider topic of punctuation, where editorial practice can have a marked effect on our apprehension of both the meaning and the style of a poem. Because of the sporadic nature of manuscript punctuation, and our imperfect understanding of its application, editors have nearly always added modern punctuation to their texts. Mostly they have ignored the manuscript punctuation, but recent editors have sometimes sought to explain and incorporate it.

How punctuation affects style can be illustrated with a passage from *The Seafarer,* which deals with bird cries as substitutes for various human pleasures:

> Þær ic ne gehyrde   butan hlimman sæ
> iscaldne wæg   hwilum ylfete song
> dyde ic me to gomene   ganetes hleoþor
> ond huilpan sweg   fore hleahtor wera
> mæw singende   fore medodrince.   (18–22)

The scheme of punctuation that we impose on this passage affects the pattern of variation. Among recent editors, both Krapp and Dobbie[18] and Ida L. Gordon make lines 19b–22 a complete sentence, which may be translated "At times the song of the swan I took for my pleasure, the cry of the gannet and the sound of the curlew for the laughter of men, the seagull crying for the drinking of mead." Mrs. Gordon points out that these lines modify the statement (18–19a) that nothing could be heard but the roaring of the sea; however, instead of linking them in one sentence, she concludes that more probably the change of sense and construction comes, as so often in Old English poetry, in the middle of the line, and she therefore begins a new sentence with *hwilum* in the middle of line 19.

A second pattern is produced by a modification of the above. As before, *hwilum* begins a new sentence which is, however, modified internally, by a common after *hleoþor* at the end of line 20. The speaker then has both the swan's song *and* the gannet's cry for his pleasure, followed by the curlew's cry for the laughter of men (21) and the seagull singing for the drinking of mead (22).

A case can be made for quite another pattern of punctuation. If we place a stop after *song* at the end of line 19, *ylfete song* becomes an additional object of *gehyrde* (18) in the first sentence, and we have a one-to-one correspondence in the second: the cry of the gannet for pleasure, the curlew's call for the laughter of men, and the gull singing for the mead-drinking. My own preference is for this version because it is more balanced and because it conforms with the only punctuation point, after *song*, on the whole manuscript page (folio 81b).

Donald Fry's punctuation in his recent revision of part of the Finnsburg episode in *Beowulf* departs markedly from the generally accepted practice:

> Gewiton him ða wigend   wica neosian
> freondum befeallen,   Frysland geseon.
> Hamas ond hea-burh   Hengest ða gyt
> wæl-fagne winter   wunode mid Finne
> *eal* unhlitme   (eard gemunde),
> þeah þe he meahte   on mere drifan
> hringed-stefnan.   (1125–31)[19]

It has been customary to put full stops, or semicolons, after *heaburh* (1127) and *unhlitme* (1129) to give a translation such as the following: "Then Finn's fighting men, bereft of their friends, departed to make their way to their own abodes and see the land of the Frisians, their homes and their lofty stronghold. But Hengest still dwelt with Finn throughout that slaughter-stained winter—most unhappy was his lot. He remembered his homeland, although he could not put out to sea his ship with the curling prow."[20] The word "not" in this last sentence is the result of the emendation of *he* to *ne*; Fry retains the manuscript *he*, and puts no punctuation after *heaburh* and *unhlitme*, but puts a stop after *geseon* (1126), a comma at the end of 1129, and parentheses round the phrase *eard gemunde*. He translates lines 1127–31 as follows: "yet Hengest, during the slaughter-stained winter, inhabited with Finn the houses and the high-fortress *eal unhlitme* ["voluntarily": Fry, p. 22] (he thought of home), although he could drive the ring-prowed ship over the sea."[21] Here I am primarily concerned with his abstraction of the phrase *Hamas ond hea-burh* (1127) from its syntactical relationship with the sentence in the preceding lines and his use of it to begin a new sentence, not as a subject, but as the object of *wunode* (1128). Now we cannot rule out this procedure on idiomatic grounds, because *wunode* can take a direct object; however, we would expect inversion of subject and verb after an initial object of the weight of *Hamas ond hea-burh*, so that *wunode* would be followed by *Hengest*. Moreover, the change in punctuation here destroys the eminently satisfactory stylistic relationship with the previous two lines, wherein we have a pleasing arrangement, with *Hamas* echoing *wica*, and both *Hamas* and *hea-burh* reflecting the scope of the survey of Frisia.

The use of capitals in Old English poetic texts varies widely, even within the same manuscript. In the introduction to their edition of *The Exeter Book*, Krapp and Dobbie give a list of the capitals in each poem.[22] They vary in frequency of occurrence from about one in every 3 1/2 lines in *Guthlac*, to one in almost 11 lines in *Christ*. Shorter but similar poems can have an equally wide variation; *The Seafarer* with 124 lines has only six altogether, whereas *The Wanderer*, with 115 lines, has twice as many. In consequence, editors have placed little reliance on them hitherto. Therefore, a great deal of interest was aroused when Dunning and Bliss suggested that the small capitals in *The Wanderer* appear to be designed to mark out independent sections in the progression of the poem.[23] Many of them in fact do correspond with divisions that have been made by scholars on syntactical and other grounds. They occur at the beginning of lines 6 and 8, marking off the two lines concerning the *eardstapa* himself as in some way parenthetic; at the beginning of the wanderer's general reflections at line 58; at the start of the impersonal elegiac passage at line 73; and to mark out what I have interpreted as the limits to the *ubi sunt* passage (88–96).

Some of the capitals put forward have been disputed, on the basis that they are too small, or at best ambiguous;[24] for, in a number of Old English letters, the capital is simply a larger form of the lower case letter. I am, therefore, confining my attention to the undisputed ones. Do they go back to the author, or are they to be attributed to a scribe—either the copyist of *The Exeter Book* or a predecessor? If they are scribal in origin, how reliable are they? The scribe may occasionally have been in error about the structure of the poem he was transcribing. In the following passage from *The Wanderer*, this may well have happened:

> Forþon wat se þe sceal   his winedryhtnes
> leofes larcwidum   longe forþolian
> ðonne sorg ond slæp   somod ætgædre
> earmne anhogan   oft gebindað
> þinceð him on mode   þæt he his mondryhten

> clyppe ond cysse   ond on cneo lecge
> honda ond heafod   swa he hwilum ær
> in geardagum   giefstolas breac
> ðonne onwæcneð eft   wineleas guma
> gesihð him biforan   fealwe wegas
> baþian brimfuglas   brædan feþra
> hreosan hrim ond snaw   hægle gemenged.[25]   (37–48)

Perhaps the scribe has mistakenly capitalized the wrong *ðonne* in one or more of a series of four: ðõn (small cap ð) in lines 39 and 45, and þõn (lower case þ) in lines 49 and 51. Dunning and Bliss depart from their adherence to the manuscript capitalization as guidance to the beginnings of new sentences, by making *þonne* in line 49 begin a new sentence, and by correlating it with *þonne* at beginning of line 51.[26] On the face of it, the two correlations of the four *ðonne/þonne* clauses are stylistically attractive, as is the editor's claim that the first grouping gives an effective picture of fitful slumber. But there are consequential problems, particularly with respect to the preceding lines, 37 and 38, which are left in isolation, without an easily discernible object for the verb *wat* (37). Dunning and Bliss put forward three reasons for denying this verb its traditional object, the noun clause *þinceð him on mode* (41). The first is admittedly that it does not fit their explanation of the syntactical implications of the four *ðonnes*. The second arises from their belief that the traditional punctuation produces a substantial anti-climax, and is of course a subjective assessment. Their third objection would appear at first sight to have more substance. They suggest that the use of the noun object *earmne anhogan* (40) in the subsidiary clause is unidiomatic, since normal usage would place a qualification in the principal clause, with a pronoun object in the subordinate clause. But the poet has in fact already departed from normal usage by putting the *ðonne* clause first. He may have done so advisedly, to get the description of the impact of sorrow and sleep out of the way first so that he could make an uninterrupted sweep through the vivid dreams that peak in the climactic ceremony before the throne that the wanderer enjoyed in former days, a ceremony whose importance to the heroic literary tradition can hardly be overestimated.

Manuscript word division presents the editor with many difficulties, for word elements and short words do not conform to modern practices in this matter. Moreover, the elements of compounds are almost always written as separate words. For example, the opening line of *The Seafarer* appears as: *Mæg ic beme sylfum soð gied wrecan* in the manuscript, and is usually rendered in modern texts as: *mæg ic be me sylfum soðgied wrecan*, "I can utter a true tale about myself."

Many elements may be linked with confidence to form compound words, often because the context is unambiguous, and the proposed first element lacks any inflection which would force us to consider it as a separate word. For example, *medo* and *drince*, and *stan* and *clifu* in *The Seafarer* folio 81b, line 15, may be linked to form compounds, but not *ganetes* and *hleopor* (fol. 81b lines 13–14), because of the genitive singular ending of *ganetes*.

Where we have an uninflected adjective followed by a noun, ambiguity may result; we then have the option of leaving the words separate or joining them to make a compound. The decision has to be made with the help of contextual clues. In the opening section of *The Wanderer* several such decisions have to be made, for example, concerning *werig* and *mod* (15), and *hreo* and *hyge* (16). Dunning and Bliss make the point that editors who join *werig* and *mod* should also join *hreo* and *hyge*, because of the obvious parallelism between the two lines:

> Ne mæg werig mod　　wyrde wiðstondan,
> ne se hreo hyge　　helpe gefremman.[27]　(15–16)

In my edition I had destroyed the parallelism between them by reading *werigmod* (15) and *hreo hyge* (16). I concede that there are no compelling linguistic or structural reasons for making the former a compound, and am glad to restore the parallelism by concurring in the Dunning and Bliss reading of *werig* and *mod* as separate words.

There is a similar situation in *The Wanderer*, with the unique sequences of *winter* and *cearig* (24) and *sele* and *dreorig* (25):

> wod wintercearig　　ofer waþe[m]a gebind,
> sohte seledreorig　　sinces bryttan.[28]　(24–25)

As a compound, *wintercearig* has two possible meanings, "worn with winter cares" or, "worn with the cares of age" (of "many winters"), either of which would fit the context well. The interpretation of the relationship between *sele* and *dreorig* is another matter. Did the wanderer, sad, seek the hall of a giver of treasure? Or, hall-sad (that is, sad at the loss of the hall company), did he seek a giver of treasure? The latter reading is probably the more acceptable one in Old English and gives a compound which can be looked upon as an echo of *wintercearig* in the previous line.

Sele occurs again, in line 34: *Gemon he selesecgas ond sincþege*, "he remembers hall-retainers and the receiving of treasure." Parallels such as the undisputed compounds, *seleþegn*, "hall-thane" (1794) and *seldguma*, "hallman" (249) in *Beowulf* justify a compound *selesecgas*. The *Beowulf* contexts indicate retainers of a rather lowly status, the servants in the hall, rather than the warriors' peers, and we can infer a similar meaning for *selesecgas*. As a compound it would appear to be supported stylistically by its balance with *sincþege*. If we do not read it as a compound we weaken the dramatic impact of the lines by having the wanderer remember "the hall, the men and the gift-receiving." The first and the last memory are connected, but *secgas*, which by itself has no connection with the hall or any of its ceremonies, is there like the unwanted guest at a party. Moreover, the balance of the line is destroyed. It is structurally a self-contained unit and needs internal balance. The *hu* clause that follows is like *selesecgas* and *sincþege*, dependent on *gemon*, but remains structurally distinct.

The Wife's Lament, Het mec hlaford min her heard niman (15), is difficult to interpret, whether we read *her heard* as two separate words or as a compound.[29] Some scholars have taken *heard*, "stern," as an adjective modifying *hlaford*, "lord," but to have a noun separated from its modifier by a possessive pronoun and an adverb is unidiomatic. Moreover, if we read *her* and *heard* as separate words, we have a metrically defective line with double alliteration in the second half. If we combine the two words, we have not only a unique compound, but one that has no parallels in Old English literature. Emendation of *heard* to *eard* can be justified by postulating accidental repetition of *h* from the previous word, and produces the idiomatic expression *eard niman* "to take up residence." Basically we have to make a decision as to whether we have two separate words or one compound. The reflection of the phrase, *her heard niman* in *on þissum londstede*, "in this country" (16b), appears to me to be a factor to be added to the other considerations discussed, in favor, not only of retaining separate words, but of the emendation of *heard* to *eard*.

As may be deduced from the foregoing analyses, the ideal editor should be part literary critic and part philologist. He has considerable powers to influence our understanding of a poem, and considerable opportunities to abuse that power. The critic in him may succumb to the temptation to come to the text with a ready-made theory about its style and meaning, and thus see only that evidence which fits his theory. That almost any theory can be made to fit a poem can be seen from the spectrum of critical assessment of *The Wanderer* and *The Seafarer*, which has ranged from seeing them as simple sea poems, through elegiac lyrics, to allegories of recondite Christian doctrine.

The philologist in the editor makes him examine small contexts in great detail. He is apt to take, and indeed should take, a worm's-eye view of the poem, submitting himself to the discipline involved in the close scrutiny of small units. By working outwards from a narrow context he may perceive what others overlook; he will be less tempted to generalize on the basis of insufficient evidence. But he must also be aware of the danger of dealing in unrelated fragments. Kenneth Sisam warned us that intensive study of a text with a strong bias towards the manuscript reading may blunt the sense of style.[30] But if we are too confident in our pronouncements on style, without due regard to our limited knowledge, we will return to the excessively subjective judgments of a former age.

Even if our knowledge of Old English poetic patterns were to increase greatly, E. G. Stanley's doubts would remain valid,[31] and we may always have to content ourselves with looking through a glass darkly. However, intensive and thorough surveys, made possible by modern technology, may go some way toward compensating us for the small volume of the literature available to us. These would include the Old English dictionary, a KWIC concordance for the whole body of Old English poetry, Bruce Mitchell's volume on Old English syntax, and other specialized studies, such as Hans Schabram's books on *Superbia*,[32] on particular concepts and specific areas of the Old English vocabulary.

Notes

1. For a summary of the whole question of "textual criticism," see Leighton D. Reynolds and Nigel G. Wilson, *Scribes and Scholars: A Guide to the Transmission of Latin and Greek Literature* (2nd ed. London 1974) 187ff. A detailed study of the causes of corruption in manuscripts is to be found in James Willis, *Latin Textual Criticism* (Urbana Ill. 1972). See also E. J. Kenney, *The Classical Text* (Berkeley 1974), and the replacement for the third edition of Paul Maas, *Textkritik* (Stuttgart 1957) requested by his publishers from Martin L. West, and published by them in 1973 as *Textual Criticism and Editorial Technique*.

2. George Kane, "Conjectural Emendation," based on a paper read to the Oxford Medieval Society in 1966, was originally published in *Medieval Literature and Civilization: Studies in Memory of G. N. Garmonsway*, ed. Derek A. Pearsall and R. A. Waldron (London 1969) 155–69. It has been reprinted in *Medieval Manuscripts and Textual Criticism*, ed. Christopher Kleinhenz, North Carolina Studies in the Romance Languages and Literatures: Symposia, No. 4 (Chapel Hill N.C. 1976) 213 (referred to below as Kleinhenz).

3. Eugene Vinaver, "Principles of Textual Emendation," published originally in *Studies in French Language and Mediaeval Literature: Presented to Professor Mildred K. Pope* (Manchester 1939) 351–69, and reprinted in Kleinhenz, 140.

4. Ibid. (in Kleinhenz) 157.

5. Kenneth Sisam, "The Authority of Old English Poetical Manuscripts," published originally in *Review of English Studies* 22 (1946) 257–68, and reprinted in his *Studies in the History of Old English Literature* (Oxford 1953) 29–44.

6. Ibid. (in *Studies*) 39.

7. Kane (in Kleinhenz, n. 2 above) 225.

8. Roy F. Leslie, ed., *The Wanderer* (Manchester 1966) 76–80.

9. Thomas P. Dunning and Alan J. Bliss, eds., *The Wanderer* (London 1969) 14, 111 (footnote to line 33).

10. Bruce Mitchell, "Linguistic Facts and the Interpretation of Old English Poetry," *Anglo-Saxon England* 4 (1975) 11–28.

11. Ibid. 11.

12. Leslie (n. 8 above) 61. "Thus spoke the wanderer, mindful of hardships, of dreadful massacres, [of] the fall of kinsmen." I believed then that *hryre* could be a genitive. I now feel that the form should be *hryres*.

13. Nora Kershaw, *Anglo-Saxon and Norse Poems* (Cambridge 1922) notes to lines 6–7.

14. "relate my journeys, how I in days of toil often suffered times of hardship, have experienced bitter breast-care, had many abodes/experiences of care on a ship." For the text see Ida L. Gordon, ed., *The Seafarer* (London 1960) 33.

15. Ibid. 33 *n.*

16. "So it happened long ago, that we tested the waves over the tumult of the surf on a ship." For the text see George P. Krapp, ed., *The Vercelli Book*, *The Anglo-Saxon Poetic Records* (hereafter *ASPR*) 2 (New York 1932) 15.

17. "Weland had for himself experience of persecution by the sword, the resolute nobleman, suffered hardships, had for his company sorrow and longing." For the text see *ASPR* 3 (New York 1936) 178.

18. Ibid. 35.

19. Donald K. Fry, ed., *Finnsburh: Fragment and Episode* (London 1974) 42–43; Introduction 20–22.

20. Translated by George N. Garmonsway and Jacqueline Simpson, *Beowulf and its Analogues* (London 1968) 31.

21. Fry (n. 19 above) 21.

22. *ASPR* 3, lxxvi–lxxxi.

23. Dunning and Bliss (n. 9 above) 4–7.

24. See review of Dunning and Bliss by Stanley B. Greenfield in *Notes and Queries* 215 (1970) 115.

25. "Therefore he knows the one who has had long to forgo the counsel of his dear lord how when sorrow and sleep both together often bind the wretched solitary one it seems to him in his mind that he embraces and kisses his liege lord and on his knee lays his hands and head as he at times before in days gone by had enjoyed the throne then the friendless man awakes again sees before him the fallow waves the sea-birds bathing spreading their feathers he sees the frost and snow falling mixed with hail." For the text see Leslie (n. 8 above) 62 (caps. and punct. omitted).

26. Dunning and Bliss (n. 9 above) 21.

27. "Nor can the weary spirit withstand fate, nor the troubled breast afford help." Ibid. 107.

28. Leslie (n. 8 above) 61; see 70 for commentary.
29. Roy F. Leslie, ed., *Three Old English Elegies* (Manchester 1961) 47.
30. Sisam, in *Studies* (n. 5 above) 39.
31. See E. G. Stanley's paper in this volume.
32. Hans Schabram, *Superbia* I (Munich 1965).

Anglo-Saxons on the Mind

M. R. GODDEN

ETER Clemoes's essay '*Mens absentia cogitans* in *The Seafarer* and *The Wanderer*'[1] drew attention to important similarities between the psychological theories of the patristic tradition and the way in which Anglo-Saxon poets present the workings of the mind. Further exploration has begun to show how rich a seam he has opened up, of interest for Old English prose as well as poetry. Anglo-Saxon writers have important and often novel things to say about the nature of the mind and soul, and their discussions touch significantly on a problem of continuing interest, the relationship of psychological ideas and linguistic expression. What follows is the product of some rather tentative researches on this subject.

Two distinct traditions of thought about the mind are evident among the Anglo-Saxons. There is, first of all, a classical tradition represented by Alcuin of York (writing in Latin and on the continent, but influential for Anglo-Saxon vernacular writers), King Alfred and Ælfric of Eynsham, who were consciously working in a line which went back through late antique writers such as St Augustine and Boethius to Plato, but developed that tradition in interesting and individual ways. In particular they show the gradual development of a unitary concept of the inner self, identifying the intellectual mind with the immortal soul and life-spirit. Secondly, there is a vernacular tradition more deeply rooted in the language, represented particularly by the poets but occasionally reflected even in the work of Alfred and Ælfric. It was a tradition which preserved the ancient distinction of soul and mind, while associating the mind at least as much with passion as with intellect.

The Classical Tradition

Alcuin

The psychological literature of the Christian Middle Ages is said to begin with Alcuin's *De animae ratione*.[2] Alcuin draws heavily on earlier writers, including Augustine, Cassian and probably Lactantius, but develops his own distinctive views, which are of considerable interest quite apart from their influence on later Anglo-Saxon writers using the vernacular. As his title indicates, his concern is with the soul, but he understands the soul as primarily an intellectual faculty. He begins, it is true, by acknowledging the old Platonic division of the soul into three parts, the rational, irascible and concupiscible:

> Triplex est enim animae, ut philosophi uolunt, natura: est in ea quaedam pars concupiscibilis, alia rationalis, tertia irascibilis. Duas enim habent harum partes nobiscum bestiae et animalia communes, id est, concupiscentiam et iram. Homo solus inter mortales ratione uiget, consilio ualet, intelligentia antecellit. Sed his duobus, id est, concupiscentiae et irae, ratio, quae mentis propria est, imperare debet.

Here Alcuin seems to accept the traditional view, passed down to him through Augustine, that the soul embraces intellect, passion and desire, and is partially shared with the animals. However, he goes on to say that the principal part of the soul is the mind (*mens*) and is soon equating the soul with the rational mind: 'Una est anima, quae mens dicitur', he says; the soul or mind (*anima uel animus*) is 'an intellectual, rational spirit'; the soul (*anima*) is 'the spirit of life, but not of that life which is in animals, lacking a rational mind'. After the initial obeisance to Plato, Alcuin takes the soul as more or less identical with the conscious, rational mind.

In equating the soul with the mind Alcuin is consciously differing from Augustine, who consistently distinguishes the two. For Augustine the mind is only the better part of the human soul, which also has lesser parts which are shared with the animals. The soul is for him more a life-spirit than an intellectual spirit. 'Not the soul, therefore, but that which excels in the soul is called mind', he says.[3] The deliberateness of Alcuin's change is clear enough if one watches him reworking Augustine on the triad of memory, will and understanding:

> Haec igitur tria, memoria, intellegentia, uoluntas, quoniam non sunt tres uitae sed una uita, nec tres mentes sed una mens, consequenter utique nec tres substantiae sunt sed una substantia. Memoria quippe

quod uita et mens et substantia dicitur ad se ipsam dicitur; quod uero memoria dicitur ad aliquid relatiue dicitur.

(Augustine, *De trinitate* x.ii)

Una est enim *anima* quae mens dicitur una uita et una substantia, quae haec tria habet in se: sed haec tria non sunt tres uitae, sed una uita; nec tres mentes, sed una mens; nec tres substantiae sunt, sed una substantia. Quod uero *anima* uel mens, uel uita, uel substantia dicitur, ad seipsam dicitur; quod uero memoria uel intelligentia uel uoluntas dicitur, ad aliquid relatiue dicitur.

(Alcuin, *De animae ratione*, ch. 6; my italics)

It is possible that Alcuin's awareness of the issue was strengthened by his reading of Lactantius, who devotes a chapter of his *De opificio Dei* to the question whether the soul and mind are the same thing and presents some arguments on both sides, without coming to a conclusion.[4] In making the equation Alcuin broadly sets the pattern for subsequent academic discussion down to Aquinas, although writers differ on the degree of identity; but as we shall see, the primitive and popular notion of a soul quite distinct from the mind and devoid of psychological powers continues in vernacular literature.

Alcuin's interest is particularly in the way that the soul's mental activity mirrors God, as a testimony to its spiritual nature and high status: the soul, he says, 'is ennobled with the image and likeness of the Creator in its principal part, which is called the *mens*'. The interrelationships of memory, understanding and will mirror the divine Trinity. The mind's ability to conjure up images of things both known and unknown mimics God's work as creator. Its ability to be mentally present in an instant at any point in the world or in time imitates the divine ability to be everywhere at all times.

What is striking about this view of the soul's mental powers is Alcuin's insistence that the soul's likeness to God resides in its engagement with the real material world. For Augustine the imagination is a dubious faculty, and the mind resembles God only in so far as it contemplates eternal truths rather than 'the handling of temporal things'; engagement with the senses belongs to an inferior part of the soul.[5] For Alcuin it is the mind's power to remember or imagine people and places that shows its God-like quality. Even dreaming is a reflection of the soul's high powers in Alcuin's view.[6] He emphasizes that the soul is invisible, bodiless, without weight or colour, but it is also, and properly, engaged with material reality and illusions of reality. There is for him no essential conflict in the soul between the activity of the rational mind and the realms of imagination and sensation. Similarly, the

Platonic and Augustinian notion of a war within the soul between reason, desire and passion finds some reflection in Alcuin's account, but he primarily sees the latter powers as spiritual forces, designed for the needs of the soul rather than the body. Vicious or irrational behaviour in man is not simply the victory of the lower elements of the soul over the reason, but reflects the free will of the conscious mind, to choose good or evil.

For Alcuin, then, there is a unitary inner self identified both with the conscious rational mind and the immortal life-spirit and God-like in its power, including (indeed especially) the creative and poetic powers of imagination and dream.

Alfred

The influence of Alcuin's treatise first appears in England itself with King Alfred's translation of Boethius's treatise *De consolatione Philosophiae*.[7] In bk III, met. ix Boethius gives an account of the universe drawn mainly from Plato's *Timaeus*. It is quite the most difficult and challenging section of the whole work, and became a focal point in the commentaries of the tenth century.[8] In the course of the poem Boethius refers in passing to the threefold soul. Most commentators agree that he is talking about the World Soul (the three parts are Same, Other and Being according to modern commentators, and earth, sea and sky according to some ninth- and tenth-century commentators), though some early commentaries also mention the Platonic notion of the threefold human soul.[9] Alfred takes it as a reference to the human soul and gives an explanation which is clearly drawn from Alcuin's account (quoted above, p. 272):

> Forþi ic cwæð þæt sio sawul wære þreofeald, forþamþe uðwitan secgað
> þæt hio hæbbe þrio gecynd. An ðara gecynda is þæt heo bið wilni-
> gende, oðer þæt hio bið irsiende, þridde þæt hio bið gesceadwis. Twa
> þara gecynda habbað netenu swa same swa men; oðer þara is wilnung,
> oðer is irsung. Ac se man ana hæfð gesceadwisnesse, nalles na oðrum
> gesceaft; forði he hæfð oferþungen ealle þa eorðlican gesceafta mid
> geðeahte and mid andgite. Forþam seo gesceadwisnes sceal wealdan
> ægðer ge þære wilnunga ge þæs yrres, forþamþe hio is synderlic cræft
> þære saule.   (81/16–25)

It is possible that the passage reached Alfred via a commentary or gloss, but no such commentary has yet been found, and in any case Alcuin's work was certainly available in England at a later date. It seems likely, therefore, that Alfred knew the whole work. His treatment of the soul and mind in his translation of Boethius shows distinct similarities to Alcuin's ideas. Boethius himself is careful to keep mind and soul separate. He nearly always refers to the centre of human consciousness as the *mens* or *animus*, occasionally as the *cor*. Desire of good is naturally implanted in the mind, he says; passions assail the mind; the mind rises to heaven to contemplate God. If he speaks of the soul, *anima*, it is for special reasons, as when he is referring to the soul which exists before and after the life of the individual, or the soul which is common to animals as well as men.[10] The soul is for him both greater than the human mind or consciousness, as pre-existing it, and less, since it is also found in animals. He seems, indeed, to suggest that the soul becomes the mind, and thereby loses some of its powers, when it becomes imprisoned within the body. Alfred, however, frequently substitutes *sawl* for Boethius's *mens* or *cor* in reference to the inner self,[11] and seems to treat mind (*mod*) and soul (*sawl*) as very closely related concepts. Boethius's seed of truth in the heart becomes Alfred's seed of truth dwelling in the soul when the soul and body are joined.[12] The health of minds, *salus animorum*, becomes *sawla hælo*.[13] *Sawl* and *mod* are interchanged in this passage, for instance, from the end of bk II, pr. 7:

> Sio sawl færð swiðe friolice to hefonum, siððan hio ontiged bið, and of þæm carcerne þæs lichoman onlesed bið. Heo forsihð þonne eall ðas eorðlican þing, and fægnað þæs þæt hio mot brucan þæs heofonlican siððan hio bið abrogden from ðæm eorðlican. Þonne þæt mod him selfum gewita bið Godes willan.   (45/27–32)

The first two sentences parallel Boethius's statement about the *mens;* the last is Alfred's addition. Alfred seems to have been content with Boethius's view of the conscious rational mind as the essential inner self but wanted to emphasize its identity with the soul or immortal life-spirit. The same equation is made in Alfred's Soliloquies, and particularly in his great affirmation towards the end of that work: 'Nu ic gehyre þæt min sawel is æcu and a lifað, and eall þæt min mod and min gescadwisnesse goodra crefta gegadrad, þæt mot þa simle habban, and ic gehere æac þæt min gewit is æce.'[14] Indeed, Alfred offers a proof that the individual *mod* has existed since Creation and will survive the body, and has his persona reply: 'Me ðincð nu þæt þu hæbbe genoh swetole gesæd þæt ælces mannes sawl nu si, and a beo, and were syððan god ærest þone forman man gescop.'[15] (This notion of the pre-existence of souls was later to be challenged by Ælfric.) The close association of soul and rational mind is also reflected in the one significant change which Alfred makes to Alcuin's statement of the Platonic doctrine of the threefold soul: where Alcuin had said that *ratio* is the special property of the mind ('ratio quae mentis propria est'), Alfred calls reason the distinctive property of the *soul* ('hio is synderlic cræft þære saule'), thus bringing the statement into line with Alcuin's later point that the soul is a rational spirit.

Perhaps because he identifies mind and soul Alfred tends to personalize the mind, treating it as a kind of inner self or personality. He frequently substitutes *mod* for the 'I' or 'me' of Boethius, and indeed creates a personification *Mod* who takes the place of the 'I' of the Latin text in the dialogue with Philosophy:

> Þa ic þa þis leoð, cwæð Boetius, geomriende asungen hæfde, þa com þær gan in to me heofencund Wisdom, and þæt min murnende mod mid his wordum gegrette, and þus cwæð . . . Ða eode se Wisdom near, cwæð Boetius, minum hreowsiendum geþohte, and hit swa niowul þa hwæthwega up arærde; adrigde þa mines modes eagan, and hit fran bliþum wordum hwæðer it oncneowe his fostermodor. Mid þam þe ða þæt Mod wið his bewende, þa gecneow hit swiðe sweotele his agne modor.						(8/15–9/1)

Mod can be used as the subject of verbs: 'ælc mod wilnað soðes godes to begitanne' (53/11). The same tendency to use *mod* rather than the first person pronoun is evident in Alfred's translation of Gregory's *Regula pastoralis*.

Like Alcuin, Alfred attributes a very high status to the mind. In this he follows Boethius, but he sometimes takes the argument further. In bk v Boethius distinguishes four levels of understanding; *sensus*, or the physical senses, which the lowest animals have; *imaginatio* (a limited ability to recognize and understand shapes and identities), which is found in higher animals; reason, which is found in men; and *intelligentia*, a direct perception of ultimate truth and forms, which is the divine understanding. Alfred follows him on *sensus*, which he calls 'andgit'; has doubts over *imaginatio*, which he renders 'rædels' (presumably meaning conjecture) but then drops from discussion; agrees in ascribing reason (*gesceadwisnes*) to men; but then attributes *intelligentia*, translated as 'gewis andgit', certain or direct understanding, to angels and wise men, not just to God. Intellectually, in his view, man can reach the level of the angels. Similarly, he elsewhere interjects a remark that only men and angels have reason: 'nis nan þe hæbbe friodom and gesceadwisnesse buton englum and monnum'.[16] What seems particularly to interest Alfred in the Platonic theory of the threefold soul is not its power to explain the interplay of intellect and passion in man, but its placing of man intellectually above the animals and close to God and the angels. Trapped within the human body is an essentially rational inner self, called *mod* or *sawl*; it has existed since the beginning of time and will survive the body till the end of time. It is in supreme control of the self, and grief, ignorance and vice are attributes of the *mod*, not of some lesser part of the soul or the body:

> Eala þæt hit is micel cræft þæs modes for þone lichoman. Be swilcum and be swylcum þu miht ongitan þæt se cræft þæs lichoman bið on þam mode, and þætte ælcum men ma deriað his modes unþeawas. Ðæs modes unþeawas tioð eallne þone lichoman to him, and þæs lichoman mettrumnes ne mæg þæt mod eallunga to him getion.   (116/29–34)

Only once in his translation of Boethius does Alfred use the word *gast*, 'spirit', and that instance is intriguing. Boethius says that some activities of the individual are the result of natural impulses rather than conscious volition, and he gives as one example drawing breath while we sleep: 'quod in somno spiritum ducimus nescientes' (III, pr. II). Alfred takes *spiritum* in a different sense and speaks of our spirit wandering abroad while we sleep, without us wishing it or having power over it:

> Swa eac ure gast bið swiðe wide farende urum unwillum and ures ungewealdes for his gecynde, nalles for his willan; þæt bið þonne we slapað.   (93/6–9)

The reference is presumably to dreaming. Alcuin mentions dreaming as an activity of the soul and also uses journeying outside the body as an image of thought and imagination, but he is insistent that the soul does not actually leave the body except at death. Alfred seems to be referring to actual journeying, and his emphasis that it is not guided by our conscious volition or control makes it unlikely that he sees it as an activity of the mind or soul as these are understood by him. Hence the use of *gast* rather than *sawl*. Alfred seems to be reflecting the common folk-belief that in dreams and trances an inner spirit or soul (usually quite distinct from the conscious mind) leaves the body and wanders about in the world.[17] The remark is prompted by a misunderstanding of Boethius's Latin text, but Alfred would hardly have interpreted the text in this way if he had not been thoroughly familiar with the idea and given it some credence. What it suggests is a distinction between the *sawl*, which is identified with the conscious mind and the immortal life-spirit, and the *gast*, which represents a kind of alien subconscious. But it may be that Alfred is referring to two quite separate traditions without seeking to reconcile them.

Ælfric

Writing a century later Ælfric draws on both Alcuin and Alfred for his own main treatise on the nature of the mind. The text exists in three versions, probably all by Ælfric, although the interrelationships (on which see Appendix, below, pp. 296–8) are complex: a Latin version, found in a Boulogne manuscript of Latin texts all associated with Ælfric; an English version, occurring as the first item in Ælfric's Lives of Saints collection; and a later English version surviving only in a twelfth-century manuscript.[18] My discussion will deal mainly with the second of these, the most familiar and accessible. The first third of the text is on the nature of God and the ways in which he differs from man and the rest of creation; several passages are adapted from Alfred's translation of Boethius,[19] others show resemblances to discussions of the same themes elsewhere in Ælfric's work. The remainder of the text is on the nature of the soul and is mainly drawn from Alcuin's *De animae ratione*.[20]

Ælfric accepts Alcuin's belief in the primarily intellectual character of the soul, and takes over his discussion of the soul's comprehensive imaginative power, its supreme control within the individual, the likeness between the Trinity and the soul's own triad of memory, understanding and will, and the soul's manifestation under different names according to its different intellectual functions. However, he seems uncomfortable with Alcuin's tendency to use soul and mind as interchangeable terms. Alcuin's reference to the mind as the principal part of the soul is omitted, and in the discussion of memory, will and understanding, where Augustine had spoken of the mind only and Alcuin had referred to the mind and the soul as equivalents, Ælfric carefully specifies the soul only:

> An sawul is and an lif and an edwist, þe þas ðreo þing hæfð on hire,
> and þas ðreo ðing na synd na ðreo lif ac an, ne þreo edwiste ac an. Seo
> sawul oððe þæt lif oððe seo edwist synd gecwædene to hyre sylfra.
> (LS, no. i, lines 114–18; cf. above, p. 272, for Augustine and Alcuin)

Similarly, Alcuin's statement that the soul or mind (*anima uel animus*) is an intellectual, rational spirit becomes in Ælfric simply 'the soul is a rational spirit' ('seo sawul is gesceadwis gast': LS, no. i, line 171). Ælfric had used Alcuin's passage on the memory, will and understanding in an earlier work and there too omitted the reference to mind.[21] The reason is not, I think, that he shares Augustine's view that the soul includes lesser elements as well as the mind, for he clearly sees the soul as an intellectual power and attributes to the soul what Augustine would ascribe to the mind. For the same reason it is not that he shares the more popular view of the soul as the treasure to be guarded by the mental faculties. The soul is distinctly the thinking power or agent in Ælfric's account. The point is perhaps rather that, while seeing a very close association between the soul and the mind, he prefers to think of the mind as the instrument or locus of the soul rather than an inner personalized spirit or self, as Alcuin and Alfred see it. Thus Alcuin says that a man pictures Rome in his mind, and he describes the process as the mind returning to the memory and the soul forming a figure or image; soul and mind seem to be, once again, variations on synonyms. Ælfric speaks of the soul creating the city in her thought ('on hire geþohte') and, again, creating in her mind ('on hire mode') whatever she hears spoken of.[22] the distinction perhaps arose from an attempt to impose clarity on an inherited nomenclature. Having identified the *sawl* as the intellectual faculty Ælfric was perhaps reluctant to treat *mod* as a mere synonym, though he acknowledges that it is the name by which we refer to the soul in its knowledge and understanding rôles.

Because the soul is, in Ælfric's view, the intellectual, rational self, its possession distinguishes man from the beasts and places him close to the angels. This is the theme of the first section of his treatise, before he begins to draw on Alcuin. Ælfric's particular interest here and elsewhere is not so much the soul's likeness to God as the theme of hierarchy; that is, the place which man's possession of mind and soul allots him in the chain of being. Thus he takes from Alfred the distinction between God, who has no beginning or end; angels and men, who have beginning but no end; and animals who have both beginning and end:

> Wast þu þæt þreo ðing sindon on þis middangearde? An is hwilendlic, ðæt hæfð ægðer ge fruman ge ende; and nat ðeah nanwuht ðæs ðe hwilendlic is, nauðer ne his fruman ne his ende. Oðer ðing is ece, þæt hæfð fruman and næfð nænne ende; and wat hwonne hit onginð, and wat þæt hit næfre ne geendað; þæt sint englas and monna saula. Þridde ðing is ece buton ende and buton anginne; þæt is God.
>
> (Alfred's Boethius, 147/25–148/3)

> Ðreo þing synd on middanearde, an is hwilwendlic, þe hæfð ægðer ge ordfruman ge ende, þæt synd nytenu and ealle sawul-lease þing þe ongunnan þa þa hi god gesceop, and æft geændiað and to nahte gewurðaþ. Oðer þing is ece, swa þæt hit hæfð ordfruman and næfð nænne ende, þæt synd ænglas and manna saula, þe ongunnen ða þa hi god gesceop, ac hi ne geendiað næfre. Ðridde þing is ece, swa þæt hit næfð naðor ne ordfruman ne ende, þæt is se ana ælmihtiga god.
>
> (LS, no. i, lines 25–32)

Similarly he takes Alfred's version of Boethius, bk v, met. v to show the separation of man from the animals, but develops it through his own successive recastings to emphasize man's intellectual place with respect to animals, angels and God.[23]

The opening of the discussion of the soul shows the same interest in hierarchy. All *catholici* agree that the soul is like God and created by him but not made of his nature. The philosophers say that the soul is threefold, partially resembling the beasts but greater than them:

> Uþwytan sæcgað þæt þære sawle gecynd is ðryfeald. An dæl is on hire gewylnigendlic, oðer yrsigendlic, þrydde gesceadwislic. Twægen þissera dæla habbað deor and nytenu mid us, þæt is gewylnunge and yrre. Se man ana hæð gescead and ræd and andgit.   (LS, no. 1, 96–100)

(Ælfric is here drawing on Alcuin by way of his own Latin adaptation, but verbal resemblances to Alfred's version of the same passage suggest that Ælfric may have recalled that version.)

The identification of the soul with the intellectual faculty and the concern with man's place in the chain of being are reflected in Ælfric's insistent denial that animals have souls. St Augustine identifies the soul with the life-spirit and naturally attributes souls to animals, and indeed to all living beings; it is the rational soul, alias the mind, that man alone possesses.[24] Alcuin generally avoids the question, but one sentence in his treatise suggests a rejection of Augustine's view: 'the soul is the spirit of life, but not of that life which is in animals, lacking a rational mind'.[25] Alfred seems prepared to follow Boethius in attributing souls to animals, though his mind was perhaps uncertain on the issue. His use of Alcuin's passage on the threefold soul does not necessarily imply that animals have souls, as Otten has suggested,[26] especially since Alfred changes the last clause so as to say that reason (the element not shared by animals) is the special property of the soul. He recasts Boethius's clearest reference to animals having souls,[27] but two adjacent passages do seem to imply that the possession of a soul extends beyond human beings:

> Ælc wuht wolde bion hal and libban, þara þe me cwucu ðincð; bute ic nat be treowum and be wyrtum, and be swelcum gesceaftum swelce nane sawle nabbað.   (91/8–11)

> Ne þearft ðu no tweogan ymbe þæt þe þu ær tweodest, þæt is be þam gesceaftum þe nane sawle nabbað; ælc þara gesceafta þe sawle hæfð, ge eac þa þe nabbað, willniað simle to bionne.   (93/24–7)

Ælfric, however, repeatedly rejects the view that animals have souls. He makes the point at least a dozen times in his various writings, always, so far as I can discover, as a personal interjection in the argument of any authority that he is following. One might note, for instance, his rendering of one of Alcuin's *Interrogationes:*

Inter omnia animantia terrae nullum rationale inueniebatur nisi ille solus.

Nan nyten næfde nan gescead ne sawle buton he ana.[28]

(The reference is to Adam.) He similarly recasts a passage from Gregory the Great which implies that animals have souls though plants do not:

Sunt herbae et arbusta: uiuunt quidem, sed non sentiunt. Viuunt dico, non per animam, sed per uiriditatem . . . [citing I Cor. xv.36] . . . Bruta uero animalia sunt, uiuunt, sentiunt, sed non discernunt.

(PL 76, col. 1214)

Gærs and treowa lybbað butan felnysse; hi ne lybbað na ðurh sawle, ac ðurh heora grennysse. Nytenu lybbað and habbað felnysse, butan gesceade: hi nabbað nan gescead, forðan ðe hi sind sawullease.

(CH I, p. 302)

The point is often linked by Ælfric with animals' lack of reason, as in these two passages, but also with their own mortality, as in this incidental exchange in a saint's legend:

Canis enim pro factis malis in ignem aeternum non mittetur, sed semel mortuus, et corpore simul moritur et flatu.

Hund is sawulleas and on helle ne ðrowað.[29]

The soul is essentially both rational and immortal, and cannot therefore be ascribed to animals. Ælfric's repeated insistence on the point suggests that he was consciously taking issue with others, perhaps his contemporaries, perhaps his patristic authorities, perhaps Alfred.

Alcuin's passing reference to the subject in De animae ratione seems unlikely to have been enough to explain Ælfric's confidence and insistence on the point. Another possible influence is Cassiodorus, ch. 3 of whose De anima begins with the words 'anima is properly applied to man, not to animals, because their life is based on the blood'.[30] One of Ælfric's statements on the subject, in fact possibly his earliest, is quite close to this:

He ne sealde nanum nytene ne nanum fisce nane sawle; ac heora blod is heora lif, and swa hraðe swa hi beoð deade, swa beoð hi mid ealle geendode.

(CH I, p. 16)

That Ælfric knew Cassiodorus's treatise is suggested by a very close parallel in his main discussion of the mind, interjected in a passage that is otherwise drawn from Alcuin:

Paruulis enim ratio crescit longa meditatione, non anima.
(Cassiodorus, De anima, ch. 7, lines 57–8)

Paruulis enim ratio crescit, non anima, et proficiendo ad uirtutem non maior fit, sed melior, nec corporalem recepit quantitatem.
(Ælfric, Boulogne text, ed. Leinbaugh)

Gescead wexð on cildrum na seo sawul, and seo sawul þihþ on mægenum and ne bið na mare þonne heo æt fruman wæs ac bið betere, ne heo ne underfehð lichomlice mycelnysse.   (LS, no. i, lines 110–12)

The latter part of Ælfric's interpolated comment resembles not Cassiodorus but the latter's source, Augustine's De quantitate animae:

. . . proficiendo enim ad uirtutem peruenit . . . quidquid anima cum aetate proficit . . . non mihi uidetur fieri maior, sed melior.
(PL 32, col. 1051)

But the first part is clearly from Cassiodorus rather than Augustine. Ælfric perhaps added the point as an answer to the problem raised by associating the soul with the intellect, which might be taken to suggest that the dimension or 'degree' of soul in an individual varies with his intellectual powers. This may be one reason why he seems to shun an actual identification of soul with mind.

One other text known to Ælfric makes a point of denying that animals have souls: namely, a passage entitled De sabbato in a work known as the Excerptiones Egberti:

Homines creat in animabus et corporibus, et animalia et bestias sine animabus; omnis anima hominis a Deo datur, et ipse renouat creaturas suas.[31]

The work shows many close parallels with Ælfric's pastoral letters, and the De sabbato passage is undoubtedly closely related to a passage in one of his homilies:

Deus Creator omnium creauit hominem in sexta feria, et in sabbato requieuit ab operibus suis, et sanctificauit sabbatum propter futuram significationem passionis Christi, et quietis in sepulchro. Non ideo requieuit quia lassus esset, qui omnia sine labore fecit, cuius omnipotentia non potest lassari; et sic requieuit ab operibus suis, ut non alias creaturas quam antea fecerat postea fecisset. Non fecit alias creaturas postea, sed ipsas quas tunc fecit, omni anno usque in finem seculi facit. Homines creat in animabus et corporibus, et animalia et bestias sine animabus; omnis anima hominis a Deo datur, et ipse renouat creat-

uras suas, sicut Christus in Euuangelio ait: 'Pater meus usquemodo
operatur, et ego operor.' . . . Et nos ipsi debemus esse spiritaliter sabbatum sabbatizantes, id est, uacantes ab operibus seruitutis, id est,
peccatis.

On six dagum geworhte god ealle gesceafta . and geendode hi on ðam
seofoðan . þæt is se sæternesdæg . þa gereste he hine . and ðone dæg
gehalgode; Ne gereste he hine for ði þæt he werig wære . se ðe ealle
ðing deð buton geswince . ac he geswac ða his weorces; He geswac ðæs
dihtes ealra his weorca . ac he ne geswac na to gemenigfyldenne þæra
gesceafta æftergengnyssa; God geswac ða his weorces . swa þæt he na
ma gecynda siððan ne gesceop . ac swa ðeah he gemenigfylt dægh-
womlice þa ylcan gecynd swa swa crist cwæð on his godspelle; Pater
meus usque modo operatur . et ego operor; . . . Oðer restendæg is us
eac toweard . . . gif we nu ðeowtlicera weorca . þæt sind synna
geswicað;   (CH II, no. xii, 274–84 and 308–11)

However, the status of the *Excerptiones* is unclear. It is a rather fluid and un-
structured assembly of mainly ecclesiastical canons and biblical and patristic excerpts on the duties of the clergy and rules for the laity, varying considerably in order and content from one manuscript to another, and
thought to have been compiled in late Anglo-Saxon England. The most recent editor[32] argues that the author was one Hucarius, a deacon of St German's in Cornwall, but the evidence is very slight. The *De sabbato* passage
occurs in only one copy of the collection, in the eleventh-century Wulfstan
manuscript, now London, BL Cotton Nero A. i, and it is so extraordinarily
close in thought and expression to Ælfric's work (there are parallels with
other homilies as well as the one quoted) that one must at least entertain the
possibility that Ælfric himself wrote it; he may, indeed, have had a hand in
compiling the whole collection. If the *De sabbato* passage is not by him it
shows that someone else in Ælfric's time took an interest in the question of
animals and souls, but it is hardly enough to have determined Ælfric's own
views on the subject.

The topic is closely associated in Ælfric's thought with his views on the
origin of the individual soul. Augustine discusses various different theories,
including the possibility that the soul is derived from the parents, without
coming to a conclusion.[33] Cassiodorus does likewise, referring back to Augustine.[34] Alcuin, in his *De animae ratione*, offers only the general statement
that the soul derives from God. Alfred, as we have seen, states firmly in his
version of Augustine's *Soliloquia* that 'each man's soul has existed since the
first man was created'.[35] I do not know where he found this idea. It is not
from his main source (Augustine's *Soliloquia*) and the editors have suggested

> Þonne wið þon gesette us sanctus Petrus syðþan ꝺ oðerra cyricena eal-
> dormen þa halgan gangdagas þry, to ðam þæt we sceoldon on Gode
> ælmihtigum þiowigan mid usse gedefelice gange ꝺ mid sange ꝺ mid
> ciricena socnum ꝺ mid fæstenum ꝺ mid ælmessylenum ꝺ mid halegum
> gebedum. ꝺ we sculon beran usse reliquias ymb ure land, þa medeman
> Cristes rodetacen þe we Cristes mæl nemnað, on þam he sylfa þro-
> wode for mancynnes alysnesse.[82]

no parallels; the pre-existence of souls is taken for granted by Boethius, but there is nothing to match Alfred's proof. Ælfric sets his face firmly against such a view, insisting that the soul does not pre-exist the body but is shaped by God in an individual act of creation and implanted in the foetus:

> Ælces mannes sawl bið þurh God gesceapen . . . Þæs mannes antimber bið of ðam fæder and of ðære meder, ac God gescypð þone lichaman of ðam antimbre, and asent on þone lichaman sawle. Ne bið seo sawl nahwar wunigende æror, ac God hi gescypð þærrihte, and beset on ðone lichaman, and læt hi habban agenne cyre.   (CH I, pp. 292)

The point recurs repeatedly in his work, sometimes—as here—in opposition to the doctrine of the pre-existence of souls, sometimes in opposition to the theory (known as traducianism) that souls are derived from parents, sometimes specifying both, as in the following:

> God gescipð ælce dæge edniwe sawle and on lichaman geliffæst, swa swa we leorniað on bocum, and þa sawla ne beoð nahwær gesceapene ær þan þe God hi asent to þam gesceapenan lichaman on heora moder innoþum, and hi swa men wurþað. Nu ge magon tocnawan þæt ure sawla ne cumað of fæder ne of meder, ac se heofenlica Fæder gescipð þone lichaman and hine geliffæst mid sawle.[36]

It even finds a place in his Latin *uita* of St Æthelwold, where the saint's mother feels the soul entering the unborn child while attending mass, and Ælfric notes that this is an argument against the traducianist view:

> Iterum ipsa mater quadam die stans in aecclesia stipata ciuibus, causa sanctam missam audiendi, sensit uenisse animam pueri, quem gestabat in utero, et intrasse in eum, sicut postea ipse sanctus, qui nasciturus erat, iam episcopus, gaudendo nobis narrauit. Ex quo ostenditur eum electum Deo extitisse etiam antequam nasceretur, et animam hominis non a patre uel a matre uenire sed a solo creatore unicuique dari.[37]

None of Ælfric's discussions of the topic comes from the sources he was following; they are mainly successive reworkings of the same main points, usually in the context of Creation. His assurance on the point is striking: when he remarks in his very first homily that 'some people wonder where the soul comes from, the father or the mother; I say, from neither . . . ', he is, after all, referring not to the idle speculations of contemporaries but to the uncertainties of such authorities as Augustine and Cassiodorus as well as rejecting the certainties of Alfred. The 'as we read in books' (*swa swa we leorniað on bocum*) of the passage quoted above (p. 284) is provocatively

vague; the source is in fact Ælfric's own Second Series homily no. xii, which
is here, if anything, drawing on his first homily in the First Series and the
passage *De sabbato*, which has just the brief but probably significant 'omnis
anima hominis a Deo datur'. (The whole passage is reworked yet again in
Ælfric's *Hexameron*.)

Both doctrines on which Ælfric takes such a firm stand have obvious connections with his views on the mind and the soul. The soul is not just a life-
spirit but a rational and immortal spirit unique to man and created specifically by God for each individual, to endow him simultaneously with life and
understanding. It is primarily an intellectual inner self, whose mental activity
imitates God and distinguishes man from the beasts. The capacity for passion
and lust is a reflection not of some lower part of the soul but of the free will,
to choose good or evil, which is granted to the soul when it is created. Soul
and mind are thus very closely associated, although as a matter of terminology Ælfric prefers, at least when being careful, to call the intellectual inner
self *sawl*, reserving *mod* for the locus or instrument of the soul's thought.

The Vernacular Tradition

What we have seen so far are ideas about the mind and soul articulated by
writers who were building on the late antique intellectual tradition and familiar with the traditional Latin terminology. That other Anglo-Saxons
held quite different notions of the soul is suggested by a passing remark in
Ælfric's *De temporibus anni*, rejecting the theory that the soul is breath: 'Nis
na seo orðung ðe we utblawað . and innateoð ure sawul . ac is seo lyft þe we
on lybbað on ðisum deadlicum life.'[38] The remark is repeated in the two
English versions of his homily on the soul,[39] but nothing in the context or
sources of either work seems particularly to have prompted it. Its absence
from the Latin version of the treatise suggests that the ambiguity of Latin
spiritus is not at issue here. Presumably the primitive identification of soul
with breath was current among Ælfric's readers or listeners.

Outside the classical tradition consciously followed by Alfred and Ælfric, views on the mind and soul are not developed in any detail or rigour by
Anglo-Saxon writers, but there are often important implications in the way
that they talk about the mind, thought and emotion, and in the terminology
they use. The intimate relationship which exists between the psychological
ideas developed by a particular culture and the language in which those
ideas are expressed was emphasized by I. A. Richards in his *Mencius on the
Mind*. More recently the anthropologist Rodney Needham has discussed
the linguistic aspects of the concept of belief, and suggested that the psy-

chological terms used by different cultures may describe quite different inner experiences:

> If the inner states hypothetically in question are universal, it is to be expected that any language will have responded to them. On the other hand, we have to contemplate the possibility that some other linguistic tradition will have established (not simply named) an inner state for which English makes no provision.[40]

This is clearly as true of the language of the Anglo-Saxons as of living languages. As an example one might take the way in which emotion is expressed in Anglo-Saxon. The Modern English use of 'feel', adapted from terms of sensory perception, does not seem to occur in Old English; there is no equivalent to *feeling* sad, angry, hostile, affectionate; the verbs *gefelan* and *gefredan* seem only to be used of physical sensation. On the other hand it is quite common to speak of 'taking' various mental states, such as anger or love, using the verb *niman:* 'nimð lufe to Gode', 'gif ure mod nimð gelustfullunge', 'nam micelne graman and andan', 'genam nið', 'nam oferhygd', 'naman ondan', 'niman geleafan', 'niman mod', 'genom wynne', 'genaman æfest' and 'niman ellen'. A few similar usages to survive in Modern English but seem to be either rather archaic, petrified phrases ('take courage') or used to suggest a rather wilful, often artificial, variety of emotion ('take delight', 'take offence', 'take umbrage'). The Old English examples do not seem to be similarly restricted in tone. There was presumably some rooted sense that passions, or feelings towards other people and things, did not just take hold of one from outside or inside but involved, at some level, an act of will. Such uses link with the prevalence of active, simplex verbs for psychological states where Modern English has to use a periphrastic form with an adjective; *modigian* 'to be proud', *yrsian*, 'to be angry', *murnan*, 'to be sad', *gladian*, 'to be happy'. Linguistically, at least, passions can resemble mental actions rather than mental states.

A different kind of example is the term *ingehyd*, as it is used by Ælfric. Literally it means inner thought or inner mind, but it translates both *scientia* and *conscientia* in Latin and it is impossible to find a close equivalent for it in either Latin or Modern English. It very often means something like 'inner disposition', a quality of will, perhaps the direction of the will, but sometimes an aspect of love: 'let us love God with good *ingehyd*'; the church opens her *ingehyd* and secret thoughts to Christ; the ascetic life and *synderlic ingehyd*, 'solitary dedication'(?), of anchorites; St Martin retained inwardly the *muneclice ingehyd* ('monastic disposition'(?), but translating *uirtus*) while outwardly maintaining the rôle of a bishop; the sinful cleric perverts the *ingehyd* of his flock.[41] When it translates *conscientia* it seems to mean the inner mind or consciousness of innocence or guilt: 'our glory is the testimony of our *ingehyd*'; the righteous is afraid on the Day of Judgement, for although he has pleased God through *ingehyd*, the *ingehyd* (= *conscientia*) trembles there, frightened by the great terror of the general judgment.[42] When it translates *scientia* it means knowledge or understanding, but the only really informative context relates it to intuitive understanding rather than learned knowledge: St Matthew reports that the Holy Ghost at Pentecost gave the apostles *ingehyd* of all wisdom and all languages.[43] The term seems to cover both cognition and volition, as well as the inner self from which they proceed. Similar uses can be found in other Anglo-Saxon writers, and the freedom and confidence with which Ælfric uses the term suggests that it did represent a precise and meaningful concept.

The Anglo-Saxon terms for the mind itself present quite the most intriguing implications. The standard word in ordinary prose is *mod*, used to designate the locus or instrument of thought and imagination and, in Alfred at least, the intellectual faculty. In Anglo-Saxon generally, however, *mod* also carries the meaning 'courage' and 'pride', and its derivatives all point in the direction of these later meanings: *modig*, 'brave', 'proud', *modignes* and *ofermod*, 'pride', 'arrogance', *modigian*, 'to be arrogant', *ormod*, 'devoid of spirit', 'hopeless'. These are quite different from the derivatives of the Latin and Modern English terms for the mind, such as 'mental', 'magnanimous', 'mindful', 'high-minded'. In so far as it refers to a power rather than a location or centre of consciousness, *mod* seems to convey to many Anglo-Saxon writers not so much the intellectual, rational faculty but something more like an inner passion or wilfulness, an intensification of the self that can be dangerous. Authors often in fact speak—especially in verse texts[44]—of the need to control or restrain the *mod*. *The Seafarer* and *Maxims I* speak in similar terms on this point:

> Stieran mon sceal strongum mode,   ond þæt on staþelum healdan.
> (*The Seafarer*, line 109)

> Styran sceal mon strongum mode.   Storm oft holm gebringeþ.
> (*Maxims I*, line 50)

A patient man is defined as one who has controlled his *mod*:

> Sum gewealdenmod
> þafað in geþylde.   (*The Gifts of Men*, lines 70b–1a)

Restraining a murderous spirit seems to be what is meant by controlling the mind in *Beowulf*, lines 1150b–1a:

> ne meahte wæfre mod
> forhabban in hreþre.

A very similar point occurs in prose, when Ælfric remarks that anger causes a man to lose control of his *mod* and thus commit murder and other great crimes:

> Se feorða leahtor is ira, þæt is on englisc weamodnyss, seo deð þæt se man nah his modes geweald, and macað manslihtas and mycele yfelu.
>
> (LS, no. xvi, line 286).

(The implication seems to be that it is the *mod* set free of restraint that initiates murder.) A more interesting example is Ælfric's presentation of *mod* as a slightly wilful, independent faculty, less rational than the self, in a discussion of temptation:

> Deofol tiht us to yfele, ac we sceolon hit onscunian, and ne geniman nane lustfullunge to ðære tihtinge: gif þonne ure mod nimð gelustfullunge, þonne sceole we huru wiðstandan, þæt ðær ne beo nan geðafung to ðam yfelan weorce. Seo yfele tihting is of deofle; ðonne bið oft þæs mannes mod gebiged to ðære lustfullunge, hwilon eac aslit to ðære geðafunge; forðon þe we sind of synfullum flæsce acennede.
>
> (CH I, p. 176)

That such expressions reflect not simply two or three distinct referents of the same word but a genuine way of thinking about the mind is suggested by the appearance of similar statements using other words for the mind:

> Hyge sceal gehealden,   hond gewealden   (*Maxims I*, line 121)
> Heald hordlocan,   hyge fæst bind   (*Homiletic Fragment II*, line 3)
> Þæt bið in eorle   indryhten þeaw,
> þæt he his ferðlocan   fæste binde,
> healde his hordcofan,   hycge swa he wille.   (*The Wanderer*,
> lines, 12–14)

Such expressions invite us to see a distinction between the conscious self and some other, inner power which we might legitimately gloss as 'mind' though it could also be translated in particular contexts as 'passion', 'temper', 'mood'.

As well as *mod*, Anglo-Saxon poetry uses for the concept 'mind' the poetic terms *hyge*, *sefa* and *ferð*, besides various compounds based on these elements. These seem to be used more or less interchangeably and are generally rendered in modern English as 'heart,' 'mind', 'spirit' or 'soul', according to context and the translator's sense of the poet's meaning. The kind of uncertainty this can create is indicated by Tolkien's comments on

Beowulf, lines 1150b–1a ('ne meahte wæfre mod / forhabban in hreþre');
this might, Tolkien suggests, refer to Finn's soul and therefore his death, to
be translated 'his soul was sped (*or rather*, he could not keep his soul from
wandering)', or it might refer to the feelings of Hengest and his fellow-
Danes, in which case it should be rendered 'the deep-stirred feelings could
not be prisoned in their breast'.[45] Tolkien rules out the former on the
grounds of narrative logic, but it could probably have been ruled out on linguistic grounds. Whatever case there might be for rendering *mod* as soul in
the sense of inner self, it does not seem to be used in poetry for the spirit
which leaves the body at death or survives death. *Sawl* is the word used for
that in *Beowulf* and other Old English poetry, and indeed in prose, along
with *gast*, while *mod* refers to thought and emotion. In fact *Beowulf* and most
other Anglo-Saxon poems seem to preserve a distinction, comparable to
that found in Homer,[46] between the *sawl* which is invoked with reference to
death and the afterlife but has no psychological powers or activities, and the
inner self or mind (*mod*, *hyge* etc.) which is responsible for thought and emotion.[47] As we have seen, Alfred and Ælfric, working consciously in a classical tradition of psychological theory, actively countered this distinction.
Something very like it, however, seems to operate in the Anglo-Saxon dialogues of the body and the soul, both in prose and verse, where the soul after death attributes to the body all the acts and decisions made during life
which have condemned the soul to its everlasting fate;[48] the soul in this view
is the helpless victim (or beneficiary) of a separate mental faculty which is
associated with the body. The same distinction is made, more explicitly, in
the Early Middle English psychological allegory *Sawles Warde*[49] where the
soul is God's precious treasure deposited in the house called Man, which is
ruled and guarded by the mental faculty Wit. (The distinction, significantly,
does not operate in the Latin source,[50] where the house is *conscientia*, the
master *animus* and the treasures to be guarded are the virtues; the soul or
anima plays no part, presumably because it is deemed as comprehending *animus* rather than being distinct from it.) In such works the existence of the
soul, like that of Homer's ψῡχή, only becomes evident under the threat or
fact of death; it is quite different from the active mental faculty.

   The classical and vernacular traditions differ on the locus of the mind.
Plato had located the rational soul in the head, the irascible or spirited soul
in the breast and the concupiscible soul in the abdomen; Cassiodorus devotes a chapter to the question of the location of the soul, and expresses a
preference for the head.[51] Nothing is said on the question in Alcuin's treatise or Alfred's Boethius or Ælfric's homily, and the omission appears to be
deliberate; Alfred in translating Boethius deletes every one of his source's

references to the heart as seat of the soul or mind, substituting *mod* or *gewit* or *sawl*, and when Ælfric argues that 'head' in a particular biblical text stands for the mind he significantly does not use the argument that the mind is located in the head.[52] The point may be that all three authors closely associate the intellectual faculty, whether called mind or soul, with the life-spirit, which has to be seen as pervading all parts of the body—a point which both Alcuin and Ælfric make. Outside these texts, however, there is ample evidence that the mind is normally thought of as residing in the heart or thereabouts. The phrase 'thoughts of the heart' (*heortan geþohtas*) occurs in the *Maxims* and in *The Wife's Lament* as well as in *The Seafarer.* The *Maxims* also place the mind in the *breostum*, and *The Wanderer* places it in the *breostcofa*. There are frequent references too to the *hreþer* as the seat of the mind or place of thought and emotion: 'I can tell you more than you, *hygecræftig*, can comprehend with *mod* in your *hreþer*' (*The Order of the World*); 'let not anger overpower you in *hreþer*' (*Precepts*). *Hreþer* is glossed as 'bosom' or 'breast' in Bosworth-Toller, but uses seem to suggest something more like 'lungs' or the part of the body containing the lungs. Possibly, as Onians argues,[53] this goes back to a traditional association of the soul with breath (a view mentioned by Ælfric, as we have seen), though it is not clear that this association extended to the mental faculty as well as the life-spirit. In texts where Ælfric is not being rigorous he too refers to the heart and breast as the seat of thought and passion, just as Alfred in his Pastoral Care seems quite happy to adopt St Gregory's uses of *cor* and *pectus*, rendered as *heorte* and *breost*, for the locus of thought and feeling. Indeed, at one point in the Boethius, where he is not following his sources closely, he introduces *heorte* as the place where man's inner self is locked up: fame 'opens the secrecy of a man's heart and penetrates the locks of another's heart'[54] (a rather cryptic extension of Boethius's point about speech).

As perhaps follows from its location in the heart, the mind is seen as both a faculty of thought and a faculty of feeling or emotion. It is common to think with the *mod* but also possible to love with it: 'ic for tæle ne mæg / ænigne moncynnes mode gelufian'.[55] In *Beowulf*, *mod* is used of wisdom ('on mode frod', 'mid modes synttrum') and the idea of building Heorot came from Hrothgar's *mod*, but the word is also much used of grief and happiness ('murnende mod', 'modes myrhðe'). *The Wanderer* refers to the *mod* darkening with despair, and Ælfric too says that someone grew dark in *mode*, probably meaning angry.[56] *Hyge* is used similarly of both thought and emotion. This perhaps helps to explain the tendency to refer to emotion as a mental action: the same 'mind' is deemed to be responsible for both conscious decisions and 'feelings' of passion. It helps to explain, too, the concept of 'mind' as an unruly, wayward, passionate faculty.

Two poems in particular, *The Wanderer* and *The Seafarer*, show a rich and complex picture of the workings of the mind, and I should like finally to turn to these.

'The Wanderer'

The Wanderer uses various apparently synonymous terms for the mind, *mod*, *hyge*, *modsefa* and *ferð*:

Ne mæg werig *mod*   wyrde wiðstondan,
ne seo hreo *hyge*   helpe gefremman.
Forðon domgeorne   dreorigne oft
in hyra breostcofan   bindað fæste;
swa ic *modsefan* minne sceolde . . .   (15–19)

Se þonne þisne wealsteal   wise geþohte
ond þis deorce lif   deope geondþenceð,
frod in *ferðe* . . .   (88–90a)

Swa cwæð snottor on *mode* . . .   (111a)

The mind's location is the *breostcofa*, 'breast-coffer' (line 18), which is presumably what is referred to metaphorically as the *ferðloca* and *hordcofa* at lines 13–14a:

    . . . þæt he his ferðlocan   fæste binde,
    healde his hordcofan . . .

Similarly, thought is located in the *hreðer* at line 72a, grief in the heart (49b) and in the breast (113a). Rather strikingly, the 'mind'-words are associated almost exclusively with emotion rather than with thought. The mind is weary (*werig mod*, 15a; *werigne sefan*, 58b), troubled or turbulent (*hreo hyge*, 16a), caught up in care or anxiety (*modcearig*, 2b) and inclined to darken (59). The mind is the source of wisdom and the place of dream-fantasies (41–4), and it can create imaginary figures and illusions (50–5). Conscious thought and understanding, however, are attributed not to the mind but to the self: 'hycge swa he wille' (14b), 'gemon he selesecgas' (34a), 'se þonne þisne wealsteal wise geþohte' (88). The most striking sentence is the one at lines 58–60:

    Forþon ic geþencan ne mæg   geond þas woruld
    for hwan modsefa   min ne gesweorce,
    þonne ic eorla lif   eal geondþence . . .

The lines sharply distinguish between the mind or *modsefa* as agent of emotion and 'I' as subject or agent of thinking. Further than that, they suggest an astonishing dislocation between the self and the mind. Ever since Descartes the mind has been the one thing that has been an open book to the self. The poet here implies that the *mod* has its reasons for not darkening (that is, becoming black and bitter or black and gloomy) but they are unknown to the possessor of the mind, who can only think about the world and be aware that his mind has unaccountably remained undarkened; or perhaps he implies that the mind has a fortitude whose origins are not the conscious thought and understanding of the speaker. The *modsefa* seems to be an inner self or consciousness which the conscious self cannot penetrate. (One could of course render *modsefa* as something like 'disposition'; we are close perhaps to that semantic element of *mod* which enabled it to develop into ModE 'mood'. Yet the sum of all the other uses of *mod* and related words within this poem force us to think of it as a substance or entity rather than a quality belonging to the mind.) Something similar is suggested by lines 70–2:

> Beorn sceal gebidan,   þonne he beot spriceð,
> oþþæt collenferð   cunne gearwe
> hwider hreþra gehygd   hweorfan wille.

That is, the thought of the heart stems from an inner self with its own volition, which a man needs to learn to understand and anticipate, since it can, presumably, dictate his actions in spite of his conscious self. Indeed, the whole poem dwells on the separation of self and mind. It speaks of the obligation to keep the mind captive, to fetter it, and also of the compulsion to send it over the sea; uncontrolled, the mind hallucinates and fantasizes. Throughout the poem there is a recognition of two levels or centres of consciousness, one associated with awareness and perception and the other (for which the 'mind'-words are mainly used) associated with emotion and volition, memory and imagination. It is a distinction that perhaps lies behind the opening paradox of the poem, as the solitary wanderer goes on waiting for, and perhaps experiences, divine favour despite all the evidence presented to his conscious mind of the fixity of his fate. It is, intriguingly, the emotional, subconscious mind, with its refusal to darken, that ultimately carries the values of the poem.

'The Seafarer'

The Seafarer similarly associates the 'mind'-words (*mod*, *ferð* and *hyge*) particularly with emotion and volition:

>   hungor innan slat
> merewerges mod . . .   (11b–12a)

>   ne ænig hleomæga
> feasceaftig ferð   frefran meahte . . .   (25b–6)

> Ne biþ him to hearpan hyge   ne to hringþege,
> ne to wife wyn   ne to worulde hyht.   (44–5)

There is again a dislocation of self from mind, with the latter functioning here as an intense inner will battering at the reluctant self:

>   Forþon cnyssað nu
> heortan geþohtas,   þæt ic hean streamas,
> sealtyþa gelac   sylf cunnige;
> monað modes lust   mæla gehwylce
> ferð to feran,   þæt ic feor heonan
> elþeodigra   eard gesece.   (33b–8)

Ic seems here to be almost identified with the body rather than the mind,
though perhaps it would be better to define it as that aspect of the self which
controls the body's actions. The poem reverses the psychological situation
of *The Wanderer*, with the mind no longer fettered by the self but escaping
and assailing it, urging it to action:

> Forþon nu min hyge hweorfeð   ofer hreþerlocan,
> min modsefa   mid mereflode
> ofer hwæles eþel   hweorfeð wide,
> eorþan sceatas,   cymeð eft to me
> gifre ond grædig,   gielleð anfloga,
> hweteð on hwælweg   hreþer unwearnum
> ofer holma gelagu.   (58–64a)

As Peter Clemoes has shown,[57] there is a striking similarity between this
picture of the mind travelling over land and sea and Alcuin's account of the
mind/soul flying over lands and seas in the act of imagination. F. N. M.
Diekstra has pointed to further parallels with Lactantius and Ambrose, who
similarly describe the act of memory or imagination as a journey of the
mind.[58] What *The Seafarer* seems to be offering, however, is an image of volition rather than imagination, calling the speaker to a journey; it develops
the point already made at lines 33b–8 (quoted above) where the *modes lust*
continually urges the seafarer to make the voyage to the land of strangers.

Like *The Wanderer*, then, the poem distinguishes two centres of consciousness: an inner, urgent, passionate personality and a more reluctant

self which controls action.[59] (Neither is explicitly identified with the soul, which is mentioned specifically only at line 100, in a reference to death and judgement; indeed, lines 94–6 imply that thinking with the mind (*hyge*) is the work of the body.) Whether the 'mind'-words refer exclusively to the inner spirit is unclear in this poem. The clause at lines 36–7a, 'monað modes lust . . . ferð to feran', is rendered by Hamer 'the heartfelt wishes urge the spirit to venture' and by Bradley 'my mind's desire . . . urges the soul to set out'.[60] If the translators intend a distinction between 'heart' and 'spirit' or between 'mind' and 'soul', it is not one in any way suggested by OE *mod* and *ferð* as they are used in the poetry generally; if such a distinction is not supplied it does seem rather odd to say that the mind's desire urges the mind. As I. L. Gordon points out,[61] it is possible to take *ferð* as subject of *monað*, parallel with *modes lust*; there is something to be said for this, with an implied *me* as object, thus distinguishing between the *mod* or *ferð* which urges and the self which is urged. Lines 50–1a, 'ealle þa gemoniað modes fusne / sefan to siþe', are similar. Hamer takes *sefan* as object and translates 'all this urges forth the eager spirit', but Bradley takes it as a genitive, parallel to *modes*, and renders 'all these urge anyone eager of mind and of spirit', which would perhaps allow us to sustain the association of the 'mind'-words with the eager inner mind.[62] It is possible, then, to read into *The Seafarer* the same linguistic distinction between an inner self called *mod* or *hyge* or *ferð* or *sefa* and an outer, conscious self that seems to operate in *The Wanderer*; but it may be that the poet used the 'mind'-words rather casually for both levels of consciousness.

The rôle of the *mod* in *The Seafarer* is incitement to a journey which is associated with the divine will and the joys of the Lord. Yet it is difficult to know what to make of lines 108–9:

> Meotod him þæt mod gestaþelað,   forþon he in his meahte gelyfeð.
> Stieran mon sceal strongum mode,   one þæt on staþelum healdan.

The notion of God stabilizing the *mod*, and of man's duty to control or restrain his strong *mod* and keep it in its place (if that is how line 109 should be construed), suggests the idea of the dangerous, rebellious inner force which the semantic field of *mod* and frequent references in other poems point to. This is not inconsistent with the earlier view of the mind's passionate, urgent quality, but it *is* inconsistent with the value placed on the *mod*'s promptings earlier in the poem. The poet seems to have drifted into a proverbial, prudential way of talking about the *mod* which neglects the fact that its passion is for things divine.

Conclusions

Anglo-Saxon views on the mind are varied and subtle. For Alcuin, Alfred and Ælfric, the mind is very closely identified with the soul, which is simultaneously the spirit of life, the immortal self and the intellectual faculty. Passion and desire are seen as conscious choices of the rational soul, proceeding from the exercise of free will or from ignorance. The emphasis is on a unitary inner self. For Alfred this inner self is a pre-existent soul-and-mind, temporarily trapped in the body; for Ælfric it is more specifically linked to the individual, for whom it is created by God after conception. In Ælfric's view this soul/mind sets man firmly apart from the beasts, whereas Alfred seems prepared to find it in at least the higher animals. The poets, perhaps here reflecting tendencies in normal Anglo-Saxon usage, are more inclined to associate the 'mind' with emotion and a kind of passionate volition and self-assertion, and to distinguish it from the conscious self. It seems to be closely associated with mood and individual personality, a kind of mixture of id and ego in opposition to a superego. The poets generally distinguish it from the soul or spirit which leaves the body in death and survives in another world. The resulting sense of multiple personality is powerfully expressed in the urgent passionate tensions of *The Seafarer*.

Appendix

*Note on the Relationship of LS, no. i, Belfour, no. ix
and the Boulogne Latin Version*

These are three versions of the same basic text, cast in the form of a homily for Christ's Nativity. For the first part of the text, on the nature of God, Ælfric draws partly on Alfred's Boethius, and the successive recastings of *De consolatione Philosophiae*, bk v, met. v show clearly the relative order of the three versions and their relationship to each other:

Boethius, *De consolatione Philosophiae* v, met. v

> Quam uariis terras animalia permeant figuris!
> Namque alia extento sunt corpore pulueremque uerrunt
> Continuumque trahunt ui pectoris incitata sulcum,
> Sunt quibus alarum leuitas uaga uerberetque uentos
> Et liquido longi spatia aetheris enatet uolatu,

Haec pressisse solo uestigia gressibusque gaudent
Vel uirides campos transmittere uel subire siluas.
Quae uariis uideas licet omnia discrepare formis,
Prona tamen facies hebetes ualet ingrauare sensus.
Unica gens hominum celsum leuat altius cacumen
Atque leuis recto stat corpore despicitque terras.
Haec nisi terrenus male desipis, admonet figura,
Qui recto caelum uultu petis exserisque frontem,
In sublime feras animum quoque, ne grauata pessum
Inferior sidat mens corpore celsius leuato.

Alfred's Boethius

Hwæt, þu miht ongitan þæt manig wyht is mistlice ferende geond eorþan, and sint swiðe ungelices hiwes, and ungelice farað. Sume licgað mid eallon lichoman on eorþan, and swa smuhende farað þæt him nauþer ne fet ne fiðeras ne fultumað; and sume bið twiofete, sume fiowerfete, sume fleogende, and ealle þeah bioð ofdune healde wið þære eorðan, and þider willniað, oððe þæs þe hi lyst oððe þæs þe hi beþurfon. Ac se mann ana gæþ uprihte; þæt tacnað þæt he sceal ma þencan up þonne nyðer, þi læs þæt mod sie nioðoror þonne ðe li-choma.   (Sedgefield, p. 147/2–10)

Ælfric, Lives of Saints

Ða gesceafta þe þæs an scyppend gesceop synden mænig-fealde, and mislices hiwes, and ungelice farað. Sume sindon ungesewenlice gastas butan lichoman, swa swa synd ænglas on heofonum. Sume syndan creopende on eorðan mid eallum lichoman, swa swa wurmas doð. Sume gað on twam fotum, sume on feower fotum. Sume fleoð mid fyðerum, sume on flodum swimmað, and hi ealle swa-þæh alotene beoð to þære eorðan weard, and þider wilniað oððe þæs þe him lyst oððe þæs þe hi beþurfon, ac se man ana gæð uprihte; þæt getacnað þæt he sceall ma þæncan upp þonne nyðer, þelæs þe þæt mod sy neoðer þonne se lichoma, and he sceal smeagen embe þæt æce lif þe he to gesceapen wæs swiðor þonne embe þa eorðlican þing, swa swa his wæstm him gebicnað.   (LS, no. i, lines 49–61)

The Boulogne Text

Creaturae uero quas unus Creator creuit multiplices sunt et uariae figurae, et non uno modo uiuunt; ex quibus quaedam sunt incorpo-

ralia et inuisibilia, ut angeli in caelo nullo terreno cibo utentes. Alia
namque corporalia sunt, ratione carentia, et toto corpore in terra
reptantia sicut uermes. Quaedam uero ambulant duobus pedibus,
quedam quattuor; quaedam pennis uolant in aere; quaedam etiam
natatilia sunt ut pissces in mari, et in amne uagantia, quae sine aquis
uiuere nequeunt, et nos in aquis suffocamus. Omnia tamen ad terram
inclinantur, de qua alimenta sumunt, et quicquid desiderant uel indi-
gent. Sed homo solus recta statura ambulat, qui ad imaginem Dei
creatus est et proprio incessu significat quod debet plus de celestibus
meditari quam de terrenis, plus de eternis quam de infimis, ne forte
mens eius fiat inferior corpore.   (ed. Leinbaugh)

The Belfour Homily

Nu beoð þa gesceaftæ þe þe an Scyppend iscop mislice heowes and
monifealdes cyndes; and heo alle ne libbæð na on ane wisæ. Summe
heo beoð unlichamlice and eac unsegenlice swa beoð englæs; heo
nabbæð nænne lichame, and heo libbæð on heofene, swiðe bliþful on
Godes isihðe, and heo eorðlice mætes næfre ne brucæð. Summe heo
beoð lichamlice, and unsceadwise, and mid alle lichame on eorþe
creopaþ; þæt is, all wyrmcyn, swa swa eow fulcuð is. Summe gað on
twam fotum; summe beoð feowerfote. Summe swimmæð on flode;
summe fleoð geont þas lyft. Þa fixas nabbæþ nan lif buton wætere; ne
we ne magon libban noht longe on watere. Ealle heo beoþ alytene and
lybbæþ bi þare eorþan, ac þe mon ane hæfð uprihtne geong, for þam
þe he is isceapen to his Scyppendes anlicnesse. He is on sawle liffæst
mid gesceadwisnesse, and his geong bitacnæð, þenne he uprihtes gæð,
þæt he sceal smeagen embe God and embe þa heofenlice þing swiðor
þenne embe ða eorðlice þing, swiðor embe þa ecan þonne embe þa ate-
oriendlice, forþi læs ðe his mod beo bineoðan his lichame.
                              (Belfour, no. ix, pp. 81/29–84/11)

Alfred is clearly paraphrasing Boethius's Latin text here, and there is no
need to posit any further source or influence for him. Ælfric adapts and expands that paraphrase in LS, no. i, while retaining many close verbal parallels that attest the directness of the debt; the Boulogne Latin text, resembling LS, no. i, rather than Alfred's version, but expanding the references to
angels and fish which Ælfric had added in recasting Alfred, must be a translation and expansion of the LS, no. i passage; Belfour, no. ix very closely resembles the Latin version of Boulogne rather than LS, no. i, and the complete absence of significant verbal similarities between the two Old English
versions suggests that Belfour, no. ix is a retranslation of the Boulogne

Latin text, not an intermediary between LS, no. 1, and Boulogne. Thus both textual development and verbal parallels indicate the order: Boethius (Latin)—Alfred's Boethius (Old English)—LS, no. i (Old English)—Boulogne text (Latin)—Belfour, no. ix (Old English). This relationship holds for the whole of the first part of the homily: LS, no i gives every sign of being the original version, with the Boulogne text being an expansion and translation of it into Latin and Belfour, no. ix certainly very like Boulogne and probably a retranslation of it.

A quite different relationship must be posited for the remainder of the homily. The ultimate source here is Alcuin's *De animae ratione*, and the very closer verbal agreement between Alcuin's wording and the Boulogne Latin text of the homily shows that no English version could have intervened between them; the Boulogne text must be an adaptation and abridgment of Alcuin's treatise. The LS, no. i English version, closely resembling the Boulogne text but showing some further slight adaptation and small additions, and revealing no independent use of Alcuin's treatise, must be an adapted translation of the Boulogne text. Belfour, no. ix, incorporating the changes made by LS, no. i and showing many verbal parallels with it, must be based on LS, no. i itself. Thus for this second and longer part of the homily, the relationship is: Alcuin (Latin)—Boulogne text (Latin)—LS, no. i (Old English)—Belfour, no. ix (Old English). Whatever explanation one offers for this complex set of relationships, it seems clear that the Boulogne Latin text, being partly based on LS, no. i, as well as serving as source for both LS, no. i and Belfour, no. ix, must have been written by Ælfric, like the two Old English texts. I would suppose that at some early stage Ælfric made a Latin abridgment and adaptation of Alcuin's treatise, probably in the knowledge that he would not be able to obtain access to the treatise at a later date. (In the same way, he made excerpts from Julian of Toledo's *Prognosticon futuri saeculi*, preserved in the same Boulogne manuscript.) Subsequently, I take it, Ælfric used this précis as the basis of LS, no. i, prefaced with new material which was partly his own and partly drawn from Alfred's Boethius. When he later was called on to produce a Latin version of LS, no. i (perhaps for a different readership; Ælfric also produced parallel Latin and English versions of his pastoral letters), he naturally used his original Latin adaptation of Alcuin for the second part rather than re-translating that part of LS, no. i. When he needed to provide a new English version of the homily some considerable time later, he naturally used the Boulogne Latin version as basis for the first part, knowing that it included the improvements which he had made since issuing LS, no. i, but used the LS, no. i version for the rest, knowing that it represented his further thoughts, and perhaps also that it was already adapted for a vernacular readership.

Notes

1. '*Mens absentia cogitans* in *The Seafarer* and *The Wanderer*', *Medieval Literature and Civilization. Studies in Memory of G. N. Garmonsway*, ed. D. A. Pearsall and R. A. Waldron (London, 1969), pp. 62–77.

2. PL 101, cols. 639–50. See K. Werner, *Der Entwickelungsgang der mittelalterlichen Psychologie von Alcuin bis Albertus Magnus*, Denkschriften der Kaiserlichen Akademie der Wissenschaften, Phil.-hist. Classe 25 (Vienna, 1876), 70.

3. Augustine, *De trinitate* xv. 7, ed. W. J. Mountain, CCSL 50 (Turnhout, 1968), 475.

4. *De opificio Dei*, ed. S. Brandt, CSEL 27 (Vienna, 1893), ch. 18. Alcuin mentions Lactantius among the authors available at York (see M. Lapidge 'Surviving Booklists from Anglo-Saxon England', *L&L*, p. 46); but since Lactantius is named in a list of Christian-Latin poets, it is probable that the *Carmen de aue phoenice* rather than *De opificio Dei* is in question.

5. See esp. *De trinitate* x. 7, xi.5 and xxi.7

6. That, at least, seems to be what is meant by his statement that the soul is not even at rest when a man is asleep. Alcuin is perhaps influenced by Lactantius (*De opificio Dei*, ch. 18) again here.

7. *King Alfred's Old English Version of Boethius 'De Consolatione Philosophiae'*, ed. W. J. Sedgefield (Oxford, 1899) (hereafter Sedgefield); subsequent references are to page and line-number of this edition.

8. J. Beaumont, 'The Latin Tradition of the *De Consolatione Philosophiae*', *Boethius: his Life, Thought and Influence*, ed. M. Gibson (Oxford, 1981), pp. 278–305.

9. See P. Courcelle, *La Consolation de Philosophie dans la tradition littéraire* (Paris, 1967), pp. 272 and 276–7.

10. Boethius, *De consolatione Philosophiae* III, pr. xi, and v, pr. ii.

11. These changes are noted K. Otten, *König Alfreds Boethius* (Tübingen, 1964), p. 173. See also H. Schelp, 'Der geistige Mensch im Wortschatz Alfreds des Grossen' (unpubl. dissertation, Göttingen Univ., 1956).

12. Boethius, *De consolatione Philosophiae* III, met. xi; Sedgefield, p. 95/13–14.

13. Boethius, *De consolatione Philosophiae* IV pr. vi; Sedgefield, p. 132/14–15.

14. *King Alfred's Version of St Augustine's Soliloquies*, ed. T. A. Carnicelli (Cambridge, Mass., 1969), p. 91/21–4.

15. *Ibid.* p. 91/9–11.

16. Sedgefield, p. 140/30–1.

17. Cf. J. Bremmer, *The Early Greek Concept of the Soul* (Princeton, NJ, 1983), esp. Appendix Two, 'The Wandering Soul in Western European Folk Tradition'.

18. The two English versions are in *Ælfric's Lives of Saints*, ed. W. W. Skeat, EETS

o.s. 76, 82, 94 and 114 (London, 1881–1900) (hereafter LS), no. i, and *Twelfth-Century Homilies in MS Bodley 34*, ed. A. O. Belfour, EETS o.s. 137 (London, 1909), no. ix. The Latin version is found in Boulogne, Bibliothèque Municipale, 63. All three versions have recently been meticulously edited by T. H. Leinbaugh, 'Liturgical Homilies in Ælfric's Lives of Saints' (unpubl. Ph.D. dissertation, Harvard Univ., 1980). I am exceedingly grateful to Professor Leinbaugh for permission to use his dissertation.

19. Ælfric's use of Alfred's translation was noted W. F. Bolton, 'The Alfredian Boethius in Ælfric's *Lives of Saints* I', *N & Q* 19 (1972), 406–7.

20. The source was identified P. Clemoes, '*Mens absentia cogitans*'.

21. *The Homilies of the Anglo-Saxon Church: the First Part, containing the Sermones Catholici or Homilies of Ælfric*, ed. B. Thorpe, 2 vols. (London, 1843–6) (hereafter CH I), i, 288.

22. *LS*, no. i, lines 130–6.

23. See below, p. 308.

24. Cf., e.g., *De ciuitate Dei* VII.29.

25. *De animæ ratione*, ch. 12.

26. *König Alfreds Boethius*, p. 175.

27. 'Nam ne in animalibus quidem manendi amor ex animae uoluntatibus, uerum ex naturae principiis uenit' (Boethius, *De consolatione Philosophiae* III, pr. xi); 'Hwæt, þa nytenu ðonne and eac þa oðra gesceafta ma wilniað þæs þe hi wilniað for gecynde ðonne for willan' (Sedgefield, p. 93/9–11).

28. *Ælfric's Anglo-Saxon Version of Alcuini Interrogationes Sigewulfi in Genesin*, ed. G. E. MacLean (Halle, 1883), ch. 33.

29. *Acta Sanctorum*, ed. J. Bolland *et al.*, Maii, I, 473; *Ælfric's Catholic Homilies: the Second Series, Text*, ed. M. Godden, EETS s.s. 5 (London, 1979) (cited hereafter as CH II), no. xviii, lines 75–6).

30. Cassiodorus, *De anima*, ed. J. W. Halporn, CCSL 96 (Turnhout, 1973), ch. 3. I owe this reference to Father Osmund Lewry.

31. Ptd *Ancient Laws and Institutes of England*, ed. B. Thorpe, 2 vols. (London, 1840) II, 97–127; the passage from *De sabbato* is found on p. 102.

32. R. A. Aronstam, 'The Latin Canonical Tradition in Late Anglo-Saxon England: the *Excerptiones Egberti*' (unpubl. Ph.D dissertation, Columbia Univ. 1974).

33. *De libero arbitrio*, ed. W. M. Green, CCSL 29 (Turnhout, 1970), ch. 21 (pp. 309–12).

34. *De anima*, ch. 9.

35. *Soliloquies*, ed. Carnicelli, p. 91/9–11.

36. *Homilies of Ælfric: a Supplementary Collection*, ed. J. C. Pope, 2 vols. EETS o.s. 259–60 (London, 1967–8), no. ii, line 220.

37. In *Three Lives of English Saints*, ed. M. Winterbottom (Toronto, 1972), p. 18 (ch. 3). The point also appears in Wulfstan's *Vita S. Athelwoldi* (ed. *ibid.* pp. 33–63, at 35–6), but it is so characteristic of Ælfric's thought as to amount to an argument for the priority of his version.

38. *Ælfric's De temporibus anni*, ed. H. Henel, EETS o.s. 213 (London, 1942), 72.

39. LS, no. i, lines 214–16; Belfour, no. ix, p. 94/11–12.

40. *Circumstantial Deliveries* (Berkeley and London, 1981), p. 59. See also the same author's *Belief, Language and Experience* (Chicago and London, 1972).

41. CH II, nos. xix, line 60, and xl, lines 194–5; CH I, p. 544; CH II, no. xxxiv, lines 119–20; and CH I, p. 514, respectively.

42. CH II, no. xxxix, lines 68 and 171–4.

43. CH II, no. xxxii, lines 102–3.

44. Verse texts are quoted from *The Exeter Book*, ed. G. P. Krapp and E. V. K. Dobbie, ASPR 3 (Columbia and London, 1936).

45. J. R. R. Tolkien, *Finn and Hengest*, ed. A. Bliss (London, 1982), p. 140.

46. Cf. Bremmer, *The Early Greek Concept*, pp. 14ff.

47. One possible exception to this pattern is the poem *Guthlac A*, where *gast* is used of both the inner self which experiences grief and the departing soul, and where *mod* is used once (line 26) with a possible reference to the soul departing in death; but the interpretation of line 26 is very uncertain (see the most recent edition of the poem by J. Roberts, *The Guthlac Poems of the Exeter Book* (Oxford, 1979), pp. 127–8).

48. See the texts ptd R. Willard, 'The Address of the Soul to the Body', *PMLA* 50 (1935), 957–83.

49. Ed. most recently in *Early Middle English Verse and Prose*, ed. J. A. W. Bennett and G. V. Smithers, rev. ed. (Oxford, 1968), pp. 247–61.

50. 'De Custodia Interioris Hominis', *Memorials of St Anselm*, ed. R. W. Southern and F. S. Schmitt (London, 1969), pp. 355–60.

51. *De anima*, ch. 10.

52. CH I, p. 612.

53. R. B. Onians, *The Origins of European Thought about the Body, the Mind, the Soul, the World, Time and Fate* (Cambridge, 1951).

54. Sedgefield, p. 28/14. Similarly, Alfred sometimes introduces *heorte* as the seat of the mind/soul when turning into verse his original prose translation of Boethius's metres.

55. *Resignation*, 106b–7.

56. LS, no. xxv, line 329.

57. Clemoes, '*Mens absentia cogitans*'.

58. F. N. M. Diekstra, '*The Seafarer* 58–66a: the Flight of the Exiled Soul to its Fatherland', *Neophilologus* 55 (1971), 433–46.

59. There are some similarities here to a Germanic conception of the spirit/soul reconstructed from mainly Norse evidence; see V. Salmon, '*The Wanderer* and *The Seafarer* and the Old English Conception of the Soul', *MLR* 55 (1960), 1–10.

60. R. Hamer, *A Choice of Anglo-Saxon Verse* (London, 1970), p. 189, and S. A. J. Bradley, *Anglo-Saxon Poetry*, (London, 1982), p. 333.

61. *The Seafarer*, ed. I. L. Gordon (London, 1960), p. 38.

62. Hamer, *A Choice*, p. 189, and Bradley, *Anglo-Saxon Poetry*, p. 333.

Sundor æt Rune:
The Voluntary Exile of The Wanderer[1]

ROBERT E. BJORK

STUDIES of the Old English poem *The Wanderer* exist, it has frequently
been noted, in great quantities. The poem has been examined in the
light of genre criticism,[2] psychoanalytic criticism,[3] and the New Criticism,[4] and has undergone iconographic,[5] structural,[6] rhetorical,[7] and stylistic[8] analysis. Some critics have looked at its dramatic features,[9] and at least
one at its romantic elements.[10] But despite the disparate cries from these
several critical voices, scholars do seem generally to harmonize on the
theme and structure of the poem: *The Wanderer* follows the development of
a troubled soul from the *eardstapa* ("earth-stepper," l. 6a), who is subject to
the vagaries of the world, to the *snottor on mode* ("wise in mind," l.111a),
who has managed to move from his personal problems to a universal, es-
chatalogical vision bespeaking an absolute hope.[11] This view, in fact, has
been so widely accepted that most scholarship on the poem now concerns
itself with working out the details of the overall scheme.[12] In one respect
the present paper does not differ radically from those that precede it, for I
feel that the poem's theme and structure have already been thoroughly and
convincingly explored. It does differ from its predecessors in its basic premise that, while we have discovered the poem's essential scheme, we have not
yet determined its exact purpose, something that we might accomplish by
viewing the wanderer's relationship to his society slightly differently than
we have typically done in the past. By so doing we can, I think, gain a new
perspective on the poem that may help clarify some of its more trouble-
some elements, including the meaning and function of *sundor æt rune*
("apart in meditation," l.111b).

The typical—and quite defensible—view of *The Wanderer* that I have in
mind can be simply stated as follows: the poem is an artifact reflecting the

culture from which it springs, and the wanderer participates—or has participated—completely in the social and cultural traditions of his age.[13] That participation and subsequent separation from his *comitatus* account for his anguish. The wanderer is an exile, the unwilling, miserable recipient of his society's worst fate. What we have not fully realized before, however, is that exile itself, as one constant tradition in the Anglo-Saxon world, can affirm that world and be as dearly clung to as the seemingly more positive aspects of life. Though perhaps the most intense and painful experience one can have within Anglo-Saxon society, exile is nevertheless an accepted (even expected) part of Anglo-Saxon life, a part that both the culture and the language accommodate. Anthropologists have made a similar point in other contexts, arguing that the negative features of a culture actually reinforce cultural stability. Roy Wagner, for example, implicitly raises the issue in discussing the importance of invention.

> Since the collective and conventional only makes sense in relation to the individual and idiosyncratic, and vice versa, collective contexts can only be retained and recognized as such by being continually drawn through the meshes of the individual and the particular, and the individual and particular characteristics of the world can only be retained and recognized as such by being drawn through the meshes of the conventional. Order and disorder, known and unknown, conventional regularity and the incident that defies regularity, are tightly and innately bound together, they are functions of each other and necessarily interdependent.[14]

In *The Wanderer*, I contend, all the cultural trappings—exile included are also "necessarily interdependent"; the wanderer's solitude is "innately bound" to the whole societal construct that he feels he has lost and becomes one more vestige of the world that he has either to divest himself of or transform to a higher purpose before reaching salvation. The poem does move between the *eardstapa* or *anhaga* ("lone-dweller," l. 1a)—and the thoroughly conventional social situation he finds himself in—and the *snottor on mode*, but that wise man sits significantly *sundor æt rune*, deliberately rejecting the entire social structure that has given rise to his pain.[15] He thus paradoxically and voluntarily seeks a more complete separation from society than the one that seemed to be his bane at the start of the poem. To attain that state of separation, the wanderer filters his experiences through a number of cultural "meshes," meshes of language, custom, and literary genre, and as he deals with each, transforming or transcending them, he also moves from basically pre-christian or pagan concerns to Christian ones.

The poem contains ample evidence that the wanderer's initial predicament ties him to the social order. Dunning and Bliss point out in their edition that the poem focuses on Anglo-Saxon life, "the life of the *gesið* in the *comitatus*. Every line," they observe, "combines with every other line to evoke this setting in our minds, and the poet never moves outside it."[16] The first seven lines alone illustrate their point. Stanley B. Greenfield has shown that lines one through five set up an extremely conventional scene focusing on exile.[17] *Anhaga*, denoting the exile's status, is a highly conventional word (seven occurences in Old English poetry) as is *wræclastas* ("paths of exile," six occurences), denoting the state "of excommunication,"[18] in l. 5a. Even the wanderer's anguish can be termed conventional, another validation of the social order. *Maxims I*, for instance, twice tells us that a lordless man must endure pain: "wineleas, wonsælig mon / genimeð him wulfas to geferan" ("friendless, the unhappy man takes for himself wolves for companions," l. 146), and "earm biþ se þe sceal ana lifgan, // wineleas wunian / hafaþ him wyrd geteod" ("Wretched is the one who must live alone; fate has decreed that he will dwell friendless," ll. 172–73).[19] Examples like these abound in Old English poetry,[20] where all wretched characters seem to abide tenaciously by the rigid rules of exile. And the wanderer is no exception. Much of the restriction (or binding or enclosure) that he feels comes from the strictures of his culture (and, by extension, the strictures of poetic convention), which determine his responses to the world and to events. The opening section of the poem even ends with a gnome (*Wyrd bið ful aræd*, "the course of events [or man's lot] is fully fixed"), a clearly pagan and Germanic[21] thoroughly conventional close for a description of this kind that also represents an entirely conventional point of view. *Wyrd*, as we learn from such poems as *Judgment Day I*,[22] is supposed to be unaffected by the world of men, is supposed to be incomprehensible, and its perpetual indifference to man's specific quandary in *The Wanderer* shows how conceptually stable the wanderer's environment is. Exile and *wyrd* both function as they should, and both bind the wanderer to the pre-Christian Germanic world. As with *wyrd*, "there can be little doubt of [exile's] pre-Christian origin and character."[23] The first five lines of the poem thus present us with a conventional situation expressed conventionally and conclude with a form of poetry basic to Anglo-Saxon culture.

Similarly, lines 6–7 bring another convention, both cultural and poetic, into play, for they establish the immediate context for the wanderer's woe: feud has taken away his kinsman and lord. Feud, of course, is a conventional, inevitable aspect of this society. And just as feuds are inevitable (and thus desirable within the culture because of their validating power), so is the grief resulting from them. One can depend on grief following a feud, and so it—like exile and the indifference of *wyrd*—becomes another paradoxical kind of consolation in itself. The wanderer thus suffers nobly and well, becoming, like *wyrd*, securely fixed in the Anglo-Saxon world at the beginning of the poem. Three patterns, however, indicate that he eventually separates himself from that world: the use of repetition; of literary genres; and of logical discontinuity and continuity within the structure of the poem.

Under the first category—repetition—we need to examine the development in the uses of *wyrd*, as well as the imagery of silence. *Wyrd* appears four times in the poem. In line 5b, as we've seen, *wyrd* "is fully fixed" and thus inhabits a specific literary (gnomic) context as the personified Germanic force ruling over or directing or simply observing the world of men.[24] We find the same concept expressed in the same syntactic pattern throughout OE poetry (e.g., *Beowulf*, 455; *Maxims II*, l. 5; *The Seafarer*, l. 115; *Solomon and Saturn*, l. 437). It is important to notice here that *wyrd* occurs in the b-line of the verse and determines the alliterative pattern of the entire line. Its placement and consequent power in the line emphasize its influence in the poem and in the world. Likewise in its next two appearances, *wyrd* still occupies the b-line and is still in its original dress as the indifferent Germanic force: "Ne mæg werig mod / wyrde wiðstondan" ("Nor may the weary heart alter the course of events," l. 15); "Eorlas fornoman / asca þryþe // wæpen wælgifru, / wyrd seo mære" ("The hosts of spears carry away the earls, weapons greedy for slaughter, fate the mighty," ll. 99–100).[25] But notice its last appearance: "Eall is earfoðlic / eorþan rice: // onwendeð wyrda gesceaft / weoruld under heofonum" ("All is difficult in the earthly kingdom: the ordered course of events changes the world under the heavens," ll. 106–7). At least two changes have occurred to *wyrd* here: it occupies the a-line, no longer determining the alliterative pattern, no longer controlling the entire line; and its case has changed to the genitive plural, putting it in a subordinate, modifying relationship to another noun. Dunning and Bliss and R. F. Leslie, pointing out that the only other occurrence of *wyrda gesceaft* in Old English poetry is in *Daniel*, l. 132, allude to the Christian underpinnings of the phrase.[26] And Leslie further observes that "certainly the picture of all creation subject to decay (106–7) indicates the subordination of creation to the creator who has instituted decay (85)."[27] *Wyrd* thus is no longer fully fixed and autonomous in ll. 106–7. It changes under the circle of the moon just as everything else does, perhaps even losing its pre-Christian associations, and the wanderer's perspective on it shifts accordingly. Significantly, that shift occurs just a few lines from the end of the poem as he nears his total dissociation from the world and his cultural surroundings.

The imagery of silence undergoes a change akin to that undergone by *wyrd*. The wanderer begins by depending on a cultural tradition and gnomic wisdom first apparent in ll. 12–14: "þæt biþ in eorle / indryhten þeaw // þæt he his ferðlocan / fæste binde // healdne his hordcofan, / hycge swa he wille" ("that is a noble custom in a man that he should bind fast his soul enclosure, hold his treasure-chamber, think as he will"). A similar emphasis on the desirability of tight-lipped stoicism appears again only a few lines later: "Forðon domgeorne / dreorigne oft // in hyra breostcofan / bindað fæste" ("therefore, those eager for fame often bind mournful thoughts fast in their hearts"). Two points are important to note here. First, we find the same insistence on silence reiterated and affirmed elsewhere in Old Germanic poetry, as in *Maxims I* ("Hyge sceal gehealdan, / hond gewealden, // seo sceal in eagan, / snyttro in breostum, // þær bið þæs monnes / modgeþoncas" ["Thought must be held in, hand controlled, the pupil must be in the eye, wisdom in the breast, where the thoughts of the man are"] ll. 121–23) and the Old Norse *Hávamál* (e.g., stanzas 6–7).[28] The wanderer thus once again abides by the dictates of his culture as he makes his actions conform to the demands of the situation. Second, the statements themselves contain expressions of two other mainstays of Germanic culture. Custom, as we know from *Beowulf* (e.g., ll. 359 ff., 1246 ff.), reinforces social stability, and the particular custom of silence gives the wanderer a measure of comfort in this poem. Fame can also give him comfort since it is the inevitable goal of a Germanic warrior (e.g., *Maxims I*, ll. 139–40). By alluding to the *domgeorne*, the wanderer initially aligns himself with them and with the earth-bound values they represent, and the resultant implication "is one of uncritical conformity to accepted codes of conduct."[29] Here in bold relief we have one of the "meshes of the conventional" that Wagner speaks of. The order and stability represented by fame and the custom of silence stand in delicate, affirmative balance with the disorder represented by exile. By enduring the latter and by abiding by one of his culture's most established tenets—reticence in the face of extreme adversity—the wanderer can attain one of his culture's most coveted goods, fame.

In the next two instances of the imagery of silence, significant changes occur. The element of knowledge enters in ll. 70–72, where we learn that a man must wait "þonne he beot spriceð // oþ þæt collenferð / cunne gearwe // hwider hreþre gehygd / hweorfan wille" ("when he would speak boast until, bold-spirited, he may clearly know where the thought of the heart will turn").[30] No longer an inflexible injunction to hold one's tongue no matter what the circumstances, this statement allows eventual articulation of one's woes once one has understood their source or meaning or context. The final expression of the theme reinforces the importance of knowledge or understanding and justifies the composition of the entire poem: "Til biþ se þe his treowe gehealdeþ. / Ne sceal næfre his torn to rycene // beorn of his breostum acyþan, / nemþe he ær þa bote cunne, // eorl, mid elne gefremman" ("Good is the one who holds his faith [or trust]. Nor shall he ever too quickly disclose his passion from his breast unless he should know beforehand, the earl, how valiantly to achieve the remedy," ll. 112–14a). This concluding statement of the theme of silence also represents the final rejection of that major tenet of the wanderer's culture. As Dunning and Bliss observe, "the man who firmly holds his faith (*se þe his treowe gehealdeþ*) need not so firmly hold his heart (*healde his hordcofan* 14), for he knows how to achieve the remedy, zealously, by reflection, in the light of that faith."[31]

The second indication that the wanderer eventually separates himself from his world is the poet's use of what we would call literary genre. Most critics agree that the poem has to do with the mind or processes of mind[32] and have pointed out its tendency both to generalize and to instruct.[33] Ida Masters Hollowell develops the point further, arguing that it is quite plausible that the wanderer is actually a court poet.[34] Though reasonable, that assertion is difficult to prove, since, as with many interpretations of the poem, it requires our imagining a specific scenario in which the "court poet" acts. What we can say, however, is that the author of *The Wanderer* makes use of various poetic forms and functions endemic to his culture. And he does so in a way that reinforces developments in his use of *wyrd* and the imagery of silence.

He begins with the most basic, Germanic, non-moral gnomic statements that bear the wisdom of the race. Lines 1–5a outline a personal situation, and then line 5b contains a generalizing gnome juxtaposed to that personal experience. We have his pattern repeated and lengthened in the next 30–40 lines (personal experience 8a–10a [hard to keep quiet], cultural generalization 11. 10b–18b [it's a noble custom to keep quiet]; personal experience, 11. 19a–29a [he lost his gold-friend], cultural generalization 11. 29b–36 [what to do when you lose one], etc.) until we reach a series of genre clusters in 11. 65b–110, representing gnome, chronicle, and homily. Lines 65b–72 are essentially gnomic, describing what a wise man should not be, but line 73 opens with, but then does not deliver, a pure gnome:[35] "Ongietan sceal gleaw hæle / hu gæstlic bið" ("The wise man must perceive how ghastly it will be"). Here we move into a tendentious observation on the nature of things which leads into a kind of chronicle or legend in ll. 80–87,[36] where we learn of the results of battles and the past destruction of this earth and the work of giants by *ælda scyppend* ("the Creator of men," l. 85b).[37] Finally we move to the extra-historical, extra-social, and decidedly moral *ubi sunt* passage in ll. 92–95a, where the poet laments the loss of things valuable in Anglo-Saxon society, the horse, the warrior, the treasure-giver, the festival halls, and the hall joys. The *ubi sunt* passage, deriving as it does from the homiletic tradition and emphasizing as it does "the vanity of the world,"[38] prepares the way for the final statement of consolation at poem's end. In ll. 108–10 ("Her bið feoh læne, / her bið freond læne, // her bið mon læne, / her bið mæg læne" ["Here is money fleeting, here is friend fleeting, here is man fleeting, here is kinsman fleeting"]), we return to the simple, declarative sentence structure of gnomic poetry, but, instead of reinforcing the social norms as gnomic poetry tends to do, these gnomic-homiletic lines affirm the ephemeral nature of all things, even the best aspects of the wanderer's own culture. A quick comparison with stanzas 76 and 77 of the *Hávamál*, which are often brought up in discussions of these lines, will emphasize the point.

> Deyr fé   deyia frœndr,
>   deyr siálfr it sama;
> enn orðztírr   deyr aldregi,
>   hveim er sér góðan getr.
>
> Deyr fé,   deyia frœndr,
>   deyr siálfr it sama;
> ec veit einn,   at aldri deyr:
>   dómr um dauðan hvern.

(Cattle die, kinsmen die, you yourself will likewise die; but fame never dies for the one who gets good [fame] for himself. Cattle die, kinsmen die, you yourself will likewise die; I know one thing that never dies: a dead man's reputation).[39]

As you can see, the Old Norse, while giving voice to natural concerns about the transitory nature of possessions and relationships, simultaneously affirms that fame, a mainstay of Germanic culture, will persevere. The wisdom here is thus time-bound, incapable of achieving the kind of lofty perspective that the wanderer has achieved as he has examined, then implicitly transformed or rejected Germanic cosmology and custom. Unlike the poet of the *Hávamál*, however, the wanderer continues to maintain and embellish his new and lofty perspective even in his use of literary genre. The movement from maxims to chronicle to homily and back to maxims in *The Wanderer* becomes part of his pathway of liberation from the world as he recasts the initial gnomic, Germanic wisdom of the poem in the light of the Christian dispensation.

The last indication of the wanderer's ultimate separation is the use of logical discontinuity in the poem. One of the most perplexing aspects of *The Wanderer* is that the poet seems at times to contradict himself, at times merely to be filling in lines. This tendency has caused some critics to see little or no unity at all in the poem[40] and has caused some editors to emend or gloss in order to achieve unity, the "*splendor formae* of medieval aesthetic" as Dunning and Bliss phrase it.[41] Some of the discontinuity derives from the culture itself or the demands the culture makes on poetic forms. Consider once more ll. 8–14.

> Oft ic sceolde ana   uhtna gehwylce
> mine ceare cwiþan   nis nu cwicra nan
> þe ic him modsefan   minne durre
> sweotule asecgan.   Ic to soþe wat
> þæt biþ in eorle   indryhten þeaw
> þæt he his ferðlocan   fæste binde,
> healde his hordcofan,   hycge swa he wille.

(Often, alone, each of daybreaks, I have had to bewail my cares—there is now no one living to whom I might dare openly reveal my heart. I know for a truth that it is a noble custom in a man that he should bind fast his soul-enclosure, hold his treasure-chamber, think as he will).

The wanderer longs in ll. 9b–11a for the conversations he used to have when he could open his heart to others. No one is alive now, though, so in an associative (and adversative) leap, he clings to another aspect of the culture that seems diametrically opposed to what he was just lamenting: he knows "for a truth" that it is a "noble custom" for a man to keep silence.[42] He clings to custom, and this particular custom fits perfectly within the larger Germanic cultural context, as we have seen. Although reticence seems at odds with the wanderer's desire at the moment, it is appropriate to his situation, and its expression takes on conventional form.

Another kind of discontinuity occurs in ll. 32–33, where the wanderer states that "warað hine wræclast, / nales wunden gold, // ferðloca freorig / nalæs foldan blæd" ("the exile track occupies him, by no means twisted gold, the frozen soul-enclosure, not at all the glory of earth"). Here he sets the exile track in opposition to twisted gold, saying that the latter does not concern him. But the two items—mainstays of Anglo-Saxon culture—are alliteratively linked, and his statement is followed by a reiteration of the importance of treasure and hall joys in his life (ll. 34–36a, 41–44). The wanderer is occupied with the exile track, as we have seen, but also with fame, as we have also seen, and with gold. The logical inconsistency is culturally consistent and shows that the wanderer acts in accordance with convention: his predictable situation produces predictable expressions of emotion. One final example should make this point clear.

> Wita sceal geþyldig:
> ne sceal no to hatheort,   ne to hræwyrde,
> ne to wac wiga,   ne to wanhydig,
> ne to forht, ne to fægen,   ne to feohgifre.
> ne næfre gielpes to georn   ær he geare cunne.   (ll. 65b–69)

(The wise man must be patient: he must not be too hot-hearted, nor too hasty in speech, nor too weak a warrior, nor too foolhardy, nor too fearful, nor too happy, nor too greedy for wealth, nor ever too eager of boast before he clearly knows.)

The lines are clearly gnomic in content but only the first half-line (*wita sceal geþyldig*) pertains to the wanderer's specific situation. What follows it is a list of conventional gnomes on what a wise man is not. Critics have tried to justify this list in terms of the theme of moderation[43] that they see in the poem, but they have not noticed that the cultural strictures on the wanderer seem to account for this odd outpouring of traditional wisdom. Associative reasoning is at work here, not a deliberate attempt on the poet's part to emphasize the theme of moderation.[44] The first gnome merely triggers a reflex reaction that produces the others, and it does not matter that they do not really fit the context. They represent "meshes of the conventional"; the form they take—and the cultural stability that that implies—is sufficient reason for their presence. The wanderer's gradual moving away from such associative reasoning, from such "meshes," shows that he also moves away from the claims of the world. The disappearance of the discontinuous in the poem coincides with the other patterns we have traced.

The overall scheme of *The Wanderer* does operate on an envelope pattern as critics generally agree, since the wanderer develops from an individual focusing on his personal quandary to a wise man, manifesting a broader perspective on the universe.[45] But in achieving that perspective, he relinquishes an unreflecting, unconscious acceptance of his culture and all its trappings—fame, gold, custom, exile—thereby divorcing himself from the temporal world. The envelope pattern that defines the poem's structure and expresses the wanderer's developing insight thus depends as much on the shifted perspective on exile expressed in the poem's opening and closing lines as on the notion of intensified wisdom evident in the change from *eardstapa* to *snottor on mode*. When the wanderer sits himself *sundor æt rune* —whether in mediation or consulting runes[46]—he actively embraces his lot, thus turning the relatively helpless *anhaga*, trapped in his earthly, cultural surroundings, into the sage who transforms the inferior, world-bound, essentially hopeless exile track of the Germanic world into the superior, heaven bound, hope-filled exile track of the Christian faith. What was his greatest torment becomes, in the end, his greatest consolation. His bane becomes his boon.[47]

Notes

1. A version of this paper was read at the annual convention of the Modern Language Association of America in Chicago, December, 1985.

2. J. E. Cross, "On the Genre of *The Wanderer*," *Neophilologus*, 45 (1961), 63–75, rpt. *Essential Articles for the Study of Old English Poetry*, ed. J. B. Bessinger, Jr. and Stanley J. Kahrl (Hamden, Connecticut: Archon Books, 1968), pp. 515–32; Stanley B. Greenfield, "The Old English Elegies" in *Continuations and Beginnings*, ed. Eric G. Stanley (London: Thomas Nelson and Sons, 1966), pp. 142–75; W. F. Bolton, "The Dimensions of *The Wanderer*," *Leeds Studies in English*, n.s. 3 (1969), 7–33; Rosemary Woolf, "*The Wanderer, The Seafarer,* and the Genre of *Planctus*" in *Anglo-Saxon Poetry: Essays in Appreciation for John C. McGilliard*, ed. Lewis E. Nicholson and Dolores Warwick Frese (Notre Dame and London: University of Notre Dame Press, 1975), pp. 192–207.

3. Mary Rohrberger, "A Psychoanalytical Reading of 'The Wanderer,'" *Cimarron Review*, 2 (1967), 70–74.

4. E.g., S. L. Clark and Julian N. Wasserman, "The Imagery of *The Wanderer*," *Neophilologus*, 63 (1978), 291–96; Elizabeth A. Hait, "The Wanderer's Lingering Regret: A Study of Patterns of Imagery," *Neophilologus*, 68 (1984), 278–91.

5. George Hardin Brown, "An Iconographic Explanation of 'The Wanderer,' Lines 81b–82a," *Viator*, 9 (1978), 31–38.

6. E.g., Stanley B. Greenfield, "*The Wanderer*: A Reconsideration of Theme and Structure," *JEGP*, 50 (1951), 15–20; Ellen Spolsky, "The Semantic Structure of the *Wanderer*," *Journal of Literary Semantics*, 3 (1974), 101–19; Rolf Breuer, "Vermittelte Unmittelbarkeit: zur Structur des altenglischen 'Wanderer,'" *NM*, 75 (1974), 552–67; Gerald Richman, "Speaker and Speech Boundaries in *The Wanderer*," *JEGP*, 81 (1982), 469–79.

7. J. E. Cross, "On *The Wanderer* Lines 80–84; A Study of a Figure and a Theme," *Vetenskaps-societeten i Lund Årsbok*, 1958–1959, pp. 77–110.

8. Stanley B. Greenfield, *The Interpretation of Old English Poems* (London: Routledge and Kegan Paul, 1972), pp. 117–22.

9. R. M. Lumiansky, "The Dramatic Structure of the Old English *Wanderer*," *Neophilologus*, 34 (1957), 104–12; John C. Pope, "Dramatic Voices in *The Wanderer* and *The Seafarer*" in *Franciplegius: Medieval and Linguistic Studies in Honor of Francis Peabody Magoun, Jr.* (New York: New York University Press, 1965), rpt. *Essential Articles*, pp. 533–70; William Alfred, "The Drama of *The Wanderer*" in *The Wisdom of Poetry: Essays in Early English Literature in Honor of Morton W. Bloomfield*, ed. Larry D. Benson and Siegfried Wenzel (Kalamazoo: Medieval Institute Publications, 1982), pp. 31–44.

10. Ralph W. V. Elliott, "The Wanderer's Conscience," *English Studies*, 39 (1958), 193–200.

11. See, for example, Thomas C. Rumble, "From *Eardstapa* to *Snottor on Mode*: The Structural Principle of 'The Wanderer,'" *MLQ*, 19 (1958), 225–30; Greenfield, "Reconsideration"; Lumiansky, "Dramatic Structure"; *The Wanderer*, ed. T. P. Dunning and A. J. Bliss (London: Methuen, 1969), pp. 78–94.

12. Some scholars, of course, do not agree with the scheme. See Bolton, "Dimensions," and Marijane Osborne, "The Vanishing Seabirds in *The Wanderer*," *Folklore*, 85 (1977), 122–27.

13. Bolton, "Dimensions," p. 27, notes that "the wanderer reacts as he does precisely because of the earth- and *comitatus*-bound notions he has of his own experience."

14. *The Invention of Culture*, rev. ed. (Chicago and London: University of Chicago Press, 1981), p. 51. See also Clifford Geertz, *The Interpretation of Cultures* (New York: Basic Books, 1973), e.g., p. 131.

15. I do not, as Rumble does ("From *Eardstapa*," p. 229), posit a specific literal scene where the wanderer sits apart from his comrades. Instead I believe that he symbolically separates himself from the culture he has described in the poem.

16. Dunning and Bliss, *The Wanderer*, p. 94.

17. Stanley B. Greenfield, "The Formulaic Expression of the Theme of 'Exile' in Anglo-Saxon Poetry," *Speculum*, 30 (1955), 200–6, rpt. in *Essential Articles*, pp. 352–62. See also Leonard H. Frey, "Exile and Elegy in Anglo-Saxon Christian Epic Poetry," *JEGP*, 62 (1963), 293–302.

18. Greenfield, "Exile," p. 354.

19. *The Exeter Book*, ed. George Philip Krapp and Elliott Van Kirk Dobbie, *ASPR* III (New York: Columbia University Press, 1936).

20. See, for example, *Genesis*, l. 1051: *Wife's Lament*, l. 10; *Resignation*, l. 91.

21. Blanche Colton Williams, *Gnomic Poetry in Anglo-Saxon* (1914; New York: AMS Press, 1966), p. 42.

22. For a discussion of *wyrd* in *Judgment Day I*, see Karma Lochrie, "*Wyrd* and the Limits of Human Understanding: A Thematic Sequence in the *Exeter Book*," *JEGP*, 85 (1986), 323–31.

23. Michael D. Cherniss, *Ingeld and Christ: Heroic Concepts and Values in Old English Poetry* (The Hague: Mouton, 1972), p. 119.

24. Dunning and Bliss, *The Wanderer*, p. 72, and R. F. Leslie, ed., *The Wanderer* (Manchester: University of Manchester Press, 1966), p. 66, point out that the initial appearance of *wyrd* in the poem is as "man's lot." See also B. J. Timmer, "*Wyrd* in Anglo-Saxon Prose and Poetry," *Neophilologus*, 26 (1941), 24–33; 213–28.

25. I disagree with Dunning and Bliss (*The Wanderer*, p. 73) in their discussion of *wyrd seo mære*, for they seem to be insisting on a particular kind of unity in the poem that we have no reason to expect. They assume, on the grounds of parallelism, that the phrase means "'the quest for the glorious destiny of death in battle'; this is something that can kill a man, and the poet is considering the glory of this death through the eyes of those who seek it." They do not consider, however, that simple juxtaposition may be involved here, the kind we see when *wyrd* is first introduced and the kind that is so typical of gnomic poetry. It is the absence of strict parallelism, in other words, that makes these lines about battle so chilling.

26. Dunning and Bliss, *The Wanderer*, pp. 73–4; Leslie, *The Wanderer*, p. 88.

27. Leslie, p. 88.

28. F. N. M. Diekstra, "*The Wanderer* 65b–72; The Passions of the Mind and the Cardinal Virtues," *Neophilologus*, 55 (1971), 77, believes that the custom of silence "of line 12 is the Christian virtue of patience and not the pagan-heroic (or British) capacity of keeping a stiff upper lip." For other expressions of the theme, see *Andreas*, ll. 1670b–71, and *Juliana*, ll. 233b–34.

29. Dunning and Bliss, *The Wanderer*, p. 45.

30. John L. Selzer, "*The Wanderer* and the Meditative Tradition," *SP*, 80 (1983), 235, notes that in this section of the poem, the wanderer "brings his understanding to bear . . . on the problem of transitoriness."

31. *The Wanderer*, p. 93. For similar points of view, see James F. Doubleday, "The Three Faculties of the Soul in *The Wanderer*," *Neophilologus*, 53 (1969), 193, and Bolton. "Dimensions," p. 30. Leslie, *The Wanderer*, p. 22, however, construes *on mode* with *swa cwæð* and notes that the interpretation "meets the objection that the wanderers' monologue violates the noble custom that a man should keep his woes to himself." Richman, "Speaker and Speech Boundaries," p. 473, concurs.

32. See, for example, James L. Rosier, "The Literal-Figural Identity of *The Wanderer*," *PMLA* 79 (1964), 366–69, and Daniel G. Calder, "Setting and Mode in *The Seafarer* and *The Wanderer*," *NM*, 72 (1971), 270–75.

33. See Ida L. Gordon, ed., *The Seafarer* (London: Methuen, 1969), p. 27; Roy F. Leslie, "*The Wanderer:* Theme and Structure" in *Old English Literature: Twenty-Two Analytical Essays*, ed. Martin Stevens and Jerome Mandel (Lincoln and London: University of Nebraska Press, 1968), p. 139; Woolf, "Genre of *Planctus*," p. 200.

34. "On the Identity of the Wanderer" in *The Old English Elegies: New Essays on Criticism*, ed. Martin Green (London & Toronto: Fairleigh Dickinson University Press, 1983), pp. 82–95.

35. Bolton, "Dimensions," p. 28, states that in this line, "the narrator takes it as a maxim (*sceal*) that the wise man will understand the implication of a *dies irae* in the evidences of commonplace decay."

36. Cross, "*Wanderer* 80–84," outlines the Christian-Latin sources of these lines.

37. John Burrow, "'The Wanderer': Lines 73–87," *N&Q*, n.s. 12 (1965), 166–68, observes that lines 73–87 deal with the historical phenomenon of the Flood.

38. Cross, "*Wanderer* 80–84," p. 85.

39. The quotation from the *Hávamál* comes from Gustav Neckel, ed., *Edda* (Heidelberg: Carl Winter, Universitätsverlag, 1962), 4th ed. rev. by Hans Kuhn. The translation comes from Daniel G. Calder, *et. al.*, trans. and ed., *Sources and Analogues of Old English Poetry II: The Major Germanic and Celtic Texts in Translation* (Cambridge and Totowa, N.J.: D. S. Brewer and Barnes and Noble, 1983), pp. 76–77.

40. E.g., P. L. Henry, *The Early English and Celtic Lyric* (London: Allen and Unwin, 1966, p. 169.

41. Dunning and Bliss, *The Wanderer*, p. 94.

42. Peter Clemoes, "*Mens absentia cogitans* in *The Seafarer* and *The Wanderer*" in *Medieval Literature and Civilization: Studies in Memory of G. N. Garmonsway*, ed. D. A. Pearsall and R. A. Waldron (London: The Athlone Press, 1969), p. 76, holds a slightly different view: "To suppose that in lines 11b–14 the wanderer is making a virtue out of the necessity of his complete isolation by proclaiming the nobility of taciturnity seems to me much less satisfactory than to suppose that, cut off from communication with his fellow men, he is reminding himself of the virtue of mental discipline."

43. See Diekstra, "Passion of the Mind," for a discussion of this theme.

44. Others have seen association at work in the poem as well. See Tony Millins, "*The Wanderer* 98: 'Weal wundrum heah wyrmlicum fah,'" *RES*, n.s. 28 (1977), 431–38.

45. W. F. Klein, "Purpose and the 'Poetics' of *The Wanderer* and *The Seafarer*" in *Anglo-Saxon Poetry*, p. 218, notes that in the final lines of the poem, "the ultimate power of human vision is located in a final context of failure . . . the principle of action in [the wanderer] has been brought to contemplative stasis." Obviously, I disagree.

46. Hollowell, "Identity," p. 93, suggests that the wanderer actually consults runes. Bolton, "Dimensions," p. 30, states that he contemplates mysteries. The vast majority of scholars, however, interpret the line *sundor æt rune* as meaning "apart in meditation." See Dunning and Bliss, *The Wanderer*, p. 123, note to line 111.

47. I would like to thank Daniel G. Calder and Theresa L. Tinkle for their insightful and helpful comments on earlier drafts of this article.

From Plaint to Praise:
Language as Cure in "The Wanderer"

MARGRÉT GUNNARSDÓTTIR
CHAMPION

IN recent years, it has become something of a critical commonplace to regard "The Wanderer" as a "Bildung" lyric, a poetic account of spiritual growth. Previous conflicts of interpretation concerning the identity of the speaker, the nature of his utterance (dramatic monologue, meditative dialogue, heroic soliloquy?) and the general ideological thrust of the poem have given way to a common reading of a quasi-didactic figure who, in the idiom of elegy, illustrates the growth of a mind, the way from pagan malaise to Christian comfort. As Robert Bjork points out, critics have come to underscore the poem's self-enclosing structure—its "envelope pattern": ". . . the wanderer develops from an individual focusing on his personal quandary to a wise man, manifesting a broader perspective on the universe." Perhaps we can assume from now on that the genre "The Wanderer" most resembles is spiritual autobiography.[1]

One of the more fruitful results of these conciliatory readings of "The Wanderer" has been a new emphasis upon the poem's dialectical movement between individual and cultural fate. The historical situation, in the guise of "Paganism," "Germanic culture" and "Christian doctrine," is no longer merely perceived as a static background against which the speaker's interior anguish can be measured but as a complex ideological fabric the individual engages with actively, emotionally and unreflectively at first, in stoic certainty at the end.[2] Clearly, the variety of relationships the speaker establishes and works through within the cultural network is open to diverse analytical positions, and it is precisely here, within the process of self-fashioning, that "The Wanderer's" chief critical interest lies for us today. Even if the problems of the poem's surface structure have been solved within the "Bildung" paradigm, the intricacies of its hidden logic, its deep structure, are only just now emerging. In this essay, I explore the poem's psychological processes as these echo in the speaker's complex use of the language of elegy.

The Work of Mourning: Theoretical Preliminaries

According to the semiotic conception of literary formations, a poetic text can most profitably be approached from a dual perspective, from the space of the "text," or the substructure, on one hand, and from the verbal construct itself, the utterance, on the other.[3] There are, in particular, two advantages obtained from this division. In the first instance, it enables a kind of movable screen to be raised between the content and the expression so that verbal communication becomes diluted, with important words highlighted as ambiguous and/or overdetermined rather than decisive and resolute. In semiotic/structuralist terms, a field of signs is staked out where meaning (the signified) continuously slides beneath the array of discrete lexical units (the signifier).

The second instance of analytic interest concerns the way in which the field of signification is superimposed upon the psychoanalytic model of the subject's place in language. In *The Interpretation of Dreams* Freud investigated dreams as linguistic mechanisms propelled by a mismatch between dream thoughts and representational structure. The crucial images in a dream, those most clearly energized by the instincts, never directly refer to the unconscious wish but stand for it obliquely, as polyvocal symbolism. Freud concluded that this surreal world is created by means of three basic rhetorical operations: displacement (and distortion), condensation (and overdetermination), and conditions of representability (metaphoric aptness). By concentrating on these configurations and on how they foreground the dream's *nodal points*, the analyst's interpretative task is made easier as s/he traces the devious connections between manifest expression and latent text.[4]

Contemporary psychoanalysis, especially the Lacanian school, has elaborated upon Freud's study of dream language and has extended that study to cover the field of discourse itself, the general principles of social communication as well as the particulars of the analytic situation. Thus, Lacan carried forward Freud's work with signifying systems—dreams, hysterical symptom, jokes, totems and taboos—to a linguistic, philosophical and anthropological investigation of the subject's place in language.[5] The overdetermined dream image or the ambiguous hysterical symptom, indeed, the self-divided structure of all pathological discourse, as well as the fact that unconscious motivation can only be detected by the other, the psychoanalyst, the auditor, the social "ear,"—all these factors indicate that there can be no subjective self-presence, only a state of permanent alienation, a split between a sense of being and the communication of that sense. To put it more simply, and into semiotic terms, there is at work within discourse a dual procedure: on one hand, there is the verbal dimension, the *utterance* (énoncé) of actual words, and on the other, the process of speaking itself, the *enunciation* (énonciation).[6] The former procedure is situated within the realm of the symbolic, within the context of convention and social communication, whereas the latter process belongs to the complex and dynamic domain of the imaginary, of subjective history and subjective meaning. From this perspective, discourse is never static; instead of a successful conflation of signified with signifier, there is a perpetual signifying glide, a process that, with respect to the poetic text, can best be described as the dialectic of form and desire. In the following reading of "The Wanderer," I will focus on that dialectic, especially on the poem's oscillation between cultural language and subjective speech. Since that movement in the poem is propelled by grief, it will be helpful first to examine in a general way the relation between elegy and psychoanalysis.

In his excellent study, *The English Elegy*, Peter Sacks argues that the common task of elegies is a project of self-consolation, a *working-through* of the crisis of loss.[7] In Sacks' account, elegiac discourse carries with it the mourner's psychological burden as he searches the adequate expression, the fitting system of figures or symbolic register, to represent his lack and his grief. Speech, in elegies, is potentially therapeutic because it mobilizes the mourner's social energies, deflecting his narcissistic malaise within dispassionate conventions.[8]

In order to labor successfully within the consolatory process, the elegist must, in Sacks' words, "withdraw affection from the lost object and reattach it to some substitute for that object."[9] Freud showed, in his essay "Mourning and Melancholia," how this is the process of mourning in general: the detachment of libido from the love object results in healthy grief whereas its continued pathological dependence leads to melancholia, a narcissistic disorder.[10] The elegiac utterance crystallizes the "work of mourning" as a process of signification; the healthy mourner improvizes a sustaining consolatory trope, or a system of tropes, which register not only the loss itself but also the awareness that the figure is quite other than the loss, a substitute, a displaced symbol. If an adequate fiction is not construed, the mourner will fall into pathology.

According to Sacks, the narcissistic dilemmas reflected in elegies recapitulate our primal experience of loss and restitution. The theoretical grounding of that view is the Oedipal narrative, told in psychoanalysis as a series of narcissistic conflicts, confrontations between the fantasizing ego and the socialized self, resolved only at the moment of the father's intervention, under the threat of castration, when the *imaginary* yields to the codes of the *symbolic*. In Lacan's account, the Oedipal resolution succeeds the major narcissistic events or crises, the first occurring at the *mirror stage* and the second during the *fort-da episode,* called so after Freud's descriptions of his grandson's play in *Beyond the Pleasure Principle*.[11]

The first blow to narcissistic integrity occurs in late infancy at the mirror stage when the child perceives the mirror image of himself, or an idealized reflection of himself in the shape of others, before his inner self has developed to any significant degree. As a result of this fantasy of fullness, the child experiences psychic fragmentation, a split within the self and between the self and the world. He can still sense the primary narcissism within, the pull of the early undifferentiated state with the mother, but this sense does not carry with it the same "jouissance," the blissful oblivion, as it did before. Now, socialized mediation in formalized exterior images dilutes the pleasure principle; narcissistic wholeness is shattered in split desire, in the rise of the conflict between originary, somatic *need* and linguistically coded *demand*.[12]

If the Oedipal resolution is successful, the subject will learn how to suppress the fantasizing ego within the nets of signifiers that come to constitute his self-image. The narcissism of the mirror stage will give way to symbolic action, to man's intersubjective experience in culture.

However, as both Freud's discussion of melancholy and Sacks' account of elegiac pathology indicate, an individual's grievous loss, especially in the form of the death of loved ones, can be the occasion of narcissistic regression, the mourner's a-social retreat into the solipsistic reveries of the mirror stage. As Sacks points out—and we will see this as a dominant force in "The Wanderer"—:

> One of the major tasks of the work of mourning and of the elegy is the repair to the mourner's damaged narcissism—but without allowing that repair to have permanent recourse either to the melancholy form of secondary narcissism or to the fantasies of the primitive narcissism associated with the mirror stage.[13]

Sacks goes on to claim that major English elegies such as "Adonais" and "In Memoriam" cannot be fully understood without the observance of their intricate work of reparations. In my opinion, the same claim can be made about "The Wanderer." Even if the Old-English poem is conceived in a different idiom from the personal elegies Sacks studies, its consolatory *passion* cannot be fully comprehended without an awareness of the underlying psychological dynamic.

In a general way, the consolatory performances of elegies can be linked to the second major narcissistic event, the *fort-da* episode, described by Freud in *Beyond the Pleasure Principle*. At this moment in a child's life, around the ages of $1-1^1/2$ years, the psychological reactions are more fully socialized than at the mirror stage and reveal more clearly the linguistic aspects of symbolic induction. The expression *fort-da* comes from Freud's account of his grandson's behavior during his mother's frequent absences. In order to compensate himself for the loss of the mother, the child invents a substitutive game, playing with a wooden reel, which he alternatively casts away, with the syllable *fort* ("there"; "away") and pulls back, with the sound *da* ("here"). The game soothes the child as he manipulates these signifiers of absence and presence, gaining a sense of self-mastery from submitting his need to their alienating representation.[14]

The *fort-da* phase is a major cultural event, registering not so much the acquisition of language as an understanding of its functioning. The young child's rudimentary language, his consolatory figure, represents his loss, grief and narcissistic desire; at the same time, this figure is at a far remove from an interiorized sense of self: it is displaced, abstract, other. The psychological compromise with the otherness of this code marks the subject's entry into language.

Since the mourner in elegy replays primal grief and the child's narcissistic crisis, and since he strives, as the child, for self-mastery, he must produce a symbol or a symbolic system that overtakes not only his personal desire but the otherness of this desire—its cultural alienation—as well. As Lacan argues in his depiction of the psychoanalytic situation, *true* speech, and thereby the process of healing, can only be generated when the analysand becomes aware of the reply of the other in his own utterance. The therapeutic ground is constituted by an intersubjective matrix, the dialectic relation between self and other. Without socialized resonances, speech either evaporates into cold, functional language or degenerates within the particular fantasy of psychotics.[15]

In great elegies, those that have truly *worked through* mourning, language may alternate between functionalism and pathology, but the final product is always *true* speech, some dispassionate image or sublime sign, which does not impose the burden of passion, but merely evokes it. We will see how this work is carried out in "The Wanderer."

Traditional Lament[16]

In the past, readers' sense of "The Wanderer's" disjunctive speech was often formulated as an aesthetic problem, entailing questions about the integrity of the poem's voice, about the number of speakers or characters and about generic class.[17] Even if these questions rarely arise today, there is no reason to disregard the intuitive perception of polyvocality in the elegy. In fact, vocal divisiveness is a defining feature of the elegiac work as the mourner's self-awareness is shattered in narcissistic crisis and then painfully reassembled in the multi-dimensional search for a consoling stability. In "The Wanderer," this search moves in three major directions which correspond to marked shifts in the poetic utterance. Thus, the first division (1–57) is characterized by the voice of melancholy, filled with sites of self-contradiction or aporias, imaginatively impotent, despite the lexical richness. The second movement (58–100) is spoken by the public voice, which at first hearing sounds entirely other than the private expression that went before. However, as we shall see, these sections are logically linked both sub-structurally, through psychological affinity, and formally, through the poem's aesthetic progress. The third and final section (111–115) borrows its full force from a superbly worked out variation on the poem's beginning lines: its voice, I will contend, is that of the artist, in full, triumphant awareness of his creative skill.

Elaborated upon in a variety of critical idioms, "The Wanderer's" three-pronged structure has often been noted. For instance, the two most recent articles on the poem develop their analysis in tune with three movements: Robert E. Bjork traces the conventional patterns or cultural meshes the speaker engages with and then separates himself from, and Patrick Cook focuses on the most abstract version of the three autobiographical stories the poem tells.[18] For the purposes of examining the different formal aspects of the poetic utterance, J. E. Cross' generic division in his essay on "The Wanderer" as "consolation" seems most pertinent.[19]

According to Cross, "The Wanderer's" achievement is self-consolation in the manner of the Latin stoics, and he points to many affinities, especially rhetorical ties, between the poem's consolatory strategies and the devices of the classical tradition. As in the standard "consolatio," the mourner in "The Wanderer" tests principally three areas for potential solace to his misery—the area of personal lament, an autobiographical solution, the area of public discourse, or philosophical council, the area of the divine, or Christian doctrine. Cross implies that these generic spheres should be considered on a progressive narrative line, as the cultural maxims gain ascendancy over the speaker and his anguish dissolves within the paradigms of ethical moderation and cosmic wisdom.[20]

What Cross draws attention to is the poem's symbolic register, the realm of social statements or official utterance. "The Wanderer's" elegiac pathos becomes the more acute as loss and narcissistic desire founder not only within the general signifying strictures of language but within the historically and culturally specific commonplaces as well. As Cross points out, even the first section of the poem—the personal lament—is, no less than the more communally oriented section, saturated with poetic "solacia," with the traditional rhetoric of comfort. The articulation of grief is restricted by the general precepts: silent suffering "is a noble mark of a man" ("biþ in eorle indryhten þeaw," 12); the loss of community, of home, of kin, of lord and *comitatus*, may be countered with hopes of new cultural ties, another "sinces bryttan" ("distributor of treasure," 25) who in the mead-hall comforts the friendless wanderer ("mec freondleasne frefran wolde, / weman mid wynnum," 28–29); the memory of former joys or lusty dreams can compensate for bleak reality (34–57). Thus, the details of the wanderer's autobiography are arranged in a general narrative pattern by the consolatory tradition and its dominant stoic and heroic precepts.[21]

Similarly, in this passage of the poem, the speaker's personality as well as the ideology he propounds are cultural and poetic commonplaces. The "anhaga" of the first line, who treads the "paths of exile" ("wadan wræclastas," 5), is an entirely conventional figure, elaborated upon in formulaic diction in a variety of Anglo-Saxon poems. Moreover, Stanley Greenfield's study of exile as an oral theme illustrates how the loners' emotional state is determined by oral-formulaic constraints: expressions of misery, wretchedness, dejection, and so on, never evolve into independent autobiographical passages but cluster in traditional semantic units—"hean" ("dejected") with "hweorfan" ("turn away"; "go"), "geomor" ("sad") with "gewitan" ("go"; "depart"), "earm" ("miserable") with "anhaga," "earmcearig" ("wretched") with "eðle bidæled" ("deprived of native land").[22] The despairing sense of personal alienation is overshadowed by exile as a cultural code and its concomitant routine images of desolate journeys, deprivation and misery.

Also, an aphoristic ideology blunts the force of personal utterance in this section of the poem. The wanderer's narrative of exile, feud, hardships and loss is punctuated by a number of gnomes reflecting pagan fatalism, the trust in mystic causality. Apparently, the speaker accepts without a doubt a fatalistic world-view that leaves no room for individual choice or desire or even for existential questioning. All experience, the most desolate wandering included, is predetermined ("wyrd bið full aræd," 5), and it is not only futile but ignoble as well to bewail that cosmic fixity ("ne mæg werig mod wyrde wiðstondan, / ne se hreo hyge helpe gefremman," 15–16). *Wyrd* is the poem's ultimate commonplace, the most banal, and therefore the most oppressive, stricture of its symbolic order.

If "The Wanderer's" genre, persona and philosophy are stock items in a standard poetic milieu, what is there to prevent the elegy from evolving into either the language of dogma, functionalist and inauthentic, or, in the case of the mourner's unbearable repression, isolated fantasy? The example of "The Seafarer" and "The Wife's Lament," often designated as companions to "The Wanderer," shows how a similar elegiac process—loss, narcissistic mourning, therapeutic drive—collapses within the rigid orders of the Anglo-Saxon symbolic. Few readers have overlooked the incongruity of "The Seafarer" where a lengthy homiletic conclusion (66–124) abruptly cuts short the imaginative (and ambiguous) account of exile, grief and spiritual quest.[23] In "The Seafarer," the work of mourning is overtaken by theological clichés; creative figuration is abandoned in favor of the stock phrases as if the speaker loses faith in his audience, in intersubjective, energetic exchange. The loss of this psychological faith and the alternative adoption of orthodoxy is, in "The Seafarer," equivalent to both emotional stasis and aesthetic bankruptcy.

The seafaring speaker seems to accept his own exclusion from the symbolic register, to opt for "empty speech" instead of the difficult word, the rich consolatory tropes of successful elegies. On the other hand, the language of "The Wife's Lament" indicates psychological betrayal of a different kind. The thick obliqueness of that poem is not solely due to a lack of reading context or intertextual milieu, as Alan Renoir suggests, but is rather the effect of the speaker's abjection, exactly the kind of narcissistic regression Sacks warns against as hindrance to elegiac recovery.[24] Indeed, the images of confinement in "The Wife's Lament"—"the gloomy cave" ("eorðsele . . . dimme," 29–39), the intractable "forest-grove" ("on wuda bearwe," 27), "the looming cliffs" ("duna uphea," 30), the mourner "sick at heart" ("is min hyge geomor," 17) in a "joyless dwelling" ("wic wynna leas," 32)—suggest that *imagos*, fantasies of the mirror state and its imaginary context, have replaced the *symbol*, the communicative, albeit alienating, social signifiers. Like the "seafarer," the "wife" surrenders her place in the chain of signifiers; however, the former erases himself in platitudes whereas the latter disappears in delusional speech.

The Psychology of Plaint

In elegies, it is the mourners' colossal task to position themselves in the alienating codes of official expression. Lacan's psychological semiotics emphasizes the troubling relation between subjectivity and positionality within signification. Because language is structured as chains of differential signifiers, one signifying unit connected to the next one in an anticipatory, linear movement, there exist no stations of subjective transcendence, no conflation of signified and signifier in a pause of full meaning.[25] There is, in other words, no pre-ordained place for the subject in language; consequently, *enunciation* or individual speech, grounded in a-temporal need, is always at odds with—sometimes painfully so—the socialized *utterance*, the language of demand, conditioned by time, place and others.

Again, elegies highlight the barrier between signifier and signified, between the language of grief and the subjective sense of loss. In "The Wanderer," the mourner faces the same dilemmas as the speakers in "The Seafarer" and "The Wife's Lament," the gap between need and demand and the struggle with symbolic exclusion. Judging from the poem's first section, the speaker's solutions seem similar to those of "The Seafarer's" conformist, riddled as the passage is with commonplaces, uttered by a stilted persona, framed by a banal philosophy. Still, "The Wanderer's" beginning is more complex than "The Seafarer's" homogeneous conclusion. The wanderer's conventionality is like a tattered blanket hurled over the urgency of need. Narcissistic speech, close to the fantasies of "The Wife's Lament," contradicts and blocks the sterile commonplaces.

As Rosemary Woolf has demonstrated, "The Wanderer" shares many formal affinities with the medieval genre of *planctus* or complaint.[26] What characterizes plaintive speech in Old-English poetry, lyrical, biblical as well as heroic, is a melancholic expression of any kind of painful loss and a socalled "ethopoetic" speaker, a quasi-didactic figure who may originate in personal experience but who tends to evolve into a universalized fictive stance.[27] Unlike elegy proper, which usually involves a particular death, planctus ranges widely in its perception of loss: in *Beowulf*, for instance, there is Hroþgar's complaint about old age (2105–14), a father's grief for the death of a son (2444) and "the last survivor's" existential lament (2247–66).[28] Thus, the causes of plaintive loss can vary between the concretely physical or libidinal and the more diffusively psychological, even metaphysical. In "The Wanderer" loss appears to emerge from both concrete and abstract causes, the death of loved ones as well as existential alienation.

Woolf indicates that the typicality of the speaker in "The Wanderer" prevents psychological conflict, that the apprehension of loss is entirely conscious and formal from the poem's beginning to its end.[29] Still, in the course of her commentary, Woolf makes many revealing suggestions about the psychological identity of the speaker, noting, for instance, the strangeness of his split persona, the constant tendency to speak about the self as if it was other. Woolf even claims that the situation in the poem is generally described as if "from the point of view of a thoughtful onlooker" and that it is "a general peculiarity of the poem . . . that the Wanderer most often describes, not how he feels, but how someone in a comparable situation would feel."[30] Surely, it is no longer sufficient to link this poetic peculiarity to the poet's artistic "intention" to typify and stylize human suffering.[31] Instead, I want to suggest that this split is a peculiarity of narcissistic speech, of *plaint*, not in the new-critical sense of stylized literary genre, but in the psychoanalytic sense of libidinal speech act. The first part of "The Wanderer" is spoken in the language of melancholia; it is the beginning phase of the poem's difficult work of mourning.

According to Freud in "Mourning and Melancholia," melancholic speech is first and foremost a profoundly self-contradictory phenomenon.[32] Although the state of melancholia may originate in genuine grief, it does not achieve the healthy mourner's detachment but remains locked in dejected lamentations. Freud draws special attention to the strangeness of the melancholiacs' accusations against themselves, which are delivered compulsively and without shame, as if in masochistic delight.[33] These outbursts, however, are far from being straightforward self-recriminations but are, in fact, the effects of an intense ambivalence toward the loved and the lost object, which the ego has internalized and identified with in narcissistic fullness. The reproaches against the self are in essence disguised attacks on the other, the ambivalent object of desire. Freud calls the melancholic speech act a *plaint*; "their complaints," he says, "are really 'plaints' in the legal sense of the word."[34] In this connection, it is interesting to note the etymological connection between "plaint" and "planctus": the former carries over some of the originary somatic meaning of the latter as the act of "striking the beast in grief." Indeed, as Freud contends, the melancholiac's expression proceeds from "an attitude of revolt," the violence of this protest muted in semantic contradictions.[35]

This delineation of the speech genre of "The Wanderer's" first section enables us to unfold its strangely evasive logic. The speaker's vascillation between convention and fantasy, between "The Seafarer's" orthodoxy and the imagos of "The Wife's Lament" is caused by his ambivalent state of revolt, his alternate sensuality and contempt for the world. Several nodal points in this section of the poem, sites of aporias or self-contradiction, illustrate the wanderer's difficult psychological dilemma. The following analysis will focus on three such nodal points.

As suggested above, loss in "The Wanderer" is a heterogeneous object, incorporating the death of a particular person, the separation from country and kinsmen as well as a more indefinite experience that can best be characterized as both cultural and existential alienation. As is the case with Anglo-Saxon poetry in general, especially *Beowulf* and "The Battle of Maldon," "The Wanderer" seems to exist in a kind of cultural twilight, within a period of a major historical transition. In his "*Beowulf* and the Origins of Civilization," James W. Earl convincingly argues that the cultural context of the Anglo-Saxon epic is itself ambivalent, caught in the shifts of religious ideologies (Paganism/Christianity) and of communal structures (the tribal/the urban; the local/the national).[36] Earl contends that *Beowulf*'s response to these transformations is neither conformist nor cynical—nor even objective—but *disillusioned* which, even if it is a "negative" reaction, is nevertheless an affirmative and a constructive one.[37]

The speaker in "The Wanderer" will learn how to achieve disillusionment, to move from destructive grief to healthy negativity. However, in the first phase of the work of reparation, in tune with melancholy logic, the ego internalizes both private and communal deprivation—the death of the heroic lord as well as the dissolution within the *comitatus*—and identifies with it in a love-hate complex of associations. On one hand, the cultural injunctions are lovingly maintained; on the other, they are rejected in nihilistic abandon.

The three major nodal areas that foreground the ambivalent blockage are those of the narrative frame itself, of the metaphoric system and of the Oedipal story the poem, at this point, tries to tell. The framer of the wanderer's autobiography is, as we have already seen, the typical heroic exile, thoroughly equipped with his culture's most valuable paraphernalia. The most insistent of these is the virtue of silence, a privileged theme in each of the poem's three sections. The beginning lines of the elegy are almost exclusively concerned with the strange contradiction between poetic desire and the cultural injunction against superfluous speech (8–21). The speaker feels compelled to recite his suffering ("Oft ic sceolde ana . . . / mine ceare cwiþan") even though he has lost his bosom-friends and confidants, exiled from his country and deprived of a lord (8–9). He knows, however, that such compulsion is morally unjustifiable; his heroic education has instilled in him a faith in stoic silence. It is no less than *nobility* in a man "to lock feelings within the breast," "to hoard them, like a treasure, within the mind"

("his ferhð-locan fæste binde/healde his hordcofan," 13–14). True manhood is bought at the price of individual speech. The wanderer knows this
intimately and lovingly repeats the stylized maxims; but no sooner has he
asserted the gnome than he defiantly breaks it in voluble fantasy, self-indul-
gent and self-commiserating. The heroic exile turns out to be a rebel. One
must, however, be careful not to mistake this narcissistic rebellion for genuine subversion. At this stage in the poem, the ego is still in a state of
thoughtless identification with the other: by attacking this other, it attacks
itself.

Breaking through the barrier of cultural silence, the self-contradictory
poetic voice generates a succession of figurative constructs, each in the
form of a wish-fulfillment fantasy (19–57). As the mourner elaborates upon
loss, his backward movement, his regression, seems to intensify, starting
with a lush memory of the heroic milieu, moving into a sensuous dream of
the lost lord, concluding with a hallucinatory experience, apparitions and
voices of the dead ("maga gemynd mod geondhweorfeð; / greteð gliwstafum, georne geondsceawað / secga geseldan," 51–53). Also, within each
fantasy, the language becomes increasingly unsettled; the relatively conventional epic of the mead-hall and its ceremonies gives way to phantas-
magoria, to the mirror-stage *imago* and to the delusional metaphor.

Thus, in his dream (37–49), the wanderer identifies narcissistically with
his former master, projecting the circumstances of what psychoanalysis
calls the "Ideal Ego," an imaginary relation, unconscious of symbolic positionality.[38] The hallucination that follows comes dangerously close to the
uprooted fantasy of "The Wife's Lament." In a kind of a waking dream, the
speaker senses the presence of his old companions so concretely that he sees
them "watch him intensely" ("georne geondsceawað," 52) and hears them
speak "joyfully" ("greteð gliwstafum," 52). Both the dream of the lord and
the vision of the departed kinsmen—"fleotendra ferhð" (54)—can be characterized in medieval terminology as "vain illusion" ("vana illusio"), false
dreams, produced by desire for what is lost. In his study of "Christianity and
Dreams," Jacques Le Goff shows how both pagan and Christian theories of
dreams recognized the category of the *phantasma*, the pure illusion, that
usually originated in some kind of physical or spiritual lack and might even,
in Gregory's the Great elaboration, tempt the dreamer into sinfulness.[39]
There can be no doubt that the wanderer's hallucination is caused by his
"sore longing" for the irretrievable ("sare æfter swæsne," 50); it is further
characterized by what psychoanalysis calls "foreclosure," an expunging of
the real world, the realm of signification, through absolute metaphoric substitution. Like the *imagos* of "The Wife's Lament," the wanderer's *phan-*

tasma tears the utterance away from its symbolic roots, replacing the difficult trope of consolation with "the voices of the dead."[40]

The narcissistic regression that characterizes the first part of "The
Wanderer" makes partly clear the speaker's desire to abandon his positionality within official signification. The mistaken search for the adequate
consolatory figure leads him away from the utterance, from his own symbolic voice, to the mirage of narcissistic enunciation. Nevertheless, in spite
of this pathological movement, the wanderer is—against need, as it were—
brought back to a communicative matrix, eventually, in the poem's next section, to take his place in the Symbolic, fully and triumphantly. How is such
recuperative work managed?

Again, psychoanalytic insight provides an explanation. As I indicated
above, psychoanalysis considers the Oedipal phase as the culminating moment in the subject's narcissistic drama. The psychic crises experienced at
the mirror stage and during the *fort-da* episode, the shocks of self-alienation, are re-ignited, now in confrontation with the *father* himself as the
representative of the Law against incest and of the prohibitions, in general,
against all the subject's misguided self-identifications. Psychological health
depends on the Oedipal resolutions: the child's fantasy of sameness must
give way to intersubjective difference.

In her fine essay "Beyond Oedipus: The Specimen Story of Psychoanalysis," Shoshana Felman argues that the major distinction between
Freud's and Lacan's reading of the Oedipus myth lies in the latter's structuralist perspective and in his insistence on the myth's significance for psychoanalytic practice.[41] Whereas Freud's interest in Sophocles' play *Oedipus
Rex* is mainly theoretical, that is, mainly tied to the discovery of unconscious desire and its general impact on psychic life, Lacan's concern is
clinical, joined with the observance of the role of speech in the analytic encounter. Where Freud emphasizes wish and its doomed instinctual trajectory, Lacan focuses upon desire in language and the question of the analytic
cure.[42] Thus, for Lacan, the Oedipal experience, the central event in psychic history, as encountered in the clinical situation, is not crucially about
the family's libidinal dilemma but about the subject's confrontation with his
own history, and cure becomes the question of *assuming* one's narrative of
oneself, of *recognizing* what had been misapprehended, the previous fatal
misrecognition ("méconnaissance").[43]

Subjective recovery in analysis happens when the analysand ceases to
repeat the old retrospective fantasies, propelled as they are by imaginary
fulfillments, and instead "names his desire" as a detached spectator of his
own destiny.[44] This naming, this full recognition, is, according to Lacan,

equivalent to the Oedipal resolution, which is first and foremost an induction into symbolic knowledge, into the epistemology of the signifier.[45] What is primarily involved in the unravelling of the Oedipus complex is not the cessation of yearning for the mother and the consequent identification with the father; at stake is what Lacan calls "the paternal metaphor," an assumption of the "*Name*-of-the-Father," the subject's anchorage to the world of signification.[46] In his role as intruder the father does not demand that the child identify with his own reality but that it should displace its wishes unto the split inherent in language, that is should, in other words, know itself as Other.

It may appear that I have strayed far from "The Wanderer," from its speaker's heavy grief and search for consolation. In fact, the paternal metaphor—The Name-of-the-Father—is an essential operation in the recuperative process of the poem. It is precisely a symbolic realization, the detached naming of desire that rescues the wanderer from anchorless retreat into narcissistic fantasy. What I want to argue is that, at the end of the first section, when the speaker is brought back from his hallucination to the icy landscape and the emptiness around him and to his own exile, he is also brought to the moment of recognition, to a kind of creative epiphany, an entrance into truthful signification. From oscillating between cultural dogma and melancholy protest, unable to figure his grief in an adequate name, the speaker is finally empowered to symbolize. The symbol he now constructs is himself as other, his own artistic mediation on the wandering exile and on exile as the human condition.

The Eschatological Artist

The new figuration starts at the opening of the poem's second section (58), a section which is in many editions presented after a break in the text, either to indicate poetic discontinuity or merely to underscore the great difference between part one and two. Indeed, readers have often been hard pressed to explain this difference and have generally wondered at the discrepancy between the private malaise of the first part and the public loftiness of the rest of the poem.[47] However, the sections are intricately connected, both psychologically and formally. The shifts from the personal to the public are effects of the speaker's Oedipal resolution. Because he wakes from imaginary plenitude to the brink of himself, to nothingness, the wanderer can no longer speak an autobiographical language, a language that assumes the subject's identification with himself. Instead, he speaks like a sage or a philosopher who delineates for mankind its true condition, its exiled state on earth. The topics of this speech are no longer the miseries of grief but existential realities—war, violence, destruction and death. Like the language of the first section, this utterance is multi-layered and polyvocal, but it is not fantastic, punctuated with mirror-stage imagos. It is true speech in the Symbolic. Possibly, the best way to characterize the whole latter section is as an eschatology, the articulation of the topic of last things (apocalypse, individual and cosmic death, the last judgment). Compared to the "self-haunted" speech of the former section this is the discourse of self-effacement, infused with otherness, almost vatic in its aphoristic exactness.

Of course, it may be objected that the confrontation with self-alienation is nothing new in the biblically inspired literature of the Middle Ages. After all, the idea of "man's exile on earth," is a Christian cliché, derived from the Old Testament account of Edenic expulsion. In fact, Old English poetry, vernacular as well as overtly religious verse, is saturated with the imagery of "paradise lost"—Grendel in the guise of Cain, the archetypal outlaw, empty mead-halls suggesting the lost idyll of the past, the desolate sea-voyage as life's allegory, the story of the Fall itself, told with didactic fervor in "The Phoenix" and the *Genesis* poems. As Dorothy Whitelock has demonstrated, "The Seafarer" can be interpreted literally as the account of a *peregrinus*, an ascetic exile who celebrates, however ambiguously, existential suffering and alienation as the natural state of being.[48] The ubiquitous diction of an exile has been analyzed by Stanley Greenfield, and we have seen it at work as a restrictive frame in the first part of "The Wanderer."[49]

What I have been hinting at throughout this essay, however, is "The Wanderer's" creative insight into a clichéd theme. At stake in the movement from private to public utterance is an enormous leap of the imagination, a kind of epiphanic glimpse into the operations of discourse, into the epistemological premise of the Name. In his "comitatus"-fantasy the wanderer's drive for self-identification is propelled by a longing not only for psychological stability but for cultural stability as well, for the lore of tradition, "the council of his lord" ("his winedryhtnes /leofes larcwidum," 38), and "the familiar sayings of kinsmen" ("fleotendra ferhð no þær fela bringeð /cuðra cwidegiedda," 54–55). It is the mourner's melancholy move away from the Oedipal resolution, the unique consolatory trope, towards narcissistic language, the soothing unified gnome.

Like Oedipus in Sophocles' *Oedipus at Colonus*, the elegist in "The Wanderer" is rescued from the misrecognition—the illusory knowledge ("méconnaissance") of himself—and, within a moment of epiphany, is ushered into a recognition, into true knowledge of the symbol, of its difficult, disjunctive, split being and of himself as its capable maker. In her discussion of Lacanian therapy, Shoshana Felman notes that the psychoanalytic cure "is radically tied up with language, with the subject's analytic speech-act, and as such, its value is less cognitive than *performative*"; and she goes on to say that "[the recognition] is, itself, essentially a speech act, whose symbolic action *modifies* the subject's history, rather than cerebrally observing or recording it, at last correctly" (Felman's emphasis).[50] Indeed, this kind of therapeutic logic is at work in the wanderer's recuperation. What distinguishes his speech act from that of the ordinary analysand is not an essential difference but a matter of "performative" degree: although both the recovering elegist and analysand come to realize the entrapment of desire by language and learn to disengage themselves from their libidinal scenarios, it is only the former who transforms this decentred knowledge into aesthetics, who dramatizes, *performs*, self-alienation, as an artist.

Thus, "The Wanderer's" next section, the recuperative speech-act, performs death as the epistemological ground of the human subject. Whereas the first section figured loss nostalgically, driven by logocentric desire, the second part elaborates an eschatology, a decentred discourse about the end of the world. Within Old English poetry, this passage is a remarkable artistic *tour de force*, a triumph of intertextual sophistication. I will indicate a few of the poem's unusual signifying ways.

As a speech act, "The Wanderer's" second section is composed of many textual strands, all linked in one way or another to death and to language. The heterogeneous object of loss of the personal lament is now contextualized, submerged within varieties of the Anglo-Saxon poetic tradition. It is as if the elegy has become an encyclopedic genre, incorporating the entire cultural utterance of grief: strains of homily, gnomic wisdom and maxims, "de excidio" ("of ruin") descriptions, images from battle poems, "ubi sunt" nostalgia, Boethian-style "consolatio." This pastiched death-song has often been criticized for what appears to be its associative logic and discontinuous movement.[51] However, the randomness is only superficial, an effect of the sustained artistic work of aligning mirror-stage fantasy with symbolic control. The melancholic protest against cultural bonds in the poem's first part has been transformed into a creative display of those bonds. The speaker neither accepts nor rejects the official codes; what he does is to figure them in his own way, to make of them his consolatory trope.

This imaginative gnomic web does not only contain topics of loss but the highly valued issue of speech and silence as well. After his initial apocalyptic image of a shrinking earth ("swa þes middangeard / ealra dogra

gehwam dreoseð and fealleþ," 62–63), the wanderer itemizes some of the
standard gnomes of wisdom and of silence. This list is suffused with stoic
philosophy:

> Wita sceal geþyldig, / ne sceal no to hat-heort ne to hrædwyrde / ne
> to wac wiga ne to wanhydig / ne to forht ne to fægen ne to feohgifre /
> ne næfre gielpes to georn ær he geare cunne.   (65–69)

> [A man should be patient; he should not be too hot-tempered nor too
> hasty of speech, nor too weak in battles nor too heedless nor too fear-
> ful nor too cheerful nor too greedy for wealth nor too eager to make a
> boast before he knows the outcome.]

The speaker then elaborates further upon ways of boasting: "A man should
wait before he makes a vow, / until he, the stout-hearted one, readily knows
/ the movement of his heart" ("Beorn sceal gebidan, þonne he beot spriceð,
/ oþþæt collenferð cunne gearwe / hwider hreðra gehygd hweorfan wille,"
70–72). The previous apocalyptic passage had noted that true wisdom
could only be achieved by a man long confronted with the destruction of
the earth (64–65). Now, balanced speech appears to be the measure of the
man, the wise utterance the outcome of apocalyptic knowledge.

As we saw in the first section, the preoccupation with the virtue of silence was dominated by the mourner's narcissism and expressed in the form
of a plaint. At that point, the speaker did not understand the trajectory of
desire and imagined a state of utopian conflation between *enunciation* (his
private woe) and *utterance* (the socialized statement). On the other hand, in
the poem's "public" section, the mourner has grown into a kind of "ex-cen-
tric" (and eccentric) wisdom: he has learned about the nature of desire as a
dissociative force in language and has realized that in order to "assume his
history," to be cured, he must speak, symbolize, within the disjunction. The
proverbial wise man—"gleaw hæle" (73)—simultaneously gazes upon destruction and death and speaks moderately. The juxtaposition is imaginatively unique, the cultural maxims exploited in order to express a profound
philosophical insight.

The images of wisdom in "The Wanderer" are thus radical elaborations, at odds with the culture's idealized depictions of personality, whether
those originate in a pagan or a pre-Christian world-view. As has often been
pointed out, the poem grapples with two ideologies, the pagan ethics of a
heroic milieu and Christian metaphysics. Usually, readers of the poem interpret it in the light of these systems of thought, proposing either their
successful synthesis or their conflict, resolved, most often, in favor of the
Church.[52] In my opinion, these views tend to be reductive because they pay

no heed to "The Wanderer's" psychology and thereby overlook its driving force, the work of mourning. As this work progresses, the poem's aesthetic awareness strengthens and with it a kind of wise detachment, the disillusioned knowledge James W. Earl notes in relation to the perspectives of *Beowulf*.[53] In a way, then, "The Wanderer" can be classified as a "Bildung" lyric, a story of the growth of a mind. This story, however, is not conventionally progressive: it neither registers heroic conformity, like so many Norse sagas do, nor religious conversion, an insight into transcendence. Instead "The Wanderer" is a story of self-creation, generically closer to modernist "portraits" of the artist as cultural exile than to either heroic legend or Augustinian autobiography.

Of course, it is not my intention to uproot "The Wanderer" from its cultural milieu and plant it in some superior universal realm, nor do I mean to overextend its artistic precociousness. In fact, the Anglo-Saxon poetic tradition itself, within which "The Wanderer" is embedded, provides a context for understanding the preoccupation with self, language and the artistic symbol. Before examining that relation, it will be necessary to look further at the elegy's figuration of self-alienation and exile.

If a post-modern perspective makes possible an account of radicalized subjectivity and facilitates a celebration of its psychological recovery, how can such a celebratory account be historically justified, especially within a poetic tradition that seems as obstinately a-psychological and foundational as Anglo-Saxon verse? In other words, how can "The Wanderer's" trope of the wise exile, who surveys transcience and "deeply ponders this dark life" ("þis deorce lif deope geondþenceð," 89), accomplish the consolatory task of elegies and "repair . . . the mourner's damaged narcissism"?[54] Does the speaker not, in the end, swerve away from his decentred discourse toward an affirmation of Christian foundationalism, placing his faith in absolute transcendence? Robert E. Bjork notes how, in the beginning of the poem, the wanderer clings to the strictures of social custom in order not to be whirled into the chaos of exile.[55] Stability is the ground of consolation: after disengaging himself from pre-Christian conformity, the speaker, according to Bjork, affirms "the superior, heaven-bound, hope-filled exile track of the Christian faith."[56] Also, R. M. Lumiansky, J. E. Cross and others have argued that the wisdom of "The Wanderer's" second section is Boethian or quasi-Boethian, stoic equilibrium in the face of universal ruin.[57] Further, Cross contends that the poem shows how the secular "de excidio" tropes are not sufficient consolations but merely prepare a mourner for the ultimate salvation, the epilogue's "*patria* in heaven."[58]

In "The Wanderer's" third and last section (111–115), the heavenly kingdom is indeed depicted as the ultimate ground of human comfort (". . . fæder on heofonum þær us eal seo fæstnung stondeð," 115). Nevertheless, a psychological reading of the poem should make clear that the "father in heaven" is neither a theological cliché nor the outcome of religious conversion. Those critical readings that overvalue the Christian implications of the epilogue, closing the poem on the note of dogma, ignore the elegist's deep psychic crisis and his difficult work toward recovery. In fact, the operative words are neither "fæder," "heaven," nor even "fæstnung," but the word *ar* or "mercy": "It will be well for him who seeks mercy (grace) for himself, / comfort from the father in heaven, where for us all stability stands" ("Wel bið þam þe him are seceð, / frofre to fæder on heofonum, þær us eal seo fæstnung stondeð" ll. 114–5). In the context of "The Wanderer's" psychological movement, its work of mourning, "ar" sparkles as—what psychoanalysis would call—"the full word," a sign resonating with its own otherness, emerging from the subject's history, conscious as well as unconscious, and from the intersubjective matrix of the Symbolic.[59] In the final stages of analysis, it is the analysand's word of cure, dialectical, suffused with the response of the Other. "Grace" represents the wanderer's cure.

In the poem, "ar" reverberates on at least three poetic and semantic levels: on a structural level, reflecting the speaker's artistic control; on the cultural level, underscoring the speaker's symbolic recovery; on the personal/spiritual level, capping the speaker's fine consolatory trope. First, the mention of God's mercy in the concluding sentence links the end to the beginning, where the lonely exile ("anhaga") waits for this mercy, apparently unsure whether he will receive it; he uses the word dejectedly ("modcearig," 2) as if it were a stock item of his culture, pagan as well as Christian.[60] Indeed, at the beginning of the poem "ar" (1) is an "empty word," cold and functionalist like "The Seafarer's" dogmatic statements. During the wanderer's epistemological education, his growing insight into the paternal metaphor, the word becomes filled with wise significance, until it is re-stated at the end in artistic triumph.

The recursive movement back to the poem's beginning alerts us to the recuperative work that has taken place, to the transformation of narcissistic grief into detached representation. Also, the semantic store within "ar" strengthens its symbolic function; on one hand, its significance is firmly tied to the wanderer's secular culture as a word of "honor," "dignity," "glory;" on the other hand, it is a Christian word, expressing the "grace/mercy" only God can bestow on believers.[61] Thus, it is an exemplary sign within the poem, registering not only the psychological experience the speaker has gone through but his interaction with both the vernacular and spiritual sides of his culture as well. "Ar" registers the wanderer's intersubjective triumph.

However, if the poem's final appeal is to the "mercy" of "fæder on heofonum," to the Christian God, does that not mean that "The Wanderer's" triumph is not so much psychological, or even artistic, but religious, the outcome of spiritual conversion? Such a conclusion would be at odds with my interpretation of the elegist's epiphanic moment, his insight into otherness. All the same, I do not think that the poem's Christianizing tendencies necessarily overturn its radical vision. It is not in the power of a traditional singer to cast off the cultural language, unless he retreats into fantasy like the speaker of "The Wife's Lament." What the wanderer accomplishes after his narcissistic breakdown is a linking of his private mourning with an activity anthropologists call *cultural work*—the construction of images or metaphoric systems that overtake the concerns of both individuals and communities. In his essay "Culture as Identity: An Anthropologist's View," Anthony Cohen makes use of this concept and shows how important it is for a culture to possess multivocal symbols that, for instance, in extreme political situations, express ethnicity or some intricate situation of communal identity. It is only the complex, open symbol, that can register both collective identity and autobiography. For instance, when a traditional symbol—some ritual, costume, even the name of an ethnic group—works effectively as protest in some exploitative situation, it is performing both in a representative and a therapeutic manner for the individual as well as the group.[62]

The consolatory trope the wanderer constructs is the outcome of such cultural work. It is the trope of himself as a traditional singer who receives grace. The "snotter on mode" ("the one of wise mind;" "the sage," 111) in the epilogue thus refers neither to a religious recluse nor a Boethian stoic but to a kind of wandering minstrel, a composite of the figures of Cædmon, praising God, and of Widsith, praising himself and his craft. In his account of Cædmon's divine inspiration, Bede demonstrates how the Anglo-Saxons considered poetic skill a gift of God:

> These verses of his stirred the hearts of many folk to despise the world and aspire to heavenly things. Others after him tried to compose religious poems in English, but none could compare with him, for he received this gift of poetry as a gift from god and did not acquire it through any human teacher.[63]

A more secular version of the glory of song is given in the minstrel poem "Widsith":

Swa scriþende gesceapum hweorfað / gleomen gumena geond grun-
da fela, / þearfe secgad, þoncword sprecaþ, / simle suð oþþe norð
sumne gemetað / gydda gleawne, geofum unhneawne, / . . . lof se
gewyrceð, / hafað under heofonum heahfæstne dom.   (135–143)

[Widely they wander as Fate may guide, / The strolling singers who
roam the world / Telling their need, returning their thanks, / And always finding, or south or north, / Some great one skilled in knowledge of song / who is open-hearted in giving of gifts / . . . He who
earns praise / Has under heaven the greatest glory.][64]

"The Wanderer's" concluding lines reflect this Janus-faced artistic
glory, heaven-bound as well as rooted in the earth. The speaker is now fully
aware of the dual function of his speech as private *passion* and public blueprint and feels confident in his role as a poetic sage: "a man should only
speak his *passion* when he knows the remedy" ("ne sceal næfre his torn to
rycene / beorn of his breostum acyþan, nemþe he ær þa bote cunne," 112–
113). He knows that it is for this speech that he will be praised, that he will
be glorious in the eyes of his culture and of his culture's God. He knows this
because his speech is true.

Notes

1. Robert E. Bjork, "Sundor æt Rune: The Voluntary Exile of The Wanderer,"
Neophilologus, 73 (1989): 119–129, esp. 126. Also, see Bjork's summary of critical approaches to "The Wanderer," 119. The classical criticism of "The Wanderer" is
marked by the debate over "voices," speaker's "identity" and the poem's religious content. For the major statements, see John C. Pope, "Dramatic Voices in 'The Wanderer' and 'The Seafarer', in *Franciplegius: Medieval and Linguistic Studies in Honour of
Francis Peabody Magoun Jr.*, eds. J. B. Bessinger Jr. and Robert P. Creed (New York:
New York University Press, 1965), 164–193, and Pope's later retraction in "Second
Thoughts on the Interpretation of 'The Seafarer'," *Anglo-Saxon England* 9 (1974):
75–86; W. F. Klein, "Purpose and Poetics of 'The Wanderer' and 'The Seafarer'," in
Anglo-Saxon Poetry: Essays in Appreciation for John C. McGalliard, ed. Lewis E. Nichol-
son and Dolores Warwick Frese (London: University of Notre Dame Press, 1975),
208–223; R. M. Luminasky, "Dramatic Structure of the Old English 'Wanderer',"
Neophilologus, 34 (1950): 104–112. For a synthesis of the "Bildung" paradigm, see
Anne L. Klinck, *The Old English Elegies: a Critical Edition and Genre Study* (Montreal:
McGill-Queen's University Press, 1992), esp. 107–126.

2. Two recent articles on "The Wanderer" are good examples of this dynamic
historicism: Robert E. Bjork's "Sundor æt Rune: The Voluntary Exile of The Wanderer," *Neophilologus*, 73 (1989): 119–129, and Patrick Cook's "The Bonds of Exile in
'The Wanderer'," *Neophilologus* 80 (1996): 127–137.

3. Semiotics articulates this division variously. Following Hjelmslev, Umberto Eco discusses the *sign*, the signifying unit, in terms of the *expression plane* and the *content plane*, in "A Logic of Culture," *The Tell-Tale Sign*, ed. Thomas A. Sebeok (Lisse: The Peter De Ridder Press, 1975), 9–17. Michael Riffaterre approaches a poem as a verbal unit, composed of, on one hand, "signs of indirection," or the poem's *significance*, and, on the other, of "mimetic information," or the poem's *meaning*, in *Semiotics of Poetry* (Bloomington: Indiana University Press, 1978), esp. 1–22. For psychoanalytic semiotics Benveniste's distinction between the "utterance" (*énoncé*), the actual words spoken, and the "enunciation" (*énonciation*), the act of speaking, has been the most important one. See Julia Kristeva, *Language: The Unknown*, trans. Anne M. Menke (New York: Columbia University Press, 1989), esp. 265–277.

4. Sigmund Freud, *The Interpretation of Dreams*, trans. & ed. James Strachey (New York: Avon Books, 1965), esp. 311–526.

5. Lacan's seminal essays on language and subjectivity are "The mirror stage as formative of the function of the I"; "The function and field of speech and language in psychoanalysis"; "The agency of the letter in the unconscious or reason since Freud." See Jacques Lacan, *Écrits: A Selection*, trans. Alan Sheridan (New York: Norton), 1–7; 30–113; 146–178. Unless otherwise noted, all references to Lacan's work are to this edition.

6. Cf. n.3. The crucial text by Emile Benveniste is *Problems in General Linguistics*, trans. Mary Elizabeth Meek (Coral Gables: University of Miami Press, 1977).

7. Peter M. Sacks, *The English Elegy: Studies in the Genre from Spenser to Yeats* (Baltimore: The Johns Hopkins University Press, 1985).

8. Sacks, 1–37.

9. Sacks, 6.

10. Sigmund Freud, "Mourning and Melancholia," In *Collected Papers*, Vol. 4, trans. Joan Riviere (New York: Basic Books, 1959), 152–170; Sacks, 155–156.

11. Sigmund Freud, *Beyond the Pleasure Principle*, trans. & ed. James Strachey (New York: Norton, 1961); Sacks, 8–17.

12. For a full account of the need/demand/desire sequence see Anthony Wilden's commentary in Jacque Lacan's *Speech and Language in Psychoanalysis* (Baltimore: The Johns Hopkins University Press, 1968), 185–192.

13. Sacks, 10.

14. Sacks, 10–12.

15. See Jacques Lacan, 85: See also Lacan's paper on psychosis, "On a question preliminary of any possible treatment of psychosis," in *Écrits*, 179–225.

16. Citations from "The Wanderer" are from *The Exeter Book*, eds. George Phillip Krapp and Elliott van Kirk Dobbie (New York: George Routledge and Sons, 1936). All references to the Exeter manuscript are to this edition. Unless otherwise noted, the translations from Old English are mine.

17. See for instance Pope, 164–193; Klein, 208–223; Luminasky, 104–112. For an influential discussion of genre see Rosemary Woolf, "'The Wanderer,' 'The Seafarer,' and the Genre of *Planctus*," Nicholson and Frese, 192–207.

18. Bjork, 119–129; Cook, 127–137.

19. J. E. Cross, "On the Genre of 'The Wanderer'," in *Essential Articles for the Study of Old English Poetry*, eds. Jess B. Bessinger and Stanley J. Kahrl (Hamden: Archon Books, 1968), 515–526.

20. Cross, esp. 524–526.

21. Cross, 517–519.

22. Stanley Greenfield, "The Formulaic Expression of the Theme of 'Exile' in Anglo-Saxon Poetry," Bessinger and Kahrl, 352–362.

23. See for instance Klinck's commentary, 139.

24. Alan Renoir, "A Reading Context for 'The Wife's Lament,'" Nicholson and Frese, eds., 224–241; Sacks, esp. 10.

25. Lacan, esp. 153–4.

26. Woolf, 192–207.

27. Woolf, 192.

28. See Woolf's examples, 194.

29. Woolf, 199.

30. Woolf, 200.

31. Woolf, 200.

32. Freud, esp. 157–158.

33. Freud, 157.

34. Freud, 158.

35. Freud, 159.

36. James W. Earl, "*Beowulf* and the Origins of Civilization," in *Speaking Two Languages: Traditional Disciplines and Contemporary Theory in Medieval Studies*, ed. Allen J. Frantzen (Albany: State University of New York Press, 1991), 65–89.

37. Earl, 76.

38. In psychoanalysis, both Freudian and post-Freudian, a distinction is made between the intrapsychic agencies of "ideal ego" and "ego ideal." Lacan relates these two structures to his orders of the *imaginary* and the *symbolic*. "The ideal ego" is a narcissistic delusion, assumed during the mirror stage; on the other hand, "the ego ideal" is formed after the Oedipal solution, indicating the subject's awareness of "the *gaze* of the other." Symbolic positions are both identifications and performances: the subject retains the narcissistic drive, but now it is modified within intersubjectivity. See Jacques Lacan, *Freud's Paper on Technique*, ed. Jacques-Alain Miller, trans. John Forrester (New York: Norton, 1988), esp. Chapter XVII. See also L. Laplanche and J.-B. Pontalis, *The Language of Psychoanalysis*, trans. Donald Nicholson-Smith (London: The Hogarth Press, 1973), 144–145; 201–202.

39. Jacques Le Goff, *The Medieval Imagination*, trans. Arthur Goldhammer (Chicago: The University of Chicago Press, 1985). See especially Chapter 5, 196–229. Also see an interesting discussion by Andrew Galloway about Gregory's the Great dream-theory and "The Wanderer." Galloway, however, does not make a distinction between the wanderer's sleeping and waking dreams; in "Dream-Theory in 'The Dream of The Rood' and 'The Wanderer'," *The Review of English Studies* 180

(1994): 475–485. Antonina Harbus argues along similar lines as Galloway in "Deceptive Dreams in 'The Wanderer'," *Studies in Philology* 93 (1996): 164–179.

40. Lacan's major statements about *foreclosure* and the three registers, the imaginary, the symbolic and the real, in relation to psychosis are to be found in "On a question preliminary to any possible treatment of psychosis," 179–225. Briefly, psychosis is a possible effect of a failed Oedipal task, a delusionary, instead of a healthy/alienated, experience of language. Lacan talks about the "delusional metaphor," an illusory stabilization of signifier and signified, which replaces the "paternal metaphor," the subject's *anchor* to the world of signification. See esp. 217–218. Also see the discussion of "The Name-of-the-Father" below.

41. Shoshana Felman, "Beyond Oedipus: The Specimen Story of Psychoanalysis," *Psychoanalytic Literary Criticism*, ed. Maud Ellmann (London: Longman, 1994), 76–102.

42. Felman, 80–83.

43. Lacan, *Le Seminaire II: Le Moi dans la théorie de Freud et dans la technique psychoanalytique* (Paris: Seuil, 1978), 58; Felman, 82.

44. Lacan, *Le Seminaire II*, 267; Felman, 82.

45. Felman, 83.

46. Lacan, "On a question preliminary to any possible treatment of psychosis," 217–218; see also Lacan, "The signification of the phallus," 281–291.

47. Such a reading is a commonplace within the criticism. See for instance Klinck's textual note, 118.

48. Dorothy Whitelock, "The Interpretation of 'The Seafarer,'" Bessinger and Kahrl, 442–447.

49. Greenfield, 352–362.

50. Felman, 82.

51. For an older criticism see P. L. henry, *The Early English and Celtic Lyric* (London: Allen and Unwin, 1966), esp. 169. More recently, a reader notes the wanderer's "self-directed discourse, with its haunting mix of associational and persuasive logics" (Cook, 127).

52. See for instance John C. Pope's commentary in his edition, *Seven Old English Poems* (New York: Norton, 1981), 80–81; see also Bjork, 126.

53. Cf. p. 12.

54. Sacks, 10.

55. Bjork, 122.

56. Bjork, 126.

57. R. M. Lumiansky, "The Dramatic Structure of the Old English 'Wanderer,'" *Neophilologus* 34 (1957): 104–12; Cross, 515–526; note S. B. Greenfield's comment that the wanderer achieves "a negative *de consolatione*," in "'The Wanderer': A Reconsideration of Theme and Structure," *Journal of English and Germanic Philology* 50 (1951): 462.

58. Cross, 524–5.

59. Lacan, "The function and field of speech and language in psychoanalysis," 40–55.

60. Klinck notes the two meaning embedded in "gebidan," "to wait" and "to experience." She also notes the element of duration in the word: the wanderer experiences a period of waiting for mercy, 106–107.

61. See definition of "ar" in Joseph Bosworth's *Anglo-Saxon Dictionary*, ed. T. Northcote Toller (Oxford: Clarendon, 1992), 47.

62. Anthony P. Cohen, "Culture as Identity: An Antropologist's View," *New Literary History* 24 (1993): 195–209.

63. Bede, *A History of The English Church and People*, trans. Leo Sherley-Price (Penguin Books, 1955), 245.

64. Charles W. Kennedy's translation from *An Anthology of Old English Poetry* (New York: Oxford University Press, 1960), 60–61.

The Form and Structure of *The Seafarer*

PETER ORTON

ONE of the accepted precepts of medieval literary studies is that texts should be interpreted against the background of the culture that produced them and for which they were composed; but some texts are not obviously associated with any specialized background, and the Old English poem *The Seafarer*—anonymous, untitled, unlocalizable within Anglo-Saxon England, and difficult to date within a period of about three hundred years—is a case in point. It is one of the poems in the Exeter Book, a manuscript written by a single scribe during the second half of the tenth century and now kept in the library of Exeter Cathedral.[1] The order in which the poems occur in the manuscript does not reveal any principles of selection or organization on the compiler's part that could be said to establish a substantial literary context for *The Seafarer*. Early connections with Exeter and the county of Devon suggest that the Exeter Book may have been written in Wessex; but this need not imply that its contents represent a compilation of Wessex poetry, and there is nothing to connect *The Seafarer* with this kingdom in particular. Like most Old English poems it is anonymous, and our one surviving text does not contain the kind of linguistic evidence that would enable us to identify the particular dialect of Old English in which it was originally composed. There are no other indications of where in Anglo-Saxon England it might have come from. The period of its composition is equally uncertain. The date of the Exeter Book means that it was probably in existence by about 950 A.D.; and as a Christian poem it cannot be earlier than the seventh century, during the course of which the Anglo-Saxons were converted. I. L. Gordon, in her edition of *The Seafarer*, would put it in the ninth century;[2] but the evidence is not conclusive by any means, and I see no reason to rule out the eighth century. The tenth seems to me less likely, for reasons which will emerge below.

Were *The Seafarer* a poem which proclaimed its own membership of some familiar literary genre, this lack of background would not matter so much. At one time, critics classed the poem, along with six others in the Exeter Book, as "elegy";[3] but it is no longer generally held that all seven of these poems belong to the same literary genre, or even that the term "elegy" is properly applied to any of them. On the other hand, there is still no agreement about what kind of poem *The Seafarer* is. There have been some definite advances in our understanding of it over the last forty years or so; but there have been just as many retrograde steps, as seemingly dead issues and long-discredited theories about it are periodically resurrected and given a slightly new slant. *The Seafarer*, for all the attention lavished upon it by critics and successive generations of undergraduates, remains a very obscure poem indeed.

What exactly are the difficulties? The condition of the text, which is not perfect, raises a few editorial problems; but the interpretation of the poem as a whole does not, one suspects, really hinge upon them.[4] There is room for disagreement over the meaning or (more commonly) the implications of certain words and expressions in the text; but these uncertainties are themselves mostly symptoms of the much more fundamental difficulty of tracing any clear line of consecutive thought through the poem. Most of the individual sentences are easy enough to understand in isolation; the problem lies in their presentation as parts of an autobiographical narrative. The rather frequent use of the connective *for þon*, the usual meaning of which in Old English is 'therefore' or 'because',[5] challenges us to make sense of the sequence of ideas; but although the poem's original audience would presumably have been able to follow it, modern readers find it difficult to see exactly how and why one thing leads to another. It is as a result of this apparent disjointedness that no agreed conception of the poem has been formed, no consensus about what one literary theorist would call its "intrinsic genre", a term defined as 'that sense of the whole by means of which an interpreter can correctly understand any part in its determinacy'.[6]

The variety of interpretations *The Seafarer* has attracted is a manifestation of the same problem. In the absence of any clear impression of genre, critics are driven to search for some hidden key to the poem's understanding, rather as if it were a riddle. But to do this is to bring into play a rough substitute for the sense of genre that the text itself fails to supply, and there are several ways in which interpretation can be compromised as a consequence. For one thing, the solution to the puzzle will be sought in those parts of the poem which are easy to understand; difficult or obscure passages will be automatically disqualified from playing any shaping role in interpretation. Furthermore, in a poem where much is puzzling, almost anything comprehensible, self-explanatory and definite can assume an air of importance for the interpreter, and be set up, so to speak, like a beacon to illuminate the surrounding obscurities. If even a few of these hitherto neglected problems begin to look less formidable in the light of it, this is eagerly accepted as confirmation of the key importance of the passage that has attracted attention. A general interpretation is then built up around this supposedly central or thematic statement, and hints or anticipations of it begin to gleam forth where previously all was dark. There is a temptation to push the meanings or connotations of Old English words beyond their normal limits, or to argue for word-play when the evidence for it is really very slender. Any outstanding obscurities are presumed insignificant and pushed to one side in the drive to knit the text into a coherent whole, and this kind of critical enterprise will typically end with a claim to have revealed a formal or doctrinal "unity" in the poem which has not been noticed before.

I doubt if anyone familiar with recent developments in *Seafarer* criticism will fail to recognize some of these trends. However, without wishing to underestimate the difficulties that fuel them, I suggest that a better understanding of *The Seafarer* is within our reach if we make a determined effort to treat all parts of the text as equally important contributions to the meaning of the whole. I think it is particularly important to abandon any notion of the poet as someone who deliberately set out to tease his audience by holding back certain key statements or information, revealing them in the course of the poem in order to clarify earlier obscurities left dangling in anticipation of them. The poem's difficulty does not mean that the poet worked in this way. Perhaps, too, we should beware of interpretations which casually assume a capacity on the part of the poem's original audience to make connections between what the poem itself says and what similar language might be used to say in other contexts. This is not to deny the poet any exploitation of literary convention; only to say that in obscure or ambiguous passages, the context in which words are used in the poem itself is the safest guide to their meaning. Difficult though it is, we must take pains to make sense of what is said in the order in which it is said, allowing meaning to accumulate or shift, but avoiding interpretations that depend heavily on looking either forward in the text or beyond it. At any rate, these are the guidelines I shall try to follow in my own reinterpretation of *The Seafarer*.

The poem opens with the speaker's insistence that what he has to tell is a true account of his own experiences, and then launches straight into a catalogue of miseries endured during solitary voyaging, apparently during the winter season. The speaker was hungry, lonely, exhausted, but above all cold; the word *cald* (*ceald*) is used five times in simplex or compound form in these early lines, and there are also repeated references to frost, ice and hail, with snow and icicles each putting in a single appearance.[7] This tale of un-mitigated woe continues up to the middle of line 33 and forms a coherent narrative sequence on its own. In a tripartite division of the poem which several critics have found useful for analysis, lines 1–33a are the first section of the poem, lines 33b–66a the second, and 66b–124 the third section. I shall adopt these terms.

There are two points in this first section where the speaker interrupts his reminiscences to draw a contrast between himself who has experienced these things and a typically conceived landlubber who has no notion of them at all. In the first of these passages, lines 12–13, this man is character-ized as fortunate in living on land rather than at sea, nothing more. The second passage, lines 27–29, repeats the point: the man who lives on land knows *lifes wyn*, 'the pleasure of life'; but also, unlike the seafarer, he has known 'few journeys of hardship' (29 *bealosiþa hwon*), doubtless an instance of the rhetorical device of litotes or understatement, the real meaning be-ing that he has never left dry land. The landlubber is further described as *wlonc ond wingal*, which Gordon's glossary indicates should be translated as 'proud (*or* splendid, *or* rich) and merry with wine'. This seems to me a just translation, though it has been pointed out that the second element of the second adjective, *gāl*, can in Old English have the derogatory force of 'wan-ton' or 'libidinous';[8] and some critics have accordingly seen in *wlonc ond wingal* a morally loaded expression, condemning the landlubber as a sensu-alist, perhaps even a swaggering, drunken, lecherous tyrant of the kind fa-miliar to students of Old English poetry in Holofernes, villain and would-be violator of the heroine in the biblical poem *Judith*. Comparison with *Judith* is invited by the poet's use of a very similar expression of Holofernes, *modig and medugal*, 'brave and merry (*or* wanton) with mead' (26). Support for the same kind of interpretation of *wlonc ond wingal* in *The Seafarer* has been drawn from a later part of the poem, where it emerges that the speaker is now planning another voyage, this time one with a clearly conceived spir-itual purpose, involving a rejection of life on land and the secular values that go with it as temporal and worthless. This attitude is explicit in lines 64–66; but it is anticipated, according to these critics, in line 29 with *wlonc ond win-gal*. Here for the first time we come up against the crucial problem of how far we should allow the attitudes the speaker expresses later in the poem to colour our response to what he says in an earlier part. The desire for coherence and a sense of unity in *The Seafarer* may seem to be better satisfied if *wlonc ond wingal* is taken as a sternly moralistic comment on the landlubber, in view of the seafarer's later resolve to abandon the kind of life he represents; but we are certainly not forced to interpret the expression in this way. For one thing, there is no supporting evidence that the speaker regards the landlubber as a bad man. For another, against the evidence of *modig and medugal* in *Judith* may be set the exact verbal parallel of *wlonc ond wingal* in another poem of the "elegy" group, *The Ruin*, which would support rather a morally neutral or even positive interpretation of the same expression in *The Seafarer*. In *The Ruin*, the narrator contemplates the remains of an old settlement, probably a Roman one (some think Roman Bath in Somerset). He imagines the place as once filled with cheerful business; but death has destroyed the men who built and inhabited it, and the buildings have crumbled. Now, piles of rubble stand where once, to quote the poet, "a host of heroes, glorious, gold-adorned, gleaming in splendour, proud and merry with wine (*wlonc ond wingal*), shone in their armour, gazed on gems and treasure, on silver, riches, wealth and jewellery, on this bright city with its wide domains."⁹ The poet is clearly impressed by the reversals that time and fate can work on such a place and the society that built it; but there is no suggestion that these reversals resulted from moral or spiritual shortcomings in the inhabitants, no attempt to identify signs of an ultimately fatal social or spiritual flaw in this old heroic society that would explain its collapse. It would not be surprising if the poet had drawn the obvious Christian inference from this state of affairs: that all the things of this world come to nothing in the end, and that only heaven holds out hope of any permanence; but he does not even do this. Is this because the moral is too obvious for words? Perhaps; but the poet was apparently content to ponder the completeness of the contrast between former prosperity and present devastation. There is no moralizing, and the expression *wlonc ond wingal* is quite happily embedded in positive imagery of heroic splendour and power. Is there any reason to interpret the same expression in *The Seafarer* any differently? It seems doubtful. As in *The Ruin*, the speaker is drawing a contrast; but it is between the happiness and prosperity of the landlubber's life and the misery and poverty of his own, not between the wickedness or folly of the former and the spiritual benefits to be derived from seafaring. The picture of seafaring in the first section of the poem is, in fact, a wholly unfavourable one. There are no consolations or benefits of any kind, and it is scarcely surprising to find the speaker thinking wistfully of the comforts of heroic society on land. In lines 18–22 he draws a series of contrasts between the social pleasures he so sadly missed during his travels, and the pathetically inadequate substitutes for them (travesties might be a better word) afforded by his marine environment: the songs of swan, gannet, curlew and seagull instead of the sounds of 'entertainment' (*gomene*) and men's laughter, enjoyed under the stimulus of mead. It is true that the seafarer later sets his face against this worldly kind of life and everything to do with it, though this is not, as we shall see, out of moral revulsion, but because he has reached a point of personal crisis. In any case, I doubt if we are justified in projecting the attitudes that this rejection implies back into the first part of the poem. Were the speaker to show the slightest awareness here that seafaring confers spiritual advantages, one might conclude differently; but I can find no sign of this awareness until much later in the poem. I shall return to the implications of treating the first section of the poem in this way, as a largely self-sufficient unit of meaning, and try to justify it in more general terms.

It is often observed, apropos of *The Seafarer,* that no Anglo-Saxon would have wintered at sea without a good reason, so it is very noticeable that the speaker does not explain exactly why he had to undergo these ordeals. It is hard to believe that he actively embraced them, even reluctantly, as a penance for some sin, for he shows no awareness of having sinned and betrays no sign of a proper penitential attitude towards his sufferings as either deserved or beneficial.[10] What the seafarer says in lines 29–30 seems to rule out some other possible explanations: he says that 'often weary' he 'had to abide on the seaway' (*ic werig oft in brimlade bidan sceolde*). There is nothing to indicate whether active coercion or mere force of circumstance is implied here; but this remark does suggest that the seafarer was under constraint to remain at sea once he was there. The lack of any mention of a destination in connection with these early voyages is consistent with what is said in lines 29–30: the seafarer shows no sign of going anywhere in particular, and so far as one can tell he may have done nothing more than drift aimlessly at the mercy of the elements. Lines 6b–12a convey an especially strong impression of his subjection to powerful natural forces. It may well be inappropriate, therefore, to speculate about the goal of these early voyages. It seems unlikely, for instance, that we are meant to think of the seafarer as looking for a new home across the sea, like the lord in *The Husband's Message,* or searching for a new allegiance following the death or departure of his lord, like the speakers in *The Wanderer* or *The Wife's Lament.* For all we are told, the whole point of his travels could have been to remain at sea, or keep away from the land. If, however, we carry inference one step further and imagine that the seafarer has been cast out from human society on land for some crime and set adrift, like certain criminals in early Irish society,[11] we face the problem of explaining why he has been permitted to return to land and tell his tale.

In view of the difficulties attendant on all these possible explanations of the seafarer's early voyages, one suspects that the whole question of their background has been deliberately left vague: that we are not meant to gain a fully realistic conception of them as having had some particular cause or motive. We would, of course, prefer to have this information; but it is questionable if we really need it, for there is much to suggest that the poet's chief aim here in the first section is not verisimilitude, but rather to establish as complete a contrast as possible between seafarer and landlubber. It is surely no accident that the two men seem to be exact, formal opposites, like black and white pieces facing each other across a chessboard. That a structural opposition is what is aimed at is strongly suggested by the contrast with the landlubber's privileges and comforts in lines 18–22, and also by the seafarer's rather artificial claim to have habitually 'dwelt' (*wunade*, 15) on the sea for long periods in conditions that certainly could not have been supported indefinitely. If the first section is viewed in this light, the question of the seafarer's reasons for being and remaining at sea seem almost as immaterial as the landlubber's reasons for staying on land. The opposition is not stable, however: only the seafarer knows both worlds, both lives. His complaint is that the landlubber neither knows (12 *wat*) nor believes (27 *gelyfeð*) how he has had to live. It has been suggested that the more widely-experienced seafarer feels a certain pride in his powers of endurance;[12] but I think it likelier that these remarks about the landlubber are expressions of a dissatisfaction arising from his inability to confer the sort of social validity on the seafarer's experiences that only "knowing" and "believing" them could confer. The seafarer's experiences cannot be encompassed within the framework of conventional life, and this alienates him from the values and priorities prevailing among his fellow-men. We shall see shortly how this sense of alienation on the seafarer's part is confirmed and finally resolved in the rest of the poem.

Interpretation of the second section of *The Seafarer* (33b–66a) must begin with the problem of *sylf* in line 35, still a much-disputed crux.[13] The meaning of *sylf* most readily suggested by the immediate context here is 'myself', in which case the first sentence of the section, 33b–5, is to be translated: 'Therefore now thoughts beat against (my) heart, that I myself should make trial of the towering seas, the play of the salt waves.' This translation implies, however, that the speaker here is not the same as the speaker of the first section; a dialogue seems indicated, with the change of speaker coming in the middle of line 33.[14] Most recent critics reject the idea of a dialogue (and with it this interpretation of *sylf*), with good reason: it is incredible that the poet would have felt able to rely on the word *sylf* alone to signal a change of speaker, especially as it could have other meanings in the context. What is needed is a meaning of *sylf* that enables us to dispense with the dialogue theory, and Kershaw's translation: 'of my own accord' has much to recommend it.[15] It does, of course, imply that the speaker was constrained to undertake his earlier voyages; but as we have already encountered evidence that he was indeed constrained, if not to go to sea, at least to remain at sea once he was there, this implication of 'of my own accord' does not militate against it.

According to this interpretation of *sylf*, the second section begins with the speaker's assertion that he 'therefore now' (33b *For þon . . . nu*) feels impelled from within to undertake another voyage 'of his own accord'; but here a difficulty arises which the dialogue theory manages to avoid: the inconsistency of the speaker's evident willingness to contemplate more seafaring after complaining about it so bitterly in the first section. The transition between the two sections has been closely scrutinized for signs of an intelligible continuity of thought not immediately apparent, and the word *hean* in 34 has been interpreted in such a way as to blunt the impression of a complete *volte face*. This coming voyage, the argument runs, will, unlike previous ones, involve travel over 'deep' seas (*hean streamas*).[16] But *hean* probably means '(towering) high' rather than 'deep';[17] and in any case, there was no reference to shallow water in the first section. The two mentions of cliffs (8, 23) have been taken by some as evidence that the seafarer's earlier voyages were confined to coastal waters, but I doubt if they provide adequate support for the supposed contrast with travel across the open or deep seas.

If, however, the first section is interpreted in the way I have suggested, and account is taken of the speaker's alienation from heroic society on land, this compulsion to undertake another voyage, though unexpected, does not seem so perverse. One can understand why the seafarer should no longer feel at home with men on land, and the sea is his only escape-route. Previously, society on land represented warmth, companionship and security—everything of which the seafarer felt most deprived in his earlier voyages; but by a cruel irony, on his return to land he finds that his isolation at sea has resulted in an equally intolerable isolation at home, where his experiences are unshared, unknown, scarcely credited, in short denied the validity I mentioned earlier, which is presumably reserved for traditional "heroic" experiences on land. All he can do is return to the sea, even though it was seafaring that led to his difficulties in the first place. The seafarer seems to be caught in a vicious circle at this stage in the poem.

If I am right in seeing the seafarer's predicament in these social and psychological terms, there still remains a problem about the relationship between the first and second sections of the poem, a problem of temporal perspective. Earlier I questioned whether we should allow the second section of the poem to shed retrospective light on the first, and suggested that we should not; that the first section was coherent in its own terms, even if it failed to provide all the information we would need to build up a wholly realistic picture of the background to the seafarer's early voyages. However, one of the implications of treating the first section in this way, as a self-sufficient unit of meaning, is that it is an expression of the seafarer's attitudes and feelings, not at the time of speaking (the present moment represented by the word *nu* in 33 and later in 58) but at the time of his earlier voyages; in other words, that the first section is something like an entry in a diary. But is this a credible interpretation? I think it is, chiefly because it seems to make the best sense of the first section in relation to the rest of the poem, but also because at least one other Old English poet whose work is known to us used the same narrative method, and for very similar purposes. In *The Dream of the Rood*, the cross, in the early part of its speech to the dreamer, gives a view of its previous experiences, particularly Christ's crucifixion, that is not fully reconcilable with its present state of theological sophistication and spiritual maturity as revealed in the final part of its speech. The description of the crucifixion gains in vividness and immediacy as a result, and we gain a deeper appreciation of the transformation the cross has undergone from wooden gallows, instrument of torture and death, to symbol of redemption.[18] I suggest that the same device is used in *The Seafarer* to give us a clear idea of the progress and direction of the speaker's psychological and spiritual development up to the time of speaking, and a more vivid impression of the actual impact his previous voyages made on him. The seafarer is, in a way, quoting himself in the first section; or perhaps one should rather say, projecting himself, as narrator, back to the time of those voyages and saying what he might have said about them when they were still fresh in his mind.

The second section of the poem opens with a description, in lines 33b–38, of powerful if rather vaguely defined inner promptings at work 'now . . . all the time' (33b *nu*, 36b *mæla gehwylce*) on the speaker to depart across the sea. But it is very clear that he does not relish the idea of another voyage: the way the pressure he is under is described, as the beating (*cnyssað*) of his heart by 'thoughts' (*geþohtas*), creates a powerful impression of helplessness, even reluctance. This is not to be wondered at, in view of his earlier experiences of seafaring; but it alerts us to the fact that in this second section, as in the first, the seafarer's situation is to be understood not solely in the retrospective light of the spiritual ambitions he expresses later on, in lines 64–6, but also in psychological terms. The seafarer is plainly in a state of conflict over his prospective voyage.

We are not told what it is that precipitates this apparently sudden compulsion to go to sea again, though it is conceivable that the coming of winter on land, described at the very end of the first section (31–33a), has something to do with it.[19] It emerged very clearly in the first section that it is the time of snow, frost and hail that the seafarer associates with voyaging; so it is possible that the winter season is a special psychological trigger for him. Perhaps all that can be said with confidence about these lines is that they are in some way transitional: like the first section, they deal with time past; but, like the second, they refer to life on land, and they may be intended as the beginning of an account of the progress of the seasons on land which is taken up later in the second section with the coming of spring (48). Winter, as I said earlier, was no time to be thinking of seafaring in the early middle ages, so perhaps we see here the first manifestation of a subversion of normal responses in the seafarer, a conditioning resulting from the terrible privations he has endured which makes him react to events in ways that would seem inappropriate or incomprehensible to landlubbers. We shall find other, more convincing evidence of this perversity later on.

An important point that emerges here, early in the second section, about this new voyage is that it is to be no mere repetition of previous ones. Evidently the seafarer has no intention of lingering on the sea in the manner of his earlier voyages; this time he has a definite goal, expressed in lines 37–8 as a wish to 'seek the dwelling-place of exiles (*or* foreigners) far hence' (*feor heonan elþeodigra eard gesece*). It should be emphasised that the meaning of *eard* in Old English generally is indeed 'dwelling-place', not 'native land' or *patria*, for which the Old English word is *eþel*.[20] The distinction is important: it means that *elþeodigra eard* almost certainly denotes a land across the sea to which men may resort as exiles, not a place from which a man may travel into exile, or to which he may return from exile. This is, I would say, an obstacle to the interpretation favoured by Smithers and others who argue that the seafarer's planned voyage is an allegory of his aspiration, as a Christian and a descendant of Adam, to regain his heavenly fatherland, because the surface-meaning does not directly correspond with (is in fact opposed to) the supposed allegorical meaning, 'heaven'.[21] Literal interpretation of the expression is to be preferred for this reason. This is not to deny, of course, that the seafarer's prospective voyage has a symbolic, Christian significance for him; later it becomes quite clear that it does, and that the seafarer's ultimate purpose is the salvation of his soul and everlasting life in heaven. But this in no way lessens the difficulty of interpreting *elþeodigra eard* allegorically.[22]

The passage from 39 to 47 continues in the same psychological vein as the second section began, though here the speaker changes to the third person and talks about the indifference that a man of his general type feels towards the pleasures and security of life on land. The change of person must, I think, be related to the fact that this passage says very much the same things about the attitudes to life on land held by the kind of man the seafarer has become as was said in the first section about the attitudes to seafaring held by the typical landlubber. It emphasises the gulf between these two varieties of men, who share no common interests or preoccupations, and places the opposition between them on a firmer structural footing. The landlubber was incapable of empathizing with the seafarer's earlier experiences at sea; and now we learn that for a man with the seafarer's experiences behind him and another voyage in the offing (perhaps inevitably, because of those experiences), heroic life on land holds no meaning, let alone attraction. For such a man—"seafaring man", as we might call him—a potent combination of feelings about the coming voyage—anxiety or sorrow (42 *sorge*) and yearning (47 *longunge*)—blots out everything else, no matter how assiduously he might otherwise (or previously) have devoted himself to the values of heroic society and conformed to its standards and ideals (39–43), or how absorbing the pleasures of heroic, domestic and sexual life on land may seem to those with the tranquility of mind to enjoy them (44–7).[23] The seafarer's identification with a type represents a mitigation of the desolate mood of the first section, for he is beginning to form a definite and more objective image of the kind of man he has become. It is, however, an essentially negative image: "seafaring man" is little more than "non-landlubber"; the seafarer has yet to re-establish a positive sense of his own place in the world.

So far there have been no Christian references in *The Seafarer*—no use, that is, of unmistakably Christian ideas or vocabulary. I may be wrong to exclude the speaker's wish to seek *elþeodigra eard* in 37–8: it is possible that an Anglo-Saxon audience would have picked up this expression as a reference to ascetic religious exile, even in the absence of any explicit spiritual motive or attitudes, though I do not think that we can assume that they did. In any case, the first unambiguously Christian remark in the poem comes in line 43: the fate of a man like the seafarer will be in the Lord's hands once he sets out. This remark does not reflect any sense of optimism or assurance on the seafarer's part: he feels anxious about his voyage, and the actual focus of his anxiety is 'what the Lord may have in store for him' (to *hwon hine Dryhten gedon wille*). There is no assumption that God will be merciful; on the contrary, he seems to fear the worst. It has been pointed out that a line almost identical in form with *Seafarer* 43 occurs in another Old English poem, *An Exhortation to Christian Living* (61 *tohwan þe þin drihten gedon wille*), also in a context of uncertainty, though here it is uncertainty about the fate of the soul after death. Some critics have been inclined to see at least a hint of this same uncertainty in *The Seafarer;* they think that here too the speaker is worrying about his soul's fate.[24] However, the basis of this interpretation is rather weak. A case for it might be made if we had reason to think that the *Seafarer* poet knew *Exhortation,* or that the form of words in question was originally or conventionally associated with anxiety about the soul's fate; but there is no basis for the first assumption, and very little for the second. Line 43 of *The Seafarer* may be slightly awkward syntactically in the sentence of which it is a part,[25] but surely not so awkward as to alert the audience to its borrowing from another context. Nor is the meaning at all obscure: the seafarer is a Christian, but he cannot be sure that God will protect him on his voyage, so he worries about his personal safety. He knows seafaring and the perils it entails. Surely it is survival, not salvation, that preoccupies him here.

There follows a passage (48–57), still in the third person, which describes the advancing year and how the various natural manifestations of spring and summer exert additional pressure on "seafaring man" to be away. As the seasons progress, time presses more and more heavily on him, and this must, I suppose, be attributed to his awareness that summer is the optimum season to begin a sea voyage. One would think that the seafarer would want to avoid the miseries of winter seafaring this time. Lines 48–9 describe the blossoming trees, the beauty they confer on the settlements of men and the meadows, and the hastening or business of the world (*woruld onetteð*). Two critics, Professors Smithers and Cross, independently had the idea that this last observation is meant as a hint of the imminence of Doomsday, an interpretation suggested mainly by a passage from *Blickling Homily* V, where the growth of natural, seasonal beauty is seen as a sign that the world is moving into its last phase.[26] The problem with all interpretations of this general kind, of course, is that they rest on assumptions about the knowledge and sophistication of poet and audience that can be neither verified nor disproved. In this particular case, everything depends on whether we believe that the poet would have felt able to rely on his hearers' familiarity with this idea from the Old English homilies they had heard, and that the diction and content of the *Seafarer* passage are calculated to trigger its recall. The verb *onettan* is probably the most distinctive dictional element in both passages; but it is not a particularly uncommon word, and discussion must surely recognize that to say that the world *onetteð* is not necessarily to say that it 'hastens towards its end' (cf. *Blickling Homily V to ende . . . onetteþ*): the verb *onettan* can mean 'to be busy', 'to be active', like the flame on Doomsday in the Exeter Book poem *Judgement Day I* (*55 leg onetteð*), as well as 'to hasten' towards some goal or end.[27] Neither Cross nor Smithers discuss the suitability of this alternative meaning of *onetteð* in *Seafarer* 49. Nor should the fact that the *Seafarer* passage is ostensibly seasonal, not eschatological, be glossed over. Translation as 'the world is busy' makes perfectly acceptable sense in the context. Smithers would disagree: he dismisses literal interpretation of the *Seafarer* lines on the grounds that it involves the "inconsistency . . . of juxtaposing a 'yearning' for a sea-voyage (which is to be full of sorrow) with a picture of the beauties of spring on land".[28] But this "inconsistency" is surely the whole point here: ironically, "seafaring man" feels pressurized to depart (50–52) by those very changes in the natural world that for the landlubber enhance the allure of life on land. The reference to the "settlements" being beautified by the blossoming trees (48b *byrig fægriað*)—surely not an indispensable element in a conventional description of spring—seems to support this idea of the poet's intended emphasis. It was to this passage that I alluded earlier when I spoke of the subversion of response (in terms of the norm established by the landlubber) that now afflicts the seafarer and his kind. The advent of the natural beauty that for others makes life on land more satisfying than ever is to them a signal that they must abandon that life.

The call of the cuckoo, sad-voiced (53 *geac . . . geomran reorde*), the guardian of summer (54 *sumeres weard*), is mentioned as a further stimulus to the sense of urgency that a man like the seafarer must feel. The song of the cuckoo was probably as conventional an element in descriptions of spring for Old English poets as it was later in Middle English; but here something like the "pathetic fallacy" seems to be at work. The melancholy quality of the cuckoo's voice seems to have been a given attribute in Old English poetry, for it appears also in *The Husband's Message*, again in association with a prospective voyage across the sea, though here the journey seems likely to have a happy outcome: the woman, to whom the poem is addressed, will be reunited with her expatriate lord.[29] "Seafaring man", on the other hand, must feel trepidation about his voyage, so for him the cuckoo's sad voice is especially piquant, boding 'bitter anxiety' (54–5a *sorge beodeð, bitter in breosthord*). The lines immediately following, 55b–7, contain the third and last remark about the landlubber's ignorance of the seafaring man's sufferings: *sefteadig*, 'blessed with comfort' (or perhaps *esteadig*, 'prosperous through inheritance', if this emendation of MS *eft eadig* is preferred),[30] he 'does not know what those endure who lay down tracks of exile most widely' (56b–7 *hwæt þa sume dreogað þe þa wræclastas widost lecgað*). These lines could denote only the miseries of exilic seafaring; but their position, right after the description of spring and summer, probably means that they refer also to the pressure exerted by the progress of the seasons: the landlubber is *sefteadig* (or *esteadig*) because he is able to take straightforward pleasure in the arrival of summer; the fresh beauty of his *burh* and the cuckoo's call do not provoke the restlessness in him that they do in a man whose previous experience of the sea has made him obsessed with the prospect of another voyage.

The climax of the second section of the poem comes in its closing lines, 58–66a, in which the speaker abandons "seafaring man" and returns to his personal affairs. First there is a memorable description (58–62a) of his mental anticipation of the voyage to come: his mind or heart (*hyge, modsefa*) actually separates itself from him and roams out across the sea, returning 'eager and greedy' (*gifre ond grædig*) to urge him to depart. I have discussed the meaning of this passage in some detail elsewhere;[31] here I only repeat that the words *hyge* and *modsefa* apply to the centres of mental or emotional activity in Old English and that it is tendentious to take them as referring to the immortal soul, for which the Old English is *sawol* or *gast*. The meaning here is psychological, not spiritual—another obstacle, I think, to Smithers's interpretation of the proposed voyage as an allegory of the speaker's desire to return to his heavenly *patria*. Despite the remarkably concrete separation of mind and body, the description is of the mental process familiar to all whereby future events are anticipated imaginatively: the seafarer rehearses the voyage he is planning in his mind, and this both reflects and sharpens his keenness to embark. External pressures on him to set forth are also at their height, with the *anfloga*, literally 'solitary flier' and in my view (as in Sieper's, Gordon's and Whitelock's, but not in any more recent critics' who have expressed an opinion on the matter) the cuckoo again, still calling, but now with an urgency which the seafarer finds impossible to resist. The way in which an external stimulus here breaks in on the seafarer's inner meditations on his voyage is remarkably reminiscent of a passage in *The Wanderer*, lines 51–5, in which the speaker's recollections of his lost kinsmen are interrupted when he notices the seabirds that surround him swimming away, and he reflects sadly on their inadequacies as 'companions of men' (*Secga geseldan*): in both passages, intrusive reality puts an end to imaginings but at the same time merges with them, as when one is woken from a dream by some disturbance.

Finally, in lines 64b–66a, the seafarer states his Christian motive for what will presumably be his last voyage: the 'joys of the Lord' (65 *Dryhtnes dreamas* are 'hotter' (*hatran*) to him than life on land, which he now rejects as 'dead' and 'transitory' (65b–66a *þis deade lif, læne on londe*). It is sometimes said that the contrast between life on land and life at sea that informs the first section of the poem and most of the second is effectively replaced here by a contrast between all worldly life, whether on land or sea, and eternity;[32] but this is only partly true. Reference continues to be made to 'life on land', and the idea of seafaring is not so much replaced as seen in a fresh light, as a means to a spiritual end which is religious exile, and ultimately salvation. The use of the adjective *læne*, 'transitory', of life on land certainly shows a new appreciation on the speaker's part of the degree to which life on land represents all mortal life, subject to decay and death; here the speaker anticipates the subject of the third section of the poem. But *deade*, with which *læne* is linked, does not mean the same thing, and is probably better interpreted in the light of the attitude to life on land that has been in evidence throughout the second section. The satisfactions, pleasures and beauties that make heroic life on land worth living for the landlubber are thoroughly obliterated by the seafarer's compulsion to return to the sea, so one can understand why he should call life on land 'dead'; for him it has indeed died.

Critics have sometimes been disturbed by the speaker's apparent delay in revealing this religious motive for his voyage until the very end of the second section. Why was this information not provided at the beginning of the section, when the new voyage was first mentioned? I think the answer must be that it properly belongs here in the scheme of the seafarer's personal development, representing as it does the remedy for the alienation from life on land that he has been describing so feelingly. For the seafarer, life on land is life in a topsy-turvy world, where his responses are completely out of step with everyone else's, and he is continually distracted by a mixture of compulsive desire and foreboding. But now, presumably under the impetus of his wish to emigrate, and his reflection that he will be completely at God's mercy if he commits himself to the sea again, his confusion is suddenly resolved by a transposition of all his desires and fears into a different, religious mode. Such a sudden surge forward in the evolution of the seafarer's way of looking at the world and his own place in it is difficult to explain except in terms of religious conversion or revelation. What appears to happen is that he discovers in his situation and feelings something of the intentions and motives of the ascetic *peregrinus*, and so is able, by a kind of conative self-projection, to replace his negative feelings with positive ones and hammer out a new identity for himself as a Christian. This confers a psychological as well as a spiritual freedom upon him which enables him to reach a fuller and wiser conception of life on land as not just "dead" but also "transitory."

This is not the first unpredictable twist in the seafarer's "true tale." The first was his compulsion to go to sea again, revealed with similar abruptness at the start of the second section. The two transitions are similar in that both are introduced by *for þon* in the middle of a line (33b, 64b); but the first was followed by the seafarer's identification with a general type of man whose experience and reactions coincided with his own—"seafaring man", as I have called him. One might expect a similar development after the second transformation: that the seafarer would go on in the third section of the poem to explore his new identity as a religious ascetic. But in fact the whole idea of voluntary exile in pursuit of "the joys of the Lord" is dropped as soon as it is introduced, and there is no further mention of the sea, seafaring or travel to foreign lands. The seafarer ceases altogether to talk about himself once he has made this gesture in the direction of *peregrinatio*, and proceeds to reflect in ways most of which are familiar from Old English prose homilies on the power of God in comparison with the feebleness of man, helpless as he is in the face of mortality and material and moral decay in the world. In his new role of homilist he speaks of the transience of worldly possessions and the inevitability of death (66b–71), the analogy between the praise of dead heroes and immortality (72–80), the physical and moral decline of mankind (80–90), the pathos of old age (91–6), the relation between Christian living and salvation, which gold cannot buy (97–102), the power of God over his creation, including men and their souls (103–6, 113–16), the desirability of Christian virtues (107–12), and ends with a prayer for all men to remember that only heaven, conceived of here as their true 'home' (*ham*), to which they may hope to return, can offer immortality (117–24).

Here, at the very end of the poem, with this reference to heaven as the Augustinian *patria* of all men, the ultimate aim of the *peregrinatio* enterprise finds expression. *Peregrinatio pro amore Dei* was a journey abroad for the soul's profit, an escape from local, secular distractions and temptations to the isolation and strangeness of a foreign country where a life devoted to prayer and contemplation might be lived and the chance of ultimate "repatriation" to heaven increased. This connection is a valuable one in the defence of the unity of *The Seafarer* against the charge of incoherence to which the sudden abandonment, half way through, of the seafaring theme lays it open; but this thematic link is not in itself sufficient to justify the whole of the third section as an appropriate sequel to the first two, because the seafarer is not urging all men to become literal *peregrini*. I think every-one would agree that he is rather trying to persuade all men to cease, as he has done, from putting any trust in the things of this world and turn to God. But how does the seafarer think this can be done? His own experiences, if taken as an example, would certainly not encourage the view that it is an easy matter for men to turn their backs on the happiness, comfort, com-panionship and sense of social security that heroic life on land affords. The seafarer himself has managed to break free from these social and psycho-logical ties by a complicated sequence of events and pressures. He has found himself in a situation where *peregrinatio* offers the only alternative to despair. But his is not an example that everyone else can be expected to fol-low. The question remains of how ordinary men can hope to achieve the same perspective on human life as the seafarer has achieved. How does the seafarer-preacher, in his new-found wisdom, advise his audience (I think we can assume that the poem is addressed to laymen) to break away from the relative narrowness of traditional, heroic ethics and priorities and replace them with Christian ones? What practical advice can he offer?

As one would expect, an important part of his strategy is to emphasise some of the more depressing and universal signs of human mortality and general earthly decline. The threat of death and doom is a powerful weapon in the battle for men's souls. So is awareness of God's infinite power, as cre-ator of the universe and final judge of souls. These are the things that dom-inate the third section of *The Seafarer*. But there is one passage which seems designed to show laymen living in the world and upholding standard heroic ideals how they too may transpose their lives into a Christian mode, rather as the seafarer himself has done. This passage (72–80) is well-known, but is worth looking at in some detail. Gordon's text of it is as follows:

> For þon biþ (*MS* þæt) eorla gehwam æftercweþendra
> lof lifgendra lastworda betst.
> þæt he gewyrce, ær he on weg scyle,
> 75 fremum (*MS* fremman) on foldan wið feonda niþ,
> deorum dædum deofle togeanes,
> þæt hine ælda bearn æfter hergen,
> ond his lof siþþan lifge mid englum
> awa to ealdre, ecan lifes blæd (*MS* blæð),
> 80 dream mid dugeþum.

Gordon translates:

> Therefore for every man the praise of those who live after him and commemorate him is the best memorial, which he may earn, before

he must depart, by good actions on earth against the wickedness of
enemies (*or* fiends), opposing the devil with noble deeds, so that the
children of men will praise him afterwards and his glory will live then
among the angels for ever, (in the) blessedness of eternal life, bliss
among the noblest.[33]

Tolkien found difficulties of syntax here (he does not say exactly what they
are) that convinced him that the passage had undergone "revision and expansion" in transmission.[34] Gordon disagrees, identifying the problem as
"the awkwardness of the reasoning which has to transform *lof,* the praise of
one's fellows, into *lof mid englum,* 'praise among the angels,'"[35] though in
her view "to one familiar from pagan poetry with the idea of fame as the
only answer to the transience of life *lof mid englum* might seem a not unnatural description of eternal life'.[36] In this way she would explain the problematic equation of this latter expression with everlasting life, *ecan lifes blæd,
dream mid dugeþum,* phrases she regards as "parallel to *lof,* amplifying and
explaining it."[37] However, although these expressions are evidently parallel
syntactically to *lof,* one would think that they were too different in meaning
from *lof* to be grammatically or logically subordinated to it in the way Gordon supposes. The awkwardness is clear from her translation, where "(in
the)" has to be inserted against the evidence of the grammar. This is no
doubt the difficulty Tolkien defined as syntactical. The glory of eternal life
amounts to much more than having one's praises sung for ever, even by angels; and this limited conception of heaven conflicts with the more conventional one we find at the end of the poem, where heaven is identified as the
true 'home' (117 *ham*) of humanity where 'eternal bliss' (120 *þa ecan eadig-
nesse*) may be enjoyed.

What seems to have happened here is that the poet has seen a valuable
analogy between two kinds of immortality: the kind which it lies in the
scop's power to confer on dead heroes (*lof*), and the Christian life everlasting, and has tried, by what one might call sheer force of syntax (by variation,
to be precise) to graft the second notion on to the first, even though they are
really too different to be run together in this way. The play on the word
feonda, 'enemies' or 'fiends', and the idea of angels' praise are meant to form
a bridge between the two, but it does not span the gulf completely. I think
that what we see here is the poet attempting to show his audience of secular
laymen how they too may, like the seafarer, turn secular experience to advantage rather than simply reject it, by using it as an intellectual foundation
for Christian awareness. The poet recognizes that men will continue to
strive for posthumous glory by brave deeds against their enemies; but their
victories can also be triumphs over wickedness and thus over the devil him-

self. Much depends on the spirit in which worldly actions are performed. The illogicality remains; execution falls short of aspiration, but it is the aspiration itself that is significant: the attempt to find some sort of typological basis for a Christian attitude to life in secular modes of thought and action must surely be connected with the fact that the seafarer's own experiences have taught him that this is feasible.

The Seafarer has been variously interpreted, so it may be helpful to conclude with a summary account of how my own interpretation of it differs from most previous ones. First, form: a crucial aspect of the poem's form has not, I suggest, been properly appreciated. The opening lines promise autobiographical revelations, and these we are given: the speaker selects amongst and presents his experiences according to his idea of himself as a product of them, as one would expect. But the narrative perspective on these experiences is not fixed; it does not reflect the full maturity and knowledge of the present moment throughout the poem, but progresses towards it in the course of the telling. The analogy I used earlier with the entries in a diary may have some value; but *The Dream of the Rood*, to which I also referred earlier in this connection, is a better one. The seafarer tells how he has come to desire a Christian life; but we are given, not just a bare sequence of incidents and episodes, but something like a running commentary by the speaker on their impact on him. The reader must follow the speaker in taking each piece of information—each event, emotion and thought—just as it comes, making sense of it in its own terms or in terms of what has preceded it. There are, I believe, no hints of what is to come, no anticipations of future developments in the speaker's life, no "seeded" revelations; in fact, one suspects that an element of suspense was part of the authorial design. Only by the end of the poem can we see how the seafarer's experiences have made him the kind of man he is, because only then do we know the kind of man he has become. The effect of this aspect of the poem's form is highly distinctive: it is as if the speaker were reliving his life rather than just relating it. *The Seafarer*, like *The Dream of the Rood*, could be called "mimetic" in this sense.[38]

The general critical assumption, however, has been that the speaker's account of his life is given from a fixed, unitary perspective, and this has tended to exaggerate certain logical difficulties presented by the poem, particularly the apparent inconsistency between the first and second sections which gave rise to Rieger's dialogue theory, and the delay in the speaker's revelation of the religious motive for his final voyage until the end of the second section. Another consequence of this insistence on a unitary perspective is the diversity and (in many cases) the extremeness of interpretations of the first section of the poem, lines 1–33a. If information from the second and third sections had not been used as a vantage-point for interpretation, it is doubtful if it would have occurred to anyone that the first section is intended as an allegory, whether of the life of fallen man in the world (as Smithers and others have tried to argue), or of a penitent sinner's confession (as Vickrey claims),[39] or a literal description of voluntary exile by an ascetic *peregrinus* (Leslie).[40] All of these interpretations, I suggest, are largely products of hindsight, of reading the poem backwards in the way I criticized near the beginning of this essay. I have tried to show that *The Seafarer* can be read forwards, as a mimetic, linear narrative, a chronicle of personal experience and developing Christian awareness.

It remains to say something about the meaning of the poem as a whole. One kind of coherent meaning can be traced in the way the poet manipulates the two sets of contrasts—"oppositions," in structuralist terminology —which inform the two halves of the poem. In lines 1–64a the main opposition is between the seafarer and the landlubber and the lives they lead, but there is also a secondary opposition, congruent with the first, between the condition of exile on one hand and the possession and enjoyment of a *patria* on the other. The seafarer himself cannot be other than a product of the kind of traditional, conventional, heroic, land-dwelling society which forms his original *patria* and from which he speaks; but protracted, solitary seafaring has revealed to him a world of loneliness, cold and pain which is the antithesis of the world he has known. His experiences in this negative realm are unmatched among men on land, so that when he returns to their society he feels alienated from them, indifferent to the things they hold most dear. He thinks only of returning to the sea, though a repetition of his earlier, aimless voyaging is no more to be contemplated than remaining where he is. His idea of emigrating to a foreign country, a 'dwelling-place of exiles', represents a desperate compromise between two impossibilities: recovery of his *patria* (or rather his sense of it as such), and perpetual, futile motion at sea of the kind he has already known. He presents himself as a representative of a certain category of mankind directly opposed to that of "landlubber" established in the first section; but this conception is too negative and abstract to be of any practical or psychological service to him; its chief value appears to be rhetorical and structural. The seafarer has now made a decision to act; but still there seems to be no positive tradition of human experience or behaviour into which he can fit himself. He remains an exile, and travel to a 'dwelling-place of exiles' would not seem calculated to relieve his condition, only confirm it.

It is at this point of crisis that the oppositions of the first half of the poem shift, as if in response to it. Up to line 64a it seems that there can be no escape for the speaker from the paradoxes into which he has fallen, as an exile in his own country, a seafarer living on land. A structuralist interpretation of his situation might see him as a figure on the margin between two states and two places who "mediates" the oppositions of the first half of the poem; and there are other aspects of structuralist theory that may be of assistance here, if we are prepared to use them. According to Lévi-Strauss's theory of mythical meaning, mediation is a dynamic process which not only identifies and resolves (or at least reduces) oppositions, but also generates fresh ones, often less extreme than those they replace, which are in their turn mediated.[41] This theory was developed as a way of interpreting myths, and *The Seafarer* has never been looked at from this point of view; but it does provide a framework for describing the consequences of the transformation the seafarer undergoes in lines 64b–66a, and offers terms in which the abandonment of the seafaring theme in the second half of the poem may be explained. The seafarer's transformation from chronic, secular exile to *peregrinus pro amore Dei* is accompanied by the appearance of a new set of oppositions. As a prospective *peregrinus*, he is able to see the traditional, secular concerns and priorities of the sort of men among whom he was born and reared in a new light. These men are no longer identifiable as landlubbers simply, but as all men who labour under the burden of these concerns, helpless in the face of mortality and decay, blind to Christian values and the possibility of salvation (they are, one imagines, the poet's audience). Although the original opposition between the speaker and other men remains, the terms of the previous categories are no longer geographical and social in a narrow sense, but universal and spiritual. The seafarer still stands apart from the benighted souls he is addressing; but he now knows that the only important respect in which he differs from them is in the possession of Christian wisdom and aspirations. The change in the terms of the opposition has thus effectively narrowed the gulf between him and them; and if, as the seafarer prays at the very end of the poem, these men can learn how to live Christian lives, this new opposition will be fully resolved. The seafarer will no longer be out of step with the rest of humanity if he can persuade others to fall into step with him.

The original secondary opposition between the condition of exile and the possession of a *patria* is still there in the second half of the poem, though again the terms of the opposition have changed radically, and it is no longer aligned with the primary opposition between the speaker and other men. The *patria* in this new opposition is heaven, the ancient, original *patria* of the human race from which it was exiled by the Fall. It thus remains a lost *patria*, like the seafarer's terrestrial homeland; but there the resemblance ends, for it is lost, not just to him but to everyone, and further more it is recoverable: all men may aspire to return to it. In structural terms, what has happened is that the category of exile has broadened to subsume both the originally opposed categories, but a new *patria*-category has emerged, restoring an opposition on the model of the original one. The implication of this development may be that the earlier opposition between exile and *patria* was "false", a mere echo or type of the true opposition between life on earth and everlasting life in heaven. The seafarer had intended (under the terms of the original, false opposition) to seek a terrestrial place of exile; but now all men are revealed as exiles in the world, and this realization must surely have something to do with the lack of any mention of *peregrinatio* in the second half of the poem: the very impulse towards it has enabled the seafarer to see that his predicament is that of all humanity; that all the world is a dwelling-place of exiles. What has now emerged is that the concept of *patria* is not properly applied to earthly existence at all, and that secular exile is therefore also something of an illusion. Heaven is man's only true *patria*, and offers the only solution to 'exile' in this new, more comprehensive sense.

If we look at *The Seafarer* as a piece of didacticism in the light of this structural analysis, another kind of distinction between the first and second halves of the poem emerges. The message of the first half might seem to be that a Christian perspective on life is achieved only at the price of thorough-going desocialization: a man must actually remove himself from his terrestrial *patria* in order to recognize his true status as an exile simply by virtue of his humanity, and come to desire heaven. A kind of rite of passage must be endured which will impress upon the initiate the precarious, relative nature of social reality. Severe as this prescription is, it has some logical force, for the contented landlubber seems to stand little chance of learning the lesson the seafarer has absorbed. However, we should bear in mind the kind of authority a man requires to be heard respectfully on the subject of the ultimately unsatisfactory nature of heroic values and ideals. The seafarer speaks as one once enthralled by these things to those still enthralled by them, not as a lifelong monk to whom secular values would doubtless have seemed simply barbaric and to be rejected as a matter of course. Who else is in a position to pronounce on the limitations of heroic social values but a man who, having absorbed them, has managed to break free of them? The seafarer's own experiences have at least demonstrated that there is nothing absolute or universal about heroic values. But still, the question that hangs in the air at the end of the second section is whether it is possible for men to live Christian lives within society, or if ascetic withdrawal is the only route to everlasting life.

The second half of the poem contemplates a less extreme alternative to the complete abandonment of the world. Here we find an emphasis on secular life in a terrestrial *patria* as the setting in which the majority of men will live and die. The kind of society depicted here should not, perhaps, be labelled "pagan", for there is no mention of pagan worship; but it is undeniably a traditional society showing some continuity with pagan times, for the old funerary customs described in lines 97–102 and 113–16—the burial of grave-goods with the dead and cremation—are presented as contemporary practices. The seafarer does not urge their abandonment, any more than he urges men to abandon their traditional quest for posthumous *lof* through daring deeds in battle. Primary conversion is not, apparently, his aim. The general context provides a comment on the futility of these rites and ideals, but the seafarer does not fulminate against them. Instead, he tries to persuade men to get these habitual ways of thinking about life and death in proportion, see them against the broader background of God's power and permanence. The omnipotence of God is a constant theme in the second half of the poem, and traditional concerns and values are made to appear temporal, provisional, insignificant when measured against the scale of eternity. But such comparisons involve juxtapositions and analogies which are, I think, meant to be instructive in a more positive way. The style of lines 72–80 implies that a man who strives for the false immortality of *lof* may at least have some inkling of how genuine immortality in heaven may be achieved; and even originally pagan funerary customs such as the burial of treasure with the dead and the strewing of gold on graves (97–102), which imply a continued existence of some sort beyond death, can give cause for reflection on the final judgement beyond even this postmortem existence, when criteria other than worldly wealth will decide the fate of the individual soul.[42] In this passage, as in the earlier lines 72–80, the tone is not dogmatic but suggestive, the misconceptions underlying these old burial rites only implied, the question of the efficacy of riches buried with the dead curiously sidestepped by the apparently irrelevant reference to gold hidden by the living. The effect is to put traditional and Christian ideas about immortality in a continuum, so that the differences between them seem not too radical, more a matter of scale and perspective than fundamental opposition. A kind of model (albeit an imperfect one) for Christian awareness is offered, and there is an analogy here with the seafarer's own education on the distinction between false and true conceptions of exile and *patria*.

Since the publication of Dorothy Whitelock's influential article on the seafarer as a *peregrinus* the general tendency has been to see ascetic ideals upheld in the poem, and to put it against a background of eremitical or penitential theory and practice. Secular, heroic values, when compared with those that motivated the *peregrinus* or hermit (better exemplified, perhaps, in accounts of the saints of the early Irish church than in Anglo-Saxon sources), are bound to appear misconceived, if not downright wicked, and *The Seafarer* has often been read as a stern indictment of secular life and the ideals that inform it, delivered from an essentially monastic standpoint. My own interpretation implies a different view: it sees the poem as showing a relatively realistic, subtle approach to the problems posed for the aspiring Christian by his attachment to traditional cultural values. It is a suggestive, dialectical work which explores analogies between two quite different attitudes to life and strives (not altogether successfully) to find some sort of evangelically viable way of bringing them into relation to each other in men's minds. The potentialities of poetic language to associate (as well as contrast) distinct conceptions, secular and Christian, both by the use of polysemes (*dryhten, feond, dream,* etc.),[43] and by the stylistic device of variation (72–80) are, I believe, exploited with this end in view. The poet's use of structural contrasts and transformations is full of meaning; but I would add that to understand *The Seafarer* properly we need to appreciate the situation of the Anglo-Saxon outsider, the problem of self-definition that the individual faced once he stepped outside the realm of conventionally received experience, and the hold over him that traditional social values exerted. The poem chronicles the fortunes of a man who, by straying into the wilderness beyond the boundaries of his own culture, loses his sense of identity, only to reach back to a different, more comprehensive vision of man and the world in order to recover it. *The Seafarer* would have struck a strong chord in the minds of the early Christian (or nominally Christian) laity of Anglo-Saxon England, and might well have been composed with them in mind.

Notes

1. On the manuscript, see R. W. Chambers, Max Förster and Robin Flower, Introduction to the facsimile edition, *The Exeter Book of Old English Poetry* (London, 1933), and N. R. Ker, *Catalogue of Manuscripts containing Anglo-Saxon* (Oxford, 1957), p. 153. *The Seafarer* is cited here in I. L. Gordon's edition (London, 1960), other Old English poems from G. P. Krapp and E.V.K. Dobbie, eds., *The Anglo-Saxon Poetic Records*, 6 vols. (New York, 1931–42), in which the Exeter Book is vol. 3.

2. See Gordon, ed., pp. 27–32.

3. The other six "elegies" are *The Wanderer, Deor, Wulf and Eadwacer, The Wife's*

Lament, *The Husband's Message* and *The Ruin*. There is no feature common to all seven of these poems, though an irregular network of serial resemblances, echoes and recurrent preoccupations might justify regarding them as a polythetic class. Three of the more significant links may be mentioned. Firstly, a characteristic nostalgia for the happiness or grandeur of days gone by, viewed from a present made depressing by an acute sense of emotional, social, moral or even universal decline and disintegration. This is the feature that has earned these poems the name of elegy, though they vary considerably in the degree to which they exhibit it, and it is scarcely to be found at all in two of them, *Wulf and Eadwacer* and *The Husband's Message*. Secondly, an intensely personal note: in several of these poems a speaker, usually anonymous and practically indistinguishable from the poet, tells a story of his or her life, often an unhappy one; but *Deor* names the speaker (the poem's modern title); *The Ruin* lacks the personal note; and in neither *The Ruin* nor *The Husband's Message* has the speaker himself suffered. The third feature is the theme of exile; more specifically, the separation of the speaker, or of someone dear to him or her, from court and *comitatus*, home and family, often by travel overseas, sometimes as a result of a specific misfortune—the death of a lord, for instance, as in *The Wanderer*; or a feud, as in *The Husband's Message* and *The Wife's Lament*, or a rivalry, as in *Deor*. Again, *The Ruin* lacks the theme of exile, though all the other "elegies" contain some version of it.

4. 63 *hwælweg* (MS *wæl weg*) is probably less crucial than was once thought. The emendation *hwælweg*, 'whale's way', first suggested by Thorpe, removes the irregularity of a finite verb (*hweteð*) alliterating in preference to a noun (*wælweg*) in the a-verse; but E. G. Stanley, reviewing Gordon's edition (*M Æ*, 31 (1962), 54–60, at 57–8), suggests that the first element of the MS form could be *wǣl*, 'ocean', giving the meaning 'ocean-way' for the compound (semantically equivalent to the emendation *hwælweg*). The question of whether or not emendation is justified thus seems to depend almost entirely on the strength of the argument from alliteration. G. V. Smithers's earlier suggestion ("The Meaning of *The Seafarer* and *The Wanderer*", *MÆ*, 26 (1957), 137–53, at 137–40) that the first element of the MS form is *wæl*, 'dead body', giving 'road taken by the dead' or 'road to the abode of the dead' as the meaning of *wælweg* should probably be rejected in the light of Stanley's more convincing defence of the MS reading, as well as for other reasons given below and in Gordon's note (ed., p. 42).

5. Ll. 27, 33, 39, 58, 64, 72, 103, 108.

6. E. D. Hirsch, Jr, *Validity in Interpretation* (New Haven, 1967), p. 86. Hirsch's discussions of genre are referred to by Stanley B. Greenfield, *The Interpretation of Old English Poems* (London, 1972), esp. pp. 11–18, and by T. A. Shippey, "Approaches to Truth in Old English Poetry" (Inaugural Lecture), *University of Leeds Review* (1982), 171–89.

7. 8, 10, 14, 19, 33 *c(e)ald-*; 9 *forste*, 17, 32 *hrim(-)*; 14, 19 *is-*, 24 *isig-*; 17, 32 *hægl*; 31 *sniwde*; 17 *hrimgicelum*.

8. Stanley, *MÆ*, 31 (1962), 57.

9. Translation from Richard Hamer, ed. and trans., *A Choice of Anglo-Saxon Verse* (London, 1970), p. 29.

10. A penitential strain is discerned in *The Seafarer* by E. G. Stanley, "Old English Poetic Diction and the Interpretation of *The Wanderer, The Seafarer* and *The Penitent's Prayer*", *Anglia*, 73 (1955), 413–66, esp. 450–52, 454, and P. L. Henry, *The Early English and Celtic Lyric* (London, 1966), pp. 21, 157. Some later writers demur: see John C. Pope, "Second Thoughts on the Interpretation of *The Seafarer*", *ASE*, 3 (1974), 75–86, at 78, footnote 1; Stanley B. Greenfield, "*Sylf*, Seasons, Structure and Genre in *The Seafarer*", *ASE*, 9 (1981), 188–211, esp. 209–10.

11. See Mary E. Byrne, "On the Punishment of Sending Adrift", *Ériu*, 11 (1930–32), 97–102.

12. Pope, *ASE*, 3 (1974), 83: "In his scorn for the prosperous landsman is there not a touch of pride in his ability to endure affliction?"

13. See Greenfield, *ASE*, 9 (1981) for the most recent consideration of *sylf*.

14. The classic exposition of the dialogue theory is John C. Pope, "Dramatic Voices in *The Wanderer* and *The Seafarer*," *Franciplegius: Medieval and Linguistic Studies in Honor of Francis Peabody Magoun, Jr*, eds. Jess B. Bessinger, Jr, and Robert P. Creed (New York, 1965), pp. 164–93; rep. *Old English Literature: Twenty-two Analytical Essays*, eds. Martin Stevens and Jerome Mandel (Lincoln, Nebraska, 1968), pp. 163–97. Pope later retracted his dialogue theory in *ASE*, 3 (1974), 75–86.

15. Norah Kershaw, ed. and trans., *Anglo-Saxon and Norse Poems* (Cambridge, 1922), p. 23. Her interpretation of *sylf* is adopted by P. L. Henry, *The Early English and Celtic Lyric*, p. 154, and by Greenfield (via Henry) in "*Mīn, sylf* and 'Dramatic Voices in *The Wanderer* and *The Seafarer*'", *JEGP*, 68 (1969), 212–20, at 217, though Greenfield now (*ASE*, 9 (1981), 205) prefers "'for . . . myself', in the sense of an act of personal recognition by and for the . . . speaker".

16. O. S. Anderson, "*The Seafarer*: an Interpretation", *K. Humanistiska Vetenskapssamfundets i Lund Årsberättelse*, 1 (1937–8), 1–49; Marijane Osborn, "Venturing upon Deep Waters in *The Seafarer*", *NM*, 79 (1978), 1–6.

17. Stanley, *MÆ*, 31 (1962), 57.

18. See Peter Orton, "The Technique of Object-personification in *The Dream of the Rood* and a Comparison with the Old English *Riddles*", *Leeds Studies in English*, N.S., 11 (1980), 1–18, at 12–13.

19. See Greenfield, *ASE*, 9 (1981), 206–7.

20. Pope, "Dramatic Voices", pp. 188–9, footnotes 33–4, points this out. He cites one instance of *eard* in the sense of 'heaven' in Ælfric's *Catholic Homilies* (ed. Thorpe, II, 214/25–7); but here the usage is, as Pope recognizes, determined by the analogy Ælfric is drawing "between the promised land of the Israelites, *þone behatenan eard*, and the heavenly destination of the Christian journey" (189).

21. Smithers, *MÆ*, 26 (1957), 151.

22. Henry's remark (p. 134) that allegory is "implicit in the *peregrinatio* project" runs the risk of confusing the description of a symbolic action with the figurative expression of meaning; cf. Pope, *ASE*, 3 (1974), 80–81.

23. Roy F. Leslie, "The Meaning and Structure of *The Seafarer*", *The Old English Elegies*, ed. Martin Green (London, 1983), pp. 96–122, at 102–4, takes lines 39–47 as

a description of a man of the same kind as the landlubber of the first section, though I cannot see how he arrives at this interpretation.

24. See Gordon, ed., p. 39, note to line 43; Greenfield, *ASE*, 9 (1981), 203.

25. Dorothy Whitelock, "The Interpretation of *The Seafarer*", *Early Cultures of North-West Europe* (*H. M. Chadwick Memorial Studies*), eds. Sir Cyril Fox and Bruce Dickins (Cambridge, 1950), 261–72, at 264, footnote 2: "Sisam doubts whether the *to hwon* clause can be taken as an indirect question . . ." (I cannot trace the reference to Sisam; doubtless it was a private communication to the author).

26. Smithers, "The Meaning of *The Seafarer* and *The Wanderer* (continued)", *MÆ*, 28 (1959), 1–22, at 7; James Cross, "On the Allegory in *The Seafarer*—Illustrative Notes", *MÆ*, 28 (1959), 104–6, at 105. For the passage in *Blickling Homily* V, see R. Morris, ed., *The Blickling Homilies*, E.E.T.S., O.S., 58, 63, 73 (1874, 1876, 1880; rep. as one vol., 1967), 56–9, beginning *Hwæt we witon þæt ælc wlite & ælc fægernes to ende efsteþ & onetteþ þisse woerlde lifes* (57/27).

27. Joseph Bosworth and T. Northcote Toller, *An Anglo-Saxon Dictionary* (Oxford, 1898; rep. 1976), s.v. *onettan*.

28. *MÆ*, 28 (1959), 7.

29. See Whitelock, p. 265, footnote 5.

30. See Gordon, ed., note to 56, pp. 40–41; cf. Stanley, *MÆ*, 31 (1962), 57.

31. "*The Seafarer* 58–64a", *Neophilologus*, 66 (1982), 450–59.

32. See Whitelock's translation of 66a, 'transitory on earth', p. 266; cf. Pope, *ASE*, 3 (1974), 81–2.

33. Gordon, ed., p. 43, note.

34. J.R.R. Tolkien, "*Beowulf:* the Monsters and the Critics", *Proceedings of the British Academy*, 22 (1936), 245–95; rep. *An Anthology of Beowulf Criticism*, ed. Lewis E. Nicholson (Notre Dame, 1963), pp. 51–103, at 93–4.

35. Gordon, "Traditional Themes in *The Wanderer* and *The Seafarer*", *RES*, N.S. 5 (1954), 1–13, at 10.

36. Ibid.

37. Gordon, ed., p. 43, note to 72–80.

38. Greenfield, *ASE*, 9 (1981), reaches a similar conclusion: ". . . the poetic form itself imitates that psychological-religious sequence of experience; and that which has disturbed critics about the poem's structure, the juxtaposition of the seafaring and homiletic halves, can in this reading be viewed as the objective correlative for the speaker's experience" (207).

39. John F. Vickrey, "Some Hypotheses concerning *The Seafarer,* lines 1–47", *Archiv*, 219 (1982), 57–77.

40. See footnote 22 above.

41. See Claude Lévi-Strauss, "The Story of Asdiwal", trans. Nicholas Mann, *The Structural Study of Myth and Totemism*, ed. Edmund Leach (London, 1967; rep. 1978), pp. 1–47. Useful discussions and criticism of Lévi-Strauss's ideas are to be found in the same book, particularly Mary Douglas's "The Meaning of Myth", pp. 49–69, and in G. S. Kirk, *Myth: its Meaning and Function in Ancient and Other Cul-*

tures (Cambridge, 1970), esp. Chap. 2, "Levi-Strauss and the Structural Approach", pp. 42–83.

42. See Gordon's note (ed., p. 45) on lines 97–102, but cf. Stanley's earlier commentary on them in *Anglia*, 73 (1955), 456, footnote. The syntax of the passage is difficult, but Gordon's discussion is open to criticism on at least two counts. First, it is doubtful if Sisam's point about the verb *byrgan* (98b) being "restricted in early use to the burial of bodies" ("*The Seafarer* lines 97–102", *RES*, 21 (1945), 316–17) carries any weight: the body will normally be the centre of interest in any burial description, but it would be surprising if *byrgan* (probably connected with *beorg*, 'tumulus') could not also denote the burial of objects beside a corpse. Second, Stanley is surely right to retain the MS reading *wille* in 99b *þæt hine mid wille*. Gordon, following Sisam, emends to *nille*, making 99b a principal clause, 'that (i.e. the gold of 97) will not (go) with him', meaning that the practice reflects a superstitious folly; but the use of *nille* to denote simple futurity would be problematic, and in any case the MS reading is intelligible if 99b is a noun clause, 'that which he (the survivor) wishes (to go) with him (the dead brother)'. Gordon defends emendation on the grounds that *wille* makes the whole sentence "awkward syntactically and logically in its blending of two separate ideas (though brother will strew the grave with gold . . . gold cannot help him when he hoarded it before)"; but this awkwardness may well be another manifestation (cf. 72–80) of the poet's attempt to correlate traditional and Christian attitudes to death and immortality.

43. See Greenfield, "Attitudes and Values in *The Seafarer*", *JEGP*, 51 (1954), 15–20, esp. 18–20.

En/closed Subjects:
The Wife's Lament and the Culture
of Early Medieval Female Monasticism[1]

SHARI HORNER

IT has long been accepted critical practice in Old English scholarship to acknowledge that the Old English elegies employ the language of the Germanic-heroic world, of retainers and lords, to articulate a Christian world-view.[2] Those elegies which are generally believed to have male speakers—in particular "The Seafarer" and "The Wanderer"—are often read as poems which explore the various tensions between spiritual and worldly desires, and which apply traditional Germanic-heroic hierarchies to the relationship between God and man. Similarly, the speaker of "The Wife's Lament" uses heroic language, yet it is not at all common to consider the language of this poem in terms of Christianity or monasticism.[3] Yet locating the "female" elegies—"The Wife's Lament" and "Wulf and Eadwacer"—within historically and culturally specific contexts of early medieval monasticism can help to re-formulate our understanding of these poems. Similarly, current work in gender theory enables new ways to read the operations of gender in these otherwise anonymous texts.

This paper will examine some connections between "The Wife's Lament" and female monasticism. In particular I will look at the poem's use of what I call as "discourse of enclosure," a system of signifying which inscribes the increasingly strict conditions of monasticism imposed on Anglo-Saxon female religious.[4] I am not interested in determining whether this poem was written by a woman, let alone a nun. Rather, my object is to examine the ways in which the gender identity of the speaker is discursively produced. By considering how a monastic discourse of enclosure regulates representation in "The Wife's Lament," I will suggest that the gendering of the speaker emerges from the cultural expressions of femininity and the female body found in early medieval Christianity.

The deployment of these discourses within the poem engenders the speaking subject.

A brief summary of "The Wife's Lament" may be helpful. Most critics now agree that the speaker is a woman.[5] She has been exiled as a result of secret plotting by her lord's relatives, and she now lives confined to an "earth-cave" under an oak tree, within a grove, surrounded by thorny branches—contained, in other words, by at least three layers of barriers. She bitterly complains of these circumstances, and concludes by grimly describing the fate of those who must wait for or depend upon a loved one. The poem remains ambiguous; many specific details about the speaker's life will never be determined, such as who she was, why she was exiled, and so forth. This analysis will not attempt to answer those kinds of questions; I am less interested in identifying the speaker as an individual woman than I am in exploring the ways the poem discursively produces its gendered subject.

To be sure, many Old English scholars have argued that grammatical gender in the poem—the feminine forms of the adjectives *geomorre* and *minre*, and of the pronoun *sylfre*—is more than sufficient evidence of the speaker's female gender. Yet strenuous arguments have been made for a masculine or even non-human speaker.[6] My analysis is an attempt to move beyond questions of grammatical gender and focus instead on what is perhaps best called "cultural gender": that is, the normative properties of gender which operate within particular socio-historical frameworks—for my purposes, the frameworks of early medieval female monasticism.

In his recent analysis of gender identities in the Old English saints' lives, Allen Frantzen draws on the work of Judith Butler to argue that traditional readers of Old English literature have suppressed or disregarded issues of gender identity in Old English texts, and therefore have not considered "gender as performance"—an unfortunate omission, considering the fluidity and ambiguity of gender identities in certain Old English texts.[7] While Frantzen's analysis is primarily concerned with "switches" of gender identity in Old English saints' lives, I would suggest that the anonymous Old English elegies also provide us with, in his words, "opportunities to explore the meaning of gender itself as a performative category that interrogates the natural positions of male and female that are opposed centers of gender anxiety" (p. 460).

Butler's formulation of gender performance is particularly useful for the analysis of an anonymous text, because it permits us to bypass questions of authority and authorship, and to examine instead the ways in which the repeated "acts" of gender in the poem produce a feminine speaking subject. Butler writes:

the appearance of an abiding substance or gendered self . . . [is] produced by the regulation of attributes along culturally established lines of coherence. . . . There is no gender identity behind the expressions of gender; that identity is performatively constituted by the very 'expressions' that are said to be its results.[8]

She argues that gender is not a stable or fixed identity; rather it must be understood as a repeated set of culturally and socially established acts, and it is this repetition which constitutes the *appearance* of a stable gendered self. The seemingly stable gender identity of the speaker in "The Wife's Lament" is, I suggest, likewise the product of culturally established "expressions" of gender.

Such gender conventions are found within the discourse of enclosure: the discursive formulation of the historically specific, essentialist views developed about the female body and femininity in the early centuries of Christianity. The writings of the early church fathers regarding female monastic enclosure identify two concomitant images of the female body: the enclosed one, the virginal, intact woman; and the enclosure, the architectural space which contains her. Just as a woman's body must be walled into a cloister, that body must *be* a cloister, must itself be impenetrable to any sort of physical or spiritual invasion. This ideology works specifically to contain the *female* body, associated by the church fathers with corrupt flesh. For the Christian woman of the early middle ages, the only hope of salvation lay in her ability to reject, dismiss, or otherwise suppress her corrupt— earthbound—female body, her sexuality, to become "male."[9] For example, Frantzen shows that the Old English transvestite saints are "manly women" who must change gender identities before they will achieve sainthood (p. 460). But the ideological motivation behind such a gender "switch" stems from the deep fear that the female body might escape its subjugation by male reason. According to Augustine (to name just one example):

The subjugation of woman is in the order of things; she must be dominated and governed by man just as the soul should regulate the body and virile reason should dominate the animal part of the being. If a woman dominates man, and the animal part dominates reason, the house is turned upside-down.[10]

While on the surface monastic enclosure can be seen to protect the female religious (and of course, this was sometimes the case), it works equally to regulate and contain her.[11]

Of all the Old English elegies, only "The Wife's Lament" and "Wulf and Eadwacer" exhibit the kind of physical enclosure which dominated cultural attitudes towards the female body; "The Wanderer" and The Seafarer," by contrast, evoke imagery of voyaging, wandering, unfettered movement. This distinction marks a crucial difference between the "male" and "female" Old English elegies. The Wanderer, as we all know, treads the paths of exile, stirs the icy sea with his arms. Like the *hlaford* in "The Wife's Lament," the Wanderer's *body* is not enclosed; though exiled, he is not imprisoned. In contrast to the female speakers, the speaker in "The Wanderer" wishes rather to enclose or imprison his "traitorous" *mind*, to fetter his thoughts, which dwell too often on his earthly misery:

> . . . ic to soðe wat
> þæt bið in eorle   indryhten þeaw
> þæt he his ferð-locan   fæste binde
> healde his hord-cofan   hycge swa he wylle

[I know truly that it is a noble custom in a man to bind fast his 'soul-enclosure,' protect his heart, whatever he may think]   (11b–14)[12]

The Seafarer, also treading the paths of exile, specifically directs his thoughts away from worldly comforts or discomforts, towards God. Yet the elegies do not provide this option to the female speakers. Their physical enclosure prohibits action but not speech; the journeys of the female speakers turn inward, as they expose thoughts and memories of their physical lives that the Wanderer would have locked away. The textual emphasis on physical enclosure, paired with such "interior" journeys, signifies their status as women.[13] Unlike the virgin saints and martyrs discussed by Frantzen, the subjecthood of these speakers is indissociable from their femininity and female bodies. The inability to escape enclosure genders their voices, and thus constitutes their primary identity.

Extant literature by Anglo-Saxon missionary nuns reveals a close textual relationship to the two Old English female elegies. The nun Egburg, writing to Boniface (ca. 716–720) occupies an isolated position similar to that of the two Old English female speakers, and her letter expresses her physical or worldly unhappiness.[14] She is particularly lonely since the departure of her sister, Wethburg, who has gone to Rome to become an anchorite.[15] Egburg contrasts her sister's more happy (because voluntary) enclosure with her own undesired position: "She is now climbing the steep and narrow path; but I lie in the depths bound by the fetters of the law of the flesh."[16] Her words recall the double bond of female claustration: within her physical or spatial isolation, she is likewise bound by "the law of the flesh," her own body. Egburg laments for lost pleasures of *this* world: her sister's departure, her brother's death, her longing for Boniface. The female elegies likewise evoke the articulation of worldly longing, and the frustration resulting from bodily and/or spatial enclosure expressed in the correspondence of the unhappy nun.

Unlike Egburg's sister, not all Anglo-Saxon women submitted voluntarily to exile or claustration. It was not rare for medieval English women or girls to be forced into the cloister for legal, social, political, or financial reasons.[17] For the women's relatives this could mean possession of the woman's inheritance, since a nun would be unable to claim legal rights, and may have been considered legally dead (Power p. 34). Such practices resonate in "The Wife's Lament:" not only does the speaker suffer exile on account of the secret plotting of relatives, but the poem carries the impression of a woman speaking from beyond the grave, a position which was at least symbolically accurate.[18] In fact, throughout "The Wife's Lament," much of the language which has caused the most critical consternation suggests culturally established paradigms of female monasticism.

The language that opens "The Wife's Lament" situates the poem and its speaker in the context of the traditional heroic elegy of exile; in particular, her opening line, *ic þis giedd wrece   bi me ful geomorre* [I recite this song about myself, very mournful], closely resembles the opening lines of "Deor," "Resignation," and "The Husband's Message." The speaker's present suffering has been caused by a past event: the departure of her *hlaford . . . heonan of leodum / ofer yþa gelac* [away from his people over the rolling waves (6–7a)]. Her use of the term *hlaford*, "lord," seems to refer to her husband, but also reflects "the conventional idiom of OE poetry which was designed to celebrate the male world of the comitatus" (Klinck p. 178). The term certainly designates a social hierarchy. Yet the letters of the Anglo-Saxon missionaries frequently use conjugal or familial terms to describe non-conjugal relationships. And *hlaford* is used elsewhere in Old English to describe an ecclesiastical leader or a spiritual lord—and, of course, to refer to God (see Bosworth-Toller, *An Anglo-Saxon Dictionary*, s.v.). Such a definition extends the usual "husband," encompassing the possibility of both a secular and spiritual relationship; if we read the lord to be the speaker's husband, we might equally read him as her spiritual guardian. The poem does not precisely define her status; the most we can know is that she is separated from a beloved man with whom she has made a formal pledge or vow.[19]

Among male and female religious, vowed spiritual friendships often resembled conjugal relationships. Boniface, of course, desired to buried in the same grave as the nun Leoba because of the deep spiritual affection he felt for her—and which he wanted to perpetuate after death.[20] And the relationship between Christina of Markyate and Abbot Geoffrey was quite domestic: "he enjoyed the virgin's company, provided for her house, and became the supervisor of its material affairs. Whilst he centered his attention on providing the virgin with material assistance, she strove to enrich the man in virtue. . . ."[21] For Christina and Leoba, such a relationship was both spiritual and pragmatic, since the spiritual leader provided real protection and material support.

In "The Wife's Lament," the speaker's somewhat ambiguous assertion, *Đa ic me feran gewat folgað secan* (9), has been interpreted to mean that she sought either financial support, or protection, or her husband (who would presumably provide both).[22] *Folgað* carries the sense of "official" service, given by a retainer to his lord, or to some sanctioned institution. Again, the term has monastic overtones: one meaning of *folgian* is "to follow the monastic profession" (Bosworth-Toller, *Supplement*, s. v.) The service sought by the wife puzzles many readers, because it seems unusual for a woman to adopt the heroic language of a retainer. Yet in fact this language echoes the Christian monastic code which includes men and women both; Aldhelm, to name just one example, describes the nuns of Barking as "soldiers of Christ" (Lapidge and Herren p. 131). Like the nuns of Barking, perhaps the Old English speaker, through the economy of language, seeks *folgað* to serve her lord—either secular or divine.

Reading this elegy as a repeated set of acts which signify a female monastic subject can illuminate other puzzling aspects of the poem. We know, for example, that the speaker felt *uhtceare*, usually translated as "grief just before dawn" and later she says that she walks alone *on uhtan*, in the (pre)dawn (35). The time she describes is that of matins, the earliest of the canonical hours, just before dawn. Typically at *uhta*, matins, the order sang *uhtsang*, the matins service. "The Wife's Lament," then, can be read as a kind of *uhtsang:* the speaker's mournful lament emulates the conventional matins song. She sings *under actreo*, under an oak tree; *treow*, of course, is a common Old English poetic metaphor for the cross. The speaker's language is the cultural expression of female monasticism: like a nun at matins singing the office under the cross (and thus lamenting her Lord), this speaker laments the loss of her lord, under a tree, at the hour of matins.

The most notable image evoked by the speaker is her enclosure itself, the so-called "earth-cave" she inhabits. The enclosed setting is emphasized through three repetitions: *eorðscræfe* (28b), *eorðsele* (29a), and *eorðscrafu* (36b). She differentiates this dwelling from her previous worldly life; the earth-cave (*wic wynna leas* a joyless dwelling 32a) contrasts with her memory of the pleasant dwellings (*wynlicran wic* 52a) of the past she shared with her lord. Yet the earth-cave may have its benefits; the enclosure has at least provided her with a refuge from the man's plotting relatives. The earth-cave may be literally a natural or man-made cave or tumulus of the sort inhabited by St. Guthlac; at any rate "grave" imagery is appropriate for a female religious, dead to the world socially and restricted from it physically.[23]

Only a handful of critics have read any elements of Christianity into "The Wife's Lament," typically viewing the elegy as an expression of love between Christ and the Church, derived from the Song of Songs. Yet the poem's very preservation in the Exeter Book places it within a Christian monastic environment, permitting us to read the multiple valences of gender and monasticism which recur in this seemingly secular poem apparently about a woman's lament for her lord.

Alain Renoir has suggested that "a mediaeval English poet may possibly have chosen to let his female protagonist draw upon popular Christian doctrine while relating her misadventures" (Renoir p. 19). He calls "The Wife's Lament" a poem of "Christian inversion" in which her "husband" is brought from a previously exalted and powerful position to a lowly one, and suggests that this process seems to illustrate a well-known biblical passage, Luke 1:52: "He hath put down the mighty from their seat, and hath exalted the humble." Renoir suggests that, regardless of whether the Anglo-Saxon poet intentionally inserted Christian doctrine into the poem, potential readers of the Exeter Book would have been "receptive" and "attuned" to its allusions to Christian doctrine (p. 23). I would like to suggest pushing this idea a bit farther, by foregrounding the context in which the passage from Luke occurs. The verse is embedded in the *Magnificat*, the song sung by Mary at the Visitation: "My soul doth magnify the Lord" (Luke 1:46–55). To pursue Renoir's line of thinking, then, "The Wife's Lament" may draw upon a biblical passage which falls within a song sung by a woman; of course, the Old English poem, too, is sung by a woman. The comparison to the biblical verse—and the significance of the comparison—emerges only when the contexts of both the elegy and the Scriptural citation are made explicit. The woman singing the Old English poem embodies the image of Mary singing the *Magnificat*—the primary example of a female speaking subject within early medieval monasticism.

Even read this way, the poem maintains its ambiguity: as a parallel to Mary, a woman singing within a monastic setting would command respect, in imitating the pinnacle of virginity. Yet this woman seems to be lamenting a beloved man on earth. Can the poem be read as Christian allegory after all? Can the *hlaford* in fact be Christ, the speaker a *sponsa Christi?* Such reading does not alter the way that the gender of the speaker is constructed in the poem, but rather confirms it. The poem becomes one ideal of expression from a female monastic community, the kind of environment which might produce such a Christian allegory. Yet the poem also rewrites that expression, since it reveals a dissatisfaction with monastic enclosure and a longing for earthly love. Ultimately, the "solution" doesn't matter; the speaker remains bound by oath to a L/lord. Within both secular and religious frameworks, she is gendered female. Singing a riddling song whose answer may even be the *Magnificat*, the woman narrator links herself at once to Mary—the socially sanctioned image of female creativity—and to the world.

Most of the questions which have traditionally puzzled readers of "The Wife's Lament" simply do not have answers; no amount of inquiry will provide hard facts about the poem's author, composition, provenance, or even its subject matter. The object of my analysis of the poem has been to ask different questions: rather than examining *what* the poem means, I am interested in *how* it means, in how it produces meaning discursively.[24] Locating the speaker of "The Wife's Lament" within the cultural contexts of female monastic enclosure permits a more complexly historicized reading of the poem. Its discursive operations produce and normalize its gendered speaking subject—a subject who is, in Judith Butler's phrase, "an identity tenuously constituted in time . . ." (p. 140).

Notes

1. The first version of this paper was presented at the 27th International Congress on Medieval Studies, Kalamazoo, MI, May 1992. The present version, in slightly condensed form, was presented at the Modern Language Association Convention, Toronto, Ontario, in December 1993. My thanks to Jane Chance and Mary Blockley, respectively, for organizing those sessions, and also to Professor Blockley for her useful suggestions. I also wish to thank Michael Bibby for his challenging and very helpful comments. This paper is still very much a work-in-progress; I offer it here in an experimental mood.

2. See, for example, Rosemary Woolf, "*The Wanderer, The Seafarer,* and the Genre of *Planctus,*" in *Anglo-Saxon Poetry: Essays in Appreciation,* ed. Lewis E. Nicholson and Dolores Warwick Frese (Notre Dame and London: University of Notre Dame Press, 1975), pp. 192–207, and more recently, Anne L. Klinck, *The Old English Elegies: A Critical Edition and Genre Study* (Montreal: McGill-Queen's University Press, 1992).

3. The four critical studies I know of which do read "The Wife's Lament" in terms of Christianity are Alain Renoir, "Christian Inversion in 'The Wife's Lament,'" *Studia Neophilologica* 49 (1977):19–24; M. J. Swanton, "'The Wife's Lament' and 'The Husband's Message': A Reconsideration," *Anglia* 82 (1964):269–290; W. F. Bolton,

"'The Wife's lament' and 'The Husband's Message': A Reconsideration Revisited," *Archiv* 205 (1969):337–351; and A. N. Doane, "Heathen Form and Christian Function in 'The Wife's Lament,'" *Mediaeval Studies* 28 (1966):77–91. Swanton and Bolton read the "husband" and "wife" as allegorical representations of Christ and the Church, and thus see the two poems as complementary.

In his introduction to his translation of the poem, S.A.J. Bradley very tentatively suggests a Scriptural interpretation as well, proposing a reading of the poem as a riddle for which the solution is either "Zion, the soul" or "*Cirice*, 'Church'" (*Anglo-Saxon Poetry* [London: Dent, 1982], p. 383). In another intriguing translation, Burton Raffel situates the speaker in "a convent of wooden nuns;" her environment is "a nuns'-nest of leaves" (*Poems From the Old English* [Lincoln: University of Nebraska Press, 1964], pp. 36–37) but gives no editorial justification for this imagery.

4. For a more detailed discussion of the discourse of enclosure, see my "Spiritual Truth and Sexual Violence: The Old English 'Juliana,' Anglo-Saxon Nuns, and the Discourse of Female Monastic Enclosure" in *Signs: Journal of Women in Culture and Society* 19 (1994), 658–75.

5. For a useful summary of the critical argument over the gender of the speaker, see Jane Chance, *Woman as Hero in Old English Literature* (Syracuse: Syracuse University Press, 1986), pp. 127–28, n. 2. See also Patricia Belanoff, "Women's Songs, Women's Language: 'Wulf and Eadwacer' and 'The Wife's Lament'" in *New Readings on Women in Old English Poetry*, ed. Helen Damico and Alexandra Hennessey Olsen (Bloomington: Indiana University Press, 1990), pp. 193–203; and Marilynn Desmond, "The Voice of Exile: Feminist Literary History and the Anonymous Anglo-Saxon Elegy." *Critical Inquiry* 16 (1990):572–590.

6. See Chance (cited above) for a brief summary of these views. While these arguments generally read the speaker as a male retainer separated from his lord, a recent article by Faye Walker-Pelkey advances the intriguing argument that the poem is in fact a riddle, and the "speaker" is its solution: "sword." "'Frige hwæt ic hatte': 'The Wife's Lament' as Riddle," *Papers on Language and Literature* 28 (1992):242–266.

7. Allen Frantzen, "When Women Aren't Enough," *Speculum* 68 (April 1993):445–71, quote from p. 460.

8. Judith Butler, *Gender Trouble: Feminism and the Subversion of Identity* (New York: Routledge, 1990), pp. 24–5.

9. In addition to Frantzen, several scholars have recently discussed this concept. See (among others) Elizabeth Castelli, "'I Will Make Mary Male': Pieties of the Body and Gender Transformation of Christian Women in Late Antiquity," in *Body Guards: The Cultural Politics of Gender Ambiguity*, ed. Julia Epstein and Kristina Straub (New York: Routledge, 1991), pp. 29–49; and Margaret R. Miles, *Carnal Knowing: Female Nakedness and Religious Meaning in the Christian West* (Boston: Beacon Press, 1989).

10. Augustine, *De Genesi contra Manichaeos*, quoted by R. Howard Bloch, *Medieval Misogyny and the Invention of Western Romantic Love* (Chicago: University of Chicago Press, 1991), p. 30.

11. On the ideology of female monastic enclosure, see Jane Tibbets Schulenburg,

"Strict Active Enclosure and its Effects on the Female Monastic Experience (ca. 500–1100)," in *Distant Echoes: Medieval Religious Women* Vol. I. Ed. John A. Nichols and Lillian Thomas Shank (Kalamazoo: Cistercian Publications, 1984), pp. 51–86.

12. All citations from the Old English are taken from George Philip Krapp and Elliot Van Kirk Dobbie, eds., *The Anglo-Saxon Poetic Records* Vol. 3 (New York: Columbia University Press, 1936). Translations are my own.

13. This juxtaposition of physical confinement with affective, expansive, or visionary mental voyaging has, of course, been frequently noted in women's literature of the later middle ages; see Elizabeth Alvilda Petroff, *Medieval Women's Visionary Literature* (New York and Oxford: Oxford University Press, 1986), especially pp. 5–30.

14. See Ursula Schaefer, "Two Women in Need of a Friend: A Comparison of *The Wife's Lament* and Eangyth's Letter to Boniface" in *Germanic Dialects: Linguistic and Philological Investigations*, ed. Bela Brogyanyi and Thomas Krommelbein (Amsterdam: John Benjamins Publishing Co., 1986):491–524, for a comparison of the poem with a letter from a different nun. Most of Boniface's female correspondents express similar themes of loneliness and sadness at times.

15. Edward Kylie, trans. *The English Correspondence of Saint Boniface* (London: Chatto & Windus, 1924), pp. 57–60.

16. Kylie pp. 58–9; see also Boniface's letter to Bugga regarding Wethburg's journey to Rome, p. 69.

17. Eileen Power, *Medieval English Nunneries* (Cambridge: Cambridge University Press, 1922), pp. 29–30. See also John Boswell, *The Kindness of Strangers: The Abandonment of Children in Western Europe from Late Antiquity to the Renaissance* (New York: Pantheon, 1988), on oblation. Boswell shows that, for the early middle ages, children—regardless of religious vocation—were legally required to remain permanently in the monasteries to which their parents "donated" them (p. 234).

Perhaps more to the point, in *Anglo-Saxon Women and the Church* (Woodbridge, Suffolk: The Boydell Press, 1992), Stephanie Hollis discusses the potential difficulties an Anglo-Saxon woman might face at the hands of unhappy in-laws after her husband's death. Such conflicts could sometimes be avoided if the woman entered a convent: "It is evident from the law codes that a widow's inheritance of her husband's property was apt to be resented by her husband's family; the church offered an alternative form of protection if her own family were dead or otherwise unable to aid her in maintaining possession of property against her husband's relatives" (p. 80).

18. For an argument advancing the view that the speaker is in fact dead, see Elinor Lench, "'The Wife's Lament': A Poem of the Living Dead," *Comitatus* 1 (1970):3–23. See also Raymond P. Tripp, Jr., "The Narrator As Revenant: A Reconsideration of Three Old English Elegies," *Papers on Language & Literature* 8 (1972):339–361.

19. From Aldhelm through Christina of Markyate, Anglo-Saxon religious use intensely personal or passionate language to express friendship. Aldhelm, for example, addresses the nun Sigegyth as "beloved and most loving," and "ten times, nay a hundred times and a thousand times beloved" [in *The Prose Works*, ed. Michael Lapidge and Michael Herren (Cambridge: D. S. Brewer, 1979), pp. 166–7]; Egburg, in a letter

to Boniface, writes, "thy love is as a bond that holds me; since I tasted it . . . the sweetness of it fills my soul" [Kylie p. 57].

Thus we need not interpret the speaker of "The Wife's Lament" as a wife; the poem simply does not precisely define her status. At any rate, the language of marriage does not preclude reading the poem within a female monastic environment—like later nuns, Anglo-Saxon nuns were considered brides of Christ; marriage terminology is therefore an integral part of their link to the monastic community.

20. See Hollis pp. 271–300, for a discussion of the relationship between Boniface and Leoba.

21. C. H. Talbot, ed. and trans., *The Life of Christina of Markyate* (Oxford: The Clarendon Press, 1959), p. 155.

22. These interpretations come from Nora Kershaw Chadwick, *Anglo-Saxon and Norse Poems* (Cambridge: Cambridge University Press, 1922), p. 33; Raffel p. 36; and R. F. Leslie, *Three Old English Elegies* (Manchester: Manchester University Press, 1961), p. 53, respectively.

23. See Karl Wentersdorf, "The Situation of the Narrator in the Old English *Wife's Lament*," *Speculum* 58 (1981):492–516 (especially pp. 498–500).

24. I draw this formulation from Gillian Overing's introduction to her *Language, Sign and Gender in Beowulf* (Carbondale: Southern Illinois University Press, 1990), p. xiv.

The Devotional Context of the Cross Before A.D. 1000

SANDRA McENTIRE

IN order to understand the milieu out of which arose crosses such as those at Ruthwell and Bewcastle and poems in Old English such as *The Dream of the Rood* and *Elene* in the Vercelli Codex, it is useful to sort out as clearly as possible the various elements of devotion, theology, and liturgy which provided the background and possible inspiration for these works. Several writers have already drawn attention to the monastic devotional traditions of the Anglo-Saxon period which influenced poetic literature and the iconography of the crosses.[1] Some have elucidated the links between the theology of judgment and eschatology and the literary and sculptural arts.[2] In the quest for an understanding of the broad devotional background which informed the spiritual milieu of the Golden Age of Northumbria, this study will focus on three additional elements. These include, first, a reconsideration of the personal devotion of the Sign of the Cross; second, a preliminary investigation of the motif of the Cross as a cosmological symbol; and, third, a brief examination of the theological and devotional meaning of pilgrimage as it relates to the Cross. The primary historical event against which this study is cast is the arrival and subsequent veneration of pieces of the True Cross in Anglo-Saxon England. I shall draw from Cross poetry and sculpture for topical examples.

In the last hundred years, scholars have provided summaries of the historical events surrounding the cult of the Cross.[3] One of the events which gave rise to a particularly popular tradition was the discovery of the Cross attested by such Church Fathers as Chrysostom and Cyril.[4] The discovery of the "true" cross of the three, its miraculous healing power, and its translation are all part of the fervently accepted tradition. Liturgical commemoration soon followed. According to the journal of Aetheria,[5] a document which describes a fourth-century journey to the holy places, Holy Cross day was already being celebrated in 335, less than ten years after the finding. The important point about the festival celebrated in Jerusalem is that it immediately drew scores of pilgrims from all over the Christian world. The pilgrim Aetheria says that they came

> not only from Mesopotamia and Syria, from Egypt and the Thebaid, where the monks are numerous, but from all other places and provinces. In fact, there is no one who would not go to Jerusalem on this day for such solemn liturgy and for such a splendid feast.[6]

Various details taken from other manuscripts of fifth-and sixth-century itineraria indicate how fervent was the devotion to the Cross.[7] Pilgrimage to the holy places was widespread and popular. The give-and-take between East and West was generous and enthusiastic. The itineraries of travelers also give us information concerning the liturgies surrounding the Cross. Veneration of the Wood of the Cross on Good Friday and attendant details with regard to the possible origin of cross reliquaries are described, again by Aetheria:

> The gilded silver casket containing the sacred wood of the cross is brought in and opened. Both the wood of the cross and the inscription are taken out and placed on the table. As soon as they have been placed on the table, the bishop, remaining seated, grips the ends of the sacred wood with his hands, while the deacons, who are standing about, keep watch over it. There is a reason why it is guarded in this manner. It is the practice here for all the people to come forth one by one, the faithful as well as the catechumens, to bow down before the table, kiss the holy wood, and then move on. It is said that someone (I do not know when) took a bite and stole a piece of the holy cross. Therefore, it is now guarded by the deacons standing around, lest there be anyone who would dare come and do that again.[8]

We can thus see that the liturgical feast of the Dedication and the devotion of the Veneration of the Wood of the Cross were already established by the mid-fourth century. Furthermore, gilded and jeweled containers for pieces of the cross functioned not only as receptacles for the sacred object but undoubtedly as vicarious objects of devotion themselves. According to the *Anglo-Saxon Chronicle*, Pope Marinus sent Alfred a piece of the true cross in 883 and another in 885. We also know that praying to the Rood had already been widely encouraged. One homily of Ælfric encourages this devotion: "forðan ðe we nabbað ða ðe he on ðrowade, ac hire anlicnys bið halig swa-þeah, to ðære we abugað on gebedum symle to ðam Mihtigan Drihtne, þe

for mannum ðrowade" (For although we have not that on which He suffered, its likeness is, nevertheless, holy, to which we ever bow in our prayers
to the Mighty Lord, who suffered for men; and the rood is a memorial of his
great passion, holy through him. . . . We ever honour it for the honour of
Christ").[9] The arrival on English soil of an actual piece of the true cross undoubtedly heightened dramatically the efficaciousness of this sentiment.
Miraculous healings with the wood could only confirm it. When we recall
that the great hymns to the Cross written by Venantius Fortunatus were inspired by relics of the true cross arriving at Poitiers in 569, we can justifiably
infer that the response of the English was likewise enthusiastic. Bruce
Dickins and Alan Ross suggest that the arrival of the fragment of the cross
in England in the eighth century occasioned the revision of the Ruthwell
Cross poem.[10] It is also worth remembering that the cross reliquary now in
Brussels served not only as a receptacle for a piece of the true cross, but that
like the Ruthwell Cross it is inscribed with phrases distinctly parallel to the
"Rood" poem: "Rod is min nama; geo ic ricne cyning bær byfigynde blode
bestemed" (Rood is my name; in times past I shaking carried the powerful
king, drenched with blood). Dickins and Ross suggest that this reliquary
was the actual work which contained the second of the pieces Pope Marinus
sent to Alfred in 885.[11] In any event, the first sections of *Elene* describe the
process of decorating crosses as a part of Constantine's revelatory experience. The poet tells us that Constantine had seen the Cross in his dream
"frætwum beorht . . . golde geglenged, (gimmas lixtan)" (bright in trappings . . . decked with gold, [gems shining]).[12] He then commanded that a
token be wrought like the Cross he had seen in the heavens. *The Dream of
the Rood* also recalls the decorated and bejeweled Cross in the dream vision
of the narrator:

> Þuhte me þæt ic gesawe   syllicre treow
> on lyft lædan,   leohte bewunden,
> beama beorhtost.   Eall þæt beacen
> wæs begoten mid golde;   gimmas stodon
> fægere æt foldan sceatum,   swylce þær fife wæron
> uppe on þam eaxlegespanne.[13]

The personal devotion which correlates with these events is the so-
called "Sign of the Cross." In the third century Tertullian had encouraged
the use of the sign of the Cross, saying, "Ad omnem progressum atque pro-
motum, ad omnem aditum et exitum, ad calciatum, ad lavacra, ad mensas,
ad lumina, ad cubilia, ad sedilia, quaecumque nos conversatio exercet, frontem crucis signacula terimus" ("At every forward step and movement, at

every going in and out, when we put on our clothes and shoes, when we bathe, when we sit at table, when we light the lamps, on couch, on seat, in all the ordinary actions of daily life, we trace upon the forehead the sign [of the cross]").[14] Cyprian and Cyril likewise proclaimed that the sign of the Cross had supernatural power.[15] The sign itself was originally a simple gesture marking the forehead by the thumb or forefinger. From the third century on it became an extremely widespread devotion, marked at times by almost magical fervor. And, indeed, the events described in the early *Life of Antony*, written in 357 by Athanasius, provide examples of the efficacious power of the sign. For Antony the use of the sign was not only an act of faith in the Redemption of Christ but a visible means of doing battle against the wiles of the devil. Antony says, "We need not fear [the devils] apparitions, for they are nothing and disappear quickly—especially if one fortifies himself with faith and the sign of the cross."[16] Furthermore, at this time crosses appear not only on coins, but in the graffiti of the caves and meeting places of the Christians.

The devotion to the Cross as a "signum" to be used in the Christian war against the devil and subsequently as an exorcism reached Britain quite early. That the sign was a widespread devotion is implied in Bede's recommendation to Bishop Egbert to remind the members of his flock "quam frequenti diligentia signaculo se dominicae crucis, suaque omnia adversum continuas immundorum spiritum insidias, necesse habeant munire" ("with what frequent diligence to use the sign of the Lord's cross and so to fortify themselves and all they have against the continual snares of unclean spirits").[17] Alcuin recommends the sign of the Cross as the first act upon awaking in the morning.[18] Ælfric, too, comments on the gesture, saying, "Ne beo ge afyrhte þurh his gesihðe, ac mearciað rode-tacen on eowrum foreheafdum, and ælc yfel gewit fram eow" ("Be ye not afraid at the sight of him [the devil], but mark the sign of the rood on your foreheads, and every evil shall depart from you").[19] But the Irish monks of the eighth-century reform movement known as the Céli Dé were the ones who translated the small sign into a broad bodily gesture. The practice of the Cross-Vigil, also known as the Breastplate of Devotion, was the devotion of praying with arms extended, as a representation of the form of the Cross.[20] This "beacna selest" may well be the same sign, physically represented, which the dreamer in *The Dream of the Rood* is encouraged to bear in his breast as a hope for salvation.[21]

The shift from the sign of the Cross as a weapon in one's personal warfare against the attacks of the devil to a miraculous means for healing others is also attested by Bede. John of Beverley's cure of the dumb boy is an ex-

ample. ". . . iussit ad se intrare pauperem; ingresso linguam proferre ex ore
ac sibi ostendere iussit, et adprehendens eum de mento, signum sanctae
crucis linguae eius inpressit."[22] Whereas previously the actual pieces of the
true cross had been widely understood to have such miraculous power, we
see here that the gesture, accompanied by authoritative command, heals
those who have faith.

The next element of devotional import I should like to consider has to
do with the motif of the cosmological Cross. From the early Church Fathers we have the description of the Cross characterized by its form, that is,
by the four directions of the wood itself: its arms extend to the ends of the
earth; its top touches the heavens; its lower extremity penetrates the abyss
below.[23] The image of the cosmological Cross also includes the concept of
Christ on the Cross embracing the whole world and taking it home to the
Father. *The Dream of the Rood* poet may well have been suggesting the resonances of just such theology in the "foldan sceatum" of line 8.[24] The concept is widespread. Borrowing from Augustine, Bede, Alcuin, and Ælfric
explain the parts of the cross as stretching out toward the four quarters of
the world, east and west, north and south, because Christ by his passion
thus draws all people to him.[25] We see here that the Cross has not only a
cosmological redemptive significance, but that the very form of the Cross
contains a deeply theological allegorical meaning. Within this context we
see the importance of such a detail as that the four dimensional stone
crosses are specifically situated with their sides facing the four directions,
north, south, east and west. The making and placing of crosses therefore
marks a specifically public devotion. The Bewcastle Cross' principal side,
for example, faces west, a detail which had to have had significance, perhaps
as a sign to the travelers going from the West to the East. Ruthwell, too,
must have originally had a directional focus.[26] Furthermore, the devotional
practice of the Cross Vigil mentioned earlier was at times also practiced
"facing the four cardinal points and also facing the ground and the heavens."[27] O'Dwyer's interpretation of this practice is that it is a prayer "for
God's help for the four corners of the earth, for the dead and finally, in the
hope of an eternal reward," turning toward heaven.[28] This interpretation
may be only partially correct. Facing the four cardinal points does indeed
recall the universality of the redemption; however, facing the ground and
then the heavens may well represent instead the vertical beam of the Cross,
which thus completes the cosmological implications.

A further parallel to this cosmological approach can be found in the so-
called boundary crosses. Archaeology has given us evidence of sites where
crosses were placed facing the four directions, probably as boundary mark-

ers.[29] The very placing of the boundary crosses for monastic properties and cemeteries strongly argues for a consciousness of cosmological theology. For example, at the consecration of the Canterbury cemetery, the cross was erected, together with smaller ones at each of the four corners of the plot, corresponding to the point of the compass, to mark the boundaries. In the consecration service, the bishop began by making the circuit of the grounds with his clergy, chanting the litany. Then he read a portion of the service at the eastern cross, did the same at the southern, western, and northern, and concluded at the cross in the center.[30] Thus the act of establishing boundaries for hallowed property contained within it the repetition of a cosmological devotion which was specifically signified liturgically.

R. E. Kaske has convincingly established that the cosmological motif is an important one in his reading of two poems from the Exeter Book, in which he also includes comments on *The Dream of the Rood*.[31] Thomas D. Hill has shown that the concept of the cosmological Cross also provides the rationale for two Anglo-Saxon cattle-theft charms.[32] A full survey of the motif, however, remains undone and would be well worth undertaking.

Closely allied to cosmological theology, however, is the importance of pilgrimage for the early Church in Ireland and Britain. We recall that the monks left home and friends as an ascetic exercise, to preach the Gospel to those who still had not heard it, traveling, at least initially, by boat. The attitude of the monks to travel, whether within the countryside of Ireland and northern England or across the sea to the Continent, was universal in character. They made, as Robin Flower puts it, the "whole world of Europe in their day into their monastery."[33] The image of the "navis crucis"—the Cross as a ship—is noteworthy. Inspired by the ark of Noah, the Church Fathers saw a ship as a figure of the Cross, carrying the chosen to salvation. The Cross is a vehicle, or instrument, by which an individual is saved. *The Dream of the Rood* poet is capturing this sense precisely when he says at the end of the poem:

> ic wene me
> daga gehwylce   hwænne me Dryhtnes rod,
> þe ic her on eorðan   ær sceawode,
> on þysson lænan   life gefetige
> ond me þonne gebringe   þær is blis mycel,
> dream on heofonum. . . .[34]

Here the Cross is the vehicle of salvation. The link to the ark of Noah is attested iconographically on several of the high crosses, especially the Armagh Cross and the broken cross at Kells. A parallel reminder of the symbolic interconnection between the Cross, pilgrimage, and the protection of Christ is found when the author of *Genesis A*, another Northumbrian poem, says that God "segnade" the door of the ark closed.[35] In this instance the signing distinctly evokes the image of the sign of the Cross.

Perhaps an even stronger representative iconographical depiction of Cross and ship can be found in an Anglo-Saxon manuscript illumination, dated by E. A. Lowe to the second quarter of the eighth century, where a stylized crucified Christ is shown above the hull of a ship in which are seen several passengers, including one central figure and another at the helm.[36] The iconography could well be the imaging of the commentary of Cassiodorus on Psalm 106, where he describes the ship which crosses the sea as having Christ as the pilot, the rowers as the apostles, and the holy pontiffs as select passengers.[37] It is in the light of just such theological and spiritual contexts that a detail in *The Dream of the Rood* should perhaps be seen. In line 91 the term "holmwudu," sea-wood, may be, not a scribal error, but the poet's attempt to capture in an Old English compound the "navis crucis" concept.[38]

The image of the ark and the Church as it signifies to the importance of preaching and admonishing the Christian faithful is widespread. Another look at the manuscript illumination indicates that the central figure in the boat is in fact Christ preaching. And we are immediately reminded that the vision of *The Dream of the Rood* dreamer is not for his own edification or spiritual growth alone. The tree commands him to proclaim what he has seen:

> Nu ic þe hate,   hæleð min se leofa,
> þæt ðu þas gesyhðe   secge mannum,
> onwreoh wordum   þæt hit is wuldres beam,
> se ðe ælmihtig God   on þrowode
> for mancynnes   manegum synnum
> ond Adomes   ealdgewyrhtum.[39]

This injunction parallels the urgency of proclamation in the first-person interpolation at the end of *Elene*: "mægencyning amæt ond on gemynd begeat . . . bancofan onband, breostlocan onwand, leoðucræft onleac, þæs ic lustum breac, willum in worlde."[40]

The relationship between catechesis and pilgrimage needs no further emphasis here. But the role of the universal Cross, a Cross perceived as a ship which reaches all mankind, north, south, east and west, would be particularly appropriate to the whole Insular spirit.

The first millennium culminates in great artistic and literary representations of the cult of the Cross. It becomes increasingly evident that stone crosses such as those at Ruthwell and Bewcastle and poetry such as *The Dream of the Rood* and *Elene* are clear and representative expressions of a devotion, spirituality, and theology having roots in a universal awareness which was being constantly renewed by historical event, personal experience, and theological development. The use of the sign of the Cross, the significance of the Cross as a cosmological symbol, and the related importance of pilgrimage all deserve further separate study. This paper presents little new material as such: rather, it proposes a direction for further consideration of the subject. The sign of the Cross, physically represented, was widely encouraged and popularly practiced in this age; what is the relationship between making the sign of the Cross on or with one's body and erecting stone crosses? We find evidence of the motif of the cosmological Cross in literature, stone sculpture, and archaeology; how universal was the understanding of this motif? The Cross is a vehicle of salvation; how do we understand the tension between the Cross taking the believer to heavenly glory and the cross reminding the believer to proclaim to the earthly community the event of the Crucifixion and its attendant redemption? Although the answers to these questions remain uncertain, we can be sure that devotion to the Cross and the expression of the Sign of the Cross were widespread from the eighth to the tenth centuries.

Notes

1. See, for example, Robert B. Burlin, "The Ruthwell Cross, *The Dream of the Rood*, and the Vita Contemplativa," *Studies in Philology*, 65 (1960), 23–43; John V. Fleming, "*The Dream of the Rood* and Anglo-Saxon Monasticism," *Traditio*, 22 (1966), 43–72; Fritz Saxl, "The Ruthwell Cross," *Journal of the Warburg and Courtauld Institutes*, 6 (1943), 1–19; Meyer Schapiro, "The Religious Meaning of the Ruthwell Cross," *Art Bulletin*, 26 (1944), 231–45.

2. See John Canuteson, "The Crucifixion and the Second Coming in *The Dream of the Rood*," *Modern Philogy*, 66 (1969), 293–97; Christopher Chase, "'Christ III,' *The Dream of the Rood*, and Early Christian Piety," *Viator*, 11 (1980), 11–33; Eleanor Simmons Greenhill, "The Child in the Tree, A Study of the Cosmological Tree in Christian Tradition," *Traditio*, 10 (1954), 323–71 and esp. 331–38; Éamonn ÓCarragáin, "How Did the Vercelli Collector Interpret *The Dream of the Rood?*" in P. M. Tilling, ed., *Occasional Papers in Linguistics and Language Teaching*, 8 (1981), 63–104.

3. Fernand Cabrol and Henri Leclercq, eds., *Dictionnaire d'archéologie chrétienne et de liturgie* (Paris, 1907–1953), III, 3131–39, v. "croix"; George Willard Benson, *The Cross, Its History and Symbolism* (New York, 1976); William Wood Seymour, *The Cross in Tradition, History and Art* (New York, 1898); Williams O. Stevens, "The Cross in

the Life and Literature of the Anglo-Saxons," in William O. Stevens, *The Anglo-Saxon Cross* (1904; rpt. Hamden, Conn., 1977), pp. 11–103.

4. Chrysostom *In Joannem Homiliae* LXXV, in *PG*, 59:459–60; Cyril *Catechesis* IV.10, in (*PG*, 33:467–70).

5. For the Latin text of Aetheria's journal see CSEL, Vol. 39 (Vienna, 1898), pp. 37–101. See also *Ethérie: Journal de Voyage*, ed. and trans. Hélène Pétré, Sources Chrétiennes, 21 (Paris, 1948). English translations include *The Pilgrimage of St. Silvia of Aquitania to the Holy Places*, ed. John Bernard (London, 1891), and *Egeria: The Diary of a Pilgrimage*, trans. George Gingras (New York, 1970).

6. *Egeria*, trans. Gingras, p. 127; "Nam ante plurimos dies incipiunt se undique colligere turbae non solum monachorum vel aputactitum de diversis provinciis, id est tam de Mesopotamia vel Syria vel de Egypto aud Thebaida, ubi plurimi monazontes sunt, sed et de diversis omnibus locis vel provinciis; nullus est enim, qui non se eadem die in Ierusolima tendat ad tantam laetitiam et tam honorabiles dies" (*Ethérie*, ed. Pétré, p. 264).

7. See the fourth- and fifth-century accounts of pilgrimages in Titus Tobler and Augustus Molinier, eds., *Itinera Hierosolymitana et Descriptiones Terrae Sanctae* (Geneva, 1879).

8. *Egeria*, trans. Gingras, p. 111; "Stant in giro mensa diacones et affertur loculus argenteus deauratus, in quo est lignum sanctum crucis, aperitur et profertur, ponitur in mensa tam lignum crucis quam titulus. Cum ergo positum fuerit in mensa, episcopus sedens de manibus suis summitates de ligno sancto premet, diacones autem, qui in giro, custodent. Hoc autem propterea sic custoditur, quia consuetudo est, ut unus et unus omnis populus veniens, tam fideles quam cathecumini, acclinantes se ad mensam osculentur sanctum lignum et pertranseant. Et quoniam nescio quando dicitur quidam fixisse morsum et furasse de sancto ligno, ideo nunc a diaconibus, qui in giro stant, sic custoditur, ne qui veniens audeat denuo sic facere" (*Ethérie*, ed. Pétré, p. 234).

9. *The Sermones Catholici or Homilies of Ælfric*, ed. and trans. Benjamin Thorpe (London, 1846), Vol. II, p. 307. See also the edition by Malcolm Godden, *Ælfric's Catholic Homilies: The Second Series*, EETS,S.S. 5 (London, 1979), p. 175 with differing punctuation and capitalization.

10. Bruce Dickins and Alan S. C. Ross, eds., *The Dream of the Rood* (London, 1963), p. 19.

11. "It is very probable that the Brussels Cross preserves the fragment of the True Cross sent to Alfred by Pope Marinus" (Dickins and Ross, p. 15). This conclusion had earlier been reached by S. T. R. O. D'Ardenne ("The Old English Inscription on the Brussels Cross," *English Studies*, 21 [1939], 145–64, 271–72). Annemarie E. Mahler has recently taken up the question in "*Lignum Domini* and the Opening Vision of *The Dream of the Rood*: A Viable Hypothesis?" *Speculum*, 53 (1978), 441–59.

12. George Philip Krapp, ed., *The Vercelli Book*, ASPR, Vol. 2 (New York, 1932), p. 68, ll. 88, 90.

13. Michael Swanton, ed., *The Dream of the Rood* (Manchester and New York, 1970), p. 89, ll. 4–9;

> I beheld, borne up on high, methought,
> a wondrous rood, bewound with light,
> the brightest of beams. That beacon was all
> overlaid with gold; lovely stood the gems at the
> ends of the earth, and up on the crossing
> were five gems more. . . .

(trans. Kemp Malone, *Ten Old English Poems* [Baltimore, 1941], p. 3).

14. Tertullian, *De Corona Militis* III, in *PL*, 2:80; trans. Peter Holmes, (*The Writings of Quintus Sept. Flor. Tertullianus*, Anti-Nicene Christian Library, Vol. 11 (Edinburgh, 1869), p. 336.

15. Cyprian, *De Lapsis* 2, CSEL, Vol. 3, Pt. 1 (Vienna, 1868), p. 238, and *Epistle LVIII*, CSEL, Vol. 3, Pt. 2 (Vienna, 1871), p. 664; Cyril, *Catechesis* XIII.36, in *PG*, 33:815.

16. *Athanasius: The Life of Antony and the Letter to Marcellinus*, trans. Robert G. Gregg (New York, 1980), p. 48. See also *PG*, 26:835–976.

17. *Venerabilis Bedae Opera Quae Supersunt Omnia*, ed. J[ames] A. Giles, (London, 1843), Vol. I, pp. 134–35.

18. "Cum a somno evigilas, et crucis signum depingis in labiis, tertio repete: 'Domine, labia mea aperies, et os meum annuntiabit laudem tuam'" (Alcuin, *De Psalmorum Usu Liber I*, in *PL*, 101:468).

19. Ælfric, *Homilies*, ed. and trans. Thorpe, I, 467.

20. Peter O'Dwyer, *Célí Dé: Spiritual Reform in Ireland 750–900* (Dublin, 1981), pp. 108 ff.

21. Swanton, p. 95, and see p. 131, n. 118. Robert B. Burlin says: "Whether 'in breostum' points to a literal crucifix 'on his breast' or a metaphorical one 'in his breast' is beside the point, for by this time it is evident that in terms of this vision the symbol and its spiritual value are indistinguishable" ("The Ruthwell Cross, *The Dream of the Rood*, and the Vita Contemplativa," p. 32).

22. *Bede's Ecclesiastical History of the English People*, ed. and trans. Bertram Colgrave and R.A.B. Mynors (Oxford, 1969), p. 458, trans. p. 459: ". . . he ordered the poor man to come in to him and then he told him to put out his tongue and show it to him. Thereupon he took him by the chin and made the sign of the holy cross on his tongue."

23. See, for example, Augustine, *In Joannis Evangelium* CXVIII, CCSL, Vol. 36 (Turnhout, 1954), pp. 654–58.

24. See the note in Dickins and Ross, p. 102, and their discussion of this equation on pp. 50–51.

25. For Bede see *In S. Joannis Evang. Expos.* XIX, in *PL*, 92:913; Alcuin, *Liber de Divinis Officiis* XVIII in *PL*, 101:1208; Ælfric, *Homilies*, ed. Thorpe, II, 254.

26. See Swanton, p. 13, n. 1: "Originally no doubt, as at Bewcastle, where the cross still stands erect, the principal face looked west so as to be seen by worshippers conventionally approaching from that direction."

27. O'Dwyer, p. 109.

28. O'Dwyer, p. 109.

29. Stevens, p. 61; Françoise Henry, *Irish High Crosses* (Dublin, 1964), p. 20.

30. John Lingard, *History and Antiquities of the Anglo-Saxon Church*, Vol. II (London, 1845), p. 52, n. 2.

31. R. E. Kaske, "A Poem of the Cross in the Exeter Book: 'Riddle 60' and 'The Husband's Message,'" *Traditio*, 23 (1967), 41–71.

32. Thomas D. Hill, "The Theme of the Cosmological Cross in Two Old English Cattle Theft Charms," *Notes & Queries*, 25 (1978), 488–90.

33. Robin Flower, *The Irish Tradition* (Oxford, 1947), p. 66.

34. Swanton, p. 96, ll. 135–40;

> . . . and everyday I hope
> the time has come when the cross of my Lord,
> which here on earth I beheld long ago,
> shall fetch me away from this fleeting life
> and bring me then where bliss is great,
> to the happiness of heaven

(trans. Malone, *Ten OE Poems*, p. 7).

35. A. N. Doane, *Genesis A: A New Edition* (Madison, 1978), p. 145, l. 1365. In his note on p. 264, Doane further relates the image to baptism.

36. *Codices Latini Antiquiores*, Vol. IX (Oxford, 1950), p. 52, Pl. 1424. The illumination is reprinted in Paul Thoby, *Le Crucifix, des origines au concile de Trente* (Nantes, 1959), Pl. XI, and in Bernard F. Huppé, *The Web of Words* (Albany, 1970), facing p. 42.

37. "'Qui descendunt mare in navibus, facientes operationem in aquis multis.' Cum dicit, 'descendunt mare,' significat sacerdotes qui saeculi istius procellosa descendunt. Nam cum dicit, 'descendunt,' ostendit inferiora loca esse saeculi, ad quae 'descendi' posse testatur. 'In navibus' autem (ut saepe diximus) ecclesias significat, quae ligno crucis mundi istius tempestates enavigant. Sic enim mare descenditur atque transitur, si tutissimus navibus insidatur, ubi gubernator est Christus, ubi remiges apostoli et sanctorum pontificum beata collectio. Sequitur, 'facientes operationem in aquis multis.' Adhuc in eadem comparatione persistit. Sacerdos sunt enim qui operantur in aquis multis, id est praedicant populis christianis" (Cassiodorus, *Expositio Psalmorum*, CCSL, Vol. 98 [Turnhout, 1958], pp. 979–80). ("They go down to the sea in ships, doing the business in many waters." When he says, "they go down to the sea," he means the priests who go down to the stormy sea of this world. For when he says, "they go down," he reveals the lower places to be of this world to which he asserts it is possible to go down. "In ships," however [as we have often said], means the churches, which sail away from the storm of this world by the wood of the cross. For thus one is brought down to the sea and brought across, if he is most safely placed in the ships where the pilot is Christ, where the oarsmen are the apostles, and the blessed gathering of the holy pontiffs. "Doing the business in many waters" follows. Still he

remains in the same comparison. For the priests are those who work in many waters, that is, they preach to the Christian nations [my translation].)

38. See, in particular, the approach to the *hapax legomenon* by Carl Berkhout in "The Problem of Holmwudu," *Mediaeval Studies*, 36 (1974), 429–33.

39. Swanton, p. 95, ll. 95–100:

> "Now I lay it upon thee, my beloved child,
> that thou tell this sight to the sons of men,
> the tale unfold of the tree of glory
> that God Almighty gave his life on,
> to save mankind from the sin of old Adam,
> and many works of wickedness"

(trans. Malone, *Ten OE Poems*, pp. 5–6). Swanton includes a summary of the critical commentary on p. 128, n. 91.

40. Krapp, *Vercelli Book*, p. 100, ll. 1247–50; The King of power taught me and poured [grace] into my mind . . . unbound my body, opened my heart, unlocked skill in song. This I have used gladly, with pleasure in the world.

Stylistic Disjunctions in
The Dream of the Rood

CAROL BRAUN PASTERNACK

THE stylistic disjunctions in *The Dream of the Rood* are not a new topic. They have been treated explicitly and implicitly for many years from several different points of view. The most frequently noted disjunction occurs at line 78 where the cross, having completed its eye-witness account of the crucifixion, commences a homily explaining the significance of its experience. But there are others as well: at 27 where the poet switches personae from dreamer to cross, at 121 where the dreamer again becomes the speaker to describe his personal reaction to his vision and at 147 where the poet begins an impersonal magnification of Christ which concludes the poem.

The earliest discussion of the disjunctions was undertaken by textual critics such as Albert S. Cook, Bruce Dickins and Alan S. C. Ross. These critics judged the poetry according to a mimetic standard and a Romantic bias in favour of spontaneous expression of feeling. As a result they considered more abstract, less emotional, passages to be inferior poetry and shifts in style to be evidence of faulty workmanship or more probably a problem in textual transmission. Albert Cook, for example, in 1905 judged the poem's last ten lines to be 'alien to the prevailing sentiment of the poem'. Whereas the preceding lines reveal the poet's 'rapture of anticipation' for a new life in heaven, the last segment 'is cool and objective in tone, and has no necessary and vital relation to what has preceded'. The lines must be the result of an 'accident' in transmission or of the poet's faulty judgement.[1] Dickins and Ross, in their 1934 edition, were also struck by the narrative's sincere feeling. In analysing the poem's textual composition, they posited an original poem, parts of which are found on the Ruthwell Cross. In this segment, the first seventy-seven lines of the poem in the Vercelli Book, 'the beauty of imagery may well come from the personal emotion felt and expressed by the poet', rather than from some specific literary source. In contrast, 'the last few lines, referring to the Harrowing of Hell, have all the appearance of an addition, and stylistically the poem seems to divide at l. 78. The latter half does not afford the assumption of an early date, and in quality it seems to us definitely inferior'. They concluded that the entire second half, therefore, is probably the work of a later poet.[2] This attitude in favour of mimetic depiction of emotion and against stylistic disjunction has such power that it has even influenced such non-textual critics as Rosemary Woolf. In 1958, in an important article on the doctrine underlying the narrative's thematic structure, she dismisses in a footnote without discussion the second half of the poem because it 'must surely be a later addition by a writer of the school of Cynewulf'.[3]

A more recent series of critics has moved away from the mimetic standard and scepticism of the text, preferring to make sense of the poem in terms of medieval ideas about the cross. Critics such as John Fleming, John Burrow, Robert Burlin and N. A. Lee have searched for thematic rather than mimetic unity.[4] One result of this different focus is that the stylistic disjunctions do not interfere in a successful reading of the poem. In fact, as Fleming has made clear, these shifts can be accounted for by standard medieval schemata like the coupling of an *explanatio* with a *narratio*.[5] These critics have not focused on the cross's speech as the heart of the poem but rather on the way the poem as a whole expresses an idea. To cite two, Robert Burlin has defined the poem's topic as '"about" vision [as] . . . a way to Life and a way of life' and N. A. Lee as 'the symbol of the cross itself and its role in the spiritual life; a contemporary, not merely an historical phenomenon'.[6] Partly in response to the earlier textual criticism which discounted the validity of much of the poem, this body of work has treated the disjunctions with an eye to demonstrating the poem's unity, the way all the parts of the poem together coherently express a central theme.

Recent critics have also worked on defining the poem's formal unity; they, too, have been able to accommodate the disjunctions within their analyses. These critics, primarily Constance Hieatt and Eugene Kintgen, have silently dismissed mimetic in favour of thematic unity and have concentrated their efforts on analysis of how the formal elements express the theme and how they create coherence among the poem's parts.[7] Although Kintgen has studied 'echoic repetition' as a device used generally in Old English poetry and Hieatt has limited her study to *The Dream*, they have both demonstrated the way 'echoic repetition' of words and formulas associates elements in the poem and connects the sections, weaving a formal as much as a thematic unity, associating the dreamer with the cross, the cross with Christ and so on. While they have not explicitly discussed the stylistic disjunctions, they have acknowledged them implicitly. The repetitions make connections and connections are made between distinct entities. Burlin, who also has noticed the poem's frequent repetition and echo, has argued quite convincingly that 'obviously the rhetoric of the poem depends upon a system of parallels and contrasts which may in turn be seen as formally congruent with the dramatic thesis—the interaction of God and man through the intermediary of the Cross. The symbolic conflict of the poem depends upon the parallelism of sympathetic responses within contrasting modes of being.'[8] Hieatt also has talked about 'parallels', 'connections . . . expressed again and again in verbal echoes', 'verbal parallels' which express 'major parallels of action, or feeling'.[9] These parallels occur not just within 'contrasting modes of being' but also within distinct sections of the poem. She has identified five topical divisions: 'Prologue' (1–27), 'Vision I, History of Rood' (28–77), 'Vision II, Explanation of Rood's Glory' (78–94), 'Vision III, Rood's Message to Mankind' (95–121) and 'Epilogue' (122–56).[10] While she has used the formal element of verbal clusters to aid in determining these divisions, she has not commented on the poet's shifts in style. We might notice, however, that the boundaries between these units coincide with the major disjunction objected to by the early critics and with other stylistic disjunctions which I shall discuss.

Certainly the parallels which unite the poem occur within contrasting modes of being and within sections which are divided topically. They also occur, however, within contrasting modes of discourse. The long discussion regarding the poem's unity is witness to these contrasts. In fact the 'echoic repetitions' and the 'system of parallels and contrasts' find their formal complement in the poem's systematic stylistic disjunctions. The next step in studying *The Dream*, the one which this article will take, is to return once again to direct examination of the poem's disjunctions, to study them not as evidence of an imperfect text but as a stylistic–structural feature of what we now consider to be a sound poetic whole.

In *The Dream* syntactic and rhetorical patterns mark the topical divisions in the narrative and in this way disjoin it into discrete segments. This formal, stylistic disjunction is the necessary complement to the poem's system of echoic repetitions and parallels. They complement each other in that both elements require the audience to recognize patterns, the repetitions and the changes in pattern. They do so in the way they function together to create meaning. The poem's meaning is created through association and contrast; that is, through analogy. An analogy, according to

common dictionary definition, is a 'resemblance in some particulars between things otherwise unlike'.[11] Instead of developing the poem in terms
of cause and effect, temporal sequence or other logical connections, the
Dream poet creates several distinct poetic experiences or strategies which
give insight into the idea of the cross. He presents the dreamer's vision, the
cross's narrative, the cross's sermon, the dreamer's personal response and
the final magnification of Christ. To describe the system in its simplest
form, the verbal echoes point to the resemblances among these parts and
the disjunctions demarcate them, pointing to the distinctions.

This non-mimetic, analogical method of creating meaning is not
unique to this poem. It complies with one of the two major conceptions of
history and, therefore, of narrative which competed in the Middle Ages.
Erich Auerbach has claimed that among medieval narratives we can find 'on
the one hand, a presentation which carefully interrelated the elements of
history, which respected temporal and causal sequence, remained within
the domain of the earthly foreground, and, on the other hand, a fragmentary, discrete presentation, constantly seeking an interpretation from
above'.[12] The latter is the one which underlies the figural interpretation of
scripture so often applied by the Church Fathers, in which one historical
event, such as Isaac carrying the wood for his own sacrifice, is seen as analogical with another, in this case Christ carrying his own cross. The same
structure of thought and expression permeates a great deal of non-biblical
and even non-allegorical medieval literature as well. Whether or not 'an interpretation from above', that is from doctrine, is available, Old English
poets frequently forgo temporal and causal sequence and present a fragmentary, disjoined narrative. The meaning in such a poem is implied
through embedded patterns of words and formulas which find their echoes
in associated parts of the poem and in traditional Germanic and Christian
motifs. The traditional ideas and the internal echoes point out the analogies among the segments and thereby unify the poem's segments and convey the poem's theme. (This method of creating meaning is the topic of
studies on echoic repetition and on themes and type-scenes as well as that
of more recent ones on formulaic language.)[13] The segments, on the other
hand, are made discrete through topical and stylistic articulation. The topic
may change, as in *Exodus*, from Moses to Noah to Abraham, or, less drasti-
cally, as in *The Dream*, from the vision of the cross to the narrative by the
cross, but the theme remains the same. Syntactic and rhetorical pattern
may reinforce as well as define such divisions. The result of such a method
is that the poet goes beyond depiction of historical event to the more abstract depiction of an idea. In the case of *The Dream* the poem is not about

what happened to an Anglo-Saxon one night or about the historical crucifixion *per se* but is about the idea of the cross, presented according to several
different perspectives. The stylistic and topical circumscription of each
perspective conveys its limitations: none of these perspectives is self-sufficient to depict the cross's absolute reality; each needs its companions to imply together something of this abstract idea.

To create the formal unity and the formal disjunction which are the architectural supports for this analogical structure, the poets exploit the same
basic resource in their audience, the ability to perceive patterns. Echoic
repetition depends on having the audience hear and recognize a keyword, a
formula or a syntactic pattern which has been used before. Disjunction depends on having the audience respond to two types of pattern, one which
contrasts with the local patterns the poem itself has established and one
which, being rhetorical, stands out in any context, including such figures as
chiasmus and variation.

Anglo-Saxon sensitivity to syntax plays a significant rôle in the poets'
exploitation of patterns, a sensitivity which has been explored rather tentatively by critics. Although there are many points of Old English syntax
about which we remain in doubt, a few salient points are certain. We know
for a fact, mostly through the work of Faith Gardner and Bruce Mitchell,
that Old English prose employs a relatively stable word order and does not
rely heavily on inflection, as was formerly thought.[14] We also know that
poetic word order is much more flexible than prose word order.[15] And it
stands to reason that, while poetic syntax is far more flexible than prose, the
Anglo-Saxons were sensitive to word order there too and the poets could
make use of that sensitivity and the flexibility that the poetry gave them. As
Stanley Greenfield has demonstrated, the poets were quite capable of manipulating individual sentences so that their syntax worked with the words
to convey meaning.[16] A major contention of this article is that they also
used syntax as an organizing feature in their poetry and a basic resource for
establishing a pattern within a poem and then changing that pattern.

The *Dream* poet draws heavily on the flexibility of Old English syntax as
well as on rhetoric to disjoin his narrative stylistically. The major resource
is the order of subject, verb and object. For example, in moving from the
poem's first section to the second, at 27, the poet switches the dominant
syntactic pattern from subject–verb to verb-initial at the same time as he
switches personae from dreamer to cross. He uses the first independent
clause to establish his word-order patterns. In all but the third section (78–
121), where compound sentences predominate, a parenthetical independent clause or one that forms a compound with a preceding independent

clause does not affect the pattern. Subordinate clauses do not contribute to word-order patterns either. They do, however, play a rôle in another way, for, in addition to word order, the poet creates patterns from the placement and type of adverbs, from the degree and extent of subordination in a sentence and from variation with its related techniques. No single method of creating pattern pervades the poem. The first section, the vision (1–26), relies on subject-initial word order; the second, the cross's narrative (27–77), on verb-initial; the third, the sermon (78–121), on initial temporal and spatial adverbs and compound sentences linked by conjunctive adverbs; the fourth, the dreamer's personal response (122–46), on initial verbs and extensive series of subordinate clauses expanded through variation; and the fifth, the magnification (147–56), on subject-initial word order, shorter sentences and a shift to the second person plural pronoun. The most important principle is contrast. Each section contrasts with the ones preceding and following. In addition, deviations from the dominant pattern within a section mark logical subdivisions which are frequently reinforced by rhetorical patterns.[17]

The first section, the dreamer's vision (1–26), stresses grammatically the subject and object, semantically the dreamer and the cross on which he gazes. The changes in the descriptive terms applied to the dreamer and the cross convey the subjectivity of the vision. Although the varied placement of the adjectives and adverbs keeps the pattern from becoming too stark, in most of the principal clauses the subject comes first, followed by the verb and the subject complement or direct object. For example, in the following three sentences the initial adjectives and adverbs 'eall þæt' and 'swylce þær' maintain a graceful variety, but the sentences are all S–V followed by a prepositional phrase:

> Eall þæt beacen wæs
> begoten mid golde.   Gimmas stodon
> fægere æt foldan sceatum.   Swylce þær fife wæron
> uppe on þam eaxlegespanne.   (6b–9a)[18]

These sentences sustain the same basic pattern of subject–verb–object and subject–verb–complement diversified in minor ways:

> Hwæðre ic þurh þæt gold   ongytan meahte
> earmra ærgewin   þæt hit ærest ongan
> swætan on þa swiðran healfe.   Eall ic wæs mid sorgum gedrefed.
> Forht ic wæs for þære fægran gesyhðe.   (18–21²)

The first sentence begins with the adverbial *hwæðre*, divides the subject and verb with the prepositional phrase 'þurh þæt gold', and follows the object with a variation, 'þæt hit ærest ongan / swætan on þa swiðran healfe'; the second begins with the adjective *eall* and divides the auxiliary and principal verb with the prepositional phrase 'mid sorgum'; and the third begins with a predicate adjective *forht* and ends with the prepositional phrase 'for þære fægran gesyhðe'. These differences, however, do not exceed certain limits. None of the S–V sentences in the vision is as long as three lines and none uses more than one variation.

Though this first section includes sentences that display V–S–O order, they fall into a tightly regulated pattern, controlled by theme and function. In all of the main clauses in which verb precedes subject and complement, the verb is the first word in the sentence and it expresses perception: 'þuhte me þæt ic gesawe' (4a), 'beheoldon' (9b) and 'geseah ic' (14 and 21b).[19] Furthermore the sentences introduced by verbs act as contrasting borders dividing the first section into four subsections. A three-line introduction and conclusion employ the dominant subject-initial syntax (1–3 and 24–6). The contrasting sentences open and close the two parts of the body: 4–12 describe the surface of the *treow* as the dreamer first saw it and 13–23 describe the dreamer's subsequent perception of contrast between the heavenly and fallen states, first in the opposite states of himself and the cross and then in the dual appearance of the cross itself.

Rhetorical devices contribute to this outline as well. The sentence that completes the preliminary description (9b–12) achieves closure in part through the use of an initial verb, *beheoldon*, but also through its chiasmic structure ('beheoldon þær engel dryhtnes . . . ac hine þær beheoldon') and its finish in a heavy three-part subject ('halige gastas, / men ofer moldan, ond eall þeos mære gesceaft').[20] To introduce the more evaluative description of the vision, the poet reverses the vision's usual subject–verb syntax by preposing the complement. The resulting chiasmus, 'syllic wæs se sigebeam, ond ic synnum fah', initiates the subsection's theme of contrast between the heavenly and the fallen, and the insertion of the third initial verb, 'geseah ic' (14b), strengthens the sense of this shift in perspective. This subsection the poet completes via the envelope 'geseah ic þæt fuse beacen' (21b), echoing the earlier 'geseah ic wuldres treow' (14b), and a tight, balanced summary of the contrast, 'hwilum hit wæs mid wætan bestemed, / beswyled mid swates gange, hwilum mid since gegyrwed' (22b–3).

These sentences which break the S–V pattern outline the vision's structure. They create a kind of bas-relief against the background of the 'normal' sentences and, in doing so, emphasize both vision and its stages, which begin with sight and expand to include a deeper perception of the cross's dual nature.[21] But for the bas-relief to be visible the background has to be maintained; nine out of fifteen of the main clauses comply with the S–V pattern and the final lines of the vision are in the basic S–V pattern:

> Hwæðre ic þær licgende   lange hwile
> beheold hreowcearig   hælendes treow,
> oððæt ic gehyrde   þæt hit hleoðrode.   (24–6)

Besides resuming the dominant pattern, these lines remind the audience where the vision began, with a night-time event—the dreamer is still lying down—and with a purpose of speaking, though his intent to speak is transferred in the last three lines to his hearing the cross speak.

With the next sentence, 'ongan þa word sprecan wudu selesta' (27), the poet breaks entirely with the vision's syntactic pattern in order to establish a new one. This initial verb emphasizes beginning and speech, and the sentence introduces both the subject-matter of the poem's second section, the cross's narrative (27–77), and its syntax norm, verb-initial. Contrasting with the looser previous section the dominant pattern here is sharply defined: thirty out of forty-seven main clauses begin with verbs, the only variation being the particle *ne* (42b and 47b). The initial verbs overwhelm: *genaman, geworhton, heton, bæron, geseah, ongyrede, gestah, bifode, ne dorste, ahof, hyldan, þurhdrifan, ne dorste, bysmeredon, geseah, weap, hnag, genamon, ahofon, forleton, aledon, gestodon, beheoldon, ongunnon, curfon, gesetton, ongunnon, reste* and *bedealf*.[22] Though several of these sentences are completed by subordinate clauses and expanded by variations, the initial verbs stand out because they contrast with the most common prose word order, in which, according to basic grammars, 'any element other than the S placed first in a clause is given emphasis',[23] and, more decisively, with the preceding section's S–V norm.

This remarkable contrast has been subjectively and objectively analysed. Burrow and Burlin have both characterized the speech's opening as highly colloquial, contrasting with 'the impersonal liturgical grandeur' and 'the awesome silence of a spacious vision' conveyed in the poem's first section.[24] The poem opens the new movement decisively by striking its peculiar chords loudly and strongly. Eugene Kintgen has pointed out the uniformity of the narrative's first sentences: with the exception of 32b, all the verses in 30–3 not only are hypermetric but also 'begin with a preterite plural verb; all follow with a pronoun in the accusative or dative case; all but one continue with *ðær*. This repetition of syntactic structures unifies the section and conveys the impression of purposeful action.'[25] The word order following the initial verbs is looser in the rest of the section and after a while the surprise of the change in pattern and tone wears off. Then, however, as in the vision, the dominant pattern becomes a background against which the poet can work.

Again, as in the vision, the sentences which contrast in their syntax with the dominant pattern divide the narrative into subsections, in this case showing four different facets of the crucifixion: 35–8 segregate the enemies' actions against the cross (30b–4) from Christ's heroic ascension on to the cross (39–43); 44a, 'rod wæs ic aræred', separates the voluntary ascent from the obverse version in which the cross raises Christ (44b–8a); and 48b–59a divide the activity of the crucifixion from its sequel, Christ's burial. The third interruption, the relation of Christ's death, appropriately emphasizes the effects of his death on others and minimizes its direct effect on Christ.[26] It is by far the longest and most important break and is itself divided into three stages by two V–S sentences. The two initial verbs relate not Christ's actions but the cross's sympathetic observation and creation's sorrow (51b–2a and 55b–6a). The description which surrounds these two sentences moves us in gentle stages up to and away from Christ's death, putting in subordinate positions all direct references to the death. The first stage (48b–51a) tells us in the main clause that the cross is covered with blood, in a participial phrase that the blood had issued from the man's side and in an adverbial clause that the blood flowed after Christ had sent on his spirit. In the second stage (52b–5a) the corpse is the direct object which darkness surrounds. In the last stage (56b–9a) Christ is finally the subject of a sentence, 'Crist wæs on rode', but this bold statement is static and recalls the hero's voluntary ascent more than his eclipse by darkness and death. The approach of the eager men who will succour the warrior–prince follows immediately. This sensitive passage completed, the poet returns to the pattern of initial verbs and to the activities they stress of relieving Christ and of removing and burying the body. A final interruption in the dominant syntax, some ten long lines later (70–4), concludes the fourth subsection by separating Christ's burial from that of the three crosses (75a), which shifts attention back to the cross.[27] At this point the poet balances 'bedealf us' with 'hwæðre me . . . freondas gefrunon', a reference to the Invention of the cross, and in so doing changes the time-frame, bringing the crucifixion narrative to a close.

From this controlled alternation between two basic ways of structuring sentences emerges the narrative's own system of fragmentation in which the verb-initial sentences relate four discrete scenes in the crucifixion: the enemies act against the cross (30b–4), Christ as hero mounts the cross (39–43), the cross raises Christ (44b–8a) and friends aid the limb-weary hero (59b–69). The sentences which contrast with the verb-initial pattern act as borders which divide these scenes from each other and control the narrative's movement. The poet defines these scenes through rhetoric as well as syntax, so that the shifting syntactical patterns act in concert with other features of design. Chiasmus plays a major rôle in this design. Besides being a recurring figure in the poem (see the discussion of 9b–11a, 13 and 44 for a few instances), chiasmus underlies the sequence of scenes which the cross narrates.[28] The pivotal point of the sequence is the chiastic 44, 'Rod wæs ic aræred. Ahof ic ricne cyning.' This line, as Macrae-Gibson has pointed out, divides the active Christ from the passive one and the passive cross from its active rôle.[29] It also bisects the four portions of the narrative so that they form a chiasmus, the central juxtaposed scenes depicting the dual acts of Christ ascending the cross and of the cross raising Christ and being pierced by the nails, the framing scenes being on the one side the enemies raising the cross and on the other side friends taking down Christ and burying the three crosses. The diagram emerges

a	*b*	*b*	*a*
enemies	crucifixion	crucifixion	friends
erecting			taking down

A second rhetorical device defining these scenes involves a closing shift in narrative focus which works as follows. Throughout the first scene (30b–4) the cross dwells on a series of actions committed by its enemies and then closes by shifting focus to the approaching 'frea mancynnes'. In the second (39–43) the series of Christ's deeds is completed by the cross's self-reflective statement that it did not dare fall. The third (44b–8a) begins with the cross acting and being acted on but finishes with the realization that Christ and the cross are derided together. In the fourth (59b–69) Christ is the object of all the men's actions, until in the last sentence he becomes the subject acting—'reste he ðær mæte weorode'. With a similar shift in focus the cross brings the dreamer out of the time-frame of the crucifixion. It begins the narrative by placing the action in the past, 'þæt wæs geara iu (ic þæt gyta geman)' (28), and ends it by moving closer towards the present to the Invention of the cross, when its friends find it and adorn it with gold and silver (75b–7).

The poem's third section, the cross's sermon (78–121), makes the shift in time more pointed, opening emphatically with 'nu ðu miht gehyran, hæleð min se leofa'. Whereas the cross's narrative had stressed active verbs and suppressed temporal adverbs,[30] the sermon does not begin any sentence with an active verb, preposing instead in most main clauses adverbs of time and place.[31] The sentences also become more complex, laden with comparisons, oppositions and reasons. It is this change that convinced Dickins and Ross and others that the poem was a composite. More recently Burrow, Burlin, Fleming and Lee have all accepted the change as rhetorical rather than accidental. Fleming, for example, has asserted that the differences in language 'mirror the tonal differences between the *narratio* of the Crucifixion episode and the homiletic *explanatio* which follows it'.[32] Lee similarly has stated that 'this stylistic change' probably 'illustrates conformity with a fairly common rhetorical scheme: a change from narrative to explanation and exhortation'.[33] He has pointed out more specifically that for the remainder of the poem 'the verses become more standardized metrically, the sentences tend to be longer and more difficult to divide . . . and there is more rhetorical organization'.[34] The poet uses the rhetorical organization and longer sentences in a specific way, to explain the relevance of the historical crucifixion to the dreamer's present life.

All the sentences between 78 and 121 make connections—either typological ones between historical events, analogical ones between historical event and Judgement Day or between contemporary man and Judgement Day, or tropological ones between historical event and contemporary man. Grammatically the sentences make these connections by using adverbs prominently to begin sentences and to join main clauses which together compare the two time periods or the temporal and the eternal. The syntactic and thematic modes of the section are clearly established in the first sentence (78–83a) by its initial adverb and sermon tag and by its statement linking the present when the dreamer must hear (78), the past when the cross suffered (79–80a) and the present when the cross is now worshipped (80b–3a). Syntactically, the present 'nu ðu miht gehyran' (78a) is weighed against the past tense in the direct object clause, 'þæt ic bealuwara weorc gebiden hæbbe, / sarra sorga' (79–80a), and that first *nu* is supplemented by the correlative 'is nu sæl cumen' (80b) and its adjective clause, 'þæt me weorðiað' (81a). Other sentences beginning with adverbs or adverbial prepositions follow. The second sentence (84b–6), like the first, shows the connection between the Passion and the cross's present rôle, *forþan* pointing to the crucifixion as the reason that the cross now (*nu* for a third time) towers in heaven and can heal any man in awe of him. The *iu* which begins the third sentence (87–9) and points to the time when the cross was 'wita heardost' is complemented by *ærþan* which points to the subsequent widening of 'lifes weg'. As the sermon progresses the Passion moves further into the background to make room for Christ's ascension and the Last Judgement. Accordingly, 'nu ic þe hate' in the fifth sentence (95–100) sets up a direct object clause, 'þæt ðu þas gesyhðe . . . onwreoh', and a variation on *gesyhðe*, still in the present tense, 'þæt hit is wuldres beam', and finally a clause modifying *beam* which points out the Passion's rôle in the past tense, 'se ðe ælmihtig god on þrowode'. The statements which follow bring us by stages to Christ's Second Coming and the significance of the cross on that *domdæg*.

Even the sentences that do not begin with an adverb are designed to stress temporal comparisons. In the first of these (90–4) the cross exclaims that the Lord honoured him over other trees just as he also honoured his mother over other women; though the sentence uses no explicit temporal references, its conjunctive adverb, 'swylce swa', compares the two extreme moments in Christ's Incarnation, the Advent and the Passion, when Mary bore him and when the cross bore him. In the second (101–2), again using a conjunctive adverb, the cross opposes the statement that Christ tasted death to 'hwæðere eft dryhten aras'. In the third (103–9 the cross contrasts the ascension with Christ's return to earth for the Last Judgement. In the fourth (110–16) the cross contemplates man's state at the Last Judgement, when Christ will ask where the man is who will taste death 'swa he ær on ðam beame dyde'. And in the sermon's final sentence (117–21) the cross claims that on this day (*þonne*) any man who 'him ær in breostum bereð beacna selest' need not be afraid. Through these temporal connections the cross explains the Passion's relevance to the cross's present rôle and to man's subsequent hope for salvation.

Two sets of parallel clauses give further order to these connections. One set (78 and 95) divides the sermon in half, the other (110–21) concludes it. In both cases the parallelisms themselves act like correlative structures, suggesting a semantic and formal interdependence similar to that created by the adverbial connectives. The two principal subsections are clearly outlined by the parallel addresses:

> Nu ðu miht gehyran,   hæleð min se leofa,
>
> . . . .
>
> Nu ic þe hate,   hæleð min se leofa . . .   (78 and 95)

They suggest that, since the dreamer is privileged to hear the cross's story and sermon, he must also relate his experience to others: the witness must become the preacher. The statements introduced by *gehyran* sum up the vision of the cross's suffering, including the result of that suffering—the cross's towering in the heavens, healing men and opening life's way. The subsection concludes in a deviant structure which shows the suffering to be an honour. The poet stresses the new perspective and creates a sense of closure by breaking the initial adverb pattern with the exclamatory *hwæt* and building a stylistically elevated sentence with variation, chiasmus and parallelism:

> Hwæt, me þa geweorðode   wuldres ealdor
> ofer holmwudu,   heofonrices weard,
> swylce swa he his modor eac,   Marian sylfe,
> ælmihtig god   for ealle menn
> geweorðode   ofer eall wifa cynn.   (90–4)

The two halves of this comparison have the same basic structure: subject, verb, object and prepositional phrase. The first half inverts the subject and object, placing 'me' before and 'wuldres ealdor' after the verb, and varies the subject with 'heonfonrices weard'. The second half follows its subject with the object and varies both the subject and object in a chiastic pattern ('he his modor eac, Marian sylfe, ælmihtig god') before repeating the verb used in the first half, *geweorðode*. Besides adding a variation on the object in the second half, the poet includes an extra prepositional phrase, 'for ealle menn', corresponding in structure to 'ofer eall wifa cynn' which parallels in function as well as structure the first half's 'ofer holmwudu'. Such a strong closure virtually requires the fresh opening of 'nu ic þe hate' (95a).

In the second subsection, introduced by 'ic þe hate', the cross demands that the dreamer explain to men the doctrinal facts which emerge from the vision and the narration. With this new focus come some modifications in syntax and content. The sentences no longer relate simple temporal connections between historical events in Christ's or the cross's life or between historical event and the cross's present rôle. Instead they relate complex moral connections between a man's state at the Last Judgement and his previous life and between man's conduct in his present life and Christ's in his suffering. To do this the poet drops the simpler temporal connectives of *nu . . . nu, hwile, forþan . . . nu*, and *iu . . . ærþan* and after 95 uses more complex chains of definition and contrast, joining clauses with *se ðe, þæt, swa, ac* and *hwæðere*, although temporal adverbs remain as well in 'hider eft', 'swa he him ærur', 'swa he ær', and 'þe him ær'. In another modification the cross no longer speaks in the first person but instead, as Kintgen has noticed, switches at 97b to the third person when it commands 'þæt ðu þas gesyhðe secge mannum, / onwreoh wordum þæt hit is wuldres beam'.[35] In concert with its theme of judgement and redemption the cross stresses Christ's transition from man to judge by first imposing an emphatic O–S–V sentence, 'deað he þær byrigde', (1012), and then balancing it with 'hwæðere eft dryhten aras' (101b), in this way juxtaposing death and resurrection, ignominy and exaltation. Once again the poet creates closure through increased variation and an unusually long involved sentence (103–9). In this case the poet balances the ascension ('he ða on heofenas astag') against Christ's descent in the Second Coming ('hider eft fundaþ') and then he expands the second clause with a variation on *hider*, 'on þysne middangeard', and one on *eft*, 'on domdæge', the main clause being completed by a delayed subject, 'dryhten sylfa', varied once by 'ælmihtig god' and expanded by the second element, 'ond his englas mid'. This main clause is followed by a purpose clause, 'þæt he þonne wile demean . . . anra gehwylcum', which itself expands with a variation on the subject, 'se ah domes geweald', and a comparison, 'swa he him ærur her . . . geearnaþ', that comparison including a variation on *ærur*, 'on þyssum lænum life', in which the phrase is pushed past the normal half-line break. Through this complex sentence the poet develops the enormity of that second journey seeking mankind and of the judgement which follows.

The second set of parallel clauses (110–21) formalizes that new element in the sermon, man's position on the Judgement Day. Although the subordinate clauses maintain the sermon's interest in time, the two main clauses deviate from the section's initial adverb syntax. The cross outlines the fear and the hope for men, uniting two with parallel structure and word echoes. The similarity in the two main clauses

> Ne mæg þær ænig   unforht wesan
> . . . .
> Ne þearf ðær þonne ænig   anforht wesan   (110 and 117)

binds the two together into an apparent paradox. Each sentence complements the initial clause with an *ac* clause (115–16 and 119–21), the first asserting that men challenged by the judge will be afraid and the second that each soul who in his life bears the cross in his breast will attain the heavenly kingdom through the cross. Each *ac* clause includes a statement on what men now think (115b–16 and 121), the repetition of *þencaþ . . . þenceð* making sharper the differences between those who have not thought 'hwæt hie to Criste cweðan onginnen' and the soul who 'mid wealdende wunian þenceð'. The tight structure of this passage, its omission of initial adverbs and its shift in subject from the Passion to the Judgement Day effectively close the sermon and create a transition to the dreamer's personal response to his dream.

This response, the fourth section (122–46), like the second section's narrative, is characterized by verb-initial sentences. But, unlike those in the cross's narrative, the initial verbs in the main clauses are not action verbs: they involve praying, being and not having. The poet also brings into this section, however, as Burrow has suggested, a sense of 'life and motion' through 'the abstract language of motion—seeking, travelling, fetching, coming, bringing'.[36] He does this through another feature which distinguishes this section from the second: extensive variation and parallelism. The verbs of motion occur in subordinate and co-ordinate clauses with initial subjects, so that, while they are multiplied through variation and parallelism, they are dependent in some way on the verbs expressing praying, being and not having. Specifically the section opens with the dreamer's declaration that he prayed, 'gebæd ic me þa to þan beame', including small variations, 'elne mycle' on 'bliðe mode' and 'mæte werede' on *ana* (122–4a). The next statement (124b–6a) consists of two clauses, 'wæs modsefa afysed on forðwege' and its adversative 'feala ealra gebad / langunghwila'. The third, more complex, sentence (126b–31a) begins the section's characteristic redundancies by declaring first

> Is me nu lifes hyht
> þæt ic þone sigebeam   secan mote
> ana oftor   þonne ealle men,
> well weorþian.   (126b–9a)

This clause already contains the variant 'well weorþian' for *secan* (which is meaningful only in relation to its variant, to its own previous occurrence in 104b and to *gesecan* in 119b). The clause is then paratactically connected to the compound clauses

> me is willa to ðam
> mycel on mode,   ond min mundbyrd is
> geriht to þære rode.[37]   (129b–31a)

This whole element says nothing that was not expressed by 'is me nu lifes hyht'. The next sentence (131b–44a) is even more expansive, stretching into twelve lines the dreamer's statement that his friends have left earth and that he expects on any day the cross to fetch him so that he may follow them to heaven. The sentence begins with the simple declaration

> Nah ic ricra feala
> freonda on foldan,   ac hie forð heonon
> gewiton of worulde dreamum . . .   (131b–3a)

but eventually it includes four variations on his friends' departure to heaven, four on the great bliss he hopes to find there and two on his hope of dwelling in glory (133b–44a).

A sound pattern emerges in conjunction with this series of subordinate clauses and variations to create a more elevated style than is found in the poem's previous sections. Verbs are used to begin or complete verses so that their similar endings form rhymes and echoes: *gewiton* initiating 133a is rhymed by *sohton* which begins the *b* verse; *lifiaþ*, at the start of 134a is rhymed by *wuniaþ* which opens 135a; *gefetige*, the last word in 138b, is echoed at the end of 139a by *gebringe*. The echoic effect grows still more intense in 139b–44a, the phrases which complete this long sentence. Here the *b* verses of 139–42 form a fourfold anaphora of 'þær is' clauses modified in the fourth to 'þær ic' and, in doing so, formalize the sentence's sound pattern, the tighter rhythm raising the passage's style from speech to chant. This series of variations and expansions carries a different structural function from those used earlier in the poem. Whereas variations were used on occasion in the cross's sermon as a device for closure, these variations and expansions typify the dreamer's reflections, swelling the passage's volume far more. Here, instead of using more variation to conclude the section, the poet breaks his pattern and, inserting the prayer itself, ends with a brief, comparatively straightforward sentence:

> Si me dryhten freond,
> se ðe her on eorþan   ær þrowode
> on þam gealgtreowe   for guman synnum.   (144b–6)

The ten lines which complete the poem with a fifth section (147–56) again use variation. But the perspective shifts from the dreamer's reflections on his present state and hopes to an impersonal, compact, doctrinal statement on Christ's grace as figured in the dual movement of the Harrowing of Hell and the Ascension. To accomplish this shift the poet employs one more stylistic disjunction. He returns to the subject-initial syntax with which he began the poem and, as Kintgen has noted, drops the personal *ic*, substituting an *us* which includes all mankind and functions as object rather than subject.[38] The poet's insertion of the *us* before the verb and his brief return to short sentences sharpens the disjunction. The completeness of this break prompted Albert Cook to analyse the conclusion as so 'cool and objective in tone' as to be 'alien to the prevailing sentiment of the poem'.[39] The first two sentences of the section show both the new style and the generalized perspective; they crystallize the purpose of Christ's suffering:

> He us onlysde   ond us lif forgeaf,
> heofonlicne ham.   Hiht wæs geniwad
> mid bledum ond mid blisse   þam þe þær bryne þolodan.   (147–9)

The last sentence (150–6) completes the statement on man's redemption with a description of the Ascension. It begins in the same pattern as the previous two, subject, verb and complement, 'se sunu wæs sigorfæst on þam siðfate', but then expands the simple statement with variation that stresses nouns and adjectives instead of verbs, first varying *sigorfæst* with 'mihtig ond spedig', then varying *siðfate* with five and a half lines divided into two separate *þa* clauses, each with its own variations. In the first, 'gasta weorode' varies 'mid manigeo', 'anwealda ælmihtig' varies *he* and 'þam þe on heofonum ær / wunedon on wuldre' and unnecessarily defines the already expansive 'ond eallum ðam halgum'. The second *þa* clause repeats the first, 'þa he mid manigeo com . . . on godes rice' becoming 'þa heora wealdend cwom / ælmihtig god, þær his eðel wæs'. These heavily repetitive, expanded, declarations of Christ's triumphant return and glory end the poem.

The stylistic disjunction of the poem's last ten lines from those which precede is important in setting up the significance of these lines. For the account of the Harrowing of Hell and the Ascension does not grow organically out of the dreamer's reflections any more than it does out of the sermon, the narration or the initial vision. The conclusion's significance becomes evident in the light of every section. Each section provides some insight, forms one strategy by which the meaning of the crucifixion can be approached. The stylistic disjunctions subliminally remind the audience that each strategy only reveals part of the meaning, the part which can be descried through that method of perceiving. It is true that the audience's experience with the idea accumulates and the poem's concluding section means far more to us at the end than it would have done at the beginning before the dynamic experience of the cross's narrative or the explanations and exhortations of the sermon.[40] Indeed the poet uses the syntax to give a feeling of overriding pattern as well as disjunction. In addition to the echoes and themes which unite the poem's sections the shifts in syntax themselves form a symmetrical pattern: the first and last are subject-initial, the second and fourth are verb-initial and the central, third, section is balanced through compound sentences and parallels. The symmetry, however, is not perfect. Among other differences the final two sections are shorter than their corresponding parts and use dramatically more variation. A pattern is there, but its lack of perfection complements the disjunction between the parts. Whether the imbalance arises from the poet's limited ability or is deliberate, it symbolizes man's imperfect understanding of the crucifixion. The dreamer or his audience can make associations among the poetic experiences, but they are only associations. For medieval man the whole truth resides in God and in doctrine as he has revealed it.[41]

Notes

1. *The Dream of the Rood: an Old English Poem Attributed to Cynewulf*, ed. Albert S. Cook (Oxford, 1905), pp. liv–lv.

2. *The Dream of the Rood*, ed. Bruce Dickins and Alan S. C. Ross (London, 1934), pp. 18–19.

3. 'Doctrinal Influences on *The Dream of the Rood*', *MÆ* 27 (1958), 153.

4. John V. Fleming, '*The Dream of the Rood* and Anglo-Saxon Monasticism', *Traditio* 22 (1966), 43–72; John A. Burrow, 'An Approach to *The Dream of the Rood*', *Neophilologus* 43 (1959), 123–33; Robert B. Burlin, 'The Ruthwell Cross, *The Dream of the Rood* and the Vita Contemplativa', *SP* 65 (1968), 23–43; and N. A. Lee, 'The Unity of *The Dream of the Rood*;, *Neophilologus* 56 (1972), 469–86. Others include Louis H. Leiter, '*The Dream of the Rood*: Patterns of Transformation', *Old English Poetry: Fifteen Essays*, ed. Robert P. Creed (Providence, RI, 1967), pp. 93–127; Faith H. Patten, 'Structure and Meaning in *The Dream of the Rood*', *ES* 49 (1968), 385–401; and O. D. Macrae-Gibson, 'Christ the Victor—Vanquished in *The Dream of the Rood*', *NM* 70 (1969), 667–72.

5. 'Anglo-Saxon Monasticism', p. 55.

6. 'The Vita Contemplativa', p. 33, and 'The Unity', p. 467.

7. Constance B. Hieatt, 'Dream Frame and Verbal Echo in the *Dream of the Rood*', *NM* 72 (1971), 251–63, and Eugene Kintgen, 'Echoic Repetition in Old English Poetry, especially *The Dream of the Rood*', *NM* 75 (1974), 202–3.

8. 'The Vita Contemplativa', p. 27.

9. 'Dream Frame and Verbal Echo', pp. 254–5.

10. *Ibid.* p. 258.

11. *Webster's Third New International Dictionary, s.v.*

12. *Mimesis: the Representation of Reality in Western Literature*, trans. Willard R. Trask (Princeton, NJ, 1953), p. 74.

13. In addition to Kintgen, 'Echoic Repetition', and Hieatt, 'Dream Frame and Verbal Echo', see Stanley B. Greenfield, 'The Formulaic Expression of the Theme of "Exile" in Anglo-Saxon Poetry', *Speculum* 30 (1955), 200–6; Alain Renoir, 'Oral Theme and Written Texts', *NM* 77 (1976), 337–46; David K. Crowne, 'The Hero on the Beach: an Example of Composition by Theme in Anglo-Saxon Poetry', *NM* 61 (1960), 362–72; Donald K. Fry, 'Old English Formulaic Themes and Type-Scenes', *Neophilologus* 52 (1968), 48–54, 'Old English Formulas and Systems', *ES* 48 (1967), 193–204, and 'Some Aesthetic Implications of a New Definition of Formula', *NM* 69 (1968), 516–22; and Randolph Quirk, 'Poetic Language and Old English Metre', *Early English and Norse Studies presented to Hugh Smith*, ed. Arthur Brown and Peter Foote (London, 1963), pp. 150–71, repr. Randolph Quirk, *Essays on the English Language; Medieval and Modern* (London, 1968), pp. 1–19.

14. Faith F. Gardner, *An Analysis of Syntactic Patterns of Old English* (The Hague, 1971), demonstrates that 'the English language of Ælfric's time and even of Alfred's relied far less upon inflections to communicate its meanings than grammarians have

thought. Even in the early Old English period, case endings were becoming redundant and position was becoming the governing syntactical factor' (p. 77); and Bruce Mitchell, 'Syntax', Bruce Mitchell and Fred C. Robinson, *A Guide to Old English*, rev. ed. (Oxford, 1982), pp. 58–117.

15. Bruce Mitchell, 'Some Syntactical Problems in *The Wanderer*', NM 69 (1968), 172–98, and 'Linguistic Facts and the Interpretation of Old English Poetry', *ASE* 4 (1975), 11–28.

16. Stanley B. Greenfield, 'Verse Form, Syntax and Meaning in Poetry', *PMLA* 82 (1967), 377–87; and 'Syntactic Analysis and Old English Poetry', *NM* 64 (1963), 373–8, among others.

17. Bernard F. Huppé, *The Web of Words* (Albany, NY, 1970) also divides the poem into sections by examination of syntax. He studies the poem's syntax by focusing on the sequence of sentences (verse paragraphs, periods and 'clausules'). Because his focus is so confined, however, he never makes summary or general evaluative statements but proceeds sentence by sentence, noting the beginning and end, chiasmus, balance, repetition of sound or word. As one would expect, then, he does not notice the stylistic shifts.

18. I use the text of *The Vercelli Book*, ed. George Philip Krapp, The Anglo-Saxon Poetic Records 2 (New York, 1932), 61–5, but I occasionally alter the punctuation in accordance with my judgement on the dominant syntax patterns. See Huppé, *The Web of Words*, for another system.

19. For other interpretations of how these repeated verbs of seeing and beholding structure the poem, see Huppé, esp. pp. 77–85, and Kintgen, 'Echoic Repetition', pp. 214–18.

20. The syntax of 9b–10a has been heavily debated, particularly with regard to 'engel dryhtnes' and 'ealle'. See W. F. Bolton, *The Dream of the Rood* 9b: *Engel = Nuntius?' N&Q* 213 (1968), 165–6; Raymond P. Tripp, Jr, '*The Dream of the Rood*: 9b and its Context', *MP* 69 (1971), 136–7; Willem Helder, 'The *Engel Dryhtnes* in *The Dream of the Rood*', *MP* 73 (1975), 148–50; and T. E. Pickford, 'Another Look at the *Engel Dryhtnes* in *The Dream of the Rood*', *NM* 77 (1976), 565–8; also the Dickins and Ross and ASPR editions. With Krapp I take *ealle* to be the subject of *beheoldon* and 'engel dryhtnes' to be the object, 'all beheld the angel of the Lord', 'all' anticipating the explicit subject in 11b–12. According to my understanding, the sentence begins at 9b and ends with 12b. 'Ne wæs ðær huru fracodes gealga' is parenthetical, an interruption in the major strain of thought which resumes with 'ac hine þær beheoldon' and the full statement of the subject. The chiasmus and the repetition of *beheoldon* help to indicate that the poet is resuming the sentence where he left off before the parenthesis. For a similar punctuation, see Huppé, *The Web of Words*, p. 64.

21. James Smith, 'The Garments that Honour the Cross in *The Dream of the Rood*', *ASE* 4 (1975), 29–35, discusses the vision as depicting the dreamer's 'discovery' of the cross and his increasing perception through the 'eyes' of the 'body', the 'mind' and 'faith'.

22. In my reading each of these begins a sentence. I omit those which are unmis-

takably variations of a preceding verb or are part of a subordinate clause. The sense of being overwhelmed by verbs comes from these verbs as well, many of which begin a half-line; see 33a, 34a, 36a, 43a, 56a, and 62a and 71a.

23. *Bright's Old English Grammar*, ed. Frederic G. Cassidy and Richard N. Ringler, 3rd ed. (New York, 1971), p. 93.

24. Burrow, 'An Approach', pp. 125–6, and Burlin, 'The Vita Contemplativa', p. 28; see also Leiter, 'Patterns of Transformation', which claims that 'repetition, parallelism, shifting of the verb of action to the semantically (though not rhythmically) important initial position . . . are fairly simple devices of a stylization that achieves emotional heightening precisely at the necessary moment in the battle metaphor' (pp. 96–7).

25. 'Echoic Repetition', pp. 219–20; Burrow notes 'the compressed paratactic syntax, the lengthened line, and the rapid sequence of verbs of action' in 30–3, as well as the repetition of *þær* ('An Approach', p. 126).

26. See Woolf, for the seminal article on the poet's depiction of Christ's death. She asserts that he 'does not speak of Christ's death: the climax of the poem is simply, *Crist wæs on rode*, and His death is thereafter described as a sleep, in terms which with cathartic effect suggest exhaustion, release and temporary rest' ('Doctrinal Influences', p. 148). For a strong argument that the poet does depict Christ's death, see M. L. del Maestro, 'The *Dream of the Rood* and the *Militia Christi:* Perspective in Paradox', *Amer. Benedictine Rev.* 27 (1976), 171–86.

27. Note that, as I have stated above, p. 408, parenthetical independent clauses and ones that form a compound with preceding independent clauses do not participate in the predominant word-order patterns. Accordingly 62b, 64b and 68b do not interrupt the verb-initial pattern. 62b explains the modifying phrase 'steame bedrifenne' (62a) and so is parenthetical (Krapp punctuates it as a case of asyndetic parataxis with a semicolon). 64b forms a compound via the conjunction *ond*. 68b, as Krapp indicates with his punctuation, is subordinated by *þa*, 'when'.

28. George S. Tate, 'Chiasmus as Metaphor: the *Figura Crucis* Tradition and *The Dream of the Rood*', *NM* 79 (1978), 114–25, demonstrates how chiasmus is metaphorically appropriate to the crucifixion tale, but he outlines a different chiastic structure for these scenes. He makes the centre of the chiasmus the crucifixion scene, which he defines as occurring in 44–56 (44 and 56b forming a chiastic frame for the episode). On the initial side of this centre, the actions of the cross 'typologically' precede Christ's and on the far side those of Christ precede the cross's. To make this arrangement work Tate has not only to resort to an admittedly 'delicate' correspondence but also to omit from the crucifixion 39–43, in which Christ climbs heroically on to the cross, and he has to insert somewhere between 67a and 75b a scene in which 'Christ is resurrected and clothed in glory' (124–5).

29. 'Christ the Victor—Vanquished', pp. 668–71.

30. In fifty-one lines the poet uses *þa* a number of times but more defined adverbs less frequently: *iu* once at the beginning (28a), *siððan* twice (49b and 71b) and *hwile* twice (64b and 70b).

31. According to Krapp's punctuation, *frineð* (112a) begins a new sentence. But, if we note the parallel structure of 110 and 117 and 115 and 119 and the complementary structure of 110 and 115, it becomes clear that 110–16 form one sentence with the same basic structure as that of 117–21. See Huppé, *the Web of Words*, p. 70, for a similar interpretation.

32. 'Anglo-Saxon Monasticism', p. 55.

33. 'The Unity', p. 470; see also Burrow, 'An Approach', pp. 130–1, and Burlin, 'The Vita Contemplativa', p. 31.

34. 'The Unity', p. 470.

35. 'Echoic Repetition', p. 222.

36. 'An Approach', p. 132.

37. The asyndetic parataxis is implied by the echo of 'is me' in 'me is', the reference of *þam* in the second part to the first part and the redundancy in content.

38. 'Echoic Repetition', p. 222.

39. Edition, p. liv.

40. For other discussions of accrued meaning, see Fleming, 'Anglo-Saxon Monasticism', p. 70; Patten, 'Structure and Meaning', pp. 385–9; and Michael J. Swanton, 'Ambiguity and Anticipation in *The Dream of the Rood*,, *NM* 70 (1969), 407–25.

41. I wish to thank Professors Daniel G. Calder and Stanley B. Greenfield for their generous help in the development and revision of this article. The concepts are clearer and the analysis more accurate because of their criticisms and suggestions.

God, Death, and Loyalty in
The Battle of Maldon

FRED C. ROBINSON

I<small>N</small> *The Battle of Maldon*, said Humphrey Wanley, "celebratur virtus bellica Beorhtnothi Ealdormanni, Offae et aliorum Anglo-Saxonum, in
praelio cum Danis,"[1] and two and a half centuries later another great
Anglo-Saxon scholar summed up the traditional interpretation of the poem
in terms which, though fuller, are not essentially different: "The words of
Beorhtwold [*Maldon*, 312–19] have been held to be the finest expression of
the northern heroic spirit, Norse or English; the clearest statement of the
doctrine of uttermost endurance in the service of indomitable will. The
poem as a whole has been called 'the only purely heroic poem extant in Old
English.'"[2] Most (though not all)[3] readers still view the poem as primarily a
celebration of heroism rather than a homiletic or hagiographical exercise,
and yet this view involves some theoretical difficulties which have hitherto
been dealt with, as far as I am aware, only indirectly if at all. The first difficulty is that *Maldon* was written out of a culture whose fundamental assumptions about God and death were incompatible with a heroic sense of
life. The second is that the ideal which motivates the heroes' sacrifice seems
(from previous interpreters' accounts of it) too narrow and parochial to sustain *Maldon*'s significance beyond its own age, a great heroic poem requir-
ing a theme of more universal significance than "comitatus loyalty." By
confronting these difficulties in the present essay, I hope to confirm *Maldon*'s status as "the finest expression of the northern heroic spirit" and to
deepen in some measure our understanding of the poem's meaning.

I

The battle of Maldon was fought and the poem about it was written at a
time when the Heroic Age of England and the conditions which made that

age possible lay in the distant past. The Anglo-Saxons had embraced Christianity centuries before, and the period of monastic reform which preceded the battle had been effective in rejuvenating men's faith and in renewing Christianity's pervasive enrichment of the vernacular literature of the Anglo-Saxons. In the range of literary conventions at their disposal, however, their commitment to the church entailed losses as well as gains. The Christian world-view, with its assumption of a just God presiding over the affairs of men and its promise of a joyous life after death for all believing and obedient Christians, was not a world-view congenial to heroic narrative. Among the cultural historians who have observed this fact, R. W. Southern, in his essay "Epic and romance," has stated the matter with particular clarity:

> [T]he monastic life—or for that matter the Christian life in any form—could never be merely "heroic" in its quality. That fatal struggle of man against superior forces, that meaninglessness of fate, and the purely resigned, defensive and heroic attitude of man in the face of fate could not, on a Christian view, be the whole story. As Europe became Christianized the epic was bound to decline, for it left out the personal and secret tie between man and God.[4]

Viewed through the uncolored lens of history, the Anglo-Saxons at Maldon in August of 991 would appear to have been anything but resigned, heroic men waging a struggle in the face of a meaningless fate. They were Christians fighting heathens, and they were led by a man who was exceptionally devout. The personal tie between these men and their God would seem to have been indissoluble, and we could imagine their looking forward to the happy afterlife which, as the Anglo-Saxon homilists so often proclaimed, awaits those who suffer martyrdom for the Lord. Indeed, as we reflect on the men at Maldon in 991, their deaths seem less and less like acts of heroic daring and more and more like a joyous witness to the faith.

But when we turn our eyes from the historical battle and consider its depiction in the poem, the dying soldiers do not seem to be Christian martyrs on the threshold of paradise but valiant warriors enacting a grim and terribly meaningful heroic sacrifice for heroic ideals. They appear to be oblivious of the Christian assurances which were available to men in their predicament, and it is this that gives the poem that curiously ancient quality remarked so often by the critics. "But for a few phrases it might, as far as the matter is concerned, have been written before the conversion of England," observed W. P. Ker in 1896,[5] and a later critic amplifies his statement to absurdity: "In *Maldon* for the last time in our literature the old epic strain is . . . revived. Once again flames out in a Christian epoch the spirit of the old pagan lays. It was doubtless the work of a Christian, but of a Christian in whom the defence of home and kindred against the Danish sea-robbers, 'the wolves of blood,' had roused the smouldering pagan fires."[6] Almost everyone who has meditated over the poem has sensed something archaic and stern in it—"the old epic strain," if you will. But the "smouldering pagan fires" are an embarrassing relic from nineteenth-century Romantic scholarship. Indeed, the central question, both for the *Maldon* poet and for us, is how can a poem revive an "old epic strain" (posited on the fatal struggle of man against superior and unfriendly forces) when there are no pagan fires smouldering? I believe an answer to this question may lie in the poet's portrayal of God and death in his narrative, for it is a portrayal which evokes an aspect of the Christian thought-world congenial to the heroic temper.

There is in the poem only one detailed account of a warrior's death, and that is the slaying of Byrhtnoth, which therefore becomes a type and emblem of all the many death-agonies suffered by Englishmen in the battle. Lines 130–72 recount the manner of Byrhtnoth's slaying, and in lines 173–80 appears his much-discussed death-prayer:

> Geþancie þe,   ðeoda waldend,
> ealra þæra wynna   þe ic on worulde gebad.
> Nu ic ah, milde metod,   mæste þearfe
> þæt þu minum gaste   godes geunne,
> þæt min sawul to ðe   siðian mote
> on þin geweald,   þeoden engla,
> mid friþe ferian.   Ic eom frymdi to þe
> þæt hi helsceaðan   hynan ne moton.[7]

"I thank thee, Lord of hosts, for all the good things I have experienced in the world. Now, gracious Creator, I have the greatest need that thou shouldst grant favor to my spirit so that my soul may travel into thy keeping, Lord of angels. I implore thee that the fiends from hell not be allowed to bring it down [into hell]." Before Morton Bloomfield's discerning essay "Patristics and Old English literature,"[8] readers paid scant attention to what this speech actually says, regarding it as no more than a vaguely pious prayer. In fact, it is a specific allusion to the *judicium particulare*—a literal, physical struggle between devils and angels for possession of the soul as it leaves the body of a dying man. Having identified the motif, Bloomfield goes on to suggest that this evocation of the "patristic" notion of the death-struggle bespeaks a religious dimension in the characterization of Byrhtnoth and that the "speech would suggest a consciousness of [Byrhtnoth's] martyr-dom." Proceeding from Bloomfield's conclusion, other scholars have arrived at allegorical or hagiographical interpretations of the entire poem.[9] In contrast to this view, I shall argue that the motif which Bloomfield identified has the opposite effect, that instead of Christianizing the poem the death-speech of Byrhtnoth subtly de-Christianizes the cosmic setting of *Maldon* and in doing so helps to create the conditions necessary for a heroic narrative.

While it is true that the supernatural struggle for a dying man's soul may be found in the writings of the Fathers,[10] it is by no means limited to patristic contexts. To the *Maldon* poet, I suspect, this curious conception would have seemed a popular rather than a patristic tradition and hence would have introduced no particular suggestion of formal Christian theology into the poem. For the motif occurs much more widely than has been noticed heretofore. It is the subject of a text called "Freondlic Mynegung" which appears in Bodleian MS Ashmole 328 at the end of Byrhtferth's *Manual*, and it is developed vividly in an eighth-century Latin letter from Wynfrith to Eadburga, which was translated into Old English in the late tenth century.[11] Many Old English homilists describe how the soul will be attacked when it passes from the body,[12] sometimes in phrasing reminiscent of Byrhtnoth's prayer in *Maldon*.[13] Several accounts of the death-struggle occur in Old English translations of Apocrypha,[14] and of Gregory's *Dialogues*,[15] while formulas alluding to it appear in the penitential texts published by Max Förster.[16] Bede's *Historia Ecclesiastica* depicts the struggle for the soul in his accounts of Furseus and Dryhthelm, and these were excerpted and translated into Old English as exempla by his countrymen.[17] Vernacular poems allude to the death-struggle, as does at least one entry in the *Anglo-Saxon Chronicle*—that for AD 959 containing the half-metrical obituary for King Eadwig.[18] A vivid illustration of St Peter fighting with a devil over the soul of a dead Christian appears in an Anglo-Saxon manuscript which has been dated to 1031—just forty years after the battle of Maldon.[19] There are many descriptions of the death-struggle in Latin works from the British Isles,[20] and the theme is attested in vernacular literature across the English Channel. The ninth-century Old High German *Muspilli*, 1–30, gives a particularly somber description of the clash of angels and devils, and there is a reference to it in *Gíslasaga*. Jacob Grimm cites numerous occurrences of the motif in later vernacular literature and suggests parallels between the Christian version of the death-struggle and pagan Germanic visions of the Valkyries descending to catch up the souls of the slain.[21] Though never as widespread as the more conventional Christian conceptions of death and judgment,[22] the contest of angels and devils at a *judicium particulare* was clearly an alternative explanation which was available in popular tradition.[23]

What is most striking about these various accounts of devils and angels struggling over the souls of the dying is the stark terror which they bring to the experience of death and their apparent negation of the usual Christian consolations for death. The souls of good men as well as of evil ones are repeatedly described as cowering in the corpses which they ought to have abandoned,[24] afraid to venture outside where "all this air is filled with hellish devils which travel throughout the world."[25] A frequent motif is the dying Christian's fear that during his lifetime he may have committed sins of which he was unaware—unwitting sins which could tip the balance of the battle between the angels and the devils in the direction of the swarming demons. This is especially noticeable in the poem *Resignation*, 75–82, where the speaker's mention *þara synna þe ic me sylf ne conn / ongietan gleawlice* brings to a climax his anxieties over the fortunes of his departing soul.[26] It is these same anxieties which moved the saintly Bede to speak "de terribili exitu animarum e corpore" when he utters his *Death-Song*,[27] and which add poignancy to the melancholy forebodings in his *Die die judicii*. If a pious man like Bede feared the moment of divine decision, then how much more terrible should that moment be to a soldier at Maldon with his enemy's lifeblood on his hands?

In the other accounts of Byrhtnoth's slaying which have come down to us along with *The Battle of Maldon* there is nothing like the disturbing image of struggle which darkens his last moments in the English poem. The nearly contemporary *Vita Oswaldi* draws on the more conventional religious doctrines when it tells us that at Maldon Byrhtnoth was supported by "the manifold love of the Lord—because he was deserving." All "the alms and holy masses he had donated comforted him," and his "prayers and his [former] good deeds lifted him up."[28] The later *History of Ely* also emphasizes his "righteous life and deeds," and, most interestingly, observes that he was "free from the fear of death" ("sine respectu et timore mortis"). The account of the monks' tender care for the corpse of "this active and pious man" brings the narrative to a close with distinct overtones of the conventional saint's life.[29] Indeed, it is the strikingly similar death of St Boniface which comes most readily to mind when we read the Latin accounts of Byrhtnoth's death. Boniface's joyous death-speech to his comrades as they are about to be cut down by the pagan Frisians is just what we might have expected Byrhtnoth to say: "Now is the day for which we have long yearned, and the moment of our release, which we have desired, is at hand. . . . Do not be frightened by these who kill our bodies, for they cannot slay the soul, which is immortal; rejoice, rather, in the Lord, . . . because in a moment He will give you a reward of everlasting recompense and a seat with the angels in the heavenly hall."[30]

Instead of these reassurances, the poet of *Maldon* evokes the anxieties of the supernatural struggle for the soul as Byrhtnoth takes leave of his life, and his last words are a pathetic plea to God not to let the demons prevail in the contest. We are not told why this good and generous benefactor of monasteries should feel so uncertain about the fate of his soul. Perhaps we are to assume that he, like the speaker in *Resignation*, feared that he might have committed unawares some grievous sins which would leave his soul prey to the rapacious devils.[31] Or again, he may have had a more immediate cause for anxiety. Anglo-Saxon penitentials state that homicide on the field of battle is not exempted from all ecclesiastical censure but must be atoned: even soldiers who have fought "pro aecclesiastica justitia" or who were defending their homeland against pagan invaders ("incursio paganorum") are forbidden entry to the church for specified periods of time.[32] Byrhtnoth and his troops had good reason to fear death at Maldon, and the poet was not violating the letter of current beliefs when he adopted as his image of death in the poem a conception which emphasizes all man's uncertainties and anxieties over dying and thus recalls a thought-world more like that of Homer or the sagas. The poet was careful, moreover, in his timing of the allusion. It is immediately after he has evoked the image of the *judicium particulare* that the cowards break and run for their lives; it is in the face of this disturbing vision of death that the heroes of the poem make their decision to stand and die.

Even before we come to Byrhtnoth's death-prayer, however, the poet has begun to hint subtly at an ominous uncertainty in God's disposition of events in this world. Besides Byrhtnoth's prayer there are but three allusions to the deity. The first occurs when Byrhtnoth, having rashly granted the Viking horde free passage through the Panta to his own army's position, muses over the outcome of the battle to which he has committed his troops: *God ana wat / hwa þære wælstowe wealdan mote* (94–5). At first glance this statement seems to be a mere formula for acknowledging an uncertainty, but in the context of the poem and of history it is darkened with tragic irony, for readers of *Maldon* have always shared God's foreknowledge of how the battle was to end: he granted victory to the heathens and allowed his faithful Christians to be massacred. This bitter irony restores to the formula some of the meaning which it bore in an earlier gnomic phrasing:

>   Meotod ana wat
> hwyder seo sawul sceal   syððan hweorfan . . .
> æfter deaðdæge. . . .
>
>   Is seo forðgesceaft
> digol and dyrne;   drihten ana wat.
>   (*Maxims* II, 57–62)

The next allusion to God occurs at the moment when Byrhtnoth drives his spear through the heart of a Viking. He rejoices briefly[33] and thanks God for the success he has had. And then, as if in sardonic reply to his prayer of thanksgiving, the next line of the poem tells us that a Viking spear immediately pierced the Christian, wounding him mortally. Here again a startling juxtaposition of narrative details throws an ominous shadow on a prayer of Byrhtnoth's. The final allusion to God is near the end of the poem where the Christian warriors offer prayers to God that he allow them to punish the heathen slayers of Byrhtnoth—prayers which, once again, God seems not to have granted. These allusions to God in the poem, along with the dying prayer of Byrhtnoth, suggest a world devoid of the certainties which orthodox Christianity is usually thought to bring and one in which heroism is achieved at a dear price and is rich with meaning.

The poet's artful evocation of a cultural attitude which makes heroic narrative possible in no way implies that he criticized or rejected standard Christian beliefs. His strategy, rather, is to select from the available Christian attitudes those which depict the world in the bleakest possible way. We should remember that pessimism and uncertainty over the divine scheme of things were not uncommon around the year 1000 and in the immediately succeeding centuries. The entries in the *Anglo-Saxon Chronicle* from the time of the battle of Maldon to the end of the twelfth century make surprisingly few references to God working through history, and such allusions as do occur often carry a tone of bewilderment at the deity's permitting the horrors which seem to prevail throughout that period. "A more sorrowful deed was not done in this country since the Danes came and peace was made with them here," says the *Chronicle* poem for the year 1036 (referring to Godwin's mutilation and murder of Alfred's retainers), and the Chronicler adds uncertainly, "Now one must trust to the beloved God that they will be happy and peaceful with Christ who were so miserably murdered without any guilt."[34] Three times in this period an entry closes with a form of the gloomy refrain, *God hit bete þa his wille beð*, and this mood culminates in the Peterborough chronicler's observation on the prevailing despair of the English: "And the land was all destroyed by such deeds, and men were saying openly that Christ and his saints were asleep."[35] Henry of Huntingdon (who is among the chroniclers who recorded the story of Byrhtnoth's death) also speaks of Englishmen saying that God slept,[36] while William of Newburgh reports the view that "the Deity seemed to be sleeping and not caring for the things of men."[37]

God's apparent condonation of human suffering had long troubled the Anglo-Saxons, of course, and the homilist Wulfstan is typical of many churchmen in his frequent insistence that England's calamities were God's punishment for the sins of the English. But as the innocent appeared increasingly to be those who suffered most, this explanation of God's purpose lost persuasiveness among some writers. The *Peterborough Chronicle* of High Candidus contains a powerful description of the horrors of the Viking invasions, in which innocent Christians were butchered by bloodthirsty pagans, and then, at the close of his account, the author turns indignantly on "men of perverse mind who persist in saying that these things are visited upon men because of their own sins." Hugh seeks among seven alternative reasons why God might afflict the innocent, but in the end he concludes stoically that Christians must assign calamities "to the mysterious judgments of God"[38]—a view which seems to bring us back to the Anglo-Saxon gnomic reflection cited above: "God alone knows . . . future destiny is hidden and mysterious; God alone knows."

It was in this world where God was inscrutable—or simply asleep—that the poet of *Maldon* recognized a viable analogue to the cosmic outlook of a Heroic Age. He portrayed the actions of his heroes against a background of divine remoteness and indifference which many Englishmen were at that time beginning to sense, and which gave deep meaning to heroic sacrifice. In doing so, the *Maldon* poet was solving in a new way the problem that an earlier English poet had solved with equal success in a quite different way. The author of *Beowulf*, who was also a Christian, used the simple device of placing his heroic narrative in the lost world of Germanic paganism, thereby lending a dark grandeur and heroic meaning to deeds which, had they been performed by devout Christians in a Christian setting, would have been merely exemplary.[39]

II

While the poet's portrayal of God and death may provide the conditions necessary for a heroic poem, it does not in itself provide a heroic poem. For no matter how bravely men die, they do not achieve heroic stature unless they sacrifice themselves for some purpose which readers can recognize as significant and worthy. To most readers there has never been doubt that it is loyalty that inspires the English to fight and die in *The Battle of Maldon*, but the poet has stressed and characterized that particular ideal of loyalty more fully, I believe, than previous students of the poem have noticed.[40] By focussing on the Viking messenger's speech, the speeches of the dying Englishmen, and other narrative details in the poem, I shall try to show first how central the theme of loyalty is in *Maldon* and second how the poet has expanded the significance of that theme so that it justifies the heroic sacrifices of the English.

It is the superb arrogance of the Viking's challenge (29–41) which is usually noticed, and that arrogance may have been given an especially sharp edge by the poet's use of Scandinavicisms to characterize the speaker (a device which would make this the first instance of literary dialect in English).[41] But these features merely supplement the central point of the speech, which is to challenge the Englishmen's loyalty to their leader. This challenge becomes clear when we attend to those grammatical forms in the speech which have troubled scholars in the past. "The use of singular and plural in this passage is puzzling," says Margaret Ashdown, and in her translation she uses modern English *you* for both singular and plural.[42] But the poet's shifts in number are his sign that the Viking does not address himself exclusively to the leader Byrhtnoth, as protocol would dictate, but speaks alternately to Byrhtnoth and to his men. Taking for granted that all Englishmen are disloyal cowards at heart, he presumes to negotiate directly with the troops themselves. The opening sharp demand is directed to Byrhtnoth alone (*þu most sendan raðe beagas wið gebeorge*), but the speech softens as the messenger turns way from the leader to speak directly with the troops (*eow betere is . . .*). At line 34, or possibly even at line 33, the Viking actually slips into a comradely first-person plural (*ne þurfe we us spillan*), implying that the soldiers in the field, both Viking and English, are united in their desire for peace, which is obstructed only by the selfish leader Byrhtnoth. When he returns to the second-person singular and addresses Byrhtnoth again, he talks as if he were the spokesman for both English soldiers and Vikings: *Gyf þu þat gerædest, þe her ricost eart . . .* , and his plea with the leader to "deliver" or "ransom" his men (*lysan*) is barbed with a stinging double entente: The sense of *ricost* addressed to Byrhtnoth is "most powerful" (that is, the one in authority), while the sense addressed to the Englishmen under arms is "wealthiest"—insinuating that it is Byrhtnoth, not they, who stands to lose the most if peace is purchased from the Vikings. The last clause in the speech is once again a friendly plural addressed over Byrhtnoth's head to his men: *We willaþ . . . eow friþes healdan.*

To these divisive innuendoes Byrhtnoth replies appropriately in the name of his army,

> Gehyrst þu, sælida,   hwæt þis folc segeð?

The ensuing plurals of his rejoinder unite the English and their leader decisively and thus answer the challenge to his men's honor. Byrhtnoth underscores the strength of the bonds of loyalty by emphasizing that he is himself but the loyal servant of his own lord, Æthelred (53), and thus expects no more from his troops than his own lord expects from him. Byrhtnoth's assertion (51), "here stands an undishonored earl with his army," affirms that the traditional bond between men and leader remains intact.

The exchange of speeches is, then, a rhetorical prelude rehearsing the test of loyalty soon to be enacted on the battlefield in deadly earnest. At another passage of high rhetoric near the end of the poem the dramatics of speech-making serve again as a vehicle for the poet's central theme. The sequence of the speakers in lines 209–60 has evoked several alternative explanations. R. W. V. Elliott perceived the speeches as "a picture of confused hurling of words as of spears" and thought of "the random style of the cinecamera."[43] N. F. Blake surmised that the variety of warriors from various regions and social stations was intended "to imply that the defenders in the battle were a microcosm of the whole of England," while O. D. Macrae-Gibson sees the speeches at the end of the poem progressing steadily from active cries for vengeance to passive statements of the speaker's willingness to die.[44] It seems to me, however, that the speeches from lines 209–60 are arranged in a sequence determined by the poem's theme of loyalty, a sequence which dramatizes the increasing power which the ideal of loyalty exerts among the loyal English at the close of the poem. The first speaker, Ælfwine, explains that in his case the claims of loyalty are the most tangible and urgent of all, for *he wæs ægðer min mæg ond min hlaford* (224). The rhetorical emphasis upon *min* forced by the meter emphasizes Ælfwine's special obligations to live up to the heroic ideal.[45] Offa, the next speaker, does not share Ælfwine's double tie of kinship and fealty, but he is clearly the most overtly obligated of all the other retainers, being portrayed throughout the poem (esp. 198–201, 289–93) as a specially close friend and lieutenant of Byrhtnoth's—probably even his second in command. Leofsunu is a less distinguished retainer, and his homely boast is that the steadfast soldiers whom he knows back at the pool near Sturmer[46] will find no reason to taunt him for disloyalty. He shares neither kinship nor close friendship with Byrhtnoth, but the principle of loyalty, conceived of in broad social terms rather than personal terms, motivates him to make the same noble sacrifice as Ælfwine and Offa have vowed to make. Next, the churl Dunnere, a fyrd man who is not even a member of Byrhtnoth's comitatus, is fired by the idea of loyalty and, in two simple verses, demonstrates that the inspiring example of the previous speakers has elevated him to the company of Byrhtnoth's comrades in performance of duty.[47] There is yet one further climax in this sequence, for the example of Dunnere seems to have been infectious itself. First, the noble *hired* is inspired by his example (261), and then the one man among the Anglo-Saxons who had least obligation of all to die with Byrhtnoth joins the loyal heroes: the Northumbrian hostage Æscferth at this point surges forward to fight and die for the fallen Essex leader.[48] At the end of this sequence of speeches the poet has demonstrated in strong dramatic terms that the remaining Englishmen on every hand have withstood the challenge to their loyalty, and we know precisely the motivation for the details in the remaining lines of the poem, where the poet records the name of each of the Englishmen as they fall under the Vikings' axes.

The force of the heroes' commitment to the ideal of loyalty is further dramatized by the poet in quite another way. Throughout the poem there emerge several partial justifications for an Englishman's taking flight. First, Byrhtnoth is clearly stated to have made an error when he committed his troops to a battle in which the enemy were allowed to have free passage across the river and take up positions before the Englishmen could begin their defense. One may argue over the meanings of *lytegian* and *ofermod* (although Professor Helmut Gneuss has provided virtually certain evidence that the latter word means "pride" and that the poet's use of *ofermod* signals a criticism of Byrhtnoth's generalship),[49] but the phrase *landes to fela* admits of no doubt. Byrhtnoth erred, and the men at Maldon were free to meditate over this fact as they considered whether or not to remain and die out of loyalty to the man whose misjudgment had brought them to this hard decision. They might further have reflected that Byrhtnoth's misjudgment was probably the basis for his retainers' decision to flee. At least some of the cowards were among Byrhtnoth's closest household thanes (see 200–1), and if these high-ranking men thought it right to leave the field, then surely the hostage Æscferth and humble fellows like Dunnere might be excused for leaving. Finally, the poet's pointed references to Æthelred throughout the poem would clearly have carried some irony, for Æthelred was at this time becoming the national symbol for English unwillingness to stand and fight.[50] A king who set an example for cravenness, a leader who had blundered, and lieutenants who withdrew from the field might well provide soldiers with a basis for reassessing the force of their own sworn loyalties. But the heroes at Maldon,

though presumably aware of these possible justifications for flight, scorned
them, and the nobility of their stand is accordingly enhanced.

However inspiring their gesture, it remains to be asked whether the
"narrow Germanic convention of honor and loyalty"[51] is a sufficiently serious theme to warrant the poet's celebration of it. Soldiers fighting loyally to
the death are not necessarily an exalting spectacle; indeed, without some
clearly perceived higher purpose their struggles might be, as Milton dis-
dainfully observed, no "more worth . . . then to Chronicle the War of Kites,
or Crows, flocking and fighting in the Air."[52] Why was the loyalty of the
Maldon Englishmen worth the poet's writing a poem on the subject, and
what is that poem's claim on our interest and sympathy today?

More than a mere tribal custom, the interlocking bonds of loyalty were
the principle on which Anglo-Saxon civilization rested, the only bulwark
against primitive chaos and anarchy.[53] Wulfstan's most famous sermon is in
large part a catalogue of the horrors that befall a people once the principle
of loyalty is forgotten,[54] and the *Chronicle* entry for 1010 illustrates how the
absence of loyalty between leaders and men induces anarchy: "Ultimately,"
says the Chronicler, "no captain would raise an army, but each man took
flight as best he could, and at the last one shire wouldn't even support the
other."[55] Like respect for the law today, loyalty in pre-Conquest society
was the *sine qua non*, and its absence marked the difference between civilization and primeval disorder. The concept in this enlarged sense was extended by poets even into the theological realm. As has often been remarked, portrayals of Christ in *The Dream of the Rood* and other Old English
poems suggest that it was not merely love, but rather that unique combination of loyalty and affection which Anglo-Saxons felt for their chosen leaders that seems to bind the Christian to his Lord. And as the poem *Genesis*
makes clear, Satan emerges in the Anglo-Saxon view as an unworthy thane
whose disloyalty to God introduced disorder and evil into the world. To
Christians elsewhere, the primal sin of Lucifer was pride; to the Christian
Anglo-Saxon it seems more often to have been disloyalty.

That disloyalty reduces human society to ungoverned misery is stated
overtly by more than one poet. The doom-laden prediction of Wiglaf
makes the connection directly:

>   Londrihtes mot
> þære mægburge   monna æghwylc
> idel hweorfan,   syððan æðelingas
> feorran gefricgean   fleam eowerne,
> domleasan dæd.
>
>   (*Beowulf*, 2886–90)

In *Maldon* the connection is dramatized rather than stated. As long as the Anglo-Saxons stand fast in their loyalty to Byrhtnoth, the English line holds, and the English warriors are as one. But at the climax of the poem, where the cowards break and run, all is suddenly transformed. The cowards' behavior is depicted not merely as a panic but specifically as personal disloyalty leading to anarchic disorder: Godric usurps the horse and trappings of his leader, and this induces immediate chaos in the English ranks, for, as Offa explains in lines 237–42, some men mistook the fleeing Godric for their lord and so were deceived into thinking Byrhtnoth was leading them in a retreat. "The people were dispersed," laments Offa, "and the shieldwall was shattered" by Godric's violation of the oaths that bound him to Byrhtnoth.

The shieldwall itself is another eloquent symbol of the link between personal loyalty and social order, for this formation was the perfect physical expression both of loyalty to the leader and of mutual loyalty among men. At the leader's command, "the front rank of men held their shields before their breasts and the ranks behind held theirs over their heads to protect both those in front and themselves."[56] As long as each man stands fast (as Byrhtnoth repeatedly urges his men to do), the formation is virtually impregnable,[57] but if a section of the rank gives way, the battle order is lost and the soldiers become isolated and helpless, vulnerable to massacre. Twice in the poem we see Byrhtnoth ordering the men to form and hold the shieldwall (19–21, 101–2), and twice we are told how it was broken by the disloyal retreat of the cowards (193–5, 241–2). The cowards' disloyalty not only severs the bond of love and obedience between men and their leaders; it also disrupts the bonds between men and men and reduces a harmonious community to primitive anarchy.

It is a comprehensive principle of human loyalty and civilized order which the English heroes choose to preserve on the battlefield of Maldon when they regroup to fight the enemy in a last desperate stand. They uphold this ideal despite the plausible rationalizations for flight which the poet suggests were available to them, and they uphold it in the face of a death to which the poem has lent renewed and ominous meaning. When the Englishmen decide to die, each man reasoning out his decision in a speech, they are not dying under orders, for their leader is dead. They are not dying in a frenzy of hatred for the enemy, for the poet has been careful to portray the Vikings as anonymous rather than hateful.[58] They are not even dying for victory, since it is clear after the rout of the cowards that no hope of victory remains. As the details and emphases of the poem make clear, the soldiers are dying together,[59] loyal both to their lord and to each other, for the principle which underlay all that was positive and good in life as they understood it.[60] The principle can be upheld on the field of battle only if man's mind and spirit are brought to assert the superior importance of the ideal over physical life and physical strength. And it is this assertion that Byrhtwold makes in the name of the fallen and falling Englishmen in words that are more meaningful the more literally they are understood: "The mind must be the firmer, the heart the stronger, the spirit must be the greater, as our body's strength declines."[61] In making this statement against the background of cosmic uncertainty which the poem's details suggest, *Maldon* is a supremely heroic poem, in a sense more heroic than the poems with which it is so often compared—the *Iliad*, the Eddic lays, and *The Song of Roland*.

Notes

1. *Antiquae Literaturae Septentirionalis Liber Alter seu Humphredi Wanleii Librorum Vett. Septentrionalium, qui in Angliae Bibliothecis extant, . . . Catalogus Historico-Criticus* (Oxford, 1705), p. 232.

2. J. R. R. Tolkien, "The homecoming of Beorhtnoth Beorhthelm's son," *Essays and Studies*, 6 (1953), 13–14. This statement of the traditional view of the poem is the starting point for Tolkien's own argument that *Maldon* specifically celebrates "the heroism of obedience and love" which is "the most heroic and the most moving" of all heroic gestures (p. 16), a view which is accepted and expanded in the closing pages of this essay.

3. Bernard F. Huppé, *Doctrine and Poetry: Augustine's influence on Old English poetry* (New York, 1959), pp. 23–38; N. F. Blake, "*The Battle of Maldon*," *Neophilologus*, 49 (1965), 332–45; and W. F. Bolton, "Byrhtnoth in the wilderness," *MLR*, 64 (1969), 481–90, all argue in varying ways that Christian doctrine has displaced concern with secular heroism in the poem, a view which is vigorously opposed by, among others, George Clark, "*The Battle of Maldon*: a heroic poem," *Speculum*, 43 (1968), 52–71. J. E. Cross supports Clark's position in general, although he differs with him over some particulars, in "Mainly on philology and the interpretative criticism of *Maldon*", in *Old English Studies in Honour of John C. Pope*, ed. E. B. Irving and R. B. Burlin (Toronto, 1974), pp. 235–53. See also Cross's essay "Oswald and Byrhtnoth: a Christian saint and a hero who is Christian," *ES*, 46 (1965), 93–109.

4. Southern, *The Making of the Middle Ages* (New Haven and London, 1953), p. 224.

5. Ker, *Epic and Romance* (London and New York, 1897), 2nd edn (Oxford, 1908), p. 55.

6. W. MacNeile Dixon, *English Epic and Heroic Poetry* (London, 1912), p. 86.

7. Quotations from *Maldon* and other Old English poems are drawn from *ASPR*.

8. Bloomfield, *Studies in Old English Literature in Honor of Arthur G. Brodeur*, ed. Stanley B. Greenfield (Eugene, OR, 1963), pp. 37–8.

9. Bolton, "Byrhtnoth in the wilderness," p. 489; Blake, "*Battle of Maldon*," p. 339. Cf. Huppé, *Doctrine and Poetry*, pp. 237–8. The first scholar to suggest a hagiographic reading of *Maldon*, however, was Bernhard ten Brink, and it is interesting to note that in his translation of Byrhtnoth's death-prayer he silently deletes any reference to the devils who will strive with the angels for Byrhtnoth's soul. See his *Geschichte der englischen Litteratur* (Berlin, 1877), vol. I, p. 120. Very likely ten Brink sensed that the squabbling demons detracted from the religious dimension which he wanted to see in the poem.

10. See G. Rivière, "Rôle du démon au jugement particulier chez les Pères," *Revue des Sciences Religieuses*, 4 (1924), 43ff., and Alfred C. Rush, "An echo of Christian antiquity in St Gregory the Great: death a struggle with the devil," *Traditio*, 3 (1945), 369–80). For a wider survey of the occurrences of the theme, see Ute Schwab, "*Ær-Æfter*. Das Memento Mori Bedas als Christliche Kontrafaktur. Eine philologische Interpretation," in *Studi di Letteratura Religiosa Tedesca in Memoria Sergio Lupi* (Florence, 1972), pp. 91–100.

11. See Kenneth Sisam, *Studies in the History of Old English Literature* (Oxford, 1953), pp. 199–224.

12. See *Wulfstan: Sammlung der ihm zugeschriebenen Homilien*, ed. Arthur Napier (Berlin, 1883), pp. 140–1, 235–7, 249–50 (also in *Byrhtferth's Manual*, ed. S. J. Crawford, EETS o.s. 177 [London, 1929], pp. 249–50); *Homilies of Ælfric*, ed. Benjamin Thorpe (London, 1846), vol. II, pp. 336–8, 350–2; *Early English Homilies from the Twelfth-Century Manuscript Vespasian D.XIV*, ed. R. D.-N. Warner, EETS o.s. 150 (London, 1917), 110–13; *Ancient Laws and Institutes of England* (London, 1840), vol. II, pp. 466–9; *The Blickling Homilies*, ed. R. Morris, EETS o.s. 73 (London, 1880), p. 209, and cf. pp. 149–51. See also *Homilies of Ælfric: a supplementary collection*, ed. John C. Pope, EETS o.s. 260 (London, 1968), vol. II, pp. 776–9.

13. Compare, for example, *Maldon*, 173–4, and *Wulfstan*, ed. Napier, p. 237, lines 4–6; *Maldon*, 180, and *The Blickling Homilies*, ed. Morris, p. 209, line 28.

14. Rudolph Willard, *Two Apocrypha in Old English Homilies*, Beiträge zur englischen Philologie, 30 (Leipzig, 1935), pp. 38ff, 126ff, and passim; and Milton McCormick Gatch, "Two uses of apocrypha in Old English homilies," *Church History*, 33 (1964), 379–91 (esp. his discussion of the Apocalypse of Paul).

15. *Bischof Wærferths von Worcester Übersetzung der Dialoge Gregors des Grossen*, ed. Hans Hecht, Bibliothek der angelsächsischen Prosa 5 (Hamburg, 1907), pp. 316–21.

16. Förster, "Zur Liturgik der angelsächsischen Kirche," *Anglia*, 66 (1942), 29 and 35.

17. *Venerabilis Baedae Opera Historica*, ed. C. Plummer (Oxford, 1894), vol. I, pp. 164–7, 303–10. For the Old English versions see *Homilies of Ælfric*, ed. Thorpe, vol. II, pp. 332–58.

18. *Two of the Saxon Chronicles Parallel*, ed. C. Plummer (Oxford, 1892–9), vol. I,

p. 115, lines 14–16. Among the poems, see *Resignation*, 49–56, and *A Prayer*, 74–6; cf. *Guthlac*, lines 6–7, 22–5.

19. British Library MS Stowe 944, fol. 7ʳ. The setting in this instance, it should be mentioned, is the last judgment.

20. Rudolph Willard, "The Latin texts of the Three Utterances of the Soul," *Speculum*, 12 (1937), 147–66; *Adomnan's Life of St. Columba*, ed. Alan Orr Anderson and Marjorie O. Anderson (London, 1961), pp. 477–9; see also n. 17, above.

21. *Teutonic Mythology*, tr. J. S. Stallybrass, vol. II (London, 1883), pp. 836–8; vol. IV (1888), p. 1551.

22. The prevailing view, as expressed repeatedly by Ælfric and others, was that the souls of good to mediocre Christians repose with God or in some kind of vaguely conceived purgatory until the last judgment, while evil Christians await everlasting punishment in hell. (See, for example, *Homilies of Ælfric*, ed. Pope, vol. I, pp. 425–8, and *Byrhtferth's Manual*, ed. Crawford, p. 249). Milton McCormick Gatch has rightly observed that the contrary view suggested by Byrhtnoth's prayer was somewhat eccentric. "By far the more usual sort of prayer," says Gatch in *Loyalties and Traditions: man and his world in Old English literature* (New York, 1971), p. 143, "is that which Cynewulf wove into the conclusion of the *Ascension:* that men would pray for him so that he might be accepted at the Judgment as a thegn of Christ."

23. The point of uncertainty which lay between the two explanations of the soul's passage to the next life was the question as to where the soul abided between death and judgment. Gregory deals with this question at some length in book IV of the *Dialogues*. For a survey of Anglo-Saxon views, see Milton McCormick Gatch, "Eschatology in the anonymous Old English Homilies," *Traditio*, 21 (1965), 124–8.

24. See for example *Wulfstan*, ed. Napier, pp. 140–1, and *Homilies of Ælfric*, ed. Pope, vol. II, pp. 776–9. Cf. *Das altenglische Martyrologium*, ed. Günter Kotzor (Munich, 1981), vol. 2, pp. 237–8.

25. *Wulfstan*, ed. Napier, p. 250: *eall þis lyft ys full hellicra deofla, þa geondscriðað ealne middangeard*. The statement occurs in the context of a description of the *mycel gewinn betweox deoflum and englum* on the day of one's death. Cf. *Byrhtferth's Manual*, ed. Crawford, p. 249.

26. Anxiety over sins unconsciously committed is also a motif in some of the prose accounts of the war with the demons for a man's soul. Thus in Wynfrith's letter (Sisam, *Studies*, p. 216) a dying man saw that *manige synna þær cirmdon swiðe egeslice wið hine þa þe he næfre ne wende þæt hio to synnum oðlengdon; and þa awyrigdan gastas wæron geswege eallum þam synnum*. See n. 31 below.

27. *Venerabilis Baedae Opera Historica*, ed. Plummer, vol. I, p. clxi.

28. "Stabat ipse, statura procerus, eminens super caeteros, cujus manum non Aaron et Hur sustentabant, *sed multimoda pietas Domini fulciebat, quoniam ipse dignus erat. . . . elemosinae et sacrae Missae eum confortabant. . . . Protegebat se . . . quem orationes et bonae actiones elevabant.*" See *Historians of the Church of York and Its Archbishops*, ed. James Raine, vol. I (London, 1879), p. 456.

29. *Liber Eliensis*, ed. E. O. Blake, Camden 3rd series, XCII (London, 1962), p. 134.

30. *Vitae Sancti Bonifatii Archiepiscopi Moguntuni*, ed. Wilhelm Levison in *Scriptorum Rerum Germanicarum in usum scholarum ex Monumentis Germaniae Historicis separatim editi* (Hannover and Leipzig, 1905), pp. 49–50 (my translation). Other good Christians of the period end their lives like Boniface and Oswald "with a happy slaying" ("felici cede" in ibid., p. 50). Thus St Edmund, who, like Byrhtnoth, was slain by Vikings and beheaded, sees his "happy soul travel to Christ" the moment he is cut down (*Ælfric's Lives of Saints*, ed. W. W. Skeat, EETS o.s. 114, vol. II, p. 32). Felix, in *Life of Saint Guthlac*, ed. Bertram Colgrave (Cambridge, 1956), p. 159, says that Guthlac at his death declared that "the spirit is eager to be carried away to joys without end," while the Old English poet in lines 1266–8 describes the saint's soul as "yearning for its exit hence to nobler homes." On every hand the contrast with Byrhtnoth's death as it is described in *Maldon* is striking.

31. Such morbid fears are but an extreme expression of the orthodox Christian view that mortals must never presume to know what God's judgment of any human being will be. Gregory the Great's interlocutor Peter gives expression to this feeling in book IV of the *Dialogues*, the Old English translation of which is this: *Hwylc man is, þe him ne ondræde, þonne he cymð to ænde, swa unasecgendlicne cwyde þære hynðe ond þæs wites, þe þu rehtest, sy swa hwylces weorces ond geearnunge man swa hit sy, forþon þe þeah he eallunga wite, hu he lifde ond hwæt he dyde ær, he swa þeah nat þonne gyt, hu smealice his dæde sceolon beon gedemde beforan Godes eagum?* to which Gregory answers, *Swa hit is swa þu sægst.* See *Bischof Wærferths Übersetzung*, ed. Hecht, p. 377.

32. See J. E. Cross, "The ethic of war in Old English," in *England before the Conquest: studies in primary sources presented to Dorothy Whitelock*, ed. Peter Clemoes and Kathleen Hughes (Cambridge, 1971), pp. 280–1. It should also be mentioned that in the instances of the war for dying men's souls which are cited above, one of the commonest motifs is the warning that men who had not confessed their sins were especially vulnerable to the host of demons who came for the soul. It seems unlikely that the men at Maldon had all been safely shriven before the battle.

33. The poet says (147) *hloh þa, modi man*, and both the phrasing and the situation are echoed elsewhere in early English literature in a way that suggests that the words are a narrative formula. In *Judith*, 23–6, Holofernes *hloh ond hlydde, . . . modig ond medugal* before Judith decapitates him. Later, in *Layamon's Brute*, ed. F. Madden (London, 1847), vol. II, p. 203, line 13, we are told that *þa king loh* at the very moment when, unbeknownst to him, Rowenna is pouring poison into his cup. This laugh may be a conventional dramatic signal that a mortal blow is imminent at the moment when the threatened person least expects it.

34. "The Death of Alfred," lines 11–15. Although Dobbie (*ASPR*, vi, 24), following Plummer (*Two of the Saxon Chronicles Parallel*, vol. I, p. 158, and vol. II, p. 211), prints the first part of this entry as prose, it is clear that the Chronicler intended it all to be poetry, the first lines in alliterative verse (of very poor quality) and the rest in a combined alliterative-rhyming form.

35. *The Peterborough Chronicle*, 1070–1154, ed. Cecily Clark (Oxford, 1958), p. 56.

36. *Henrici Archidiaconi Huntendunensis Historia Anglorum*, ed. Thomas Arnold (London, 1879), p. 277.

37. *Historia Rerum Anglicanum*, in *Chronicles of the Reigns of Stephen, Henry II, and Richard I*, vol. I, ed. Richard Howlett (London, 1884), p. 45.

38. *The Chronicle of Hugh Candidus, a Monk of Peterborough*, ed. W. T. Mellows (London, 1949), pp. 23–7. Hugh lived more than a century after the battle of Maldon, but, as the editor has shown in his introduction, his Chronicle often draws on Old English sources.

39. The classic work on this subject is J. R. R. Tolkien's "*Beowulf:* the monsters and the critics," Sir Israel Gollancz Memorial Lecture, 1936, *Proceedings of the British Academy*, 22 (1936), 245–95.

40. Most previous discussion of the ideal of loyalty in *Maldon* has centered on the question whether it was a poetic anachronism (suggestive of the customs described in Tacitus's *Germania*) or an actuality of the late tenth century. Edward B. Irving, "The heroic style in *The Battle of Maldon*," *SP*, 58 (1961), 460, speaks of "the antique virtues husbanded over the centuries in the worn formulas of poetic diction," and this seems to me to account adequately for the highly traditional form which the theme assumes in the poem. T. D. Hill, "History and heroic ethic in *Maldon*," *Neophilologus*, 54 (1970), 291–6, and M. J. Swanton, "*The Battle of Maldon*: a literary caveat," *JEGP*, 67 (1968), 441–50, see the ideals governing the heroic action as genuinely anachronistic and argue that the poet is critical of Byrhtnoth for adhering to them. Hans Kuhn, on the other hand, feels that the comitatus was a living system which the Essex Englishmen had adopted from their Scandinavian neighbors in the Danelaw: see "Die Grenzen der germanischen Gefolgschaft," *Zeitschrift der Savigny-Stiftung für Rechtsgeschichte*, Germ. Abt. 86 (1956), 1–83, esp. p. 45, as well as the rejoinder by Walter Schlesinger, "Randbemerkungen zu drei Aufsätzen über Sippe, Gefolgschaft und Treue," *Alteuropa und die Moderne Gesellschaft: Festschrift für Otto Brunner*, Herausgegeban vom Historischen Seminar der Universität Hamburg (Gottingen, 1963), pp. 21–41. Frantšek Graus's startling claim, "Eine typische germanische Treue gibt es (ausser in der Historiographie) nicht," in "Über die sogenannte germanische Treue," *Historica*, 1 (1959), 120, is effectively rebutted by Schlesinger, pp. 41–59.

41. My evidence for this supposition is set forth in "Some aspects of the *Maldon* poet's artistry," *JEGP* 75 (1976), 25–4a.

42. Ashdown, *English and Norse Historical Documents* (Cambridge, 1930), p. 74.

43. Elliott, "Byrhtnoth and Hildebrand: a study in heroic technique," in *Studies in Old English Literature*, ed. Greenfield, p. 64.

44. Blake, "*Battle of Maldon*," p. 338; Macrae-Gibson, "*Maldon:* the literary structure of the later part," *NM*, 71 (1970), 192–6.

45. See John C. Pope, *Seven Old English Poems* (Indianapolis, 1966), p. 78.

46. See Gordon, ed., *Battle of Maldon*, Methuen's Old English Library (London, 1937), p. 85, on the meaning of *Sturmere*.

47. The name *Dunnere* may be related to *Dunne*, which Henry Bosley Woolf cites as the name of a peasant in his *Old Germanic Principles of Name-Giving* (Baltimore,

1939), p. 140. W. J. Sedgefield, *The Battle of Maldon* (Boston, 1904), inadvisedly emends the name to Dunhere, thus obscuring its humbler origins.

48. Sedgefield, finding it incredible that a hostage held by Byrhtferth should die fighting for him, reasons that "Æscferð was doubtless a hostage who had escaped from the enemy" (*Battle of Maldon*, p. 38). That a hostage could be inspired by the example of his captor's loyal retainers to join in the fight for their leader is demonstrated, however, by the British hostage in the famous *Chronicle* entry for 755.

49. See H. Gneuss's discussion in "*The Battle of Maldon* 89: Byrhtnoth's *ofermod* once again," *SP*, 73 (1976), 117–37.

50. In "Some Aspects of The *Maldon* Poet's Artistry", I argue that *The Battle of Maldon* was composed long enough after the death of Byrhtnoth for its audience to have appreciated the historical ironies created by Æthelred's ineffectual warfaring in succeeding decades. The frequent assumption that *Maldon* was composed almost before the dust of battle had settled has little to support or recommend it. As Tolkien observed ("Homecoming," p. 16), the poem "is certainly not a work of hot haste."

51. *The Oxford Anthology of English Literature*, vol. I, ed. J. B. Trapp et al. (London, 1973), p. 106: "The poet's theme turns on this narrow Germanic convention of honor and loyalty." See n. 40 above.

52. *The History of Britain* in *The Works of John Milton*, ed. F. A. Patterson et al. (New York, 1932), p. 191. The reference is to earlier wars of the Anglo-Saxons.

53. See Dorothy Whitelock, *The Beginnings of English Society* (Harmondsworth, Middlesex, 1952), pp. 29–47, and Gatch, *Loyalties and Traditions*, pp. 129–41. Gatch's discussion of *Maldon* on pp. 129–35, which anticipates in part some of my own arguments, seems to me to be the best existing account of the theme of loyalty in the poem.

54. *Sermo Lupi ad Anglos*, ed. Dorothy Whitelock, reprinted with additions to the bibliography (New York, 1966).

55. *Two of the Saxon Chronicles Parallel*, ed. Plummer, vol. I, pp. 140–1. Clark, "*The Battle of Maldon*," p. 59, cites this passage.

56. Gordon, ed., *Battle of Maldon*, p. 50.

57. Albert S. Cook, *Judith* (Boston, 1904), p. 26, collects passages from Roman historians attesting to the difficulty of penetrating a Germanic shieldwall. (Gordon, ed., *Battle of Maldon*, p. 50, calls attention to Cook's note.)

58. Clark ("*The Battle of Maldon*," p. 58) has stated this point well: "The vikings are simply a force impelling the decisions to pay or fight, to flee or die; they are not objects of interest in themselves." See also my remarks in "Lexicography and literary criticism: a caveat," pp. 141–2, and in "Some aspects of the *Maldon* poet's artistry," pp. 121–137, both in *The Tomb of Beowulf and Other Essays in Old English* (Oxford, 1993).

59. The orderly solidarity of the dying heroes stands in eloquent contrast with the pell mell, *sauve qui peut* flight of the deserters. Brave men die in good company; the oldest proverb in English tells us how cowards die: *suuyltit thi ana*.

60. In their speeches the Englishmen do not, of course, enunciate an abstract principle of loyalty. They speak rather to the particular vows which are the concrete manifestations of that principle of loyalty within their own lives.

61. *Maldon*, 312–13. F. Th. Visser, *An Historical Syntax of the English Language*, part 1 (Leiden, 1963), pp. 162–3, makes the interesting suggestion that *sceal* is gnomic in this passage. But his translation of the verb ("is proper," "ought to be") seems weak. Context implies the normal meaning "must be." I have benefited from suggestions and encouragement generously offered by Professors Robert Farrell, Thomas D. Hill, and Robert E. Kaske of Cornell University.

Maldon and Mythopoesis

JOHN   D.   NILES

How are we to read *The Battle of Maldon?* A thousand years after the battle that this poem commemorates was fought, historians and literary scholars are no nearer consensus on this issue than ever, and for good reasons. Like most Old English verse, the poem does not explain itself. Long before twentieth-century theorists announced, with some satisfaction, the death of the author, the unknown author of *Maldon* was indeed quite dead, having left no trace of his identity or his reasons for composing this work other than what can be inferred from the text.[1] Mutilated by the chances of manuscript transmission, the poem in its present state consists of a single brightly-lit narrative into which speeches are introduced. There is no introduction, no conclusions or aftermath. Absent are historical digressions, gnomic asides, elegiac passages, homiletic interludes—in short, almost all the involutions that add shadows to the complex art of *Beowulf.* Despite its tenth- or eleventh-century date, *Maldon* thus displays a form that scholars often have associated with the *urgermanisch* heroic lay, and for this reason it has appealed to readers who like to take their literature straight.[2]

Taking Old English literature straight, however, is not as easy as may seem. Even in its brisk, somewhat brusque demeanor, the narrative of *Maldon* embodies complex messages. Like any historical fiction, it does ideological work that requires exegesis with reference to the tensions of the period when it was composed.

One way to read the *Maldon* story—not the only way, to be sure, but one that has the virtue of attempting to ascertain what work the poem has done in history—is as an example of mythopoesis in late Anglo-Saxon England. Whatever else it is, *The Battle of Maldon* is a myth-like story that tells im-

plicitly of the origin of one of the notorious aspects of Anglo-Viking relations during the realm of Æthelred II (reigned 987–1016), namely the policy whereby the English paid large sums of money to waves of Viking
raiders in the vain hope of stabilizing the realm. In splendid alliterative
verse, the poem recounts a tale of defiance and loss that makes clear the sad
necessity for this policy of buying the Vikings off. Nor is this the end of the
story. In much later time, during the clash of modern nation-states, *The
Battle of Maldon* has come to represent something slightly different to a new
set of readers, and a myth of suicidal devotion has grown up around it. This
myth too has done ideological work in that it has served to justify sacrifice
in a patriotic cause on the field of war. But more of this latter myth later.

The thesis that the poem makes manifest the need for something resembling Æthelred's policy of accommodation, rather than serving as an
implicit condemnation of this king's pusillanimity, poses a challenge to a
critical consensus that has emerged over many years, and I shall have to argue it carefully if I am to cut through these habitual ways of reading.[3] First,
though, I should clarify that the thesis depends to some extent on a theory
of the poem's approximate date; and it is offered within the context of recent research that, without rehabilitating Æthelred's reputation altogether,
has shown the inadequacy of historical judgments that are based on an uncritical acceptance of some early sources. Although Simon Keynes has recently remarked that it is difficult to conceive of Æthelred "outside the
context of the myths that have developed around his name," Keynes's own
research (as well as that of other scholars) has done much to make this statement no longer valid.[4] As for the question of dating, I should state my
agreement with the conclusion that the poem is not a timeless piece of fiction, but rather raises issues that have a specific application to the reign of
Æthelred.[5] According to the poem's most able editor, there is no good linguistic, literary, or historical reason to favor a date much later than the battle, and Nicholas Brooks has recently provided a fresh argument for reading the poem in the context of Anglo-Saxon military service in the 990s.[6]

Adding to the weight of arguments for dating *Maldon* soon after the battle is the nature of the poem's three references to Æthelred. The first of
these is Byrhtnoth's proud declaration that Æthelred is his "ealdor" ("lord,"
53) in the passage where he defies the unnamed Viking messenger.[7] The
second and third occur in the part of the poem where Byrhtnoth is first
pierced through by a Viking spear and then, after additional wounds, falls
dead on the field of battle. Here Byrhtnoth is specified to be Æthelred's
"þegen" ("thegn," 151), then his "eorl" ("ealdorman," 203). Some readers,
influenced by the knowledge of Æthelred's ill reputation that they have

gained from sources outside the poem, have concluded that these references to the king are ironic. According to this view, Byrhtnoth's boast of being Æthelred's thegn would have struck an audience of Anglo-Saxons as an almost comically empty gesture, given Æthelred's well-known ineffectiveness as king. This view leads to a theory of dating the poem long enough after the battle for Æthelred's ill reputation to have become established.[8]

If the references to Æthelred are taken as ironic, it follows that Byrhtnoth is portrayed as uttering his great words of defiance, then giving up his life, in what we know to be an act of devotion to a worthless king. While this way of reading the poem may have a certain appeal, to the disenchanted at any rate, it requires that we read two of the most memorable and moving passages of the poem with an attitude of superior detachment.[9] The perspective that is required here makes it difficult to see Byrhtnoth's death as having exemplary force as a display of courage in a high cause. My alternative suggestion is that Æthelred is invoked as a figure in serving him. Æthelred's ill reputation, after all, largely postdated the Maldon campaign. He was no more than twenty-five years old at this time and may have been somewhat younger. The realm was wealthy and stable, and the miseries that were to afflict it later could by no means have been foreseen. Æthelred was not to earn his sarcastic epithet "Unræd" ("Ill-Counsel") until the twelfth century, as far as one can tell—the earliest recorded reference to it is by Walter Map, writing in the 1180s[10]—and the entries in the CDE versions of *The Anglo-Saxon Chronicle* that lament the disastrous course of events during his reign were likewise composed retrospectively sometime in the first half of the eleventh century, not contemporaneously with the events described.[11] Regardless of their date, these entries do not necessarily reflect a sentiment that was felt universally at any time.

The three references to Æthelred are significant, for they transform what might otherwise seem a merely local encounter into an issue of national importance. As George Clark has remarked, "The narrator portrays Byrhtnoth as the defender and spokesman of England, not as a provincial earl of Essex."[12] The references have a proud ring to them, if I am not mistaken, for invocations of his king, his homeland, and the English people make it clear what Byrhtnoth is fighting for. They fit with what seems to be an attempt to represent the troops under Byrhtnoth's command as a microcosm of the English people. Among the warriors are men with ties to many geographical locales besides Essex, men of Scandinavian as well as English descent, and members of various social classes ranging from the upper nobility to the rank of ordinary freemen.[13] The poet presents Byrhtnoth as the lynchpin of a five-part hierarchy of command that links the English *fyrd* or general levies; the *heorðgeneatas* or elite troops; Byrhtnoth as a representative of the high aristocracy; Æthelred as King of England; and Christ as Lord of Hosts.[14] As field commander of the English troops, Byrhtnoth is portrayed as an experienced, forceful leader who responds to the Viking threat with a vigor of which his young king would have approved, though also with a touch of arrogance that goes beyond the limits of prudence.

To return to the central issue of *Maldon* as an example of mythopoesis, what I mean to suggest is that the poem is not just a celebration of English heroism on the occasion of Byrhtnoth's death. The poem can be read as an attempt to conceptualize major social issues relating to Æthelred's reign and to resolve them, or at least hang them in suspension, in the form of a story. In particular, the poet orients the first part of the narrative around a pressing pragmatic question: how should the English nation respond to the threat posed by an aggressive army of Vikings, by offering fight or tribute? And it poses an answer to this question not discursively, but rather in the form of a myth.

Since the term myth means different things to different people, I should make clear how I am using it. By a myth, I mean a story, well known among a people or a group, that tells about larger-than-life figures from the recent or distant past in such a way as to confirm one or more essential ideas pertaining to the culture of the people or group in question. A myth in this sense is not a term for someone else's false belief, nor is it a sacred narrative. On the contrary, it is regarded as a true account of events, true in its conformity to a set of accepted ideas concerning the way that the world is shaped and has unfolded in time.[15] The myth is underpinned by a quasi-logical structure that is based on a distinction between time past and time present, events *in illo tempore* and *in hoc tempore*. "Because event *A* happened in former times," the myth implicitly affirms, "we do (or think, or experience) *B* today."[16]

Myths in this sense are rather more common than most people think. In Great Britain, for example, one can speak of the myth of Arthur, which served to justify imperial ambitions both in the fourteenth century and in the nineteenth, or the myth of Robin Hood, which for seven centuries has confirmed popular animosity directed against institutional corruption in church and state. In this country one can speak of the myth of George Washington, which justifies a certain patriarchal structure of governance, or the myth of John Henry and the steam drill, which gives narrative form to one of the chief issues of late industrialism, namely the plight of manual laborers (blacks in particular, in this country) who have been made redundant by automation. Often though not always, the subjects of myth are historical persons, and the mythopoeic impulse takes the form of auxesis. The myth magnifies real or imagined people or events into something grand, tragic, or inspiring, and it turns them into the central icons and focal points of stories that, built on archetypal patterns and believed in as articles of faith, serve to explain a current reality or validate a people's customary attitudes, habits, or beliefs.

Myths of this kind need not be hundreds of years in the making. They can develop surprisingly quickly, depending on the ideological climate of the moment and a people's appetite or need for them. A sudden death or spectacular killing, especially at a time of crisis, can provide the kernel from which they spring. Martyrdom can be one key element in the mythopoeic process, for violence, myth, and the sacred are sometimes grim sisters. To refer again to North America, one wonders if such heroes of the popular imagination as Abraham Lincoln, Jesse James, James Dean, Marilyn Monroe, John Kennedy, or Martin Luther King, Jr., could have achieved quasi-mythic status so readily if they had not met with a sensational death.[17]

In the turbulence of late tenth-century England, the killing of Ealdorman Byrhtnoth at Maldon—the culmination of a sudden and apparently devastating Viking campaign in Essex—likewise lent itself to mythopoesis. Today, it is hard to imagine the shock-waves that this death must have touched off among Byrhtnoth's contemporaries. In the preceding decades, ever since the battle fought at Brunanburh in 937 had confirmed the rule of the West Saxon kings over all of what was now England, the new nation had seen power grow into confidence. In many ways it had become the envy of Europe in its efficient administration, which was based on an amalgam of English and Anglo-Danish power. Beginning with the traumatic campaign of 991, the nation was thrust into a new era of insecurity, wracked by renewed Viking invasions and torn by internal divisions. In the opinion of Eric John, the battle at Maldon was probably no insignificant clash, as used to be thought, but rather occurred at a moment of intense crisis and may have been a turning point in the history of the times.[18]

The poem we know as *The Battle of Maldon* marks an early stage in the emergence of a myth that made Byrhtnoth's death the centerpiece of a tale of dramatic reversal in England's fortunes. In a series of scenes that inscribe themselves on one's imagination, the poem displays the courage of Byrhtnoth as an uncompromisingly hawkish leader, excoriates the breach of faith shown by those who fled the battle, and celebrates the heroic loyalty of those who stood firm after his death, even at the cost of their own lives.

The issue on which the battle is imagined to hinge is highlighted early on. Should the English accept the terms of peace that the Vikings offer them, by which they are to pay an unspecified amount of money as tribute, or should they refuse these terms and fight? The poet presents us with a Byrhtnoth whose emphatic response, backed by the imagined shouts of his troops, is to reject any negotiation whatsoever:

> Gehyrst þu, sælida,   hwæt þis folc segeð?
> Hi willað eow to gafole   garas syllan,
> ætrynne ord   and ealde swurd,
> þa heregeatu   þe eow æt hilde ne deah.
> Brimmanna boda,   abeod eft ongean,
> sege þinum leodum   miccle laþre spell,
> þæt her stynt unforcuð   eorl mid his werode,
> þe wile gealgean   eþel þysne,
> Æþelredes eard,   ealdres mines
> folc and foldan.   (45–54a)

Do you hear, seafarer, what this army is saying? They want to give you spears as tribute, deadly spearpoints and time-tested swords, a payment of war-gear that will do you no good in battle. Messenger of the Vikings, report back to your people; tell a much less welcome tale, that here stands with his warriors an ealdorman of unstained reputation, one who intends to defend this homeland, its people and its turf, the kingdom of Æthelred, my lord.

In a voice laced with irony, Byrhtnoth declares that his troops will indeed offer gifts—of weapons, points first.[19] He himself, a nobleman who has never been disgraced ("unforcuð eorl," 51), will stand firm in defense of the land and its king. Indeed, he goes on to say, he would find it shameful ("heanlic," 55) if his northern guests were to return home unchallenged after they had gone to the trouble of coming so far. Before the English pay tribute, the play of war ("guðplega," 61) will "reconcile" ("geseman," 60) the two opposing parties.

As the annals of the composite work known as *The Anglo-Saxon Chronicle* make clear, the choice that is dramatised in this fictional exchange between Byrhtnoth and the Viking messenger was one that the English faced repeatedly during the years from 991 to 1013. Their decision, time and again, was to pay tribute: £10,000 in 1991, £16,000 in 994, £24,000 in 1002, £36,000 in 1007, £48,000 in 1012, and an undisclosed sum in 1013.[20] Perhaps these payments were craven, as used to be assumed. Perhaps, at first, they were one part of a strategy whereby Æthelred gave material aid to Olaf Tryggvason and other Norwegian Vikings in the understanding that they would accept the Christian faith and help guard England against the ascendant power of Swein Forkbeard's Denmark.[21] In either case, the results were depressingly the same. No matter what payments were made, no last-ing peace emerged. The harrying continued, growing worse as time went on, until eventually Swein drove Æthelred into exile and Swein's son Cnut assimilated England into a Danish empire that spanned the North Sea.

The poem thus foregrounds the key issue of these years before the fall of Æthelred: buy the peace, or fight? Trust, even if uneasily, in the *pax nordica* that the Vikings propose, or hold out defiantly against them?

The entries for the year 991 in the CDE versions of the *Chronicle* make clear that the death of Byrhtnoth at Maldon was the key factor in persuad-ing the English to follow the less resolute of these courses:[22]

> Her wæs Gypeswic gehergod, 7 æfter þon swiðe raðe wæs Brihtnoð ealdorman ofslegen æt Mældune, 7 on þam geare man gerædde þæt man geald ærest gafol Denescum mannum for ðam miclan brogan þe hi worhton be ðam sæ riman, þæt wæs ærest x ðusend punda. Þene ræd gerædde ærest Syric arcebisceop.

> In this year Ipswich was ravaged, and very soon after Ealdorman Brihtnoth was killed at Maldon. And in this year it was decided that tribute should first be paid to the Vikings because of the great terror they wrought along the coast. This first payment was £10,000. Arch-bishop Sigric first advised this course.

In typical fashion, the annalist links the two events by parataxis alone: Byrhtnoth was slain, and a decision was made to offer the Vikings tribute. The causative element here is left understood. As happens frequently in oral narrative as well as in annalistic writing of this kind, the juxtaposition, in sequential order, of two related elements is enough to imply the work-ings of causality. Byrhtnoth was the third-ranking nobleman in the realm. His inability to defeat the Viking force in a pitched battle seems to have had such a strong psychological impact on the English that they decided to be-gin paying tribute. According to the myth, the sums of money paid in sub-sequent years have this first payment as their precedent. They are exten-sions, in similar circumstances, of the same process of thought that led Archbishop Sigeric and other leading advisors to urge accommodation with the Viking force to forestall further damage. Whether or not the bat-tle fought at Maldon was the key event that initiated this reversal of fortune, it was believed to be so, as is made evident by the annalist's threefold repe-tition of the verb "ærest" ("for the first time"), even though these payments were not in fact the first ones offered by the English.[23]

To judge from the number of sources that testify to Byrhtnoth's death, a mythopoeic impulse was at work soon after Byrhtnoth's death and did not play itself out until late in the twelfth century, as numerous writers mulled over the themes of defiance and loss and worked out their significance in various ways.[24]

The entries in *The Anglo-Saxon Chronicle* provide evidence that parallel and conflicting accounts of what happened at Maldon were in circulation not long after the battle was fought. Versions CDE state curtly that Ipswich was harried, that Byrhtnoth was slain at Maldon, and that £10,000 in trib- ute was paid. Version A, the Parker Chronicle, specifies that Folkestone, Sandwich, and Ipswich were all harried, that it was Anlaf (Olaf Tryggvason) who led the Vikings, that he commanded 93 ships, that peace was made with him, that Æthelred stood sponsor to him at his confirmation, and that all this took place in 993, not 991. No mention is made of tribute. The A an- nalist thus departs from CDE in his more favorable portrait of the truce and in his conflation of events that in CDE are divided between 991 (the battle at Maldon) and 994 (additional harrying and Olaf's confirmation). In the words of David Dumville, the A version is "a retrospective annal, written after the fame of the battle of Maldon (991) had spread and contaminated the recollection of other encounters."[25] In other words, at play in this ac- count is a mythopoeic impulse that consolidated the events of history into a unified narrative, one that incidentally is not hostile to Æthelred.

A different development of the myth is evident in the Latin *Life of St. Oswald*, attributed to Byrhtferth of Ramsey and probably written during the years 997–1005.[26] Obvious in this account are the workings of hyper- bole. The campaign now encompasses the whole of southern England, as the Vikings are said to have begun their harrying in the west, in Devon, be- fore moving east to Essex. Much is made of Byrhtnoth's large stature and commanding appearance: he stands tall above the rest, with swan-white hair. Similarly impressive is the number of men said to be involved in the battle, "for an infinite number of them and us fell." The English warriors flee after Byrhtnoth's fall, but the Danes' victory is a pyrrhic one, for they suffer losses so great that "they were scarcely able to man their ships." No mention is made either of tribute or of the courage of retainers who chose to stand firm in the midst of the general flight. Curiously, however, a heroic theme similar to what we find in the last half of *The Battle of Maldon* occurs in the context of the Devonshire battle. In this conflict "one of our men, a valiant soldier called Stremwold, was killed along with several others who chose to end their lives by death in battle rather than to live on in shame" ("qui bellica morte magis elegerunt uitam finire quam ignobiliter uiuere"). It is not clear what the shame of these men would have been if they had cho- sen to live on, for the men of Devon, unlike those of Essex, are said to have won their battle. One wonders if lost poems comparable to *The Battle of Maldon* celebrated the deeds of Stremwold and his companions, or if the theme of heroic resistance to the Vikings was displaced from the warriors in Essex to their Devonshire counterparts, or vice versa. In any event, the theme was in the air.

Later accounts, based chiefly on the information given in the *Chronicle* as supplemented by knowledge of the treaty known as II Æthelred, which dates from 991 to 994, show the emergence of a canonical version of what happened in 991. The twelfth-century Anglo-Norman historians John of Worcester, Henry of Huntingdon, and Symeon of Durham all repeat the information given in *Chronicle* versions CDE, stressing that tribute was given and that a great number fell either on both sides (John) or on the English side alone (Henry). By this time, Æthelred's unfortunate reputation was confirmed, and Henry accordingly specifies that tribute was paid "on the disastrous advice" ("consilio infausto") of Sigeric.[27]

One other twelfth-century account, the *Liber Eliensis*, stands as an important witness to an independent tradition about Byrhtnoth and Maldon. This anonymous work may well draw on local legends current at Ely, the site of Byrhtnoth's tomb. Byrhtnoth and his widow were well remembered here on account of their benefactions to the monastery, and the *Liber* uses the account of his death as a means of confirming the specific grants he made to Ely. It does this by way of a story of how the abbot of Ely offered Byrhtnoth and his men generous hospitality when they were on their way to Maldon after having been rudely turned away from the rival house of Ramsey. As improbable as this story may seem, given its obvious bias for Ely, the *Ramsey Chronicle* confirms it in its essentials.[28] The tale may thus be based on actual events, though not necessarily ones that occurred on the eve of the battle in 991.

As might be expected in a document of this kind, the *Liber Eliensis* includes fulsome praise of Byrhtnoth's courage, stature, and generosity, together with approving comments on his support of the tenth-century monastic reform. With slight hyperbole, it adds that Byrhtnoth was protector not only of his own men, but of all the leaders of the shires, who chose him as their leader on account of his great worth and faith. Just as Byrhtnoth is raised in stature, the battle at Maldon is amplified into a two-part campaign extending over a period of years. First, in 887, Byrhtnoth is said to have met a party of Vikings "at the bridge over the water." He kills nearly all of them. Four years later, in 991, a Viking army returns to avenge this defeat and boldly challenges Byrhtnoth, who agrees to join battle against them with only a small force. This is the only account that specifies that

Byrhtnoth was outnumbered at Maldon. Given the likelihood that a lord of his stature would have assembled a large force of men from the eastern counties before engaging a Viking army of this kind, this statement of his underdog status may be taken as mythic adornment rather than historical fact.[29] Similarly fanciful is the statement that the ensuing battle lasted fourteen days. The English are said to fight valiantly, inflicting great slaughter on their enemies, but the Vikings finally win, decapitating Byrhtnoth. The monks of Ely recover his torso and bring it back to the church for burial. No mention is made of three themes that figure prominently in *Maldon:* an attempt at extortion, the flight of cowardly retainers, and the heroic resistance of warriors after their leader's death.

In the main, the account in the *Liber Eliensis* is likely to have accorded with the narrative content of the textile hanging that Byrhtnoth's widow, Ælfflæd, gave to Ely in his memory. In the words of the *Liber,* this hanging, now lost, was "embroidered and figured with the deeds of her husband" ("gestis viris sui intextam atque depictam").[30] If this embroidery was on display for long at Ely, an in-house chronicler is not likely to have contradicted it in its important features. On the contrary, he would probably have made a point of including reference to the deeds that figured prominently on it. To judge from the later, more famous narrative hanging that is preserved at Bayeux, the Ely hanging would have included Byrhtnoth's death among its featured scenes. Though surely less grand than the one commissioned after 1066, it might well have been ample enough to include such other incidents, mentioned in the *Liber,* as the skirmish at the bridge, the Viking army's landing near Maldon, Byrhtnoth's reception at Ely, the general melee, and the recovery of Byrhtnoth's body for burial. Like the tomb, the textile at Ely would have done much to promote Byrhtnoth's reputation as a great warrior and a martyr for the faith.

The Battle of Maldon thus is noteworthy not only for its length and detail, as compared with these other sources, but also for its apparent independence from these accounts. It is a separate witness to the growth of a myth-like story focussed on the battle fought in Essex in 991.[31] Of course, all we have is a fragment. If the beginning and end of the poem had survived, its departures from these analogues might be less striking. Still, the physical evidence suggests that not much is lost.[32] What the fragment does include suggests that the poem had a pivotal place in the development of memories of Byrhtnoth's death into a myth that accounts for why the English paid for peace again and again during the latter part of Æthelred's reign.

In a unified narrative, the poem as we have it arrays four main themes around the kernel element of Byrhtnoth's death, the main event from which these elaborations must have sprung. While each of these themes plays a part in one or more of the analogues, only in the poem are they brought together in a seamless sequence. Leaving aside the initial lines that set the stage for action, the poem thus displays a five-part structure that can be summarized as follows:

1. *The debate about tribute* (lines 25–61). The poet foregrounds this issue and dramatizes it in the form of a superb exchange of words between Byrhtnoth and an unnamed Viking messenger. The Viking offers the English protection ("gebeorge," 31) and a truce ("grið," 35; "frið," 39) in exchange for an unspecified amount of treasure ("beagas," 31; "gafol," 32; "gold," 34; "feoh," 39; "sceattas," 40). Byrhtnoth responds to this offer with splendid disdain. Whether or not such an offer was made at Maldon in fact, the poet has reasons to include it in his dramatization of events. Everyone knew that tribute was paid after the battle was lost. By presenting Byrhtnoth as scorning the path of accommodation, the poet is able to show what the alternative to payment was. By this means, the grievous English losses that ensue are presented as by no means an inevitable consequence of the Vikings' presence. Instead, they are the result of a policy decision. While in principle, the decision can only command admiration, its results are bitter indeed. The effect of the passage is thus complex. On one hand, one cannot help but admire what some readers might call the *chutzpah* of the English host. The commanding rhetoric of Byrhtnoth's response almost compels readers to share in his choice, as I have observed on many occasions when teaching the poem to university students, who invariably delight in Byrhtnoth's defiant stance. On the other hand, the ensuing course of events is sobering, to say the least. One by one, Byrhtnoth and a group of his best retainers are cut down. In retrospect, such an unremitting sequence of losses, even if glorious ones, casts into doubt the practical wisdom of a purely hawkish response to the Viking threat.[33]

2. *The fight at the ford* (lines 62–95). As in the *Liber Eliensis*, which tells of a preliminary battle fought at a bridge over a body of water, this initial combat is portrayed as a clear victory for the English. The victory remains inconclusive, however, in that it leaves the main army of Vikings intact. The vivid images associated with this incident—the tide flowing in and out, the men waiting impatiently at each shore, the holding of the causeway by three named warriors—provide the kind of circumstantial detail that has led some readers to believe that the poet must have been a witness of the events described. A narrative logic governs this section, however. Byrhtnoth's success in this initial skirmish has a fatal effect, for it reinforces his confidence in his ability to resist any challenge. When the Vikings then

make a second offer, namely that they be allowed to cross over the ford to engage the English in a general combat, Byrhtnoth in accepting it commits his second tactical mistake. As before, he is shown making a magnificent gesture that commands admiration, for it issues from a superabundance of courage. On its face, there is nothing foolish about this choice. Byrhtnoth had apparently never opposed an enemy he could not subdue. The Vikings were known to shun pitched battles, and, though we are not told of Byrht-noth's motives, one may imagine his satisfaction at being granted this op-portunity to cripple the invaders. At the same time, as events prove, Byrht-noth underestimates both the Vikings' power and his own vulnerability. The narrator, blessed with hindsight, is explicit in condemning his choice: Byrhtnoth offers "too much land" to the Vikings ("landes to fela," 90), and the Norsemen advance as a direct result of his pride, or excess of courage ("for his ofermode," 89). The meaning of the key term *ofermod* has been fought out in the critical literature, and there is no point in reiterating this debate here. M. R. Godden has pointed out that the semantic field of the word *mod* frequently encompasses the idea of a "dangerous, rebellious in-ner force" in Anglo-Saxon literature; the intensifying prefix *ofer-* clearly magnifies this sense here.[34] Few readers today doubt that in the context of the narrator's negative judgment concerning the wisdom of allowing the whole Viking army to advance, the term carries at least some pejorative force.[35]

     3. *Byrhtnoth's last fight and death* (lines 96–184). All the medieval sources agree on one feature of the battle, if only on this one: that in it Byrhtnoth met his death. One can scarcely praise overmuch the narrative skill with which the *Maldon* poet dramatises this incident. From the narrator's initial evocation of the advance of the "slaughter wolves" over the causeway ("wælwulfas," 96) to Byrhtnoth's final request for peace at the hands of God, his eyes raised toward heaven, while for a brief time out of time all narrative action is suspended (172–80), the passage moves inexorably to-ward its end. If the poet knew of the legend of Byrhtnoth's decapitation, he gives no sign. Instead, rather than introducing this gruesome detail to the narrative, he focusses attention on the man's undaunted spirit as he strikes down one enemy after another, receives three dire wounds (each one of which might have been enough to fell a lesser man), and then, on the verge of death, still urges his companions on and prays to God for his personal salvation. The narrator makes clear that Byrhtnoth dies every inch a hero, a man of supreme piety as well as courage, whose only fault was an excess of confidence. If there was ever a man to fight off the Vikings, the poet im-plies, this was the one. Also implied in Byrhtnoth's fall is a corollary ques-

tion: where now in England is there a man who can succeed where Byrht-noth failed?[36]

4. *The flight of the cowardly retainers* (lines 185–201). Among the various accounts of the battle, only the *Life of St. Oswald* agrees with the *Maldon* poet in mentioning a flight that followed after Byrhtnoth's fall. In the *Life*, how-ever, the flight is a general one. In the poem, a contingent flees after three named men (Godric, Godwine, and Godwig, the three sons of Odda) turn for the woods and ride away, the first of them on Byrhtnoth's own war-horse. In the poet's eyes, the flight of these brothers represents not only cowardice but treachery as well, for he specifies that they abandoned their good lord ("þone godan forlet," 187b) in the heat of the fight, with no thought for the gifts that they had received at his hands. Later, one of the thegns who stays at the front condemns their act as a "betrayal," in that it touches off a general flight: "Us Godric hæfð, / earh Oddan bearn, ealle beswicene," Offa laments: "Godric, the cowardly son of Odda, has betrayed us all" (237b–38). Several readers have seen this breach of faith as so central to the poet's design as to regard it as "the turning point and central issue of the poem."[37]

In the annals of *The Anglo-Saxon Chronicle* for the later years of Æthel-red's reign, complaints about such breaches of faith, verging on treason, are reiterated with distressing frequency.[38] In 992 Ealdorman Ælfric sent warning to the Vikings in advance of an attack, then "absconded by night from the army, to his own great disgrace." In 993 the three leaders of an En-glish army that was mustered to fight Viking invaders at the mouth of the Humber fled, starting a general flight. In 998, whenever the English set forth to fight the invaders, "a flight was always instigated by some means." In 999 the Kentish levy turned and fled. In 1001, according to the Parker chronicle, Swein's brother-in-law Pallig deserted Æthelred in spite of all the pledges that he had given him, as well as the gifts he had received. In 1003 Ealdorman Ælfric, "up to his old tricks," feigned illness and refused to lead his army forth. In 1010 "there was no leader who would collect an army, but each fled as best he could." In 1011 Ælfmær, Abbot of Canter-bury, allowed the Vikings inside this monastery by treachery. Rarely during these years was there a time, it seems, when Æthelred could count on un-ambiguous support.

Those English noblemen who were of mixed Anglo-Danish heritage were particularly vulnerable to the charge of treason on account of their possibly mixed loyalties. Significantly, Odda, the father of the three broth-ers who are said to flee at Maldon, bears a name that is only slightly angli-cised from its Scandinavian source, Oddr. Since his sons bear English names, there are two possibilities. If he is fictive, then the poet invented him as a representative of the class of assimilated Danes. If he was a real person, then he must have married into the English lesser nobility. In either case, the poet's allusion to him calls attention to the issue of trust, or the lack of it, between Englishmen and anglicized Danes.[39] Few issues were so critical during the long period from Alfred to Cnut. The St. Brice's Day massacre of 1002, when Æthelred is said to have ordered all Danes in England to be killed "because the king had been informed that they would treacherously deprive him, and then all his councillors, of life," brought this issue to an infamous head.[40] The *Maldon* poet introduces the theme of betrayal to his narrative for much the same reason, evidently, as he introduces the theme of tribute: to encapsulate in one grand story the pressing political issues and tensions of his time.

5. *The heroic stand of the loyal retainers* (lines 202–325). Once the sons of Odda ride for the woods, touching off a large-scale flight, those who stay at the front are in desperate straits. The rest of the poem recounts the exemplary resistance of twelve named warriors, each one of whom is shown choosing to stay and fight, whatever the personal cost. Here in particular is evident what Dolores Frese has called the poem's "dazzling varieties of impersonated consciousness," as more than a third of this part of the poem consists of direct speech in the form of monologues imagined to be uttered by one or another of these men.[41]

Many readers of the poem accept that some if not all of these named warriors were real persons who died in this battle and who are therefore given an exemplary role. As George Clark has suggested, the men may be named precisely because their death at the front, assuming that they were actual warriors, would have exempted their heirs from repayment of the heriot and possible loss of their land. According to section 78 of part two of the *Laws of Cnut*, "the heriot is to be remitted for the man who falls before his lord in a campaign, whether it is within the land or outside the land; and the heirs are to succeed to the land and to the possessions and divide it very justly."[42] Similarly, the poet's naming of Godwine and the other sons of Odda may be significant in the light of section 77 of the same code, which specifies that "the man who, through cowardice, deserts his lord or his comrades on a military expedition, whether by sea or by land, shall lose all that he possesses and his own life."[43] Although the *Laws of Cnut* postdate the battle fought at Maldon, they probably codify customs that were honored at least in principle in earlier times. The poet's specificity concerning who stayed and who fled the battle is understandable, given the practical rewards and punishments that awaited those who either died beside their lord or deserted him on a campaign.

In evoking the heroic stand of the loyal retainers, the *Maldon* poet again shows his originality. Among the analogues, only the *Life of St. Oswald* raises this theme, and this is in the context of the Devonshire battle, not the one fought in Essex. In *Maldon* we thus again see the results of narrative compression. Dramatic examples of flight and of heroic resistance are put on exhibit as two sides of the same coin, two contrasting responses to the same existential dilemma. What is of greater value, the poet implicitly asks: life, or the way one lives it? The veteran warrior Byrhtwold, whose name as well as whose age implies an affinity with Byrhtnoth, answers this question most directly. In the present circumstances, a long life alone, if achieved at the cost of flight, will only mean lasting grief at the thought of a dear lord's death and a great opportunity missed to avenge him. This, at any rate, I take to be the meaning of his remark "A mæg gnornian / se ðe nu fram þis wig-plegan wendan þenceð" ("Ever will he have cause to mourn who intends to turn now from this battleplay," 315b–16).

The Battle of Maldon can then be read as a work that uses a particular event, drawn from history though rendered schematically, as the core of a story that gives coherent literary expression to major issues of the poet's day. In the stylized fashion that is characteristic of hagiographic and heroic poetry, the poem treats its subject with grand extravagance. Everything is made larger or more vivid than life. As is habitual in heroic narrative, the conflict is polarized into extremes.[44] The heathen wolves of war are arrayed against the pious English warriors; the faithless sons of Odda are juxtaposed with the loyal retainers who stand firm; there is a cowardly Godric (186–90) and a brave Godric (320–24). The game of war ("guðplega," 61; "wig-plega," 316) is choreographed into a deft dance as pairs of Norse and English warriors face one another and make deadly exchanges of blows. Favorite lines and half-lines punctuate the narrative with iterative force: "wæl feol on eorðan" ("the dead fell to earth," 126b, 303b); a certain warrior stands firm "þa hwile þe he wæpna wealdan moste" ("as long as he was able to use weapons," 272; cf. 83). The favorite numbers of traditional narrative are preferred. Three men defend the causeway; three times Byrhtnoth is wounded; Byrhtnoth and two companions fall dead side by side; three brothers flee; twelve named warriors stand firm after Byrhtnoth's fall.[45]

In its schematic way, the poem thus turns a key incident drawn from the Viking troubles of the 990s into a showpiece of contemporary ethics and politics. In this showpiece, the cause of the English defeat is overdetermined. The point of the poem, unlike that of the annals, is not just that Byrhtnoth dies and tribute is given. Rather, Byrhtnoth's refusal to pay tribute, coupled with his lack of discretion in permitting the Vikings to advance past the causeway, leads directly to his death. Both his conduct and that of his thegns is exemplary, whether for good or for ill. Stage by stage, as the poem progresses, the actions and motives of the men who figure in the action exemplify the two great issues of this period of English history: the need to negotiate peace with the Vikings versus the will to resist them by force, and the centrifugal drift toward separate survival strategies among the English and Anglo-Danish nobility versus the charismatic, centripetal power of overlordship.

The messages encoded in this narrative are complex to the point, perhaps, of seeming contradictory. The poet gazes with longing at a vanished world when choices were simple, when all a great lord needed to do when confronted by roving bands of marauders was to shout "Noli progredi," or its Old English equivalent, then clear the way for a knockdown fight. Byrhtnoth makes this choice, and it is a grand one, and it leads to a splendid disaster. For his world is already the flawed one of historical contingency. Instrumental in the defeat at Maldon is the role of those English warriors who make a separate peace by showing their backs. The poem thus prepares the ground for the sad conclusion that whatever Byrhtnoth did, no other English lord should attempt. If even the legendary Byrhtnoth, backed by his elite troops as well as the *fyrd* of the men of Essex, all of them armed and in good array, could not defeat an army of Vikings on their home turf, then how could any other leader be expected to do so?

In this manner, the poem uses the counterexample of Byrhtnoth's *ofermod*, spiced by the treachery of the sons of Odda and the heroic but futile resistance of the other named warriors, to show the practical necessity of a policy of peacemaking that Æthelred pursued for many years, no matter how painful and repugnant this policy must at times have been. The poem did this work, probably, with little consciousness on the part of its author that this was what the story signified; but such is the usual way of myth, which routinely encodes ideological messages in the form of a simple account of past deeds. Psychologically speaking, the pain and humiliation that attended England's appeasement of the Vikings were probably the driving forces that brought the poem into being in this form. Certainly the striking thing about the poem is how much more it has to say, in images that display what Edward Irving has called "the crushing burden of individual choice," than the bare theme of Byrhtnoth's death required.[46]

What the poem does not do, or does not chiefly do, on the other hand, is to celebrate a death wish on the part of the English warriors, a kind of collective lemming-like impulse toward self-destruction. And yet this misapprehension is at the heart of a modern myth that has grown up around the poem, a myth that is in some ways as interesting as the medieval one that turned the incident of Byrhtnoth's death into a showpiece of contemporary issues.

This modern myth could be called "the Balaklava syndrome," in that it calls to mind the ideology that provided a justification for the heroic sacrifices and the sometimes brutal expenditures of human life that were attendant upon nineteenth-century imperial politics: "Theirs not to reason why, theirs but to do and die."[47] According to a way of viewing *The Battle of Maldon* that has become popular in recent years, the conflict described in the poem has a timeless meaning that transcends the historical context of the late tenth century. The poem is important as presenting a test of character against which any man can measure himself.[48] The headnote that introduces the poem in Bruce Mitchell's and Fred C. Robinson's *Guide to Old English* expresses this view succinctly:[49]

> The fighting men at Maldon, no less than those at Balaklava and Dunkirk, triumph in this test of character in a manner of which Englishmen have always been especially proud. The Anglo-Saxons who fight to the bitter end are portrayed by the poet as glorious in defeat, and their valour redeems the honour of their country.

The key terms invoked in this kind of appreciation—"pride," "glory," "valour," and "honour"—are precisely those that define the ideal of gentlemanly conduct as seen through nineteenth- and early twentieth-century English eyes, as Mark Girouard has remarked in his fine book *The Return to Camelot: Chivalry and the English Gentleman*. For countless young men who grew into manhood during that era, glory in a noble, lost cause was the object of one's highest ambition. Girouard not only points out some of the delightful idiosyncrasies that sometimes attended the late Romantic quest for honor and its pseudo-medieval chivalric trappings. He also notes how the idealism that was associated with the concept of the gentleman led directly into the unparalleled disaster of World War I: "One conclusion is undeniable: the ideals of chivalry worked with one accord in favour of war."[50]

When I teach *The Battle of Maldon* to university students today, I find it difficult to pierce through this accretion of chivalric vocabulary to engage directly with the issues posed in the text. Thanks in part to the impact of rhymes like "Into the valley of Death rode the six hundred," with their exaltation of a military fiasco into an instance of sacrifice in a noble cause, the strings of modern readers' sensitivities tend to vibrate so sympathetically to the theme of suicidal devotion that it is sometimes hard to perceive that there is no death-wish in *Maldon*, or at least that this is not a dominant theme. A noteworthy death, yes. Byrhtnoth provides this. Heroism? Yes, and plenty, in the words and conduct of both Byrhtnoth and his loyal followers. But as for a collective impulse toward suicide, or what in an influential article has been called "the ideal of men dying with their lord," there is little trace of it here, despite a chorus of declarations to that effect that have been made by a number of scholars.[51]

An approach to the poem as a work in praise of suicidal self-sacrifice is fraught with difficulties. First, although some of the men are killed, the group of loyal retainers is not necessarily wiped out at Maldon, despite statements to that effect that are found in the critical literature.[52] The idea that the poem ended with the courageous last stand of the remaining English warriors, in the manner of Roland's men at Rencesvals or Custer's at the Little Big Horn, is part of a modern myth that has grown up around the story, for the poem breaks off before the fate of the English is made clear. This imagined annihilation of the warriors is confirmed by neither the *Chronicle*, which does not specify the extent of English losses, nor the *Life of St. Oswald*, which states that at the end of the battle there were scarcely enough Vikings left to man their ships. The idea that the poem ended by describing the annihilation of the loyal retainers is one striking illustration of how *The Battle of Maldon* has been drawn out of the orbit of practical vengeance literature and has been made a prime exhibit in the post-romantic cult of suicidal devotion.

Second, the narrator never states that the loyal thegns know that the battle is lost, nor does any one of them reveal such knowledge through his own words. True, they know that their situation is critical: Byrhtnoth is dead, and the English ranks are broken thanks to the flight of the sons of Odda. It is for this reason that the retainers urge one another on, exhorting one another to put away thoughts of saving their lives through flight so that they may achieve their goal of inflicting grievous losses on their enemies (see for example lines 257–64, which focus on the need for action in indifference to the threat of death). The point is that the danger the men face gives them all the more reason to stand firm, or their cause will indeed be lost.

Third and most important, despite this stress on the importance of indifference to death, Byrhtnoth never speaks of a positive desire to die, nor do any of the retainers express an inclination to die beside him with the exception of Byrhtwold and, possibly, Leofsunu.

Byrhtwold is a special case. He is aged, as the narrator states—"se wæs eald geneat" ("he was an old retainer," 310)—and as he himself declares: "ic eom frod feores" ("I am advanced in years," 317).[53] His inspirational speech to the retainers should be seen in the context of both his advanced age and his strong personal devotion to Byrhtnoth, whom he calls "leof" ("well-beloved," 319). To be blunt, geriatric warriors have little to lose by a death only slightly hastened by the spear. They may have much to gain if their conduct earns them lasting fame, as Byrhtwold's does. Knowing full well that he is soon to die in any event, Byrhtwold scorns flight and declares his intention to stand firm, urging his fellow warriors to new heights of heroic action to make up for the deaths of their companions. What he calls for is *mod*, not martyrdom. If he should fall, still, he knows he will have the consolation of lying beside his dear lord "ðegenlice" ("in a manner befitting a thegn," 294), as his comrade Offa has done.

As for Leofsunu, his speech directly follows Offa's condemnation of Godric's breach of faith, and it must be read in the context of this betrayal. Leofsunu declares that unlike the cowards, he will not yield a single foot. No one in his home village of Sturmere will have cause to taint him for turning away, he vows, but on the contrary, "me sceal wæpen niman, / ord and iren" ("weapons, the spear and the sword, are destined to take me," 252b–53a). Assuming that the poet introduces Leofsunu because a man of this name did indeed die at Maldon, the words that are ascribed to him have prophetic value. Conscious of his imminent death—note the verb *sculan*, which characteristically denotes necessity or fate—Leofsunu chooses to carry on with the fight rather than be disgraced like Godric. No word indicates that he actually wishes to die. What we are told is that he desires to avoid the ignominy of flight—"fleam he forhogode" ("he scorned flight," 254b)—and that, like the other loyal retainers, he hopes above all to avenge Byrhtnoth: "ic . . . wille . . . wrecan on gewinne minne winedrihten" ("I wish to avenge my lord in the fight," 246–48).

Statement after statement in the poem makes clear that it is this desire for vengeance, not a desire for death, that drives the loyal retainers on. At the beginning of this section of the narrative, the poet makes the terms of their choice explicit:

> Þa ðær wendon forð   wlance þegenas,
> unearge men   efston georne;
> hi woldon þa ealle   oðer twega,
> lif forlætan   oððe leofne gewrecan. (205–08)

Then the proud thegns pressed forward there; the courageous men pushed on eagerly. They all wished one [that is, the second] of two alternatives: to lose their lives or to avenge their beloved lord.

One of the oddities of the criticism of *Maldon* is that every editor and translator whose work I have been able to consult has interpreted the key phrase "oðer twega" in a neutral sense, with the meaning "one of two alternatives," rather than in the more specific sense "the second of two alternatives," which seems to be required here. Clearly the phrase can have the former meaning.[54] That it need do so, particularly in the poetry, is open to question. In innumerable instances in Old English poetry and prose, the word "oðer" serves as the ordinal numeral and can be translated "second" or "other." As the poem progresses, the warriors who stand firm at Maldon proceed to gain this second, more welcome end. They neither wish to die, nor do they necessarily do so. Some of them clearly fall in battle: Edward, Offa, Wistan, and Godric do, and apparently Leofsunu, Æscferth, and Byrhtwold do as well. Others may survive. Ælfwine, Dunnere, Æthelric, Oswold, and Eadwold all urge their companions on without the poet giving any explicit indication as to their fate.

The effect of the poet's naming the first of these two alternatives, "to lose their lives," is to underscore the heroic resolve of the men who stand fast. Even though they know that their lives hang in the balance, these men prefer vengeance to a life of shame. First Ælfwine, Byrhtnoth's blood relative, presses forward, remembering his feud ("fæhðe," 225), until he strikes down one of the Vikings. Then Offa castigates the fugitives and urges his companions to press on. Leofsunu vows that he will push forward to avenge his lord ("wrecan," 248). Dunnere, a simple yeoman, calls on each of the warriors to avenge Byrhtnoth ("wrece," 257b; "wrecan," 258b). Fighting hard in response to this plea, the warriors then pray to God that they may avenge Byrhtnoth ("gewrecan," 263) and bring destruction on their enemies. Æscferth, using his bow, strikes down many a Viking. Edward the Tall breaks through the Norse shieldwall and nobly avenges his lord ("wurðlice wrec," 279a). Æthelric fights determinedly as well. Offa cuts down a Viking before he falls. Wistan kills three men before he too succumbs. Oswold, Eadwold, and Byrhtwold all urge on their comrades, and Godric—the brave one, not the coward—does much damage before he too falls in battle. Here the fragment breaks off, with no clue as to the number of men who survive and with no statement as to which army wins control of the battlefield. While the English suffer grievous losses, the poet makes clear that they have at least partially succeeded in their great desire to avenge their lord.[55]

The theme of vengeance that dominates the last part of the poem is not a congenial one to modern readers, and perhaps it is for this reason that one hears little about it in the critical literature about *Maldon*. In the chivalric world of the English gentleman, the urge to bathe one's hands in the blood of one's enemies is a vulgar one. What a gentleman wants is to suffer poignantly in a noble cause. The history of the vulgarization of the concept of vengeance would make the fascinating subject of a different paper.[56] What is important to note here is that in the early medieval world, vengeance was still sometimes a social duty. In theory, and apparently sometimes in practice, it was the great peacekeeper. The Icelandic sagas show us no lack of acts of vengeance that are undertaken reluctantly, by decent people who experience no tumult of passion in their hearts but who feel impelled to act because of their duties to their kindred. According to the early Germanic code of conduct, it was a *failure* to exact revenge that was potentially destabilizing, for a family that did not gain recompense for an injury was offering an open invitation for others to repeat the crime.[57]

In late tenth-century England, the influence of the Church and the advancing hegemony of the West Saxon royal line had weakened the code of vengeance somewhat as far as affairs within the realm were concerned. The payment of wergild under protection of the king's peace was supplanting the blood-feud as the basis of social order.[58] But in international affairs, then as now, acts of violence tended to be both perpetrated and punished outside the workings of a stable system of law. When tribe meets tribe or nation meets nation, as when child meets child on the inner-city playground, what tends to count is deterrence: massive retaliation, if you will. Often, in these contexts, the threat of violence is enough to forestall violence. The ideal deterrent is one that is never used. When deterrence fails, however, a handsome thrashing of an aggressor may lend credence to earlier threats and may work wonders in forestalling additional injuries; or this, at least, for better or for worse, is the theory that has governed most conduct since time immemorial in contexts where the rule of law is insecure.

The *Maldon* poet asks us to visualize the kind of disaster that can ensue when deterrence fails and some rather insolent Viking raiders, living outside English law, attempt to extort money from the men of Essex and their leader, Byrhtnoth. The Vikings would never make such an attempt at extortion, we may assume, if they were not confident in their own abilities and reputation in war. The action of the poem confirms how well founded this confidence is, for the men succeed in striking down not only Byrhtnoth but a number of his elite troops as well. In turn, the Norsemen suffer grievous casualties. The result, according to all that survives of the poem, is a terrible set of losses on both sides. While evidently the English warriors punish the Vikings enough to compensate for their lord's death, their success clearly falls short of what would be required for them to retain their reputation as a people best left alone. In the future, the poem implies, the English will have to negotiate their relations with the Vikings delicately if they are to overcome the legacy of this loss.

When we study mythopoesis in *The Battle of Maldon*, then, we have to study two phenomena: first, how the story of Byrhtnoth's death was elevated into a myth-like narrative of defiance, betrayal, loyalty, vengeance, and loss, and second, how a different myth of suicidal devotion grew up around this poem in recent times. Without denigrating the chivalric code and the stunning sacrifices that it has at times inspired, I would claim that the message of the earlier myth of Maldon has less to do with the ideal of suicidal devotion than with the pragmatics of violence and accommodation in a world that was spinning rapidly out of English control. The myth tells us that Byrhtnoth's policy of frontal resistance to the Vikings failed, so that it ceased to be a viable option with his death.

As we know today, Æthelred's policy of buying the peace was also to fail in the face of rising Danish power. Æthelred's failure became evident only gradually over many years, however, while Byrhtnoth's was manifest in a day. As Eric John notes, thirty-four years passed between the first Viking attacks and the acceptance of Swein as king of the English people.[59] Perhaps the poet composed his work too soon after 991 to have knowledge of Swein's and Cnut's eventual conquests. For whatever reasons, the poem seems almost opaque in its refusal to present the story of what happened at Maldon within an overt political frame. All we can say with confidence is that *The Battle of Maldon*, in common with many other works of imaginative literature, presents a complex vision of reality whereby conflicting desires and codes of conduct meet and clash. At the same time as the poem looks with longing eyes at a vanished world where heroes could act like heroes, secure in the knowledge that their sufferings would make a song for people to come, it also points ineluctibly to the need for leadership of a more supple kind than Byrhtnoth is shown to offer.

Notes

1. See in particular Roland Barthes, "The Death of the Author," and Michel Foucault, "What Is an Author?" The two essays, which were first published in 1966 and 1969 respectively, are reprinted in English translation in *Modern Criticism and Theory*, ed. David Lodge (London, 1988), pp. 167–72 and 197–210, respectively.

2. Note for example the comments of Walter John Sedgefield, ed., *The Battle of Maldon and Short Poems from the Saxon Chronicle* (Boston, 1904), p. vii: "Very striking is the absence of ornament from the *Battle of Maldon;* all is plain, blunt, stern. Yet this directness, this simplicity produce on the hearer or reader a deeper effect than mere verbosity would have done." W. P. Ker's admiration for the poem likewise derives in part from his appreciation of its direct style: "The poem of Maldon, late as it is, has ut-

tered the spirit and essence of Northern heroic literature in its reserved and simple story and its invincible profession of heroic faith": *Epic and Romance* (New York, 1908), p. 57.

3. See for example R. W. V. Elliott, "Byrhtnoth and Hildebrand: A Study in Heroic Technique," in *Studies in Old English Literature in Honor of Arthur G. Brodeur*, ed. Stanley B. Greenfield (Eugene, 1963), pp. 53–70: "Perhaps the poem is intended as a deliberate criticism of the policy of appeasement so characteristic of Æthelred's reign" (p. 69). J. E. Cross, "Mainly on Philology and the Interpretative Criticism of *Maldon*," in *Old English Studies in Honour of John C. Pope*, ed. Robert B. Burlin and Edward B. Irving, Jr. (Toronto, 1974), pp. 325–53, suggests that the poem, if composed during the reign of Æthelred, "could be an indictment by implication of the policy of buying off the Danes," as well as a criticism of Englishmen who lacked loyalty during these times (pp. 247–8). John Scattergood, "The Battle of Maldon and History," in *Literature and Learning in Medieval and Renaissance England*, ed. Scattergood (Dublin, 1904), pp. 11–24, argues more forcefully that the poem is "essentially propagandist" in its hard line against accommodation with the Danes: "The poet defines how, in his opinion, the Danes should be opposed. His attitude is clear: he believes in military opposition, a refusal to pay tribute, decisive leadership and a determination to see battles through to the end" (p. 22).

4. "The Declining Reputation of King Æthelred the Unready," in *Æthelred the Unready: Papers From the Millenary Conference*, ed. David Hill, British Archaeological Reports, British Series 59 (Oxford, 1978), pp. 223–53 (p. 229). See in addition Pauline Stafford, "The Reign of Æthelred II, a Study in the Limitations on Royal Policy and Action," ibid., pp. 15–37, and Keynes, "A Framework for the Reign of King Æthelred," Ch. 4 of his *The Diplomas of King Æthelred "The Unready" 978–1016* (Cambridge, 1980), pp. 154–231.

5. Most early commentators accepted a date soon after the battle, some of them in the naive belief that the poem is an eye-witness record rather than a carefully crafted work of art. John McKinnell, "On the Date of The Battle of Maldon," *Medium Aevum*, 44 (1975), 121–36, proposes a date not earlier than circa 1020 on the grounds of the poet's use of the noun *eorl* as a title in the poem. His argument has been countered by (among others) Cecily Clark, "On Dating *The Battle of Maldon*: Certain Evidence Reviewed," Nottingham Medieval Studies 27 (1983), 1–22. Earl R. Anderson, "The Battle of Maldon: A Reappraisal of Possible Sources, Date, and Theme," in *Modes of Interpretation in Old English Literature*, ed. Phyllis R. Brown, Georgia Ronan Crampton, and Fred C. Robinson (Toronto, 1986), pp. 247–72, while finding McKinnell's linguistic test "inconclusive," proposes a date as late as the reign of Edward the Confessor (1042–65) on the basis of possible literary influence on the poem. He grants that this evidence is "not really conclusive either," however (p. 249). Scattergood, "The Battle of Maldon and History," p. 16, argues for an early date on the basis of the poem's definition of period-specific issues: "[The poem] seems to me to belong to a distinctively historical context because it deals with problems which were relevant to Englishmen in the reign of Æthelred—three problems in particular: what is it that makes a good leader, espe-

cially a good war-leader; whether it is better to confront the Vikings with military force or to pay them tribute; and whether it is better to fight battles through to the bitter end and risk one's life or to ensure safety by flight." W. G. Busse and R. Holtei, "*The Battle of Maldon:* A Historical, Heroic and Political Poem," *Neophilologus,* 65 (1981), 614–21, speak in similar vein of how *Maldon* illustrates "the mastering of contemporary problems by means of literature" (p. 619). For them the key issue raised in the poem is that of heroic resistance versus flight, for this issue relates to real-life choices made by members of the class of thegns during Æthelred's reign.

6. Donald Scragg, ed., *The Battle of Maldon AD 991* (Oxford 1991), p. 32 (henceforth referred to as "Scragg 1991"). Brooks, "Weapons and Armour," in Scragg 1991, pp. 208–19.

7. Quotations from the text of the poem in the present essay are from Scragg, ed., *The Battle of Maldon* (Manchester, 1981), henceforth "Scragg 1981." Translations are my own unless otherwise indicated.

8. Fred C. Robinson, "Some Aspects of the *Maldon* Poet's Artistry," *Journal of English and Germanic Philology,* 75 (1976), 25–40, claims that "Each of the poet's allusions to Ethelred the Unready carries a rich and powerful irony if we can assume that the poem was composed long enough after the battle for the audience to know that the king had proved unworthy of the sacrifices that were made in his name" (p. 28).

9. I use the term in the general sense in which H. Marshall Leicester, Jr., employs it in *The Disenchanted Self: Representing the Subject in the Canterbury Tales* (Berkeley, 1990). Chaucer's ironic stance in a disenchanted world stands in sharp contrast to the narrator's stance in any Old English literature that has survived.

10. Keynes, "Declining Reputation," p. 240.

11. This wide span of time represents the dating of Janet M. Bately, "The *Anglo-Saxon Chronicle,*" in Scragg 1991, p. 42. Eric John, "War and Society in the Tenth Century: The Maldon Campaign," *Transactions of the Royal Historical Society* 27 (1977), 173–95, notes that the CDE annals of the *Chronicle* are a retrospective account, "written when defeat had become a habit" (p. 184). Keynes, "The Declining Reputation," pp. 229–32, argues for the probability that these annals date from the period 1016–23.

12. George Clark, "*The Battle of Maldon:* A Heroic Poem," *Speculum,* 43 (1968), 52–71 (p. 58).

13. On the idea of the microcosm see N. F. Blake, "The Battle of Maldon," *Neophilologus,* 49 (1965), 332–45 (p. 338). Margaret A. L. Locherbie-Cameron, "The Men Named in the Poem," in Scragg 1991, pp. 238–49, summarizes what information is known about the individuals whom the poet mentions by name.

14. See A. N. Doane, "Legend, History and Artifice in *The Battle of Maldon,*" *Viator,* 9 (1978), 39–66 (pp. 54–55). While Doane sees the relationship between the men who figure in the poem and Christ in hierarchical terms, other readers have examined this relationship in terms of allegory. See Scragg 1981, references on p. 35, and note Richard Hillman, "Defeat and Victory in *The Battle of Maldon:* The Christian Resonances Reconsidered," *English Studies in Canada,* 11 (1985), 385–95.

15. Compare Doane's slightly different approach to the kind of writing that is rep-

resented by this poem: "What strikes one immediately about the period in question is that historical and fictive narrative are not markedly distinct. Poetry, history, encomium, hagiography tend to merge into a single all-pervasive method of narrative which I will call 'legendary'. The legendary method is on its surface historical, and all narrative claims to be historical, since fiction has little status. . . . In such writing historical events must conform to established ideological, typological, anagogical ways of looking at them." ("Legend, History and Artifice," pp. 42–43.)

16. For various essays defining myth and exploring its functions, see Alan Dundes, ed., *Sacred Narrative* (Berkeley, 1984). Most of these essays are written from an anthropological perspective and are concerned with the role of living myths ("sacred narratives") in primary oral cultures. The role of myth-making in the literature or mass media of complex societies is another question, one that has not been dealt with systematically as yet, to my knowledge. The best case study of such myth-making with which I am familiar is Bruce Rosenberg, *Custer and the Epic of Defeat* (University Park, PA, 1974); see especially pp. 209–16 for a discussion of *The Battle of Maldon* in terms of mythic patterning. George Clark, "Maldon: History, Poetry, and Truth," in *De Gustibus: Essays for Alain Renoir*, ed. John Miles Foley (New York, 1992), pp. 66–84, while never using the word or concept "myth," writes about Maldon in a somewhat comparable vein. In his view, the poem "epitomizes a history of Anglo-Saxon England's defeat" (pp. 74–75); it is "a poetic idea of an age" (p. 83).

17. See Rosenberg, pp. 271–78, for a discussion of popular myth-making with regard to the deaths of Lincoln and Kennedy. Rosenberg shows how the myth-making process can begin "within days, perhaps hours of the event" (p. 269).

18. "War and Society," pp. 173 and 190, respectively.

19. Irving, "The Heroic Style in *The Battle of Maldon*," *Studies in Philology*, 58 (1961), 457–67 (pp. 460–61), and Anderson, "Flyting in the *Battle of Maldon*," *Neuphilologische Mitteilungen*, 71 (1970), 197–202, stress the masterful irony that is achieved through verbal echoes in Byrhtnoth's speech to the Viking messenger.

20. Keynes, "The Historical Context of the Battle of Maldon," in Scragg 1991, pp. 81–113, summarizes these payments and assesses their significance in the overall pattern of Anglo-Viking relations during this period (p. 100).

21. This argument is advanced by Theodore M. Andersson, "The Viking Policy of Æthelred the Unready," *Scandinavian Studies*, 59 (1987), 284–95.

22. Scragg 1991, p. 38.

23. Payments were made in 865 and, apparently, in 872 and 876, as is noted by Cross, "Mainly on Philology," pp. 235–53 (p. 241). Keynes, *The Diplomas of King Æthelred*, p. 202 note 181, notes that in the earlier part of the tenth century, King Eadred alotted £16,000 "to be used for the good of his people, should they need to purchase relief from hunger and from the heathen army."

24. The sources are edited and translated with admirable clarity in Scragg 1991, pp. 1–78.

25. David N. Dumville, *Wessex and England from Alfred to Edgar* (Woodbridge, Suffolk, 1992), p. 59.

26. For the dating see Michael Lapidge, in Scragg 1991, p. 51. My quotations are from Lapidge, pp. 51–55 (his translations).

27. Alan Kennedy, "Byrhtnoth's Obits and Twelfth-Century Accounts of the Battle of Maldon," in Scragg 1991, pp. 59–78 (p. 63).

28. Kennedy, pp. 63–70.

29. Curiously, students of mine who have never read the *Liber Eliensis* have referred to Byrhtnoth as being outnumbered at Maldon. They have been surprised to discover that there is no basis for this idea in the poem. As Rosenberg notes (*Custer and the Epic of Defeat*, pp. 238 and 266–67), a mythopoeic impulse identifying Byrhtnoth as an underdog is still at work in current times.

30. Mildred Budny, "The Byrhtnoth Tapestry or Embroidery," in Scragg 1991, pp. 263–78 (p. 263), and see Dolores Warwick Frese, "'Worda and Worca': *The Battle of Maldon* and the Lost Text of Ælflæd's Tapestry," *Medievalia* 17 (1994 for 1991), 27–51.

31. For a different view see N. F. Blake, "The Genesis of *The Battle of Maldon*," *Anglo-Saxon England* 7 (1978), 119–29. Blake's argument that the poem is best taken as "a literary creation based entirely on the *Vita Oswaldi* and imagination" (p. 129) has not been accepted by other critics.

32. Scragg 1991, p. 16, finds it "tempting to assume, though it cannot be proved, that the poem was written on one such booklet [a quire of four double sheets], the outer sheet of which has been lost." This theory, admittedly speculative, would allow for a loss of not more than 50 or so lines at either end of the poem.

33. Heather Stuart, "The Meaning of *Maldon*," *Neophilologus*, 66 (1982), 126–39, offers the most thoroughgoing anti-heroic reading of the poem that has yet been advanced in the critical literature. So as not to be misunderstood, I should stress that the differences between her view and mine are many and significant. According to Stuart, for example, the flight of the deserters is a triumph of realism, while the decision of Byrhtnoth and his loyal retainers to fight to their death is a heroic fantasy that emanates from feelings of fear and panic. The poem exposes the folly of war. As I read the poem, the cowards are berated for their desertion, while Byrhtnoth and his loyal retainers are portrayed as noble in defeat. The poem is no pacifist document that condemns warfare *per se*; rather, it is a myth-like account of the tragedy that results from a decision to fight a force that, as events prove, is too formidable to be resisted.

34. Malcolm Godden, "Anglo-Saxons on the Mind," in *Learning and Literature in Anglo-Saxon England: Studies Presented to Peter Clemoes*, ed. Michael Lapidge and Helmut Gneuss (Cambridge, 1985), pp. 271–98 (p. 295).

35. A definitive statement in this debate has been offered by Helmut Gneuss, "*The Battle of Maldon* 89: Byrhtnoth's *Ofermod* Once Again," *Studies in Philology*, 73 (1976), 117–37; see this article for references to earlier studies.

36. Scragg has made this point with reference to history, not just the fictionalized account of history that the poem presents: "Partly through long life and partly through force of personality, Byrhtnoth had established military sway in England second to none. The loss of so experienced a commander must have had a significant effect on the aristocracy, both spiritual and lay, and the decision to buy off the invaders

may have been taken on the assumption that if Byrhtnoth could not contain them, no one could" (Scragg 1981, p. 19).

37. Anderson, "*The Battle of Maldon:* A Reappraisal," p. 259. See also Judith Johnson, "The Real Villains of *The Battle of Maldon,*" *Michigan Academician,* 17 (1985), 409–15, and cf. Busse and Holtei, p. 616.

38. See Dorothy Whitelock, ed., *English Historical Documents, Volume I: c. 500–1042,* 2nd ed. (London, 1979), pp. 234–44 (henceforth cited as *EHD*). References in my present discussion are to versions CDE of the *Chronicle* unless otherwise noted; due allowance for this chronicler's characteristic bias should be made (see Keynes, "The Declining Reputation of Æthelred 'The Unready,'" pp. 229–36).

39. See Anderson, "*The Battle of Maldon:* A Reappraisal," pp. 258–59. Interestingly, John of Worcester adds to his *Chronicle* source for the year 993 that the three English leaders who fled during a campaign near the mouth of the Humber at this time did so "because they were Danes on their father's side." One of these leaders is named Godwine, like his counterpart in *The Battle of Maldon.* It could be that memories or oral reports of the flight of men of Anglo-Danish heritage in 993 came to be attached to Maldon and the battle fought there in 991. If so, we see here another striking instance of mythopoesis at work, as events originally separate in time and space are conflated into a single unified story.

40. *EHD,* pp. 238–39 (versions CDE).

41. Dolores Warwick Frese, "Poetic Prowess in *Brunanburh* and *Maldon:* Winning, Losing, and Literary Outcome," in *Modes of Interpretation in Old English Literature,* pp. 83–99 (p. 83).

42. Clark, "*The Battle of Maldon:* A Heroic Poem," p. 60; *EHD,* p. 466; for the Old English text see *Die Gesetze der Angelsachsen,* ed. Felix Liebermann (Halle, 1898), 1:364.

43. Richard P. Abels, *Lordship and Military Obligation in Anglo-Saxon England* (London, 1988), p. 149; for the Old English text see Liebermann, p. 364.

44. See Rosenberg, *Custer and the Epic of Defeat,* Ch. 9, "Laws of Contrast," pp. 253–86. Jerome Mandel has stressed how fully the principle of rhetorical and structural contrast governs Old English verse in general: "Contrast in Old English Poetry," *Chaucer Review,* 6 (1971), 1–13.

45. Hillman ("Christian Resonances," p. 392) notes that the number twelve recalls the paradigm of Christ's disciples. Here again (as with Charlemagne's *douze pers* in Old French epic poetry) may be seen the results of mythopoesis, as a local battle is represented in terms congruent with the central story of Christendom.

46. Irving, "The Heroic Style," p. 464. Cf. the point made by Busse and Holtei that amplification and repetition in the speeches of the loyal retainers serve "to pose the critical problem of decision over and over again" ("*The Battle of Maldon,*" p. 617).

47. Tennyson wrote "The Charge of the Light Brigade," from which this immortal line is taken, to honor men who died in an accident of the Crimean war that took place on October 25, 1854. Like *The Battle of Maldon,* the poem is better remembered today than the incident it commemorates.

48. The masculine pronouns here are deliberate; the test is gender-specific.

49. Bruce Mitchell and Fred C. Robinson, *A Guide to Old English*, 4th edition (Oxford, 1986), p. 225.

50. Mark Girouard, *The Road to Camelot: Chivalry and the English Gentleman* (New Haven, 1981), p. 276.

51. Rosemary Woolf, "The Ideal of Men Dying with Their Lord in the *Germania* and in *The Battle of Maldon*," *Anglo-Saxon England* 5 (1976), 63–81. Woolf notes that this imputed ideal is not found elsewhere in the surviving poetry of England: "this idea was not an ancient and traditional commonplace of Old English heroic poetry but was new and strange" (p. 81). Elsewhere in Germanic heroic poetry "what is required of a lord's retainer after his death is not that he should die with him as an end in itself but that he should effectively avenge his lord" (p. 69). The only way Woolf can account for the supposed presence of this ideal in *Maldon* is by postulating literary influence from the lost *Bjarkamál*, which is known only from Saxo Grammaticus's verse paraphrase. Roberta Frank, "The Ideal of Men Dying with Their Lord in *The Battle of Maldon*: Anachronism or *Nouvelle Vague*," in *People and Places in Northern Europe 500–1600: Essays in Honour of Peter Hayes Sawyer*, ed. Ian Wood and Niels Lund (Rochester, 1990), pp. 95–106, argues (against Woolf) that the ideal of dying with one's lord was not a Germanic survival, borrowed into English from Old Norse, but rather represented an aspect of emergent medieval vassalage, informed by religious idealism.

I have not been able to trace the Woolfian vein in *Maldon* criticism back beyond 1943, at which strategic time, when Churchill's wartime broadcasts to the English nation were still a vivid memory, it was given voice in two influential publications. Charles W. Kennedy, *The Earliest English Poetry* (London, 1943), pp. 347–48, refers to Byrhtwold's words to the other retainers as a "clarion call to fortitude and heroic death" and speaks of the retainers as "devoting themselves to death." F. M. Stenton, *Anglo-Saxon England* (Oxford, 1943), p. 377, states that Byrhtnoth's loyal thegns, "knowing that the fight was lost, deliberately gave themselves to death." This assertion has been repeated without correction in the 1947 and 1971 editions of Stenton's great history. In more recent years many critics have taken this dubious point for granted. G. V. Smithers, "Destiny and the Heroic Warrior in *Beowulf*," in *Philological Essays: Studies . . . Herbert Dean Meritt*, ed. James L. Rosier (The Hague, 1970), pp. 65–81, defines the Germanic heroic ethos in terms like these, though without explicit attention to Maldon. George Clark, "The Battle of *The Battle of Maldon*," *Neuphilologische Mitteilungen*, 69 (1968), 374–9, states that "every member of the English army chooses to flee and live or advance and die" (p. 378). Woolf, "The Ideal of Men Dying," speaks both of the retainers' "determination to die" and of their "decision to die" and characterizes Maldon as a story "in which paradoxically it is better to lose than to win" (pp. 67, 81, and 81, respectively). Robinson, "Some Aspects," refers to Byrhtnoth's "election" of an honorable death (p. 28), and in "God, Death, and Loyalty in *The Battle of Maldon*," in *J. R. R. Tolkien, Scholar and Storyteller*, ed. Mary Salu and Robert T. Farrell (Ithaca, 1974), pp. 76–98, Robinson not only states that the retainers "decide to die" (p. 97) but implies that Byrhtnoth too desires to die for the sake of entry to a better world (p. 83). John M. Hill, "The Good Fields of Grief: Remnants of Christian Conversion," *Psychocultural Review*, 2 (1978), 27–43, speaks of the warriors "suicidal commitment" (p. 36), their "suicidal loyalty, a glorious commitment to smite the foe and then join one's lord in death" (p. 39), and of their "suicidal heroism leading to transfigured existence" (p. 41). Stuart, "The Meaning of *Maldon*," speaks of Byrhtnoth's "desire for self-destruction" and of his retainers' acceptance of the idea of "group suicide" (pp. 132 and 136, respectively). Hillman, "The Christian Resonances," declares that after Byrhtnoth dies, his men "go forward . . . determined to fight until they meet a similarly glorious end" (p. 391). Anderson, "A Reconsideration," sees as the poem's central theme "the ideal of suicidal fighting as an expression of loyalty" (p. 264); in "The Roman idea of a *comitatus* and its application to 'The Battle of Maldon'," *Medievalia* 17 (1994 for 1991), 15–26, however, he offers an important modification of this statement. Finally and most recently, Katherine O'Brien O'Keefe, "Heroic Values and Christian Ethics," Ch. 6 of *The Cambridge Companion to Old English Literature*, ed. Malcolm Godden and Michael Lapidge (Cambridge, 1991), p. 123, speaks of the "suicidal military virtues" that are ascribed to the English, perhaps on the model of those of their Viking opponents.

52. For example, by George K. Anderson, *The Literature of the Anglo-Saxons* (Princeton, 1949), p. 93: "From our superior vantage-point of history we know that the brave English forces were annihilated before the Viking Danes got possession of the field."

53. Robinson, "Some Aspects," pp. 38–40, reviews and rejects the claim that has been made by several critics that the adjectives *eald* and *frod* imply only experience or trustworthiness, not age.

54. See James Bosworth and T. Northcote Toller, *An Anglo-Saxon Dictionary* (Oxford, 1898), s.v. "oðer," heading I.1 ("oðe twega").

55. Macrae-Gibson, "*Maldon:* The Literary Structure of the Later Part," *Neuphilologische Mitteilungen*, 71 (1970), 192–96, speaks of a "steady change of emphasis as the poem proceeds from loyalty expressed by vengeance to loyalty expressed by death" (p. 195). While there is some basis for this conclusion, the poet does not make clear that the retainers who are named first are able to avenge Byrhtnoth without dying, nor that the retainers who are named later die without avenging him; the three themes of loyalty, death, and vengeance are subtly intertwined.

56. In secular literature, as far as I can judge, it is not until the seventeenth century that one can see strong evidence of the deflation of vengeance as an honorable ideal. In Webster and Tourneur's lurid play "The Revenger's Tragedy," for example, the urge for revenge is represented as a personal passion, and hence as something unruly and socially destabilizing. Hamlet has his problems with revenge precisely because he is sensitive enough to see it as a tainted enterprise, especially in a universe governed by a God with a strong stake in the sixth commandment. The warriors depicted in *The Battle of Maldon* have no such qualms.

57. On the theory and practice of the feud within the medieval Icelandic social context, see Jesse L. Byock, *Feud in the Icelandic Saga* (Berkeley, 1982), Theodore M.

Andersson and William Ian Miller, *Law and Literature in Medieval Iceland: Ljósvetninga Saga and Valla-Ljóts Saga* (Stanford, 1989), pp. 22–51, and Miller, *Bloodtaking and Peacekeeping: Feud, Law, and Society in Saga Iceland* (Chicago, 1990).

58. Note however Dorothy Whitelock's contention in *The Audience of Beowulf* (Oxford, 1951), pp. 13–17, that "killing for the sake of vengeance was not felt to be incompatible with Christian ethics at any period in Anglo-Saxon times" (p. 13).

59. "War and Society," p. 183.

Contributors

EARL R. ANDERSON is professor of English at Cleveland State University.

ROBERT E. BJORK is professor of English at Arizona State University.

MARGRÉT GUNNARSDÓTTIR CHAMPION is lecturer in English literature at the University of Gothenburg.

SARAH FOOT is lecturer in history at the University of Sheffield.

M. R. GODDEN is Rawlinson-Bosworth Professor of English at the University of Oxford.

STEPHANIE HOLLIS is professor of English at the University of Auckland.

SHARI HORNER is associate professor of English at Shippensburg College, Pennsylvania.

NICHOLAS HOWE is professor of English at Ohio State University.

SUSAN KELLY is Research Fellow in the Department of Medieval History, University of Birmingham.

KEVIN S. KIERNAN is professor of English at the University of Kentucky.

CLARE A. LEES is professor of Medieval Literature and the History of the English Language at King's College, London.

ROY F. LESLIE was professor of English at Victoria University, British Columbia.

SANDRA McENTIRE is professor of English at Rhodes College.

JOHN D. NILES is professor of English at the University of Wisconsin.

KATHERINE O'BRIEN O'KEEFFE is professor of English at Notre Dame University.

PETER ORTON is lecturer in English at Queen Mary, University of London.

GILLIAN R. OVERING is professor of English at Wake Forest University.

CAROL BRAUN PASTERNACK is associate professor of English at the University of California, Santa Barbara.

FRED C. ROBINSON is Douglas Tracy Smith Professor of English (emeritus) at Yale University.

STEPHEN D. WHITE is Asa G. Candler Professor of History at Emory University.

JOCELYN WOGAN-BROWNE is professor of English at Fordham University.

Index